W9-BVL-304

Duty, Honor, Applause

Duty, Honor, Applause

America's Entertainers in World War II

Gary L. Bloomfield and Stacie L. Shain,
with Arlen C. Davidson

The Lyons Press
Guilford, Connecticut
An imprint of the The Globe Pequot Press

The Lyons Press is an imprint of The Globe Pequot Press.

10 9 8 7 6 5 4 3 2 1

Printed in the United States of America

ISBN 1–59228-550–3

Library of Congress Cataloging-in-Publication data is available on file.

Contents

1. The Great War and the Prelude to WWII

"WHILE THE STORM CLOUDS GATHER FAR ACROSS THE SEA
LET US SWEAR ALLEGIANCE TO A LAND THAT'S FREE.
LET US ALL BE GRATEFUL FOR A LAND SO FAIR
AS WE RAISE OUR VOICES IN A SOLEMN PRAYER . . .
GOD BLESS AMERICA."

—*Irving Berlin*

OPPOSITE: *Despite repeated attempts to remain neutral, the U.S. entered military action in World War I on the Lorraine front in France. Here, Battery C of the 6th Field Artillery fired America's first shot of the war.*
U.S. Army Photo

THE SMOLDERING ACCOUTREMENTS OF BATTLE LAY shattered and discarded along the ragged front of the Meuse-Argonne offensive of 1918. Stretcher-bearers collected up the wounded and the dying, some begging for the widowmaker to end it all, while scavengers retrieved anything salvageable, ignoring the unmistakable smells of the battlefield. Heaven help any enemy soldier, fallen and broken, looking up at the sharp end of a bloody bayonet and asking for mercy.

During a lull in the skirmishing, more ammo was handed out, the lines were reinforced with anyone who could hold a weapon, and the weary combatants caught a few precious moments of rest, ignoring the roar of biplanes overhead and the clatter and rumble of hundreds of field guns and behemoth tanks repositioning for the next engagement. Combat engineers worked their magic in rebuilding bombed-out fortifications and trench lines, ducking and crouching low so enemy snipers couldn't get off a clean shot, an easy kill.

The skirmish lines moved back and forth, surging, collapsing, shifting, retreating to regroup and advance again. Both sides could gloss over the setbacks and embellish the day-to-day victories, each wanting to believe they were winning the fight. But the scrappy American Expeditionary Force, fighting alongside other Allied ground units, clearly had the initiative over the battle-weary Germans, who were just prolonging the inevitable.

The German frontline soldiers were ravaged by influenza, and many of the older cynics in the trenches, who'd been in the thick of it for four long years, sensed the futility of continuing on, especially with so many untested, scared-shitless teenaged recruits mustered into combat in recent months. And with another brutal winter just weeks away, many thought about simply giving up the will to live, choosing to die just to avoid one more day of hell.

At the time, the Battle of the Meuse-Argonne was just another major campaign of

BELOW: *American tanks rolled through the Argonne Forest toward the front lines on September 26, 1918.*
U.S. Army Photo

what was known as the Great War. In fact, it was the final offensive of World War I, for Germany had had enough and was willing to accept whatever punishment the Allies felt was warranted.

A Lovelorn Soldier's Lament

Germany had plunged into the fight in August of 1914, dispatching its forces in all directions within the year—at Liege in Belgium; and Lille, France; Tannenberg in East Prussia; and Warsaw, Poland—stretching its army to the breaking point, digging in for the long haul, willing to sacrifice an entire generation of men—and nearly accomplishing it. Budding author Erich Maria Remarque was one of those young soldiers who experienced the misery of trench warfare, and he wrote about it in his classic novel, *All Quiet on the Western Front*:

"The front is a cage in which we must await fearfully whatever may happen. We lie under the network of arching shells and live in a suspense of uncertainty.

"In a bomb-proof dug-out I may be smashed to atoms and in the open may survive ten hours' bombardment unscathed. No soldier outlives a thousand chances. But every soldier believes in Chance and trusts his luck."

For the fortunate few, those who survived the war without a scratch, Lady Luck was a constant companion. But for thousands more, she stood off in the distance and smirked as the Grim Reaper rushed in and claimed a few more hundreds for his own personal army . . . in the fiery depths of hell.

While on sentry duty in Switzerland in 1915, knowing he was about to head to the Russian Front—possibly the worst living hell on Earth—another apprehensive young German soldier, Hans Leip, wrote a poem to his girlfriend, Lili, back home in Hamburg. He composed the verses for "The Song of a Young Sentry," wondering if Lili would wait for him, not knowing if he would ever see her again, wondering if she would still want him if he returned to her less than whole. A pretty nurse he'd met that night while guarding his compound happened to pass by, and, watching her walk away into the evening's fog, he imagined she was Lili. He knew only the nurse's first name, Marlene, but she inspired him to add another verse to his poem. His words, those of a lonely soldier, would immortalize both the nurse and his girl back home when they were later adapted and put to music in the simple, haunting song, "Lili Marlene."

"At the barracks compound, by the entry way
There a lantern I found and if it stands today
Then we'll see each other again, near that old lantern we'll remain
As once Lili Marlene.
Well she knows your foot steps, your own determined gait
Ev'ry evening waiting, Me? A mem'ry of late.

Should something e'er happen to me, who will under the lantern be,
With you Lili Marlene?"
—From the poem "The Song of a Young Sentry"

Another German soldier who fought on the Western Front and who survived a poison gas attack had been a struggling artist in Austria before the war. In his book, the title of which is translated as *My Struggle*, he wrote about his experiences in battle and recalled the initial exhilaration of certain victory that somehow turned horribly wrong, transforming his feelings into bitter disillusionment:

". . . and then came a damp, cold night in Flanders, through which we marched in silence, and when the day began to emerge from the mists, suddenly an iron greeting came whizzing at us over our heads, and with a sharp report sent the little pellets flying between our ranks, ripping up the wet ground; but even before the little cloud had passed, from two hundred throats the first hurrah rose to meet the first messenger of death.

"This was the beginning. Thus it went on year after year; but the romance of battle had been replaced by horror. The enthusiasm gradually cooled and the exuberant joy was stifled by mortal fear."

These were the words of a bitter, broken war veteran, Corporal Adolf Hitler, in his book, *Mein Kampf*. His anger, as one of the defeated combatants, a sentiment shared by thousands of German war veterans, would turn into a maniacal rage that propelled him on an all-consuming quest to dominate the world, a quest that possibly only he envisioned after his discharge.

Those Glorious Flyboys

In early August of 1914, France mobilized its forces just as Germany declared war on its neighbors and the world. The French Foreign Legion was

Left: *Fighting for freedom and justice in World War I didn't mean American troops received just treatment. This 1st Army Post "All Colored" Band entertained in Souilly, France, in 1918. This band was one of the first Army entertainment groups and played for soldiers of all races and ranks.*
Army Air Forces Photo

accepting all able-bodied men—fellow countrymen and foreigners, including six hundred Americans. One of those was a black expatriate, Eugene Bullard, a successful boxer who frequented the many nightclubs in Paris, especially those where American performers sang and played up-tempo tunes unlike any heard on the continent.

BELOW: *Pilot William Wellman scored three confirmed kills and earned France's Croix de Guerre with two palms and five U.S. medals during World War I. He learned to fly when he left the U.S. in 1917 to join the Lafayette Flying Corps, part of the French Foreign Legion. His style earned him the nickname "Wild Bill." Wellman directed the first Oscar-winning motion picture,* Wings, *which won a Statuette in 1927.* National Archives Photo

For eighteen months Bullard would serve with a machine gun crew in the 170th Infantry Regiment, enduring trench warfare and all its misery at the Western Front. He would be wounded at Verdun, recuperate for six months, and then volunteer for the French Army Air Corps, where he would become the first black combat pilot, with the Nieuport Squadron 93, flying a wood and canvas Spad avion de chasse.

When the American doughboys started arriving many months later, the biplanes and swashbuckling airmen of the fledgling U.S. Army Air Corps followed quickly after. Like many American flyers serving with the French Foreign Legion and Air Service, Bullard requested a transfer, but his was the only one not accepted—because he was black. Reluctantly he continued to fight for the French forces.

Eugene Pallette was a Hollywood extra who had worked his way up to leading man by 1917, when he enlisted in the Army Air Corps and was dispatched to the front.

William Wellman initially volunteered for the Ambulance Corps in France, assigned to stumble across the bomb-pocked battlefields to pick up wounded soldiers and hustle them back to field hospitals in the rear. It was a miserable task and he quickly realized the glamour boys were the ones flying those biplanes roaring and sputtering overhead, so, like Bullard, he joined the French Foreign Legion and flew pursuit fighters with the Lafayette Flying Corps. (After the war he became a stunt pilot and, a decade later, directed the Academy Award–winning movie *Wings,* about combat pilots and their war machines engaging in spectacular dogfights overhead. One of the actors in *Wings* was Buddy Rogers, who would learn to fly with aviation pioneer, Hoyt Vandenberg.)

When the United States entered the fray, Wellman was one of the many American pilots serving with the French who requested a transfer to the U.S. Army Air Service. Other Yank pilots included Howard Hawkes, who would later direct the movie *Sergeant York*; and James N. Hall, who would write the classic, *Mutiny on the Bounty*.

Vernon Castle, who had teamed with his wife, Irene, to form the United States' top

LEFT: World War I pilot William Wellman directed this scene from his 1927 Oscar-winning film Wings, *which showed air combat between biplanes and zeppelins. The director won numerous medals as an aviator and had the War Department's complete support on this extravagant film. Paramount Studios took a major risk on the 29-year-old Wellman, who earned $250 a week for directing the film and shouldered the responsibility of pulling together nearly 3,500 Army personnel, 60-plus pilots, and approximately 165 planes. Studio executives almost fired him on multiple occasions as the film continued to go over its budget and schedule. Wellman took nearly a year to make the movie, partially because he insisted on near-perfect cloud formations. Despite winning the 1927 Oscar for the film, Paramount chose not to renew the director's contract, and he was not invited to the Academy Awards ceremony.*
National Film Archives, London, Photo

dance couple, had joined the Royal Flying Corps in 1916. The couple had planned to resume their standing as America's sweethearts of the ballroom once the fighting was over, but before he could complete his hitch, Vernon was killed in February of 1918 at Fort Worth.

The Yanks Volunteer for the Big Fight

In mid-1917, when it became evident that the United States would end up getting involved, and that revered Army General John "Black Jack" Pershing would be heading up an expeditionary force bound for Europe, thousands of American men signed on, lured by the excitement of battle, the adventure of going overseas, and the gallantry of fighting for one's country.

Future radio star Rudy Vallee, still in high school, quickly decided to drop out and join the Navy, wanting to get a taste of the action, but he was

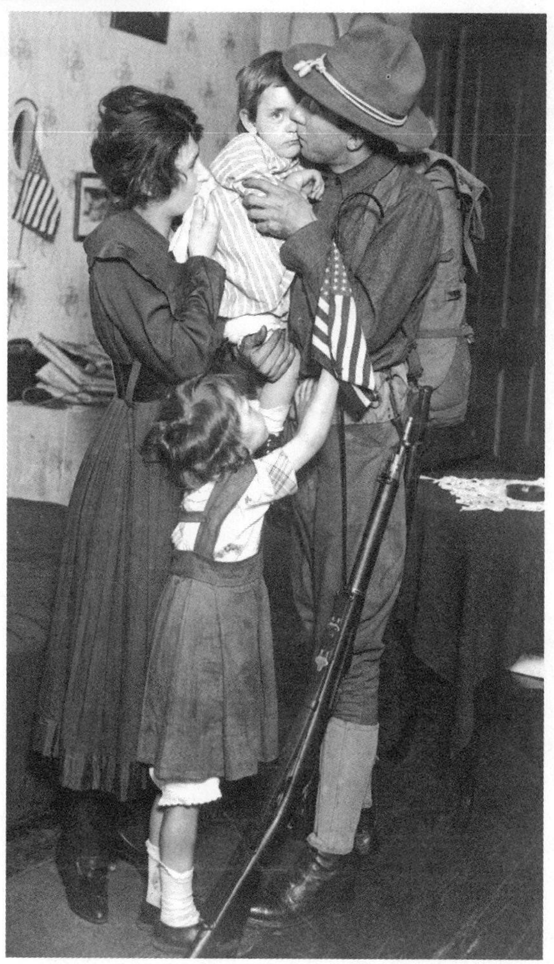

Above: *In what looks like a poster for a would-be movie called* Daddy Goes to War, *Private T. P. Loughlin of the 69th Regiment of the New York National Guard kisses his child one last time before departing for World War I battle fronts.*
War Department Photo

considered underage and was sent home before he could get into the fight.

Benjamin Kubelsky didn't have much use for high school either, but he could play an adequate violin, and teamed up with pianist Cora Salisbury to work the East Coast vaudeville circuit long before Rudy Vallee pounded the boards. Kubelsky—wanting a catchier stage name—changed his to the simpler Ben Benny, and joined the Navy in 1918. During his free time he and a group of other new recruits at the Great Lakes Training Station north of Chicago would play ragtime and popular tunes on Saturday nights. After finding out there was another violinist with a similar name, he changed his name once again, settling on Jack Benny. Though he never made it overseas, Benny did hone his stage patter during his hitch, starring in the Great Lakes Revue, raising funds for Navy Relief.

Another future star was Humphrey Bogart, who didn't drop out of high school; he was dismissed for "high spirits" and "infractions of the rules" from the prestigious Phillips Academy in Andover, Massachusetts. He underwent training in New York, then served in the Navy as a helmsman on the troop transport *Leviathan.* Although he never made it to the far side of the Atlantic while the war was still raging, he continued to disobey orders at every turn.

Like Bogie, future actor Pat O'Brien left high school and joined the Navy near the end of the war. He served at the Great Lakes Training Station with Jack Benny, but never got overseas for the "good fight."

Doughboys Do the Grunt Work

Future actor Melvyn Hesselberg wanted to get in while the battle against "the Huns" was still going on overseas, so he joined the Army at seventeen, but he got stuck stateside as a medical aide in Wyoming. Percy Helton had been a child actor with song-and-dance man George M. Cohan, then signed on with the American Expeditionary Force and saw action in France, enduring the miserable existence in the trenches that crisscrossed the fighting front.

Basil Sydney learned his stagecraft in England and then in 1914 toured U.S. theaters. When hostilities broke out in Europe, he caught a transport ship home and served with the British Royal Army.

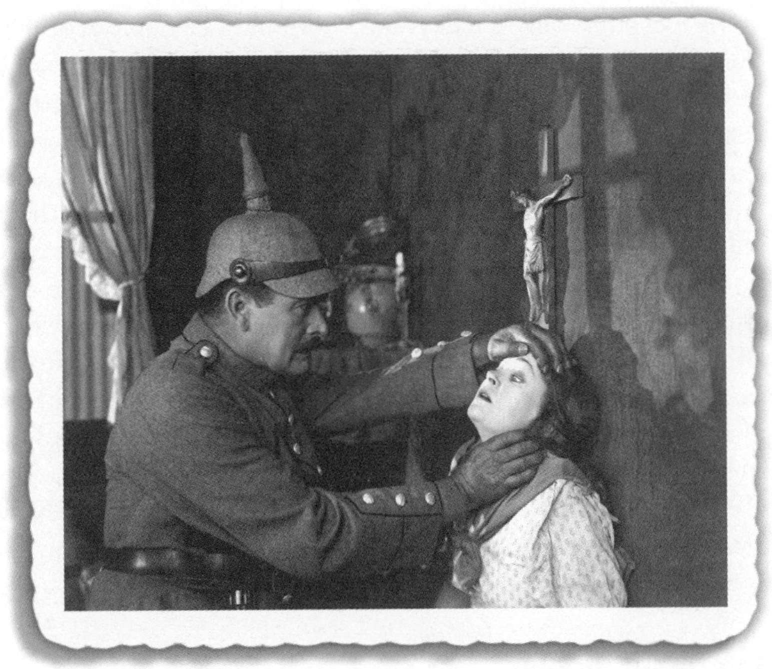

Left: *Hollywood often portrayed Germans as "dastardly Huns," even as early as this 1918 release,* Stake Uncle Sam to Play Your Hand. *In the movie, a German soldier, played by A. C. Gibbons, attacks a Belgian girl, played by Mae Marsh. While films about the Japanese portrayed everyone as "evil," movies often showed both "good" and "bad" Germans.* Bureau of Public Debt Photo

One reluctant Tennessee farmer, who was a pretty darn good shot with a Springfield rifle, knew he would be going overseas. Alvin York was a God-fearing man who had only used his rifle for hunting and target shooting. He had never fired at a man before and wasn't sure he could do it, even in battle. But at Meuse-Argonne, York watched as enemy bullets ripped into his buddies, fellow doughboys who didn't want to be there any more than he did. To stop the killing, York had to silence the killers, scrambling from one position to the next, picking off the enemy soldiers one at a time. Near the end of the campaign, assigned to the 82nd Division, he killed 25 German soldiers and captured another 132. (Once his exploits became known and documented, York's superiors recommended him for the Medal of Honor, and Hollywood came calling, but York was not interested in seeing his story splashed across the big screen. He just wanted to get back home to Tennessee and live a simple life, away from the celebrity status he wanted no part of.)

The Americans paid a heavy toll in the closing months of the war at the battle of Meuse-Argonne—where more than 26,000 were killed and another 95,000 wounded, mounting statistics in a war some felt was nothing but a massacre of lunatic proportions. But even amidst the human tragedy of war, a small glimmer of life miraculously survived the bombing and the devastation, and would go on to play an important role in future battles still many years away.

A young doughboy patrolling the bombed-out houses and buildings of Lorraine heard a faint yelping from near a collapsed stone wall of a dog kennel in the village. He discovered among the rubble a frightened German shepherd nursing her five pups, only ten days old. Corporal Lee Duncan of the Army's 136th Aero Division had seen enemy soldiers using shepherds as war dogs; he immediately knew these newborns could be trained in similar roles for the American Expeditionary Force, and was willing to take on the task. (In fact, the Germans utilized more than 30,000 war dogs, as sentries, ammo and supply carriers, scouts, and couriers.) Duncan adopted two of the pups—a male and his sister—and other members of his unit took in the rest of the litter.

Two months later, on November 11, Germany surrendered, giving up the fight after four long years of misery and destruction. The world rejoiced; finally, the guns were silent and the Earth stopped trembling. Like thousands of other doughboys of the American Expeditionary Force, Corporal Duncan knew that finally he'd be heading home soon, and he got permission to take the shepherd pups with him. But the female developed distemper during the two-week transatlantic trip, and died soon after arriving in New York. Corporal Duncan continued on to California with the frisky male pup in tow, a pup he'd named Rin Tin Tin.

The Aftermath of War

The picturesque regions of Europe were devastated by hundreds of thousands of artillery shells both sides had lobbed at each other during the Great War. Vineyards, forests, and pastureland were turned into minefields and

RIGHT: *Much to Germany's chagrin, U.S. troops marched through the streets of Paris on Independence Day, 1917.*
U.S. Information Service Photo

wasteland, crisscrossed by a labyrinth of collapsed trenches, broken spans of concertina wire, and the wreckage of gun emplacements, bomb craters, and other battle debris.

Schoolhouses and churches used as makeshift hospitals and command centers were also targets of enemy field guns and tanks, leaving entire villages destroyed and abandoned. And when the two sides moved on, back and forth, attack and counterattack, they left behind scorched rubble that would take years to rebuild.

The terms of the Versailles Treaty, which officially ended the hostilities of WWI, forced a defeated Germany to downsize its military to minimal levels. Thousands of demands were dictated to the defeated country, including:

- no more than seven infantry divisions and three cavalry divisions
- a standing army of fewer than 100,000 troops
- the abolishment of universal compulsory military service
- naval forces would not exceed six battleships, six light cruisers, twelve destroyers, and twelve torpedo boats
- naval forces would include no submarines
- naval personnel would not exceed 15,000
- no military or naval air forces, though Germany could maintain up to one hundred seaplanes or flying boats to be used only to search for submarine mines; these planes could not carry arms, munitions, or bombs

The treaty also determined "the maximum number of guns, machine guns, trench-mortars, rifles, and amount of ammunition and equipment"; forbid "the manufacture of arms, munitions, or any war material"; "the manufacture and importation of aircraft, parts of aircraft, engines for aircraft, and parts of engines for aircraft," and "the use of asphyxiating, poisonous, or other gases [and] their manufacture and importation"; and declared that "educational establishments, the universities, societies of discharged soldiers, shooting or touring clubs . . . must not occupy themselves with any military matters," to name just a few of the hundreds of restrictions imposed on a defeated Germany, which had little option but to accept the terms.

The Treaty also required Germany to pay the damages incurred by all of the victorious nations. Other financial obligations included:

- damage caused by any maltreatment of POWs;
- all pensions and compensation to naval and military victims of war;
- 20,000,000,000 Marks gold bearer bonds without interest;
- 40,000,000,000 Marks gold bearer bonds bearing interest; and
- an additional 40,000,000,000 Marks gold 5 percent bearer bonds.

To understand the miniscule point-by-point detail listed in the Treaty, the following is included in Annex IV of Article 244 of Part VIII, Reparation:

- To France, 500 stallions, 30,000 fillies and mares, 2,000 bulls, 90,000 cows, 1,000 rams, 100,000 sheep, and 10,000 goats.
- To Belgium, 200 stallions, 5,000 mares, 5,000 fillies, 2,000 bulls, 50,000 cows, 40,000 heifers, 200 rams, 20,000 sheep, 15,000 sows.

These terms, if allowed to remain in force until fulfilled, would have constricted Germany for thirty years, plunging it into economic depression, with unemployment running rampant in the 1920s and well into the next decade.

The disillusionment Corporal Adolf Hitler felt at the end of the never-ending conflict and wrote about in *Mein Kampf* and stood on street corners screaming to anyone who would listen, was shared by millions of German citizens and thousands of demoralized veterans, both the physically wounded and the mentally scarred. That bitterness would turn to rage as the angry Hitler openly criticized his own spineless government for allowing the "stab in the back" agreement "dictated" by the victors of WWI. This borderline lunatic—some considered him the greatest actor in German history, while others ridiculed him as little more than a boorish loudmouth—was saying exactly what the German masses were feeling, demanding that they deserved a strong leader who could restore Germany's national pride and rebuild the Fatherland into a world power once again.

With the National Socialist German Worker's Party providing the muscle—the Nazis in the late '20s and early '30s were little more than street thugs—Hitler's political aspirations grew, and he developed a loyal following among the disenfranchised, the unemployed, and the easily duped. In 1933 he seized power via coalition. The untimely death of Germany's revered leader, war hero Paul von Hindenburg, followed quickly, in mid-1934. Suddenly, before anyone could step forward to oppose his leadership, Hitler abolished all free elections and used extreme violence to silence his critics, who didn't have the muscle to protect them from the Nazi goon squads. He then set out to rectify the perceived wrongs of the Versailles Treaty by rebuilding Germany's military might and by promising to retake disputed territories, such as the Alsace-Lorraine region of France.

Hitler also sought to create an Aryan super race by eliminating all "undesirables"—such as Slavs, Jews, Gypsies, and the handicapped—from the German population. This included the boycotting of Jewish merchants and the looting of their shops, the firing of all Jewish teachers, lawyers, doctors, and the like. Many Jews had lived through similar threats and purges before and defiantly remained vigilant, which proved to be a fatal error, as millions were rounded up and sent "away," never to be seen or heard from again.

Their neighbors watched the many departures but knew not to ask where they might have gone. Many other Jews chose to find safe harbor in neighboring countries. As those too came under Nazi control, the refugees desperately fled to Britain and the United States.

American Heroes Return to Civilian Life

Rudy Vallee had wanted to serve in the Navy but was too young. After returning home, he would eventually become a huge vaudeville singer and musician, before NBC snatched him up for a variety show on network radio. Then his career took off. Like the younger Vallee, Jack Benny got out of the Navy, returned to vaudeville, and eventually got his own radio show, sponsored by Canada Dry ginger ale.

The cantankerous Humphrey Bogart continually challenged naval authority, and would take his bad-boy image to Hollywood and buck the system there, refusing to kowtow to the studio assembly line. After getting his discharge in 1921, Pat O'Brien returned to high school, then went on to Marquette University and caught the acting bug, which led to countless movie roles in Hollywood. In 1919, newly discharged flyboy Eugene Pallette returned to Hollywood, hoping to resume the leading man roles he was offered prior to the war. But he found he was a forgotten man, and he became a rotund character actor to stay in show business.

LEFT: *Film pioneer D. W. Griffith featured Dorothy Gish in* The Greatest Thing in Life, *which was a motion-picture appeal to end the war. Griffith was no stranger to war movies, having made* Birth of a Nation, *a film about the Civil War that was released in 1915—the war's 50th anniversary.*
War Department Photo

After the war Melvyn Hesselberg changed his name to Melvyn Douglas and took up acting, establishing himself in Hollywood as a debonair leading man. Former child actor Percy Helton returned from the fighting in France and sought roles on Broadway, then headed to Hollywood as an established character actor.

Basil Sydney received his discharge from the British Army and returned to the States after the war. He had offers from Hollywood, but he insisted that he would act only in adaptations of works by Shakespeare and Bernard Shaw. Hollywood scoffed at his demands, and Sydney headed back to Broadway and British theater. He eventually eased off his self-imposed demands and finally made it in Hollywood, appearing in several movies.

Right: *D.W. Griffith made* Hearts of the World *in 1917 to show "the evil Huns" mistreating people living under German rule. In the film, actress Lillian Gish receives cruel treatment from German soldiers. The film realistically portrayed war's horrors and ironically served as a recruiting tool for the U.S. military, as thousands enlisted after its release.*
National Archives Photo

Heroes of Derring-Do

Every generation of boys and girls has its heroes, whether real life or make-believe. In the 1920s and into the '30s, many of those heroes could be traced to the combat exploits of WWI, on the ground, across the seas, and in the air.

"Most exciting to me in those days were the pulp magazines about flying aces of the First World War, always available on the magazine racks for a dime," remembered Carroll O'Connor in his book, *I Think I'm Outta Here*.

"War on foot was not much romanticized in fiction magazines because it was muddy, bloody, and proximately deadly. A war was coming, and at sixteen I did not want to be denied a war, presuming it would be as thrilling as the movies made it. Some credit for this is due to the World War movies of the '30s, like *The Dawn Patrol* starring Errol Flynn, that made us long to fly fighter planes and shoot vicious-looking Germans out of the skies."

Like hundreds of youngsters, nine-year-old George Roy Hill was fascinated with the WWI pilots who barnstormed across the country in the '20s. He'd read about the exploits of Jimmy Doolittle and Eddie Rickenbacker, and went to all the local air shows to see the barrel rolls and loop-de-loops and wing walkers, and spent his afternoons at the local airport near Minneapolis. By the time he was sixteen, Hill was learning to fly on his own. (In the early '50s he would became a writer for television, and then graduate to the big time as a movie director.)

As a boy in the 1920s, Brian Keith read about the exploits of the Marines in WWI in the "War Dog" magazine column and John W. Thomason's book, *Fix Bayonets!* For Keith it seemed like a thrilling way to see the world, conquering the belligerents and saving the damsels in peril, and it is what he wanted to do when he grew up, if there were still belligerents to rid the world of by that time. Little did he know what was brewing overseas in Germany and Japan.

Set in another time, *The Lone Ranger* was first heard on the radio, with a hearty "Hi-Yo Silver," in 1933—a champion for the downtrodden, the underdog. The show's popularity grew, and Lee Powell took the role to serial films in 1938. Then it was easy for moviegoers to tell who the bad guys were . . . they all wore black hats! Along with his faithful sidekick, Tonto, and valiant steed, Silver, the masked man became a hero to thousands of youngsters, inspiring them to send away for the official six-shooter cap guns and pint-sized ten-gallon hats, but most importantly, to always do what's right, no matter the odds.

(Lee Powell would later join the Marines and continue to do what's right, for his country, against some of the worst "bad guys" ever born.)

The comic strip *Don Winslow of the Navy,* created by Frank Martinek, made it to radio in October 1937 for NBC. The show followed naval intelligence officer Frank Martinek and his best buddy, Red Pennington, as they pursued the despicable Scorpion and his daughter, Tasmia, over two seasons. (By October 1942, the show was dusted off and rewritten to reflect a global war footing. The evildoers were Japs and Nazis threatening our sovereign shores, and young listeners were briefed on how to protect their homeland in their own small way, no matter where they lived.)

Captain Midnight was another hero of the airwaves, captivating youngsters every weekday afternoon through the 1940s. Developed by WWI aviators Robert Burtt and Wilfred Moore, *Midnight* detailed the many confrontations with the despicable Ivan Shark and his daughter, Fury, plus assorted other criminal elements. And, of course, there were numerous gadgets that youngsters just had to have, such as the official Captain Midnight Code-O-Graph to unscramble the hidden message at the end of each episode.

Ominously, one episode signaled what no one would have believed at the time. "In the fall of 1941 the plot concerned an unnamed foreign power that was attempting to sink a ship in order to block Pearl Harbor in preparations for an air attack," revealed Richard Lamparski in his book, *Whatever Became of . . . ?* "Weeks later the Japanese bombed Pearl Harbor and the FBI visited the producers for a long and grueling interrogation about the striking coincidence." They wanted to know if maybe the writers of *Midnight* had prior knowledge of Japan's intentions and could have prevented the attack by warning authorities.

The Green Hornet was another radio superhero who probed into the underworld of evil and espionage. With his trusted Japanese sidekick, Kato (whose nationality would be changed to Filipino after Pearl Harbor), the Green Hornet may have been bruised and battered by all manner of despicable villains, but he was always victorious by the time each adventure had run its course.

The Shadow came to life on radio in September 1930. Initially, with his mystic chuckle and booming voice, the Shadow was the host of the *Detective*

Story Magazine Hour. But he soon became the lead character, spinning tales of "crime detection, romance, and espionage, all enhanced by the sound man's weird effects," wrote Barry Farrell and Maureen Baron in the compilation book, *The Swing Era: 1944–45*. "As we crowded around the set, waiting eagerly for the nameless terror that lurked behind the door, we created the menaces, as awful as we could make them, that faced our heroes. No storm was so terrible, no haunted house so spooky, no villain so grotesque that we couldn't make things worse."

Wallace Beery was no youngster when he became fascinated with naval aviators Jimmie Thach, H. S. Duckworth, and T. D. Southworth. The real-life pilots were on the set of the movie *Hell Divers,* teaching dive-bombing tactics to forty-nine-year-old Beery and fellow actors Clark Gable and Cliff Edwards. Beery was hooked, and he soon joined the Navy Reserve as a proud pilot. He would never be asked to fly into combat, but like thousands of Americans inspired by the exploits of their favorite real-life heroes, Beery was certainly ready to do his part if ever called.

Europe between the Wars

Decorated war hero Eugene Bullard, the black expatriate who served with the French Army Air Corps, returned to Paris and became a nightclub entrepreneur and jazz drummer around town. He also worked at the Zelli nightclub, the hottest of hot spots in Montmartre, booking the most popular musicians, singers, and dancers around.

The French capital was a hotbed for German spies, and, because of his proficiency with the German language, Bullard was recruited to eavesdrop on pro-Nazi patrons in Paris nightclubs, including his own club, L'Escadrille. Sassy and provocative Folies Bergères headliner, Josephine Baker, known as the "eternal Mistinguett," was also involved with underground activity, passing crucial information about Nazi actions to local partisan groups.

As the Nazi threat grew in the 1930s, many foreigners were urged to flee, but Bullard and Baker withstood the pressure and held out, though not without great peril. But among the many who failed to escape the Nazi crackdown in time were two black American musicians, Charlie Lewis and Art Briggs, who were rounded up by the Nazis and imprisoned, along with their families.

European Exiles Flee to America

The unrelenting, unforgiving Nazi effort to eliminate the Jews from Europe, cutting off all aspects of their livelihood, forced many to consider safe

Left: *A smartly dressed Hedy Lamarr immortalizes her autograph in concrete outside the USO's Hollywood Canteen in December 1942. Lamarr fled Germany between the World Wars, not in fear of the Nazis but because of response to her nudity in* Extase. *Although her husband tried to purchase all known copies of the film, she moved to France and was discovered by MGM Studio's executive, Louis B. Mayer, who changed her name from Hedwig Kiesler and made her a silver screen star.*
Associated Press Photo

passage to England and beyond. Sadly, far too many waited until it was too late to leave.

Instead of boarding transport ships westward, those who tried to wait out the Nazi harassment were rounded up and sent east, herded into cattle cars bound for one of the many camps established to handle the "Jewish Question."

One Austrian Jew who fled the Nazis was Billy Wilder, whose mother would perish at the Auschwitz Death Camp in Poland. (The Nazis built four other massive extermination or death camps in the eastern territories: Treblinka, Majdanek, Chelmno, and Sobibor.) When the Nazis came to power, Wilder had been working at the UFA film studios, which immediately released blatantly pro-Nazi newsreels, ignoring internal protests from its own Jewish contingent of actors, directors, writers, and other employees. The names of Jews were even deleted from film credits released earlier by UFA. Behind the scenes, powerful arms manufacturer Alfred Krupp, who owned controlling stock in the UFA studios, had quickly realized his future fortunes would be enormous if he aligned himself with the war-hungry Nazis, and so he opened the gates of his movie studio and allowed the Nazis to determine what the German masses would be permitted to see.

Wilder and hundreds of others quickly realized their livelihood in the film industry was dying, at least in Germany. Many fled to Paris, including composer Friedrich Hollander, stage actor Peter Lorre, author Erich Maria

Remarque, and screenwriter Max Kolpe, to name just a few. From there they made it to the coast, or found safe passage down into Spain and Portugal, or crossed the Channel to England. It didn't matter where they went as long as they went, staying one step ahead of the Nazi tidal wave rolling into neighboring countries.

After making it to southern California, Billy Wilder learned to speak English by memorizing twenty new words every day. Soon he was again writing movie scripts, but in English. (He would eventually become one of the most successful writers and directors in film history.)

John Wengraf had been a repertory actor in Vienna, Austria, until Nazi forces annexed his homeland. He fled to London, then moved on to Broadway, and finally settled in Hollywood, where he starred in numerous WWII movies. Carl Esmond also left Vienna and ended up in Tinseltown, playing Nazi roles in a variety of movies, including *Dawn Patrol* and *Ministry of Fear*.

Otto Preminger was another Austrian actor who fled the Holocaust. New York stage actress Tallulah Bankhead used her influence—asking her own father, William B. Bankhead, who was Speaker of the U.S. House of Representatives—to pull some strings for Preminger and his family, and other European refugees in the film and theater communities. Otto soon made it to Hollywood and became a renowned director.

Sig Arno was a well-known comedian in German theater until the Nazis came to power in 1933. He then bounced around Europe, staying ahead of the Nazi expansion, then departed for America, where he resumed his acting career in musicals and comedies.

Danish comic and pianist Victor Borge took jabs at the Nazis in his concerts and mocked the laughable antics of Adolf Hitler, infuriating the Führer. Borge was on Hitler's list of Enemies of the Fatherland, and he barely escaped capture after Nazi forces invaded Denmark. He boarded the refugee ship SS *American Legion* to New York. (Borge learned English by sitting through marathon sessions of movies. He worked at odd jobs in New York and California and was discovered by vaudevillian Rudy Vallee for his radio show.)

Author Erich Maria Remarque first incurred the wrath of Nazi thugs in 1931. That year, at the premiere of the movie *All Quiet on the Western Front*, which was adapted from Remarque's WWI literary classic, they unleashed white mice in the Nollendorfplatz Theater, creating a panic. After Hitler came to power, the Nazis condemned Remarque's literary works, removing them

Below: *Silent film star Charlie Chaplin poked fun at Germans and military life in* Shoulder Arms, *which debuted only four weeks before the war's armistice. The movie costarred half-brother Sydney Chaplin, who plays the raving maniac Kaiser and an American soldier. Charlie Chaplin later had fun lampooning Adolf Hitler in* The Great Dictator.
National Film Archives, London, Photo

from all public and school libraries. Dr. Joseph Goebbels, the Nazi propaganda minister, singled out *All Quiet on the Western Front*, declaring, "Against literary betrayal of the soldiers in the world war, and in the name of national education in the spirit of self-defense, I consign to the flames the work of Erich Maria Remarque." The author reluctantly left his beloved Germany. He fled to Hollywood, although he did travel to Europe surreptitiously whenever he could. (Ironically, when word of the book burnings leaked out of Nazi Germany, sales of *All Quiet on the Western Front* soared in countries outside of Axis influence.)

While listening to heated debate among the hundreds of European refugees who made up the Hollywood colonies (segmented by country allegiance), realizing that to defend Nazi Germany's actions would be indefensible, Remarque made a staggering prediction, one that would ring true in the coming years: "The Germans for the next century will be the most hated people in the world."

Thirteen-year-old Werner Klemperer fled Germany with his family in 1933, soon after the Nazis began their crackdown on the Jews. His father, noted conductor Otto Klemperer, had been grooming his two children to be master musicians. (Young Werner ended up in California and studied acting in Pasadena, then joined the U.S. Army in 1942 and served as an MP and with Special Services doing stage shows in the Pacific. In the mid-sixties he would take on his most noted role, as Colonel Klink in the popular television show *Hogan's Heroes*, with one stipulation: that the inept Colonel Klink would be little more than a Nazi buffoon.) John Banner was another Austrian Jew who barely escaped the Nazi persecution in 1938. (He too went on to star in *Hogan's Heroes*, as the roly-poly Sergeant Schultz.)

Another blossoming teenaged thespian who departed Germany before the Nazi crackdown was Maria Lilli Peiser. She reluctantly turned down a contract with the prestigious Darmstadt State Theater in Germany, then went to Paris, changing her name to Lilli Palmer to mask her Jewish lineage. She and her sister found work performing as Les Soeurs Viennoises in Parisian nightclubs. Soon after a London producer saw Lilli on stage, he encouraged her to cross the Channel, both for her safety and for more theatrical work. (She would eventually become a respected actress on the silver screen.)

German actor Felix Bressart fled to the United States in 1936. He too found work in Hollywood, playing German characters in several war-related films. Ludwig Donath made it to Hollywood, playing both despised Nazis and elderly Jews in the '40s. Otto Reichow was also stereotyped for his menacing portrayals of Nazis in more than one hundred movies, including *Five Graves to Cairo*, *The Hitler Gang*, and *Desert Rats*. But his motivation stemmed from personal tragedy when he was a young actor in Berlin. Soon after they came to power in 1933, Nazi thugs killed Reichow's brother.

Peter Van Eyck appeared in *Five Graves to Cairo* with Reichow. A German concert pianist, Van Eyck had toured Europe before fleeing to Hollywood. He played a rare role in the movie *The Moon is Down*, as a sympathetic Nazi officer who refused to kill Norwegian civilians, committing suicide instead.

Sig Ruman left Germany before the Nazi crackdown, acting in German-language stage roles in New York. By the mid-1930s he was in Hollywood and appeared in a variety of pictures, including the war classics *Casablanca* and *Stalag 17*. Another actor who appeared in *Casablanca* was S. Z. "Cuddles" Sakall, who had fled from the Nazis in 1939.

French actor Jean Gabin saw his film work dwindle to nothing as the Nazis occupied his homeland and escalated their control over the cultural community. Through the centuries, France and Germany and England had tormented each other, and any tenuous alliance among any two of them—during WWII it would be France and England—would include an underlying sense of distrust. But early on, France's only hope for liberation was Great Britain. Upon arriving in New York, ultra-Frenchman Gabin explained the dilemma he and all his countrymen were facing:

"Those who are pro-British say every night in their prayers 'Dear God, let the gallant British win quickly,' and those who are anti-British pray, 'Dear God, let the filthy British win very soon.'"

Lithuanian Kurt Katch studied theater in Germany and founded Berlin's Kulturbund Deutschen Juden Theater. Like so many other Jewish artists, he fled to Hollywood and appeared in countless war movies, including *Watch on the Rhine*, *Berlin Correspondent*, and *The Seventh Cross*.

Actress Hedwig Kiesler was forced to flee Germany after 1933, but not because of Nazi pressure. That year she had appeared nude in the silent film *Extase*, which included several provocative scenes. Her husband attempted to buy up all copies of the film but failed. The resulting scandal forced her to flee the country. During a brief stay in France she met MGM boss Louis B. Mayer, who was captivated by her ravishing looks—but wasn't excited about the name Hedwig Kiesler.

After a few suggestions, she changed her name to Hedy Lamarr. She moved to Hollywood and starred in movies well into the 1950s.

Noted German stage director Kurt Weill had suffered personally and creatively when the Nazis came to power and forced him to flee to New York. But by 1936 he had written the musical *Johnny Johnson* and was hailed as the new sensation on Broadway. Two years later he wrote the play *Knickerbocker Holiday*, eventually made into a movie.

Popular British actress Gracie Fields appeared in the 1936 film *Queen of Hearts* and ended up marrying Italian director Monty Banks. Three years later, after Britain declared war, Banks would have been imprisoned as an enemy agent if he had remained in the country, so Fields chose to move with him to Los Angeles, where she found more film work. Unfortunately, her countrymen considered her a deserter, and her popularity back home nose-dived.

Four years after leaving France on a transport bound for New York, the German shepherd pup Rin Tin Tin and his owner, Lee Duncan, were walking from one studio to the next along Hollywood's poverty row, looking for film work, when they came to the set of the film *Man From Hell's River*. A temperamental wolf refused to cooperate on cue, and the trainer was catching heat from the director and the film crew. After watching the goings-on, Duncan stepped forward and boldly stated that his shepherd could do the trick in one take. The director ignored the offer, even though he wasn't having any luck with the stubborn wolf, which reminded him of a few persnickety actresses he'd dealt with in the past. Finally, exasperated, the director looked over at Lee Duncan and pointed to where he wanted the mutt to stand.

As promised, with no rehearsal, Rin Tin Tin needed only one take to complete the scene, and the rest is film history. He was hired to complete the film, and *Man From Hell's River* became a hit. (Rin Tin Tin went on to make twenty-six pictures for Warner Brothers and received thousands of fan letters every week. It would be a few more years before he and Duncan "enlisted" to help the war effort that was brewing in Europe and the Pacific.)

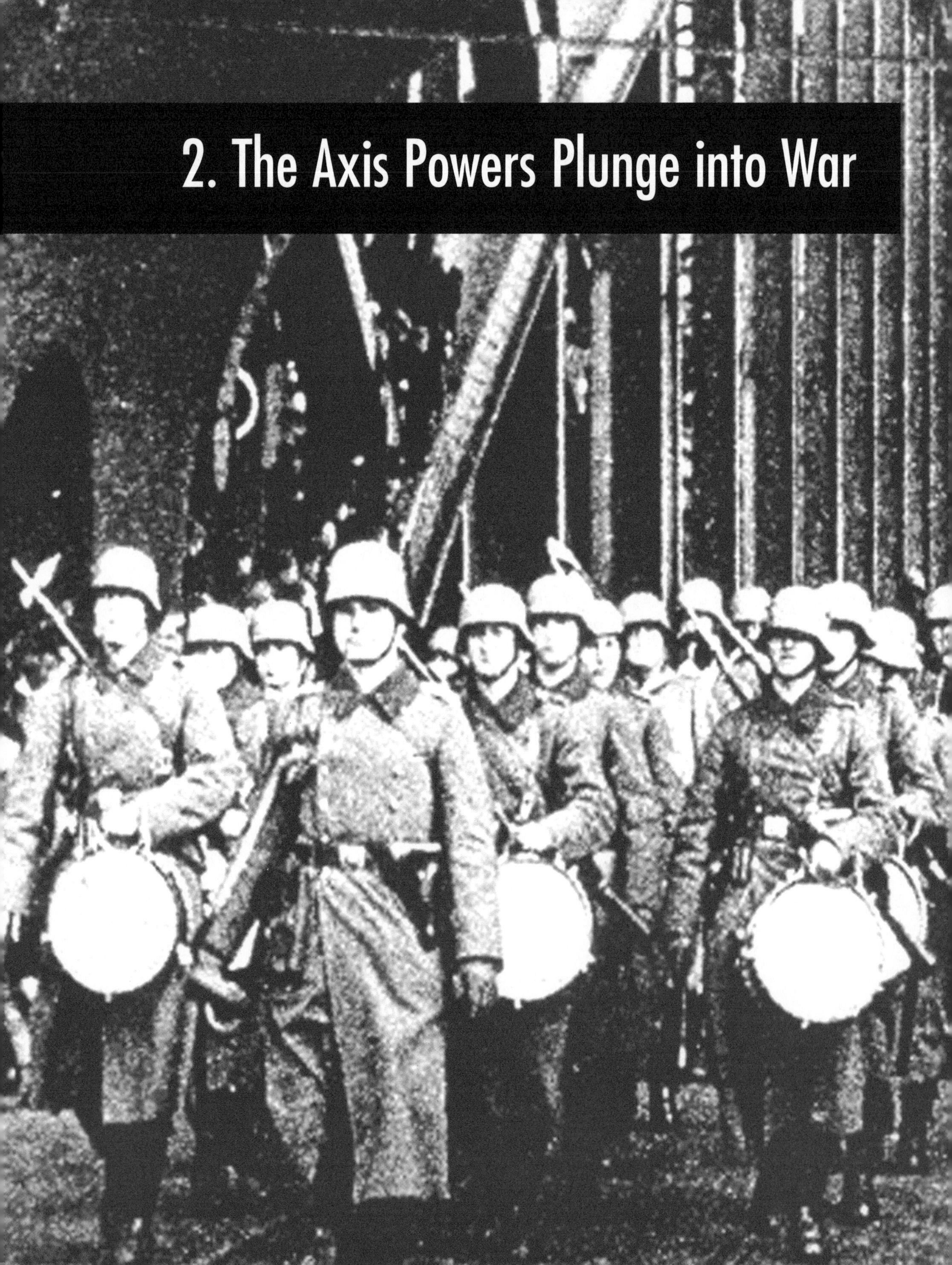

2. The Axis Powers Plunge into War

"In every great world-shaking movement, propaganda will first have to spread the idea of this movement. Thus, it will indefatigably attempt to make the new thought processes clear to the others, and therefore to draw them over to their own ground, or to make them uncertain of their previous conviction."

—*Adolf Hitler in* Mein Kampf, *1927*

FORMER GERMAN WWI VET ADOLF HITLER AND THE National Socialist Party seized control in 1933 and immediately set out to expand Germany's sphere of influence throughout Europe, intent on creating a Thousand-Year Reich. They quelled all internal opposition, swiftly and brutally, then intended to steamroll any neighbor who foolishly dared to challenge them. Like toppling dominoes, the countries and regions of Europe collapsed with barely a whimper: first the Sudetenland and Austria, then Czechoslovakia and Poland (although the Poles did try to repel the Nazi Blitzkrieg with outdated armaments and tactics, such as pitting cavalrymen on horses against German tanks), followed by the march north into Denmark and Norway, the Netherlands, Luxembourg, and France, then the push farther east, into Yugoslavia and Russia, and south across the Mediterranean toward North Africa.

Opposite: *On March 7, 1936, Nazi troops corrected a perceived "wrong," by reclaiming the industrialized Rhineland. As part of the Treaty of Versailles to end World War I, Germany ceded the land to France. Lacking access to natural resources such as coal, Hitler defied the treaty and seized the demilitarized Rhineland. Hitler later explained that had the French resisted, Germany would have retreated because of a lack of military resources.*
Imperial War Museum Photo

Nazis Unveil Blitzkrieg Tactics

When Germany and Italy dispatched military forces to support Franco and his fascists in Spain, the Loyalist government forces could not withstand the overpowering onslaught of Hitler's new military tactic, the Blitzkrieg—or lightning strike—a concentration of combined military forces, most notably bombers and fighter aircraft, tanks, artillery, and highly mobile infantry, all in a coordinated attack.

Movie producer Walter Wanger was interested in spotlighting the conflict, and produced the United Artists film *Blockade*, starring Henry Fonda as a Spanish farmer caught up in the conflict. The lines were intentionally blurred between the good guys and the bad, but audiences knew that movie hero Fonda must be on the side of righteousness, even if he and

Actor Henry Fonda joined the U.S. Navy in 1942 and earned promotions up to lieutenant on staff duty. He traded playing a hero, in movies such as Blockade, *for living the role of a seaman.*
U.S. Navy Photo

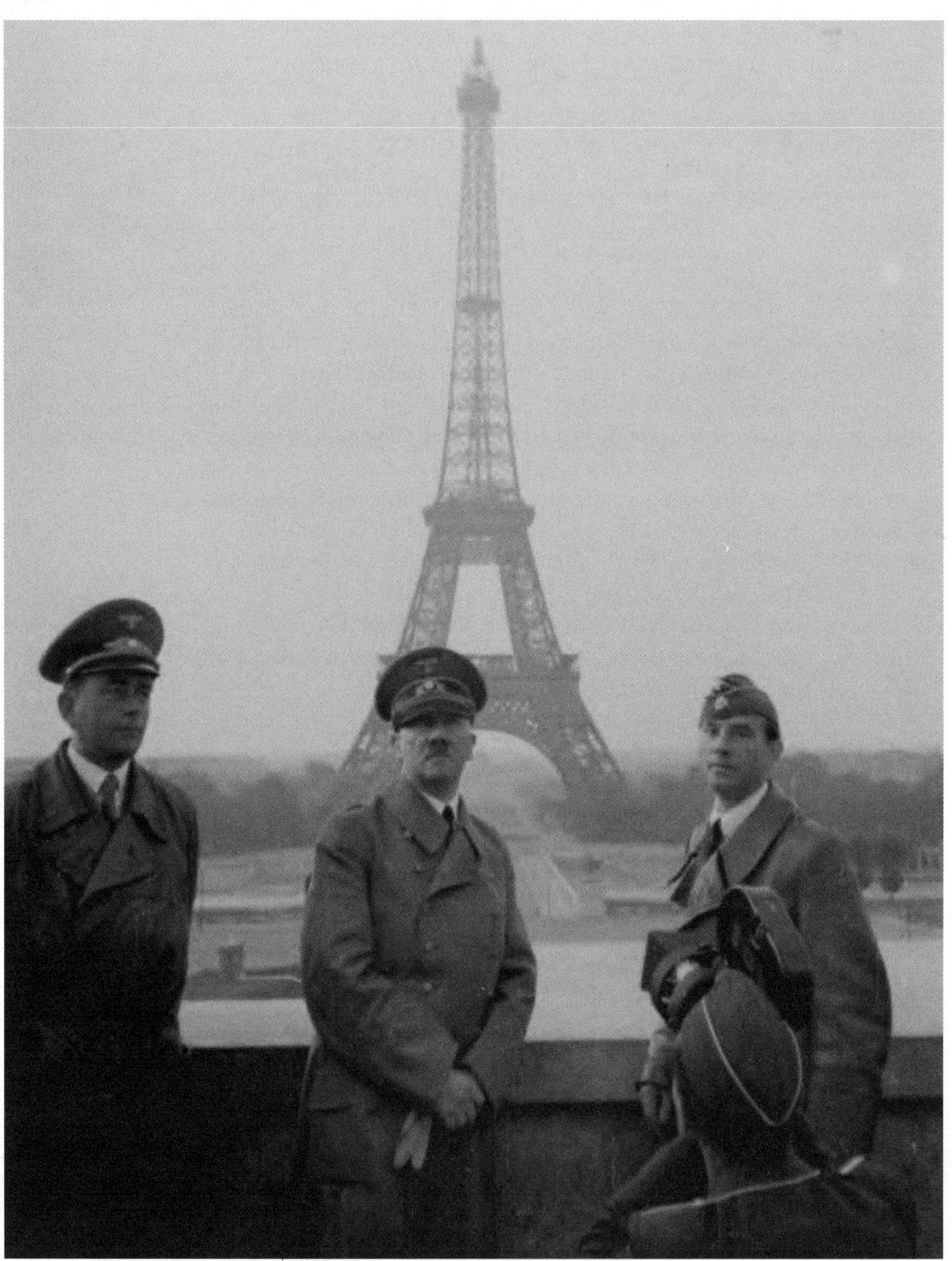

his fellow partisans were soon defeated by the combined firepower of the despised fascists.

In a concluding appeal for help, Fonda looked into the camera and said: "Where can you find peace? The whole country's a battleground. There is no peace. There is no safety for women and children. Schools and hospitals are targets. And this isn't war, not war between soldiers. It's not war, it's murder. It makes no sense. The world can't stop it. Where is the conscience of the world? Where is the conscience of the world?"

When it was released, *Blockade* provoked pickets and boycotts in the United States. The movie became both a touchstone for heated debate and a cautionary message to other filmmakers contemplating war-related movies. But in hindsight, the Spanish Civil War, whether on film or the front pages, gave the world a glimpse of the overwhelming firepower of the Nazis' revolutionary blitzkrieg tactics.

The movie *Arise, My Love* tackled another aspect of the Spanish Civil War, shocking the audience from the start. "The film begins on an overhead shot of a prisoner being led to his execution in a sun-baked courtyard," wrote Kevin Lally in his book, *Wilder Times*. In a nearby cell, captured pilot Tom Martin, played by Ray Milland, is playing cards with a priest. "The guns explode, and the shadow of Tom's dead comrade darkens the ground outside the window. The priest tries to persuade the pilot to repent for shooting down twelve enemy planes in the Spanish Civil War, but Tom's only regret is that he wasted his life 'in some palooka preliminaries in Spain just before Hitler and [Great Britain's Neville] Chamberlain warm up for the main event.'" (*Arise* was written by Austrian exile Billy Wilder, with Charles Brackett.)

In a twist, where real life had an impact on Hollywood, actor Robert Montgomery volunteered to serve as an ambulance driver with the American Field Service in France, until the Nazi occupation. MGM was not very pleased that one of their box office stars was gallivanting overseas, dodging live bullets, instead of playing make-believe in the movies. Montgomery escaped to Spain and Portugal and should have caught the next transport bound for the States, but instead he heard that actress Madeleine Carroll was about to be cornered on the French Riviera, so he dashed off for a hasty rescue mission. Once they both were back in Lisbon, they boarded a ship for America.

(When the Nazi invasion of Poland was announced, on September 1, 1939, Bob Hope and hundreds of others were on the luxury liner *Queen Mary* in the mid-Atlantic. The news unnerved many passengers, so Hope quickly put on a show to calm the jitters. It would be the first of many performances he would do during the war years.)

A year later, America was concerned that Nazi influence was probing into South America, so in early 1941, Navy lieutenant Douglas Fairbanks Jr., who

Opposite: *Despite his demonic tendencies, under his Aryan skin Hitler was also a tourist at heart. After invading France and seizing control, he asked that his photograph be taken with the Eiffel Tower as a backdrop.* National Archives Photo

Right: *Hollywood celebrity-turned-Navy lieutenant Douglas Fairbanks Jr. visited South America on a trip arranged by the U.S. Department of State. Under the auspices of friendship, the actor covertly uncovered plans that the Nazis wanted to use the region as a southern front and exploit the area's natural resources to build their evil empire.*
U.S. Navy Photo

had recently starred in *Gunga Din* and *The Dawn Patrol*, was sent there by the State Department on a supposed "goodwill tour" to clandestinely assess Axis activities in the region. In fact, the Nazis were opening a southern front there, attempting to tap into South America's natural resources. (After WWII, with the fall of the Third Reich, many high-ranking Nazi officials fled Europe to South America and attempted to live there under new identities.)

Nazi U-boats prowling in the Caribbean made it possible to sneak through Allied naval patrols undetected and menace shipping lanes in the region. Wolf Packs also reached the northern waters of Scandinavia and Russia's Bering Sea, further increasing the number of countries wary of the Nazi advances.

After several meetings, Hitler and Italy's Benito Mussolini formed a Pact of Steel that threatened all of Europe. Imperial Japan would later join in to form the Axis powers, with its tentacles reaching into every corner of the Far East and Central Asia.

As Japanese soldiers swept southward through China, they celebrated victory in Singapore.
Japanese Imperial War Museum

Japan didn't need any help from Der Führer or Il Duce in occupying Manchuria, then Southeast Asia, and exploiting its vital resources of rubber, coal, oil, and tin. In fact, by the 1930s Japan's military muscle rivaled Nazi Germany's. Certainly both countries had more seasoned combat units than any other world power, including Great Britain and the United States. They were also modernizing their arsenals of ships, planes, and tanks.

ABOVE: *Japanese troops fought in Shanghai in 1937 as part of the empire's plan to control the continent. Under the plan, Japan invaded Manchuria and swept through China in an attempt to occupy all of Asia. Japan wanted to use each country's manpower for labor and seize control of all natural resources.* National Archives Domei Collection Photo

The Propaganda Merchants

Both Hitler and Mussolini understood the power of propaganda as a way to indoctrinate the masses, instill fear, and incite hatred. Of the two maniacal leaders, Hitler was the undisputed master of manipulation, controlling all aspects of the craft, from posters and literature, music and art, to radio and film.

Even before coming to power, Hitler turned to the film company Fox-Tonende-Wochenschau to document his message. "Millions of Germans would not have heard his hypnotic oratory if Fox's German subsidiary, a weekly newsreel, hadn't disseminated propaganda favorable to Hitler in such short films as *Der Führer* (*The Leader*) and *Hitler's Kampf um Deutschland* (*Hitler's Fight for Germany*)," wrote Hector Arce in the book *The Secret Life of Tyrone Power*. "The Fox subsidiary also loaned sound trucks to the Nazis, so that Hitler could speak to the increasing multitudes." During the weeks leading up to the elections, these newsreels were shown throughout the country, reaching those citizens who couldn't see the rantings of the ex-WWI corporal in person. By coalition government, Hitler would be elected chancellor in 1933.

Leni Riefenstahl had been an actress before her landmark work behind the camera, documenting the Nazis' early days in the hypnotic film, *Triumph of the Will*. Though it would later be labeled one of the era's most blatant examples of propaganda, *Triumph* was filmmaking artistry that would inspire countless directors for decades after.

"Hitler himself had partly designed the 1934 Nuremberg rally as a cinema spectacle. In place of Hollywood's all-talking, all-singing, all-dancing musicals, here was the Nazi equivalent—all-shouting, all-stomping, all-saluting.

Right: *The Nazi mystique was so pervasive in Germany that even children stood awestruck by Hitler and his henchmen. Youngsters, such as this girl, did not understand politics and racism and therefore bought into the Nazis' "Aryan nation" mentality.* British Imperial War Museum Photo

For Hitler knew that potent images and the emotional fury of his speeches had far more power to persuade than any rational argument," wrote Geoff Brown for the book *Movies of the Forties*, a compilation from numerous film aficionados. In the same book, Clyde Jeavons revealed exactly what messages the Nazis were trying to deliver to the masses at every opportunity: "anti-Semitism, Aryan superiority, war heroism, Germany's glorious past, loyalty to the Fatherland and worship of the Führer," all via propaganda newsreels and shorts, typically shown prior to escapist movies.

Riefenstahl never joined the National Socialist Party, yet she was considered a Nazi because of *Triumph of the Will* and her documentary of the 1936 Summer Games in Berlin, titled *Olympia*. This film would be lumped in with other propaganda movies commissioned, controlled, and completed to complement the overriding message, that the Nazis were destined to rule the world because of their Aryan superiority. Riefenstahl never fully understood why *Olympia* would be considered pro-Nazi, stating, "I'm an artist, not a politician. *Olympia* doesn't glorify any one nation. It glorifies the athletic body."

Il Duce's fascination with the movies may have started when he was paid the grand total of two dollars a day as an extra on the set of *The Eternal City* when it was on location in Rome. His propaganda efforts weren't as pervasive as Der Führer's, but it wasn't for lack of trying. "By the mid-'30s, Benito Mussolini looked toward Germany and realized what his fascist regime in Italy was lacking: a propaganda machine," wrote Chris Mashawaty in the article "Cinema's Paradiso" for *Entertainment Weekly*.

"Il Duce dispatched his son to Hollywood to take notes on America's dream factories so he could replicate them in Rome." Within two years the sprawling Cinecitta studios were established over ninety-plus acres near Rome and were cranking out many of Mussolini's pet projects.

Cinecitta would later be seized by the Nazis, bombed by the Allies, and closed down after American forces liberated the country. (In later years many of Hollywood's biggest stars would gravitate to Italy's City of Cinema, including Liz Taylor and Richard Burton, Charlton Heston, and Audrey Hepburn.)

One of Mussolini's film ideas was a depiction of the great Italian master Michelangelo. Hollywood's Jack Warner was contacted by an Italian film associate, who stated that Il Duce would provide a million dollars for the project, if it would be filmed in Italy, on location and at Cinecitta. Warner was interested and even traveled to Italy to research the feasibility of the project. But once there, he was informed that Mussolini would put up only half the amount and expected under-the-table kickbacks for his associates. Warner declined the offer—and lived to tell about it!

Movies Scream to the World

A decade after WWI ended, the classic novel *All Quiet on the Western Front* by German war veteran Erich Maria Remarque was made into a movie by Universal, directed by Lewis Milestone. Released in 1929 and starring Lew Ayres, the film portrayed German teenaged boys who fall for the thrill and glory of war

BELOW: *German storm troopers guard Jewish shops such as this one in April 1933. Nazis allowed no one to shop and Jews were not allowed on the street, meaning they could not work, shop, or socialize outside the home.* Archiv Fur Kunst and Geschichte, Berlin, Photo

RIGHT: *As Paul Baumer, the main character in the film version of* All Quiet on the Western Front, *actor Lew Ayres shows audiences the horrors of trench warfare during World War I. German soldier Erich Maria Remarque penned the book as a protest to the war's bloodshed. Nazis banned most books, and writers such as Remarque sought exile. Remarque, rumored to be a love interest of actress Marlene Dietrich, departed for France. German audiences missed Lewis Milestone's 1929 movie because Nazis thought American soldiers cast as German soldiers symbolized anti-nationalism.* National Film Archives, London, Photo

and volunteer to fight for the Fatherland, then became disillusioned by the reality of battle. Honored with an Oscar for Best Picture, it was dubbed a pacifist film. (Ayres would be so affected by the experience of portraying a soldier in combat that, when hundreds of fellow actors volunteered for military service after the Japanese attacked Pearl Harbor, he declared himself a conscientious objector and suffered the sting of criticism for his decision.)

Another Remarque novel was reworked by F. Scott Fitzgerald, Edward Paramore, and Joe Mankiewicz for the 1938 political tearjerker *Three Comrades*, set between the Great War and the dawn of Nazi Germany.

Like Remarque's *All Quiet on the Western Front*, the 1939 movie *Pastor Hall* portrayed a WWI veteran who saw the horrors of war and turned against it. This film brought to life the story of U-boat captain Martin Niemoller, who became a preacher railing against war and its suffering. "The film vividly illustrated Nazi storm troopers moving into a German village, conducting a campaign of terror, sending Niemoller to a concentration camp," wrote Clayton Koppes and Gregory Black in *Hollywood Goes to War*. The film became a hot potato that no studio would distribute, until the filmmakers added a disclaimer and deleted or toned down several scenes.

Europe was already neck-deep involved with the Nazi juggernaut by the late '30s, while America continued to resist getting involved. But by now much of the Hollywood community was made up of refugees from Germany, and France, Russia, and Poland, and they pushed forward with numerous pro-war, anti-Nazi movies.

The Long Voyage Home, released in 1940, combined four Eugene O'Neill plays and spotlighted the travails of a lone munitions transport running the gauntlet of a Nazi U-boat blockade in the North Atlantic. The movie paralleled the vigilance of Great Britain standing alone without assistance, against enormous odds.

The plight of French POWs under Nazi occupation was captured in Jean Renoir's 1937 classic, *Grand Illusion*. Renoir had fled the Nazi purges of his beloved France and set out to tell the world what was unfolding in his homeland. Alfred Hitchcock turned the autobiography of correspondent Vincent

Sheehan into the Nazi thriller *Foreign Correspondent*, starring Joel McCrea and Laraine Day. The film suggested that spies could be anyone, lurking anywhere. "The final scene is an impassioned radio appeal to America not to turn its head away but to get involved in the soon-to-be universal fight for freedom," wrote John R. Taylor in *Hollywood 1940s*. (It was later rumored that Winston Churchill had personally requested that Hitchcock move to Hollywood to make first-class movies in support of the British war effort.)

The movie's final appeal wasn't just a wake-up call to the United States—it was a sledgehammer: "It's as if the lights were all out everywhere, except in America. Keep those lights burning there! Cover them with steel! Ring them with guns!" shouted Joel McCrea as Vincent Sheehan. "Build a canopy of battleships and bombing planes around them! Hello, America! Hang on to your lights. They're the only lights left in the world."

A more subtle sea tale that still carried an anti-Nazi punch was 1940's *The Sea Hawk,* starring Errol Flynn as a privateer and featuring Queen Elizabeth I issuing the denunciations during the defeat of the Spanish Armada in 1588. Hollywood was still maintaining a neutral stance concerning the conflict in Europe, but this film tilted the scales toward supporting the war effort. An even more blatant period piece was the 1941 pro-British film *That Hamilton Woman*, starring Laurence Olivier as British naval legend Lord Nelson. Some insiders suspected that director Alex Korda, another associate of Winston Churchill's, was dispatched to Hollywood to make the film to curry support for the British war effort.

Hollywood attempted all genres and combinations to deal with the war. Some worked; others failed miserably. *One Night in Lisbon*, released in 1941, was adapted from the play *There's Always Juliet*, about a British lady who acts as a decoy for enemy agents, and starred Madeleine Carroll and Fred MacMurray. "It tried to blend sophisticated romance, wacky comedy, and wartime topicality, and the mix fell pancake flat," wrote John D. Eames in *The Paramount Story*.

Mocking a Maniac

If not for his warped ideas about racial cleansing and living space, Adolf Hitler's theatrical buffoonery might have been laughable. In fact, Hollywood actor Charlie Chaplin pounced on the idea of lampooning Der Führer in the late '30s, and worked on mimicking Hitler's speech patterns and mannerisms. "With *The Great Dictator*, [Chaplin's] worries proliferated along with his ideas," wrote Garson Kanin in his book, *Hollywood*.

"In 1938 to joke about Adolf Hitler was no joke. It was a nervous world in which anything might happen at any given moment. There might come a sudden time when Hitler might prove to be an impossible subject for comedy. There was something magnetic and irresistible about the subject and Chaplin's creative juices were flowing."

Chaplin toyed with developing two similar-looking characters, a tyrannical dictator—Adenoid Hynkel, the diabolical leader of Tomania—and a helpless Jewish laborer, a simple barber. According to Julie Gilbert in the book *Opposite Attraction,* Chaplin explained to director Alexander Korda that he would play both characters. "As Hitler I could harangue the crowds in jargon and talk all I wanted to. And as the tramp I could remain more or less silent. A Hitler story was an opportunity for burlesque and pantomime." But Chaplin was also concerned about giving the Nazi dictator credibility, even while lambasting him. He wavered about doing the film, asking everyone what they thought, to the point of friends' exasperation. Finally, his good friend Douglas Fairbanks set him straight: "You don't have a choice. This is one of the most fortuitous tricks in the history of civilization . . . that the greatest living villain in the world and the greatest comedian should look alike. Now stop asking 'if' and get on with it."

While Chaplin had pinned a bull's-eye on Hitler's chest, he also zinged the other Nazi leaders, creating Dr. Garbitsch (for propaganda minister Joseph Goebbels), Marshall Herring (for Hermann Goering), and Benzino Napaloni, the dictator of Bacteria (for Il Duce, Italy's Benito Mussolini).

Chaplin's soon-to-be ex-wife, Paulette Goddard, would appear in the movie as the village washerwoman, Hannah, representing the downtrodden Jewish masses. (She had lobbied for the role of Scarlet in *Gone with the Wind*, but Chaplin clandestinely pulled strings to prevent her getting that part, freeing her for his project.)

At the end of the film, still very much concerned about how the public might accept (or reject) the movie, Chaplin added a final speech, addressing not only the hope of the world's future, but as a final plea to his lovely wife: "Hannah, can you hear me? Wherever you are, look up! Look up, Hannah! The clouds are lifting! The sun is breaking through! We are coming out of the darkness into the light! We are coming into a new world, a kindlier world, where men will rise above their greed, their hate, and their brutality. Look up, Hannah! The soul of man has been given wings and at last he is beginning to fly. He is flying into the rainbow . . . into the light of hope. Look up, Hannah! Look up!"

The ending seemed spliced on in response to recent events at the time. In fact, Edward G. Robinson explained this problem, common among films, in his autobiography *All My Yesterdays*, cowritten with Leonard Spigelgass: "That is the true dilemma of propaganda in a democracy. The even-handed approach is the only one possible, except that it's impossible in the movies. The time lag alone is against it; it takes a minimum of a year between the assignment of a script and the preview; in that year even-handedness, certainly relevance, can become as old-fashioned as the hoop skirt. Events, unpredictable and catastrophic, can turn a film from a serious investigation of a social phenomenon into a ludicrous farce.

"Take Chaplin's *Dictator*; he started out to make a farce, to show Hitler and Mussolini as idiots. By the time the film was released, Hitler and Mussolini were hardly idiots; rather, they were potential inheritors of the Earth. I've often wondered if Chaplin did not add that last oration, so inconsistent with the rest of the picture, at the last moment."

The film premiered in New York on October 15 of 1940, and was immediately panned. "The public didn't want a serious Chaplin film," wrote Julie Gilbert. "They found it too long, redundant, and pious. They resented being force-fed propaganda at the end when Chaplin as Hitler makes a humanist speech for brotherhood."

Time reviewed the film two weeks later: "*The Great Dictator* is the story of a little, persecuted Jewish barber living in a state ruled by a nasty dictator and how the two finally find their roles reversed. Mr. Chaplin put into it four infallible ingredients: slapstick (Chaplin as a soldier of World War I firing an antiaircraft gun in all heavenly and earthly directions); satire (one magnificent scene in which Dictator Chaplin lifts a globe of the world from a stand and does a bubble dance, exquisite and grotesque); pathos (the homely lives of the Jews in the Ghetto); and melodrama (storm troopers as brutal, a dictator as pathologically ruthless, as human sadism could desire)." The *Time* review considered this jumbled concoction practically impossible to comprehend, though Chaplin considered it a personal triumph.

Another black-humored film in production at the time was *To Be or Not to Be*, starring Jack Benny and Carole Lombard. In the film, Benny and his troupe are performing Hamlet in a theatrical tour of Poland, despite the Nazi occupation. Lombard is having an affair. And all the while she and Benny are sparring with the fascist soldiers.

At the movie's premiere (released only weeks after Lombard was killed in a plane crash), the audience was enjoying the banter until a caustic comment from the character of a Gestapo officer brought reality crashing down. Benny's portrayal of Hamlet was circumspect, and the Nazi quipped, "What he did to Shakespeare we are now doing to Poland." It was a comment that had crossed the line, and from that point, the audience forgot how to laugh for the remainder of the film.

Saboteurs Get Caught

With the large influx of immigrants fleeing Europe, concern grew that some "undesirables" might slip through the screening process and cause problems on behalf of the Axis powers, possibly even receiving orders to sabotage key industries, such as petroleum refineries, ammunition plants, and weapons manufacturers. (It would later be revealed that in fact guidance was passed to

German-American operatives via couriers on transatlantic passenger ships.) Evidence gathered and submitted to the House Un-American Activities Committee (HUAC) revealed that, by 1938, five years after the Nazis came to power, there were in fact 135 subversive or questionable organizations with ties to Germany operating within America's borders. One of the most visible was the German-American Volksbund, most commonly known as simply the Bund, with origins going back to 1924. The Bund had its own newspapers, which provided current information about Germany but also supported and regurgitated Nazi policy. A related, but more militaristic, group was the Ordungs Dienst, or OD.

"Members wore uniforms almost identical to their German counterparts and met for German-style drills each week," reported Kathleen Karr for *WWII History* in September 2002. "The OD denied having any involvement with firearms. However, the need to become familiar with such equipment was easily satisfied through strategies such as setting up target ranges for weekend sporting purposes at Bund camps, hiding rifle ranges on outlying farms, and more significantly, having Bund members join their local National Guard." To further indoctrinate these Bund members into the Nazi way of thinking, key members were allowed to take a "vacation" back to Germany, where they would undergo two months of paramilitary training. One of these key members was Fritz Kuhn, who would head up a youth program in the States and target boys and girls of German heritage to learn how to fire a weapon, operate a shortwave radio, and perform other paramilitary tasks. Kuhn would later be described as the "Führer" of the Bund.

A vast covert network was rapidly building, preparing for the now-inevitable war Hitler was instigating. These un-American groups knew they might play a key role in disrupting U.S. efforts when this country finally joined the fight alongside its ally, Great Britain. By 1938 the network began to unravel, though, and several key leaders ratted out the covert organization

Below: *The American Nazi Party had strong support in 1939, with many German immigrants secretly delivering information to their homeland. From Miami to Maine, German spies used freighter ships to carry messages.* Confessions of a Nazi Spy *chronicles the story of a German immigrant captured as he tried to send messages to the Party. Hans Pogel (center) bore the flag during a Camp Siegfried parade in 1939. This camp and many others across the U.S. attempted to indoctrinate children and teens into the Nazi values.* National Archives Photo

in exchange for lesser sentences. Some fascist leaders beat a hasty retreat to Germany before they could be caught in the ever-widening trap. The unraveling of this clandestine network was played out on the front pages of metropolitan dailies by reporters such as Heywood Broun, and heard every night on the radio by commentators like Walter Winchell, and many other media bloodhounds.

Capitalizing on this groundswell was FBI agent Leon Turrou, who headed up the investigation. His involvement, including his testimony when the case went to trial, led to an offer from the *New York Post* for Turrou to write a book, which went on to become a powerful movie, *Confessions of a Nazi Spy*, produced by Warner Brothers.

"Warner had closed down its German office in 1936 after its local representative, Joe Kaufman, a Jew, had been murdered by Nazi thugs in a Berlin back street," reported Kathleen Karr. "The Warner brothers, also Jewish, had been searching for a suitable property to use as a wake-up call to America."

Once Warner secured the rights to Turrou's book, *Confessions* became a lightning rod. Warner Studios in Hollywood received hate mail, death threats, and unrelenting pressure from pro-fascist groups and individuals to abandon the project, which only reinforced their conviction that Americans had to know just how dangerous the Nazi underground had become in this country. The film was released in April 1939 under tight security, with a blatantly incendiary promotional campaign: "Made behind locked doors because it is the most daringly fearless and breathlessly awaited picture ever to come out of Hollywood!"

Among loyal Americans, the film was a wake-up call to the fascist poison that was infecting all of Europe and spreading to our shores. It became a box-office blockbuster in the States, though there were concerns around the other studios that it would have serious repercussions overseas, most notably in those countries under Nazi control.

"Luigi Luraschi, of Paramount's Censorship Department, wrote that if the film were 'in any way uncomplimentary to Germany, as it must be if it is to be sincerely produced, then Warner will have on their hands the blood of a great many Jews in Germany,'" noted Koppes and Black in *Hollywood Goes to War*. Germany banned the film from all territories under its control. Boldly (some would say foolishly), and despite Nazi occupation of their country, many Polish theater owners attempted to show the film. Those who were caught were hanged and left on display in their own movie houses as a warning to others who attempted to defy the Nazis.

An Unexpected Invasion

Nightly news broadcasts informed listeners of the deteriorating efforts to halt the Nazi advance across Europe. Hitler rebuffed all diplomatic initiatives to abide by the terms of the Versailles Treaty and demobilize his massive war machine. Instead, he directed his forces to prepare for war, to steamroll any neighbor who dared put up any feeble effort to stop what would not be stopped.

The Red Cross heard the rumors of the mass transport of all undesirables to camps in the east, and demanded to inspect these sites. Hitler welcomed the inspectors with open arms, inviting them to tour his showcase village of happy Jewish residents. He wouldn't allow them to visit any of the walled-off ghettos or concentration camps where the true horrors were occurring. European exiles in the States knew the sad truth about what was going on, about a vast network of camps and ghettos meant to contain the Jews, members of their own families. The disheartened exiles huddled around the radio every night and tuned in faithfully, hoping for a glimmer of good news from home. But the news just kept getting worse.

During these dark times, radio remained the primary source of entertainment for the American public, entertaining millions of families every night with adventure serials, comedies, and music showcases. But then on the night of October 30, 1938, during a broadcast of *La Cumparsita* by Ramon Raquello and his orchestra, a CBS announcer broke in with sketchy details about "several explosions of incandescent gas, occurring at regular intervals on the planet Mars." He warned that experts at the Mount Jennings Observatory in Chicago were concerned about the fiery gas spheres rushing toward Earth "with enormous velocity," and "like a jet of blue flame shot from a gun."

Just as abruptly the broadcast returned to the performance, but minutes later the news was worse. A suspected meteorite, like a fireball, had hit the Earth near Grover's Mill, New Jersey. But the meteorite was quickly discovered to be a "metal cylinder"—one containing strange creatures wielding "deathrays." A reporter who was rushed to the location attempted to describe the hideous sight of creatures never before seen on Earth, "wriggling out of the shadow like a gray snake. They look like tentacles to me. It's large as a bear and it glistens like wet leather. But that face. . . . The eyes are black and gleam like a serpent."

State police were dispatched to contain the invaders, but then, "There's a jet of flame . . . and it leaps right at the advancing men. It strikes them head-on! Good Lord, they're turning into flame!" The reporter continued to tell listeners about the spreading inferno, engulfing everything in its path, but then his microphone went dead, and listeners could only imagine what was happening.

The in-studio announcer received an update from the scene and relayed the horrific, unimaginable news to his listeners: "Those strange beings who landed in the Jersey farmlands tonight are the vanguard of an invading army

On October 30, 1938, 23-year-old Orson Welles and his fellow Mercury Theatre actors terrified millions with their loose interpretation of H. G. Wells's War of the Worlds. *Welles placed the story in Grovers Mill, New Jersey, and structured to sound like an orchestral program with interruptions for "breaking news."*

Wells introduced the program by explaining that the story was fiction, but most listeners missed his introduction. War of the Worlds *played opposite the more popular ventriloquist Edgar Bergen and his sidekick, Charlie McCarthy. Bergen held 35 percent of the audience, while Mercury Theatre averaged approximately 4 percent. On any given night, Welles's performance would not have caused such widespread panic. But on this night, Bergen and McCarthy completed their opening jokes and introduced Nelson Eddy, who began singing. Nearly four million listeners turned the radio dial and found themselves listening to CBS coverage of a Martian invasion. They had missed Welles's disclaimer, and by the time the next one came 40 minutes into the show, people across the country had flooded streets, jammed phone lines, and sought hospital treatment for shock.*

What early listeners heard was a "live performance" by the Ramon Raquello Orchestra. An announcer interrupted the band's tango with, "Ladies and gentlemen, we interrupt this broadcast," wording listeners found familiar when breaking news was reported.

The announcer and reporters continued to interrupt with descriptions of an explosion on Mars, testimonies from "eyewitness townspeople" and "astronomers from Princeton Observatory," and strategy discussions by "military men." The interruptions were always followed by the return to the orchestra music.

A 1940 study by Princeton University found that 1.2 million of the 6 million listeners who heard Welles's broadcast panicked and believed the U.S. had been invaded by Martians. Associated Press Photo

from the planet Mars. The battle which took place tonight at Grover's Mill has ended in one of the most startling defeats ever suffered by an army in modern times, seven thousand men armed with rifles and machine guns pitted against a single fighting machine of the invaders from Mars." The monster continued on, cutting communications all along the Eastern Seaboard, ripping up railroad tracks, forcing everyone to flee via clogged roadways. The broadcast cut to an operator in Newark, who gave the ominous warning: "Poisonous black smoke pouring in from Jersey marshes. Gas masks useless. Urge population to move into open spaces. . . ."

Bells and sirens in New York warned of the approaching invaders. Millions were attempting to flee the city. But there was more than just one hulking monster. In fact, there were nineteen, and in the next two days they had made their way to the middle of an eerily deserted New York. A Princeton astronomer, Professor Pierson, was the lone brave soul tracking these creatures to Central Park: "I could see . . . those great metal Titans, their cowls empty, their steel arms hanging listlessly by their sides. I looked in vain for the monsters that inhabit those machines. Suddenly my eyes were attracted to the immense flock of black birds that hovered directly below me. They circled to the ground, and there before my eyes, stark and silent, lay the Martians, with the hungry birds pecking and tearing brown shreds of flesh from their dead bodies. Later, when their bodies were examined in laboratories, it was found that they were killed by the putrefactive and disease bacteria against which their systems were unprepared. . . ." The broadcast concluded with Professor Pierson recalling the haunting events of the last two days, contrasted with the tranquil scene now outside his window.

Radio listeners were mesmerized by the broadcast and truly believed the Mars invasion was unfolding at that very hour. Some—at least, those in the path of the marauding invaders—immediately began boarding up their windows. Thousands fled their homes, certain that to stay would lead to hideous death. But those panicked hordes had missed several telltale clues—why was no other radio network covering the invasion? How could it be happening in real time and then, within the hour, jump forward two full days, as if the events were now over? Most listeners had missed the disclaimer that opened the show and was repeated in the middle, identifying the program as a dramatization of the H. G. Wells story, "War of the Worlds," presented by Orson Welles and the Mercury Theatre (many had probably been turning the dial on their radio, searching for something worthwhile to listen to, and then had become captivated by the sensational news coming from someplace called Grover's Mill in New Jersey.)

Welles and company had intended the show to be a Halloween prank, and in fact, they had scrapped the first version as too dull, and sensationalized the rewrite by moving events to the present tense, changing the location of the invasion from Britain to America's East Coast, adding the news bulletin cut-ins, and including the names of supposedly real people. (CBS censors had ordered minor changes to the script, mostly eliminating the names of some people, including President Roosevelt.) No one felt the broadcast would literally scare the heebie-jeebies out of an entire nation that was hooked on radio for its immediate news.

But within the first half hour, phone lines across the country were jammed as worried listeners called their local newspapers and radio stations to see what the teletypes might be saying (and then they didn't believe the reporters when they said there was no mention of any East Coast invasion, by the Nazis or the Martians), asking the police what they should do, and pleading with their clergy to provide divine intervention. Due to the jammed phone lines, many systems did shut down—including power outages—which only fed the hysteria. Many authorities had no clue what the panic was about, since only CBS was detailing the Martian invasion. But soon, not wishing to be scooped by the competition, other radio stations and newspapers ran with the story, providing their own elaborations.

In Cleveland, radio announcer Jack Paar was monitoring the national broadcast when the phone lines lit up. He attempted to reassure listeners that the broadcast was merely science fiction. " . . . [T]he calls kept pouring in, many of the panicky callers charging that I was covering up the truth," he wrote in his book, *I Kid You Not*. "Finally, I phoned the station manager." But the manager's advice to Paar downplayed the event's urgency: "'Calm down, Jack. You're always so emotional. Just take it easy. It's all a tempest in a teapot.'" Obviously, Paar's boss had no idea what was taking place either in Cleveland or across the country.

The mass exodus from the cities overwhelmed major arteries, creating massive gridlock, which led to paranoia and speculation that it was all caused by the hulking, metal creatures from Mars, rampaging at will, with no possible way to stop them.

Like thousands of others, stage actor John Barrymore was certain Martians were invading, careening down Madison Avenue and cutting off all means of escape from New York. Barrymore rushed outside to a kennel housing his beloved Saint Bernards—twenty in all—and cast open the barrier, pleading for them to "Fend for yourselves!"

In the CBS studio, Welles and company were completely shut off from the chaos they were creating outside, and they continued with the sham. CBS affiliates across the country were fully aware of the havoc, though, and they contacted anyone still at work at CBS New York. After grasping the gravity of the situation, the CBS staffers rushed down to Studio One, barely ahead of policemen storming the building, just as Welles concluded the program with a tongue-in-cheek

BELOW: *Americans like these young Schulstad lads from South Dakota initially thought news reports of the Pearl Harbor attack were a hoax, likening the reports to Orson Welles's* War of the Worlds, *which had frightened Americans with its fictitious accounts of a Martian invasion.* Office of War Information Photo

sign-off, explaining to listeners that his retelling of the Mars invasion had "no further significance than as the holiday offering. It was intended to be the Mercury Theatre's own radio version of dressing up in a sheet and jumping out of a bush and saying *boo!*"

For the next few hours Welles faced a barrage of questioning from the police and the press, and was forced to explain over and over that it was just a radio show—maybe a little over the top, but certainly no harm was intended. He was beginning to wonder if maybe his radio career was ruined, but in fact the nationwide notoriety catapulted him from obscure elitist to media darling overnight. Still, CBS had to do a lot of backpedaling over the next several days, apologizing for the mass panic one of its shows had instigated.

When he was informed about the mock invasion and the resulting panic it caused, Adolf Hitler denounced the silly Americans for their instability and hysterical bent.

A Humble Hero

One movie that screamed the loudest when Europe was boiling over was the anti-war saga, *Sergeant York,* starring Gary Cooper and released in 1941. This tale, about a devout southern gentleman who is forced to make life-and-death decisions in the heat of battle to save his fellow soldiers, was first pitched to the very reluctant doughboy, Alvin York, soon after he returned to his Tennessee home in the Cumberland Mountains. But at that time all this Medal of Honor recipient wanted to do was resume his simple, uncomplicated life, without further fanfare. By 1940 Alvin York had seven children, and was trying to raise enough money to build a Bible school for the region, known as the Valley of the Three Forks of the Wolf. After years of relentless badgering from Hollywood, and with a promise that he would receive more than enough funding to complete the school, York said he would grant permission for the filmmakers to use his story—but only if three conditions were met: The lead actor would be Gary Cooper or no one; York didn't want any "oomphy" starlet to portray his wife; and he wanted the film to be a true depiction, without all the Hollywood glitz. But Gary Cooper had reservations about playing a larger-than-life hero. In his book, *Gary Cooper,* Hector Arce notes that Cooper said, "York himself came to tell me I was his own choice for the role, but I still felt I couldn't handle it. Here was a pious, sincere man, a conscientious objector to war, who, when called, became a heroic fighter for his country. He was too big for me, he covered too much territory."

When Coop was told that York would not agree to have any other actor portray him, and after going back and forth, he took the role, and portrayed York with such simple honesty that he won an Oscar for his subdued portrayal of this true American hero, the most decorated doughboy of WWI. Joan Leslie was chosen to play his wife, and she did so without glamorizing the part.

The film's premiere, at the sprawling Astor Theatre in New York, was a spectacle rivaling all others. "The Astor was adorned with a four-story caricature of Cooper/York in which 15,000 flashing red, white, and blue lights changed from a hillbilly carrying a squirrel gun to a soldier carrying a rifle," wrote Clayton Koppes and Gregory Black in the book *Hollywood Goes to War*. "For the premiere York marched down Broadway, escorted by an honor guard of World War I veterans."

And in its August 4 issue that year, *Time* magazine reported, "*Sergeant York* does not glorify war, does not try to horn in on World War II. It stays scrupulously within the bounds of one man's part in another war. But by showing what he found in the U.S. worth fighting for, it becomes Hollywood's first solid contribution to national defense. Result: one of the cinema's most memorable screen biographies."

LEFT: *World War I Medal of Honor recipient Alvin York's entering into combat paralleled closely the military action in 1917. Neither wanted to fight, both were forced into it, and both had to fight. York, a God-fearing Tennessee farmer, portrayed here by Gary Cooper, reluctantly went into military service. He ended up hunkered down in trenches near the Argonne Forest in 1918. When a German sniper picked off his buddies one by one, York's hand was forced, and he fought back to keep his other friends from dying. He and other American soldiers fought to overrun a German position. In the fighting, York relieved a German officer of his Lugar and single-handedly captured 100 Germans.*

When director Howard Hawks made Sergeant York *in 1941, York did not want to help with the film unless three demands were met: (1) his portion of the profits would be donated to construct a Bible school York wanted built; (2) an actress who smoked cigarettes could not play his wife; and (3) only actor Gary Cooper could portray York in the movie. While producers complied easily with the first two conditions, York himself had to plead with Cooper to play the role. The movie was distributed five months before the Japanese attack on Pearl Harbor. Vice Admiral "Bull" Halsey showed sailors aboard his* Enterprise *the film as the aircraft carrier made its journey back to Pearl Harbor later on December 7.*

Cooper later performed in USO shows, but audiences best remember him for his Pride of the Yankees *role as Lou Gehrig.* National Film Archives, London, Photo

The film's relevancy to America's own soul-searching at this time of uncertainty is further described in John Belton's *American Cinema/American Culture*: " . . . as world events slowly converted America to a wartime mentality, Hollywood served as a tool of anti-fascist filmmakers and the Roosevelt administration for the reeducation of an isolationist and pacifist populace into reluctant warriors." Belton continued, "The conversion that takes place in *Sergeant York* of the born-again Christian Alvin York from a conscientious objector into a patriotic soldier serves as apt metaphor for the film industry's project during the months immediately preceding American entry into the war; Americans are, like York, uncertain about war."

On the Eve of War

Under Lend Lease agreements with Great Britain and China, the United States sent planes, ships, supplies, and munitions to both countries to help in their fights against Germany and Japan, respectively. The States sent additional outdated warships and aircraft to Australia and New Zealand to blunt Japanese expansion into Indonesia and the southern territories. This commitment was meant as a show of support for America's allies, allowing the country to delay direct involvement in overseas confrontations that had been raging since the mid-'30s.

Many British stars who had moved to Hollywood were now torn emotionally. They saw the huge influx of refugees from Europe, a creative tidal wave of writers, directors, artists, actors, and actresses all trying to remain active in a business constricted or closed down altogether by the Nazis back home.

In fact, as Britain braced for war, it sent out a worldwide appeal for all able-bodied men to return home and rally around the Union Jack. Actors David Niven and Leslie Howard departed the glitz and glamour of Hollywood, despite uncertainty about what they would face back home. (Leslie Howard would not survive the war; he was killed when his passenger plane was shot down by German fighters. David Niven joined the Rifle Brigade and eventually was a lieutenant colonel in the British Commandos. He later returned to Hollywood and spent thirty years as a leading man.)

Many British actresses also wanted to do something to support the war effort. Joan Fontaine led efforts to raise funds and collected materiel goods in Los Angeles under the Bundles for Britain and Thumbs Up programs. "I joined a group of women mobilized into sewing units, making endless shirts, mufflers and mittens," Fontaine recalled in her book, *No Bed of Roses.* She joked, "The pajamas I sewed would have crippled the wearers long before they ever walked through a minefield."

The chief concern of European immigrants was for their family and friends still in danger back home. They did whatever they could, sending clothes and money (for passports, tickets, and bribing officials), writing letters, urging everyone to leave as soon as possible before it was impossible to leave. In Washington, D.C., the federal government was tracking the day-today activities of the Axis powers and seeing all diplomatic efforts deteriorate, leaving limited options for turning back the tide. Many politicians wanted to stay out of the war, preaching isolationism—the war was a European problem. Others felt we needed to stand beside our British brothers-in-arms and stamp out the fascists before they infected our own country.

People were also deeply concerned about Japan's aggressive maneuvering in the Far East. Soon Japan's expansion would have to be stopped too, if not through diplomacy, then with armed force.

Japan's military commanders knew that if they truly wanted full control of all of Asia and every island chain in the Pacific, they would have to eliminate any foreign opposition in the region, and that meant the inevitable confrontation and destruction of the U.S. Pacific Fleet. The Japanese made plans to take on the U.S. armada when it was most vulnerable—in port, nestled among the volcanic mountains of the Hawaiian Islands, at Pearl Harbor.

3. A Despicable Act

"TO THROW BOMBS FROM AN AIRPLANE WILL DO AS MUCH DAMAGE AS THROWING BAGS OF FLOUR. IT WILL BE MY PLEASURE TO STAND ON THE BRIDGE OF ANY SHIP WHILE IT IS ATTACKED BY AIRPLANES."

— *Newton Baker, U.S. Defense chief, 1921*

OPPOSITE: *President Franklin Delano Roosevelt signed the declaration of war against Japan on December 8, 1941, the day after the vicious attack on Pearl Harbor. Although the U.S. had taken an isolationist stance when war broke out around the world, the "day that will live in infamy" thrust Americans into battle.*
National Archives Photo

BY LATE 1941, NAZI BUZZ BOMBS AND NIGHTLY BOMBING raids were devastating London and demoralizing its citizenry huddled in underground shelters. Germany was already infecting large territories of occupied Europe with its poisonous propaganda about racial purity and expanded living space, intent on creating Hitler's Thousand-Year Reich populated by blue-eyed, blond-haired Aryans. (Has anyone ever wondered what Aryan trait Adolf Hitler possessed, if any?)

In the Far East, news of the savagery of Japanese soldiers was filtering out of Manchuria and China proper. Japan was looking to exploit other countries in the region, knowing it could take what it wanted with little or no opposition.

Both Axis powers had naval armadas powerful enough to cripple shipping lanes in the Atlantic and Pacific, hamper any Allied movement by sea, and thus threaten America's shores, in essence isolating the isolationists. The power brokers and military strategists in Washington knew that a confrontation was brewing, but at the time the major threat appeared to be Nazi Germany, which was already menacing Allied ships in the North Atlantic. The United States rushed aid, which included antiquated transport ships, planes, supplies, and munitions, to Great Britain. Many of those transport ships were manned by American privateers with the Merchant Marines or sailors of the Navy Armed Guard, braving the treacherous waters where Nazi U-boats sought out easy targets. Many seamen perished delivering goods and armaments to Great Britain. They were some of the first Americans to be killed during WWII, months before the United States was finally and officially dragged into the fight. Hundreds of other Americans also rushed to the British Isles and signed on with one of the armed services there, including the Eagle Squadron of the Royal Air Force.

RIGHT: *Newspapers from Connecticut to this one in Redding, California, published extra editions in the days following the Japanese attack on Pearl Harbor. Newsboys hawked papers on most streets, as Americans sought every detail of the December 7 assault and its aftermath. With only newspaper accounts and radio reports, the public hungered for facts and had a nearly insatiable appetite for news.*
Office of War Information Photo

Preparing to Defeat the "Barbarians"

As early as 1927, Prime Minister Giichi Tanaka of Imperial Japan held a conference in Tokyo to formulate the exploitation of the entire Pacific. The meeting's innocuous-sounding title: the Greater East Asia Co-Prosperity Sphere. The Tanaka Memorial was created from that meeting, and stated, "In Japan her food supply and raw materials decrease in proportion to her population. If we merely hope to develop trade, we shall eventually be defeated by England and America, who possess unsurpassable capitalistic power."

"The Tanaka Memorial, first published and revealed to the world in 1929 by the Chinese, may well have been, as charged by the Japanese, a clever forgery," reported Louis Snyder in his book, *The War: A Concise History, 1939–1945*.

During the next ten years the relationship between Japan and the United States deteriorated beyond repair. After Japan invaded Manchuria, and after all diplomatic pressure was rebuffed, the U.S. dropped the 1911 trade agreement with Tokyo in 1939. The next year, Japan's financial assets in the United States were frozen; then FDR halted the export of critical machinery and materials to Japan.

RIGHT: *Bleary-eyed sailors gather around a radio to listen to President Franklin Delano Roosevelt declare war on Japan. FDR's declaration hit airwaves at 11 A.M. on the East Coast, but Americans in every time zone stopped what they were doing—even sleeping—to listen to the President.*
National Archive Photo

The belligerents in Japan saw these moves as grounds for war, and when Crown Prince Konoye continued to press for a diplomatic solution, his senior military adviser, General Hideki Tojo, stressed that a confrontation with the United States was inevitable. Tojo ordered all military forces to prepare for battle immediately.

In 1940 an "Export Control Act authorized President Roosevelt to regulate or interdict the export to Japan of machine tools, chemicals, and strategic materials," Snyder continued. "A blockade established by the ABCD powers [America, Britain, China, and the Dutch East Indies] soon cut off some 75 percent of imports into Japan." If the blockade had been allowed to continue, Japan's military muscle would be standing still without petroleum and rubber from Indonesia or the scrap metal bought up in recent years from the United States to be melted down for new tanks, planes, and warships.

Japan secretly declared war and made plans to cripple the United States naval forces at Pearl Harbor with overwhelming firepower. Heading up the plan was the chief of the Imperial Japanese Navy, Admiral Isoroku Yamamoto, who "had an intense hatred for America and the West," wrote Snyder in *The War*. "It was said that he imbibed this resentment from his father, who told him bedtime stories of 'the barbarians who came in their black ships, broke down the doors of Japan, threatened the Son of Heaven, and trampled on the ancient customs.'"

Despite the escalating rumble of war clouds in the Pacific, Asian "authorities" in the United States downplayed the threat. Noted writer Bennett Cerf recalled the hazards of preparing a weekly publication in the midst of this simmering crisis: "One of our best-known magazines appeared with a lead article designed to prove that Hawaii never could be attacked successfully," Cerf wrote in his book, *Good for a Laugh*. "Another periodical was featuring a piece by an 'expert' who proved conclusively that the Japs were worthless as air fighters because their planes were antiquated puddle-jumpers, their pilots were cockeyed, and their bombs were duds."

After several weeks of training at Tankan Bay in the Kurile Islands—selected for its resemblance to Pearl Harbor and its surrounding mountains—conducting mock bombing runs on scale models of the American warships of the Pacific Fleet, the Japanese armada—with its "antiquated planes and cockeyed pilots"—was ready to unleash its fury. The attack was planned for a lazy Sunday morning in December of 1941, when a lot of servicemen there would either be on shore leave, hungover, sleeping in, or a combination of the three. The last thing they would expect was the last moment of their life.

Heading toward the Hawaiian Islands in the central Pacific was a tidal wave of Japanese warships, including six aircraft carriers and sixty-six escorts, which included battleships, cruisers, submarines, and support vessels, plus more than four hundred aircraft aboard the flattops.

Battle in the Islands Starts Early

Saturday night in Honolulu was hopping, especially at the naval station's Bloch Arena, packed with servicemen from around the islands and local girls, all of them looking for a great time. The Navy's "Battle of Music" pitted the musicians from the battleships *Pennsylvania* and *Tennessee* and the auxiliary ship *Argonne,* named for the campaign that ended WWI, the Meuse-Argonne. (A fourth band, from the USS *Detroit,* couldn't compete that night because they were at sea.)

Each band played a variety of tunes in the elimination tournament—ballad, swing, and a specialty piece, their own secret weapon with which to dazzle the crowd and impress the judges. A jitterbug contest pumped up the sexual energy and kept the crowd interested. The combo from the *Penn* captured the honors for the evening and taunted their next "victims," the powerful musicians from the warship *Arizona,* who were looking on, checking out the competition. (The two bands were slated to go at it a week later, on December 13, for bragging rights as top band in the Pacific Fleet.)

The twenty-one musicians of the USS *Arizona* band were typical of others in the Fleet. Most of the members had been together less than six months, after graduating from the Navy School of Music in May, traveling to Hawaii, and getting assigned to the battleship a month later. They knew all the military and patriotic marches, but they really enjoyed playing the most popular big band tunes of the day, including those recorded by Glenn Miller, Tommy and Jimmy Dorsey, Count Basie, Duke Ellington, and Artie Shaw. For the weekly battle of the bands at Pearl, all of the Navy combos sizzled and had the audience jumping.

The *Arizona* hep cats had their own nicknames, much like the big boys back home. Bill "Killer" Morehouse was on trumpet, Alexander "the Swooze" was next to him trading off horn licks, Nadel Harry "The Mad Russian" Chernucha played clarinet and sax, as did Frank "Flat-Foot Floogie" Floege, and Wendell "Lady Killer" Hurley was also on clarinet. They all had monikers and reputations, too, and could often be found at one of Honolulu's night spots, jamming with other musicians assigned to this Pacific paradise.

Promptly at midnight on December 6, the national anthem was played in the Arena and in every bar and nightclub in Honolulu, and somehow even the drunkest of servicemen staggered to attention, then promptly dashed off to any available taxi or bus or hoofed it or hitched back to their ships. Airmen returned to one of the various bases surrounding Pearl, while soldiers headed back to Schofield Barracks next to Wheeler Air Field. After packing up their instruments, the musicians from the *Pennsylvania* headed back to Pearl for a few hours of shut-eye. All of the Fleet's capitol ships had their own bands, and they had to be up at "oh-dark thirty" and assembled on deck for Morning Colors.

Honolulu Radio station KGMB normally signed off at midnight, but had been instructed to play Hawaiian music through the night as a homing beacon for the incoming flight of aircraft. On board those planes, radio operators scanned the frequencies for any message traffic, searching for the well-known hula music of Hawaii. Some weren't exactly sure what that really sounded like.

Sunday Morning Calm Explodes into Chaos

The Army's radar site at Kahuku Point on the northern tip of Oahu detected a large blip on the screen more than one hundred miles away early that Sunday morning, but the two soldiers monitoring the screen were told not to be concerned, because a flight of B-17 Flying Fortresses from California's Hamilton Field were in-bound. The radar watchers tracked the blip as it continued on from the northwest, assuming it was the heavy bombers that would soon be landing at Hickam Field. At daybreak they shut down the radar site and headed back for a few hours of sack time.

But at 7:55 that morning, the worst of all nightmares began to unfold, as the incoming flight of planes wasn't the expected American bombers, but the first wave of Japanese attackers, which splintered into separate groups, then dropped down to hug the horizon. The swarm of 183 enemy planes converged on the neatly arrayed Battleship Row at Pearl Harbor, and the planes lined up at nearby Hickam and Wheeler airfields, appearing from out of the clouds over Diamond Head just as hundreds of sailors stood at attention on the decks of the *Arizona,* and the *Nevada,* the *Pennsylvania,* and many other ships for the playing of the national anthem. Others were attending sunrise services dockside and on the beach.

Before the bands could finish the anthem, torpedo bombers swooped in and released their deadly "fish," which churned through the water toward the unsuspecting American warships. Dive-bombers broke through the clouds and swooped down on their targets, without any opposition from anti-aircraft guns. Even after the first explosions, some Americans still thought it was just a drill—odd for a Sunday morning, but what else could it be? It wasn't until the stunned sailors spotted the large red "meatball" on the sides and the wings of the enemy planes, and heard the explosions all around them, and felt the heat of hell erupting, that they scrambled to their battle stations.

For the musicians on the *Arizona,* their task was not to jump overboard and swim to safety, but to dash belowdecks to the ammunition magazine and haul the gunpowder bags and 14-inch shells and other armaments to the gun crews now trying desperately to defend their ship. Some of the musicians never got to their post below the second gun turret before the *Arizona* was ripped apart by a spread of torpedoes and bombs. The most devastating blow was an armor-piercing shell that penetrated belowdecks and exploded in the

ammo hold, setting off all of the ordnance and instantly killing everyone, including every one of the *Arizona*'s band members. All told, more than 1,100 sailors and Marines on board the mighty warship perished that morning, many of them trapped belowdecks, unable to escape the rush of water pouring in.

Other vignettes of service musicians caught up in the maelstrom at Pearl Harbor were described in "World War II Plus 55" by David H. Lippman: "On *West Virginia* Marine Corps Field Musician Dick Fiske blows General Quarters into the loudspeaker. On USS *Maryland* the bugler tries to do the same, but the officer of the deck, finding the bugle too make-believe, tosses the trumpet into the harbor and yells into the mike instead.

"A *Nevada* bandsman, manning his anti-aircraft gun, puts his trumpet to even worse use . . . he loads it accidentally into the gun and shoots it at the Japanese. At Schofield Barracks, bugler Frank Gobeo can't even remember the call for Stand To, so he blows Pay Call instead, which brings the men hustling out of the barracks." Those soldiers scrambled outside and saw off in the distance billowing black clouds of smoke, fiery explosions, and those damnable Japanese planes, some hugging the horizon, others diving at steep angles, seemingly taking turns and picking out their targets at will. It all played out like a well-choreographed action film, but one with horrible consequences.

Army soldiers at Schofield Barracks scrambled into combat gear, dispatched to lookout points across the island, watching for an anticipated invasion force of Japanese assault troops. Army doctors and medics braced for the influx of wounded servicemen. Still other GIs—firefighters, stretcher-bearers, welders, traffic control—helped out as needed, some for several days with very little or no sleep.

Certainly there were countless acts of heroism and tales of sorrow at Pearl Harbor, not for just the musicians and entertainers stationed there, and every one is worth remembering and retelling.

It took barely an hour for the Japanese attackers to lay waste to America's naval armada in the Pacific, which could have been much worse if the Japanese had launched a third wave of attacks as planned, but they withdrew to safer waters. The toll was devastating enough: 18 warships sunk or severely crippled, 188 fighter and bomber planes destroyed, with another 159 damaged. Of the 2,400 service members killed, nearly half were lost on the *Arizona*, with more than a thousand injured, plus another thousand missing. Amidst the carnage and the death toll, there was a bit of good news for the U.S. Pacific Fleet: the Japanese had failed to damage or destroy any of their primary targets, the elusive and prized aircraft carriers, those crown jewels of every naval battle group. America's two ladies of the sea—the *Sara* and the Lady *Lex* (the *Saratoga* and *Lexington*)—were deployed, while the Big E (the *Enterprise*) had left Hawaii a week earlier to dispatch Marine Fighter

OPPOSITE: *Japanese bombers hit Pearl Harbor's Naval Air Station as well as battleships and destroyers at dock. Radar operators spotted a large "blip" headed toward Hawaii from more than 100 miles away, but attributed it to 16 American B-17 Flying Fortress bombers that were heading to Hickam Field from Hamilton Field in California as the Japanese arrived. These American planes, however, carried no bombs or guns, as they were coming in from the West Coast. Most made emergency landings at alternate airfields, lacking the fuel to return to the mainland. The movie* Air Force *depicts the attack on Hawaii, one of the first non-documentaries on the subject.* National Archives Photo

Right: *The USS* California *billowed dark, oily smoke after being bombarded with Japanese explosives. The* California *was one of six ships that did not sink but was refurbished and re-commissioned. Only the USS* Oklahoma *(to the* California*'s extreme right) and the USS* Arizona *sank and failed to return to service. Many sailors died aboard the* Arizona *because they were belowdecks. The ship's band serves as a good example (all large vessels had their own bands). Every Sunday morning the sailors gathered on deck, and the band played "The Star Spangled Banner." As band members played on December 7, they saw the planes and sped up the tempo. Once finished, they put aside their instruments and raced belowdecks to haul gunpowder, shells, and other ammunition to the gun crews in the turrets. All band members on the* Arizona *died when bombs and torpedoes struck, including one that hit belowdecks and broke through the ship's ammunition storehouse and set off all the ordnance.* Office of War Information Photo

Squadron 221 to Wake Island before returning home. The Big E and its escorts pulled into Pearl midmorning of the following day, the crews solemnly surveying the smoldering rubble of what used to be Battleship Row. The light cruiser *Northampton* was part of the *Enterprise* task force that arrived at Pearl the day after. On board was an eighteen-year-old radio operator, Jason Robards, about to be thrown into the thick of naval engagements in the Pacific Campaign. Like every service member headed into combat during the war, Robards would put his future plans on hold, unsure if he would ever make it home again.

After seeing the carnage at Pearl, Admiral William "Bull" Halsey on the mighty *Enterprise* made a promise echoed by millions of Americans: "When this war is over, the Japanese language will be spoken only in hell."

Americans Hear the Unbelievable

News about the attack in Hawaii hit around midafternoon in Washington, D.C. Flash reports from Pearl were sent to the War Department. Within

Left: *Japanese planes hit eight battleships, including the USS* Tennessee *and the USS* West Virginia, *shown here, taking them out of commission. The squadron under the command of Japanese Admiral Chuichi Nagumo also attacked hundreds of other naval vessels, such as destroyers, cruisers, and smaller craft. The attack fell short of its goals, however, as no U.S. aircraft carriers docked at Pearl Harbor, and their location at sea spared thousands of other lives and numerous aircraft.* U.S. Navy Photo

minutes, concerts and movies, afternoon socials, church services, and sporting events were interrupted as government leaders and all essential military personnel were summoned back to work immediately.

Onlookers could sense something serious was happening as they watched countless others rushing out to who knows where, but no one could or would provide any information. Hasty phone calls were made to newspapers, to radio stations, to home. Reporters and broadcasters checked the teletypes clattering from wire service reports, with sketchy details and unconfirmed reports of hundreds of casualties and the entire Pacific Fleet wiped out and . . . "where the hell is Pearl Harbor?"

Radio stations interrupted their regular programming—Sunday religious service and mellow music for prayer and meditation—to break the news. But millions of listeners remained skeptical. They weren't about to be fooled again by another of Orson Welles's black-humored pranks, about invasions and Armageddon and "how long would it take them slant-eyed bastards to get to California if it was an invasion?"

Jack Paar had been a budding comic while working at a radio station in Cleveland the night Orson Welles scared the bejesus out of the entire country with his "War of the Worlds" broadcast. "I began picking up phones and telling the alarmed listeners that the invasion was fictional," Paar recalled in his book, *I Kid You Not*. "I also broke into the program to announce this, but the calls kept pouring in, many of the panicky callers charging that I was covering up the truth."

Two years later, Paar had the misfortune of being on duty that Sunday night when "again fragmentary reports began coming in on the network

Right: *While one squadron attacked Hawaii, other bombers and fighter planes hit American bases in the Philippines. Blasts took out American Air Force assets, leaving troops without air cover. When fighting broke out on the ground, Coast Guard sailors suddenly became infantrymen. Japanese soldiers celebrated the fall of the Philippines in 1942.*
U.S. Army Photo

about a mysterious attack—this time on a place called Pearl Harbor. The first reports were sketchy and again the station switchboard lit up with listeners asking about the attack." Paar even called the station manager and informed him of the situation. "'All hell is breaking loose. The network is broadcasting about an attack on a place called Pearl Harbor.'

"'Oh no, Paar,' the manager sighed. 'Not again. You're always so panicky. What is this . . . another Man from Mars attack?'"

"In Topeka they were listening to 'The Spirit of '41' and napping on their sofas after dinner," reported *Time*. "In San Francisco they were listening to the news, the Philharmonic and 'Strings in Swingtime.'"

But as the disbelievers frantically flipped the dial on their Philcos from one radio station to the next, and all of them were broadcasting the same horrible news, and the reality hit like a sucker-punch to the gut. Just as quickly, that disbelief turned to white-hot rage.

Anthony Dominick Benedetto was at a family get-together that Sunday afternoon. On the way home, "we heard the newsboys in the street shouting, 'Extra! Extra!' The big news was that some place we'd never heard of—Pearl Harbor—had been attacked by the Japanese. One minute it was a peaceful Sunday afternoon, and the next we were at war." (Anthony Benedetto would soon join the Army, be discovered as a singer, and perform for his fellow soldiers on stage and on the radio, eventually changing his name to Tony Bennett.)

Hollywood starlet Shelley Schrift wrote in her autobiography, *Shelley*: "I was sitting in front of our Philco when suddenly the Sunday opera was interrupted by the announcer. Japanese planes had attacked Pearl Harbor and wiped out our fleet. Everyone came running in from various parts of the house, and we stared at each other in stunned disbelief. America had always seemed so strong and invulnerable; how could anyone do that to her? And why were most of our warships in Hawaii?" That same afternoon, her fiancé, Paul Miller, joined the Army Air Corps. (On New Year's Day of '42 they got married. Shelley Winters, the new bride, wrote about honeymooning in Brooklyn: "What I remember most is holding Paul in my arms and knowing he was scared, yet he had to be a pilot and avenge Pearl Harbor and the concentration camps we were hearing about.")

Lana Turner had recently signed a new contract with MGM and bought a house in the hills overlooking Los Angeles. That Sunday afternoon she hosted a party that included her close friends, Susan Hayward and Linda Darnell, and musicians Buddy Rich and Tommy Dorsey. Her mother stopped by and was shocked that the group hadn't heard the news about Pearl Harbor. "During that whole fun-filled afternoon we hadn't had an inkling that the country was about to go to war," Lana wrote in her memoir. "I got the musicians quieted down and turned on the news. As we listened I looked around at the stunned young men in my living room, and thought how drastically our lives were going to change."

The Andrews Sisters—Patty, Laverne, and Maxine—were in Cincinnati on December 7, slated to give a concert that night. Typically, people would be lined up for hours for one of their shows, and, according to advance sales, Cincinnati would also have been a packed house. "It didn't matter how cold it was or how high the snow, people [would be] lined up for blocks," Maxine told Studs Terkel for his book, *The Good War*. "This Sunday morning, I walked over and there were no lines. I thought, now, this is funny. I walked onto the stage, which was very dark. The doorman and the stagehands were sitting around the radio. They had just one light on. They were talking about Pearl Harbor being bombed. I asked the doorman, 'Where is Pearl Harbor?'"

With continuous updates overloading newsroom teletype machines, radio stations stayed on all through the night, broadcasting live concerts of well-known big bands. One of those was Stan Kenton's, playing at the Hollywood Palladium. "Because we were the last in the time belts, we were the only ones still playing when the New York and Chicago bands were finished. So sometimes we'd be on three networks at once," Kenton remembered.

Hollywood star Buddy Ebsen had been sailing with a close friend in Santa Monica Bay that Sunday afternoon when a Coast Guardsman waved them in and cautioned them not to pick up any Japanese fishermen or tourists. That's when they found out about the attack on Pearl and that there was concern about an invasion of the West Coast. The next morning Ebsen trooped down to the Navy Armory and volunteered his boat and his services as a coast watcher. He even suggested that the Navy could outfit the vessel with a deck gun and depth charges to ward off enemy submarines. The Navy politely rejected his bold offer.

That Monday morning the prevailing anger had turned to action, as hundreds of thousands of American men lined up outside armed forces recruiting offices across the country, intent on some heavy-duty payback. They signed on "for the duration." No one knew for certain how long that might be.

Reaction Overseas

In Tokyo the masses took to the streets and cheered when Prime Minister Hideki Tojo announced the attack, but with a cautionary tone: "The West has been trying to dominate the world. To annihilate the enemy and to establish a new order in East Asia, Japan must anticipate a long war. The hundred million people of the Japanese Empire must pledge all of their energies, their lives, to the state."

Japanese actor Sessue Hayakawa wasn't quite as confident as his fellow countrymen. He was on location in Paris when the news broke, and he decided just to lay low with his French lover until the war was over, unsure of how the conflict would turn out. (His wife endured the hardships of the war in Tokyo and would not hear from him until five years later, when he nonchalantly returned home in 1946.)

Japan's Foreign Office exaggerated the attack via the *Times* and *Advertiser*, trumpeting, "'U.S. Pacific Fleet is wiped out!' The paper asserted that Japan had reduced the United States to a third-class power overnight," wrote Louis Snyder in *The War*. "Adolf Hitler went into one of his rare

moments of euphoria when he heard the news from Pearl Harbor. To the Reichstag Hitler proclaimed: 'A historical revision of unique scope has been entrusted to us by the Creator.' He went on to denounce 'the unholy trinity of capitalism, Bolshevism and Jewry.' He was elated at Japan's bold move, stating, "We now have an ally who has never been vanquished in 3,000 years. Now it is impossible for us to lose the war." While Japan claimed to have reduced the United States to "a third-class power overnight," Hitler joked that the only thing America was capable of doing well was producing chewing gum, razor blades, and Hollywood starlets.

When war-weary Britons heard the news of the attack at Pearl Harbor they knew it would finally drag a reluctant America into the fight. Winston Churchill addressed Parliament soon after: "Now that the issue is joined and in the most direct manner, it only remains for the two great democracies to face their task with whatever

ABOVE: *Sailors laid wreaths on the graves of shipmates who died at Pearl Harbor. The Japanese attack killed nearly 3,000 people, many of them on the USS* Arizona. *Most of the* Arizona *dead lay entombed there today. The Japanese strike was ill timed; because the attack occurred on a Sunday morning, many sailors had not reported back to their ships after having had a weekend pass or Saturday night liberty. Had the Japanese launched an attack on a weekday, more sailors would have met a fiery, watery grave.*
National Archives Photo

strength God may give them. It is of the highest importance that there should be no underrating of the gravity of the new dangers we have to meet, either here or in the United States.

"We have at least four-fifths of the population of the globe upon our side. We are responsible for their safety and for their future. In the past we have had a light which flickered, in the present we have a light which flames, and in the future there will be a light which shines over all the land and sea."

FDR Talks to the Country

The day after the attack, President Roosevelt issued his Day of Infamy speech. Two days later he spoke to the country in a radio address from the White House. After recapping the escalating provocations by all three Axis powers—Germany, Italy, and Japan—he stated with full candor, "We are now in this war. We are all in it all the way. Every single man, woman, and child is a partner in the most tremendous undertaking of our American history. We must share together the bad news and the good news, the defeats and the victories, the changing fortunes of war."

Roosevelt explained what would be required of the country during the coming years: "In these past few years and, most violently, in the past few days we have learned a terrible lesson. It is our obligation to our dead, it is our sacred obligation to their children and our children that we must never forget what we have learned. And what we all have learned is this: There is no such thing as security for any nation or any individual in a world ruled by the principles of gangsterism. There is no such thing as impregnable defense against powerful aggressors who sneak up in the dark and strike without warning. We may acknowledge that our enemies have performed a brilliant feat of deception, perfectly timed and executed with great skill. It was a thoroughly dishonorable deed, but we must face the fact that modern warfare as conducted in the Nazi manner is a dirty business. We don't like it, we didn't want to get in it, but we are in it, and we're going to fight it with everything we've got."

Roosevelt wanted everyone to understand that the entire free world was now looking to the United States to right the wrongs of the belligerents: "We are now in the midst of a war, not for conquest, not for vengeance, but for a world in which this Nation, and all that this Nation represents, will be safe for our children. We expect to eliminate the danger from Japan, but it would serve us ill if we accomplished that and found that the rest of the world was dominated by Hitler and Mussolini. We are going to win the war, and we are going to win the peace that follows."

In Hollywood, the cast and crew had just arrived for the first day of filming the movie *Yankee Doodle Dandy,* starring Jimmy Cagney. Decked out in makeup and costumes, they listened to the radio, stunned as President

Left: *Rather than begin production for* Yankee Doodle Dandy, *film star James Cagney called together the cast when he heard President Franklin D. Roosevelt declare war on Japan. Standing together in full costume and makeup, the actors and actresses prayed before director Michael Curtiz cheered them on to "make a really wonderful picture."*
Associated Press Photo

Roosevelt declared war on Japan. Many cried and weren't sure if it was appropriate to work that day. Cagney pulled the cast together and announced, "It seems to me, this is the time for a prayer." Then director Michael Curtiz rallied everyone, saying, "All right now, let's go to work and make a really wonderful picture."

Three days after the news hit the States, the Texaco Star Theatre altered its normal Wednesday night broadcast, which usually opened with fire alarms and sirens. After the attack on Pearl, the producers felt the startling opening might cause alarm among already-on-edge listeners.

Hollywood Takes on Pearl Harbor

Japan's sneak attack on the Pacific Fleet was labeled everything from underhanded, evil, and duplicitous to sheer cowardice. The gloves were off, and, as thousands of Americans joined the military, remembering the heroes of Pearl Harbor, the film community swung into action, with portrayals of the Japanese that reeked of racism. For example, in a poster for the 1942 movie *Menace of the Rising Sun*, "a huge Japanese figure, blood dripping from its buck-toothed fangs, rose from the sea. His octopus tentacles swatted

American planes from midair and crushed American ships on the high seas," wrote Clayton Koppes and Gregory Black in *Hollywood Goes to War*.

Koppes and Black explained that *Menace of the Rising Sun* "would tell Americans for the first time how 'Japs repaid kindness with ruthless murder,' how 'Jap militarists played their filthy game of treachery,' and how the 'Japs had planned for years to stab the United States in the back.' Hollywood's instant analysis embroidered the 'stab in the back' thesis. The drama of Pearl Harbor . . . was gangsterism on an international scale with America cast in the role of outraged innocent."

Republic Studios had been the first to do a film project on the Japanese attack, rushing out within a year of the attack the feeble *Remember Pearl Harbor*, which included a grand total of zero footage of the actual lopsided battle or even any staged reenactment using model ships and planes. Instead, the attack occurred "off-screen." Audiences were not impressed—incensed, yes, but they didn't need a lame movie to foment hatred for the Japanese.

In contrast with depictions of the Japanese as "slant-eyed bastards," Hollywood studios went to great lengths to show the melting-pot ethnic mix of American bomber crews and infantry squads, overlooking the fact that blacks were excluded from most combat units. (The few exceptions were all-black units commanded by white officers.) Another common stereotype purveyed by films of the era was the maverick on the team who in the end perishes so his battle buddies can live on.

Director John Ford headed up the Field Photographic Branch of the Office of Strategic Services (OSS). Soon after the Japanese sneak attack, he was summoned by the secretaries of the Navy and the War Department to travel to Honolulu and produce a factual account of what had taken place. Ford and his crew arrived in Hawaii in mid-January. Later, in an interview with the Naval Historical Center, he recalled, "We found Pearl Harbor at that time in a state of readiness. Everybody had learned their lesson from Pearl Harbor. The Army and the Navy, all in good shape, everything taken care of, patrols going out regularly, everybody in high spirits, was courageous." (Instead of working on the documentary about Pearl, John Ford would be sent to Midway Island where he would see firsthand—and film—the Japanese aerial bombardment.)

A year after the attack on Pearl Harbor, Air Corps commander Henry "Hap" Arnold approached his good friend Jack Warner about doing a film featuring the flight of B-17s that had the misfortune of leaving California on December 6, 1941, bound for Hawaii. In 1942, Warner Brothers released the Howard Hawks film, *Air Force*, which followed the crew of the Flying Fortress *Mary Ann* from California, arriving in the middle of the attack on Battleship Row.

"Here were all the stenciled characters: the high-minded captain; the chip-on-the-shoulder sergeant [the Pole, Sergeant Winocki, played by leading man John Garfield], destined to be the bravest of heroes; the Bronx kibitzer; the jittery son of a famous military figure; the seasoned veteran, and the raw recruit," noted Ted Sennett in *Warner Brothers Presents*. The *Mary Ann*'s crew included a cross-section of American society, including a Swede, a Jew, and a WASP. After landing briefly at Pearl and seeing the carnage there, the crew is filled with rage.

"It is difficult to avoid wincing at George Tobias's remark as a Japanese plane plummets to the earth in flames: 'Fried Jap going down!' or to keep from noticing that although Americans are killed in battle, their deaths are bloodless and almost gentle. It is the Japanese plane that explodes in midair, with the bleeding pilot slumped unconscious in his cockpit, and the Japanese ship that is bombed into oblivion, with enemy sailors drowning or blown to pieces by shrapnel. Curiously, too, only the Japanese are cruel (they machine-gun a parachuting pilot), while the American flying men kill only out of revenge, blind fury,.or simple duty." In the end, Sergeant Winocki makes the ultimate sacrifice to save the rest of his crew, which was a common ending for the war movies of the early 1940s, as if the American public needed constant reminders that to win the war would take everything everyone had to give, with little thought to their own well-being.

Even songwriters jumped on the "Remember Pearl Harbor" bandwagon—

"On December the seventh, nineteen hundred and forty-one
The Japanese flew over Pearl Harbor, dropping bombs by the ton.
Some say the Japanese is hard fighters, but any dummy ought to know
Even a rattlesnake won't bite you in your back,
He will warn you before he strikes his blow."
— *From the song "Pearl Harbor Blues," written by Peter Clayton*

"Let's remember Pearl Harbor as we go to meet the foe.
Let's remember Pearl Harbor as we did the Alamo.
We will always remember how they died for Liberty.
Let's remember Pearl Harbor and go on to victory."
— *From the song "Remember Pearl Harbor," words by Don Reid, music by Don Reid and Sammy Kaye*

"We're gonna have to slap the dirty little Jap
and Uncle Sam's the guy who can do it."
— *From the song "Remember Pearl Harbor," by Carson Robinson*

Rampaging across the Pacific

Almost immediately after laying waste to the Pacific Fleet, the Japanese headed for other Allied strongholds in the region, including the Philippines,

Midway, Singapore, and Wake Island, where American forces had already been alerted and deployed. The Allies braced to turn back the onslaught, underestimating the armada headed their way. The only air cover available to the Philippine Defense Forces were 35 B-17 bombers and 60 P-40 fighter planes "lined up like ducks on a pond" at Clark and Iba Fields.

Japanese bombers quickly wiped out nearly all of the Allied planes as easily as they had taken out Battleship Row at Pearl. But unlike the air assault on Hawaii, Japan's conquest of the Philippines also involved naval firepower and the 150,000-man Imperial Japanese Army.

Despite enormous odds against them, the Americans blunted the initial invasion force and held out on Bataan Peninsula for as long as possible, believing reinforcements were on the way. The weary American and Filipino forces, who became known as the "battling bastards of Bataan," wrote a tongue-in-cheek ditty about their plight:

"We're the Battling Bastards of Bataan,
No mama, no papa, no Uncle Sam,
No aunts, no uncles, no nephews, no nieces,
No pills, no planes, no artillery pieces,
And nobody gives a damn!"

For four months the "battling bastards" withstood constant bombardment and enemy ground attacks, but finally they surrendered in early April. Some defenders refused to give up and swam the shark-infested waters to Corregidor, two miles away and guarding the entrance to Manila Bay. Others fled into the mountains and jungles and would participate in guerrilla activities during the next several years. For twenty-seven days, the defenders on Corregidor came under artillery and bomber attack and fought off disease and dehydration. Among the holdouts of "the Rock" were American airmen without any planes and sailors without ships, who stood side by side with soldiers and Marines, nurses and civilians stranded there. An intricate maze of tunnels and gun emplacements allowed them to duck incoming artillery fire, although many couldn't stand the tunnel rat environment and would rather remain topside, exposed to anything the Japs threw at them. But on May 5, an enemy invasion force stormed ashore, and soon Corregidor fell.

The weary survivors were rounded up, shipped across the bay to the Bataan Peninsula, and force-marched northward along a winding mountainous road. Many fell by the wayside or were singled out by sadistic guards and wantonly killed for pleasure. Those who survived the Death March were crammed into boxcars and transported to Camp O'Donnell further north, where they would be imprisoned for the remainder of the war.

At Wake Island, situated 2,300 miles west of Hawaii and barely big enough to accommodate an airfield, American forces repelled repeated attacks and invasion attempts for twelve days but could not hold off the Japanese Fourth Fleet.

When Wake Island's Marine commander sent out a flash radio message informing Pearl Harbor of the attack and his units' successful rebuff, he was asked if he needed anything. Boastfully, the commander quipped, "Send us more Japs!" It was one of the last radio transmissions sent from the besieged outpost before it was overrun. It would be America's first land battle in the Pacific, and even though Wake eventually fell, the resolve of the American defenders there, and at Bataan and Corregidor, bolstered morale back home.

The "Bastards" and the Angels Make It to Film

"Within fourteen months of Bataan's fall, Hollywood put a movie version of the event into the nation's theaters," wrote John Wukovits for *WWII History* magazine in September 2002. "*Bataan* attempted to convey the unified effort exerted by American and Filipino soldiers in their futile struggle to halt the Japanese advance. The movie's scriptwriters even made sure that most of the United States' ethnic groups received representation—a Jewish soldier, an

Left: *The "battling bastards of Bataan" fended off Japanese attacks on Manila Bay for months before being captured and marched to prison camps for the war's duration. Many of the Americans manning the coastal guns had never expected to leave the boundary waters of the United States as members of the U.S. Coast Guard but found themselves fighting without adequate guns, ammunition, planes, or ships. The trek to the camps became known as the Bataan Death March, where hundreds of Americans died and countless Filipinos gave their lives in liberty's defense.*

U.S. Army Photo

Italian, a Pole, a Latin American, an African-American, and a white middle-class individual comprise the platoon that dominates the action. Japanese stereotypes reinforced the image of sneaky, devious men and the image of thirteen Americans fighting to the last man."

BELOW: *Robert Taylor, who portrayed one of the survivors in* Bataan, *lauded dying for freedom's sake in the movie but never saw combat action as a U.S. Navy pilot during World War II. His movie and aviation experience made him a natural in aviation training films, his major contribution to the war.* National Archives Photo

The film starred Thomas Mitchell, Lloyd Nolan, Robert Walker, Tom Dugan, Kenneth Spencer, Desi Arnaz (who won a Photoplay Award for his role), and Robert Taylor, who stood at the end, among his fallen soldiers, exhausting his weapon as a horde of Japanese infantry close in. His final words were a clarion call to American audiences back home: "It doesn't matter where a man dies, so long as he dies for freedom."

The movie's dedication reemphasized the sacrifices made by the valiant few at Bataan, sacrifices that would have to be made by everyone to be victorious in the Pacific: "When Japan struck our desperate need was time . . . time to marshal new armies . . . ninety-six priceless days were bought for us . . . with their lives . . . by the defenders of Bataan, the Philippine Army which formed the bulk of MacArthur's infantry, fighting shoulder to shoulder with the Americans. To those immortal dead, who heroically stayed the wave of barbaric conquest, this picture is reverently dedicated."

The angels of Bataan and Corregidor—the nurses who volunteered to stay and treat the wounded and dying—were brought to the screen by Paramount in 1943 in *So Proudly We Hail*. Starring Paulette Goddard, Veronica Lake, and Claudette Colbert, with Sonny Tufts, Barbara Britton, Mary Servoss, Kitty Kelly, Ann Doran, and Mary Treen, the film blended entertainment with propaganda, the hell of combat with the tug at the heartstrings of a pained lover seeking revenge against a cruel enemy. "A group of nurses ship out for the Philippines in November 1941, only to get caught in the aftermath of Pearl Harbor," wrote Koppes and Black in *Hollywood Goes to War*. "Their camp is shelled by the Japanese, despite their prominently displayed Red Cross flag. They make a successful retreat only because Olivia (portrayed by

Veronica Lake), whose fiancé was killed by the enemy, sacrifices herself for the larger group—a frequent movie wartime gesture.

"She arranges her long blond hair over her shoulders so that the Japanese will think she's an innocent woman, pulls the pin on a grenade, stuffs it into her clothing, and walks toward the oncoming Japanese. The grenade explodes, wiping out the enemy as well as Olivia, and her comrades escape. Eventually the order comes to evacuate to Corregidor; they are finally plucked from the island fortress and returned home."

Colbert as the head nurse was the recognized star of the film, but Paramount wanted to also showcase its new sultry starlet, Veronica Lake, in a dramatic role. But it was Goddard, despite almost daily bickering with Colbert, who got the accolades, including an Oscar nomination. "The surprise of the group is Miss Goddard, until now not much more than a fluttery pretty-pretty but this time an actress of vigor and zest for life," wrote reviewer Alton Cook for the *New York World-Telegram*.

A similar film about the courageous women on Bataan was *Cry Havoc*, also released in 1942, adapted from a Broadway play and starring Margaret Sullavan, Joan Blondell, and Ann Sothern. And, like the movie *Bataan*, this one featured a diverse group representing the various socioeconomic classes of American women: sisters studying art and music, a stay-at-home southern lady, a fashion writer, a Filipino villager, a switchboard operator, the tough-as-nails commander, a factory supervisor, a stripper, a nurse, a cook, and a volunteer. They all band together, caring for the men wounded in battle, in a futile situation, with the enemy closing in all around them.

Another film situated near Bataan and Corregidor was 1942's *Manila Calling*, with Carole Landis, Lloyd Nolan, and Cornel Wilde, who attempt to hold off the Japanese until enemy bombers obliterate their position. Near the end they attempt to get a message out, to warn the rest of the world about the brutal Japanese.

The battle for Wake was turned into a chest-thumping recruiting film for the Marines in *Wake Island,* starring Robert Preston, Macdonald Carey, Brian Donlevy, Rod Cameron, and William Bendix, directed by John Farrow, and rushed out less than a year after the island fell. The American defenders on Wake, both civilian and military—377 Marines and civilian contractors—bicker and spar during the days leading up to December 7, but they must band together if they want any chance of repelling the inevitable Japanese onslaught. "The Japanese are seen in close-ups as real flesh and blood people, not some distant inhuman thing," wrote Jeanine Basinger in *The World War II Combat Film*. "The film obviously seeks to stir up the viewer's hatred for this enemy, by presenting him as a frightening figure who would shoot a radioman in the back, and who would gun down a brave pilot who had to parachute out of a burning plane."

The doomed garrison refuses to surrender, withstanding enemy attacks for two weeks, choosing to fight to the last man. "It includes a patriotic reference to our historical battles . . . 'Don't fire till you see the whites of their eyes,' Brian Donlevy tells his men, pointing out that he is quoting Colonel Prescott from the Battle of Bunker Hill," continued Basinger. "*Wake Island*, like the war films which follow it, concerns itself not only with history and battle, but also with the underlying issue of what it means to be an American: Here is a nation that seeks to whip its populace into patriotic fervor by showing them films based on defeat, not victory.

"As the introductory words of *Wake Island* indicated, both Valley Forge and Custer's Last Stand, not to mention the Alamo, represent great moments in American bravery or folly (or both), depending on your point of view. The clouds of smoke that blur the final images of the deaths of the last men alive on Wake Island are cut by hundreds of marching Marines emerging out of the fog. We may be losers, but we never give up—and losers who never give up will finally win."

This movie took a bit too long to establish the characters and prepare for the enemy attack, but once the action scenes started, they cascaded to the foregone defeat of America's finest. The facts were not distorted for the sake of a happy ending, and as such, *Wake Island* "had medals pinned on its chest by the critics, the public, and the Academy (four nominations) as the first realistic movie about World War II in the Pacific," wrote John Eames in *The Paramount Story*. "In the end it was a defeat, but a glorious one. But it was the real-as-newsreel action in this uninhibited patriotism-rouser that made it one of the year's most potent successes."

"*Wake Island* showed audiences that war in the Pacific was going to be a tough, dirty war fought with few rules and even fewer heroes," wrote Clayton Koppes and Gregory Black in *Hollywood Goes to War*. It was the first of many combat films from WWII that didn't have a happy ending, that clearly informed the viewing public that there would be more sacrifices and more defeats along the path to eventual victory, and Americans would be victorious only if they had the resolve to stay the course.

Not only did this movie inspire thousands of average Americans to enlist in the Marines, the film's crew, including Macdonald Carey, signed up. (Carey was initially rejected due to color blindness, but he was later accepted for duty.)

Tin Pan Alley Sings Red, White, and Blue

"Ah God! How pretty war is, with its songs and its rests."

—*Guillaume Apollinaire,* L'Adieu du Cavalier, *1918*

THE CREATIVE ENERGY OF AMERICA'S SONGWRITERS worked at a fever pitch from the early 1900s through the 1940s in New York's Tin Pan Alley district, located on Manhattan's West 28th Street between 5th Avenue and Broadway, where many music publishers set up shop. There, hundreds of American classics were written by some of the most well-known composers ever, including Irving Berlin, Cole Porter, and Jerome Kern. Over time Tin Pan Alley would produce all forms of American music, including jazz, blues, swing, ragtime, Dixieland, and pop. The meaning of the phrase would move beyond its Manhattan setting and refer to all published music unique to America.

Turn of the Century newspaper writer Monroe Rosenfeld "coined the term Tin Pan Alley to symbolize the cacophony of the many pianos being pounded in publishers' demo rooms which he characterized as sounding as though hundreds of people were pounding on tin pans," wrote Rick Reublin in March 2000 for ParlorSongs Association. "The lyrics of music from this period (1900 to 1910) suggest that the USA was a peaceful, happy, and prosperous place. The many songs about the past describe warm memories of happy and innocent times in rural or small town settings. The persistent image of the 'Gay Nineties' as one of the happiest and least troubled times in American history has been derived largely from these songs."

But as storm clouds began brewing in Europe by 1914, threatening to drag America into the fight, songwriters from Tin Pan Alley and elsewhere echoed the sentiments of the time. One of the most blatant anti-war songs was "I Didn't Raise My Boy to Be a Soldier" by lyricist Alfred Bryan and composer Al Piantadosi:

"Ten million soldiers to the war have gone,
Who may never return again.
Ten million mothers' hearts must break,
For the ones who died in vain.
Head bowed down in sorrow in her lonely years
I heard a mother murmur through her tears —
I didn't raise my boy to be a soldier."

Background: *Japanese Zeros took off from carriers very early on Sunday, December 7, 1941, surprising American forces in Hawaii and the Philippines. Japanese military leaders planned to launch two bombing flights, but they were afraid U.S. aircraft carriers would track the second series of flights. Still, approximately 170 Japanese planes took part in the attacks.*
U.S. Navy Photo

This tune was recorded by Morton Harvey in 1915 and was a huge hit at the time. But two years later, American forces were headed to the front and patriotic sentiments took a turn, and Harvey and his anti-war song were ostracized for years afterward. Another anti-war tune was "Stay Down Here Where You Belong," penned by Irving Berlin and recorded by Henry Burr prior to the American Expeditionary Forces departing for France. This song, too, disappeared overnight.

Other war-themed songs from WWI included "All of No Man's Land is Ours" and "How Ya Gonna Keep 'Em Down on the Farm after They've Seen Paree?", both released by James Reese Europe's 369th Regiment Hell Fighters Band; the Irving Berlin classic "Oh, How I Hate to Get Up in the Morning" (as a doughboy, Berlin certainly knew how to capture the humor amid the misery of soldiering), Jack Caddigan's and James Brennan's "We're All Going Calling on the Kaiser," and Dana Burnet's and James H. Rogers's "When Pershing's Men Go Marching into Picardy."

One of the most popular patriotic songs of the Great War was the classic "Over There," written by George M. Cohan and published by Leo Feist, Inc., in 1917:

"Over there, over there
Send the word, send the word, over there . . .
That the Yanks are coming, the Yanks are coming
The drums rum-tumming ev'rywhere.
So prepare, say a prayer
Send the word, send the word to beware.
We'll be over, we're coming over
And we won't come back till it's over, over there."

Cohan would receive a Congressional Citation for "Over There," a song that would be recorded by hundreds of artists through the years. (It would be dusted off and revived for WWII, just as appropriate, just as patriotic.)

The Patriotic Tunesmith

Israel Baline was born in Mohilev, Russia, but by fourteen he was singing in New York saloons for tips, and at sixteen was writing song lyrics for Tin Pan Alley. He changed his name to Irving Berlin and became one of the most prolific composers ever. Amazingly, he never learned to play music, and he confined most of his work to the black keys of the piano. A transcriber would listen to his songs and write them down. One of his earliest hits was "Alexander's Ragtime Band" in 1911. A decade later he was a veteran of the Great War and put on stage revues at his own theater on Broadway.

His style wasn't as sophisticated as Cole Porter's or George Gershwin's, but Berlin's music was just as popular. Two of his songs were sentimental favorites during World War II.

World-famous composer and World War I veteran Irving Berlin spent years entertaining troops in two global conflicts. During World War I, Berlin created Yip, Yap, Yaphank, *a show that he performed for troops and war bond drives. For World War II, he wrote* This is the Army, *a Broadway-style musical based on his World War I play, that was first used to raise funds for the military and later toured cities around the nation and the world.* This is the Army *also became a hit movie in 1943, starring Ronald Reagan.*

Berlin was fifty-three when the Japanese attacked Pearl Harbor, and had already written classics like "God Bless America" and "White Christmas." But he felt compelled to write the play for This is the Army *and the songs to accompany it. Berlin said in a Summer 1996 article by Laurence Bergreen in* Prologue, *a National Archives quarterly publication, "Songs make history and history makes songs." The play was an all-soldier show and integrated black and white soldiers, which even the Army itself did not do at the time.*

National Archives Photo

His daughter, Mary Ellin Barrett, recalled for *Newsweek* in its June 28, 1999, issue, "In the fall of 1938, he came back from a business trip to Europe and said there's going to be a war. That's how everybody was talking here. He began thinking about the possibility of writing a song that would have something to do with the really very frightened feelings of the time. That was the moment when he remembered 'God Bless America.'

"He put a verse on it—which is not always sung, but which goes, 'While the storm clouds gather far across the sea, let us swear allegiance to a land that's free'—and made a few changes in the lyric and melody, and there it was. Kate Smith introduced it on Armistice Day, and she closed her program with it every week, week after week, for months and months.

"By the following summer, people were talking in Congress about making it the new national anthem, and my father and Kate Smith said no. My father said, we have a national anthem which should never be replaced." That debate still continues today.

In December of 1941, thousands of American men had postponed the holidays to enlist in one of the armed forces. A year later they were deployed to the inhospitable climes of the South Pacific, far from evergreen trees, and

Right: *Singer Kate Smith belted out "God Bless America" in concert halls around the nation, many times with millions of radio listeners enjoying the live performance. The song was so popular in the 1930s that many citizens wanted the tune to replace "The Star-Spangled Banner" as the national anthem. Both Smith and the song's composer, Irving Berlin, lobbied against such a change.*
National Archives Photo

snow and icicles, Christmas carols, and crackling fireplaces. By Thanksgiving of 1942, Bing Crosby was crooning a bittersweet Irving Berlin tune from the movie *Holiday Inn* that captured the feelings of all those homesick GIs:

> "I'm dreaming of a White Christmas,
> just like the ones I used to know.
> Where the treetops glisten and children listen
> to hear sleigh bells in the snow."

"White Christmas" immediately became a sentimental holiday favorite of WWII and would become one of those "evergreen" tunes that has never lost its appeal. "So many young people were away and they'd hear this song at that time of the year and it would really affect them," Crosby recalled in *Bing*. "I sang it many times in Europe in the field for the soldiers. They'd holler for it; they'd demand it and I'd sing it and they'd all cry. It was really sad."

Berlin also put together the popular stage show *This is the Army*, a rousing collection of patriotic numbers with a star-studded cast, which began on Broadway but soon went on the road, cross country and even overseas to England, with all the proceeds going to Army Relief programs.

The GI Composer

Frank Loesser was already an established composer when war began, but he didn't hesitate to toss aside a lucrative career to join the Army. At the time he

Left: *Frank Loesser, who wrote songs like "That Ain't Hay (That's the USA)" and "Praise the Lord and Pass the Ammunition," served in the Radio Productions Unit and produced shows with Bing Crosby, Danny Kaye, and Dinah Shore that promoted recruitment. He moved to New York's Special Services Unit in 1943 to create pre-packaged shows called "Blueprint Specials" for soldiers to perform.*

Loesser gave the royalties from "Praise the Lord and Pass the Ammunition" to the Naval Relief Society, which amounted to a hefty sum from the sales of two million records and one million copies of sheet music. Americans loved the song so much that the Office of War Information allowed its play only six times a day so the public would not grow tired of hearing it.
YANK Magazine Photo

had no idea he would continue with his craft while in uniform, writing a virtual songbook of patriotic tributes to all the armed services. "For the Army Air Forces he wrote such tunes as 'The Sad Bombardier,' 'On the Beam,' and 'It's Great to be in the Air Corps,'" wrote Sergeant Richard Harrity for *YANK* magazine. "For the Women's Army Corps he came up with 'The WAC Hymn.'

"'Occasionally,' he explains, 'I had a hard time convincing a zealous character that 'The 1233rd Machine Records Unit Camp Withlacochee Forever' was not a particularly good title or theme for a march.'"

After surviving the rigors of basic training, where recruits do a zillion push-ups and march everywhere, Loesser wrote:

"There is many a fall in the Cavalry but never a fallen arch.
And what do you do in the Infantry? You march, you march, you march."

Humor was a common element of many Loesser songs. A good example is "They're Either Too Young or Too Old" (music by Arthur Schwartz), which Bette Davis sang in the movie *Thank Your Lucky Stars*. The song was a lament that all of the most eligible men were now in the military, leaving very few cast-offs to choose from:

"They're either too young or too old.
They're either too gray or too grassy green.
The pickings are poor and the crop is lean.
What's good is in the Army, what's left will never harm me.
I'm either their first breath of spring,
Or else, I'm their last little fling,
I either get a fossil or an adolescent pup,
I either have to hold him off, or have to hold him up.
The battle is on, but the fortress will hold.
They're either too young or too old."

Swing Music Gains Worldwide Appeal

After the down years of the Great Depression, the up-tempo tunes of the big bands swept through the 1930s like a breath of fresh air. Swing music was back in style.

RIGHT: *Captain Glenn Miller was not only popular with servicemen and women, but civilian fans flocked to his shows and rushed to buy his records, popularizing such tunes as "In the Mood" and "Tuxedo Junction"—music that worried parents feared would jeopardize their children's health with tempos faster than the human pulse.*
United States Air Force Museum Photo

"The famous bands arose at a time when entertainment was an integral element in America's emergence from hard times, as well as a salve for increasing anxiety about the distant rumble of war," wrote Owen Edwards in the article "Magic Wand" for *Smithsonian* magazine, March 2004.

Glenn Miller was at the top of the class, but numerous groups challenged him as everybody's favorite. Duke Ellington, Tommy and Jimmy Dorsey, Woody Herman, Harry James, Lionel Hampton, Artie Shaw, Bob Crosby, Count Basie, Jimmie Lunceford, and Benny Goodman—the "King of Swing"—all had a following who bought their records, and listened to their radio performances, and bought tickets to their shows. Even the schmaltzy Guy Lombardo could pack a ballroom. As their popularity grew, these instrumental groups added vocalists, such as Marion Hutton and Ray Eberle with the Miller Orchestra, "Liltin' Martha Tilton" with Benny Goodman, Helen O'Connell with the Jimmy Dorsey crew, the then-unknown Billie Holiday with Artie Shaw in '38, and Ella Fitzgerald with Chick Webb.

Les Brown and his Band of Renown discovered seventeen-year-old Doris Van Kepplehoff in 1940. Doris changed her name to the catchier Doris Day, and together they recorded another tug-at-the-heartstrings song that appealed to servicemen and their lady loves back home. "Sentimental Journey," which yearns for another place and a happier time, soared to the top of the charts upon its release in 1945, and remained there for an amazing seventeen weeks.

Vocal groups such as the McGuire Sisters, the Mills Brothers, and the Andrews Sisters all vied for position at the top of the charts, revealed every week on the radio show, *Your Hit Parade*.

Ellington captured the mood when he teamed with Irving Mills to pen:

"It makes no difference if it's sweet or hot.
Just give that rhythm ev'rything you got.
Oh, it don't mean a thing, if it ain't got that swing."

LEFT: *Part of Glenn Miller's service to his country was touring with his military orchestra throughout the U.S.—and eventually to England—to perform for soldiers, seamen, airmen, and even leathernecks. Miller lost his life over the English Channel on December 15, 1944.*

Miller had left England headed to France to plan a long tour of the continent. When weather in London shut down airports, Miller hopped on a chartered flight between Bedford and Bordeaux. Historians speculate that as military bombers returned to England after a mission to Germany, crews dropped their extra payloads over the Channel and one bomb hit Miller's lower-flying charter plane, causing it to explode into unrecoverable pieces.
National Archives Photo

Some authorities felt the allure of swing, the hyper movements of jitterbugging (and toe-tapping?) were dangerous to the long-term health of America's youth. *The New York Times* solemnly suggested that the craze was getting out of hand, quoting a psychologist on the 'dangerously hypnotic influence of swing, cunningly devised to a faster tempo than seventy-two bars to the minute—faster than the human pulse."

Obviously, with such "poison" infecting America's youth, it was only natural that swing music should be exported! One offshoot of the big band era was the secretive popularity of swing records in Germany, despite the Nazi regime's crackdown on all "subversive cultural influences."

"There was a group of [German] teenagers who were rejected and who began to reject the system. Their affinity was for English and American records. Jazz especially," Hans Massaquoi told Studs Terkel for his book, *The Good War*. "If they caught you playing these records, [the Nazis would] confiscate them or take you to jail and keep you overnight. The swing boys, as we were called . . . identified with English and American

LEFT: *Jazz and swing ushered in the happier days of the 1930s, with orchestras packing hotel ballrooms like this one at Chicago's Savoy in 1941. Even would-be Nazi youth caught "swing fever" in Germany and secretly listened to banned American music.*
Office of War Information Photo

culture. More American. We would crave listening to jazz. Almost fanatics. Every other night, some band would be arrested because they were egged on by the swing boys to play 'Some of These Days' or one of those numbers. A Gestapo man in the audience would arrest the whole band."

Novelty Tunes Hint at Racism

If it weren't for Adolf Hitler's deadly and despicable acts, his rantings and ravings might be considered humorous, at least to the outside world, those a safe distance from the long arm of the Gestapo. It was only natural that Hitler would be a target of American and British comics. Charlie Chaplin spared nothing when he starred in the film, *The Great Dictator*. Songwriters also took their shot, with such ditties as Cole Porter's "Let's Not Talk About Love":

"Let's heap some hot profanities on Hitler's inhumanities
Let's argue if insanity's the cause of his inanities . . .
But let's not talk about love."

Other Nazi put-downs included "Lord Haw-Haw and the Humbug of Hamburg," "I'm a Flying Wreck" ("I'm a flying wreck a riskin' my neck. I'd circle over Germany and spit in the Führer's eye!"), and "Let's Knock the Hit Out of Hitler." "Round and Round Hitler's Grave," written by Woody Guthrie, Millard Lampell, and Pete Seeger, included these "wishful" lyrics:

"Now I wished I had a bushel, wished I had a peck,
Wished I had old Hitler with a rope around his neck."

In 1944, two soldiers, Sergeant Joe Bushkin and Private John De Vries, penned the popular "There'll be a Hot Time in the Town of Berlin," which included the verse

"They're gonna take a hike, through Hitler's Reich
And change the 'Heil' to 'Whatcha know, Joe?'
There'll be a hot time in the town of Berlin,
When the Yanks go marching in."

The cowardice of "those slant-eyed bastards" when they attacked Pearl Harbor led to a flood of tunes tinged with racism. After the attack, Congressman J. Parnell Thomas appealed to the country's tunesmiths to hustle out something appropriate: "What America needs today is a good five-cent war song . . . a good, peppy marching song, something with plenty of zip, ginger, and fire." But the first ditty to hit the airwaves was Burt Wheeler's "We'll Knock the Japs Right into the Laps of the Nazis."

"Following in quick order were the following songs: 'Goodbye Momma, I'm off to Yokohama,' (which included the lyrics "A million fighting sons of Uncle Sam, if you please, will soon have all those Japs right down on their Japan knees,"), 'The Japs Haven't Got a Chinaman's Chance,' 'They're Going to be Playing Taps on the Japs,' 'We Are the Sons of the Rising Guns,' "Oh, You Little Son of an Oriental,' 'Slap the Jap Right Off the Map,' 'To be Specific, it's Our Pacific' and 'When Those Little Yellow Bellies Meet the Cohens and the Kelleys,'" reported Bob Greene in the *Jewish World Review* on November 21, 2001. "Clearly, once war was declared, anything was considered fair game. From a song introduced by Eddie Cantor on his network radio show: 'Take the nip out of the Nipponese and chase 'em back to their cherry trees . . .' From the song 'You're a Sap, Mr. Jap,' which was written and copyrighted before Congress even declared war: 'You're a sap, Mr. Jap, to make a Yankee cranky . . . Uncle Sam is gonna spanky . . .'"

None of these novelty songs would become classics, but they certainly reflected the mood in America at the time. Other assorted satires included "We're Gonna Have to Slap the Dirty Little Japs," and Hoagy Carmichael's "I'm a Cranky Old Yank in a Clanky Old Tank in the Streets of Yokohama with a Honolulu Mama, Singin' Those Beat-oh, Flat on His Seat-oh, Hirohito Blues." And a few slams were directed at the Axis trifecta—Germany, Italy, and Japan—including "The Jap and the Wop and the Hun" and "Let's Put the Axe to the Axis." One of the most memorable songs to take a shot at the Big Three Buffoons was written by Paul Roberts and Shelby Darnell: "There's a Star-Spangled Banner Waving Somewhere."

"In this war with its mad schemes of destruction
Of our country fair and our sweet liberty,
By the mad dictators, leaders of corruption,
Can't the U.S. use a mountain boy like me?
God gave me the right to be a free American,
And for that precious right I'd gladly die
There's a Star-Spangled Banner waving somewhere.
That is where I want to live when I die."

Other tunes appealed to females across the country, asking them to sacrifice their virtues and to do their part for the war effort. "'You Can't Say No to a Soldier' was a training manual for the companion arts of promiscuity and infidelity; 'I'm Doin' it for Defense' was doubtless written in a courtroom during one of the ensuing divorce proceedings; 'As Mabel Goes so Goes the Navy' was practically a rallying cry for organized prostitution," wrote Steve Kluger in *YANK.*

4. Thousands Sign Up "For the Duration"

"OLDER MEN DECLARE WAR, BUT IT IS YOUTH THAT MUST FIGHT AND DIE."

—*President Herbert Hoover*

"EVERYBODY IN A MOVIE IS PART OF A FAMILY THAT CAN NEVER BE INVADED BY OUTSIDERS, INCLUDING REAL FAMILY MEMBERS. SOME CALL IT SUMMER CAMP. FOR OTHERS IT IS LIKE MARINE BOOT CAMP. MAKING A MOVIE IS ALSO LIKE A WAR, AN INTENSE, EMOTIONAL EXPERIENCE FOR CAST AND CREW. EACH DAY YOU PRESS ON. THERE IS NO STANDING STILL AND GOING BACK IS EXPENSIVE AND DANGEROUS TO THE COMMON EFFORT."

—*David Brown in* Let Me Entertain You

OPPOSITE: *Navy recruits crawled through log obstacles as part of the torture called boot camp.*
U.S. Navy Photo

IMMEDIATELY AFTER PEARL HARBOR, TENS OF THOUSANDS of young men raised their right hand and swore their allegiance to Uncle Sam, signing on with one of the armed forces, for however long the war was going to last. But which of the services would they choose, as long as they still had a choice?

The Army was mud and pouring rain, or choking dust and sweltering heat, or freezing cold, and foxholes and C-rations . . . and that damnable mud.

The Marines were first to storm the beach and that Bulldog growl and blood in the sand and never leave anyone behind.

The Navy had tin cans and submarines and flattops and a helluva long way to swim if someone yelled "Abandon Ship!"

And the flyboys had all-night bombing raids and "Enemy fighters at twelve o-clock high" and ball-turret gunners and flying through a gauntlet of anti-aircraft fire. And it didn't matter much if anyone got one of those "safe" jobs—like bomber mechanic or clerk typist—because when the casualties mounted, and they certainly would, it was some poor unlucky REMF who got "volunteered" as a replacement for the frontline units, thrown into the thick of it.

Sure, there were a few lucky saps with talent who got plucked after basic to play in one of the many service bands, or sing and dance in a camp show, or "spin platters" on the radio (which in some remote locations was little more than a record player and screechy loudspeakers), all in an effort to boost morale in just the right doses.

BELOW: *Soldiers carry anxiety as heavy as their duffel bags while boarding ships bound for war. Men departed for the duration of the war, not knowing when, or if, they would return home.*
U.S. Army Photo

RIGHT: *Army basic trainees at Camp Edwards, Massachusetts, swing through the final obstacle on a rigorous course. In many movies, basic training was played for laughs. Abbott and Costello made several sixty- to ninety-minute comedies about basic training, often poking fun at activities, such as crossing a horizontal ladder, but most of it was not "fun and games," especially anything involving drill sergeants.* Office of War Information Photo

And not everyone who was intent on some serious payback was taken . . . seriously. "Pops [Gene Fowler] called Lionel Barrymore and W. C. Fields on the telephone, asking what they might do for the war effort," noted Will Fowler in *The Young Man from Denver*. "The three met at Fields's home. Shortly thereafter, the three went to sign up at the local recruiting station. Taking one look at the three volunteers, the recruiting officer exclaimed: 'Who sent you? The enemy?'"

Whipping Army Recruits into Fighting Condition

No matter what they signed on for, all service members went through basic training or boot camp before heading to their unit stateside or being thrown into the fight overseas. This was their first taste of reality, with a drill sergeant breathing down their necks at every turn, whipping them into shape, instilling in them that fighting spirit that just might keep them alive. Many also learned how to smoke like a chimney, drink like a lush, and cuss a mean streak with the best of them.

Some recruits were foolish enough to test their drill sergeants, but this defiance only led to pain and suffering. That's what doing a zillion push-ups will do! Peeling a hundred

RIGHT: *Army troops trained for combat by mastering a Browning .50-caliber flexible machine gun.* U.S. Army Photo

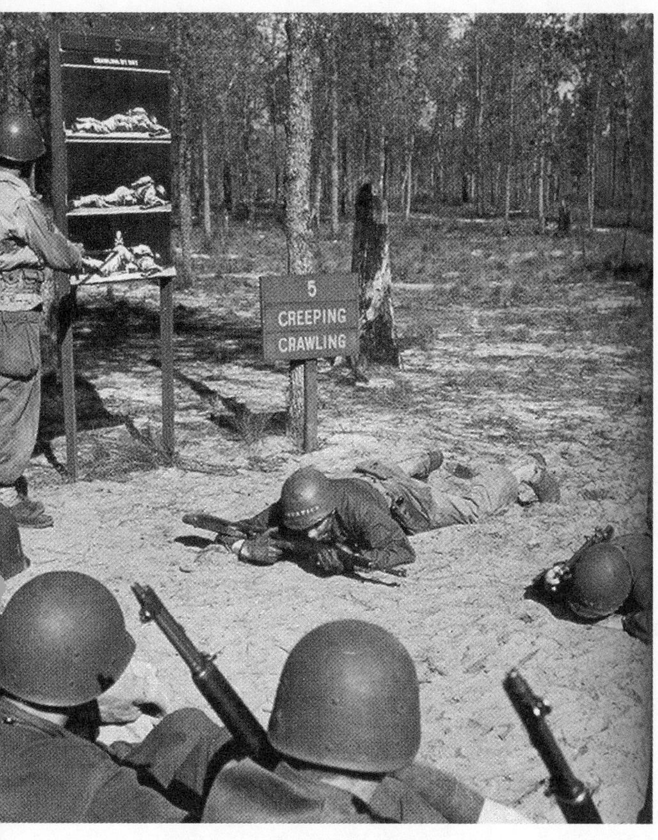

pounds of potatoes while on three days of KP can also make a strong impression on the most rebellious of recruits. Peeling twenty pounds of raw onions can convince anyone that drill sergeants are always right . . . ALWAYS.

For many it was their first time away from home, first time sleeping in open bays with fifty other guys snoring and making other strange noises and having bad dreams, first time with no privacy anywhere, not even while taking a dump or a shower.

Frank Loesser and Peter Lind Hayes captured that feeling in their song "Why Do They Call a Private a Private?":

Left: *Army trainees practice low crawling at Fort Benning, Geogia, as real bullets whiz over their heads. They all knew better than to stand up, especially since the guy firing the machine gun was usually one of the cantankerous drill sergeants.*
U.S. Infantry Museum, Fort Benning, Georgia, Photo

"A hundred other rookies, enjoy his mother's cookies
and read his mail and borrow his underwear.
And in the morning when he wakes, with every shower that he takes
There's seven other fellows standing there
Why do they call a private a private when his life is a public affair?"

British actor Stewart Granger had joined the Gordon Highlanders and described his first night in the barracks as a new recruit: "a private, the lowest form of animal life in the British army. That night as I lay dazed in bed I was more homesick and scared than I'd ever been in any of my schools. The blackout boards were up, so no air could enter the room, and the smell of unwashed bodies soon became overwhelming. And the noises! The different types of snoring, the muttering and groaning, the farting and belching. Oh Jesus! But eventually, overcome by exhaustion, I slept." It may not have been Fort Polk, Louisiana,

Left: *New Marines learned to navigate obstacles with M1s at Mont Ford Point, North Carolina. Recruits often trained with wooden weapons during boot camp.*
Marine Corps Photo

ABOVE: *Infantrymen faced a field inspection on the Hawaiian Islands in January 1941. During these exercises, troops used broomsticks and threw rocks because there was a shortage of modern weapons. A month after the inspection, the Islands saw the arrival of troop reinforcements and new equipment.*
U.S. Army Photo

or Fort Sill, Oklahoma, but sweaty recruits in stagnant barracks in Aberdeen, England, stink the same and make those same noises as American troops anywhere.

Jack Paar was one of those recruits who had difficulty adjusting to the U.S. Army's way of doing things. "I'm afraid I was never meant to be a soldier," he wrote in his book, *I Kid You Not*. "I never understood the Army and the Army seemed to make no effort to understand me. I said 'Good Morning' instead of saluting and, despite my best efforts, I'm sure there were times when the Army wondered which side I was on."

Mel Torme, known as "The Velvet Fog" for his silky smooth voice, joined the Army and was sent to Fort MacArthur in California. He could have joined the Army Air Corps Band, but his highly attuned hearing made him a perfect candidate to learn Morse code for the Signal Corps. Continued force marches while still at basic training caused an injury to his feet, and he was given a medical discharge before graduation.

Steve Allen was living in Arizona to keep his asthma in check and was promptly drafted after passing his physical. He was inducted at Fort MacArthur on the way to basic, where he trained to be in a heavy weapons unit, which included mortars and machine guns. But after five months in the Army, his asthma flared up again, and, like Mel Torme, he was discharged.

Audie Murphy was a runt of a recruit at 5'4" and 110 pounds dripping wet. He tried to train with the airborne troops but was rejected because of his size. Even after bulking up he still couldn't get a combat job that utilized the hunting and tracking skills he'd learned as a boy. His commanding officer was trying to steer him toward cooking and baking school, but Audie persisted and finally qualified as an infantryman. (After exploits overseas that made him the most decorated soldier in the Army, he would later be offered movie roles in Hollywood.)

Anthony Benedetto (the future Tony Bennett), who watched his older brother go into the Army Air Corps and wind up in England, was drafted into the Army to be an infantryman. "Everything you've ever heard is true, only worse. I was in training to be an infantry rifleman and man, it was tough," he wrote for his autobiography, *The Good Life*.

"They'd send us out on bivouacs, mock-battle training missions that consisted of endless marches through wild terrain and muddy trails. These exercises were supposed to break us in for the rigors of battle. The biggest shock was the level of bigotry. Our sergeant was an old-fashioned southern bigot and he had it in for me right from the start because I was an Italian from New York City. I wasn't the only one who experienced prejudice—it was just as bad for other ethnic groups, especially the Blacks and Jews."

Sammy Davis Jr., who was both black and Jewish, went through the Infantry Basic Training Center near Cheyenne, Wyoming, and experienced the same harassments Tony Bennett wrote about. Davis and another black recruit were assigned to one of the first integrated units in the military, and not everyone welcomed the change. "The physical grind wasn't as rough on me as on some of the others because as a dancer I was in good shape. I didn't even mind the food. I'd had far worse and far less," he wrote in his book, *Yes I Can*. But basic was not a cakewalk for him or for any of the other black recruits who had to endure racial taunts and physical harassment from the other trainees. "I had been drafted into the Army to fight, and I did. We were loaded with Southerners and Southwesterners who got their kicks out of needling me. I must have had a knockdown, drag-out fight every two days and I was getting pretty good with my fists." Fortunately for Davis, his background as an entertainer led him to the post service club, where he performed on Friday nights, and parlayed that exposure into a job with Army Special Services.

Mickey Rooney was initially rejected by the military because of high blood pressure, but after asking for a reevaluation, he was classified 1-A; soon after, he was at Fort MacArthur to get his clothing issued, and then it was on to Fort Riley, Kansas. "Army training was tough, but I had no problem with the forced marches, the heavy packs, the work on the obstacle courses, or the hours on the rifle range," he recalled in his book, *Life Is Too Short*.

"By the end of two weeks' training, I found myself a squad leader. Some of [my fellow soldiers] thought the Army gave me special treatment because I was a movie star." Like Sammy Davis Jr., Rooney had to use his fists to prove he belonged there, and he soon won over his fellow recruits.

Burt Lancaster had been a circus acrobat and rigger and a vaudeville performer in the 1930s before joining the Army in January 1943. He wanted to join the combat engineers, but because of his athleticism and entertainment experience was instead assigned to Special Services duty as a sports instructor and organizer at Camp Sibert in Alabama. (Lancaster would eventually deploy to North Africa and then on to Italy, in charge of entertainment and morale building.)

Actor John Craven appeared in the 1944 movie *Purple Heart,* and then joined the Army, learning how to set up and operate communications gear,

Right: *Actor John Craven served as an Army private at Fort Benning, Georgia. The son of actor Frank Craven learned to operate a portable radio as part of his training.* *YANK* Magazine Photo

including field radios and phones, at Fort Benning, Georgia. His dad was actor Frank Craven, and young John had spent a lot of his boyhood on movie sets. After deciding he'd like to try acting, he started with stage work and then moved on to Hollywood.

One prominent movie star who trained new recruits for combat was Rin Tin Tin, son of his namesake, the German shepherd pup that Corporal Lee Duncan had found in the rubble of a bombed-out French village at the end of WWI. Duncan had seen how German frontline units used war dogs and brought Rinny back with him. Twenty-five years later, Duncan and Rin Tin Tin III spearheaded the effort to train several thousand dogs and their handlers for a variety of frontline duties, including sentries, couriers, explosives detectors, and tunnel rats.

Training to Dance among the Clouds

Many of the Army Air Corps officer candidates and enlisted recruits had grown up listening to and reading about the daring exploits of WWI fighter aces, such as Eddie Rickenbacker and Hap Arnold. In the '20s and '30s, children's radio shows about barnstorming aviators in America and freedom fighters seeking to right various wrongs overseas reinforced the fantasy that of all the armed forces, of all the adventuresome occupations the military had to offer, flying must be the best of the best. But before they could climb into the cockpit of a fighter plane, or blast an elusive enemy with the tail guns of a heavy bomber, or wriggle into that tiny bubble underneath the Flying Fortress as the ball turret gunner, these budding "cloud-dancers" first had to survive basic training.

Actor Tim Holt was slotted for B movies at Universal and RKO Radio Pictures prior to joining the Army Air Corps. After basic he moved on to Victorville Air Base to learn how to be a bombardier. He was then selected to train

Below: *Air corpsmen trained with bayonets, usually made of wood. All Army and Army Air Forces soldiers had to learn hand-to-hand combat, although they hoped they would never have to use it.* Office of War Information Photo

high-altitude bomber crews for the Marine Corps at El Centro in California. After a short tour to Washington, D.C., for liaison work with naval aeronautics, he returned to the West for additional bombardier training on the sleek silver B-29s. Three years after joining the military, Tim Holt was finally sent to the Pacific Theater for the closing of the air war with Japan.

Another established actor who joined the Army Air Corps was Robert Cummings, appearing in numerous light comedies in the late '30s. He joined prior to Pearl Harbor and went through aviator school, eventually becoming a flight instructor. Country music singer Tennessee Ernie Ford was also sent to Victorville Air Base in California, where he too was a flight instructor. Folksinger Pete Seeger was training to be a B-24 bomber crewman when his left-wing political leanings caught the attention of military intelligence snoops. He was quickly transferred to Army Special Services, where he entertained the troops with his left-wing folk tunes sprinkled among more standard Army fare. (Seeger would later write one of the most popular protest songs of the Vietnam War, "Where Have All the Flowers Gone?")

Actor Ray Milland tried to join the Air Corps, but a badly injured left hand bumped him from consideration. He did work as a civilian flight instructor and continued to make movies during the war.

Walter Palahniuk was destined to follow in his father's footsteps as a Pennsylvania coal miner when the world erupted and pulled the United States into the conflict. Palahniuk was training as a B-24 bomber crewman in Arizona when his plane crashed and he was critically burned. Cosmetic surgery would reduce the scarring but would leave him permanently disfigured. (After the war, Palahniuk chose to become an actor instead of a coal miner, changed his name to Jack Palance, and parlayed his craggy face into a stellar career in the movies.)

Not many of his fellow recruits at the Army Air Force Training Command Radio School at Sioux Falls, South Dakota, were aware that Private Bernard Hardesty had been one of the most famous child actors of the late '20s. Back then he was better known as Wheezer in the *Our Gang* comedy series of short films. Waddling around in an oversized diaper, hanging on to his ever-faithful companion Pete—the black-and-white mongrel with the black circle around one eye—Hardesty retired as Baby Wheezer at the fine old age of five when he outgrew his white cotton wardrobe! Understandably, Hardesty wasn't too keen on letting drill sergeants know about his thespian past or his cutesy moniker.

A classmate of "Wheezer" at the AAF Radio School was Private Byron Harker, an amateur harmonica player, who "amuses his buddies by sending fourteen words a minute in code on a harmonica," reported *YANK* magazine. "'I had just passed my 16-word check at school and returned to good old Barracks 916 when I had a fiendish idea. Why not send some code on my harmonica and see how many eyebrows would be raised in the barracks? After a few words, I looked up and saw that a few fellows were transcribing it. I kept it up, faster and faster. Pretty soon almost all the fellows were taking my code. One thing I haven't tried is sending a message and playing a tune at the same time.'"

Sabu Dastagir, was known as "Elephant Boy" on the silver screen, when he joined the Air Corps in Los Angeles, then transferred to Greensboro, North Carolina, where he trained to be an aerial gunner. Sabu had been discovered in India at age eleven, plucked from other youngsters trying out for the British-produced movie about a local boy and his elephant. He moved to London to finish the film and attended school there between movie roles. From there he moved on to Hollywood, where his goal was to get his American citizenship. Then war was declared, and, with the Japanese threatening his native India, Sabu joined the Air Corps to do his part in winning the fight in Asia.

Alfred Cocozza had had an undisciplined childhood and didn't care to be told what to do. He had aspirations to be a professional singer, using the stage name Mario Lanza, and so getting his draft notice was the worst possible obstacle to fulfilling his dreams. During basic in Miami he distinguished himself by his indifference to maintaining his gear, to keeping his uniforms clean and presentable, to defying the drill sergeants, and by ignoring wake-up calls—and on and on. While other entertainers in uniform were sent to Special Services units where they could make the most of their talents, Cocozza (he didn't use the name Mario Lanza again until he was discharged) was assigned as a military policeman to patrol the Mexican border near Marfa, Texas. In the book *Mario Lanza: Tenor in Exile,* Roland Bessette wrote about the defiant airman: "He was not the worst soldier in the Air Force, though he could have held his own if such a competition had been held. His uniform was unkempt, his belt missing or barely cinched, the shoes frequently minus laces, the knot of his tie several inches below an unbuttoned collar, and the hat frequently where he was not."

RIGHT: *Child movie actor Sabu Dastagir – better known as just Sabu—initially worked in the war effort by selling bonds for the Treasury Department. Sabu traveled around the U.S. and spoke on radio shows to encourage Americans to buy bonds. Once he gained his U.S. citizenship in 1944, Sabu became an aerial tail gunner for the Army Air Forces, earning staff sergeant's rank and a Distinguished Flying Cross for his services.*
Army Air Forces Photo

As a result, the young Private Cocozza, who felt his talents were his ticket to the big time, allowed his attitude to build barriers, delaying performing opportunities that could have been his from the start if he'd just tried to be a better serviceman.

Two former members of the Chicago Opera Company ran into each other while stationed at Camp Swift in Texas. Private Edward Grabinski had been a tenor during the 1938–41 performances, while PFC Richard Holtzclaw (whose stage name was Richard Wentworth) was a baritone before enlisting as a surgical technician. Grabinski served as a driver for a Quartermaster unit.

Hollywood Hunks Sign Up

Clark Gable was stunned in early 1942 when his fun-loving wife, Carole Lombard, was killed in a plane crash returning to Hollywood from a successful war bond drive. His friends, concerned for his well-being, tried to pull him out of his depression, and when he volunteered for the Air Corps that summer, many wondered if he was fulfilling Carole's wishes to join the military, or seeking dangerous missions intent on dying a war hero.

With much fanfare, the King of Hollywood (along with MGM photographer Andrew McIntyre) shipped off to Officer Candidate School at Miami Beach. Once the news of Gable's signing up got out, hundreds of adoring fans migrated to the southern tip of Florida to meet their favorite Hollywood heartthrob. But Gable was having difficulty with the grueling regimen, both the physical and the mental demands. "At forty-one, he was ill-equipped to compete with men half his age . . . awakened at 4:15 every morning and required to march a mile or two before breakfast," Warren G. Harris wrote in *Gable and Lombard*.

"Gable was almost undone, however, by the academic side of his training. Never a good student, he found it extremely difficult to adapt to a classroom routine. If he failed, Gable was subject not only to being transferred to the infantry, but also to national humiliation if the truth was ever revealed."

He finally mastered the curriculum by treating each lesson

Below: *Clark Gable, Hollywood's reigning king in the early 1940s, fled Hollywood and set aside fears of flying for the Army Air Corps. He joined when his wife, Carole Lombard, was killed in a plane crash returning home from a 1942 bond drive. The actor accepted Gen. Henry "Hap" Arnold's request to make a movie about aerial gunners to recruit more men to the air forces. Although Gable was only to make documentaries, every plane he flew on to film combat action was fired on by Luftwaffe fighter pilots and anti-aircraft gunners.*
Army Air Corps Photo

the same way he had movie scripts, by memorizing them. Every night after lights out, he got the "urge" to go to the bathroom, with a textbook in hand, and he would camp out in one of the stalls for hours, prepping for the next day's work. His method obviously worked; because on October 28, 1942, Clark Gable was commissioned as a second lieutenant, 700th in a class of 2,600, far from being the distinguished graduate, but because of his celebrity status, his classmates asked him to speak for all of them:

"I've worked with you, scrubbed with you, marched with you, worried with you over whether this day would ever come. The important thing, the proud thing I've learned about us is that we are men. . . . Soon we will wear the uniforms of officers. How we look in them is not very important. How we wear them is a lot more important. The job is to stay on the beam until in victory we get the command 'FALL OUT.'"

Another out-of-shape "entertainer" who had difficulty keeping up with much younger recruits in the continuous marching and drilling was Harry Holubiak's retired circus horse, who was put out to pasture near a training base outside South Bend. The post band would occasionally rehearse their marches on the adjacent parade field at the same time massed recruits practiced the various facing movements—forward march, to the rear march, wheel right, and so forth. Unfortunately, the feeble circus horse in the nearby field was used to promenading around whenever he heard music and nearly collapsed from exhaustion one day when the damn band just wouldn't call it quits!

Unlike the King of Hollywood, Clark Gable, who dreaded dancing among the clouds, Jimmy Stewart was an avid flyer, who had grown up fascinated by the tales of WWI fighter aces. (He had also been a fan of aviation pioneer Charles Lindbergh, but disagreed with his pro-isolationist stance during the Nazis' rise to power. Lindbergh even had the audacity to suggest that if Americans went to war in Europe, the Nazi blitzkrieg tactics would beat them.) In 1935, whenever time allowed between movie projects, Stewart took flying lessons in a two-seat biplane, and he eventually bought his own Stinson 105.

In 1940 he starred in *The Mortal Storm*, "an early propaganda film which prophetically warned of the Nazi menace while German-American storm troopers were still goose-stepping around Soldier Field in Chicago," wrote Frank Sanello in *Jimmy Stewart: A Wonderful Life*.

In early 1941, just as *The Mortal Storm* was being shown around the country, Stewart tried to enlist and battle the Nazis for real, hoping to become an Air Corps pilot, but the review board felt he was too skinny and underweight to meet the minimum requirements. It didn't matter that he was an accomplished pilot—he needed to gain fifteen pounds. Stewart promptly hired a trainer and added another ten pounds, but it still wasn't enough. He appealed to an Army official to maybe look the other way and ignore his weight. Finally, on March 22 he was accepted for duty and reported to Fort MacArthur's induction center. He was offered "star treatment," including permission to sleep in every morning, but Private Stewart wanted to be treated just like everyone else, which meant wake-up calls at "oh-dark thirty."

"Reveille was at 5:45 A.M., which didn't faze him at all, since he was used to getting up only slightly later—6:30—for early morning calls to the movie set. Autocratic directors and 12-hour shoots to save money had a boot camp flavor of their own." After his training, war had been declared, and Stewart was anxious to get overseas, but instead he was transferred to New Mexico's Kirtland Field, where he became a bombardier instructor.

Even Dummies Try to Get In

As part of a publicity stunt to bolster enlistments, comedian Charlie McCarthy joined the Army Air Corps while doing his weekly radio show. He demanded to be promoted to master sergeant even though he had never served in the military, but that wasn't the main hurdle to accepting him in the service. Charlie couldn't pass the physical for a variety of reasons: he was too short, he wouldn't speak on his own, and oh, by the way, he was made of wood—white pine to be exact! Charlie McCarthy, of course, was renowned ventriloquist Edgar Bergen's dummy. But he wasn't just any ordinary dummy.

BELOW: *To encourage enlistments, popular radio dummy Charlie McCarthy tried to join the Army Air Forces but was turned down for being too short, mute, and made of wood. To further bolster sign-ups, McCarthy (led by his ventriloquist pal, Edgar Bergen) also attempted to join the Marines when the Army turned down his request. Here McCarthy and Bergen visit with actor W. C. Fields (left) and starlet Paulette Goddard.* Armed Forces Radio Services Photo

"In the minds of millions of Americans, Charlie McCarthy became a real person," wrote John Dunning in *Tune in Yesterday*. "His character took on three-dimensional qualities. Charlie was America's most lovable bad boy."

Of course his acceptance into the Army Air Corps was denied, so "the following week, Charlie tried to obtain another commission by joining the Marines. It culminated in a highly publicized 'military trial' on location at the Stockton, California, Army base. Lieutenant James Stewart was brought in to defend Charlie, who, in the end, was found as guilty as he was."

Leathernecks Looking for a Few Good Men

In the Universal Studios film *Gung-Ho*, Marine recruits have payback on their minds as they undergo rigorous training, prepping them to go into battle against an inferior enemy.

"The film opens at a Marine base in San Diego where a special unit is being trained to conduct secret raids on Japanese bases," wrote Clayton Koppes and Gregory Black in *Hollywood Goes to War*. "The call goes out for volunteers, and each man is asked during an interview: 'Why do you want to kill Japs?' Each has his reason. Says one: 'My brother was killed at Pearl Harbor.' Another: 'I fought in Spain—we're still fighting fascism.' And a third: 'I don't like Japs.' The men are anxious to get an opportunity for revenge. Randolph Scott is in charge of training for the raiders. The Pacific war will be won by teamwork, he tells his men. They must work together, and in order to do so, they must each eliminate all prejudice from their system. Ironically, *Gung-Ho* proceeded to be one of the most rabid 'hate the Jap' films made in Hollywood."

Numerous Hollywood stars signed on with the Marine Corps, none bigger than Tyrone Power, who trained in San Diego. Movie mogul Darryl Zanuck tried to talk him out of enlisting but was rebuffed. Then Zanuck encouraged him to accept an officer commission, but again, Power didn't feel it should be given to him because of his star status. He wanted to earn it first.

Right: *Hunky Hollywood actor Tyrone Power initially enlisted in the U.S. Naval Reserves in April 1942, but was angered when he inquired about seeking active duty status and was denied the chance to be a fighter pilot. Not satisfied with the opportunity to be an ordinary Navy seaman, he joined the U.S. Marine Corps four months later, despite the pleading of Fox Studio executive Darryl Zanuck, then a U.S. Army colonel. Power earned naval aviator status and saw combat action in March 1945 as he delivered supplies and transported casualties out of Iwo Jima and Okinawa. This photo showed Power in his last make-believe role, as naval Lt. Ward Stewart fighting Nazis in 1943's* Crash Dive.

Associated Press Photo

Zanuck did urge Power to delay his enlistment for six months so he could complete the film *Crash Dive*, a naval yarn in the North Atlantic.

Soon after shooting wrapped, Power headed down to San Diego to become a leatherneck. "When later asked if he'd had a rough time in boot camp, Ty replied, 'In a way. They made me do everything twice. I guess they never believed me the first time.' He welcomed the opportunity to prove he was as tough as his swashbuckling image," wrote Hector Arce in *The Secret Life of Tyrone Power*. Like many of the so-called "pretty boys," Power was challenged early and often, at least until he used his fists to prove he belonged.

After completing boot camp, Power was selected for Officer Candidate School at Quantico in Virginia. From there he went on to flight training, where he learned to fly DC-13 transport planes.

As a youngster Hugh Krampe had joined the Pup Marines, made up mostly of children of Marine Corps officers and NCOs, who did quasi-marching drills, community service work, and learned first aid and map reading. As a teenager young Krampe attended Roosevelt Military Academy in Illinois and then Kemper Military School in Missouri. It was only natural that as soon as he could join the armed forces, he would become a leatherneck, qualify as an expert shot, and become an honor graduate. At only eighteen, he was the Corps' youngest drill instructor, barking out orders to men as much as twice his age.

"Let me tell you, some of those guys were tough as nails and I was the one that had to whip 'em into shape. I learned early on that without strict discipline and following the rules, you could lose control of your troops quickly," he recalled on his Web page. "You had to be tough, smart, and fast to weed out the 'law-breakers' and malcontents, or you risked paying the ultimate price in battle." He was offered an appointment to the Naval Academy at Anapolis, but declined. (After completing his military service, Krampe turned to acting after the war and changed his name to Hugh O'Brian.)

Robert Ryan had tried numerous occupations after graduating from Dartmouth with a degree in English Literature, including newspaper reporting, coal stoking deep in the sweltering bowels of an Atlantic freighter, cowpoking in Montana, modeling in Chicago, bill collecting, and panhandling for gold. He had been an extra in two silent movies in the late twenties, and decided to give that profession a try. A decade later he was studying acting in Hollywood, which garnered an offer from Paramount that wasn't renewed for a second year. He was unemployed again. Then,

Below: *Marines in North Carolina take a break from their intensive training. Instructors maintained a grueling pace to prepare young men for combat.*

Office of War Information Photo

while on stage with *Clash by Night*, Ryan received favorable reviews and an offer from RKO Radio Pictures, which immediately cast him in numerous film projects, including *Marine Raiders*. After filming was completed, he joined the Marines for real, first as a recruit at boot camp, and then as a drill instructor at Camp Pendleton.

Another Marine Corps training instructor was Ed McMahon, who had been with the Civilian Military Training Corps in high school. "It was in the CMTC that instructors first recognized my natural leadership qualities and promoted me to sergeant. Those qualities consisted primarily of the fact that I was the tallest person in my squad and had the loudest voice," he recalled in *For Laughing out Loud*.

After listening to his father talk about fighter aces of WWI and barnstorming in the years after, McMahon was hoping to be a Marine Corps fighter pilot. Instead, he was landlocked, training other aviation candidates on how to take off and land on aircraft carriers. (By 1950 the showbiz bug had bitten, and he was performing as a circus clown; many years later, he was best known as Johnny Carson's sidekick on *The Tonight Show*.)

Sterling Hayden had salt water in his blood, and as a boy yearned to sail the Seven Seas, reading library books about pirates and adventurers, learning about sails and their functions, ropes and knots, the many types of boats, weather and creatures of the deep, and everything nautical. He visited the docks and the dockmen and badgered them for a job aboard anything afloat. "Friendly, leathered sailors invited him aboard, where they regaled him with tales of afar. Sterling soaked it all in. Someday, he knew, these would be his exploits," wrote James E. Wise Jr. and Anne Collier Rehill in *Stars in the Corps*.

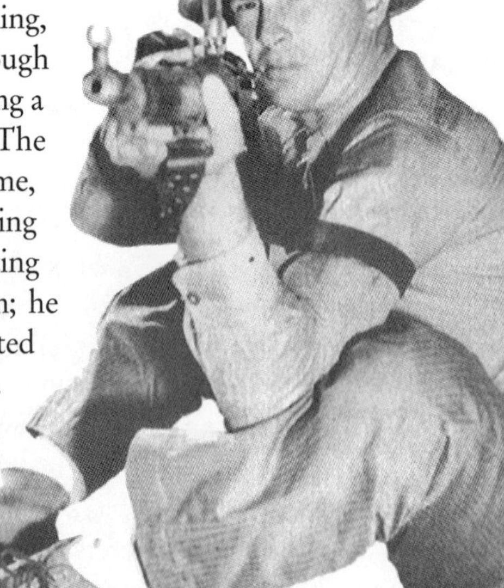

RIGHT: *Sterling Hayden always wanted a life at sea, but without a high school education, the Navy only offered the would-be actor a position on a PT boat, where casualty rates were high among these "expendables." He settled for an enlistment in the Marine Corps in 1942, and, after excelling during boot camp and gaining the attention of his commanders, was commissioned an officer the following year. Hayden served in the Navy's Office of Strategic Services (OSS), the precursor to the modern Central Intelligence Agency. He maneuvered behind enemy lines to collect data, move supplies, and rescue downed Allied airmen.*
Marine Corps Photo

Others called him the Viking, handsome and rugged, and through acquaintances he wound up signing a contract with Paramount. "The studio, like many others at the time, groomed lookers such as the Viking for stardom. They gave him acting lessons and sent him to the gym; he got the full treatment, and he hated it all," noted Wise and Rehill. "He was sent on publicity tours, which he found ridiculous."

Aware of the escalating turmoil in Europe,

Hayden knew he couldn't remain an actor while the rest of the world was turned topsy-turvy. He offered his services to the Office of Strategic Services—an eclectic group of spies and mercenaries and assassins and eavesdroppers—and they shipped him off to Great Britain for training in commando operations. But when he broke his ankle and wracked up his knee on a parachute jump, they sent him home to recuperate and rehab.

As soon as he could pass the physical and stand up to the rigors of military training, Hayden joined the Marines and did boot camp in South Carolina, at Parris Island. He too would serve briefly as a drill instructor and then move on to Officer Candidate School at Quantico. "Hayden was a good Marine on the surface, but he loathed the discipline and the fact that he was so easily recognized, which worked against him in the Corps," continued Wise and Rehill. "He no longer wanted to be associated with Hollywood; Hayden wanted to be thought of as just another Marine." He thus changed his name to John Hamilton.

Above: *Second lieutenant Macdonald Carey served in the Marine Corps as an ordnance officer, despite being rejected initially for service. The actor's color blindness nearly prevented him from being a leatherneck. Here he practiced his weapons skills in Cherry Point. After the war, Carey played many movie and television characters, including the role of Dr. Tom Horton, patriarch of the* Days of Our Lives *soap opera family.*

Marine Corps Photo

Macdonald Carey was a popular actor on both radio and Broadway, and then Hollywood came calling. He appeared in 1942's *Wake Island*, about a small contingent of Marines holding out against impossible odds. Carey and numerous other cast members felt a fondness for the leathernecks and enlisted soon after filming wrapped. He too would go through boot camp at Parris Island, then on to OCS at Quantico and a commission with the Marine Corps Reserve. With his radio broadcasting background, Carey was tabbed as an air controller and underwent radar training in Florida.

Jacques O'Mahoney was a former collegiate swimming champion and avid equestrian when war dragged the United States into the fight. Three days after Pearl Harbor, he volunteered to serve as an instructor with the Army Air Corps. Then he decided to enlist in the Marines where he went through boot camp at San Diego. (After his service, he would change his name slightly to Jock Mahoney and make it to Hollywood, primarily as a stuntman and mostly in westerns.)

Jazz drummer Buddy Rich was already well known in music circles, sitting in with some of the most popular big bands of the day, including Tommy Dorsey and Artie Shaw. And so it was only natural that when he joined the Marines, he became a . . . judo instructor? Actually, Rich wanted to get overseas and see a little combat, but higher-ups wanted him to assemble his own jazz combo. He wasn't interested.

Going to Sea

Navy boot camp wasn't any easier than for the other services, and many landlubbers who had never even seen the ocean let alone been on a boat were inducted into the maritime service.

Bernard Schwartz had done community theater during his high school years in the Bronx, but soon after graduation, with the war raging, he signed on with the Navy and was trained as a signalman. He eventually was deployed to the Pacific, where he would be injured. (After the war he studied acting, changed his name to Tony Curtis, and headed for Hollywood.)

Above: *Handsome actor Robert Stack took his dead-eye shooting skills he had honed as part of 1936's five-man skeet shooting national championship team and used them to teach others aerial gunnery in the U.S. Navy. Although he'd set his sights on being a fighter pilot, Stack lacked depth perception, and instead taught several future fighter aces.*
U.S. Navy Photo

Robert Taylor was one of Hollywood's hottest leading men, starring in thirty-seven movies between his start in 1934 and his enlistment in the Navy in 1943. He earned his aviator wings and then became a flight instructor in New Orleans.

Another Hollywood hunk was Robert Stack, who was part of the five-man skeet team that won the National Championship in 1936, and who won the singles 20-gauge champion the following year. As it became evident the United States was about to get entangled in war, Stack considered following in his uncle's footsteps as a Navy fighter pilot. Despite his eagle eyesight as a skeet shooter, he failed the depth-perception exam and thus was denied cockpit duty. He would get through Navy boot camp and then become an instructor in aerial gunnery, which was extremely dangerous. On a pitching aircraft trying to evade enemy fighters swooping in with their own guns blazing, it was the young tail, side, and ball turret gunners who had to blast them out of the skies, and maybe live another day. Simply learning how to fire these guns was perilous for the gunners, for the instructors like Stack, and for anyone else within striking distance, such as nervous pilots towing flying targets behind them.

Actor Robert Montgomery had seen action in both the European and Pacific theaters when he was sent to the Naval Small Craft Training Command in California. His task was to develop radio-controlled drone aircraft that could be used as targets for the aerial gunners in training. Actor Reginald Denny was also involved with this development program, which contributed greatly to the accuracy of naval gunners on planes and warships.

Frank "Junior" Coghlan had starred as Billy Batson—" known to radio listeners as the world's mightiest mortal"—in the *Captain Marvel* episodes in 1941. He served in naval aviation, learning to fly the Kingfisher floatplane, which could be used to search for downed pilots, land on the water, and rescue them. It could also carry ordnance, such as depth charges and bombs. After graduating with high marks, Coghlan was asked to stay on as a flight instructor for incoming "slingshot aviators," as Kingfisher pilots were dubbed.

At age thirty-seven, Henry Fonda could have spent the entire war making movies, but he felt he had to do his part and didn't think his fans would remain loyal if he watched the whole show from the grandstand seats. Like his good friend Jimmy Stewart, he bulked up with an MGM trainer prior to enlisting, then joined the Navy. He survived the rigors of boot camp at San Diego and was trained to be a communications operator, learning to use signal flags and blinker lights.

MGM star Gene Kelly was another old-timer at age thirty-two when he endured boot camp in San Diego. His dancing on screen had kept him in shape for early morning calisthenics and endless marching drills, but he often questioned the reasoning behind the three-month madness. Another recruit at San Diego was Robert Ozell Moseley, whose unit, Fleet Air Wing 14, prepped other Navy units deploying to the Pacific, training air crews. During his free time he pulled lifeguard duty at San Diego's North Island. (Like so many other servicemen with big aspirations in southern California, Moseley got out of the Navy, changed his name to Guy Madison, and hit it big in Hollywood, staking out the title role for the television series *Wild Bill Hickok* from 1951 to 1959.)

Robert Keith Jr. excelled at the marksmanship range during boot camp and was soon teaching officer candidates at Quantico how to shoot. (After the war he would find work in stock theater and change his name to Brian Keith.)

Radio performer Mike Douglas tried to join the Navy but broke his ankle and was put on ninety-day convalescence. Once his foot had mended, he enlisted and was sent to the Great Lakes Naval Training Station in Chicago, "then on to Madison, Wisconsin, for officer's training as a naval radioman," Douglas wrote in *I'll be Right Back*. "Typical government logic—since I was a

BELOW: *Guy Madison's photo appeared in an on-base publication while he was spending his precious little free time working as a lifeguard at Naval Air Station North Island in San Diego. Movie mogul David Selznick came across the picture and signed Madison—then named Robert Ozell Moseley—to a contract upon his honorable discharge from the Navy in October 1945. Madison would trade a sailor's hat for a cowboy hat, becoming television's Wild Bill Hickok from 1951 to 1959.*
U.S. Navy Photo

singer on radio, it made perfect sense that I should transmit coded radio signals from warships on the high seas."

While many other bandleaders joined one of the armed forces and established their own group of military musicians, pianist Eddy Duchin saw his talents used for other purposes. After surviving boot camp at Great Lakes, he moved on to Northwestern University's Naval Training School and Sub-Chaser School in southern Florida, relying on his perfect pitch in mastering sonar detection, the pinging echoes created by nearby ships and submarines.

One sailor whom the military used for his musical skills was the King of the Banjo, Eddie Peabody, who also served at Great Lakes and trained hundreds of musicians for the many bands scattered wherever the Navy was deployed around the globe. Jazz saxophonist John Coltrane was one of those seamen who played concerts, ceremonies, and parades during his hitch.

Strother Martin had been a collegiate swimmer at the University of Michigan and after joining the Navy became a swimming instructor at St. Mary's Navy Pre-Flight School. (After getting out of the Navy, he would find work in Hollywood as a swimming coach to the children of the stars; he would later offer up small swimming roles in films. This led to bigger speaking roles.) One of his students at St. Mary's was future *Gunsmoke* sidekick, Dennis Weaver.

Another well-known swimmer who helped train Navy recruits was Tarzan—Johnny Weissmuller—who was too old to serve in the military but still volunteered his talents by teaching sailors how to hold their breath underwater and swim away from oil and petroleum burning on the surface.

RIGHT: *Eddie Peabody (with banjo) trained Navy bandsmen at the Great Lakes Naval Training Center in Chicago. He thought music was important to troop morale, and in addition to popular music, he also played patriotic and march tunes. Peabody entertained soldiers at officers' and NCO clubs around the world.* U.S. Naval Historical Center Photo

Jackie Cooper had grown up in Hollywood, in front of the cameras, with insufficient time for proper schooling. This would be an enormous liability for him, and he

had difficulty with the Navy's V-12 program at Notre Dame. And the Navy wasn't into grading on the curve for any Hollywood glamour boys.

Unlike Clark Gable, who snuck off to the latrine late at night to study, Cooper was assessed demerits every time he was caught doing the same. His grades suffered while the demerits piled up, and soon he was dropped from the program, banished to boot camp at Great Lakes Training Center, where he eventually connected with senior band instructor Eddie Peabody. Cooper couldn't keep up with the academic demands of the V-12 program, but he excelled as a percussionist and, after graduating from boot camp, he headed for Los Angeles to link up with bandleader Claude Thornhill, who was assembling a small ensemble to tour the Pacific. (At the Army Air Base in Miami Beach, Private Ewen McNaron claimed he was Jackie Cooper, then got thrown in the stockade for four months for going AWOL.)

Above: *Former child actor and Seaman Second Class Jackie Cooper not only served his country in the U.S. Navy but also entertained troops and gave the ladies, such as these women serving in the Marine Corps in Hawaii, some eye candy to look at.* Marine Corps Photo

Jack Lemmon was another reluctant student in the Navy's V-12 Reserve Officer Program. In fact, he distinguished himself by having the lowest possible marks of any graduate in the program! For a class skit Lemmon did pen a forgettable little ditty about every serviceman's unknown future:

"I'm in the U.S. Army
and if Hitler ever sar me
he would never dare to harm me."

Obviously Lemmon would not have much future as a lyricist, whether in the Navy or out, but his comedic talents would serve him well, most notably in Hollywood.

Entertainers Bolster Troop Morale

"... But then his number came up
and he was gone with the draft.
He's in the Army now, a-blowin' reveille.
He's the Boogie Woogie Bugle Boy of Company B."

From the song "Boogie Woogie Bugle Boy," by Don Raye and Hughie Prince, MCA Music Publishers, 1941

Background: *Every new recruit had to pull guard duty. This sentry stands alone at Fort McClellan, Alabama*
YANK Magazine Photo

AMERICA'S PERFORMERS, FROM BROADWAY TO VAUDEVILLE to Hollywood and everywhere in between, stepped forward to entertain the troops undergoing training stateside. Hundreds of entertainers were eventually in uniform also, assigned to morale-building units that put on concerts, plays, and variety shows.

After weeks of nonstop, grueling drills, classes, physical exercise, and on and on, piling into a cramped theater or jamming into bleacher seats, or just sitting in the mud to watch entertainers strut their stuff was a much-needed break for the weary recruits.

The most visible difference between United Services Organizations (USO) and Special Services entertainers was immediately obvious. USO starlets could wear flashy outfits and stylized hairdos, while those women in any of the armed forces were under stricter guidelines, suffering with frumpy, baggy, unflattering uniforms and clunky shoes. The only service members who could get away with campy fashions—feather boas, thigh-high and plunging evening gowns, and stiletto heels—were guys dressing in drag! Of course it was all done in fun, and practically every service show had at least one cross-dressing vamp who could do the bump and grind better than any stripper.

Two entertainers who were literally rescued from dismal military life were Sammy Davis Jr. and Alfred Cocozza (who later performed as Mario Lanza).

Davis had learned to tap dance practically before he could walk. Soon after, he learned to sing and play several instruments, and he was performing in vaudeville shows by age four. His act included impersonations, jokes, and lightning-fast feet. On stage he heard the applause and lived for the spotlight.

Below: *Singer Faye McKenzie aimed a gun at Utah's Wendover Field as comedian Billy Gilbert looked on.*
Army Air Forces Wendover Field Photo

ABOVE: *Sometimes the luckiest guy in the camp became the most envied. Glamour girl Carole Landis plucked PFC Joseph Schneeberg from the audience and asked him to jitterbug with her. The dance was part of a USO show touring training camps across the Midwest.* Fort Crook, Nebraska, Public Relations Office Photo

But in the Army, where he joined one of the first integrated basic training units at Fort Warren in Wyoming, he experienced the never-ending ugliness of bigotry. His only sanctuary was the post service club, where he could step back into the spotlight for the Friday night talent shows. "My talent was the weapon, the power, the way for me to fight," Davis remembered in his book *Yes I Can*, cowritten with June and Burt Boyar.

After one appearance, he was approached by another soldier, who introduced himself as George M. Cohan Jr., son of the renowned showman. Davis recalled the conversation with Cohan: "'That was one hell of a show you just did,' he said. 'You've heard about the big show every camp's going to be doing for the inter-camp competition? Well, with all the stuff you know and with my dad's special material, which I know backwards, I'll bet we could get that assignment. You know as well as I do that all the guys who'll be trying for it will just be using stuff out of the Special Services books. But with us writing our own, something fresh, we couldn't miss.'"

And they didn't miss. Davis was picked up for duty with Army Special Services and toured the country, "gorging myself on the joy of being liked, killing myself to give back as much as they were giving me. I dug down deeper every day, looking for new material, inventing it, stealing it, switching it, any way that I could find new things to make my shows better, and I lived twenty-four hours a day for that hour or two at night when I could give it away free, when I could stand on that stage, facing the audience, knowing I was dancing down the barriers between us."

A Stumblebum in Uniform

There was no hiding the fact that Private Alfred Cocozza was one lousy soldier. The Army had snatched him up just as his singing career was taking off (under the name Mario Lanza, the tenor with the golden voice), and he had no interest in serving his country. Millions of other men could take his place and let him get back to what he did best. He certainly didn't want to be in the military, and intentionally looked like a stumblebum in an effort to get kicked out, without any luck.

When a service-wide call went out for former entertainers, Cocozza was rescued from his miseries, most of which were his own doing. "Johnny Silver, a noncommissioned officer who had been a comic in burlesque was scanning service records in search of candidates for variety shows that would be presented at military bases throughout the country," Ronald Bessette wrote in *Mario Lanza: Tenor in Exile*. Cocozza was summoned to try out for the job.

Soon after, another former entertainer, Peter Lind Hayes, was hopscotching from one base to the next looking for talent to fill out the cast of a new musical show he had written with songwriter Frank Loesser, to be called *On the Beam.* Cocozza soon joined the cast of the loosely written, vaudevillian-style show, and once again, as he had done before enlisting, he heard rousing applause whenever he took center stage and unleashed a voice that was heaven sent.

Another offer came in, when playwright Moss Hart assembled a massive cast for his *Winged Victory* musical extravaganza about the Air Force. Unfortunately, because of his portly and rumpled appearance, Cocozza was buried among the masses of the men's chorus instead of out front in the spotlight.

"The cast of *Winged Victory* included impressive names from the stage and motion pictures: Alan Baxter, Red Buttons, Marc Daniels, Ray Middleton, Karl Malden, Gary Merrill and screen actor Barry Nelson, Edmond O'Brien, George Reeves and Don Taylor," Bessette continued in *Mario Lanza*.

The show ran for six months at the 44th Street Theatre in New York, pulling in $600,000 for Army Relief. Even though he was finally back on stage and singing again, Private Cocozza was little more than another face among the many, practically ignored and underappreciated.

Other Entertainers in the Services

Private Leota Lane Pitts was part of the Lane family singing troupe, who had appeared on radio, the silver screen, and theater. When war broke out they felt obliged to do their part in some way. "All of us Lane sisters sat down one day and conferred over who was to represent the family in the armed services," she explained to *YANK* magazine. "We figured that, since we came from Indianola, near WAC headquarters in Des Moines, Iowa, at least one of us should be in." Leota stepped forward and signed up as a singer with the Second Air Force Band in Colorado Springs. During her off-duty hours she also sang at the local USO and surrounding military posts and bases, arranged sing-alongs, and frequently appeared on local radio programs.

Even fictional characters had a chance to work for the war effort. *YANK* magazine revealed how a popular cartoon character occasionally led cadence at Boca Raton Field in Florida: "When the monotony of close-order drill begins to get the boys down, drill sergeants let Donald Duck—or rather his voice—give the commands the way the feathered film star might give them if he were drill sergeant. The voice is that of Corporal Theodore Gurtner, who for five years before he came into the Army was a narrator for the Walt Disney Studio. Though Gurtner's face has never appeared on the screen, it was his voice that accompanied the antics of Donald Duck in *Der Fuehrer's Face*."

Spicing up the monotony of mandatory training was also the intent of Special Services personnel at Fort Hamilton in New York. One week prior to scheduled orientation courses on Monday mornings, the entertainment staff would latch onto the training manual, rip it apart, jazz it up with a skit, toss in liberal doses of humor written by comedian Ziggy Lane, and music composed by Harold Rome. Rehearsals sorted out any problem areas and added polish. The productions even included costumes and stylized sets and props. Monday morning at 10:30 sharp, with the audience—basic trainees—in their seats at the base theater, the curtain rose, the lights went up, and it was showtime again.

Actor Burgess Meredith was not yet in the service when he narrated the radio show, *The Spirit of '41*, which soon became *The Army Hour*. He then took *Hour* around the country, explaining to recruits what was happening overseas and how the United States was bracing for the impending conflicts. (Shortly thereafter, Meredith and an actor he shared a house with received their draft notices. That roommate was Jimmy Stewart.)

Tech 4 Luanne Spurgeon played baritone with the WAAC Orchestra at Fort Des Moines. Martha Settle was among the initial forty black women who were sent to Fort Des Moines. She would become an officer and remain at the post to train other female recruits. Even though integration was opening up the armed forces to blacks, it didn't curtail prevailing prejudices. Settle noted that "black musicians were routinely banned from the base band, so they formed their own—maybe the first all-black, all-female military band in the world," wrote Tom Brokaw in *The Greatest Generation*.

"Martha recalls that Army officials in Washington sent word to Des Moines: 'We don't need two base bands. Get rid of the black band.' Martha . . . raised the band issue with her superior officer. Others got involved as well, including the musicians' guilds, and eventually word reached the White House and Eleanor Roosevelt. Not long after, the black band was back in business."

Comedian Joey Bishop was tabbed to be a recreation director for the Army at Fort Sam Houston in San Antonio, Texas. Former big band singer Ruth Johnson performed at Camp Bowie, Texas, where she always capped her show with the song "He Wears a Pair of Silver Wings," dedicated to her husband, an Army Air Corps officer overseas in the China-Burma-India Campaign.

Senior actor and WWI veteran Walter Brennan was too old to serve after Pearl Harbor, but he was very active throughout the war, entertaining the troops. Comedian Sid Caesar joined the Coast Guard and spent his war years guarding the Brooklyn docks. Every chance he got, he sat in with the service's orchestra and wrote comedy routines, performing in the "Tars and Spars" variety show that crisscrossed the country.

On his eighteenth birthday Aaron Spelling joined the Army Air Corps. Soon thereafter he was at Fort Worth in Texas, "where I started submitting sketches to the camp revues," he wrote in his autobiography. "The first offerings were rejected, but I kept at it and finally scored with something called 'Wacky-Khaki,' your basic barracks-room humor. I knew immediately after hearing the applause that this was what I wanted in life—to entertain an audience."

Army Private Mary Louise Ellington—the Duke's niece—was stationed at Fort Riley, Kansas, assigned to the WAC detachment's drum and bugle corps. She was the band's percussionist and drum majorette.

Ozzie Nelson and his orchestra were the featured performers on the Red Skelton radio show, as part of NBC's powerful Tuesday night lineup. By the end of 1941 they had several songs near the top of the charts. Ozzie noted in his autobiography, "With the advent of World War II in December of '41, however, one by one the boys in our band were drafted into the service bands. By February of 1942, we had experienced about a 90 percent turnover in personnel from the previous year." Nelson's plight was shared by every big band across the country.

Movie star Mickey Rooney was at Camp Sibert in Alabama, training to be a chemical warfare specialist, when the Army solicited information about any performers in uniform who could deploy overseas to entertain the troops. "It seems that entertainers attached to the USO didn't want to have any part of the action on the front lines," Rooney wrote in his book, *Life Is Too Short*. "So the Army said, 'That's okay, we've drafted some entertainers of our own. We'll entertain our own troops.' My commanding officer tapped me, and soon word came through: I'd be headed for an Army base near New York City."

Actor Victor Mature was initially considered just a pretty boy by his Coast Guard shipmates on the cutter *Storis*—understandable, since fan magazines had dubbed him a "beautiful

Below: *Chief Boatswain's Mate Victor Mature was easily recognized both in and out of his U.S. Coast Guard uniform. The actor tried to join the Navy but was denied an enlistment because they claimed he failed the color-blindness test. When the Coasties administered a rarer test—using the Navy's equipment—Mature passed with flying colors. He served on the* Storis, *which sailors called the "Galloping Ghost of the Alaskan Coast."* U.S. Coast Guard Photo

hunk of man." But he never used his star status to shirk any "shit details" in the military, and was quickly accepted as just one of the guys. Good-naturedly, they nicknamed him the Coast Guard's "Hunk of Junk."

Radio disc jockey Jack Paar was working at WBEN in New York when he enlisted. Because of his background he was assigned to Army Special Services, where the unit's function "was to bolster morale by furnishing entertainment, publishing camp newspapers, providing books and periodicals and the like," he explained in *I Kid You Not*. "Our motley group included everything from a former burlesque comedian to a string quartet."

One high-profile entertainer who fortunately refused a cushy assignment with Special Services was leading actor Jimmy Stewart. Sure, he knew how to play the accordion . . . barely. In fact, it was joked his musicianship might do more harm to the war effort than anything the Nazis could throw at the Allies in Europe!

Performers Tour the Country

Six months before war was declared, 370-pound Tiny Hill and his swing band toured the country, playing shuffle-rhythm tunes that had the boys at Army and Navy camps hopping. "Tiny" had wanted to enlist, but the Army felt he was just slightly overweight—like, maybe 150 pounds over. "The Army made a mistake," Tiny quipped to *YANK* magazine. "It would have gotten two men for one."

James Cagney was chairman of the Hollywood Victory Committee and led the charge as more than twenty-five thousand members of the Screen Actors Guild volunteered to make personal appearances at training camps, bases, and posts throughout the country. "He would be leading the Hollywood Victory Caravan . . . accompanied by Pat O'Brien, Merle Oberon, and a host of others," wrote Michael Freedland in *Cagney*. "It was the toughest job he had taken on in years, but he knew he really was doing more good than just stepping into uniform for the benefit of a crowd of photographers."

Cagney was the tireless hoofer, often performing as many as twelve shows in a single day, whether the audience was several thousand recruits or a hospital ward of only a handful of servicemen on the mend. And when the massive influx of recruits stretched existing training facilities to the bursting point, Cagney generously allowed the Army to use his sprawling Martha's Vineyard estate for field training exercises. (His neighbors may not have appreciated the simulated gunfire and explosions and smoke clouds that smelled of sulfur, or the early morning calisthenics and ten-mile road marches complete with those famous Jody Calls, but everyone in the country had to make sacrifices, so being "invaded" by a few thousand soldiers-in-training was not a lot to ask.)

Another tireless entertainer was Bing Crosby. "On one trip in 1942 Bing and composer-friend Jimmy Van Heusen traveled more than 5,000 miles in the U.S. performing a two-man show for servicemen and visiting hundreds of hospital wards," Charles Thompson wrote in *Bing*. "On another trip, he took a large troupe of dancers, a band, and comedian Phil Silvers, as well as Van Heusen. They averaged three shows a day at camps all over the States and these shows would continue throughout the war years."

During his swing through training camps and bases in the southern states, Der Bingle (as he was dubbed by German soldiers who heard his records) and other entertainers, along with the thousands of servicemen there, heard a new style of music. Some called it hillbilly, others dubbed it country. "Ferlin Husky recalled serving in the Merchant Marine with 'lots of boys who had never really heard country music before, and it was interesting to see how fast they acquired a taste for it,'" Joshua Zeitz reported in the article "Dixie's Victory" for *American Heritage* magazine, August/September 2002. "By the 1940s 'Grand Ole Opry' was perhaps the most admired radio show in the United States, with a cast of songsters and comedians that included Roy Acuff, Bill Monroe, Minnie Pearl, and 'Uncle Dave' Macon."

It was only natural that as more and more servicemen heard this new type of music, whether at the recreation centers and service clubs on posts in the south or collapsed on their bunks listening to it on the radio, its popularity would spread. Soon even crooners like Bing Crosby were singing country songs. (He recorded "Don't Fence Me In" with the Andrews Sisters and

Left: *The Andrews Sisters frequently toured with USO shows around the country. Here, they pay homage to the Hollywood Canteen in the Broadway musical,* Over There.
World USO Photo

ABOVE: *The Western Signal Aviation Unit at Camp Pinedale, California, "adopted" showgirl Beryl Wallace. Soldiers presented her with honorary sergeant's stripes.*
Army Air Forces Photo

"Deep in the Heart of Texas" with the Woody Herman Orchestra during the early '40s.)

Fort Sill near Lawton, Oklahoma, was one of the largest Army training posts and a frequent stop for entertainers. One of those troupes was Ada Leonard and her All-American Girl Orchestra. Ada was born in Lawton, and when she was growing up her parents, themselves entertainers, would haul her out to Fort Sill while they performed for the recruits during WWI. It was only natural that Ada would do the same during the Second World War, taking her all-girl entourage around the country on six-month tours.

As with any combo there was bound to be occasions when someone couldn't make it. During a show at Camp Edwards in Massachusetts, the horn player wasn't feeling well, so the call went out for any recruit who could play. There was only one catch: they had to wear a wig and a skirt! "He was the best trumpeter that ever played for me," Ada laughed.

Even established stars were willing to hit the road for hours on end to go wherever the troops were training.

"We traveled most in buses, the programs were hastily put together, but the enthusiasm of the artists helped to overcome a lot of the difficulties," recalled Marlene Dietrich in her autobiography. "Great comics like Jack Benny or George Jessel led groups and also performed themselves. The awareness of being on native ground gave them a feeling of security."

Benny bled red, white, and blue. As a former vaudeville comic and WWI veteran, he understood how important it was to bolster troop morale. By 1942 he had his own radio show and would frequently go on the road during the week, visiting as many camps as time allowed, then rush back to Los Angeles to rehearse the next show and do it live on the air. Then he'd head back on the road again.

For Hollywood's comedians, dancers, and singers, going on the road and performing for the troops was just more of what they'd done in the past, whether it was up and down the East Coast and the Borscht Belt of clubs and resorts or cruising the Pacific Coast Highway and the numerous nightclubs along the way. But actors and actresses were handicapped, because they didn't have a repertoire that translated easily to a stage appearance, going solo without boring the audience.

Left: *Rosalind Russell enjoyed dinner with her brother, George (left). The actress dined with her brother and his friends at Camp Bowie, Texas, in 1942 when he served in the 6th Armored Division.* U.S. Army Photo

Rosalind Russell explained this dilemma in *Life is a Banquet*, cowritten with Chris Chase: "We knew what to do with the musical people, they could be sent directly to Army camps to entertain the boys—Ginger Rogers can go, she can tap dance, and Fred Astaire would obviously be in demand and Joan Crawford, she sings, yes, she can do songs—but nobody knew what to do with the straight actors, people like Irene Dunne, Claudette Colbert, Loretta Young and me.

"It was George Murphy who suggested the routine I wound up doing all over the country. He gave me a couple of jokes, advised me to build a Gracie Allen-style act around an invented brother who joins the Army and is a total idiot, does everything wrong. I did, and it worked fine; I'd never thought of myself as a stand-up comic, and Bob Hope I wasn't, but soldiers are generous audiences."

In fact, Roz did have a brother, but he was no idiot, and when he signed on with George Patton's Sixth Armored Division, Russell planned a Christmas party for the soldiers. She turned to her fellow stars at RKO Studios, collecting funds to pay for everything, including food, gifts from "Santa," transportation for the entire Hollywood entourage; "enlisting" other performers and starlets to put on a show; asking female assistants, secretaries, wardrobe and makeup gals to dance with the boys and mingle. "We had a meeting on an RKO soundstage, and I told the girls what I wanted them to wear. Flat heels and warm clothes," she recalled in *Life is a Banquet*. "Not one of them paid any attention; they came with the tall spike heels and the short flimsy dresses and nearly froze to death. We took a whole show with us, orchestra and all. Red Skelton came and played Santa Claus."

Merv Griffin was another performer who gave the GIs exactly what they wanted, before he signed up for the service himself. "I put together a small musical revue, three of the prettiest girls at San Mateo High all wanted to be singers so I taught them to harmonize; I knew having pretty girls behind me in a USO show meant a certain encore," he recalled in his autobiography, co-written with Peter Bassocchini. "Getting to our performances was really a cloak-and-dagger affair. The Army sent trucks to bring us to the bases, and since many of them were top-secret installations, we had to ride in canvas-covered troop carriers. They would back the truck right up to the stage door, we would do the show; then we had to climb right back into the truck, never knowing where we'd been."

The Hollywood spin machine was running full tilt when Jane Russell suddenly popped up out of nowhere, literally and figuratively. Her buxom figure was attracting a lot of buzz in screen magazines, even though she had yet to appear in even a walk-on role. In fact, she was more popular as an unknown actress than many other established movie stars. And what better way to raise the temperature even further and entice every man in the country than to troop around to as many Army camps as possible.

RIGHT: *Private Don Byrnes surprised dancer Alice Swanson as she performed during a tour of Army training posts across the South when he hopped on stage to twirl her. But he was no ordinary recruit—he had danced with her for 13 years before joining the Army. The two quickly fell into their old routines without missing a beat.* *YANK* Photo

Acrobat Milo Linwood Jones had made a career doing handstands and other balancing tricks as part of the "Three Milos" troupe. Soon after a show at the Trenton Fairgrounds in New Jersey, he enlisted at nearby Fort Dix and then went on to Camp Davis in North Carolina where he was training to be an airplane mechanic.

It was there that Jones performed in the show "Furlough Time" for his fellow GIs. He did elbow lifts and tiger bends and a two-arm planche, capping his routine by playing the trumpet while balancing on one hand.

Fort Dix had its own Army revue show, known as "Hi, Yank," which starred former Borscht Circuit performer Bobby Faye, who joined the Army under his real name, Isidore Falick. Portraying the befuddled pencil-pushing Sad Sack, Corporal Falick hoped to parlay the role into a Broadway audition after his Army stint was over.

The show was put together by Special Services producer Captain Hy Gardner, who recruited Dave Fitzgibbon as director of the show and teamed up fellow soldiers Frank Loesser and Alex North to write the score. (Loesser was already well known for his numerous patriotic and military tunes.)

Left: *Lena Horne often performed at camp shows, singing for soldiers and signing autographs. At Fort Huachuca she visited with members of the 92nd Infantry Division. Installations often offered two shows – one for white officers and enlisted men, and another for blacks and prisoners of war. A few shows were integrated, although not many. Horne caused a sensation one time though, when after being told of the separate shows, she went over and entertained for the black recruits and POWs, then left without performing for the white officers and enlisted men.*
92nd Infantry Division Public Affairs Office Photo

When asked about his Army experiences, Falick told a reporter with *YANK* magazine, "I was a Sad Sack right from the start. A year and a half ago, when I got my induction notice, my pals on Broadway offered me six to one that I would never wear khaki except on the stage." In fact, Falick wore very baggy khaki for the show and would have lost that bet.

Lena Horne first caused a sensation when she danced at Harlem's Cotton Club as a teenager. Then she went on the road with the all-white Charlie Barnet band and frequently faced bigotry. After being discovered and signed by MGM, she went on tour during WWII and caused a minor uproar but stood her ground when she was asked to give separate performances at Fort Dix and other posts. The first show at the New Jersey post would be solely for the white soldiers and the officers. The second would be for German prisoners of war and all of the black troops undergoing training and stationed there. Miss Horne declared that she would do only one show, and then she headed to where the black recruits and German POWs were waiting. Immediately after dazzling the crowd, she departed, leaving behind a subtle message about segregation.

Another black entertainer whose career got a boost by playing for service members was Pearl Bailey. Within a month after the Japanese attack, she was touring several camps in Texas with a small combo. "The camps weren't even set up for soldiers yet. We spent five weeks in Texas; then we crossed over a few states and reached the land of sunshine, California," she wrote in *The Raw Pearl*. "There were six of us on my second USO tour: Fetaque Saunders (a magician and the emcee), Freddie and Flo (comedy, song, and dance), a pianist named Basil Spears, Bobby Wallace doing imitations, and myself. Fort Huachuca, Arizona, became our home for thirty days. There were so many soldiers there they made us a home-based troupe. We had a good time with the 92nd Division."

Actor George Raft was a big fan of boxing and baseball and put together his Cavalcade of Sports to tour the country. "'I was too old for the service, so the Cavalcade was my contribution to the kids who were fighting for me,'" he told Lewis Yablonsky for the book, *George Raft*. "The Cavalcade consisted mostly of a traveling team of fighters who put on bouts at Army and Navy bases. I'd referee the fights, unless such ring greats as ex-heavyweight champ Jim Jeffries or Henry Armstrong were scheduled to officiate. Then I'd entertain."

Arlene Francis was the sultry "femcee" for the popular summer radio show, *Blind Date*, which plucked "died-and-gone-to-heaven" lucky servicemen—the envy of every man in uniform listening in—to go on a blind date with Hollywood's most desirable starlets, models, and singers. The potential GIs had to convince the young ladies in hiding to pick them for a memorable night on the town. Some of the guys pumped up their gentlemanly manner, or their down-home southern charm, or their worldly intellect, or their previous career in showbiz. Others wanted just "one last memory" to tide them over during the next few years of peril and uncertainty.

The lucky couple then enjoyed the hot spots of LA, with the date ending promptly at 3 A.M., when the sponsors were off the hook. What happened after that was nobody's business but the starstruck GI and his beautiful escort.

Ethel Merman, along with her accompanist Walter Gross, spent a lot of time at New York's Camp Shanks, even when she was pregnant. "Obviously the soldiers enjoyed it. I was made an honorary top sergeant," she remembered fondly in *Merman*, cowritten with George Eells. "Many of the boys would march right out of the staging area to a boat train heading for their ship and overseas. That staging area was the last sight of the States that they would have."

Screen Roles Portray Training

Movies about basic training and boot camp in the 1940s typically were either madcap comedies or overdramatizations of the rigors and the uncertainty, the bonding of a disparate cross-section of American society, preparing young men to go into battle. The former was played for laughs by Bob Hope, the Three Stooges, the Marx Brothers, and Abbott and Costello, to name just a few.

The dramas featured practically every leading man in Hollywood, playing the crusty, cantankerous drill sergeant, or the reluctant squad leader pulling his disgruntled recruits together to get through it all, or maybe the commanding officer who inherits the platoon and gives them the bad news that they are tabbed for an impossible mission, one doomed to fail, but still, someone's got to do it and it might as well be them. Then they ship off to the Pacific or the Mediterranean or an air base in England, and find out what hell is really like.

The Paramount Picture *I Wanted Wings* followed three all-American boys as they underwent training to be aviators, anticipating high-flying exploits in the coming war. William Holden portrayed a simple garage mechanic, Wayne Morris was the collegiate jock, and Ray Milland was a New York dandy. Upon its release in 1941, the movie was a precursor of what would unfold overseas.

Columbia Pictures got approval from the War Department to start production on *Officer Candidate School*, with Lieutenant Walter O'Brien, an OCS graduate from Camp Davis in North Carolina, slated to serve as technical adviser for the film.

If his schedule wasn't already crammed enough—with almost-constant touring capped by his weekly radio shows broadcast from bases and posts across the country—Bob Hope starred in *Caught in the Draft* as an actor doing everything he can, desperately trying anything to get out of the Army after accidentally signing up. Like all recruits through the ages, he quickly learns that KP and peeling a ton of potatoes ain't much fun. *Time* magazine film critic Richard Schickel said of Hope in this film, "he was jumping off a piano so he could flatten his feet. They would shoot guns off near him and he'd faint. It works out: he accidentally does something heroic and he gets the girl." His love interest was Dorothy Lamour, the colonel's daughter. In another Hope film, *Off Limits,* a doctor is giving Mickey Rooney a physical, but when he shines a light in the young recruit's ear, somehow the light can be seen shining out the other ear! Just then Bob Hope passes by, sees the anomaly, and quips, "This man is officer material!"

In *True to the Army,* Judy Canova is a gender-bending fugitive on the run, hiding out at a military post. Concealing the fact that she's a she is complicated in an all-male environment, leading to plenty of comical situations. One of her many costars was Jerry Colonna, Bob Hope's sidekick on his many USO tours, both stateside and abroad.

Pat O'Brien starred with Dick Powell and Ruby Keeler in *Flirtation Walk*, filmed exclusively at West Point Military Academy. O'Brien wrote about the movie in *The Wind at My Back*: "I had the role of the hard-hitting sergeant. Always a sentimental slob, on graduation day I was deeply touched and wept unashamed tears as the cadets marched by on parade—a stirring, magnificent sight."

Bud Abbott and Lou Costello had fun in *Buck Privates*. "Here Bud and Lou go through all kinds of familiar slapstick situations and in the end emerge with a new respect for themselves, each other, and all the patriotic values of Army and country," wrote John Russell Taylor in *Hollywood 1940s*.

BELOW: *Box office star Carmen Miranda learned magic tricks from Sergeant Anthony M. Lopilato at Fort Benjamin Harrison's Billings General Hospital in Indianapolis. He founded a magic club for servicemen in the city while he was an instructor at the hospital's laboratory school.* National Archives Photo

Films for the Troops

Director Frank Capra was asked by the War Department to create a series of training films titled *Why We Fight*, to be shown to basic trainees, providing overviews on a variety of topics the government wanted every service member to understand, such as world events, how the United States could impact favorably on democracy, and how each service member played a vital role in the inevitable victory. Eventually the series was also released to the general public for viewing.

Hollywood frequently loaned new films to the military for showing to the troops months before theatrical release in the States. Kingsley Canham and Sally Hibbin noted in *Movies of the Forties* that "at home and overseas, movies formed a staple part of the troops' ration of entertainment. Statistics in 1943 show that 630,000 men in the armed services were seeing Hollywood films each night, with those numbers increasing as the war geared up by 1944 and '45.

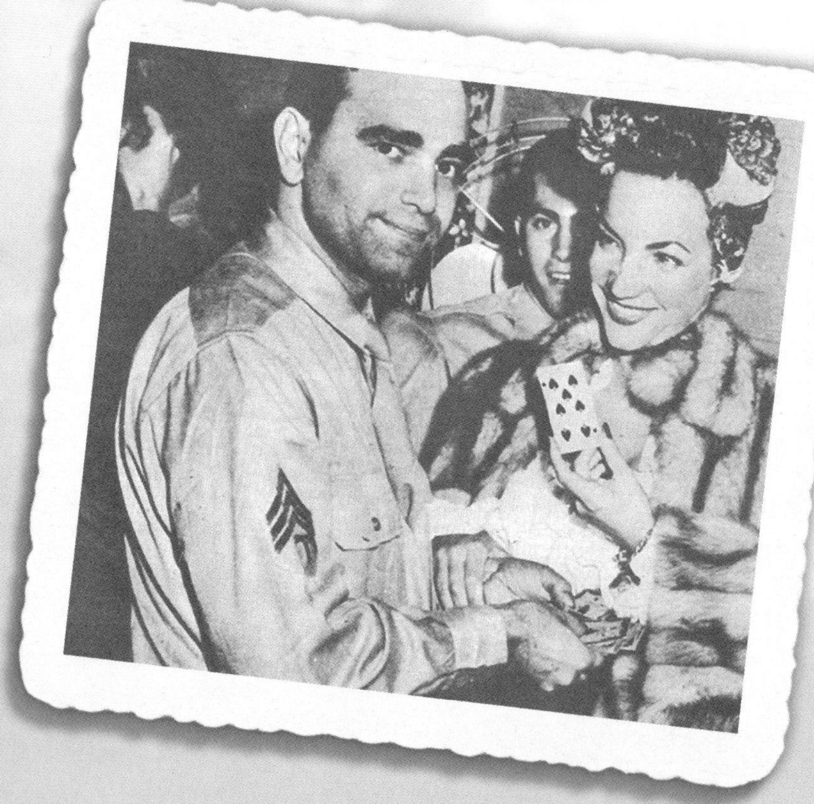

"Some of these—including *Saratoga Trunk* (1943) and *The Two Mrs. Carrolls* (1945)—were viewed by them quite a few years before their commercial release." It was all a part of Hollywood's efforts to sustain morale among the armed forces.

Of course, every once in a while, legislators have to stick their snooty noses into things. In Mississippi a long-standing blue law prohibited all forms of entertainment on Sundays, including the showing of movies. For the more than 100,000 recruits training there every year, Sundays were typically the only day of the week they might get some badly needed time off, maybe take a break, catch up on some sleep . . . or see a movie (and not one of those boring training films about venereal disease, or heat stroke, poisonous snakes, or how to assemble and disassemble their rifle). But state politicians in Ole Miss felt that allowing movies on the Sabbath would "open the gates of hell." State Senator Joe Daws even used the Japanese attack on Pearl Harbor to prove his point, saying that instead of being at their posts, service members in Hawaii "were attending Sunday movies!"

But a breath of common sense drifted into the chambers, starting with Senator Earl Richardson, who asked the assembled legislators: "Do you know what time Pearl Harbor was attacked? It was about 7:15 in the morning. That's a mighty funny time for soldiers or anybody else to be in the movies." The debate raged back and forth, but in the end the measure passed, twenty-nine to ten. The soldiers stationed in Mississippi would have their movies on Sundays.

Background: *Hollywood starlet Marguerite Chapman signed autographs for Army Air Corps GIs in Salt Lake City, Utah. Soldiers, sailors, airmen, and Marines loved to be entertained by the pretty ladies, who often became pen pals with the guys while they were overseas.*
Army Air Forces Photo

War Bonds: Americans Chip in to Support the Cause

"Any bonds today?
All you give, will be spent to live in the Yankee way.
Scrape up the most you can.
Here comes the freedom man
Asking you to buy a share of freedom today."

—From the song "Any Bonds Today?" by Irving Berlin

LONG BEFORE PRESIDENT ROOSEVELT DECLARED WAR, Americans across the country, who were outraged by the Japanese attack on Pearl Harbor, were already doing whatever they could to support the war effort overseas. Raising funds to help European Jews flee Nazi persecution, paying for passports including exorbitant amounts for forged passports, bribing officials, booking safe passage on the next available ship bound for England or New York or anywhere but where they were then.

"The Hollywood Committee, which had been founded when the Nazis seized power, was all ready for action. Its chief organizers were [former European refugees] Ernst Lubitsch and Billy Wilder," wrote Marlene Dietrich in her autobiography. "We sent sums of money to a contact man in Switzerland . . . for the purpose of liberating hundreds of prisoners from the German concentration camps and bringing them to America."

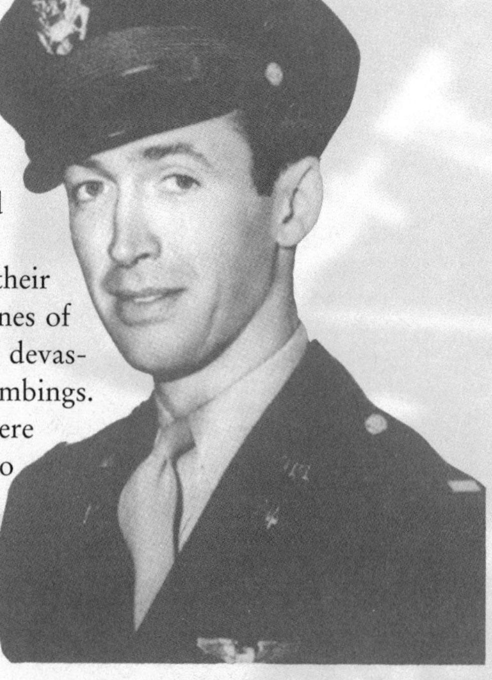

Right: *Airman and actor Jimmy Stewart once played his accordion at a Houston fund-raiser to support Great Britain's war efforts before the U.S. entry into the conflict. The performance was actually a duet, with pal Henry Fonda accompanying Stewart on the cornet.*
Army Air Forces Photo

American children gave up their dolls and other toys for the wee ones of London and other English cities devastated and displaced by the Nazi bombings. Often spearheading the efforts were former refugees who had made it to the United States and knew they could count on their American friends to help out.

Jimmy Stewart and Margaret Sullavan were working on the

anti-Nazi movie *The Mortal Storm* when they took a side trip to Texas in August of 1940, along with his good friend Henry Fonda (who was also Sullavan's former husband) to raise funds for England, "which was about to begin the battle for its life in a near Götterdämmerung called The Blitz the very next month," Frank Sanello wrote in his book, *Stewart*. "At a Houston fund-raiser, the Coliseum was sold out to see real-life stars like Jimmy and Henry Fonda do hokey magic acts and play a duet, with Fonda on the cornet and Jimmy on his lethal accordion."

ABOVE: *British-born Cary Grant drew sharp criticism for not returning to his homeland to defend Mother England against the Nazis. Instead, the actor donated his earnings from two movies to the English war efforts. Grant (left) chatted here with Jean Arthur, Ronald Colman (far right), and a Russian military representative outside Columbia Studios in 1942.*
National Archives Photo

British actor Cary Grant was catching flak from the press back home, criticizing him for not leaving Hollywood and joining his countrymen in the fight against Nazi Germany. But fellow British film star David Niven had already done just that—returning home to enlist—and had promptly been ripped for doing so by British journalists, who felt he only did it for the publicity. Grant decided to remain in the United States and applied for American citizenship. He did donate his salary from *Arsenic and Old Lace* and *The Philadelphia Story*—more than $300,000—to British War Relief.

An unexpected contributor to the British War Relief effort was the Nazi Führer's sister-in-law, Bridget Hitler, who was living in New York by 1941. Already sensing the attitude among America and its millions of citizens with European ties, she told *Time* magazine: "Adolf should be killed by slow torture, a little bit every day."

Actress Tallulah Bankhead was asked to donate blood for the war effort, but quipped, "I told them that I was so damned anemic, my blood would kill a good American soldier. I told them that I'd give them quarts of the stuff if they would put it into the right places—into Japanese soldiers!"

Swedish movie star Ingrid Bergman volunteered her time to tour the United States to entertain the troops and raise funds for war bonds. And when the Office of War Information asked her to make the short film *Swedes in America*, she traveled to Minnesota, where she was greeted by thousands of Swedes as a local heroine. The film was later shown to her countrymen back home to bolster their will to hang tough despite the Nazi threat.

Tyrone Power and his first wife, French actress Annabella Power, hosted a massive fund-raiser at their estate, selling off some of their prized possessions along with items donated by other stars and friends, all in an effort to raise money for the Free French Relief Committee.

When the king of jazz, Duke Ellington, celebrated his twentieth anniversary and *Down Beat* magazine selected his band as tops in the country, he held a sold-out concert at New York's Carnegie Hall. The money raised was donated to another of America's allies during WWII, for Russian war relief.

Hollywood Rallies Immediately

The stab-in-the-back sneak attack on Pearl Harbor was a wake-up call, and the entire country mobilized for the long haul to defeat Nazi Germany and Imperial Japan. Rationing was implemented, collection points were established for vital goods—including rubber, tin, and metal—and bond drives were held, with Hollywood stars as the drawing cards, attracting thousands of fans.

Within days of FDR's declaration of war, actors and actresses got together to form the Hollywood Victory Committee, which coordinated the Caravan of Stars, dispatched across the country for personal appearances, performances, and bond rallies. "A committee of fifteen, headed by Clark Gable, was chosen to coordinate talent for bond rallies, camp shows, and hospital tours. Serving with Gable on the committee were Myrna Loy, Claudette Colbert, Charles Boyer, Bob Hope, Rosalind Russell, John Garfield, Bette Davis, Tyrone Power, Gary Cooper, Ginger Rogers, Ronald Colman, Cary Grant, Irene Dunne, and Jack Benny," wrote Warren G. Harris in *Gable and Lombard*. "One of the first requests received [by the committee] was to send a film star to Indiana to help promote the launching of the state's campaign to sell U.S. Defense Bonds. Gable . . . nominated his own wife for the tour. Since [Carole] Lombard was a native of Indiana, he was sure she would be delighted to return to her home state for this patriotic mission."

RIGHT: *Composer Irving Berlin and director Michael Curtiz discuss their movie,* This Is the Army, *which was based on a play the songwriter developed during World War I. The movie began as a Broadway-style musical, with both civilians and servicemen performing. The show's success in raising money for the war effort prompted the two to turn the stage performance into a film.*
National Archives Photo

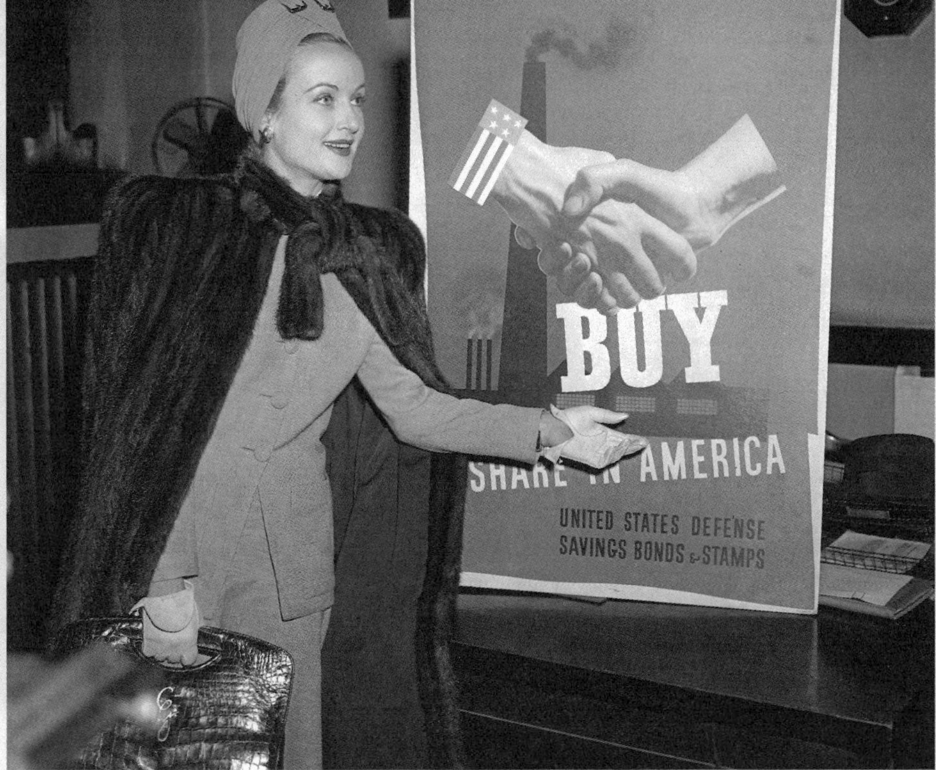

LEFT: *Happy-go-lucky Hoosier Carole Lombard became the first celebrity to die in World War II when she perished in a fiery plane crash outside Las Vegas while returning from a war bond rally in her home state of Indiana. The comic actress took the train from Los Angeles to the Midwest, making stops in Salt Lake City, Utah, and Chicago along the way to Indianapolis. In Indy alone, Lombard raised $2 million for the war effort. Rather than return on the train, she decided to fly back to California so she could see her husband, Hollywood hunk Clark Gable, sooner.*
Associated Press Photo

A Deadly Change of Plans

Carole Lombard was a free-spirited, fun-loving screwball actress, who had moved from Fort Wayne, Indiana, to Hollywood when she was just a child. She soon found work in movies and grew up on screen, holding her own in dramatic roles as well as the comedies she loved. When her husband asked her to do the bond drive in mid-January of 1942, she had just finished filming *To Be or Not to Be* with Jack Benny, who played a Shakespearean actor fleeing the Nazis. Gable wanted to go on the fund-raising trip with her, but filming was about to start on his next film, *Somewhere I'll Find You*, with Lana Turner.

The whistle stop tour would leave Los Angeles on January twelvth with layovers at Salt Lake City and Chicago, with time for her to be in Indiana by the fifteenth. Lombard was certainly well aware of her husband's roving eye and philandering reputation, and she left behind a subtle reminder for him to stay away from his sultry costar. When he got home from filming on the thirteenth, waiting in bed was a well-endowed blonde mannequin with a note, reading, "So you won't be lonely." He got the message, although he wouldn't allow anyone, not even his wife, to dictate who he slept with or when. And of course, Carole Lombard knew that, too.

"Her tour had been incredibly successful. In Indianapolis alone, she sold over $2 million worth of bonds. She had signed thousands of autographs, shaken thousands of hands," wrote Lyn Tornabene in *Long Live the King*. "When she led the singing of the Star-Spangled Banner in the Cadle Tabernacle, backed by three military bands, she broke, for the first time, and cried. After a powerful farewell victory salute, she listened to the loving cheers of her fellow patriots, prouder of herself than she had ever been."

Instead of boarding the train for the return trip to Los Angeles, Lombard decided to fly home, canceling planned whistle stops in Kansas City and Albuquerque. She wanted to get back to Clark as quickly as possible, obviously because she missed him, possibly in part because she didn't trust him. But the twin-engine DC-3 was plagued with problems all along the way and required maintenance at each stop. Tragically, flying out of Las Vegas at seven o'clock on the night of January 16, the plane plowed into Potosi Mountain. Due to blackout conditions, beacons along the top of the mountain had been turned off—beacons that would have warned the pilots before they slammed into the vertical rock face of the peak.

As soon as he heard that the plane was down, Clark Gable flew to Vegas. There he had to wait for three agonizing days while search and recovery teams brought the badly burned bodies down from the mountain.

President Roosevelt immediately sent Clark Gable the following message by telegram: "Mrs. Roosevelt and I are deeply distressed. Carole was our friend, our guest in happier days. She brought great joy to all who knew her and to millions who knew her only as a great artist. She gave unselfishly of her time and talent to serve her government in peace and in war. She loved her country. She is and always will be a star, one we shall never forget nor cease to be grateful to. Deepest sympathy."

Because she was on a government-sponsored mission, the War Department felt Lombard should have a military funeral with full honors. Many of her closest friends planned to build a mausoleum, but Clark Gable refused both offers. He gave her what she had wanted; a very simple, very private service.

Carole Lombard's death cast a black cloud over the Hollywood Victory Committee's efforts. Now the sacrifices of WWII were personal, for they had lost one of their own. Unanimously they vowed to carry on, as Carole would have wanted it.

Going Out on Tour

Many stars participated in the Caravan of Stars. In 1942 the tour included Laurel and Hardy, Bob Hope, Bing Crosby, Charles Boyer, Frank McHugh, Claudette Colbert, and Pat O'Brien, with Rise Stevens opening each show with the National Anthem, and the great Jimmy Cagney bringing the house down with "Yankee Doodle Dandy."

Cagney understood the importance of getting the stars out for meet-and-greets, to put on a show, to give the fans their money's worth. "No matter how tough the going is, [the American people] still find something to laugh at. That's why we feel entertainment is so valuable in wartime."

"With all of the greatest stars on hand, the greatest ovation and reception all across the country were always for Laurel and Hardy," recalled Pat O'Brien in his book, *The Wind at My Back*. "Every time they made their entrance, there were loud bursts of applause and cheers." (It was estimated that at every performance, the Victory Caravan pulled in at least $50,000 in donations. In its first year alone the Caravan's efforts raised more than twelve billion dollars in donations and bond sales for the various armed forces, relief agencies, and other charitable causes.)

Like Laurel and Hardy, the comedy team of Bud Abbott and Lou Costello was immensely popular everywhere they went, and very successful on bond drives. In fact, New York Mayor Fiorello LaGuardia recognized the duo after a three-day effort pulled in $89 million.

Comedy may have been the key to a successful bond rally, but feisty actress Bette Davis was not about to let anyone off the hook easily if she felt their participation wasn't sufficient. "If she didn't sell enough bonds by signing autographs, selling memorabilia, and being gracious, Bette would harangue an audience until they were cowed into shelling out their money—

LEFT: *At most USO shows and bond rallies, the guys couldn't wait for the girls to perform. But comedy duo Laurel and Hardy often closed the show, and it was an act nobody wanted to miss. Ending with laughter encouraged folks to dig deep for spare change, loose bills, maybe even for $100 or more to support the war effort. The comedy team was also popular on the USO circuit and always sent the soldiers, seamen, or airmen back to barracks feeling better, if only for a few hours. Here, the pair entertained in the Caribbean in 1943.* Office of War Information Photo

Right: *"Diamond Lil," actress Mae West, donated jewelry to the war effort. The proceeds from the sale of the sparkling gemstones helped pay for supplies, proving that although diamonds are a girl's best friend, there's nothing more valuable than freedom.*
Associated Press Photo

'Do what you can do—to the level you can do!' she'd rasp, her voice about to go, 'or you're not my idea of an American,'" James Spada revealed in the Davis biography, *More Than a Woman*. "When press reports likened Bette to a drill sergeant . . . she snapped, 'I'm the one who has to deal with the public. The only way to get them to contribute, to develop enthusiasm, is to let 'em have it straight, no holds barred!' When Bette sold two million dollars' worth of bonds in two days (and a picture of herself in *Jezebel* for $250,000), criticism of her sales pitches ceased."

The CBS Radio show *Screen Guild Theatre* became a weekly watering hole for Hollywood's biggest stars; among them were Joan Crawford, Bob Hope, Jack Benny, Robert Taylor, Bette Davis, James Stewart, Humphrey Bogart, Mickey Rooney, Tyrone Power, Gary Cooper, Eddie Cantor, Clark Gable, George Burns and Gracie Allen, Gene Autry, Loretta Young, Basil Rathbone, Marlene Dietrich, Ginger Rogers, Helen Hayes, Charles Laughton, Paulette Goddard, Fredric March, Fred Allen, Jeanette MacDonald, Judy Garland, and James Cagney. Instead of paying these and many other stars an appearance fee, the show's sponsor, Gulf Oil, donated $800,000 to the Motion Picture Relief Fund, which paid for the construction of a home to care for movie stars in need. Bogie also used his tough guy image on Edgar Bergen's radio show to "threaten" listeners to buy war bonds . . . or else!

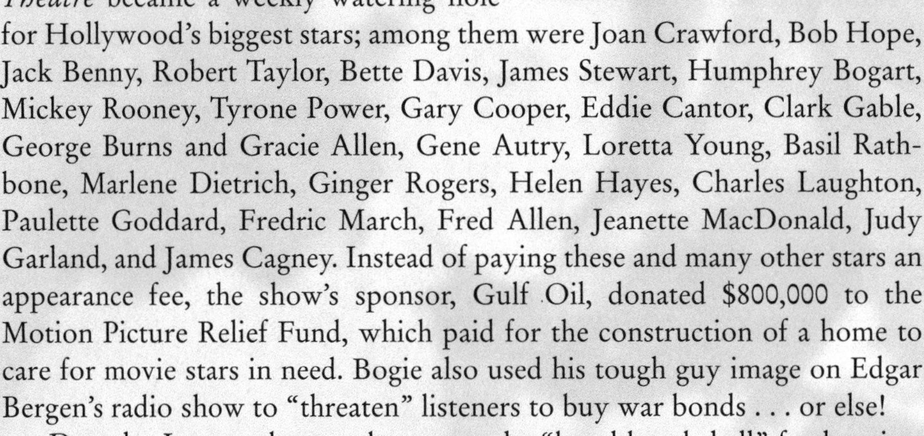

Dorothy Lamour became known as the "bond bombshell" for her tireless efforts to raise money during the war years—$300 million worth. The armed forces so appreciated her work that whenever she went out on tour, they came up with a private rail car solely for her use.

Another popular radio show for CBS was *Millions for Defense*, sponsored by the Treasury Department and first aired during the summer of 1941, five months before the attack on Pearl Harbor. "It was a 60-minute variety hour and, typical of these wartime bond shows, had its pick of top Hollywood talent on a gratis basis. Bob Hope, Bing Crosby, and Dorothy Lamour appeared on the second show; subsequent guests included Bette Davis, Lily Pons, Bud Abbott and Lou Costello, Tyrone Power, and Claudette Colbert," wrote John Dunning in *Tune in Yesterday*. "It became very popular during the waning months of the summer owing to its lavish format. . . . then came Pearl Harbor and Treasury shows were everywhere."

Above: *Jane Wyman, Mrs. Ronald Reagan during the war years, hounded Los Angeles-area moviegoers for spare change and other donations for local military relief organizations.*
Photo Courtesy of the Reagan Presidential Library

Actress Jane Wyman kept busy while her husband, Ronald Reagan, was making training films for the Army. She worked as a volunteer at a kiosk outside a local theater in Hollywood, coercing passersby to purchase stamps and bonds for the war effort. Inside the theater, Phil Harris was on stage, giving the audience a pep talk before the lights went down and the movie came on. But in the middle of Harris's brief skit, Wyman would barge in and commandeer the microphone, appealing to everyone's patriotism, asking them to donate any spare change they had. And oh, by the way, she would be hanging around outside until after the movie, still trying to get patrons to part with a few bucks more.

Reagan himself was in Burbank, assigned to the First Motion Picture Unit, tasked with making training films and documentaries. Due to his proximity to Hollywood, he frequently participated in local bond rallies whenever he could get a pass. He also took time out to star in the benefit movie, *This Is the Army*. Other actors did likewise, including Victor Mature, who was in the Coast Guard show *Tars and Spars*; Mario Lanza, whose performances in the Army Air Corps benefit shows *On the Beam* and *Winged Victory* earned him the nickname "Caruso of the Air Force"; Coast Guardsman Cesar Romero, who was assigned to an attack transport ship but was allowed shore leave to speak at bond rallies; and Burgess Meredith, who was granted leave to star in a theatrical benefit that ran for six weeks in the Big Apple and two more weeks in D.C.

Not too far from Los Angeles, another young performer on the outside looking in was struggling to make it in showbiz, willing to try anything to get noticed. Merv Griffin was already entertaining the troops at local bases and camps with three girls from San Mateo High School as his backup singers. Soliciting money for war bonds was merely another opportunity to possibly be "discovered." "The local fund-raisers built a platform for me on a street corner in San Mateo, and there I played piano, sang songs, and heckled pedestrians until they coughed up some cash," Griffin recalled.

Right: *Blonde bombshell Lana Turner often donated personal items, including nylons and kisses, to raise money. At rallies from coast to coast she promised "a sweet kiss" to anyone who purchased a $50,000 war bond. She credited herself with single-handedly raising millions of dollars for the War Department.*
Office of War Information Photo

Bing Crosby crooned "Buy, Buy Bonds" for the film short, *All-Star Bond Rally,* produced for the War Activities Committee. In Houston, the city's symphony orchestra performed at the Municipal Auditorium while professional wrestlers pounded on and tossed each other around the stage, all to raise money for war bonds. In major cities, bond rallies were held at least every month to varying degrees. "Breathed no man alive in the 48 states who was not almost daily exhorted, begged, and bewitched into buying war bonds," reported *Time* magazine in its August 24, 1942, issue. "Bathing beauties did it. Big, beautiful eyes and slim, wonderful legs did it. The supreme Empress of Cheesecake, the very Marlene Dietrich herself, was fittingly crowned by the Treasury as the champion bond seller of all. On three cross-country trips she upped the pulses and unsnapped the purses of thousands of U.S. males."

Actress Lana Turner remembered those days, traveling cross-country, sometimes by bus, sometimes by train—if the promoters could find a rail car that wasn't carrying newly trained troops to the East or West Coasts. "When I had time between pictures I boarded that long train that rolled into cities where munitions plants were located. At every stop we were greeted by wildly cheering crowds, often mostly women. That sea of female faces—you knew the men had gone to war. I wrote my own little speech to deliver at those rallies, and I added a special touch. When there were men in the crowd, I promised a sweet kiss to anyone who bought a $50,000 bond. And I kept that promise—hundreds of times. I'm told I increased the defense budget by several million dollars."

Marlene Dietrich certainly knew how exhausting those bond tours were—"six to eight hours a day, and sometimes also an evening performance. I had to go into factories and call upon workers to give a certain percentage of their salaries as a loan to the government. I also worked in nightclubs in the evening. Spurred on by my bodyguards from the Treasury Department, I turned to the half-drunk audience with the zeal of a traveling salesman."

But not all Hollywood starlets who toured the country for war bond rallies had long legs and batted their eyelashes. Fourteen-year-old Jane Powell, who had a cousin in the Navy, was described in *YANK* magazine as "the kind of cute, blue-eyed brunette you'd like to have for your kid sister. She's as natural as any teenage, bobby-sock girl. After a tour across country and back, during which she appeared at WAC recruiting drives, war bond rallies, canteens, and the like, Jane was chosen Victory Girl by the Oregon Victory Committee and toured [her home state of] Oregon, the adjoining states, and Canada to help the sale of War Bonds with her songs."

ABOVE: *The armed services rewarded actress Gene Tierney's efforts to sell war bonds by presenting her with a medal and making her an honorary drill sergeant.*
National Archives Photo

For some entertainers the constant touring took its toll, though, and some returned home exhausted. "Rita Hayworth and Greer Garson collapsed on grueling bond-selling tours, but Paulette Goddard, who is smart as well as oomphy, doesn't intend to have that happen to her," Julie Gilbert wrote about the starlet's upcoming support for the war in *Opposite Attraction—The Lives of Erich Maria Remarque and Paulette Goddard.* "Paulette's getting into condition to do the country for the Treasury Department." And then off she went, on another whirlwind, 'round-the-clock tour for the war effort.

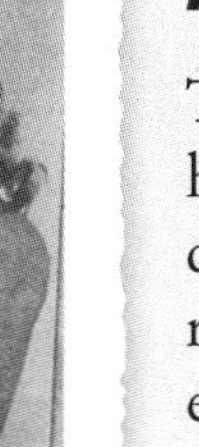

LEFT: *In addition to being a fabulous entertainer, Danny Kaye was a talented auctioneer. He successfully ran the Gimbel's auction in New York City to raise money for war efforts, garnering $1 million for Jack Benny's violin alone.*
Armed Forces Radio Services Photo

Auctioning Off the Ridiculous

Those who bought war bonds at $18.75 each would have to wait ten years to cash them in at $25. (All told, during the war years, more than $185 billion was raised through bond sales alone.) Another way to generate big bucks was for Hollywood stars to offer up personal mementos, and by selling kisses or dances. Lauren Bacall recalled in *By Myself*, "Young actresses were stationed at various nightclubs around the city to sit at tables and try prettily to collect money."

Stars also helped auction off everything from tickets to a Broadway show to a slab of bacon. Well,

it wasn't exactly a slab of bacon—it was the entire pig—and even though no one would get to keep it, they offered up thousands of dollars to be the top bidder at each auction site. Beth Py-Lieberman described this fund-raiser in *Smithsonian* magazine:

"Take a 700-pound pig, paint its toenails bright red and dangle silver bangles from its ears. Put that porker up for auction and what would it fetch? How about $19 million? By some reports that's what 'King Neptune,' the war bonds hog, made between 1942 and 1946, after the animal was auctioned off again and again as part of what has been called the biggest selling campaign in history. Once the pig was purchased, patriotic duty required the owner to donate him to the next sale."

One of the most alluring attractions for WWII fund-raising was Betty Grable and those killer legs. At a bond drive in Pulaski, Virginia, a pair of stockings that had once adorned those beautiful gams was auctioned off for $110,000! Topping that, sultry Veronica Lake allowed a lock of her silky blonde hair to be auctioned off, and it brought in $200,000!

ABOVE: *Deadpan comedian Jack Benny was dead serious about supporting the war effort. He once donated a violin for a Gimbel's department store auction. A Russian immigrant paid $1 million for the fancy fiddle.*
National Archives Photo

Pinup queen Betty Grable was also the "captain" of the Hollywood Comedians football squad, which played against Rita Hayworth's Leading Men at Los Angeles Coliseum, with all the proceeds going to local charities.

Jack Benny never claimed to be a virtuoso on the violin. He wasn't even halfway decent at it, nor was his instrument much to rave about, although he claimed "Old Love in Bloom" was a priceless Amati. (In fact, it was a twenty-year-old, seventy-five-dollar fake.) But that didn't stop comedian Danny Kaye from bumping up the price of Benny's precious prop during an auction at Gimbel's bargain basement in March of 1943.

There were some truly priceless items up for bid, such as a letter written by George Washington and a Bible that had belonged to Thomas Jefferson. But it was Benny's fiddle that created the biggest sensation, when a sole buyer opened the bidding at a mere $1 million!

Stars Promote Rationing and Recycling

At the numerous rallies he attended around the country, comedian Ed Wynn had a favorite joke he liked to tell about recycling efforts: "I told my audiences, 'Ladies and gentlemen, the government wants all the old tin cans from your kitchens. The simplest method is to cut the ends out of the can, put it on the floor, jump on it to flatten it out, and then hand it in to the government. I tried it this morning. I cut each end out of the can. I put it on the floor. I jumped on it hard. It flattened out beautifully. Of course, it took me three hours to scrape the beans off the wall.' I must say, that story always got a great laugh. You'd be surprised to know how much tin it raised too."

Jack Benny was touring the Midwest when he ended up in St. Joseph, Missouri, to do his weekly radio show. Instead of charging admission to the show, Benny put the word out that anyone who donated a pint of blood to the Red Cross would get into the show for free. That night, ten thousand pints of blood were collected, soon to be shipped off for troop hospitals in the European and Pacific Theaters.

5. Defense Plants Gear Up for War

"It will not only be a long war, it will be a hard war. That is the yardstick by which we measure what we shall need and demand; money, materials, doubled and quadrupled production . . . ever-increasing. On the road ahead there lies hard work—grueling work—day and night, every hour and every minute."

—*President Franklin D. Roosevelt, Radio Address to the Nation, December 9, 1941*

Opposite: *Actress Paulette Goddard portrayed a female welder in* I Love a Soldier, *where her role closely mirrored these women at Ingalls Shipbuilding Corporation, in Pascagoula, Mississippi Goddard refrained from playing up her movie-star appearance, choosing to look like a real welder. By not glamorizing her character, she realistically showed the hardships and accomplishments of these defense workers.*
Women's Bureau Photo

WHEN FDR DECLARED WAR ON JAPAN, HE STRESSED THAT winning the fight for freedom and democracy would require the all-out efforts of every man, woman, and child in America. But at the same time that factories retooled to make howitzers and tanks, aircraft carriers, battleships and submarines, fighter planes and heavy bombers, and all the accoutrements each service member needed to fight and survive, millions of factory workers trooped down to local recruiting offices and enlisted, for the duration. Thousands of those men would have been exempt from military service because their jobs were classified as vital to the war effort, but still they signed on, out of patriotism, out of a desire for revenge, or because it was the only right thing to do at the time. So, just as those factories were ready to run 'round-the-clock, many didn't have enough trained workers to run the equipment, let alone handle a second and third shift.

In Detroit alone the manpower demands were staggering as automakers shut down their car lines and converted to tanks, vehicles, and aircraft: "General Motors expects to employ 450,000 persons, Ford—200,000 (including 25,000 women among the 100,000 employees of the bomber plant), Chrysler—130,000. [Newspaper] correspondents wrote about production lines miles long—Chrysler making at least $675 million worth of tanks, planes, and guns in 1942 . . . Ford with eleven miles of airplane runways at Willow Run," reported *Time* magazine in February of 1942.

Instead of competing for American car buyers, Detroit automakers rallied together for the common good, to win the war, to do whatever it took to achieve that goal.

For example, besides tanks, planes, and guns, Chrysler also produced steel-mesh anti-submarine barrier nets, ambulances, anti-aircraft guns, motorboat engines, and armored weapons carriers; Cadillac cranked

Below: *President Roosevelt watches as the Liberty ship* Joseph N. Teal *was launched. Workers built the boat in a mere ten days, testament to their dedication to defend the nation against the evil Axis powers.*
U.S. Navy Department, National Archives Photo

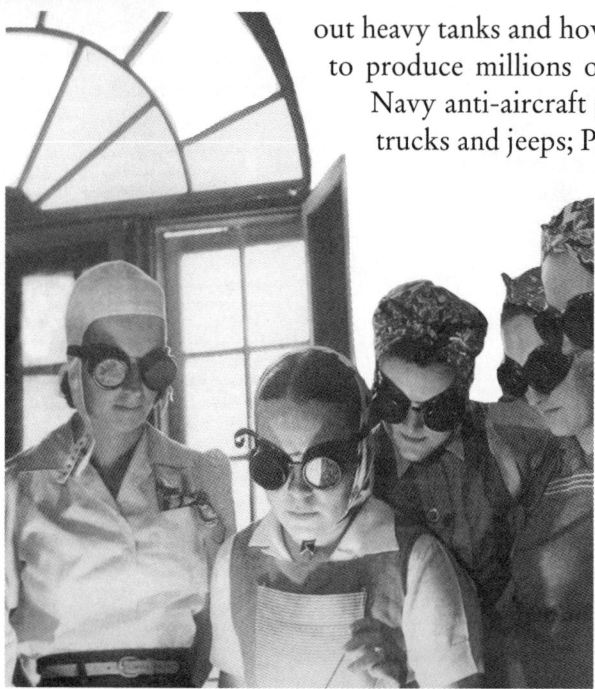

Above: *Many American women gained their first jobs outside the home during the war, showing they had talents beyond making dinner and ironing clothes. These women learned how to weld and helped U.S. factories make 300,000 military planes, nearly 90,000 tanks, and machine guns and rifles by the millions.*
National Archives Photo

out heavy tanks and howitzer motor carriers; Fisher Body Works retooled to produce millions of parts for everything from bomber aircraft and Navy anti-aircraft guns to Army tanks; Ford rolled out thousands of trucks and jeeps; Packard concentrated on motors for various aircraft and the Navy's "expendables"—the swift and deadly PT boats that would be shipped to the South Pacific to harass and torpedo much larger enemy warships; and Chevy churned out gears for aircraft engines and axles for a variety of Army trucks.

Nationwide the output was staggering: more than 290,000 aircraft (everything from small scout planes to heavy B-17 and B-24 bombers, and later the sleek silver B-29s); up to 100,000 tanks and armored vehicles (88,000 of those were tanks for the Army); more than 76,000 naval craft (from PT boats and submarines, to battleships and aircraft carriers); and on and on, including 41 billion rounds of munitions, including pistol, rifle, and machine gun bullets, bombs, grenades, mortar rounds, naval shells, and torpedoes.

To understand just how American industry stacked up against its enemies, Louis Snyder wrote in *The War: A Concise History, 1939–1945*, "Within a year after Pearl Harbor the United States was equaling the entire Axis war production, though the latter had a decade's head start." Nazi Germany and Imperial Japan had started preparing for war as early as 1933 and clandestinely manufactured planes, warships, and tanks to overwhelm all enemy forces, in both Europe and Asia. By the end of the decade, American industrialists began to formulate plans in preparation for conflict with the two (and their bastard little stepbrother, Mussolini), but it took the staggering news about Pearl Harbor to convince the American magnates to convert their factories almost overnight to a war footing. Yet by the end of 1942, America had surpassed the combined output of Germany, Italy, and Japan.

The Human Element

Men between the ages of twenty-one and thirty were the first required to register for the draft. That group was immediately expanded to eighteen and sixty-four after Pearl Harbor. Male workers were classified according to whether their job was vital to the war effort—including those jobs in armaments plants, shipyards, aircraft factories, and vehicle manufacturing. Farmers and ranchers were also slotted as war essential.

Many others with ailments and limitations were considered 4-F, or physically unfit, most likely willing to fight, but disqualified during their induction physical. They may not have been able to withstand the rigors of basic training and eventual combat, but they could work, and they did work, in whatever capacity was needed.

But soon the dual manpower requirements of the military and American industry were hampering the latter. "The giant industries of the Midwest, from Chicago and Detroit, right down through the center of heartland America to New Orleans and Houston, cried out for workers, more workers, as their production facilities were strained to capacity," wrote Donald Rogers in *Since You Went Away*. "From the farms and plantations and pine tree country of the South whole families responded, white and black alike, leaving some sons on the way at the Army and Navy reception centers."

The call went out for retirees, older teenagers, those handicapped who had some work skills, and women to fill the void. And as more and more women started punching time cards, any of their able-bodied male counterparts still working were pressured to ditch their work clothes and tool belts and join the military.

Among the many former and future entertainers who pulled their weight in one of America's factories included actor Earl Rowe, who was a student at Philly's School of Dramatic Arts. He worked at an aircraft plant, then joined the Army, and would be wounded in Germany near the end of the European Campaign. (In 1958 Rowe appeared in the cult sci-fi movie *The Blob*; then he bounced around from TV to Broadway, soap operas, and commercials.)

Movie actor and Spanish American War veteran George Bancroft, also from Philadelphia, was dubbed the "smiling villain" for his film roles. Another journeyman actor, he started in vaudeville and on Broadway, then appeared in silent movies and "talkies." In 1942, at the age of sixty, he called it quits to help the war effort as a rancher. Hollywood performer Charles Bickford had a hog farm in Massachusetts and provided meat to all of the armed forces.

University of California drama student John Russell wanted to join the Marines in 1941, but at six foot four was considered too tall, so he worked as a mechanic's assistant at Interstate Aircraft in southern California. (After

Left: *The romanticism of a man in uniform provided a powerful aphrodisiac. Men were handsome in their insignias, and very gallant-looking soldiers made the ladies swoon. Some were caught up in making a man's last days happy—in case he didn't return home. No one knows how many illegitimate children resulted from these romantic send-offs, but the nation saw a baby boom directly after the war from 1946 to 1964.*
Library of Congress Photo

Pearl Harbor, when there was an immediate need for every able-bodied man to be in the military, Russell was allowed to join, and he saw combat in the South Pacific. After the war, he was discovered by Universal-International and starred in numerous westerns on the big screen and television.)

BELOW: *As men went off to war, women entered military service to take over maintenance jobs. Women like these Marines working in a North Carolina airplane repair shop were treated more like an auxiliary unit than regular military. Unlike men, they had no benefits and no authority, even if they held higher ranks. At first men were all too happy to have the ladies join them at work. But they later resented the women and their abilities to do the jobs as well as—or better than—the men they replaced. The resentment was short-lived, however, because many men left support roles when they received draft notices.*
U.S. Marine Corps Photo

Maverick Robert Mitchum had tried writing gags and patter for nightclub performers and had taken some nonpaying acting gigs in little theater in Los Angeles, but with his newlywed bride already pregnant, he knew he couldn't panhandle for free drinks and leftovers like he used to. He found work as a sheet metal worker for Lockheed Aircraft in Burbank, working the graveyard shift. He pulled in twenty-nine dollars a week minimum but frequently earned twice that much in overtime. One of his co-workers was an affable Irishman, Jim Dougherty.

"Bob was a good guy. Somebody you like to know. Very easygoing. And a fantastic storyteller. During the lunch break he would always have a new one. About boxing. And riding the rails. They sounded like tall tales but we all enjoyed them," Dougherty recalled for the book, *Robert Mitchum—"Baby I Don't Care,"* by Lee Server. Because they worked side by side, it was only natural the two would spend their after-hours time together, and that's when Mitchum met Dougherty's girlfriend, fifteen-year-old Norma Jean Baker. The two would soon get married. After Pearl Harbor, Dougherty and many of his co-workers at Lockheed joined the military, but Mitchum held out and soon had an acting offer, as an extra in the Hopalong Cassidy series of films. (Mitchum would later play a variety of combat roles during the war years, and Norma Jean Dougherty only became one of the world's most recognized female icons, the yet-to-be-discovered Marilyn Monroe.)

The Lockheed plant in Burbank where Robert Mitchum and Jim Dougherty worked was only a few blocks from Warner Brothers Studio. During the weeks after war was declared, there was deep concern that the Japanese might invade the West Coast, or bomb key installations in southern California, including Lockheed. Jack Warner was so concerned about Japanese bomber planes confusing his sprawling soundstages for the aircraft plant that he ordered his workmen to climb up on one of the roofs and paint a massive sign and arrow guiding any potential enemy planes in the right direction: LOCKHEED—THATTA WAY!

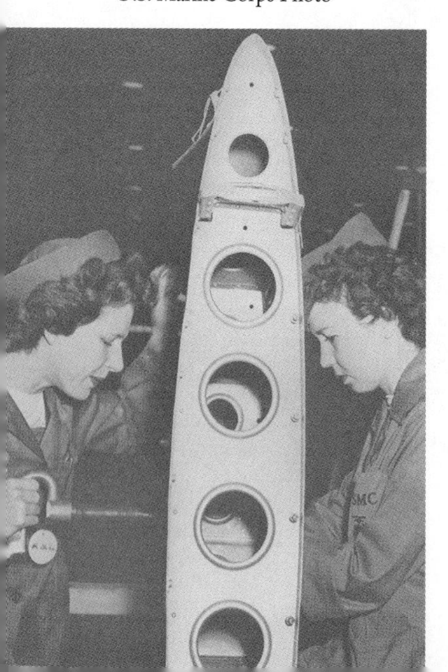

Women Get Tough

To entice as many women as possible, the government released the documentary film *The Hidden Army,* which showed worried moms and wives receiving the worst of news . . . that their son or husband in uniform had been killed in battle. The film dared to ask women what were they doing at home, besides waiting and worrying, to end the war and bring the men back safely? The narrator cautioned, "There is no such thing as a slight falling off of production because there's no such thing as a slight death." Another documentary, with a similar message, was *Women in Defense*, narrated by Katharine Hepburn and written by Eleanor Roosevelt. These films succeeded in encouraging millions of women to seek employment, sometimes traveling to the northeastern steel mills, the East Coast shipbuilding ports, the Midwest aircraft plants and subsidiary suppliers, and the Northwest logging crews.

LEFT: *With women as the largest labor reserve in the country, posters such as this one encouraged women to practice patriotism and work outside the home to support the war effort.*
National Archives Photo

Just as many women remained closer to home, able to commute to work, often pulling double shifts and working weekends to make extra money. And the money certainly was good, an honest wage for a hard day's work. All told, five million women donned dungarees and hard hats, swelling the total of female workers to nineteen million. Collectively they were affectionately referred to as "Rosie the Riveter," no matter what their job was.

Rosie was immortalized when Redd Evans and John Jacob Loeb wrote a song in 1942, recorded by Kay Kyser and his band:

> "All the day long, whether rain or shine, She's a part of the assembly line, She's making history, working for victory, Rosie the Riveter."

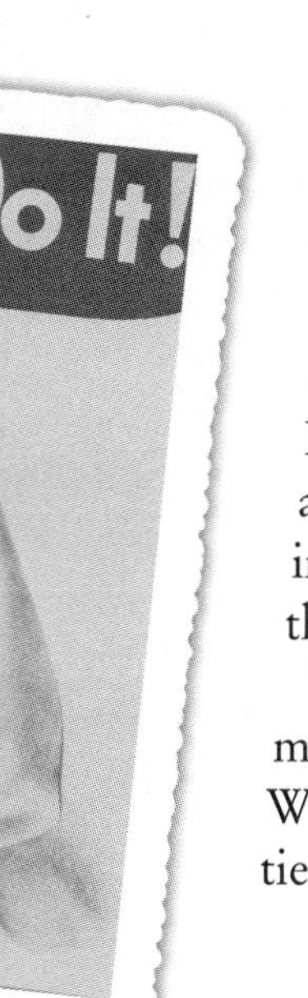

LEFT: *By 1944 women comprised more than 35 percent of the American workforce. For many women, this was their first employment outside the home. In other cases, younger women were getting their first jobs. This image became the most famous poster to recruit women workers. "Rosie the Riveter" implied that any job men could do, women could do better.*
National Archives Photo

The government quickly jumped on the bandwagon and plucked a bona fide Rosie from the assembly line at Ford Motor Company: Rose Will Monroe was handling a rivet gun on Ford's aircraft production line in Detroit when she was discovered by Hollywood actor Walter Pidgeon, who was touring the plant during a promotional tour. Soon she was starring in a film short about women at work for the war effort.

Rosie the Riveter may have been the most recognized female worker during WWII, but many other real-life personalities were right there beside her.

RIGHT: *Black women faced the worst discrimination in America during the war years. At the workplace, they were hired behind whites—men and women—and black men. But as more men left to fight, more black women seized the opportunities to learn a skill and earn a steady income. They joined the ranks of "Rosie the Riveter" and sought better lives with a new trade.*
Library of Congress Photo

"Portland was filled to the bursting point; shipyard workers attended 'swing-shift matinees' at movie houses from midnight to 4 A.M. Among those working for Douglas Aircraft at its six plants in California, Illinois, and Oklahoma were tennis champion Dorothy Bundy, dancer Ruth St. Denis, actress Betty Grable's sister, actress Carole Landis's mother, and a corps of midgets who were found invaluable for work in confined places," reported William E. Leuchtenburg in *New Deal and Global War*.

With her husband overseas, Norma Jean Dougherty found work at the Radioplane Corporation, painting fuselages and working on an assembly line that manufactured radio-controlled target practice planes for anti-aircraft gunnery training. In early 1945 an Army photographer showed up at the plant to do a feature on Women in War Work and spotted Norma Jean. Army Private David Conover shot a few photos of her, along with any of the other attractive female workers at the plant. But there was something about the fetching Norma Jean, and Conover caught up with her later and shot more photos during her lunch break. She seemed to light up while posing for him. Soon after, Conover would be sent to the Philippines, and he thought nothing more of the photos . . . that is, until years later, when she suddenly burst onto the Hollywood scene as Marilyn Monroe.

The United Services Organizations, or USO, "extended its social programs to include the hundreds of thousands of workers in defense plants across the nation who had been relocated to distant communities," reported Frank Coffey in *Always Home: 50 Years of the USO*. "For women defense workers with small children and with husbands who were away from home in the armed forces, the USO provided some of the country's first-ever day care services."

Hollywood leading lady Joan Crawford was concerned about the children of defense workers and stepped in to help. "I was up to my ears, organizing a day nursery for fifty youngsters whose mothers were working in war plants," she wrote in her autobiography, *A Portrait of Joan*, cowritten with Jane Kesner Ardmore. "In the papers you read constantly of children 'abandoned' in cars while their mothers worked. I promptly joined the American Women's Voluntary Services, uniform and all. The Board of Education supplied a principal and assistant teachers and we had a wealth of volunteer workers. We found an old house near the aircraft factories and the volunteer workers and I scrubbed it from top to bottom. It took us a week to get it in shape, then we were ready for the children. During the war years, I cooked the meals, took care of the children. While they slept I scrubbed floors, washed diapers, lined shelves with paper, scrubbed cupboards, and still wasn't tired."

Without the total commitment to the cause, without the millions of women who stepped forward and performed admirably on assembly lines across America, the outcome of WWII might have taken years longer and cost thousands more lives in combat . . . thousands more fathers and sons, husbands and brothers.

ABOVE: *Bolstering troop morale became critical to the war effort. Americans, including this "G.I. Cookie Girl," looked for any way to contribute. Whether it meant working in a factory, knitting mittens, sewing shirts, or baking sweets, everyone looked for a way to lend a hand.*
Chicago Historical Society Photo

Movies and Plays Highlight the Home Front

Hollywood's portrayal of the war effort focused on two themes: the 'round-the-clock unity of the workplace and the sacrifices of home life . . . and usually featured a happy ending, although some films leaned more to the bittersweet. There were few attempts to expose such hot-button issues as extramarital affairs brought on by opportunistic and lecherous bosses propositioning young married women in the workplace, racism against southern blacks who moved to the industrial North looking for work; racketeering as greedy landlords and store merchants raised prices to gouge the enormous influx of workers to the big cities; and depression, especially for the thousands of wives who waited patiently for that happy ending that so many actresses experienced on-screen when their men in uniform returned from the war.

Expecting the same outcome as they'd seen countless times on screen, and then getting the worst of news—that their man wouldn't be coming back alive—plunged countless wives into the depths of despair, wondering how to cope with work and children, in a strange city.

While the movie studios for the most part avoided these issues, movies played a vital role in bolstering morale and keeping the populace on course toward the only acceptable goal that mattered—the defeat of Nazi Germany and Imperial Japan. Internal issues could be dealt with after the war was over and the boys were back home again. "It's no surprise that Hollywood chose to celebrate its heroines during WWII: A preponderance of women on the home front during that four-year span surely accounted for a disproportionate share of the box office," wrote Michael Barson for *Entertainment Weekly*'s April 4, 2003, issue.

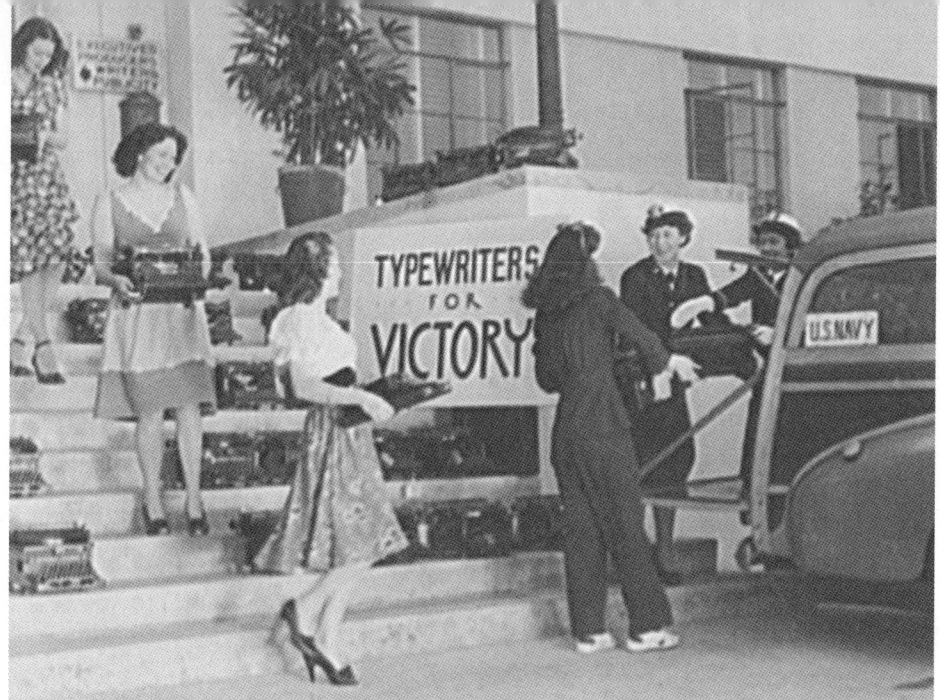

RIGHT: *The U.S. military found itself in short supply of typewriters, so Hollywood studios offered some of theirs. Here, workers at 20th Century Fox turn over their spare equipment to WAVEs.*
National Archives Photo

"Thus, in addition to contemporary folk hero Rosie [the Riveter], moviegoers were treated to such rousing female-themed entertainments as *She's a Soldier Too* (Shelley Winters and pals carry their lunch boxes daily into war-product factories) . . . and *Tender Comrade* (Ginger Rogers moves in with a bunch of other wives whose husbands have been shipped overseas to fight)."

RKO Studios brought out *Tender Comrade* in 1943, with Ginger Rogers as Jo, the mourning widow, toiling in an airplane plant, trying to scratch out a decent living for herself and her newborn son. Feeling melancholy, with a photo of her fallen hero close by, Jo tells her baby that the dad he's never seen "went out and died so you could have a better break when you grow up. He only left you the best world a boy could ever grow up in. He bought it for you with his life . . . a personal gift to you from your dad."

The housing shortage became fodder for big-city romance in 1943's *The More the Merrier*, starring Jean Arthur, who opens her flat to strangers, played by Charles Coburn (an industrialist) and Joel McCrea (an aircraft technician), the latter an aggravating thorn in her side—that is, until she falls hopelessly for him.

Spencer Tracy and Katharine Hepburn appeared in the 1945 film *Without Love*, which dealt with the housing shortage in Washington, D.C. (Hepburn first brought the role to the stage and reworked it for the screen.) She is a war widow renting out a room to a government scientist who is conducting secret tests. He needs an assistant, she needs a job, and along the way they fall in love. Two comedic foils were Keenan Wynn and Lucille Ball.

Another film that told the story of America's families, by portraying a single household coping with separation, uncertainty, and loss, was *Since You Went Away*, released in 1944 and starring Claudette Colbert, Jennifer Jones, and Shirley Temple as a blossoming teenager. First, Anne's husband, Tim, goes off to war and ends up missing in action; then her daughter Jane's boyfriend, Bill, is killed at Salerno. Both women receive telegrams about the bad news, and then have to endure lectures, handle the hurt, and continue on.

Anne (Claudette Colbert) deals with Tim's absence (and possible death) by finding work as a welder in a local factory. There she meets other women, some immigrants, who have also endured sacrifices and hardships, and made the best of life, no matter how crappy it gets. Anne holds out hope that her husband is still alive. But in the closing scene, Christmas Eve is hardly worth celebrating and the women sit solemnly remembering their world before it was shattered by the war. Suddenly the phone rings and Anne hears the great news: Tim has been found, alive, and he will be home very soon. The film's final message was a clarion call to all Americans: Hold on to hope no matter how dark it gets. The news may not always be the best for everyone, but in the end the world will be better for all. The arsenal, and the armada, and the air power that were rolling off the assembly lines across the country would spearhead the eventual defeat of the Axis powers, but the true foundation of Fortress America was the American family.

Critic Philip Hartung felt this movie ended on a false note, writing in *Commonweal*: "There are many of us who are of good courage and have strong faith, but who will not receive cables on Christmas Eve telling us our sons or fathers are safe after all."

Mickey Rooney had the difficult task of delivering those unwelcome telegrams in 1943's *The Human Comedy*, written by William Saroyan (who earned an Academy Award for best original story) and costarring Frank Morgan, Van Johnson, and Marsha Hunt. Like so many home-front movies, this one was also set in small-town America, a cross-section representing the whole.

LEFT: *This mother, like many other American moms, sent her sons off to fight the evil of the Axis powers. As she stared into their smiling faces, she certainly wondered which sons, if any, would come home again. Women all across the U.S. were "blue-star mothers," displaying in their window a white flag with a red border and a blue star to represent a son sent off to fight. It was not uncommon for homes to display flags with multiple blue stars, as many families watched all of their young men go to battle. When a son died during the war, the mother would hang a gold-star flag. Unfortunately, many women become "gold-star mothers" as the war raged.*
Library of Congress Photo

Bette Davis took on the role of a neurotic, frumpy spinster, embittered by an overbearing mother in the 1942 Warner Brothers film, *Now Voyager*, for which she received her fifth Oscar nomination.

"The film's theme of sacrifice and redemption through selfless love, touched a deep chord in the hundreds of thousands of women whose husbands, fathers, boyfriends, brothers, and sons were fighting a war in Europe and Asia," wrote James Spada in the Davis biography, *More Than a Woman*.

Don Ameche played the distraught but stoic father in 1943's *Happy Land*. He receives news that his son, Rusty, has died in battle while serving in the Navy. "He never had a chance to live . . . never went anywhere, just went to school, worked for his dad, never had a home of his own or a boy of his own to worry about, or make a scooter for. It isn't right. It isn't fair." Then, in a series of flashbacks, prompted by reminders from his grandfather, Rusty is shown in vignettes, as a Boy Scout, a school athlete, helping his dad at work, just a terrific kid, like so many other American boys who were cut down before they even had a chance at life. Gramps tells the audience:

"As long as kids can play cowboys and Indians, join Boy Scouts and do a good deed every day, eat ice cream, go to high school, play football . . . it'll be worthwhile."

Thousands of immigrants, especially those from Europe, pursued the American dream and believed wholeheartedly in democracy and what it took to preserve it. In the film *An American Romance,* Steve Dango arrives in New York at the end of the 1800s, then moves on to Minnesota, where his cousin helps him get a job in an iron pit mine. The work is hot and it's difficult, but at the end of the week, Dango gets paid six dollars, and he feels like a rich man. He sets his sights on bigger and better things: a wife, a family, and maybe someday, he can be foreman of the plant's steam shovel. All of his dreams eventually do come true, but with them comes that price for democracy that he feels obliged to pay.

With the Great War raging, his firstborn son—George Washington Dango—becomes a doughboy. While studying to become an American citizen, Dango senior receives a telegram that George has been killed in Europe, and he suddenly realizes that often the price for freedom is very painful.

Released by MGM, "*An American Romance* idealizes the America of heavy industry. Blast furnaces, belching locomotives, elongated ore boats, rivers of molten metal, infernos of steam and smoke—all become a visual representation of the might of an industrial society whose war-making capacity surpasses that of all others," wrote Clayton Koppes and Gregory Black in *Hollywood Goes to War*. But also, "the movie instructed the audience in how to bear the grief of the loss of sons—stoically and with the knowledge that death was meaningful." The message was clear: "Stay the course; everyone must do their part for the country, no matter how personally painful the war becomes."

John Wayne portrayed Pittsburgh Markham—a ruthless industrialist who steps on his workers and is only interested in padding his bank account—in the 1942 film *Pittsburgh*, coincidentally also set in Steel Town. But after severing ties with his partner (played by Randolph Scott), his personal life comes crashing down, he loses everything, and he is forced to take a job at the bottom rung of the ladder, using a false name. When the company struggles to meet the demands of the war effort, all is eventually forgiven between the feuding partners, and Markham returns to the head office. Given a second chance, he makes the most of it, and almost overnight the company makes a dramatic turnaround, exceeding its production goals.

While the film's documentary style did not go over well in movie theaters, the movie continued to hammer the theme that everyone must set aside their personal differences and work together for the good of the country.

There was real concern among national safety officials when it was announced that Paulette Goddard would be portraying a shipyard welder in the movie *I Love a Soldier*. "The National Safety Council . . . began to worry [and] Colonel John Stilwell, president of the council, requested that the studio cover her up safely because 'the problem of getting women to wear proper protective clothing has been a very real one.' The studio retorted with 'She'll set a fine, shapeless, all-inclosed example.' The colonel responded diplomatically, saying that safe clothing 'need not detract from feminine charm.' Paulette wore an authentic, all-covering welder's uniform," reported Julie Gilbert in *Opposite Attraction—The Lives of Erich Maria Remarque and Paulette Goddard*.

Time magazine explained the problem of having women in a male-dominated workplace when it reported in its September 14, 1942, issue: "A very shapely sweater girl wanders in to take her place in the swing shift. Low whistles follow her as she ambles down the aisle between machines. But a few minutes later a gray-haired factory chaperone catches her in the ladies' room. The chaperone admires the sweater girl's figure but says it would be a shame if because of her some man lost a hand under a punch press. Next night the girl comes back in other clothes. Most women now wear slacks, but rebel at keeping their hair covered. Occasionally one gets scalped when the hair gets caught in a machine."

Knowing these workplace mishaps were increasing as more and more

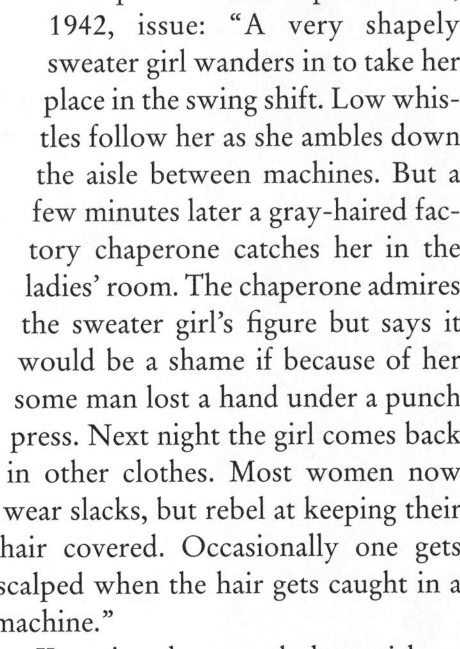

LEFT: *Wanting to help in the war effort but not wanting to check their femininity at the factory door, women often wore dresses, fancy sweaters, and scarves to both feel pretty and to attract the attention of the men left at work. But the frilly fashions got caught in equipment, and machines grabbed mohair sweaters that became statically charged. Hundreds of women were injured and factories lost valuable production time because of damaged equipment. Defense plants quickly engaged in an advertising plan to encourage women to dress in safer clothes. These Los Angeles workers modeled the latest coveralls, hats, safety glasses, and plastic bras, all designed to prevent injuries.*

Women's Bureau Photo

women filled vacancies on the assembly line and operated dangerous and unforgiving equipment, it was only natural for the National Safety Council to be concerned that the beautiful Paulette Goddard might glamorize her role as a welder and thus influence thousands of real-life workers.

Another glamorous sight amid the gritty war industry scene was leggy dancer Ann Miller playing one member of a musical troupe that works at a plane factory during the day and performs after hours in Paramount's 1942 film, *Priorities on Parade*. The lineup also included Bob Hope's sidekick, Jerry Colonna, playing trombone and leering at Miller.

In a much more sinister vein, *Joe Smith, American* focused on a vulnerable worker on a munitions assembly line who is seized by Nazi spies and tortured but cannot be broken. He will not give up vital information about the country's armaments plants. This theme is echoed in 1942's *Saboteur*, when another blue-collar worker, a common patriot, snubs the dastardly efforts of another evil Nazi.

In 1943 composers Oscar Hammerstein and Georges Bizet collaborated with Broadway producer Billy Rose to debut an adaptation of the classical *Carmen*. The updated musical, *Carmen Jones*, was set in a parachute factory in the deep South during WWII, where an Army corporal falls in love with the sultry Cindy Lou. (Ten years later, an all-black cast led by Harry Belafonte, Diahann Carroll, and Dorothy Dandridge would bring this love story to the silver screen.)

BELOW: *Black women, like Martha Bryant (left) and Eulalie Hampden, used the war to gain skills and work their way out of abject poverty. These women learned how to use a bolt-cutting machine at Todd Erie Basin in 1943.*
Library of Congress Photo

The arsenal of America's military was forged with the blood, and the sweat, and the tears of millions of men and women, all pulling together toward the same goal. Maybe Hollywood did gloss over the deplorable housing conditions and the less-than-harmonious racial tensions and the thousands who were maimed or killed in the mandated rush to overproduce. The movies may even have implied a "Whistle While We Work" unity on every assembly line across the country. But the studios had a mandate not only to entertain the masses, but to keep them focused and working as one well-oiled machine. Reality may have fallen far short of that myth on screen, but everyone knew it. Yet while American workers laughed about the whitewash they saw from one movie to the next, America's enemies felt the roar and the thunder when that laughter disguised a rock-solid resolve to get the job done and turned hostile emotions into heavy bombers, and armored tanks, massive aircraft carriers, and deadly silent but lethal submarines.

Left: *Folk singer Pete Seeger performed at the Washington, D.C., labor canteen opening. Despite the Federal Workers of America, Congress of Industrial Organization sponsorship of this show, he was later labeled as a communist and blacklisted. Seeger frequently sang about and spoke in favor of equal rights and better pay and working conditions.* Office of War Information Photo

Tribute to a Golden Goddess

Shipbuilders at California's Terminal Island in late 1943 took special interest in one 10,500-ton Liberty ship, slated to be launched in January of '44. Maybe it was just another of the several hundred churned out in California during the war, but this one had a sentimental bond with the Hollywood community, for it was to be christened the USS *Carole Lombard,* named for the tireless and vivacious actress who had died while returning from a successful war bond drive two years earlier.

Lombard's husband, Clark Gable, was on hand for the ceremony, dressed in his Army Air Corps uniform, and he spoke to the 15,000 shipbuilders and their families, stressing the importance of their work. Still grieving over the loss of his wife, he kept his remarks short, unable to even speak her name. As the ship was christened and slowly slid into the water, the King of Hollywood stood at attention and saluted, facing away from the crowd, who could not see the tears flowing from his eyes.

Maybe Hollywood did miss the mark more often than they got it right, and maybe the biggest stars didn't face the sacrifices the rest of the country endured during the war years, but no one felt the pain of losing a loved one to the war more than did Clark Gable. He was a king who would have traded it all to turn back the clock two years and have his wife beside him again.

Radio Reinforces the Message

"Bing Crosby became a secret weapon in his own right. From London he was persuaded to broadcast to Germany and particularly to the enemy soldiers. He talked and sang in phonetic German and expressed the hope that soon Germany would know the freedom that Americans and Britons enjoy. And the enemy fondly called him Der Bingle . . ."

—*Charles Thompson in the book,* Bing

Background: *Singer and comedian Bob Hope not only traveled with touring entertainment shows, but he also performed frequently on radio to reach GIs in every corner of the globe. Often his camp shows, such as this 1944 Hawaii appearance, were taped and broadcast to troops over Armed Forces Radio.* USO Photo

DURING THE WAR YEARS, RADIO WAS THE QUICKEST AND most effective way to reach out to the masses. The Nazis perfected it as a powerful and incendiary weapon to infect listeners with their poisonous propaganda. Orson Welles used it in his "War of the Worlds" dramatization of an invasion from Mars to scare the crap out of a gullible American public, causing widespread panic across the country.

Just as it oversaw movie scripts—reviewing them, suggesting changes—the Office of War Information got involved in radio, exploiting it to keep the entire nation focused on the only thing that really mattered in the early '40s—defeating the Axis powers. The OWI monitored radio programming, from children's after-school adventure serials to evening soaps, from Sunday sermons to Red Skelton's silliness, to ensure that all broadcasts followed agency guidelines and weren't in any way compromising the war effort.

Right: *Gene Autry gave young radio listeners his "Ten Cowboy Commandments," and later the popular Christmas tune, "Rudolph the Red-Nosed Reindeer." The Singing Cowboy served in the China-Burma-India Theater before returning to Hollywood and his numerous show-business pursuits.* Army Air Corps Photo

More than a decade before the United States was plunged into WWII, Gene Autry, the Singing Cowboy, created his own "Ten Cowboy Commandments" and presented them on his popular show, *Radio Rangers*:

Do not take unfair advantage of an enemy.
Be a patriot.
Be gentle with children, elders, and animals.
Do not possess racially or religiously intolerant ideas.
Don't drink or smoke.
Help people in distress.
Respect women, parents, and your nation's laws.
Be a good worker.

Always tell the truth.
Never go back on your word.

(Too bad the militant leaders in Berlin and Tokyo didn't listen to or abide by Autry's Commandments.)

Dramatizing the War Effort

"Once war was officially declared, it became everyone's job to pitch in and get on with it, and radio went to war in every conceivable way. Comedians, singers, musicians, and every variety of entertainer joined in one vast chorus of patriotic response," reported Barry Farrell and Maureen Baron in *The Swing Era: The Golden Age of Network Radio*. "War themes inundated the dramas, the soap operas, the adventure serials. *The March of Time*, already a successful series of dramatized news events and analysis, reached even greater popularity."

The Friday night series, developed by CBS and *Time* magazine, depicted real-world events, some of which spiraled out of control by the end of the decade, including the Spanish Civil War and the provocative rise of Nazi Germany. By constantly monitoring the news wires, the show's producers could change direction and focus and remain topical and riveting, often cutting away to *Time* correspondents dispatched around the world, reporting events as they happened.

Cavalcade of America, the radio series presented by Du Pont, presented vignettes of the country's most compelling historical events.

"*Columbia Presents Corwin* was a special series of 30-minute plays by Norman Corwin, CBS resident poet," wrote John Dunning in *Tune in*

LEFT: *As the most powerful medium in the U.S. during the war, radio exerted immense influence on listeners. Programs such as "You Can't Do Business with Hitler" never missed an opportunity to speak out against the Nazis and those who would ally with them.*
Office of War Information Photo

Right: *Actress Eve Arden performed in radio plays as sailors, leathernecks, airmen, and soldiers around the world listened.*
Armed Forces Radio Service Photo

Yesterday. "Corwin, one of the big guns of American radio, had had many other specials, one-shots and mini-series before and after *Columbia Presents Corwin* came to the air. That was simply his best, most sustained showing."

On Saturday mornings, *Report to the Nation* brought to life reenactments of current news events, with actors portraying world leaders. One of those actors was the "Man of a Thousand Voices," Art Carney, who "wore dozens of vocal hats: FDR, Wendell Wilkie, Harry Truman, George Marshall, and Dwight D. Eisenhower among them," wrote Michael Seth Starr in the biography, *Art Carney*. "Art's impersonation of FDR was so realistic that FDR's press secretary, Steven Early, was forced to write *Report to the Nation*'s producer. 'Don't have any more imitations of the President on your show,' Early wrote. 'That man who imitates the President is too good. We don't want people to think the President is going on your show.'"

Among the many other radio shows that brought the war into living rooms across the country was *I Was There*, which profiled true accounts of adventure and was narrated by newscaster Chet Huntley. "Dedicated to the fighting men of the United States and the United Nations" and presented by CBS was *The Man Behind the Gun*, spotlighting America's finest and their individual acts of bravery in the face of adversity and certain death. "*The Army Hour*, a giant wartime extravaganza first heard on NBC, gave Americans their first in-depth look at the war and how it was being fought," reported Dunning in *Tune in Yesterday*. "The format was sweeping; the canvas as large as the world. When the Army took a village, *Army Hour* correspondents were there; listeners heard the sniper fire and machine guns in the background."

Rallying the Home Front

In the early 1940s, television was still several years away from being available to the masses, so radio was the messenger of choice, day after day, urging everyone to do whatever they could, from collecting and turning in materials that could be recycled, to limiting their use of valuable commodities, from working in manufacturing plants to volunteering as civil defense wardens, nursing assistants, auxiliary firefighters, and USO supporters, from watching out for enemy activity in every town in America to donating blood for the wounded boys overseas. Some of these radio shows were serials that portrayed "typical" Americans coping with the war's demands. Others more blatantly spewed out patriotism in heavy doses.

Against the Storm was first broadcast in October of 1939, two years before the Japanese attack on Pearl, but six years after the Nazis came to power. "It premiered . . . to the growing tempo of war, and quickly established in its theme a resistance to that war, and to all war," wrote Dunning in *Tune in Yesterday*.

"Its central characters were the Allen family [including] Professor Jason Allen [who] taught at a college campus and was an outspoken opponent of Hitler and of warfare. Even President Roosevelt accepted a speaking appearance on *Against the Storm*." (Ironically, Roosevelt's appearance was cancelled by the bombing of Pearl Harbor.)

Above: *Mickey Rooney—pictured here with Sergeant Bill Stewart, an unknown Signal Corps officer, and actor and Armed Forces Radio Services member Tom Poston—often performed in USO shows and on Armed Forces Radio programs.*
Armed Forces Radio Service Photo

Mutual Radio and the Office of Emergency Management produced *Keep 'Em Rolling* one month before Pearl Harbor, to bolster any flagging sentiments about America's resolve. Not only was Great Britain counting on ships and planes and munitions produced in the United States, but our own WWI-era ships and planes needed to be upgraded to keep pace with the German and Japanese military muscle. Ethel Merman sang the theme song for *Keep 'Em Rolling*, titled "The Flame of Freedom is Burning," while numerous entertainers, writers, actors, and actresses volunteered their time to the thirty-minute Sunday night program.

In mid-1942 there was still concern about Japanese carrier-launched planes hitting the West Coast. NBC aired *Eyes Aloft* for its Pacific radio stations, urging citizens to be vigilant in securing the coastal regions, watching all air and sea approaches from the West and reporting any suspicious activities such as blinking beacons or spotlights, signal flares, coded radio messages, and strangers lurking in the dark near airports and docks. Not only was there concern about a Japanese invasion force just beyond the horizon, but the many aircraft manufacturing plants along the West Coast were considered under threat, and the military took precautions to protect them. "In California the air was so heavy with war planes being tested near aircraft factories, and causing such unrelenting noise, that Hollywood studios had to rewrite scripts to eliminate outdoor shooting locations," wrote Joseph Julian in *This Was Radio*.

One of the suspense serials on ABC's Blue Network was *Counterspy*, which warned of an underground movement in America, controlled by Nazi Germany's Gestapo and Imperial Japan's Black Dragon. It was the job of U.S. agents to rout them out before they could damage the country's infrastructure.

BELOW: *Armed Forces Radio announcer Jack Brown (center) talked to famous movie duo Humphrey Bogart and Lauren Bacall during a broadcast to American troops across the seas.* Armed Forces Radio Service Photo

Mr. District Attorney profiled a tough-as-nails crime-buster who went after the racketeers and black-market hustlers, the organized networks that bilked hard-working Americans. The narrator proclaimed:

> "Mister district attorney, champion of the people.
> Guardian of our fundamental rights to life, liberty,
> and the pursuit of happiness."

Many of the program's scripts were taken directly from front-page scandals. The DA upheld the oath of his duties, which he restated at the beginning of every show: "It shall be my duty as district attorney not only to prosecute to the limit of the law all persons accused of crimes perpetrated within this country, but to defend with equal vigor the rights and privileges of all its citizens."

Jim and Marian Jordan started in radio in 1924 as the O'Henry Twins. Fifteen years later they were on nationwide radio for the Red Network, every Tuesday night, as *Fibber McGee and Molly*. Though he earned his nickname for telling whoppers, Fibber McGee had actually toned down his act by 1940, and while he frequently bumbled his way into calamities in their neighborhood at fictitious Wistful Vista, he never strayed too far from the hardships of mainstream America, especially during the war years.

"Fibber and Molly were always hustling for the war cause, pleading with their audience to save gas and rubber, to pitch into the soap drive with a little more elbow grease, to keep away from black market meat. But it was always developed as entertainment, well within the context of the story," Dunning reported in *Tune in Yesterday*. Other actors in the ensemble cast included Bill Thompson, who wound up in the Navy, and Gale Gordon, bound for the Coast Guard.

The soap opera *Lonely Women* aired on the NBC radio network for only one season, during the summer after Pearl Harbor. The show featured several women, including a housekeeper, a model and her sister, a secretary, and an elevator girl, and all the travails they encountered.

The Better Half was a good-natured, on-air challenge of the sexes. Thousands of women had already displaced men in the war factories and had proven to be just as competent with heavy tools and backbreaking work. Could men be just as adept in the kitchen? The show's creators intended to find out every Sunday night, pitting husbands and wives against each other in a variety of tests that played off age-old stereotypes of what was "men's work" and what was "women's work." Typically, the final tally was a toss-up, allowing both sides to claim the upper hand.

Local radio stations also shifted programming to accommodate those supporting the war effort. In Philadelphia, Democratic Party workers bought airtime on radio station WIP from midnight to 1 A.M. to reach potential voters during a shift change at local war plants. In Akron, several local bands including those led by Jan Garber, Tommy Tucker, and Richard Himber regularly performed for second- and third-shift workers at the local armory, dubbed the Swing Shift Canteen.

ABOVE: *Popular songstress Lena Horne belted out tunes on* Jubilee, *which served as a forum for African-American entertainers to reach servicemen via radio. Her music was recorded and sent to stations that broadcast to military men and women overseas.* Armed Forces Radio Service Photo

Performer Alvino Rey and his bandmates played both sides of the fence in Los Angeles, working the midnight-to-dawn shift at Lockheed, then performing at the nearby Aragon Ballroom and other night spots during the evening hours. They also found gigs in several Hollywood musicals—that is, until some of the musicians got their draft notices. In Denver, one downtown theater hosted a "Dawn Jamboree" every Wednesday night at 1 A.M. for swing-shift workers just getting off but not too tired to do a little jitterbugging before heading home. Local radio stations sometimes aired these performances "live" for late-night listeners.

Reaching Out to Young Listeners

Hap Harrigan started as an adventure hero in All American Comics, and then became a popular children's radio character on the Blue Network. *The Hap Harrigan Show* featured the daring exploits of America's "Ace of the Airways," and his dim-witted sidekick, Tank Tinker. But even while ranging far and wide, often on clandestine missions in enemy territory, Hap took time to remind his young listeners that they should do their part to help him, by encouraging their parents to turn in recyclable goods, such as tin, and rubber, paper, and even cooking fat, all of which could help defeat America's enemies. And whenever Red Cross blood supplies ran low, Hap prodded his listening audience: "The blood given by your family and friends may be responsible for bringing back alive your brother, father, cousin, or neighbor. So keep on punching, gang. Don't even for one minute relax in your efforts to help speed victory."

LEFT: *Martha Wilkerson became GI Jill on the Armed Forces Radio show* GI Jive. *Thousands of servicemen stationed in the U.S. and abroad listened to Jill daily.* Armed Forces Radio Service Photo

RIGHT: *Entertainers Betty Hutton and Jimmy Durante cooked a steak on radio's* Command Performance *after a serviceman said he wanted to hear a big porterhouse sizzle, even though he knew it could be months before he got to eat such a juicy piece of beef.*
Armed Forces Radio Service Photo

BELOW: *Ann Sheridan performed on Armed Forces Radio frequently. Hearing performers sing, dance, or act in plays made GIs feel a little closer to home despite being thousands of miles away.*
Armed Forces Radio Service Photo

Another popular children's radio hero was Jack Armstrong, the All-American Boy, who "enlisted" millions of fans in his "Write-a-Fighter Corps" program, each one promising to write a letter every month to a serviceman overseas. The show's creators realized the influence the program had, and urged listeners to plant victory gardens and collect reusable goods

Hundreds of teenaged boys were fascinated by exciting tales heard over the airwaves, clustered around the family radio. *Terry and the Pirates* debuted in November of 1937 and ran three times a week. Situated in the exotic locale of the Orient, Terry Lee and his sidekicks Flip Corkin, Hotshot Charlie, and Pat Ryan, along with provocative ladies of mystery, took on a motley assortment of evildoers, who sounded a lot like the real-life Japanese forces rampaging across Manchuria and threatening other regions of the Far East by 1937.

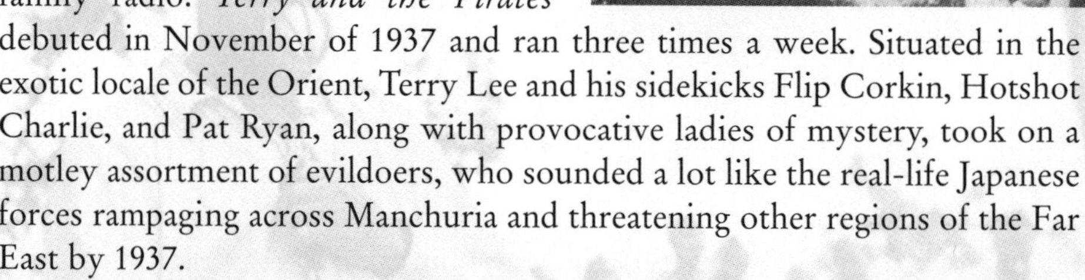

The Air Adventures of Jimmy Allen, which first aired in 1933, documented the fictional yet very dangerous around-the-world missions of the title hero and his fellow aviator, Speed Robertson. In the show's heyday, more than three million kids—with visions of one day skipping among the clouds and protecting the world from all comers with bad intentions—"enlisted" into Jimmy Allen Flying Clubs.

Of course, another superhero who struck down evil at every turn, including menacing Nazis and Japs, was the Man of Steel—

". . . faster than a speeding bullet, more powerful than a locomotive,
able to leap tall buildings at a single bound.
"Look! Up in the sky . . . it's a bird . . . it's a plane . . .
it's . . . SUPERMAN!"

Mild-mannered Clark Kent, reporter for the *Daily Planet*, was ever watchful for sinister characters and their devious plots, and at the first whiff of trouble, he would rush to the nearest phone booth (or any unoccupied room, alleyway, or parked car) to strip off his business attire and step out as Superman, the number-one righter of all dastardly wrongs.

The National Aeronautic Association teamed up with the military services to develop *Scramble*, a Blue Network radio show that attempted to interest young people in the exploits of bona fide war heroes rather than the fictitious tales of Superman and Terry Lee and the like. Whenever possible, *Scramble* brought the actual aviators on the air to talk about their experiences.

Dedications from Loved Ones

Popular female singers such as Dinah Shore, Doris Day, and the Andrew Sisters tugged at the heartstrings when they sang about missing their fella fighting overseas. It was a message played 'round the world, rebroadcast via shortwave radio over ship intercoms and on camps' scratchy loudspeakers.

Some of the most popular weekly shows were those that played dedications: "This next tune is from Sweet Sue in Kalamazoo to her GI Joe near Palermo."

Servicemen could send in requests to *Command Performance*, and Hollywood stars would do their best to grant them, like when Ann Sheridan grilled up a thick, juicy steak, with the microphone held close enough to pick up the mouthwatering sizzle of that delectable hunk of meat. First broadcast to the troops in March of 1942 and produced by the Armed Forces Radio Services (AFRS), *Command Performance* was a weekly thirty-minute variety show that "enlisted" Hollywood's top stars, including Bob Hope, Bing Crosby, Judy Garland, and Red Skelton, to name just a few.

LEFT: *Because* Command Performance *allowed servicemen and -women to send in requests, singers like Janet Blair could dedicate songs to great guys and gals serving in the U.S. military all over the world.*
Armed Forces Radio Service Photo

"The show was written to the specifications of homesick fighting men," reported Dunning in *Tune in Yesterday*. "By request listeners heard Carole Landis sigh, the sounds of Fifth Avenue, a slot machine hitting the jackpot, and other personal oddities."

LEFT: *Popular entertainers appeared weekly at the servicemen's request on* Command Performance. *Here, Major Mann Holiner visited with singers Dinah Shore and Bing Crosby.*
Armed Forces Radio Service Photo

"Bob Hope ended one session with the gag that if the boys wanted lilting songstress Ginny Simms to sing another number, they had only to tear off the top of a Zero and send it in," wrote Donald I. Rogers in *Since You Went Away*. "Bit by bit the wing of a Japanese plane was sent through the mail to 'Mr. Bob Hope, Hollywood, California.' Assembled, it showed

RIGHT: *Bob Hope and "Sweetheart of the Fighting Fronts" Frances Langford entertained troops at USO camp shows, and many performances reached millions of GIs stationed around the world through radio broadcasts. According to a February 9, 2002, article in* The Washington Post, *Langford said she forgot all about show business when she was on stage in front of troops. "We were there just to do our job, to help make them laugh and be happy if they could," she said. Langford always sang her signature tune, "I'm in the Mood for Love," which drew a huge response from the crowd. "Everywhere I went, it was the same thing," she told* The Washington Post *reporter. "I got up and sang about eight bars and way in the back some GI would stand up. He's say, 'You've come to the right place, sister.' They responded to everything, they were such a wonderful audience."* U.S. Air Force Museum Photo

the Jap symbol of the rising sun. Ginny Simms hurriedly prepared another special program of favorite songs for the boys."

Another show that appealed to women was *The Breakfast Club*, and a special moment on every morning's installment was Prayer Time, when host Don McNeill solemnly recited,

> "All over the nation, each in his own words, each in his own way,
> For a world united in peace, bow your heads and let us pray."

The show was a blockbuster for morning radio, and McNeill's rallying cry was such a hit, he continued it long after the war was over.

While early morning wake-ups were never quiet routines for most GIs, the radio show *Reveille with Beverly* was a hit, six days a week, starting at 5:30 A.M. on Denver's radio station, KFEL. Hosted by former starlet Jean Ruth, the one-hour show played big band music by request, and "Beverly" answered fan mail on the air. "I tried to make it the girl next door, warm, and maybe semi-sexy," Ruth explained years later.

"When a story about the show appeared in *Time* magazine, Ruth was hired by KNX in Los Angeles," reported Owen Edwards for *Smithsonian* in May of 2004. "The newly formed Armed Forces Radio Service picked up the show and began sending it to bases all over the world, and before long Ruth was waking up some 11 million GIs stationed in 54 countries."

Background: *One of the nation's most popular singing acts, the Andrews Sisters belted out the crowd-pleasing "Boogie Woogie Bugle Boy of Company B" to a packed Hollywood Canteen.*
National Archives Photo

Hollywood and the Canteen

"With the advent of war, the complexion of the city changed almost overnight . . . there was real danger. There was great fear by our leaders that California might be invaded."

—*Yvonne DeCarlo, in her autobiography,* Yvonne

LONG BEFORE COMING TO POWER IN GERMANY, THE National Socialist Party spewed forth a barrage of incendiary propaganda, setting forth an agenda unparalleled in history. Once in control of the Fatherland in 1933, Adolf Hitler and the Nazis cracked down on anyone with an opposing viewpoint. Jewish writers, composers, and movie directors were blacklisted as enemies of the state, and publishing houses and film studios were seized and silenced. Books were burned, movies were confiscated and destroyed.

Jewish writers, directors, actors, and actresses were suddenly out of work, caught up in the Nazis' purging of all traces of their culture and influence. All Jewish intelligentsia, including doctors, lawyers, and teachers, were threatened, first with their livelihood, then with their lives. Not only were they being silenced, Europe's Jews were selected for elimination. Those who persisted, who ignored the warning signs, who chose to stay behind and ride out the storm, just as Jews had done for centuries, didn't realize that this time it was different—this time it was more than just bluster. This time their decision to stay would be a fatal one.

Right: *Hollywood fifth-graders at the Cheremoya Public School pledge allegiance to the flag during* Three Thirds of a Nation, *a play designed to influence every man, woman, and child to do what he or she could to support the war.*
Office of War Information Photo

Hundreds who could afford to flee the rising storm sought refuge in England, and from there on to America, where freedom of expression was guaranteed. As Nazi Germany spread its poison to other countries, those occupied territories also saw a mass exodus from their publishing, film, and theatrical communities. Those immigrants who made it to America were just glad to be alive, and out of harm's way, but they were also apprehensive about how to live in their new country and still continue to be successful as artists—on stage, on screen, in print, on the air. As strangers in a strange land, they sought out friends and associates who had arrived before them and established themselves on Broadway and in Hollywood. Those refugees who followed them, who fled the Nazis, represented some of the greatest creative talents of that era, and Hollywood benefited from the influx.

Tinseltown quickly became a kaleidoscope of foreign colonies, each an eclectic group of actors and actresses, fashion designers, directors, screenwriters, makeup artists, cameramen, and other craftsmen, plus their families and hangers-on.

They all wanted to pursue the American dream, yet they could not ignore or easily toss aside their heritage—French, German, English, Russian, Austrian, Polish, Italian, Belgian, Chinese—and were frequently cast in roles based on their ethnicity, roles that may have been abhorrent to them. Some German Jews portrayed Nazi prison guards, or Chinese actors might don Japanese Army uniforms. (In the months immediately after Pearl Harbor, fearing a fifth column of spies, all of the Japanese along the West Coast, including actors and actresses, had been rounded up and sent to internment camps in the southwest, so by mid-1942 there were no Japanese actors in Hollywood. Casting directors turned to Chinese actors, or to the laughable makeup gimmick of giving white actors almond-shaped eyes and black hair.)

The movie *Across the Pacific* was underway when the attack on Pearl Harbor disrupted filming. "It features the slimiest Japanese villains who had ever appeared on the screen," wrote Jeffrey Meyers in *Bogart: A Life in Hollywood*. According to Meyers, actress Mary Astor remembered, "'The government started shipping out our Nisei cast. A little indignation and some wire-pulling held them at least until the picture was finished.' But her memory was unreliable. All the Oriental roles were played by Chinese actors, made to look as ugly and sinister as possible and to reflect the current hatred of the Japanese enemy."

After America declared war on the Axis powers, California Guardsmen were deployed to Hollywood's many movie studios to protect them from sabotage. They also confiscated all functioning firearms to be reissued to civil defense patrols. "All studios were ordered onto a daylight shift of 8 A.M. to 5 P.M. so that employees could get home before the blackout began, and, as a result,

BELOW: *Star Janet Blair showed audiences how to conserve fat, which could be taken to a recycling center and turned into nitroglycerin. The U.S. government urged housewives to save one tablespoon of waste kitchen fat each day to meet the nation's needs.*
Office of War Information Photo

night filming was temporarily halted," reported Colin Shindler in *Movies of the Forties*. "Most of these instinctive measures were only imposed in the early days of the war when it was still feared that the Japanese were preparing to invade along the vast, undefended coastline of California."

The government considered movie production as war essential, and even though they would not be called up to serve in the military, hundreds of Hollywood craftsmen and stars also sought work at one of the many defense plants in the Los Angeles area. "The 1940 population figure of 210,000 mounted to 235,000, and nearly all the newcomers worked in war jobs," reported Army Private James O'Neill for *YANK*. "Over 40,000 workers were employed in some 200 small-scale war industries that sprung up in Hollywood since Pearl Harbor. These plants made plastics, precision instruments, gauges, and airplane hydraulic valves." These numbers did not include the many film industry professionals who joined one of the armed forces and continued to do the same jobs in developing training films and combat documentaries for the military.

There were still plenty of beauties and handsome hunks hanging outside all the popular night spots, hoping to be discovered, but few had the free time to go on auditions all day, every day, and line up for casting calls. The urgencies of the war had changed all that.

"Though [Hollywood] Boulevard still boasts the most concentrated array of beautiful young women to be seen anywhere in America, now the ladies rush down the street with a jerky, tense jauntiness, a lot of them wearing aircraft-employee identification discs on their blouses," noted O'Neill. "Nowadays a beautiful doll often is seen walking along the Boulevard lugging a lunch pail."

Building a Place for the Boys

Leading actor John Garfield was listed as 4-F, disqualified from service, but he knew he had to do something for the war effort besides make movies. He saw the hundreds of servicemen passing through southern California bound for the Pacific, and he knew what they needed. He approached Bette Davis with the idea of opening a club where these GIs could meet and dance with starlets, listen to great entertainment, enjoy a good meal, and not pay anything for it. Everything would be gratis. The stars and the bands would donate their time—both on stage and behind the scenes, even if it meant washing dishes and mopping floors; local restaurants would donate the food and the cooks. Davis tapped her close friend and MCA chief Jules Stein to head up the fund-raising efforts to defray anything they couldn't get for free. Doris Stein, Jules's wife, would be in charge of ensuring a sufficient number of starlets would be on hand every night once the club was open.

The Hollywood Canteen would rival the hottest of hot spots in town, and anybody who was anybody or who someday wanted to be a somebody would want to be seen there, doing his or her part, giving the boys an evening they'd never forget. Okay, so maybe the dilapidated livery stable over on Cahuenga Boulevard wasn't exactly the place they had in mind, and at a hundred dollars a month for the lease, somebody was getting snookered. It certainly wasn't anywhere anyone would want to be seen, but it was the best of what was available. Through the years it had housed a community theater and several failed nightclubs. Bette Davis envisioned something no one else could see, but that didn't stop her. She plunged headfirst into the project, mustering an army of workers from the various guilds and unions in town—carpenters, plumbers, electricians, painters, glaziers, decorators—to donate their time and any supplies and equipment the studios could part with.

With a little magic and maybe some glitter dust, it took only three weeks to turn the place into a showcase, including a Gay-Nineties-meets-Old-Frontier motif, painted by some of the best cartoonists in the business.

Davis even coerced her fellow stars to chip in. Studio head Jack Warner paid for the flooring, and Cary Grant came through with a piano.

Opening night was October 3, 1942, and it was treated like a movie premiere, with massive spotlights, and hundreds of GIs inside, and just as many spectators jammed outside. Bette Davis, who was to provide the opening remarks, couldn't even get near the front door and ended up crawling through a window just to get to the stage. Rudy Vallee headed up the procession into the Hollywood Canteen and was just one of the many performers. Other entertainment included Abbott and Costello and the big band music of Duke Ellington and Kay Kyser.

Below: *Hollywood hotties Ann Sothern, Hedy Lamarr, and Linda Darnell served coffee and sandwiches at the Canteen, which was always packed with servicemen. The USO club was only a block away, and soldiers and sailors would beat a path between the two. The Canteen's popularity forced the rule that guys were permitted to stay only a short time to eat, drink, and dance with the stars. Time limits allowed more men to visit on any given night.* USO Photo

A steady stream of stars showed up that night—Betty Grable and Rita Hayworth, Marlene Dietrich and Carole Landis, to name a few—and they danced till their feet hurt, then danced some more because they didn't have the heart to turn anyone down. (And the stars danced every night the Canteen was open, through the end of the war.)

Other regulars during the war years included Freddy Martin and his band, singer Dinah Shore, comedian Red Skelton, actresses Dorothy Lamour, Olivia de Havilland, and Hedy Lamarr, and actors Humphrey Bogart and Spencer Tracy. Bette Davis, who could be counted on to be there five or six nights of every week, noted in her autobiography, *This 'n That*, "On any given night a serviceman might dance with Betty Grable to Harry James's band. Betty and Harry met and fell in love at the Hollywood Canteen and were eventually married. A soldier might ask Hedy Lamarr to pour another cup of coffee, while Marlene Dietrich served sandwiches, and Basil Rathbone carried a tray of used dishes back to the kitchen. The master of ceremonies might be Eddie Cantor, Fred MacMurray, or Bing Crosby. Saturday was Kay Kyser's night. I cannot remember Kay and his band ever missing one Saturday, even though sometimes it was necessary to fly the band back from some distant engagement."

BELOW: *Actress Olivia de Havilland enjoyed coffee with a soldier, a leatherneck, and a sailor at a USO club. The servicemen didn't seem to mind burnt java in Styrofoam cups while in the presence of a beautiful woman.*
USO Photo

Yvonne De Carlo was one of the movie stars who frequented the Canteen. "Every night hundreds of GIs would wait in around-the-block lines to glimpse a movie star or dance with a starlet, but many of them just wanted someone to talk with, to help soothe their homesickness. The sadness of war was all around us, but so was the electrical charge of the common cause," she wrote in her autobiography.

"With the USO and the Canteen located within a block of each other, the strip between Hollywood and Sunset boulevards swarmed with military personnel passing through town on their way to unknown destinations. I never failed to keep my twice-a-week date with the lads at the Hollywood Canteen."

Joan Crawford could be found at the Canteen on Monday nights, pulling waitressing duties and talking with the boys, even jotting down their home addresses so she could send postcards to their loved ones. Young Roddy McDowall frequented the joint, doing busboy duties without complaint. Jeannette Oden pulled duty on Sunday afternoons. "I tell people that I danced my way through the war."

It is rumored that Marlene Dietrich had a voracious sexual appetite and that her appearances at the Canteen led to more than just meeting and talking with the servicemen. "Dancing with the young heroes, offering the handsome one sexual consolation, sweating in the kitchen over their scrambled eggs, scraping and washing their dishes, she found herself in her element," wrote Diana McLellan in *The Girls*. "She laid all her talents at the boys' feet, or a little higher. She played her musical saw for them at every opportunity. She and her great new chum Orson Welles developed a mind-reading act to entertain them, as part of his 'Wonder Show.'"

On another occasion Miss Dietrich left the set of the movie *Kismet* and went straight to the Canteen, still decked out in gold paint. She was always very popular with the troops, but this night she nearly caused a riot.

One of the many "sailors" who got to dance with Marlene Dietrich was Johnny Carson, who had just graduated from high school and acquired a Navy midshipman's uniform to get into the Canteen. He was later arrested for impersonating a Navy recruit and was fined fifty dollars. The arrest didn't keep him from later enlisting in the Naval Air Corps.

Singers, dancers, musicians, and comedians were used to performing and knew what audiences liked, but actors like Gary Cooper, though encouraged to stop by the Canteen, felt they couldn't offer any kind of performance that the troops would enjoy. "Those guys don't want to see me," Coop told gossip columnist Hedda Hopper. "They want some pretty girls. What in the world can I do?" But Hopper wouldn't let him off the hook so easily.

"Against his better judgment, he consented. Standing before a microphone [on stage at the Canteen], Hedda sensed that Cooper was squirming uncomfortably behind her," wrote Hector Arce in *Gary Cooper*. "She began asking him questions, which he answered in a mumble. The audience laughed uproariously. Puzzled by the explosive response to the innocuous words, she nevertheless continued. The wave of laughter resumed as Cooper mumbled another reply. Curious, Hedda turned around to see Cooper spit out a mouthful of feathers. He'd been eating the plumage on her hat! So gratifying was the response of the servicemen that Cooper returned often to the Canteen."

Above: *Celebrities, such as starlets Maria Montez and Gloria Jean, did more than entertain during World War II. They also collected supplies for the armed forces, worked in war bond drives – even turned in their nylons – and encouraged all their fans to support the war effort, too.*
National Archives Photo

The holidays were the hardest to take for the boys, so far from home and headed overseas. The stars did their best to bring a festive mood to the Canteen, but it was difficult, knowing that many of the young men wouldn't be coming back. One Christmas Eve Bing Crosby and his sons stopped by to sing carols. "There was not a dry eye in the Canteen," Bette Davis recalled in *This 'n That*. "Watching the faces of GIs trying so hard to be cheerful made all of us die a little. Bing's sons represented everything the GIs were fighting for—a country without war in the future of little boys like these."

Los Angeles Welcomes the GIs

LA welcomed many thousands of servicemen, and when the boys got a weekend pass or a few hours of liberty, they couldn't just wander the streets until dawn. The local Riverside Theater opened its doors after the twilight show, allowing up to 1,500 GIs to grab a pillow and sack out for the night. It may not have been a comfy bed, but at least the theater had heat and the boys were in a secure environment. *YANK* reported that as many as 60,000 GIs might be in town any Saturday night. "Moviedom's contribution, the Hollywood Canteen, received national publicity, but the unsung people of this town—the homeowners, the workers, the apartment dwellers—handle the major part of Hollywood's effort to make visiting GIs happy. A local 'Bed for Buddies' Committee has scraped up regular weekend sleeping accommodations for as many as 12,000 servicemen. Each weekend the Hollywood High Gym takes care of 1,000 GIs." On Sunday mornings, the school provided breakfast for twenty-five cents, with students serving as waitresses, cooks, and dishwashers.

Many years after the war, an anonymous veteran wrote to *Dear Abby* about one actor's generosity before the young recruit shipped off to basic: "The party [at the Hollywood Canteen] was a huge success. However, finding shelter for the evening was next to impossible at any price during the war years. After the gala event was over, I was dozing in a chair when I was awakened by a petite elderly lady who said she would get me a place to sleep that night. An auto awaited, and with two other servicemen, I was driven to Beverly Hills. Abby, we were in the home of the movie actor Edward G. Robinson. He had turned over his home to the USO while he was in New York."

The Canteen Hits the Silver Screen

In the Warner Brothers movie, *Thank Your Lucky Stars*, song-and-dance man Eddie Cantor played dual roles—as himself the performer, and as a tour bus driver roaming around Hollywood. The musical was basically a series of numbers done by Warner's top singers and dancers (and several who couldn't sing or dance but gave it their best effort). The lineup included Alan Hale, Ida Lupino, Dinah Shore, Errol Flynn, Jack Carson, Olivia de Havilland, Dennis Morgan, and Ann Sheridan. Actor Humphrey Bogart portrayed an unshaven tough-guy gangster who gets unceremoniously escorted out of the theater. The bouncer was "Cuddles" Sakall, the lovable waiter Carl from *Casablanca*. Bette Davis sang a lament common to many single women during the war years: the Frank Loesser and Arthur Schwartz tune, "*They're Either Too Young or Too Old.*"

The film's top entertainers waived their $50,000 salaries, donating a combined $2 million to the Hollywood Canteen. Warner Brothers kicked in another $1.5 million in profits from the film.

The musical's success, plus the popularity of radio shows broadcast on location at the Canteen, led Warner Brothers to produce the musical *Hollywood Canteen*, utilizing practically every star and player the studio had under contract.

"The story dealt with two soldiers [Robert Hutton and Dane Clark] who come to the Canteen during sick leave," wrote Whitney Stine and Bette

Davis in *Mother Goddam*. "Hutton perchance happens to be the millionth GI to cross the threshold of the Canteen, and the prize is a date with Joan Leslie." The flimsy storyline connected the comedy skits and production numbers that dominated the film and made it a hit with audiences.

The importance of the Hollywood Canteen and the movies that sustained the club led to the establishing of New York's Stage Door Canteen, supported similarly by Broadway's entertainment community. It too became a stopover for GIs headed overseas, in this case to England or the Mediterranean or the fighting front of Fortress Europe.

6. The Pacific Rim

"From the Far East I send you one single thought, one sole idea—written in red on every beachhead from Australia to Tokyo: There is no substitute for Victory!"

—*General Douglas MacArthur*

IN A COUNTERCLOCKWISE ARC, THE ENTIRE PACIFIC RIM was threatened as Imperial Japan's tentacles strangled Manchuria, then probed far beyond the coastal regions of China to menace Burma and India. Those probing tentacles invaded the Aleutians, hoping to hop-scotch an invasion force over to Alaska, then swoop down into Canada, and prepare to attack America's Pacific Northwest. And they reached down into Indonesia, attempting to seize vital oil and rubber resources in the region. But to do so Japan would have to cut off and eliminate the rapidly growing Allied threat in nearby Australia and New Zealand, where thousands of Americans were massing, steeling themselves for a little payback in the South Pacific.

Australia's and New Zealand's ports were vital as refueling and resupply depots and to repair any Allied ships damaged in the Pacific. The Japanese, knowing these ports were strategically important, bombed Darwin, Australia, on February 19, 1942. A dozen Allied ships there were sunk by torpedoes and bombs. It would be the only attack on Australia, although Japanese forces continued to menace Allied air and naval forces in the surrounding waters.

After the rigors of basic training or boot camp, the thousands of GIs deployed to the lands down under must have felt they were on vacation. (The first American troops arrived only days before Christmas of 1941, with up to a million spending time in the region during the war years.) They still had to drill and take classes during the day, but their nights were mostly free, except for the unfortunate few on guard duty. Being halfway around the world surely was lonely and boring for some—at least, that's what they wrote in their letters home—but thousands of other Yanks had the good fortune to fall in love for the first time, with an Aussie or a Newzee girl, thousands of whom became war brides. (Best estimates are that as many as 12,000 Americans—including nurses and

Opposite: *The deck of the* Hornet *buzzed with excitement as B-25 bombers prepared to take off for a bombing raid on Tokyo. The attack caught the Japanese by surprise because they never imagined that bombers could take off from an aircraft carrier. These planes were bigger and slower than fighters, and they normally required approximately 400 more feet of runway to lift off. One pilot on the raid, Ted Larson, penned* Thirty Seconds over Tokyo, *which detailed the mission and aftermath. Lawson's plane crashed, and he fractured his leg. Fortunately one of the crewmen was a doctor and amputated his leg to stop the bleeding and save his life.*
U.S. Navy Photo

Left: *The character of Flip Corkin in the popular 1940s comic strip,* Terry and the Pirates, *was modeled after Colonel Philip "Flip" Cochran, who served with the Army Air Forces in the China-Burma-India Theater. In the strip, Terry Lee and his sidekicks, Corkin, Hotshot Charlie, Pat Ryan, and a team of provocative ladies, battled a variety of evildoers in the Orient.*
Army Air Forces Photo

members of the Women's Army Corps—found wedded bliss with local citizens.)

One of the sailors bound for Australia was Mike Douglas, who had helped raise war bonds in southern California as an up-and-coming entertainer. He was assigned to the recently launched Liberty ship, the *Carole Lombard,* named for the Hollywood glamour queen who died on her way home from a fund-raising trip in early 1942.

"It was a good ship, but the crew didn't consider it such a great honor to be on board," Douglas recalled in his book, *I'll Be Right Back*, written with Thomas Kelly and Michael Heaton. "The *Carole Lombard* was a munitions transport headed out on the long Pacific route to Australia. My first day on board, I asked my CPO [chief petty officer] where our destroyer escorts were. He got a good laugh from that question.

"'Escorts? Son, we are one big floating stick of dynamite. If we get hit, everything within a mile is going straight up to Kingdom Come, and it don't take more'n a warm match to do it neither.'" Fortunately, the transport made the journey and back without any enemy sightings.

American movies were shown every night in Australia and New Zealand, in the mess tent, or any makeshift theater in camp. And American entertainers braved the perilous Pacific to strut their stuff on stage, even if that "stage" was nothing but the back end of an open Army truck. To show their appreciation, local entertainers with varying degrees of talent performed for the troops. They ranged from teenaged magicians honing their craft and hoofers (tap dancers) to a geriatric comedian whose recycled jokes were so old the GIs groaned and tossed him the punch lines whenever he forgot them. Some of the local acts included the Kinky Campboy Club, the Ozark Mountaineers, seven-year-old Leigh Brewer (dubbed "Sweetheart of the Marines"), and the Arcadian Revellers Revue. Miss Matilda's Gospel Choir and the Bible-Thumping Brass Quartet weren't big hits either, at least not on Saturday nights when the Yanks were looking for a little action.

The U.S. Army's 37th Division was initially based at Auckland, New Zealand. In this region alone there were eighteen musical groups that put on 140 concerts for the division's numerous encampments in the area, from Papakura and Mangere Crossing to Wellington and Opaheke. Some of the more talented GIs returned the favor and "formed a vaudeville group,

BELOW: *Actress Merle Oberon posed in 1941 for a snapshot by Corporal Charles Savage and his GI buddies in China. She starred in U.S. and British films and earned an Academy Award Best Actress nomination for her role as Kitty Van in the 1935 film,* Dark Angel.
National Archives Photo

calling themselves 'The Fourragere Follies,' [which] entertained different units of the Division as well as at civilian concerts," wrote Denys Bevan in *United States Forces in New Zealand.* "Several performances were given to capacity houses at the Wellington Opera House."

LEFT: *Comedian Joe E. Brown often led the way for entertainers into theaters of war. And the China-Burma-India Campaign was no different. Brown was once again one of the first Americans to entertain troops, such as at this 1944 show in China.*
National Archives Photo

The U.S. 2nd Marine Division was also stationed at New Zealand before plunging into the thick of the fighting in the Pacific. "Amongst the over 20,000 men of the Division were two well-known film personalities," continued Bevan.

"Louis Haywood, a South African-born screen actor, was married to British actress Ida Lupino. He starred in British films before moving to Hollywood in 1935 and gaining U.S. citizenship. While serving in the Marines, he used the surname of Richards. During a tour of Mt. Cook, Christchurch, and various scenic locations, he and the other film personality, Milton Sperling, a 20th Century Fox executive, produced a film about the New Zealand people and environs as seen through the eyes of a GI."

To further cement the bond between New Zealanders and the Americans stationed there, local radio stations broadcast a variety of shows, including *The American Hour* every Sunday night. This show spotlighted many of the local GI groups, but also included American entertainers touring the region, such as comedian Joe E. Brown and composer Johnny Mercer. The 2nd Marine Division Band performed on *The Radio Theatre Show,* with the gate receipts from the live audience being donated to the Wellington Patriotic Fund. *The Marine Corps Program* was broadcast on Sunday nights, and the Mighty Marine Matinee Players with Lieutenant Fred Babo pulling the strings performed for *The Semper Fidelis Show.*

LEFT: *Band leader Artie Shaw and his musicians performed nonstop in the Pacific Campaign. The humidity dulled performers and musicians. Many men became sick, brass instruments rusted, and woodwinds had shredded reeds and disintegrated pads. Despite wanting to entertain more GIs, the band flew back to the States to recover and refit their orchestra. They were too exhausted, though, and did not return to the Pacific.*
Library of Congress Photo

Artie Shaw and his Navy band "invaded" the southern reaches in July of 1943 and played at both military camps and civilian concert halls throughout New Zealand and Australia. Though the GIs were hungry for big band jive, the locals in Wellington thought the band was just "too swingy and too loud." The band was on such a demanding schedule, often performing several times a day, that by November they were physically exhausted and their instruments were breaking down. Shaw and several of his bandmates were so spent, they were medically discharged from the Navy.

Song-and-dance man Ray Bolger did his usual shtick for the GIs, and sang his popular hit from *The Wizard of Oz*: "We're off to see the Wizard, the wonderful Wizard of Oz." The 9th Division, getting acclimated to the South Pacific while training down under, made the song their own as they prepared to go off and fight the "little munchkin men" of Imperial Japan somewhere on some unheard-of Pacific island. Bob Hope, John Wayne, Una Merkel, Phyllis Brooks, and Gary Cooper all made the trek down under to entertain the troops stationed there.

The Trip From Shangri-la

Ever since the Japanese raid on Pearl Harbor, Americans had spoken with one voice. Somehow, someway, sometime soon the U.S. military would avenge the sneak attack by delivering a haymaker on Japan, though no one knew how, or how soon.

The Japanese felt that a "divine wind" protected their home islands from all hostile invaders, and they had confidence that their vastly superior naval armada—with the U.S. Pacific Fleet in shambles—would never allow enemy warships to approach in any direction, or that enemy planes could ever penetrate the gauntlet of anti-aircraft gun batteries ringing Tokyo, capable of blasting any "imperialist" war birds foolish enough to fly overhead.

U.S. military planners determined there was only one enemy target in the Pacific Theater they should hit that would shock the world: Imperial Japan's capital city. That would certainly get Tojo's attention and shatter this "divine wind" crap! More importantly, it would boost morale in America, where every citizen was desperate for good news.

The improbable was easy—bomb Tokyo and maybe a few other industrial cities along the way. The impossible was going to take a little figuring out, but by the spring of '42 a mission was well under way, although its odds for success were dubious. The plan was to do what had never been done before: to get within 450 miles of Japan and launch sixteen B-25 Mitchell bombers off the pitching flight deck of a carrier. At that distance the bombers could get to Tokyo, and then fly on to China and land at a remote airfield for refueling before continuing on to friendly territory.

Left: *Lieutenant Colonel James Doolittle and his bombers' crews and men of the* Hornet *before final preparations in April 1942 for the first air attack on Japan. When the War Department dreamed up the plan, they knew the aviator would be the only man with the chutzpah to carry out the mission. The plan called for Doolittle to lead a group of bombers off an aircraft carrier, head for Japan, refueling after in China. He took his team to a Florida airfield to practice takeoffs on a shortened runway.*

The day of the attack, a Japanese boat spotted the Hornet *and its deck of B-25s. Afraid the Japanese captain had called in their position, the* Hornet's *escort ships attacked the vessel before it could escape, and Doolittle ordered the mission to begin immediately. For the pilots, it meant near-certain death, as the* Hornet *was 250 miles away from where the raid would begin. This meant that the planes would not make it to China for refueling.*

All planes took off safely and dropped bombs over Tokyo, doing minimal damage. But the raid was more symbolic than destructive. Doolittle intended to send a message that the air around Tokyo was not mystically protected, as the Japanese had claimed. The planes sought safe landings, but many were lost at sea or crashed behind enemy lines. Luckier airmen, such as Doolittle, found safe havens in the hands of Chinese partisans. Others were captured, killed, or died in the crashes.

National Archives Photo

Noted aviator Jimmy Doolittle was picked to lead the raid, one only a diabolical widowmaker could have concocted. Many thought he was the only one crazy enough to believe he could pull it off.

In late February of '42, the airmen assigned to the mission were sent to Eglin Air Force Base in Florida to practice short takeoffs. Instead of building up speed to 95 mph and using a minimum of 1,000 feet of concrete to get aloft, the pilots were given confusing instructions: throttle up and lift off in under 500 feet, even though there was plenty of runway left. And they practiced until they got it right. No one except Doolittle was aware of why that short distance was so damned important. Their Mitchell bombers were stripped of their heavy radio transmitters and the bottom gun turrets. Even the super-secret Norden bombsights were taken out for fear that one might fall into enemy hands. Additional gas tanks were put on board, obviously for long-distance missions deep into enemy territory. To ward off enemy fighters they were given tail guns: broomsticks painted black! None of these signs was very assuring, but the crews trusted Doolittle and were willing to stick it out if he was going to be there with them. A month later the bomber crews flew cross-country to San Francisco, where a crane loaded their B-25s onto the carrier *Hornet.*

After provisions and munitions were put on board, the flattop pulled away, its decks crammed with aircraft, and passed under the Golden Gate Bridge, which was lined with cheering onlookers. Those few on board who were aware of the secret mission were concerned there might be an enemy sympathizer along that broad span, who would see the heavy bombers in clear view and promptly notify Tokyo, or Japanese agents in Hawaii, or an enemy ship or sub lurking just beyond the horizon. And the American air-crews wouldn't know if they were flying into a trap until it was too late.

Out in the vast Pacific, the *Hornet* linked up with the carrier *Enterprise* and its escorts, which included eight destroyers, four cruisers, and two oilers, and continued on. But on April 18, still more than two hundred miles from the takeoff point, the task force was spotted by an enemy picket ship, which sent an alert message back to Japan. The enemy scout was blown to bits but it was already too late: The warning had been sent, and Doolittle had no choice but to take off immediately.

Not only would the bombers not have enough fuel to make it to that isolated airfield in China, but anti-aircraft gun batteries around Tokyo would know the bombers were coming.

"The carrier was pitching so much as it headed into a 30-knot wind that waves tossed water over the flight deck, drenching deck crews," wrote James A. Cox for *Smithsonian* magazine in its June 1992 issue. "Waiting Mitchells revved their engines before takeoff. In plane No. 7, the *Ruptured Duck,* Captain Ted Lawson [who would write the best-selling book, *Thirty Seconds over Tokyo,* later a Van Johnson-Spencer Tracy film] was outraged at having to burn up 40 gallons of this precious 1,150 gallons of fuel before the mission had even started."

BELOW: *Actor Spencer Tracy portrayed Lieutenant Colonel Jimmy Doolittle in* Thirty Seconds Over Tokyo, *a 1944 movie about the surprise bombing raid on the Japanese city. The movie marked the first "good news" film about the war and used footage from the actual raid.* Associated Press Photo

Miraculously, the B-25s flew over the coastal territories of Japan unopposed, but in Tokyo, air raid sirens went off and everyone rushed to designated safe areas. But in another stroke of luck, the air raid was just a practice, and when the bombers roared by at rooftop level, everyone thought it was part of the drill. The bombers did encounter scattered ground fire, but nothing of consequence. Each of the Mitchells dropped its four bombs—an incendiary cluster and three five-hundred-pounders—on Tokyo, Nagoya, Kobe, and Yokohama. The targets included an aircraft plant, oil refineries, ship docks, ammo and supply depots, and a steel factory.

The aircrews had little time to celebrate the mission's success, because now they were on their own, flying on in bad weather, on empty fuel tanks, headed into hostile territory. Fifteen crashed in China, and one diverted to Siberia. Most of the flyers eventually made it back to safety with the help of Chinese partisans, but three died, and eight were captured by Japanese patrols.

Those POWs were tried and convicted as criminals. Three were executed, and one died in prison. (The other four would endure horrific conditions for three years in camps and hang on until they were liberated at the end of the war.)

Captain Ted Lawson, who had his face mangled and his leg splintered and ripped open when his plane crashed, would have been one of the fatalities if not for the tireless efforts of local Chinese sympathizers and the mission's doctor, Lieutenant Thomas White, who learned of Lawson's condition, made his way to the injured pilot, and tended to his wounds. He would eventually have to amputate the shattered leg.

When news of the attack reached the States, front-page headlines announced "TOKYO BOMBED! DOOLITTLE DO'OD IT!" The raid was called "a daring and spectacular mission."

A few days after the attack, when he was asked where the bombers came from, FDR quipped, "They came from our secret base at Shangri-la!" without further explanation. Was that a carrier? A remote island? (Actually, it was little more than the fictitious location of a utopian village in James Hilton's book, *Lost Horizon*.)

The damage done by the bombing raids was more psychological than physical. Japanese leaders were humiliated by the act, and the populace now realized their "divine wind" could not prevent the war from reaching their homeland, that maybe there were a few cracks in their invincibility. Tactically the blow had a domino effect, as Japan pulled back some of its forces, including two aircraft carriers, to ward off any future attacks.

Removing those two flattops from the fight would prove a crucial error in the next naval confrontation with the United States, at Midway. It would turn the tide in the Pacific and blunt the Japanese advances.

After returning to the States, and during his rehabilitation, pilot Ted Lawson wrote the best-seller, *Thirty Seconds over Tokyo*. MGM pounced on the project, securing film rights and signing up stars Spencer Tracy as Jimmy Doolittle and Van Johnson as Lawson, with Phyllis Thaxter as Lawson's wife. The studio rushed the film into production.

"The Doolittle raid had all the elements necessary for a dramatic war picture," wrote Clayton Koppes and Gregory Black in *Hollywood Goes to War*. "Training and teamwork of American combat men were stressed. The film follows the real-life situation closely with relatively few Hollywood dramatics, free of racial slurs directed against the Japanese. Several good chances for rousing anti-Japanese speeches are passed over. At one point Lawson muses about the upcoming mission. He concedes he does not like the Japanese; but on the other hand, he does not hate them either. This was a rare confession by an American fighting man in films dealing with the Japanese."

One of the story's secondary characters was played by one of Tinseltown's many faces in the crowd, Robert Mitchum, who had appeared in nineteen movies yet was little known outside of Hollywood. After thirty screen tests with MGM, bad boy Mitchum got the part of Bob Gray, one of the Doolittle pilots.

"This gig had big time written all over it, a top-of-the-line MGM movie, with Mitchum working beside Metro's most distinguished employee, Spencer Tracy, and the popular bobby-soxer favorites Van Johnson and Robert Walker," wrote Lee Server in the Mitchum biography, *Baby, I Don't Care*.

"Bob and much of the cast and crew arrived by train from California and transferred to Eglin Field where they were housed in the utilitarian barracks. They took their meals from the mess line, showered communally, shat in the immodest group latrines, and basically enjoyed all the movie actor perks of the average enlisted man."

The regimentation and restrictions of military life imposed on the set and after hours were shunned by the rebel Mitchum, who defied authority at every opportunity. Yet he would go on to "serve" in every branch of the armed forces, even if it was on film.

The CBI: Confused Beyond Imagination

Japan's occupation of Manchuria in the early '30s was nothing less than genocide, massacring thousands of innocent Chinese peasants, including defenseless women and children. Partisan groups attempted to antagonize their Japanese occupiers but were hampered by outdated weapons, depleted ammunition, and scarce food stocks. American and British resupply efforts bolstered the rebel Chinese Nationalist forces, but overland routes were scarce or impassable.

American aviator Claire Chennault led the Allied effort long before the attack on Pearl Harbor, serving as a consultant to the fledgling Chinese Air Force and using his connections to have one hundred Curtiss P-40 fighter planes flown over. He also recruited seventy-five former Army Air Corps and Navy pilots and two hundred ground support volunteers to sign on with his American Volunteer Group, nicknamed the Flying Tigers, partly for the sharks' teeth painted on the nose of their planes, but also for their courageous daredevil antics in the skies over China. Their role would be to antagonize the Japanese from the air, swooping down on ground forces, blasting enemy planes out of the skies, and strafing Japanese transport ships along the coast.

Above: *Flying Tigers leader Major General C. L. Chennault met starlets Ann Sheridan and Mary Landa in the Pacific Rim theater.*
YANK Magazine Photo

Allied aircrews from the U.S. Air Transport Command also flew in from remote bases in India and Burma to drop relief supplies, modern firearms, and munitions to the Chinese guerrillas. But these perilous flights had to negotiate the treacherous Himalayans, nicknamed the Hump. That gauntlet included freezing rain and blinding snowstorms, sudden wind gusts that could slam a plane into a mountainside, Japanese fighter planes on the prowl for the lumbering transports, and of course, the risk of mechanical failure from overextended use. During the course of the China-Burma-India Campaign, more than four hundred supply planes were lost. Many pilots used the glare from the wreckage below as checkpoints as they negotiated the Aluminum Trail, given that moniker for all the planes that didn't make it. As Allied forces gained a foothold on mainland China, the U.S. 10th Air Force was successful in destroying enemy railways, docks, bridges, and ports. By mid-1943, the U.S. 14th Air Force was also operating in the region with equal success.

Left: *Popular cowboy actor Gene Autry (right) moved from the saddle to the cockpit when he trained as a pilot during his service in the Army Air Forces. He enlisted on the radio during his highly rated weekly program. Autry is well known for his Westerns and for range-riding songs.*
Army Air Forces Photo

One of the most famous entertainers to fly the Hump was Gene Autry, the singing cowboy, who hosted the CBS radio show *Melody Ranch*, which first aired in 1940 and was sponsored by Wrigley Gum. In July of 1942 he decided to join the service, after taking flying lessons, and he did his swearing-in ceremony on his show. At the time he was earning $600,000 a year, but decided there were more important things he needed to do during the war. He signed on with the Army Air Corps, was commissioned an officer, and earned his wings. Autry served as copilot on numerous planes, but flew primarily C-47 transports in the CBI Theater. (After the Japanese surrender, in September of 1945, Autry transferred to Special Services and toured the Pacific to entertain the troops; then he returned to Hollywood and was back on radio with CBS.)

American, British, and other Allied ground forces were thrown into the fight, clandestinely brought in along unguarded coastlines of China by PT boats or submarines, dropped in behind enemy lines, linking up with Chinese partisans to conduct hit-and-run operations against the Japanese. Lieutenant General Joseph "Vinegar Joe" Stilwell was sent to command all U.S. Army Forces in the CBI Campaign, working hand in hand with Chinese Nationalist leader, Chiang Kai-shek. The most notorious of Stilwell's commanders was Frank Merrill, who headed up the 5307th Provisional Regiment, a feisty group of commandos dubbed Merrill's Marauders, thrown into the thick of fighting. Another awesome commando unit arriving in northern Burma was the Mars Task Force, the 5332nd Provisionals, which included the 124th Cav and 475th Infantry regiments. They unleashed enough firepower in concentrated doses to convince the Japanese that a much larger field Army was in country.

Former CBS radio announcer Bert Parks joined the Army in 1942 and served as an infantryman in China, going out on commando patrols behind enemy lines to set up radio linkups, vital for calling in air strikes on Japanese positions and for resupply drops to Allied units. During infrequent R&R stops, he worked part-time as a radio announcer at local bases and camps. (After the war, Parks returned to CBS and hosted a variety of game shows.

BELOW: *General Daniel Sultan led his 124th Cavalry Regiment across a bridge at Burma's Pandu Ghat in 1944. This unit fought covertly behind enemy lines, mostly at night sabotaging enemy operations. With such clandestine fighting, the unit had to be resupplied behind enemy lines, forcing the men to put their lives on the line to get food and ammunition. The radio operator often climbed to a hill to transmit the team's location, and soldiers held their collective breath in hopes the enemy would not pick up the signal or see the supply drop. Unlike other units, these GIs had to leave behind fallen comrades because they could not afford to carry dead weight. Each soldier killed was buried in a marked grave, but in haste and under the cover of darkness.*
National Archives Photo

Left: *This platoon from Merrill's Marauders—the precursor to today's Army Rangers—operated covertly in Burma. Here they crossed the Chindwin River seeking to attack the Japanese from behind enemy lines.*
U.S. Army Photo

Below: *Mule skinners for the 2nd Battalion 475th Infantry Regiment led their animals through a Burma river. Although some units used native guides, many chose mules because they made no noise and were the sturdiest pack animals.*
U.S. Army Photo

His most famous gig, though, was host of the Miss America Pageant, beginning in the mid-1950s.)

When he was just nine years old, Jackie Coogan was one of Hollywood's biggest box office stars. In early 1941, at age twenty-seven, he joined the Army Air Corps, initially as a glider instructor. Then in March of 1944 he volunteered to take in the lead glider on a night commando raid behind the lines in the buildup of Allied forces in northern Burma. "'He had some horrific war experiences,' recalls John Astin, who heard Coogan's war stories while traveling on promotional tours with him. 'One time he had a crash. He was in the front of the transport glider, of course, and everyone that he was flying with was shoved up against him. He was sort of at the bottom of the pile. The Japanese soldiers came in and bayoneted everybody in the plane. And Jack was the only one that they missed. He lay alone at the bottom of this pile of dead and dying men, and

LEFT: *Hollywood star Jackie Coogan served as a glider pilot and worked with units like Cochran's Air Commandos in Burma. Glider pilots faced enormous dangers trying to place troops in enemy territory. These planes flew 50 feet behind a larger aircraft, attached by a tether. Once aloft, a crew member cut the tether, and the glider carrying many soldiers sought a clear landing behind enemy lines. Gliders often disintegrated. Gliders were one-use plywood-and-glue planes with no controls other than for landing.*

Coogan once came down in hostile territory and landed on the bottom of a human pile when the plane crashed. Japanese soldiers bayoneted the men to death but left Coogan for dead without stabbing him. Coogan said that he often experienced nightmares following this incident.
Army Air Forces Photo

eventually he got out and escaped. But he was plagued with nightmares much of his life,'" wrote Neil Grauer in "The Kid," his piece for *American Heritage* magazine, December/January 2001.

Another young actor who saw action in the CBI Campaign was Sabu Dastagir, born in Karapur, India. At age twelve, while working as a stable hand tending to his uncle's two hundred elephants, Sabu was discovered, not only because of his good looks but also his deft skill with the large beasts. He was flown to England and had the lead in the film *Elephant Boy* in 1937. Three years later he was in Hollywood and studying to become a U.S. citizen. He then enlisted and became a B-24 ball turret gunner with the 13th Air Force, flying missions over China and in other Pacific campaigns.

A huge logistical problem was resupplying the Allied patrols harassing the Japanese forces. Sporadic air drops sometimes reached the Allied forces, but Japanese soldiers were on the lookout for the huge and noisy transports, and anytime they spotted parachutes with crates and canisters underneath, they quickly converged on the drop zones and waited in ambush for the precious supplies to be picked up. Just radioing for replenishments was difficult, with signals obscured by dense jungles, steep mountains, and thick cloud cover. Child actor Sidney Lumet was a radar operator and repairman with the Army, responsible for tracking enemy aircraft and guiding in Allied planes and their precious cargo. (Years after the war, Lumet became a respected movie director.)

As the air resupply missions continued, a massive construction project was under way to cut a meandering path from India through Burma and on to southern China. Japanese occupation in Burma had severed the overland route into China, and so an alternate had to be found and cleared. In contrast to flying the Hump—where the bitter cold led to a myriad of problems—efforts to building the 1,044-mile Ledo Road, the "toughest road in the world," were plagued by sweltering heat, monsoon rains, dense impassable jungles and swamps, impenetrable mountains, and tropical diseases such as malaria and typhus, dengue fever, and on and on. The monsoon rains alone hampered construction, sometimes only allowing progress to advance less than a mile for every month of rain. Conversely, the builders could advance a mile a day when the rains finally subsided. Japanese patrols and planes frequently attacked the construction crews and destroyed their efforts along the route. (The first caravan of trucks didn't christen the Ledo Road until February 1945, with Japanese forces already abandoning China and pulling back to defend the home islands.)

Thousands of American, British, and Chinese fighters lost their lives in the CBI Campaign, but many more enemy forces died in the futile offensive to bring China under Japanese domination.

Entertainers in the CBI

Even frontline soldiers had to be pulled off the line for rest and recuperation, to eat a few decent meals, sleep on a cot with a pillow, and maybe catch a movie or two. The simple pleasure of doing absolutely nothing was a relief. With a little luck, they might even see a halfway decent stage show put on by some of the guys from Special Services or see a *great* show when the real entertainers from Hollywood and Broadway stopped by. (Actually, many of those "halfway decent" entertainers in uniform were former stage and screen stars, and Special Services frequently put on a dazzling spectacle that rivaled anything stateside. And of course, after enduring the hardships of combat on the front lines, the guys in uniform were hungry for any diversion that didn't require diving into a foxhole or shooting back at someone who was shooting at them.)

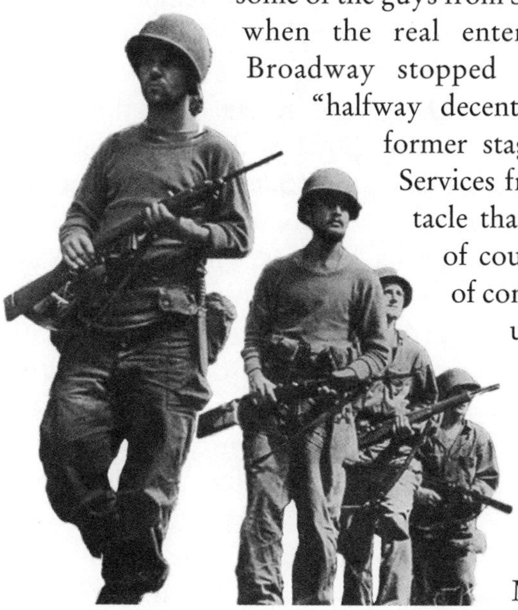

One time when battle-weary soldiers from Merrill's Marauders were sent back to New

LEFT: *Merrill's Marauders, named for unit leader Brigadier General Frank Merrill, faced 11 months of combat in the Pacific Rim, fighting in 20 skirmishes and marching more than 600 miles through enemy territory.*
Imperial War Museum Photo

Right: *Not all camp shows featured the usual variety of popular songs and dancing. In January 1945 opera star Lili Pons and her husband, conductor Andre Kostelanetz, entertained soldiers in China.*
National Archives Photo

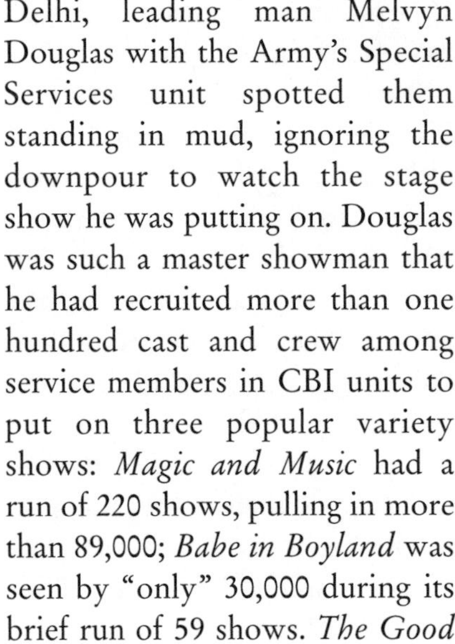

Delhi, leading man Melvyn Douglas with the Army's Special Services unit spotted them standing in mud, ignoring the downpour to watch the stage show he was putting on. Douglas was such a master showman that he had recruited more than one hundred cast and crew among service members in CBI units to put on three popular variety shows: *Magic and Music* had a run of 220 shows, pulling in more than 89,000; *Babe in Boyland* was seen by "only" 30,000 during its brief run of 59 shows. *The Good Old Days*, a sentimental revue, hit the boards 129 times and was seen by more than 120,000 troops. (During this same time, numerous Broadway shows premiered and closed with less success.) And whenever USO shows arrived in country, Douglas and his troupe were there to coordinate their visit. Some of the luminaries who braved those perilous flights over the Hump included Noel Coward, Pat O'Brien, Paulette Goddard, Keenan Wynne, Joe E. Brown, Carole Landis, Ann Sheridan, and Lily Pons with her husband, Andre Kostelanetz.

Above: *Soldiers often gave starlets gifts during their appearances at camp. Without shopping centers or flower stores nearby, GIs relied on their creativity. In many cases, they gave away souvenirs they'd collected on enemy battlefields. Actress Ann Sheridan showed off a Japanese flag a GI presented to her during a 1944 visit to Burma.*
National Archives Photo

Sometimes Douglas wondered if producing variety shows was really what he should be doing while other servicemen were in combat. But morale-building played an important role in sustaining the emotional well-being of frontline troops. He saw the emotional bond these hardened combat veterans still had for a little something from home, like a brief ray of sunshine in the form of a Hollywood starlet, or a favorite song that could quickly get the eyes to tear up. This was especially true during the holidays, when such standards as "White Christmas" and "Silent Night" triggered memories of another place and another time, with someone they loved.

One of those sentimental softies was Mike Douglas, who in the book *I'll be Right Back* recalled "walking the streets of Calcutta, India, on shore leave one lonely night, so far from my home. I needed something to lift my spirits. As I passed a Hindu man sitting at a street corner, I heard something strikingly familiar. I turned to see the man cranking one of those ancient Victrolas, and I heard Bing Crosby singing 'Accentuate the Positive.' I stopped and smiled in appreciative recognition. The Hindu man nodded and smiled back."

Another Special Services entertainment coordinator was Major Clark Robinson, formerly a director at New York's Radio City Music Hall. In

India he put together the fast-paced *Hump Happy* revue. *YANK* correspondent Sergeant Ed Cunningham reported on the troupe: "Broadway stage shows don't usually rehearse their songs, gags, and sketches against the roar of a transport plane's motors, 5,000 feet above the Assam jungles. But a group of airborne soldier-showmen in India have been practicing their numbers in the clouds ever since they first started their swing around this country to entertain U.S. troops."

The *Hump Happy* soldiers traveled mostly by transport planes, sometimes taking hours to get to remote outposts. With little or no time for rehearsals, they practiced their songs and comedy skits high above the Himalayas.

"So far, they haven't figured out a way to go through their dance routines while in flight. It isn't just that their 'stage' is somewhat wobbly; it's because the cabin is jampacked with a piano, stage curtains, props, footlights, and public address system, leaving little room for the hoofers to practice their steps."

Originally the entertainers in *Hump Happy* could get together only after hours because they were cooks and mechanics, radio repairmen and truck drivers. But after the first show, a one-star general was so impressed that he immediately had the GIs transferred to Special Services so they could hone their show business skills full-time.

"The cast had its baptism in 'the show must go on' tradition when Major Robinson was killed in a plane crash. The accident happened at a remote air base where a performance was scheduled the next night. Major Robinson had gone on ahead to make advance arrangements. When his men arrived the next day, they were told the tragic news. Although grieved by his death, the cast decided to go on with the show that night rather than disappoint their audience."

The twelve-member cast was a motley bunch of performers, with varying levels of skill and education. The emcee was Private George Davis, who developed his banter on Brooklyn radio; Sergeant Dalton Savage had played bass fiddle with the Melody Cowboys in Oklahoma and Texas; Al Roth had been a theatrical agent in New York and served as stage manager; Larry Fishman was a former piano instructor in the Big Apple; Sergeant Jack Sydow did some stage work while going to the University of Illinois; Sergeant Jack Newman had been a tenor with the Chicago Opera Company; Sergeant George Winston did a stint with the Sal Turner Orchestra in St. Louis; PFC Robert McCollom was a singing cowboy and even appeared in a few Gene Autry flicks; PFC Al Holden had been a violinist with Bert Malheim's band; and Creth Lloyd, who took over after Major Robinson was killed, played guitar. Three of the performers who managed to hold their own despite no professional training or experience were Master Sergeant John Cobb, who played guitar, impersonator Al Pestcoe, and singer John Hupfel.

The highlight of every show was a special appearance by the Andrews Sisters—Sydow, Hupfel, and Cobb in drag. "The next best applause-getter is Sydow's strip tease act," quipped Ed Cunningham for *YANK*. "GIs who haven't tested their tonsils on 'Take It OFF!' since they last visited burlesque theaters really get in some wolf-calling practice during Sydow's 'delayed peel.' Sydow uses an AAF emblem instead of a G-string. In fact, the whole show, with its latrine lyrics and gents-room jokes, makes Minsky burlesque look like a Legion of Decency selection."

While most of the Special Services entertainers performed for U.S. military audiences, they occasionally invited local civilians to their shows. One unique performance happened when Pops Hollowell and his V-Boys visited the India-Burma border region in mid-1943 and local Haga headhunters, who served as guides and pack-bearers for the U.S. ground patrols, were in the crowd. Every member of the V-Boys troupe was with an all-black engineer unit and played with the regimental band. Their specialty was foot-stomping boogie-woogie, and the headhunters hadn't heard anything like it. In fact, their only form of music was war drums!

Hollowell was quite the impresario, assembling a twelve-man choir, a twenty-member glee club, his fifteen-piece V-Boys troupe—and he still found time to play the organ for Sunday services. Only a handful of these musicians and singers had any previous experience. Most learned to read music from Hollowell.

Below: *Entertainer Pat O'Brien admired a Chinese weapon on his visit to Luchow. His stay was cut short, however, when the Allied position was threatened by enemy attack and entertainers were evacuated. Despite the dangers, actors, comedians, singers, and musicians tried to reach as many camps and bases as possible to share their talents with the men and women fighting the war.*
U.S. Army Photo

The dangers of flying the Hump were certainly well known to the aircrews who were stationed there and flew everyday, but entertainers—even those well-seasoned travelers who had been to Europe and the Mediterranean, the Pacific Rim, and all of the little islands in between—were not prepared for the white-knuckle terrifying flights they survived in the CBI.

Veteran performer Pat O'Brien wrote about his experiences in his book, *The Wind at My Back*: "Asia, from the air, is ruins, sand, dust, jungle, wild rivers and vast mountain ranges and unending space. Upon arrival in Kunming, China, we gave a show in one of the big hangars. It was quite a sea of lonely far-from-home faces. It was a rough primitive life and we entertainers got the best there was of it. But it was a strange, unreal, dangerous world, far from all we knew, valued, or understood. On all sides a few miles away, a few yards even, were the enemy, cruel little men with deadly tools of war, and fearful habits of torture and experimenting with death in all its dismal forms."

O'Brien and his troupe went to regions of the CBI that were still considered "hot zones," but they wanted to perform for as many servicemen as possible. "Luchow, one of our outposts, was extremely close to enemy territory. It was not a good flight; much of the ground below was already in enemy hands. We arrived at Luchow, a raw, open battlefield. We six performers, frightened as we were, proceeded to do the show. There were many patrols out on active duty who could not see the first show. Like heroes we decided to stay and do another show. By this time we could see the flashes of gunfire on the horizon and the sound of firing real close. In spite of our trembling, we gave another show for the men who came off duty later that night. It was nerve-wracking and I wonder if we really were amusing and entertaining. The girls on the tour held up fine. They were tireless, brave, and rarely lost their sense of humor or hair waves during all those trying, weary months. With Jinx Falkenburg, Ruth and Jimmy Dodd, Betsy Eaton [and] Harry Brown, I shared the satisfaction of knowing we played places where no other entertainers in their right minds had ever ventured. I knew why I was over there. I was trying for one crazy moment to make life worth living for these poor kids who maybe were never going to get back home."

A close friend of Jinx Falkenburg was actress Paulette Goddard, who also made it to the Far East and visited fourteen military bases in the CBI: "I brought back thousands of messages from soldiers to their loved ones. I made a point to kiss one GI—just one—at every place we stopped. I just walked up to the first GI I saw, kissed him on the cheek, and said, 'This is for all you swell guys.' Most of the time our arrival at a camp wasn't announced in advance, and the look on those boys' faces was something I'll never forget. In their honor I wore pinup dresses for every show, whether it was for ten men in a hospital tent or seven thousand in an outdoor hillside theater. Once a boy came up and asked if he could smell my hair. Everyone sent me expensive perfume before I left. I took it all along with me. I'd heard that GIs love perfume and I was going to give them the best smell they'd had in the South Pacific. We went to a zone in China where dead Japs still littered the ground; there were bodies all over. They needed to smell something sweet."

Movie Depictions of the CBI

To outsiders, China was a mystical land that should have been unified in its fight against the Japanese occupiers. But there was internal strife as two strong leaders emerged: Mao Tse-tung led the Communists, while Chiang Kai-shek broke away to lead the Chinese Nationalists. The two sides should have combined forces to drive out the Japanese, but in fact, Chiang considered the Japanese "a disease of the skin," while he viewed the Communist Chinese as "a disease of the heart." (After the war, Mao set out to destroy Chiang and his followers, who would flee to the island of Formosa, now Taiwan.)

Hollywood's portrayals of the Chinese typically avoided the factional confusion, lumping them all into one massive army of patriotic allies, saddled with antiquated equipment and ragtag tactics. "Movieland China was a far-off land of mystery, teeming with millions of people who spoke a strange language, ate with sticks, and worshipped their ancestors. [It] consistently was pictured as backward, poverty-stricken, and unfamiliar with modern science and technology," wrote Clayton Koppes and Gregory Black in *Hollywood Goes to War*. "China, it seemed, needed Western help to modernize and prosper."

The Office of War Information's Bureau of Motion Pictures wanted to educate the American populace about this most valued of allies in the war against Japan. With oversight control on all film projects during the war, the OWI gave the green light to several pro-Chinese movies, including *Escape from Hong Kong*, *Flying Tigers*, *China Girl*, *Bombs over Burma*, *A Yank on the Burma Road*, *The Good Earth*, *Objective Burma*, *Night Plane from Chungking*, and several Charlie Chan films.

A documentary in Frank Capra's *Why We Fight* series, 1944's *Battle of China* explained the importance of American, British, and Chinese forces fighting as one unified juggernaut: "The oldest and youngest of the world's great nations, together with the British Commonwealth, fight side by side in the struggle that is as old as China herself. The struggle of freedom against slavery, civilization against barbarism, good against evil."

In the 1943 Paramount film, *China*, Alan Ladd is an American oil merchant exploiting China's untapped resources for his personal gain, ignoring the threatening overtures from Japan as he sells that country the black crude. Loretta Young is trying to help Chinese women flee from the sadistic Japanese and appeals to the American profiteer, begging him to join the country's freedom fighters. After seeing one of the young women raped and her family butchered, his rage takes over, and he links up with local partisan groups, becoming a virtual one-man army as he kills hundreds of enemy soldiers. In a final symbolic act, he boldly stops a Japanese convoy on a mountain road and is told about the attack on Pearl Harbor. He tells the convoy commander that their efforts in the Pacific will eventually fail because "millions of little guys all over the world have freedom in their blood." Then suddenly a dynamite charge planted higher on the slope explodes, wiping out everyone in the convoy, our valiant hero along with them. (By the time *China* was released, Alan Ladd was in uniform and preparing to fight the Japanese for real.)

Whether intentional or not, 1944's *Dragon Seed*, starring Walter Huston as a Chinese farmer, with Katharine Hepburn as his free-thinking Chinese daughter-in-law, comes off as a blatantly racist film. The OWI approved the script, feeling it portrayed the Chinese as willing to sacrifice everything for the common good, for the preservation of their way of life, to rid the world

Left: *British actor Errol Flynn drew fierce criticism from his countrymen for portraying an American soldier in* Objective Burma. *The film leads viewers to believe that the U.S. troops won the conflict single-handedly, when the Brits had taken the brunt of the punishment for years before the Americans stepped in to fight. One editorial cartoon depicted Flynn in a director's chair sitting atop a mass grave of British dead, showing displeasure with the actor's role.*
Associated Press Photo

of the evil occupiers. On film it was simply "an unimaginably bad movie," wrote critic James Agee. All of the Chinese characters were played by Caucasians with their eyes pulled back in a macabre oriental slant. And all of the evil Japanese were played to the hilt by Chinese actors trying to make them look as awful as possible. They succeeded . . . it was an awful movie!

In *Objective, Burma*, starring dashing Errol Flynn and released in 1945, a squad of American commandos parachute behind the lines to blow up an enemy radar station. Once they complete the mission, they make their way to the rendezvous point to be picked up, but the place is swarming with Japanese, so now the good guys have to trek through the jungle and send as many enemy soldiers to the hereafter as possible. A correspondent accompanying the patrol spews venom after seeing the mutilated bodies of American infantrymen:

"I thought I'd seen or read about everything one man can do to another, from the torture chambers of the middle ages to the gang wars and lynchings of today. But this . . . this is different. This was done in cold blood by people who claim to be civilized. Civilized! They're degenerate, immoral idiots. Stinking little savages. Wipe them out, I say. Wipe them off the face of the Earth."

While this film bolstered America's involvement in the CBI Campaign, it incensed the British. "Apart from one or two passing references, the film managed to omit any mention of Allied involvement in the Burma campaign, least of all the British 14th Army, made the Burmese jungle look like a national park, and so offended the British public and military personnel alike that Warner Brothers were forced to remove it from English screens," wrote Clyde Jeavons in *Movies of the Forties*. The casting of Flynn, their former countryman, rankled the Brits even more. While other British actors returned home when the war flared, Flynn chose to stay in Hollywood and become an American citizen. Back home, though, "the 4-million circulation *Daily Mirror* depicted Flynn in a half-page cartoon, dressed in battle dress, seated in a studio chair with his name stenciled on the back and in his hands the script of *Objective Burma*," recalled fellow Brit David Niven in *Bring on the Empty Horses*. Niven was one who returned home to serve in uniform. "On the

Right: *Planes of the Flying Tigers landed in the southern part of China before the U.S. officially declared war on Japan. The all-mercenary team of pilots and ground crews were Americans but not military aviators. Major General C. L. Chennault developed a team concept to air combat, which allowed planes to fly in formation and to cover each other during engagements with enemy aircraft. During a break in missions, crewmen reloaded a Tomahawk.*
YANK Magazine photo

studio grass beneath his chair was a multitude of tiny crosses and, beneath the jungle trees, stood the ghostly form of a soldier. The caption read: 'Excuse me, Mr. Flynn, but you're sitting on some graves.'" It was a brutal indictment.

Warner Brothers added a prologue to the movie, stating that the film depicted only one mission in a lengthy campaign and in no way downplayed the vital role of British forces—but the damage had already been done, at least in the eyes of the Brits.

Three films that glorified the exploits of American aviators were *Flying Tigers*, *God is My Co-Pilot*, and *The Purple Heart*. Released in 1942 amid nothing but bad news coming from the Pacific, *Flying Tigers* starred John Wayne and depicted the early days of the ragtag American volunteer aviators taking on the Japanese invaders and coming out victorious at every turn. It was a rousing flag-waver that continued to paint the Japanese as evil scum who must be eradicated.

"Through its two heroes, *Flying Tigers* demonstrates the conflict of individualism that will be resolved within the new definition of the combat film," wrote Jeanine Basinger in *The World War II Combat Film*. "The two men are played by John Carroll and John Wayne. Carroll's character is jaunty, irresponsible, a wolf with women, and a daredevil. Wayne is sober and responsible, a good and true leader of men. The film implies that the skills of both are needed to win the war by establishing that, to accomplish the final mission, both men must be in the plane which sets out on a suicidal objective.

"America, a maverick country that was started, settled, and built by a rebellious group of religious dissidents (and also by a ragtag group of misfits and outlaws), always contains the elements of rebellion and outlawry in the national persona."

Despite their differences, the two heroes pull together to defeat their enemy, just as Americans with different viewpoints must unite for the ultimate goal: defeat of the Axis powers.

God is My Co-Pilot, released in 1945, was a fictionalized adaptation of a book by aviation colonel Robert Scott, told in flashback, starring Dennis Morgan, Alan Hale, Raymond Massey, and Dane Clark. The movie follows Colonel Scott from a boyhood spent dreaming about adventure, going to West Point, and then on to Kunming, China, where he turns to God to help him get through the daily grind of dangerous missions.

A Yank on the Burma Road was wrapping up production when the Japanese attacked Pearl Harbor. Released in 1942 and starring Barry Nelson, Keye Luke, Laraine Day, and Philip Ahn, *Yank* follows a former New York cab driver who hears about the Japanese aggressions in China and decides to get involved, leading a group of Chinese partisans in their fight against the invaders. The film's hero drives a truck loaded with badly needed medical supplies, avoiding enemy patrols while dealing with damaged bridges and roadways, finally getting through to help local villagers.

"This is the first film about fighting the Japanese after Pearl Harbor. What is suggested is that we civilians, like the hard-driving hero, will have to get involved, sacrifice our selfish needs, and fight a tough war," wrote Basinger in *The World War II Combat Film*.

The Purple Heart was released in 1944, after the news about the captured Doolittle Raiders leaked out, but before their fate was known. As a warning to viewers, the film opened with the following narrative: "Out of the dark mists of the Orient have come no details of the actual fate of the heroic American aviators forced to Earth in the bombing of Tokyo. Perhaps those details will never be known. The Japanese Government, in mingled hate and fear, announced only that some were executed. This picture, therefore, is the author's conception of what may well have happened based on unofficial reports."

The film depicted a bomber crew led by Captain Harvey Ross, played by Dana Andrews, shot down behind the lines and seeking Chinese partisans to help them reach friendly territory. Instead they are hustled to a safe house by a local traitor who turns them over to the Japanese. The American POWs are put on trial in an attempt to force a confession from them, to admit their bombing mission originated from an aircraft carrier, not a distant airfield.

But even under sadistic torture, the airmen in *Purple Heart* refuse to crack. Captain Ross is permitted to address the court and uses the opportunity to warn the Japanese just how persistent American resolve will be, no matter how long the war drags on: "It's true we Americans don't know very much about you Japanese, and never did, and now I realize you know even less about us. You can kill us . . . all of us, or part of us. But if you think that's going to put the fear of God into the United States of America and stop them from sending other fliers to bomb you, you're wrong . . . dead wrong. They'll blacken your skies and burn your cities to the ground and make you get down on your knees and beg for mercy. This is your war . . . you wanted it . . . you asked for it. And now you're going to get it . . . and it won't be finished until your dirty little empire is wiped off the face of the Earth!"

By the 1944 release of *The Purple Heart*, American bombers from both aircraft carriers and island bases were in fact blackening Japan's skies, burning its cities, and humiliating its leadership. It was only a matter of time before the "dirty little empire" would be beaten into submission.

Confrontation in the Frozen Frontier

More than two hundred years ago Russian outdoorsmen traversed the Bering Sea and the chain of islands stretching west from Alaska—the Aleutians—searching for an overland bridge to the Canadian north. They wanted to tap into the abundance of North America's fur animals before other hunters and trappers could stake their claim on the continent. Japanese military strategists in the late 1930s had more sinister plans than fur hunting when they looked at the Aleutians' proximity to their own Kurile Islands stretching to the east. The United States Congress recognized the threat to the Aleutians and increased funding to establish military bases from Dutch Harbor to Anchorage. Seven months before the attack on the Pacific Fleet at Pearl, U.S. ground forces were diverted from their original destination—of

BELOW: *When Japanese troops tried to land on the shores of Massacre Bay in the Aleutians, American mortar crews stationed atop a hill launched rounds to defend their position in May 1943.*
National Archives Photo

Guam—and arrived at Dutch Harbor in the frigid north, fully equipped . . . with tropical gear.

The Japanese escalated their interest in the islands off the Alaskan mainland after President Roosevelt boasted that the Doolittle bombers came from "Shangri-la." Those bombers were too big to have been launched from any aircraft carrier, or so assumed the best military minds in Tokyo. And the Japanese held every island within range (except for the Aleutians), so the American bombers couldn't have flown from the West Coast and landed somewhere for refueling on their way to Tokyo. In June of 1942, Imperial Japan dispatched two carrier task forces and thousands of men to the "frozen frontier."

Soon after news of the enemy deployment to the waters near the Aleutians reached the West Coast, all radio stations stretching from Canada and down to Mexico shut down for eight hours as a cautionary measure so that bomber aircraft couldn't swing south and use the signals as beacons, much as they had when attacking Pearl harbor seven months earlier.

Japan's strategy was twofold: to threaten North America's West Coast and to divert U.S. forces from other locations in the Pacific, tipping the balance of power in Japan's favor. But American code-breakers cracked enemy communications and were able to determine that the Japanese were using the Aleutians offensive as a diversionary tactic. Still, neither side could afford to ignore the strategic location of the northern frontier. The thousands of troops who spent any time there quickly came to the same conclusion: Mother Nature was an undiscriminating bitch! Subfreezing temperatures took a heavy toll on the soldiers themselves, who were unable to dig foxholes in the frozen tundra or keep fires going in the bitter winds. The cold also turned lubricants to jelly, drained batteries of any power, rendered vehicles and planes useless. It was a frozen, miserable hell for all combatants no matter which flag they fought for.

Despite the hardships, the American forces endured. It would take fourteen months to drive off the Japanese invaders, but once the Aleutians were secured and under American and Canadian protection, construction crews began building and repairing airstrips. Soon after, bombing raids on Tokyo—just 2,100 miles away—were launched.

Few among the Many

Of the thousands of American servicemen who endured the Aleutians campaign, two would later distinguish themselves as leading men in Hollywood.

Drama student and New York stock theater actor Ira Grossel enlisted in the Army on December 8, 1941, the day President Roosevelt declared war on the Axis powers. Grossel would be sent to the Aleutians and spend most of his hitch there. (After getting out of the Army, he found regular work on the radio show *Our Miss Brooks* with Eve Arden. He was soon discovered by Universal Studios and made his big screen debut in the 1947 film, *Johnny*

O'Clock, but not with the name Ira Grossel. He would forever after be known as Jeff Chandler, one of Hollywood's most popular "hunks.")

Charlton Carter (who would later change his last name to Heston), also a drama student, signed up for the duration with the Army Air Corps. While training at several air bases in the States, his training squadron prepared for deployment to the China-Burma-India Theater, getting shots, sitting through orientation films about the region, and receiving lightweight tropical uniforms and gear. Then, like something out of a bad espionage movie, Heston, the rest of his crew, and approximately twenty other bomber crews were woken up in the middle of the night, escorted onto a civilian passenger liner docked in Seattle, and whisked off . . . to Alaska, totally prepared to freeze their asses off, until cold-weather gear caught up with them. They wound up at Attu with the 77th Bombardment Squadron, flying B-25 Mitchell bombers. In a freak accident, while rushing to the aid of another bomber that crashed, Heston slipped on the ice and was knocked unconscious. He would be evacuated to the mainland and then returned to Alaska for duty at Anchorage's Elmendorf Air Base as a flight controller. (He was discharged in 1946 and knocked around between Chicago, New York, and North Carolina, struggling for acting gigs on stage and television. Heston vaulted to the top rank of movie stars with his 1956 portrayal of Moses in *The Ten Commandments*, followed four years later by his Best Actor effort in *Ben Hur*.)

While not stationed in the Aleutians, former vaudeville entertainer Christian "Buddy" Ebsen served on the Navy patrol frigate *Pocatello*, which prowled the waters 2,500 miles north and west of Seattle for up to a month at a time. As unofficial morale officer, Ebsen also coordinated variety revues for the crew whenever time allowed. (He would get his discharge in early '46 and make it back to Broadway that same year, in a revival of *Show Boat*.)

The American outposts in the Aleutians were not popular destinations for Hollywood entertainment troupes, not so much because of the frigid temperatures, but because it remained a largely forgotten campaign. But there were a few entertainers who would go wherever American troops were stationed. "Joe E. Brown, Al Jolson, and the Bob Hope-Jerry Colonna-Frances Langford triolet have bobbed about to the military establishments within the confines of Alaska's 586,400 square miles," wrote Army Sergeant Georg Meyers for *YANK* on October 21, 1942. "Hope even volunteered to give a special performance on Attu Island as a possibility for ridding the Aleutians of the only winged pests in the world larger than Alaska Mosquitoes. Hope said all he wanted to do was Kiska Japs good-bye."

Joe E. Brown was the first entertainer to brave the frozen north, touring the region in 1942. Brown, in fact, was the first entertainer to get to many combat zones around the world, and he maintained a whirlwind schedule throughout the war years.

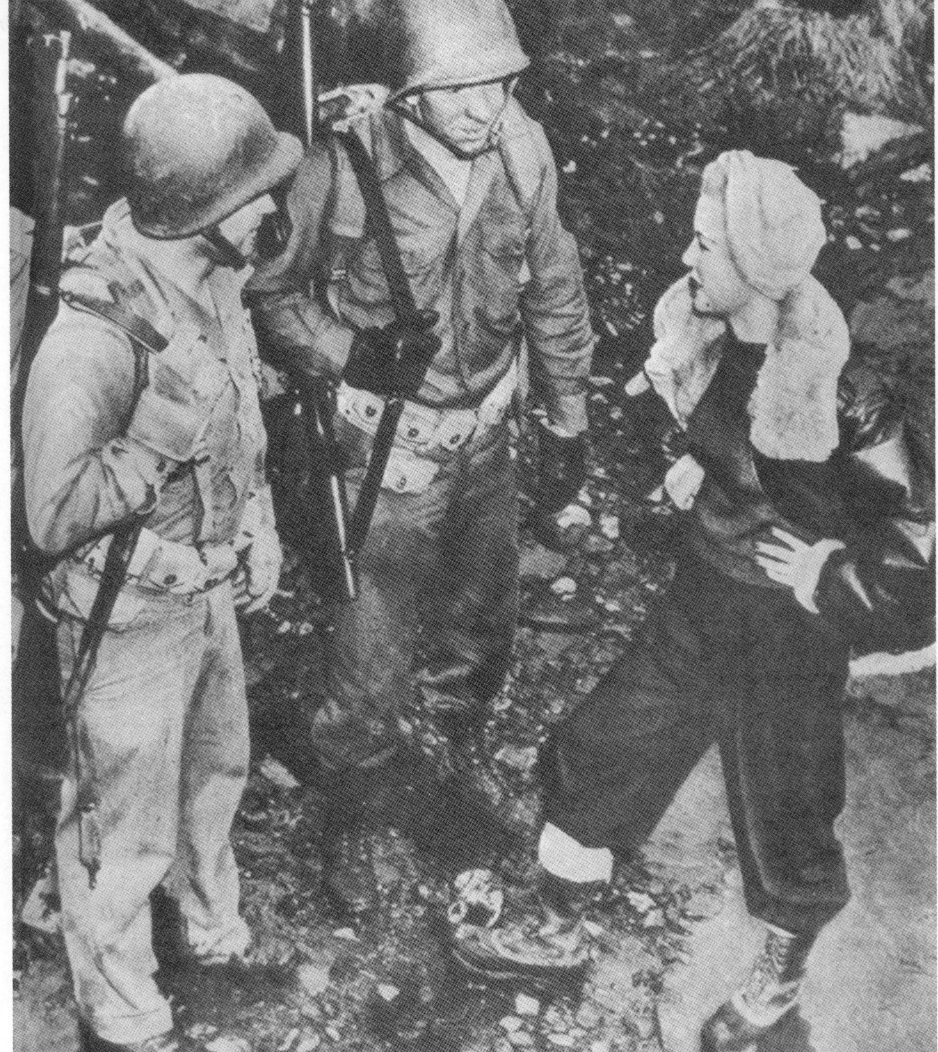

Left: *Bundled up for the cold weather, Hollywood starlet Marjorie Reynolds visited with two troops during her stop in the Aleutians.*
YANK Magazine Photo

Army PFC Gene O'Donnell had a few minor film roles with Monogram and Warner Brothers, and was a regular on national radio shows like *Big Town, Sherlock Holmes,* and the *Lux Radio Theater* prior to his hitch in Alaska. Because of his radio experience, O'Donnell was asked to emcee a fashion show featuring beauties from the various Allied units and the Red Cross in the region.

Because of the lack of female competition in the Aleutians, the few female volunteers at the Fort Richardson service club were extremely popular. One of them was Margaret Becker, "who was in the road company of *Boy Meets Girl* and worked for George Abbott on Broadway," reported Sergeant Georg Meyers for *YANK* on Christmas Eve of 1943. "Sunday is the toughest day on the calendar for the girls at the club. They invite the soldiers in for an afternoon dance and then return for another couple of hours in the evening. Margaret estimates that she dances with 150 men during the two-hour evening session. 'It's all a blur,' she says. 'One of the girls kept count once. She passed into the arms of 55 men during a single tag dance.'"

63

Hollywood Director Films the Frontier

John Huston was wrapping up the filming of *Across the Pacific* with Humphrey Bogart when he was asked to report to Washington, D.C., in April of 1942. He turned the production over to Vincent Sherman and then linked up with the Army Signal Corps. It was the typical Army gripe of "hurry up and wait." Itching to get overseas and do what he did best, Huston waited out the sweltering summer in D.C. It would be late summer before he found out what his mission would be. "I was to proceed to the Aleutian Islands and document that theater of combat," he recalled in *An Open Book*. "I met my five-man crew on Umnak Island and we moved right on out the chain to Adak, [which] was less than 500 miles from Attu and only 250 to Kiska—both of which were Japanese-held; it was nearer to the enemy than any other American territory anyplace in the world."

Huston and his crew flew on numerous bombing runs, often under fire. "On my second flight to Kiska, Zeros attacked us. I was trying to photograph over the shoulder of the waist gunner. Presently my camera wound down and I lowered it to rewind. The waist gunner wasn't there. I looked down and saw him lying dead at my feet."

Prior to another mission, Huston listened to a briefing by Colonel William Eareckson, leader of the bomber command in the Aleutians. "He filled in all the details, then said, 'Don't take evasive action on the bomb run. You're just as likely to turn into the stuff as away from it. Keep going in a straight line. And if someone plucks your sleeve and you look around and he's got a long white beard . . . why, you'll know you haven't another care in this sad world.'"

OPPOSITE: *When the first U.S. troops landed on Kiska Island in the Aleutian chain, they were ill prepared. The soldiers—originally destined for Guam—arrived with tropical gear, such as jungle boots, mosquito nets, and lightweight uniforms. The cold weather paralyzed the first units: the ground was too frozen to dig foxholes, automobile batteries died, and regular motor oil congealed. Troops lacked cold-weather experience, particularly in some seemingly commonsense situations, including building shelter. The first huts had doors that opened out, and snowdrifts blocked men inside when they could not open the doors.*
National Archives Photo

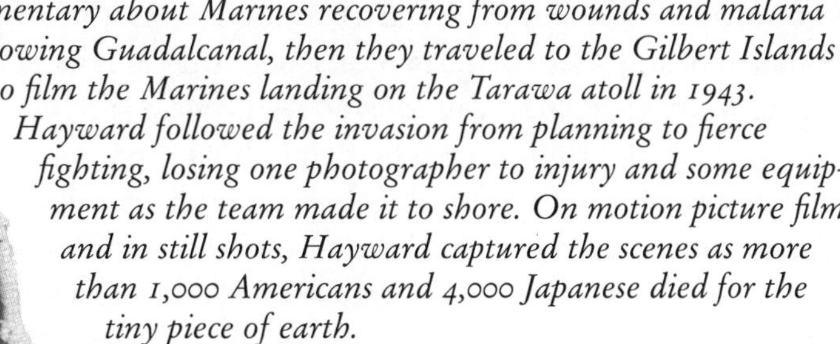

BELOW: *Marine Corps Photographic Field Officer Louis Hayward shot film of two very important battles and their aftermath during World War II. His crew made a documentary about Marines recovering from wounds and malaria following Guadalcanal, then they traveled to the Gilbert Islands to film the Marines landing on the Tarawa atoll in 1943. Hayward followed the invasion from planning to fierce fighting, losing one photographer to injury and some equipment as the team made it to shore. On motion picture film and in still shots, Hayward captured the scenes as more than 1,000 Americans and 4,000 Japanese died for the tiny piece of earth.*

Later, Hayward sent his film to Washington, D.C., and the Joint Chiefs of Staff passed it along to Hollywood director Frank Capra, who was serving in the Army Signal Corps. Capra put together With the Marines at Tarawa, *which won the 1944 Oscar for best documentary.*
U.S. Marine Corps Photo

The USO "Drafts" Soldiers in Greasepaint

BACKGROUND: *Everyone loved comedian Joe E. Brown. One thing soldiers, sailors, Marines, airmen, and Coasties agreed on was the funny man's way of making them laugh, even in troubled times. Brown traveled endlessly to all corners of the world to put smiles on servicemen's faces.*
U.S. Navy Photo

"THANKS FOR THE MEMORY AND STRICTLY ENTRE-NOUS,
DARLING HOW ARE YOU?
AND HOW ARE ALL THE LITTLE DREAMS THAT NEVER DID COME TRUE?
AWFULLY GLAD I MET YOU, CHEERIO AND TOODLE-OO
AND THANK YOU SO MUCH."

—*From the song "Thanks for the Memory" (from the movie,* The Big Broadcast*)*

HOLLYWOOD'S STARS AND STARLETS WERE QUITE ACCUStomed to making movies in exotic locales. Okay, so maybe it was only on the back lots at MGM, and Paramount, or Fox, and RKO, but with a little wizardry and a halfway decent budget, set designers could transform a quaint Coventry village in 1620 to a Russian city in flames during the Revolution, from the dark days of New York after the stock market crash to the revelry of Oktoberfest in Munich.

After the Japanese attack on Pearl Harbor, Hollywood rallied 'round the flag and mobilized its forces for the biggest production ever undertaken. Singers and dancers, musicians and comics, magicians, acrobats, and models all volunteered to do what they did best: entertain appreciative audiences throughout the United States and overseas.

In the early months of the war, stateside training posts were strained to the max as thousands of new servicemen poured in from around the country. For many of these wide-eyed recruits, it was their first time away from home, and they were uncertain of where they might be in six months, wondering if or when they would ever see home again, hoping they would survive with all their limbs attached and all vital organs and precious jewels in all the right places. But first they had to survive weeks of crawling in the mud and eating dust, "drop and knock out ten," and oh-dark-thirty wake-up calls. And sometimes, in the midst of all that chaos and insanity of basic training (or boot camp), a ray of sunshine might peek through the dark clouds in the form of showgirls and singers and starlets on a makeshift stage. They danced and showed off the prettiest legs God ever created, and they purred into the microphone and stole a hundred hearts forever just by batting their eyelashes.

And they pulled one lucky sap out of the crowd and mussed up the hair he didn't have and gave him lipstick kisses he didn't ever plan to wash off (at least until Drill Sergeant Savage showed him the error of his ways, with a wire scrub brush and lye soap!).

Anywhere GIs trained, the entertainers made every effort to show their appreciation, to let the boys know everyone back home was missing them. And when the soldiers went overseas, from the Solomon Islands to Sicily, from Tunisia to Tarawa, from the Aleutians to Australia, the road show wasn't far behind them.

Wherever the troops were sent is where the entertainers wanted to be—often even risking their lives to perform as close to the front as commanders would allow.

Origins of the USO

While President Roosevelt is credited with mustering support from six humanitarian agencies in early 1941 and combining them under one umbrella—as the United Service Organizations, or USO—in fact its origins can be traced back to the Civil War and Virginia's 1862 Battle of Fredericksburg. There a community service group pulled together volunteers to serve coffee to the soldiers massing in the area. Utilizing huge boiler kegs mounted on horse-drawn wagons, the volunteers were able to serve ninety gallons of coffee every hour. In its own way, this small gesture was an opportunity to tell the soldiers they were cared about and their sacrifices were appreciated.

More than fifty years later, as American doughboys deployed to France as part of the Allied Expeditionary Forces, hundreds of civilian volunteers followed them close to the front. These volunteers represented the original six agencies that would eventually become the USO: the Young Men's Christian Association (YMCA) and its female counterpart, the YWCA, the Salvation Army, the National Catholic Community Services, the National Jewish Welfare Board, and the National Travelers Aid Association. Each of these groups deployed its own "armies" of tireless workers, who often lived in miserable conditions perilously close to the battlefield, certainly within enemy artillery range.

Near the end of the Great War these humanitarian groups began to coordinate their efforts to better serve the frontline troops, but when hostilities ceased and the Armistice was signed, the hundreds of volunteers returned home. The agencies quickly scaled back their operations.

BELOW: *USO clubs were important, no matter the location. Here at Fort Bragg, North Carolina, soldiers took a break from training to listen to music with a hostess. Local USO clubs often lacked the glitz and glamour of their big-city brothers, yet they were full of girls "who braved mashed toes and table tennis elbow to brighten up the lives of America's GIs," wrote Mollee Kruger in a December 25, 1994, article for* The Washington Post.

She added that senior hostesses recruited girls to serve cookies and coffee, play Ping-Pong with shy guys, and dance from 8 to 11 P.M. every weekend. And there were never enough girls—often soldiers outnumbered the gals 25 to 1. Still, Kruger called it a "utopia where no matter how many pimples or crooked teeth you had, you never lacked admirers. Some evenings you couldn't finish a single dance without having another soldier cut in."

Office of War Information Photo

RIGHT: *Wartime romance was in full bloom, as USO hostesses tried to make soldiers' last days in the States happy ones. Ladies often recounted stories of falling in love over and over again and bidding dramatic farewells to the men in uniform. Many reported that the good-byes were like ones a person saw in movies but never experienced in real life.*
Library of Congress Photo

In 1940, as the United States geared up for the impending conflict in Europe and the Far East, new Army basic training posts were quickly established, with barracks, classrooms, firing ranges, and parade/calisthenics fields built in a matter of weeks when existing posts couldn't handle the increase. But the sudden surge of recruits often overwhelmed the local communities and church groups struggling to provide comfort and support. (The Air Corps, Marines, Navy, and Coast Guard had similar problems.) Roosevelt asked the six humanitarian groups, which had been so important to troop morale during WWI, to formally band together under one name, and the USO was launched on February 4 of 1941. Naturally, the task of pulling together the manpower and resources of so many agencies would have a few glitches, but by the time war was declared in December of that same year, the USO was for the most part running as a well-oiled machine.

Wherever the troops were being trained, while they were in transit from one post to the next or waiting on the East or West Coast to deploy overseas to the war front, USO

RIGHT: *Even war-weary GIs didn't forget their manners when there was a pretty girl around. Martha Tilton stood in line for chow at a field hospital in Cape Gloucester in July 1944.*
National Archives Photo

workers and volunteers were there with coffee or cocoa, with cookies and donuts, with a friendly smile and best wishes from home, establishing hospitality clubs, working out of tents or mobile kitchens, converted churches, barns, marinas, castles, museums, warehouses. They were there.

An organization this immense would require a massive budget to keep things running. Amazingly, the USO relied solely on private donations and volunteers giving their time freely. "With its fund comprised of pennies from little children as well as large sums from labor unions and business corporations, the USO is the newest and most up-to-date example of American democracy at work," stated the USO's campaign chairman in 1941, Thomas E. Dewey. "It is an example that shows conclusively that, regardless of whatever difference of opinion there may be on American foreign policy, our people stand squarely behind their people in uniform."

At its wartime peak, the USO was maintaining more than three thousand clubs throughout the world in 1944, with more than 1.5 million volunteers, most of them giving freely of their time after working at full-time jobs.

The most celebrated addition to the USO effort was the creation of Camp Shows, Inc., in 1941. The entertainment community stepped forward even before they could be asked, some seven thousand strong (actors and actresses, musicians, singers and dancers, magicians and comedians), and traveled to every combat zone throughout the world, wherever American servicemen and -women were deployed. Those entertainers stood center stage for thousands but would also take time out at every compound to visit one on one with wounded GIs (although many stars admitted that seeing such young men bandaged and broken was emotionally draining for them).

From 1941 through '47, Camp Show entertainers logged more than 425,000 performances. Tragically, thirty-seven entertainers died while representing the

Left: *Eddie Bracken and his USO entertainers traveled to Palau in the summer of 1945 to entertain troops weary from a long war.*
U.S. Marine Corps Photo

USO, including big band leader Glenn Miller, who was lost at sea while flying from England to Fortress Europe to coordinate his Army band's tour of the continent.

A Few of the Many

Entertainers who volunteered with the USO were often asked to wear military-style uniforms, without unit patches or ranks, when they were traveling. The starlets would shuck the unflattering olive drab uniforms and jumpsuits backstage in favor of glitz and glamour for the boys. Those entertainers who joined one of the armed forces were service members first, and entertainers second. Typically they were stationed in one theater, such as the CBI, Italy, or the Aleutians, and entertained only fellow GIs within the region.

A few national touring shows, such as *Winged Victory* and *This Is the Army,* had a huge cast and crew of service members, many of them nationally known recording stars, comedians, and actors. The major difference between USO and military shows, such as those put on by Army Special Services, was the latter's lack of women. Oh sure, there was typically at least one buxom babe in the all-guy revues, but "she" could hardly be called a beauty, especially with a five o'clock shadow! Guys in drag just didn't quite have the same sex appeal as Betty Grable and Rita Hayworth.

Among the many entertainers who performed on behalf of the USO or one of the military entertainment units was comedian Joe E. Brown, who maintained a nonstop schedule, yucking it up from the Aleutians and China to England, North Africa, and Italy. His love for the troops was true red, white, and blue, but Brown had a personal affinity for those in uniform; his own son, a flyer, was killed in action.

Below: *Heaven for Tech-4 Leon Blackley was a hug from starlet Jeanne Darrell in Liberia.* *YANK* Magazine Photo

Dolly Loehr was an accomplished pianist and child star in Hollywood. She changed her name to Diana Lynn, and her big break came in *The Major and the Minor*, in which she played Ginger Rogers's roommate. When she toured the country to entertain the troops, Lynn frequently played the piano. She later released an album of piano songs.

Mladen Sekulovich started his acting career on Broadway and appeared in one movie before he signed on with the Army Air Corps. Along with Red Buttons and Edmond O'Brien, he would join the *Winged Victory* cast. He also performed in *This Is the Army*. (After the war he became one of the great character actors in Hollywood, known better as Karl Malden.)

Gower Champion teamed with his wife, Marjorie, to dance in numerous movie musicals. He joined the Coast Guard and toured with USO and service shows until he got out in '46. (He soon returned to the big screen and the new medium known as television, continuing to sing and dance, often choreographing the program's musical numbers.)

Big band leader Kay Kyser pulled double duty, performing on Saturday nights at the Hollywood Canteen and then going out on the road, across the country and around the world, playing more than five hundred concerts for the troops.

Bing Crosby and Bob Hope, Mickey Rooney, Marlene Dietrich and Martha Raye, the Andrews Sisters (Maxene sang the high parts, LaVerne was way down low, and Patty was the perky one in the middle), and the McGuire Sisters were all road warriors during the early '40s. Some of the old-time performers who held up with them were Rudy Vallee, Pat O'Brien, and Jack Benny.

In the mid-1930s the Boswell Sisters—Martha, Helvetia, and Connee—had appeared on Bing Crosby's *Woodbury Hour* radio show, but in 1936 marriage broke up the trio. Connee Boswell continued on by herself, keeping a grueling schedule to sing for the troops, taking time out after every show to meet and greet as many GIs as possible. The Andrews Sisters later revealed that they had grown up idolizing the Boswells.

Time magazine reported in 1943 on just a few of the stars who were overseas: "In the Middle East were Jack Benny, Larry Adler and his harmonica, Al Jolson with a harmonium, Ray Bolger was in the South Pacific, Judith Anderson in Hawaii. A while back Martha Raye went to the foxholes of Tunisia; and in New Guinea a show went on within earshot of the Japs." (At age thirteen Larry Adler had won the Maryland Harmonica Championships, and he headed for Hollywood the next year, appearing in *Clowns in Clover* at just fourteen.)

Left: *Entertainers faced certain danger traveling from one USO show to another. Flying the Hump—over the Himalayan Mountains—was particularly treacherous. Updrafts and downdrafts made the trip bumpy, and the lack of radar caused pilots to navigate the perilous path with only a few controls and their five senses. On this trip, Mr. and Mrs. Jim Dodd (far left), a very green-looking Pat O'Brien, and starlets Betty Yeaton and Jinx Falkenburg made the rough ride from China to India.*
U.S. Army Photo

Pat O'Brien wrote about Hollywood's crucial role in building and sustaining morale during the war years, in his book *The Wind at My Back*. "The dismal war was still raging. Again came the summons to entertain on the battlefronts. The war was at its worst, and all over the globe our troops were just holding and suffering, engaged in bloody encounters, and in need of entertainment and hope. There weren't actually, to be truthful, too many in the USO who volunteered for dangerous assignments. Joe E. Brown and Bob Hope were always ready. They covered more mileage than most of us combined."

In her book *By Myself*, Lauren Bacall recalled being a budding model on a train bound for New York filled mostly with servicemen in December of '42: "Word was passing through the train that Martha Raye was in the club car entertaining the servicemen. She had been traveling overseas to do that. I was dying to see her.

"Martha Raye was sitting with a drink in her hand, talking to everyone in the car, cracking jokes, singing songs." Bacall, who watched as the comic with the big mouth captivated her impromptu audience of GIs in that club car, would eventually become a star herself.

Other future stars who plied their craft in the military included composer Hal David—"I always wanted to write songs. The Army was where I had the opportunity;" Carl Reiner, who performed with producer Maurice Evans's troupe in the Pacific; and Ossie Davis and Don Knotts, both of whom hit the stage for the Army.

GI Bob

But of all the entertainers who did what they did best for GIs all over the world, Bob Hope was by far king of them all.

Soon after the USO came into being, it asked Hope, then a radio host and comedian, to put on a show at nearby March Airfield in Riverside, California, in May of 1941. Hope was apprehensive, unsure of how the servicemen would respond, but he was willing to give it a try, once, opening the show with a plug for his radio sponsor: "How do you do, ladies and gentlemen. This is Bob 'Army Camp' Hope telling all soldiers they may have to shoot in the swamp or march in the brush, but if they use Pepsodent, no one will ever have to drill in their mush."

But it was his self-deprecating humor that won the boys over: "But all these fellows were glad to see me today. One rookie came running up to me, very excited, and said, 'Are you really Bob Hope?' I said 'yes,' but they grabbed his rifle away just in time." Hope's doubts were dispelled

RIGHT: *Comedian Jerry Colonna, who traveled often with Bob Hope to USO shows around the world, took the troops' minds off fighting for a few minutes as he joked with them in New Guinea in May 1944.*
National Archives Photo

immediately and he soon came to realize that GIs are "the best audience in the world."

After his March Airfield show, Hope began to tour military bases throughout the country, broadcasting his weekly show with several favored sidekicks, including Jerry Colonna, and songbird Frances Langford, guitarist Tony Romano, and comic Jack Pepper.

"In addition to the four hundred radio shows, we played three or four shows for camps or bases every day while we were on the road," Hope wrote in *Have Tux, Will Travel.*

Over the next few years, Hope and company made it to every combat theater and countless campaigns in between, willing to sacrifice the creature comforts of life in Hollywood for the hardships and miseries the "boys" had to endure for months on end. One of Hope's friends and rivals wasn't quite so certain Hope really had it as rough as many believed:

"He traveled everywhere in the world just to bring a little cheer to lonely Americans serving their country far away from home," wrote George Burns in *All My Best Friends*. "It was a terrible struggle for poor Bob, all alone except for a few members of his crew, and people like Ann Sheridan, Carole Landis . . . year after year, Hope and some of the most beautiful women in the world went off to isolated outposts of civilization where they huddled together to keep warm. So I think you can imagine how much sympathy I have for him. I mean, alone with just these women to keep him company. And Bob never took advantage of it either."

Time magazine caught up with Hope on one of his whirlwind tours in 1943, and reported in its September 20 issue: "Hope was funny, treating hordes of soldiers to roars of laughter. He was friendly—ate with servicemen, drank with them, listened to their songs. He was indefatigable, running himself ragged with five, six, seven shows a day. He was the straight link with home, the radio voice that for years had filled the living room. . . ."

When asked to explain why the tireless Hope continued to perform such a nonstop schedule, spokesman Ward Grant explained, "It's not the war or politics or even patriotism . . . although God knows Hope is a patriot. It's the guys."

LEFT: *Frances Langford toured extensively with USO shows to sing for soldiers, sailors, and airmen. She recalled in a March 12, 1989,* San Francisco Chronicle *article that she once slept in a small tent set up in camp next to other tents for soldiers. An armed GI guarded the entrance to prevent any frisky fellas from trying to bother her. The problem, Langford said, was that the guard sang her signature tune, "I'm in the Mood for Love," all night and she got no sleep.*
U.S. Air Force Museum Photo

LEFT: *A dog-faced soldier gave actress Ann Sheridan two of his most prized possessions: a hug and a bloody Japanese flag. The starlet toured around the world with USO shows.*
U.S. Army Signal Corps Photo

7. Nazi U-boats Terrorize the Atlantic

"When we have our victory and we've added to
our history
It will be right there to see how sweet and simple
life can be
When the lights go on again all over the world
And the boys are home again all over the world."

—*From the song "When the Lights Go on Again," by Eddie Seiler, Sol Marcus, and Bennie Benjamin, Porgie Music Corporation, 1942*

Background: *Most people think attacks in the Atlantic took place in the ocean's northern portion. But many assaults occurred south, all the way to the Caribbean. This tanker took a torpedo hit off Florida's coast in 1943. German U-boats loved to attack tankers—they lumbered through the water and were easy targets, they sank quickly, and they carried essential cargo.*
Army Air Forces Photo

SOMEWHERE OUT IN THAT DARKNESS, JUST BEYOND THE horizon of the Eastern Shores, lurked underwater predators roaming in packs, lying in wait for the Allied convoys departing safe harbor for the treacherous waters of the vast Atlantic.

Despite signing the Versailles Treaty, which ended the hostilities in WWI and restricted Germany from possessing U-boats or building new ones, the country clandestinely began designing a new series of submarines as early as the 1920s. These prototypes were built for Finland, Turkey, and Spain and were modified over the next decade. After the Nazis came to power in 1933, Hitler set out to defy every agreement of the Treaty and began building modern U-boats which were launched two years later. (His rearmament program also included tanks, bombers, and fighter planes, and warships and the mobilization of men in the various armed forces, all of which had been banned at Versailles.) Churchill condemned the action as a "brazen and fraudulent" violation of the Treaty, but Hitler scoffed at the bluster, daring anyone to do something about it. By September of 1939 the Nazis had fifty-seven U-boats, although only twenty-six were seaworthy in the Atlantic. (A total of 1,153 German submarines would be deployed during WWII, along with many more midget subs.)

Right: *These Avengers based in Norfolk, Virginia, protected ships along the East Coast from German U-boat attacks. Because the planes could go no more than 500 miles away from shore, American vessels relied on other aircraft out of Scotland, England, Iceland, and Greenland to protect them in the final portion of their journey. Still, a "black hole" existed in the middle of the sea, where ships had no air protection from either side of the Atlantic. To guard against Nazi submarine attacks, American vessels traveled in a convoy with tankers and troop transports on the inside and all other warships around them in a grid-like pattern.*
National Archives Photo

In mid-June of 1942, ignoring the territorial boundaries of U.S. waters, Nazi U-boats brazenly probed the coastal defenses for any weaknesses and landed saboteurs at Amagansett, off Long Island. "Shortly after midnight the conning tower of a German U-boat broke through the surface of the black ocean water offshore. A hatch swung open, and the commander of the U-202 and several crew members climbed topside," wrote Joan Miller in the article "Nazi Invasion!" for *American History Illustrated*, November 1986.

Above: *Miss America 1945, Bess Myerson, was a Jewish heroine to Jewish war veterans.* Associated Press Photo

"The submarine slowly moved into shallower water until it lay only fifty yards from the beach, but shrouded by the fog, it remained invisible to anyone on land." (Four days after the landing at Long Island, another Nazi commando team slipped ashore in Florida, at Ponte Vedra.)

Nazi Germany's espionage unit, the Abwehr, trained agents for specific missions and formulated a list of strategic targets across New England and reaching all the way to Cincinnati and St. Louis. These targets included aluminum and magnesium plants, rail yards and bridges, waterways and ports.

In addition to the very real threat of Nazi saboteurs coming ashore, the U.S. military was concerned that the illumination from East Coast cities would silhouette any ships heading out to sea, making them easy targets for the Nazi armada's silent assassins. When Atlantic City, New Jersey, hosted the Miss America Pageant during the war years, the hoopla was toned down, especially after dark. "The security forces insisted that at night all the Boardwalk shop windows be covered with blue cellophane, which made the coastline stores as iridescent as the night sky and all but invisible to German vessels lurking only a short distance out to sea," wrote Susan Dworkin in *Miss America 1945*. But despite the blackout efforts, the war was still going on in Europe, and those Allied transport ships had to traverse the gauntlet, in massive flotillas with warships guarding the flanks.

Shipping Aid to Allies

During the Atlantic campaign more than 2,400 seamen died as 120 ships were sunk along the East Coast, nicknamed Torpedo Junction. In fact, many of those brave men died *before* President Roosevelt declared war on Japan and Germany.

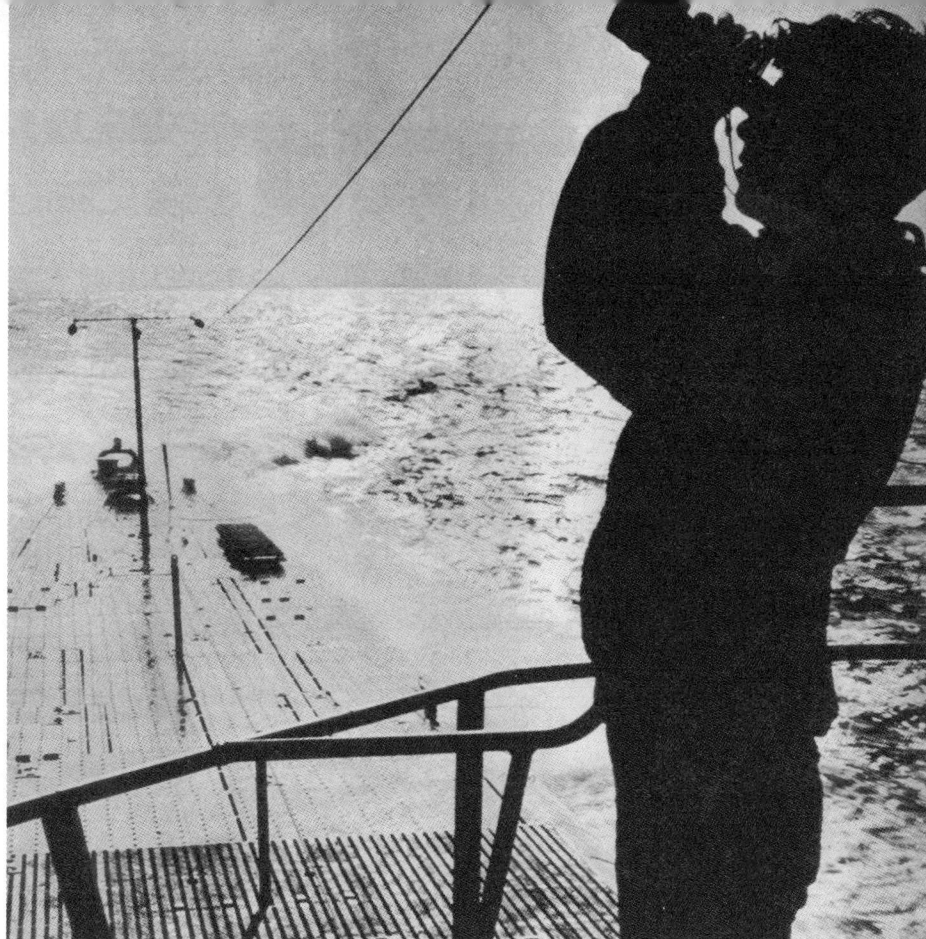

LEFT: *Because of frequent German Luftwaffe attacks on convoys leaving the East Coast, vessels always posted a lookout.*
U.S. Navy Photo

BELOW: *These sailors worked to douse a tanker fire. Convoy ships looked out for each other, and in this case, saved the lives of sailors who abandoned ship when the torpedo hit.*
U.S. Navy Photo

Under the Lend Lease agreement, the United States had sent planes, ships, and supplies to Britain to sustain her fight with Nazi Germany and postponed American involvement. In June of 1940, after British forces were routed from Dunkirk, the United States rushed a shipment of $43 million in surplus bombs and bullets to England. Three months later, under the Destroyers for Bases agreement, the U.S. sent fifty WWI-era destroyers in exchange for access to British airfields and naval bases in its colonies. Churchill felt that Britain would need at least twenty transport ships loaded with supplies and munitions arriving every day throughout the war to sustain and achieve eventual victory. That support effort would require a continuous flow of transport ships and their guardians from America's East Coast to England. Of course, the Nazis were fully aware of this massive oceanic effort, and they deployed their Wolf Packs directly in the transport ships' most likely path.

As the Allies stepped up convoy protection, improved their radar and sonar capabilities, and provided better aerial cover, they were able to

Right: *By the time many men arrived in England, they thought they'd already been through hell. GIs traveled on small, cramped ships that were tossed about on the ocean's waves. Most became seasick. Others also suffered from claustrophobia, which was not surprising given how men were stacked in bunks and had to do nearly everything sitting down in the tight confines. Black soldiers had it worse—their berths were belowdecks and by the boiler room, making for a steamy, noisy voyage. Trips to England often lasted 16 to 23 days because transport vessels traveled in a zigzag path to avoid detection and attacks by Nazi wolf packs.*
National Archives Photo

ward off the U-boat threat and turn the tide, but it was still a costly endeavor. (All told, Nazi U-boats sank more than 3,500 transports and 175 warships in the Atlantic at a cost of thousands of American and British lives.)

Entertainers in Uniform

Some entertainers' careers were interrupted by World War II; others were just starting out and had yet to achieve their dreams of making a living by performing, acting, or singing. Whether in the Merchant Marines, the Coast Guard, or the Navy Armed Guard, they braved the dangerous North Atlantic. Few made the transatlantic trip without incident.

Carroll O'Connor served with the Merchant Marine, on fourteen transports and auxiliaries. He wrote later in *I Think I'm Outta Here*: "I never knew Humphrey Bogart, but he convinced me and every merchant seaman that what we were doing in the war was a heroic way to help win that war. That was the message of a movie starring

Right: *Crossing the Atlantic meant cramped quarters and few amenities. Some ships broadcast abbreviated radio shows and sports programs to help men pass the time.*
YANK Magazine Photo

Left: *There's nothing better then milk and cookies with a lovely lady. This airman enjoyed his visit with actress Joan Blondell during her camp show visit in the North Atlantic in 1943.*
Office of War Information Photo

Bogart called *Action in the North Atlantic*; it was about American sailors, civilian seamen, aboard freighters on the suicidal Murmansk run. No service seemed more dangerous, more glamorous, more desirable. I had been very lucky during the war. Convoys I sailed in were attacked, ships were hit and sunk, but never one of mine."

Another effective recruiting tool for the Merchantmen was the CBS radio program *We Deliver the Goods*, broadcast on Sunday nights and created by bona fide Navy veterans and active duty servicemen, including the Maritime Service Band led by Lieutenant Curt Roberts, announcer Bosun's Mate Sam Brandt, and singers CPO Ray Buell and Ship's Cook Joe Sylva. Each week the cast dramatized a real-life sea adventure, often inviting the actual hero on the air to share his experiences with captivated listeners.

Rebel folksinger Woody Guthrie joined the Merchant Marine to avoid the draft. During those dangerous Atlantic crossings he frequently went belowdecks and played his guitar for his shipmates and the soldiers being sent to the European Campaign. On board with him were fellow folksinger Cisco Houston and amateur singer Vincent "Jimmy" Longhi. During a U-boat attack, they would pull out their guitars and sing for the troops belowdecks; the white soldiers on one level, the black troops farther below. Despite strict segregation rules, the three would sometimes gather the troops together for a sing-along. They would survive a mine explosion just off the coast of France.

Jimmy Dean was just sixteen when he quit school to join the Merchantmen, serving for two years. (He would become a country singer after getting out of the service.) Peter Falk wanted to join the Marines, but he'd lost his right eye due to a tumor when he was a boy, so he joined the Merchant service, as a cook. (He would later use his haggard appearance to become a great character actor.)

Jack Warden had the back-breaking job of working in the engine room during Atlantic crossings. "My romance with the life of a sailor ended in 1942 while working as a water tender in the engine room of a freighter thirty feet belowdecks listening to repeated attacks by German bombers." After surviving a particularly frightening enemy attack, Warden decided that maybe jumping out of airplanes was safer than being trapped belowdecks of a sinking ship. He joined the Army's fledgling 101st Airborne Division.

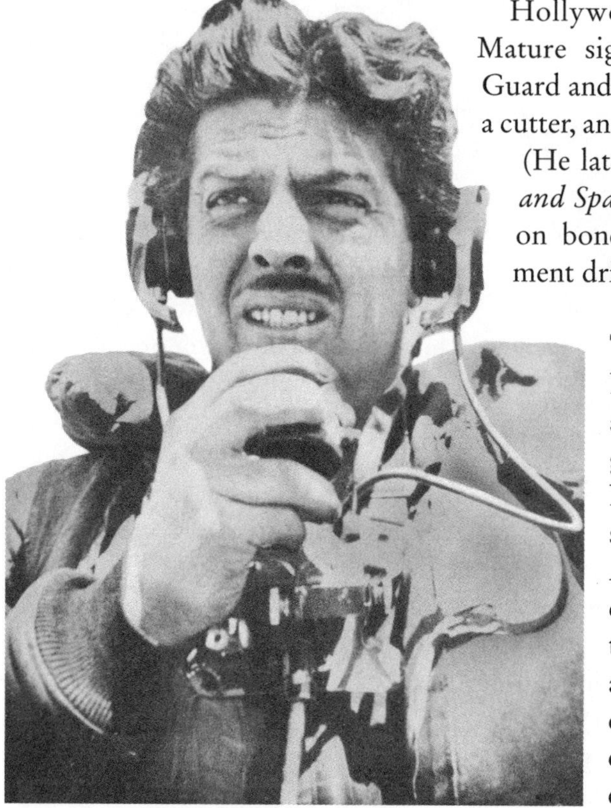

RIGHT: *Hunky Victor Mature served on a Coast Guard cutter during the war before he joined a touring show to encourage Americans to support the war effort by buying bonds or enlisting in the armed forces.*
U.S. Coast Guard Photo

Hollywood heartthrob Victor Mature signed on with the Coast Guard and spent fourteen months on a cutter, an icebreaker, in the Atlantic. (He later joined the musical *Tars and Spars* and toured the country on bond promotions and enlistment drives.)

Former child actor Tom Ewell enlisted in the Navy Reserve in early 1942 and then was activated as a gunnery officer with the Navy Armed Guard, assigned to escort duty with Atlantic convoys. Comedian Norm Crosby was on the deck of a sub-chaser and suffered hearing loss due to the explosive repercussions from dropping depth charges whenever suspected enemy U-boats were detected. The detonations "made a terrific sound, very loud and you could feel it through your bones. The hearing loss came about slowly, over time." (Crosby would be fitted with a cumbersome hearing aid and become a proponent for assisting those with hearing loss over the years.)

Big band leader and clarinetist Artie Shaw joined the Navy and was stationed on New York's Staten Island, assigned briefly to a minesweeper prowling the coast. Soon he was transferred to Rhode Island, where he took charge of a Navy band, attracting some of the best musicians to join the service. Douglas Fairbanks Jr., son of the famous silent film star, was also at Staten Island, assigned as executive officer on the minesweeper USS *Goldcress*; then he pulled duty

RIGHT: *Big band leader Artie Shaw started his naval career working on a minesweeper before being transferred to Rhode Island to put together a top-notch band. Here, the musician played his clarinet with the orchestra in the Pacific on a hastily assembled "stage" aboard a U.S. ship.*
U.S. Navy Photo

on the battleship USS *Washington* and the carrier *Wasp,* escorting transports loaded with planes and supplies bound for Malta and Murmansk.

Leading actor Robert Montgomery served as the naval attaché at the American embassy in London in mid-1941, tracking the Allied convoys. After Pearl Harbor, he volunteered for extremely dangerous PT boat duty.

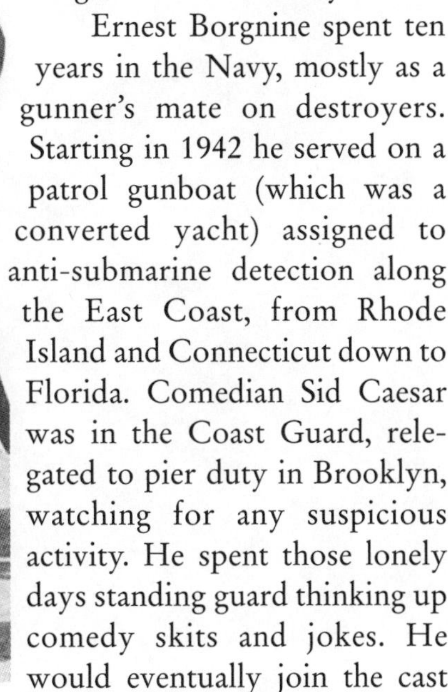

LEFT: *Actress Marlene Dietrich posed with her USO team in Greenland before boarding their C-47 transport. Dietrich spent much of her free time entertaining soldiers and sailors, always willing to share a song and a kiss (or more). Dietrich's signature tune was "Lili Marlene," a song penned during World War I. German General Erwin Rommel loved it, and had it played for his troops during the North Africa campaign. The British heard the song and adored it, too. It became the only song that Axis and Allied fighters shared an affinity for.*
National Archives Photo

Ernest Borgnine spent ten years in the Navy, mostly as a gunner's mate on destroyers. Starting in 1942 he served on a patrol gunboat (which was a converted yacht) assigned to anti-submarine detection along the East Coast, from Rhode Island and Connecticut down to Florida. Comedian Sid Caesar was in the Coast Guard, relegated to pier duty in Brooklyn, watching for any suspicious activity. He spent those lonely days standing guard thinking up comedy skits and jokes. He would eventually join the cast of the Coast Guard musical *Tars and Spars* and tour the country, and he later appeared in the movie version of the show. (After his discharge, he would study acting on the GI Bill.)

Perilous Journeys to Perform for the Troops

Entertainers who volunteered to go overseas may not have known about Nazi Germany's Grey Wolves lurking just below the surface of the Atlantic, but they quickly found out even before leaving safe harbor. Actor Ray Milland recalled in *Wide-Eyed in Babylon*: "As we started out across the Atlantic I noticed that [the *Normandie*] was tracking way north of the normal steamer lanes and that men were covering all ports and windows with black paint. On the third day we began to sight icebergs. The atmosphere on board became more ominous as lifeboat drills were meticulously carried out and the people became more silent. I figured there was not much point in worrying unless they started playing 'Nearer My God to Thee.'"

Edward G. Robinson was in Europe with his wife and son when the threat of war boiled over in 1939. "The acrid smell of war was in the air, and as it grew closer, I began making frantic efforts to get us all back to safety. We had return tickets on the *Athenia,* but apparently our reservations were canceled out," he

remembered in *All My Yesterdays*, cowritten with Leonard Spigelgass. Instead they were booked on the *America*, and learned later that the *Athenia* was one of the first passenger liners torpedoed in the Atlantic.

Pat O'Brien had traveled to all quarters of the world and knew the dangers the young sailors faced on every trip. He wrote about their sacrifices in *The Wind at My Back*: "The American Merchant Marines were making their valiant voyages, often death runs, night in and night out. Many of them went down to an oil-spread death in their torpedoed ships."

Opposite: *The Women's Air Corp, or WAC for short, served near all battle zones in World War II. Most worked as nurses, although not all were registered medical professionals. Some had merely been hospital clerks or nursing assistants back in the States. But in wartime, the government valued any experience. These WACs boarded a transport ship to France, where women worked on hospital ships during D-Day and later moved onto the beachhead to treat the wounded.*
U.S. Signal Corps Photo

Protecting the Southern Flank

Military strategists and political leaders in Washington, D.C., were concerned about Nazi influence spreading toward the Caribbean and South America. In mid-1941 actor Douglas Fairbanks Jr. was asked by the U.S. State Department to go on a "goodwill tour" to South America, to supposedly foster good relations within the film community and promote American-made movies in untapped foreign markets. This became especially important to Hollywood after the Nazis put a blanket over European distribution of American and British films. His real mission, though, was to assess Nazi influence in the region, politically, economically, and militarily. He was to collect intelligence data and report back immediately to the State Department.

After determining that the Nazi threat was very real, the United States dispatched military units to the region, establishing outposts in such exotic locales as Trinidad and Panama, with Navy patrols looking out for those elusive U-boats and other German warships.

Lee Van Cleef served on one of the many Navy sub-chasers in the Caribbean. (Years later he would drift into acting, being cast in the touring

Left: *Up-and-coming actress Ilana Massey toured Caribbean bases to entertain troops. A tour in the theater was a soldier's dream come true—there were no land battles, and German U-boats posed only a minor threat. It was essentially a pleasure tour, giving GIs time to enjoy pretty sights, like sunsets and starlets.*
YANK Magazine Photo

production of the WWII Navy play, *Mister Roberts*. It was the start of a lasting career playing sinister characters, mostly in Westerns.)

Military duty in the region was certainly not without peril, but the off-duty hours were worth it. At Trinidad, GIs learned about Calypso music. With such popular singers as Attila the Hun, the Roaring Lion, and Lord Executioner, American servicemen fell for the improvisational style of up-tempo music. "A Calypso singer is a kind of Bing Crosby who makes up his own words as he sings and covers a lot of subjects besides love—politics, war, food, and international affairs, for example. He's just as popular in Trinidad as Crosby is in the States, and a lot more influential," reported Sergeant Burtt Evans for *YANK* magazine. "They've played enough GI shows to have many American soldiers humming such Calypso ditties as 'Rum and Coca-Cola,' 'Small Island,' and 'Some Girl Something.' The favorite is 'Rum and Coca-Cola' as sung by the Invader.

"Love making in wartime is the theme of many current Calypso songs. King Radio sings this one about air-raid shelters:

'I thank the government wholeheartedly,
Believe they really did a good to me
By digging holes underground
In case of air raids for us to run.
I hear they are calling them air-raid shelters
But they made them for me to romance my lovers.'"

GIs stationed in Panama's Canal Zone were frequently serenaded by the Panama National Symphony Orchestra, made up of musicians from numerous Central American and South American countries, European refugees, and American soldiers and sailors, many of whom were accomplished musicians prior to joining the military. Founder and director Herbert de Castro had invited GIs stationed in the region to audition for the troupe and even included compositions by American songwriters in the repertoire, such as the many folk songs of Stephen Foster.

In an interview with *YANK*, de Castro spoke for many Panamanians when he said, "We all hope this war will be won quickly, but when it is, we are going to miss these men. These soldiers and sailors who join with us in making music are, indeed, good neighbors in the truest sense."

Movies Portray the Battles of the Atlantic

The threat of U-boats landing saboteurs on the East Coast became a reality, and Hollywood rushed *Confessions of a Nazi Spy* to the screen. But this early film was short on the naval intrigue, playing up the courtroom drama instead. Other movies informed the viewing public that North America's shores were vulnerable to Nazi exploitation.

Leslie Howard, Laurence Olivier, and Raymond Massey starred in 1942's *The Invaders*, about a crippled U-boat and the crew that must abandon it. They trek across Canada, eluding their pursuers while seeking safety. (This movie won an Oscar for best original screenplay.)

The British played the heightened awareness along the East Coast as a comedy in *Sailors Three*, released as *Three Cockeyed Sailors* in the United States in 1940. The film follows three Limeys after their ship docks in the States, they're granted liberty, and they go about partaking in all the American vices they can before reporting back to their ship. But with the fog of alcohol clouding their vision, the British sailors somehow stumble onto a Nazi warship, the *Ludendorff,* and by the time they realize where they are, it's too late to backstep down the gangplank.

As word reached Tinseltown that the Nazis were moving south into the Caribbean, Paramount released *Mystery Sea Raider* in 1940, starring Carole Landis as an innocent American who helps an old salt acquire a tramp freighter. But he turns out to be a German naval commander who uses his ship to cripple Allied shipping in the region.

The battle of the Atlantic was taking a heavy toll as the Nazi U-boats struck again and again with deadly accuracy. Hundreds of sailors and Merchantmen perished and many more were injured, but still the manpower pipeline had to be sustained as more transports and their accompanying warships were built and launched. The Office of War Information thus asked the movie studios of Hollywood to produce films glamorizing and glorifying the perilous occupations on the high seas, hoping to increase enlistments for the Navy, the Coast Guard, and the Merchant Marine.

"*In Which We Serve* was the first really great picture of World War II. It is the story of a British destroyer, from her launching in 1939 to her sinking off Crete in 1941," reported *Time* in late December of 1942. "So real is her story and that of the men who sailed in her that when the film was first shown in London, tears poured down the cheeks of bluejackets and hardened critics who saw it."

The film was written and directed by Noel Coward, who also played the lead character, Captain Edward Kinross. While Coward denied the similarities, many felt this was a fictional portrayal of his good friend, Lord Louis Mountbatten, who had survived a similar loss of a warship yet rebounded to become Royal Navy commander. The story is told in flashback as the survivors cling to a life raft and reflect on their lives. "Aboard Coward's fictional HMS *Torrin* there existed forties British society in microcosm. Here everybody knew his place," wrote film critic Barry Norman. "The one thing they all had in common was the knowledge that each of them, high or low, was expected to show unswerving loyalty and devotion to duty."

Alfred Hitchcock tackled human interactions and the North Atlantic in *Lifeboat*, the tale of a passenger ship torpedoed by a U-boat, also damaged in the exchange of fire. After the survivors from the liner—representing all strata of society, from the rich tycoon to a nurse tending to the others, a sailor who knows the hazards of life at sea, and a foreign correspondent who has the insights of the world at war—make it to a life boat, they struggle with the dilemma of rescuing the U-boat commander who ordered the attack on their ship. "The Nazi then betrays their trust, stealing more than his fair share of food and water and piloting them into enemy territory," wrote John Belton in *American Cinema/American Culture*. "When the others learn of what he has done, they denounce the fascist philosophy that inspires his actions and kill him."

Tyrone Power had enlisted in the Marine Corps in August of 1942, but he was granted a four-month leave of absence to star in and complete the Technicolor movie *Crash Dive*, which won an Oscar for its special effects. With costars Dana Andrews and Anne Baxter, Power was caught up in a love triangle that only added to the tension as the two men put to sea in an American submarine on a secret mission to destroy a covert Nazi base.

"The picture took on the look of a Navy recruiting film and ended with a patriotic montage of all the impressive military hardware that could be borrowed by Twentieth [Century Fox]," wrote Hector Arce in *The Secret Life of Tyrone Power*. The story skirted the issue of "taking two men in love with the same girl, having them go off into battle together, yet refusing to give them any significant interplay—selfless rescues, selfish reprisals, inspirational teamwork—that would create any drama from their basic rivalry. What resulted was such a romanticized view that it prompted Bosley Crowther of *The New York Times* to remark, 'It leaves one wondering blankly whether Hollywood knows we're at war.' Movie audiences wondered the same thing. Since the United States was now in the war for real, families with boys overseas were beginning to resent the sugar-plum fantasies they had turned to Hollywood for all through the Depression."

Once filming was completed, Ty Power returned to duty for boot camp at Camp Pendleton, followed by officers' training at Quantico in Virginia.

Pat O'Brien, George Murphy, and Jackie Cooper starred in 1942's *The Navy Comes Through*, a less-than-credible depiction of maritime life on the Atlantic. In a review, *The New York Times* dismissed it, saying "a picture dealing with such a hazardous occupation as getting munitions through the submarine zone of the Atlantic calls for something more inspiring than the comic-strip daring that the script writers unblushingly thought up in this case."

Director John Ford teamed up with leading man John Wayne for 1940's *The Long Voyage Home*, adapted from four Eugene O'Neill short plays about life on the high seas. Gregg Toland's cinematography "wraps the film in a sensual, ghostlike shroud, the air of death hovering over the sailors has a palpable presence," wrote Lynne Arany, Tom Dyja, and Gary Goldsmith in *The Reel List*. "A saga of men at sea, this is a tribute to Britain in its darkest hour against the Nazi hordes."

In *Stand by for Action*, released in 1943, Robert Taylor "is assigned to a destroyer that saw service in World War I and that has been lovingly cared for by a civilian watchman who once served on her crew in active combat [Walter Brennan]," wrote Jeanine Basinger in *The World War II Combat Film*. "The story of how both Brennan and the old ship are refurbished to fight and win anew makes an obvious metaphor about America's preparation to fight the Germans a second time in a great World War."

Above: *Actor and officer Robert Taylor (left) played several roles in the U.S. Navy, including working as an aircraft inspector at Naval Air Station Glynco in Georgia.*
U.S. Navy Photo

When the crew spots a life boat with survivors on board, they pull up alongside to take on two very pregnant women and several hungry, crying babies. The crew now has to scramble to find diapers, and more diapers and milk, and if that's not enough for men to deal with, soon they have to deliver a baby . . . and then another.

Edward G. Robinson played the crusty old salt from WWI in 1943's *Destroyer*, trying desperately to get back in action as the battle for the Atlantic heats up. On board the relic warship is the typical cross-section of American society, representing most ethnic groups. In addition to battling the Nazis, Robinson also does battle with Glenn Ford, who attempts to woo the old grump's daughter, played by Marguerite Chapman.

After filming of *Casablanca* wrapped, Humphrey Bogart plunged into *Action in the North Atlantic* (originally titled *Torpedoed*), released in 1943 and also starring Raymond Massey and Alan Hale. The movie opens with a declaration from President Roosevelt, who promises: "The goods WILL be delivered by this nation, which believes in the tradition of DAMN the torpedoes. Full Speed Ahead!"

Bogart plays First Mate Joe Rossi on board a merchant ship—the *Northern Star*, bound for Murmansk—that is torpedoed by a Nazi raider. "The German submarine [that] sunk it comes in, taking a film of them, and tries to run them down, showing no mercy to those in the icy water," wrote Jeanine Basinger in a review of the film. "In *Action* the Germans are heartless and cold, laughing at the hapless men in the water. 'We'll pay ya back,' shouts Massey defiantly.

"After eleven days at sea, they are rescued, brought ashore and assigned to a cargo ship in a convoy bound for northwest Russia," wrote Jeffrey Meyers in *Bogart: A Life in Hollywood*. In the rough seas, this transport becomes separated from the safety of the convoy and is pounced on by Nazi planes and a spread of torpedoes from another U-boat. After his captain is injured, seaman Bogart takes charge of the ship and uses it to crash into the U-boat. Once the threat is eliminated, he navigates the brutal seas of the North Atlantic and makes it to Murmansk, where he declares to his Russian comrades (and the viewing public): "A lot more people are going to die before this is over. And it's up to the ones that come through to make sure that they didn't die for nothing." The film concludes with an armada of American-built transports braving the high seas as President Roosevelt declares, "We shall build a bridge of ships. Nothing shall prevent our complete and final victory."

Broadway and the Stage Door Canteen

Background: *Soldiers preparing to ship off to Europe marched up New York City's Fifth Avenue. Because New York was a major port city, many men left for war through the Big Apple. Many New York theaters provided free tickets for any serviceman in uniform.*

Office of War Information Photo

> "When the lights go on again all over the world
> And the ships will sail again all over the world
> Then we'll have time for things like wedding rings
> and free hearts will sing
> When the lights go on again all over the world."
>
> *From the song "When the Lights Go On Again," by Eddie Seiler, Sol Marcus, and Bennie Benjamin, Porgie Music Corporation*

FOR A CITY THAT NEVER SLEEPS, IT WAS A BLOW WHEN NEW York's Great White Way extinguished its marquee lights in late April of 1942 due to the threat that Nazi U-boats prowling offshore might use them as beacons. (It would be three years—not until after the defeat of Nazi Germany—before the lights of the Roseland, the Astor, Lindy's, and the Paramount, to name a few, twinkled brightly again.)

Just as Hollywood saw a continuous stream of actors and extras, technicians and assistants leave for the military, whether by choice or by chance, Broadway also felt the sting as some of its most prominent stars trooped off to war, some to entertain, many to join the fight.

"The manpower bugaboo put some crimps in the professional theater. The armed forces had more than 1,150 members from the New York roster of Actors' Equity alone," wrote Army Sergeant Georg Meyers for *YANK* magazine. "'We lived in a cross-fire between the draft board and Hollywood,' says Broadway producer Brock Pemberton, speaking of his road company of *Janie*, a play calling for several young men of military age. 'Every time we'd get some man who was doing well in a part, the Army would grab him or Hollywood would like his looks and steal him.'"

The War Comes to Broadway

"During the 1943–44 season on Broadway there were 41 comedies, 30 straight dramas, 25 musicals, four melodramas, one farce, three spectacles and two variety shows," noted Meyers in *YANK*. "Seventeen of the straight dramas and five of the musicals had a war slant."

Those plays included *The Eve of Saint Mark*, a drama about a group of GIs in the Pacific. The story line follows a young farm boy, Quizz West, as he says good-bye to his girlfriend, endures basic training, and gets sent off to a remote isle in the Pacific, where he and his buddies withstand all the horrors the jungle, Mother Nature and the Japanese can throw at them, remaining steadfast even when death is their only option.

In *Jacobowsky and the Colonel,* the Nazi occupation of France became a "half satiric, half-fantastic comedy," reported *Time* in its March 27, 1944, issue. "Its comic thesis is that flight from the Nazis makes strange carfellows." The farce follows an uppity Polish officer and a Jew on the run thrown together in a car as they attempt to flee Paris before the Nazis close off all escape routes.

One of the earliest war-related productions was *There Shall Be No Night*, in 1940, which dramatized the Russian invasion of Finland and depicted a Nobel recipient and his American wife, played by Broadway's leading couple, Alfred Lunt and Lynn Fontanne. The characters' son, who goes off to fight despite his father's objections, was played by Montgomery Clift. The play consisted mostly of rambling, incendiary speeches, railing on war's injustices, reflecting author Robert Sherwood's hatred for the Russian aggression. (After its run on Broadway, this production went on an eight-month U.S. tour but folded after Pearl Harbor when President Roosevelt appealed to Sherwood, saying the message was too controversial in light of war and the sensitivities of America's Russian allies.)

BELOW: *Irving Berlin's* This is the Army *toured the country as an all-serviceman show to raise money for the military. Roles, such as these "chorus girls," were played by GIs in drag!*
National Archives Photo

John Hersey's novel about a reporter covering the action on Sicily was brought to the stage in *A Bell for Adano*, which opened in December of 1944 and later was made into a movie.

Two of the biggest Broadway spectacles included *Winged Victory*, produced by Moss Hart, and Irving Berlin's *This Is the Army*, both of which were fund-raisers for military war relief. When Berlin took his show to England in 1943, it "knocked London sideways," reported the *Daily Herald*, raking in hundreds of pound sterling for several local charities.

Carmen Jones, which opened in 1943, took the classic opera *Carmen* and dropped it into a southern town, with an all-black cast. The alluring heroine works in a parachute factory. Her ill-fated lover is a hard-luck military policeman who loses her to a boxer (he was a bullfighter in the original opera.)

The Voice of the Turtle, which also opened in 1943 and ran for five years, follows the comic misadventures of a hapless soldier on a weekend pass who gets stood up.

LEFT: *Singer Ethel Merman presented a goat to the crew of the USS* Pensacola *as part of the ship's commissioning ceremony on February 6, 1930.*
U.S. Naval Historical Center Photo

"*Something for the Boys* gives Broadway the music comedy it has been thirsting for," critiqued *Time* on January 18, 1943. "It reveals songblitzer Ethel Merman at her absolute peak and songwriter Cole Porter well above the timberline. It tells of three uninhibited cousins (Merman, Paula Laurence, Allen Jenkins) who inherit a Texas ranch next door to [the Air Corps'] Kelly Field and set up a boardinghouse for soldiers' wives. In their spare time they also make defense gadgets out of carborundum. The hostelry turns into a scandal, and actress Merman, by getting some carborundum in her teeth, turns into a radio receiving set. After that nothing even tries to make sense."

Merman also appeared in the all-star cast of *Stage Door Canteen*, along with Gypsy Rose Lee, Katharine Hepburn, Tallulah Bankhead, Judith Anderson, Helen Hayes, and virtually every other Broadway star available. Proceeds from the show benefited the American Theater Wing, Broadway's wartime service organization.

Simply keeping the pipeline stocked with worthwhile scripts became more difficult as the war progressed, and some producers were forced to put on the classics and remakes. "Finding material worth producing has been as neat a trick as finding somebody to play in it, with men like Warrant Officer Irwin Shaw and Private William Saroyan overseas and several other top-drawer writers in the service," reported *YANK*'s Sergeant Meyers. Sidney Kingsley, an Army sergeant, won the 1942–43 New York Drama Critics' Circle award for his play, *The Patriots*. Composer Frank Loesser, one of Broadway's shining lights, was busy writing ditties and marches and ballads for the Army and various military units that asked him. Army Private Harold Rome, stationed at New York's Fort Hamilton, wrote a musical revue cast with soldiers stationed in the Big Apple that was scouted favorably by Broadway producers.

In every season there were a few stinkers, including some so-called war dramas written by hacks whose only experience in battle was fighting to get the miserable mess produced. But audiences attuned to letters from loved ones fighting overseas could see through the gloss and the falsehoods, and once word spread, they stayed away, helping another bomb fade into oblivion.

With so many GIs in the New York area, most of them waiting to ship out to Europe, plus sailors in town on liberty before heading back out to sea, the American Theater Wing made hundreds of show tickets available every day to the servicemen, for all shows, not just the war-themed productions. Those troops training and stationed in the New York area, who wanted a little culture, were also treated to ballet. "They may very likely enjoy it, for they will see nothing dainty or esthetical in *Fancy Free*, the surprise hit of Manhattan's booming ballet season," reported *Time*, May 22, 1944. "It is a lusty piece of knockabout vaudeville . . . The bored sailors tank up and pursue three slick chicks."

After touring Europe the previous six weeks in 1944, dancer Fred Astaire stopped by one of the theaters in Manhattan and fielded questions from servicemen. All they wanted to know was, "How does it feel to hold Rita Hayworth? How about Ginger Rogers?"

He responded as only a hoofer could: "Fine . . . they're swell dancers." Of course the GIs were hoping for juicier information than how the beautiful stars with the gorgeous gams danced.

Doing Time at the Stage Door Canteen

The American Theater Wing was instrumental in setting up and running the Stage Door Canteen in New York, along with similar clubs in six other cities stateside and another in London. Patterned after its popular Hollywood counterpart, the Stage Door Canteen relied on actors, actresses, technicians, and assistants to volunteer their time to perform, to help out, to dance with the guys, and sign autographs. Some stars could be counted on several nights every week.

RIGHT:: *Alfred Lunt and Lynne Fontanne were among the stars who started the Stage Door Canteen. As Broadway's power couple during the war years, the two secured donations of food, money, and entertainers' time. Actors and actresses rarely declined Lunt's or Fontanne's requests to serve in the Canteen. If these would-be stars wanted roles on the Great White Way, they knew they had to keep the couple happy. Starlets saw it as an opportunity to cozy up to Broadway's elite and use the Canteen as a springboard to stardom.*
Office of War Information Photo

Left: *The American Theater group ran the Stage Door Canteen for servicemen in New York City, giving them a place to eat, drink, and enjoy performances by some of the city's top stars. Broadway's big names staffed the little place in Times Square, serving up sandwiches and dishing out delicacies for those with a sweet tooth. In addition to working at all jobs to keep the Canteen open, celebrities toiled tirelessly to secure donations, including free food from some of the city's best eateries.* National Archives Photo

Model and budding starlet Lauren Bacall was a regular on Monday nights whenever she was in the New York area. She wrote in her biography, theater *By Myself*: "Only theater folk qualified. I was to dance with any soldier, sailor, or Marine who asked me, get drinks or coffee for them, listen to their stories. It was really very sweet and sad and fun. There was always music, and stars would appear each night to entertain or talk to the boys from the small stage.

"My first night there I couldn't believe it. . . . Alfred Lunt and Lynn Fontanne were washing dishes and serving coffee. Helen Hayes too. On Monday nights there was fierce jitterbugging. Many a time I found myself in the middle of a circle . . . everyone clapping to the music . . . while I was being whirled and twirled by one guy, then passed on to another, nonstop, until I thought I would drop. It wasn't much to do for the war effort, but it was something. At least the boys had a place to go that was clean and fun and a relaxing change for them."

Future author Art Buchwald was still in high school when he got an after-hours job in the mailroom at Paramount Pictures on Broadway, only half a block from the Stage Door Canteen. "I volunteered, and because I worked for a movie company, I was accepted. I was a busboy and a dishwasher and did anything they asked of me, with other busboys such as Alfred Lunt, Bert Lahr, and Ethel Merman," he wrote in *Leaving*

RIGHT: *Chorus girls like these volunteered at the Canteen to sing and dance for the troops.* Office of War Information Photo

Home. "I found rubbing shoulders with the famous and talented a very good experience. . . ."

With a bevy of stars and a toe-tapping lineup of entertainers stopping by every night, it didn't take long for CBS to find a spot in its weekly radio programming for a show from the Canteen.

"That happened in 1942. The show opened July 30th as a Thursday night variety entry, moved to Fridays in 1943, and ran for most of the war's duration," wrote John Dunning in *Tune in Yesterday: Old Time Radio*. "Jane Froman, Orson Welles, Wendell Willkie, Madeleine Carroll, Connie Boswell, Mary Martin, Rodgers and Hammerstein, Helen Hayes, Merle Oberon, and George Burns and Gracie Allen were a few who appeared. Bert Lytell was master of ceremonies, opening the show with 'Curtain going up for victory!' The cast, decked out in red, white, and blue, closed each broadcast with the singing of the National Anthem."

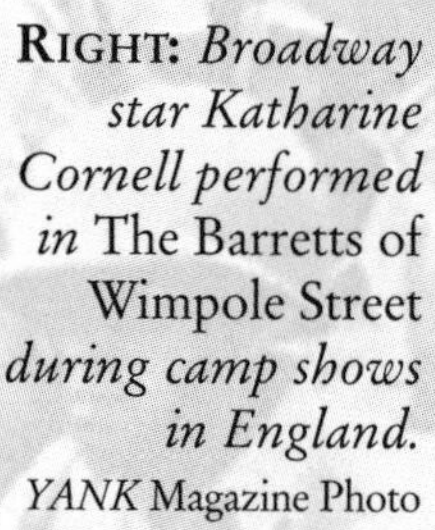

RIGHT: *Broadway star Katharine Cornell performed in* The Barretts of Wimpole Street *during camp shows in England.* *YANK* Magazine Photo

Performing for the Troops

It was common practice for popular shows to hit the road and tour the country, playing for a full week or more in select cities. The American Theater Wing arranged for some Broadway shows to head overseas and perform for the troops, including Katharine Cornell's *The Barretts of Wimpole Street*.

"Other theatrical entertainment committees have sent professional players, usually girls, to overseas bases where they form the nucleus of casts for shows staged by soldiers. Italy and North Africa have had such a troupe, and GIs in the Aleutians have seen *The Doughgirls* and *Kiss and Tell*," reported Georg Meyers for *YANK*.

Toward the end of the war, stage actor Tom Ewell was pulled from Navy Armed Guard duty with Atlantic convoys and dispatched to Broadway and the Navy Liaison's entertainment branch, where he scouted performers who wanted to go overseas to entertain the troops.

8. Fighting in the Mediterranean

"The troops that come out of this campaign are going to be battle-wise and tactically efficient."

—*General Dwight D. Eisenhower, on the invasion of North Africa*

"This is not the end. It is not the beginning of the end. It is perhaps the end of the beginning."

— *British Prime Minister Winston Churchill*

Opposite: *Four months prior to the invasion of North Africa, American B-25 bombers were striking Nazi fortifications in the region, including Matruh in Egypt.*
Army Air Corps Photo

FOR THOUSANDS OF YEARS THE LANDS ALONG THE Mediterranean have been fought for and conquered, plundered and liberated, and conquered again many times over.

As that two-headed monster of Hitler and Mussolini extended its sphere of influence to include virtually all of Europe, it looked south beyond the Mediterranean for more to devour. North Africa became its next target for exploitation.

Noted German composer Norbert Schultze frequently wrote patriotic songs, and he seized on the light poem "The Girl under the Lantern" by WWI veteran Hans Leip to create the beloved song "Lili Marlene" in 1938. The song was recorded by Lale Andersen and initially failed to receive much notice. But after General Erwin Rommel and his vaunted armor corps invaded North Africa in 1941, German Forces Radio began playing the song for the homesick soldiers there.

Though Propaganda Minister Joseph Goebbels hated the tune because it was meek when stacked against the pomposity and patriotism of Richard Wagner compositions, it gained popularity among the soldiers of the Afrika Korps, who requested to hear it aired every night.

Rommel and his tanks continued with the same blitzkrieg tactics that had overwhelmed the highly regarded Polish cavalry in the early days of September 1939. The Desert Rat and his rumbling armor units soon had a reputation of mythic proportions, bordering on pure military genius. Such was the opponent facing Allied commanders in late summer of 1942 as they formulated how to blunt the Nazi occupation of Africa's northern regions, hoping to confine the Afrika Korps between Britain's Eighth Army forces in the east and the invasion force coming in from the west, dubbed Operation Torch. Other Allied objectives were to establish bases for the eventual invasion of southern Europe; squeeze Axis shipping in the Med and protect Allied

Below: *Used in combat for the first time, paratroopers from the 509th Parachute Infantry Battalion were tasked with jumping behind enemy lines for Operation Torch, the invasion of North Africa.*
U.S. Army Photo

Right: *When they came ashore at various points of North Africa, American forces weren't exactly certain of what type of "reception" they might get, so they announced their arrival with red, white, and blue fireworks and the Stars and Stripes waving. Opposing them, besides the Nazis, were three disparate factions of French forces—pro-Allies, or pro-Nazi, or the neutrals—and the GIs had no idea which was which. They were met with either a hail of bullets, or hugs and handshakes, or the typical French attitude . . . indifference!*
Imperial War Museum Photo

transports; and convince the French to quit flip-flopping and side with the Allies, not the Axis.

The Allied leaders decided on a three-pronged attack, with two separate convoys of ships—one from America's eastern ports and another from England, with more than 107,000 troops crammed on board—along with untested paratroopers of the 509th Parachute Infantry Battalion jumping at night behind the lines.

But for the North Africa campaign, the lines were not clear-cut. Thrown into the mix were disparate French forces already on the continent. Some were pro-Allies, others were pro-Nazi, and others attempted to stay neutral. This bewildering quagmire was mockingly called "the God-damned French political mess." The Allied invasion force would not know which French units were "friendly" until they were already ashore and either ducking bullets or trading hugs.

By November 8 of 1942, the separate task forces had merged into one mighty armada consisting of 850 warships, transports, oilers, and cargo ships poised within sight of the African coastline.

In their compounds farther east, German soldiers could

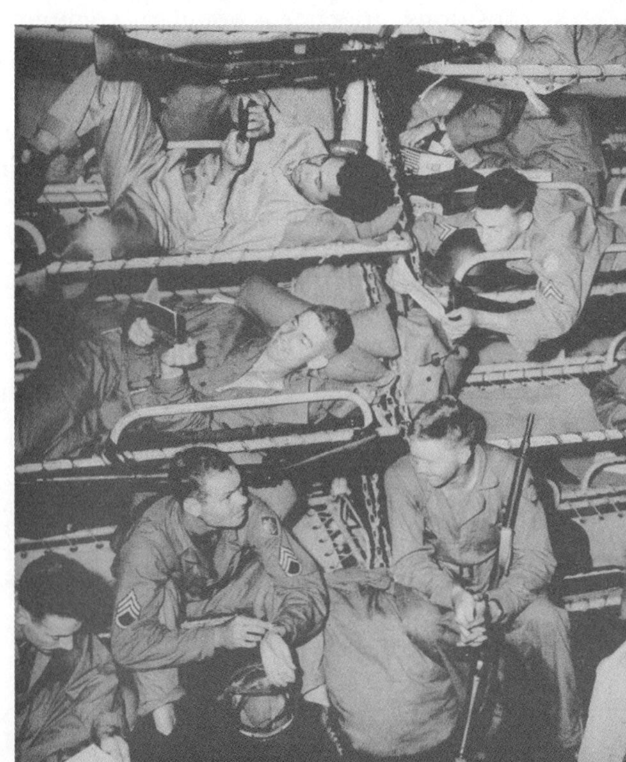

Right: *It was a long and miserable trip across the Atlantic crammed deep in the bowels of a transport ship. The hours seemed like days, and the days never ended, as thousands of American and British troops headed for North Africa, for Operation Torch.*
U.S. Navy Photo

Left: *Two tidal waves—from America's Eastern shores and from Great Britain—converged in early November of 1942 on the northern coast of Africa, forming one massive armada of 850 warships and auxiliaries, with thousands of Allied troops aboard.*
U.S. Army Photo

pick up Radio Yugoslavia from Belgrade, aired by fellow Nazi broadcasters who played patriotic music and read the news laced with propaganda. Every night at 9:55, the last song was always "Lili Marlene," as requested by Rommel. British soldiers waging war against the Nazis in Eastern Africa also enjoyed the song whenever they could tune it in, even if it was in German. Radio monitors on the Allied ships scanned the airwaves for local French and African broadcasts out of Casablanca and Algiers. Whenever they came across halfway decent music, they'd flip on the ship's loudspeakers so everyone on board could hear it. Every once in a while they heard "Lili Marlene," and soon it became popular with all combatants, both the Axis and the Allies.

Before the Allied troops went ashore or descended from overhead, naval warships unleashed their big guns, softening up the Nazi fortifications along the coast. Then it was time to board the smaller transport ships and scramble onto the beaches, sometimes unopposed, other times under fire.

"Algiers, the center of French military, political, and economic activity in North Africa, and the easternmost of the three major Allied objectives, surrendered on the first day," wrote Louis Snyder in *The War*. "At Oran, 130 miles west of Algiers, resistance was stiffer. Within two days the assault force was in control of Oran and the important nearby naval base. Most difficult of all were the Casablanca landings, on the Atlantic coastline of Morocco. From their coastal batteries in Casablanca the French fired on the assault boats which came ashore. But resistance ceased on November 11th."

Within the month, the Allies poured 185,000 combatants into North Africa and prepared for the push toward the Persian Gulf, dismantling or driving off the Afrika Korps along the way.

Entertainers Caught in the Fight

Several future stars of stage, and screen, radio, and records served with one of the Allied naval forces of the African coast, or ended up fighting the good fight on land.

RIGHT: *Douglas Fairbanks Jr. played an active role in the Mediterranean operations, serving on board the carrier* Wasp, *which delivered British fighter planes to Royal Air Force bases in the region. The actor maintained the operations log for all flights and would later serve in other key campaigns in the European theater. Here, he shook hands with King George of England.*
Royal Navy Photo

Army Private Sol Parker occupied his time during the transatlantic crossing by writing the song "Ship at Sea," which was later sung by Evelyn Knight on CBS radio.

Douglas Fairbanks Jr. could have had a cushy job on the staff of Britain's Lord Louis Mountbatten or worked clandestinely at the request of President Roosevelt, but instead he volunteered for combat. Among his many assignments, he served on the carrier *Wasp,* delivering Spitfire and Hurricane fighter planes to Royal Air Force units in the Med at Malta, a vital outpost directly along the naval resupply route for the Afrika Korps. His job was to keep a log of flight operations, and he also took his turn standing watch as communications officer.

British actor Alec Guinness joined the Royal Navy and endured convoy duty on the Atlantic and the Mediterranean. (He would later command a landing ship in other beach assaults in southern Europe.) Fellow British stage actor Anthony Quayle set aside his aspirations to join the British army and served on the Allied staff of General Eisenhower, who followed the invasion of North Africa from nearby Gibraltar.

Future stage and television actor Jan Merlin was still a teenager when he enlisted in the Navy as a torpedoman on a destroyer that earned campaign streamers for actions in support of the North Africa landings and the Middle Eastern conflict. (After getting out in April 1946 he would study acting in New York and then debut on Broadway in the WWII Navy yarn, *Mister Roberts.*)

Movie mogul Darryl Zanuck volunteered for the Army and headed up a film unit that made training shorts in England. He later documented the invasion of North Africa. Ossie Davis was assigned to the Army medical unit that would establish the first field hospital to handle casualties from the North Africa campaign. (Davis would later become a distinguished actor, writer, and director on Broadway.)

Army corporals Sal Ficcitto and Don Layton belonged to an anti-aircraft gun battery at Tunisia, and when they weren't busy blasting Axis planes out of the skies, the two were playing the guitar and bass fiddle, jamming on the front lines and on stage with a soldier troupe there. Another group of GIs at a nearby ammunition depot that kept the frontline units supplied with bullets and explosives and harmonized in their spare time soon became known as the Four Commanders. The popular quartet—Grady Porter, Paul Favors, Booker Harris, and Amos Lundy—even performed for President Roosevelt and Prime Minister Churchill when they met at Casablanca.

Below: *New Jersey boy Joe Pellegrino had the misfortune of visiting his parents' homeland when war broke out and he was mustered into the Italian Army. He was rushed into the fighting in North Africa but was soon taken prisoner. At a POW camp at Bizerte in Tunisia, he led an ensemble of musicians made up of fellow Italian prisoners of war.*

Fortunately for "Jersey Joe," his case was evaluated and he was released as a POW, with the stipulation he switch sides and suit up for Uncle Sam instead!
Army Signal Corps Photo

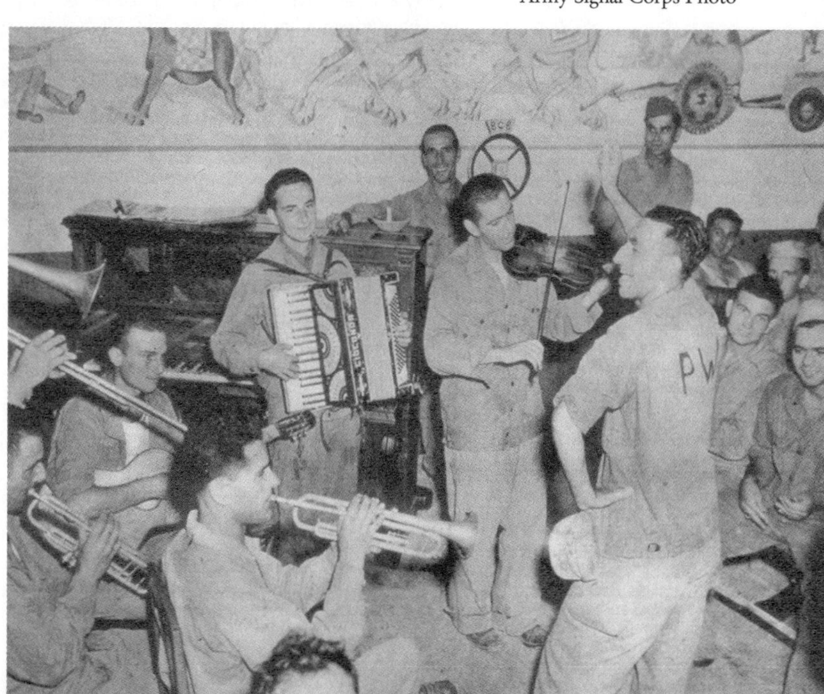

Performing for the Troops

Soon after Army units secured the region and staked out new compounds in the rear, Special Services personnel swung into action, setting up libraries, intramural sports, recreation centers, and clubs. Former circus performer Burt Lancaster was with the 21st Special Services Unit and was tasked with coordinating stage shows for the troops in the area.

Lancaster ended up a triple threat, writing the skits, acting, and directing the show *Let's Go* in Casablanca; then, he put on the popular revue *Stars and Gripes* in Tunisia, stocked with professional talent within the Army ranks. British comic Sterling Holloway played the new recruit, complete with gags and pratfalls, in the soldier show, *Hey Rookies*.

Child actress Sybil Jason was born in Capetown, South Africa. As a precocious youngster she was first noticed for her impressions of Jimmy Durante, Mae West, and Maurice Chevalier. By the time she was ten she had already appeared in numerous Hollywood movies. In late November of 1941, 20th Century Fox sent her on an international publicity tour, but after the Japanese attacked Pearl Harbor, she returned to South Africa and remained there throughout the war. In addition to hosting her own radio show, she entertained Allied servicemen with her song-and-dance routines and comical impressions. Another former child star who supported the troops stationed in the Mediterranean during WWII was Jean Darling, former pixie in thirty-five *Our Gang* shorts.

The Special Services mobile unit of the 9th Air Force in Cairo took the stage show *Sky Blazers* on the road, traveling the dusty roads and riverbeds of North Africa to get to as many Allied units as they could find. The small caravan included professional musicians, comedians, and singers, plus truck drivers, stagehands, electricians, and carpenters needed to perform magic on a daily basis as they built hasty stages from wooden pallets, crates, and shipping containers wherever they could find them. All of the soldiers were recruited from the ranks of servicemen in the Middle East. Performing members of the *Sky Blazers* included Bob Panachi, who performed with Artie Shaw's big band prior to enlisting; Baltimore radio announcer Jacques Kahn; former NBC Studio singer Alston Townley; Chicago club musician Jack Wolfe; Bernie Neirenberg, who danced in Cole Porter's *Jubilee*; Frank Smith, a musician from Cleveland; big band trumpeter Murray Davidson; Pittsburgh showman Reg Schlegel; New York nightclub musician Jack Jacobson; another Steel Town musician, Bob Clements; Woody Perrin from San Antonio; and Maurice Delse, who performed in Baltimore dance bands. Two of the troupe's signature numbers that GIs in North Africa closely identified with were "Blackout Boogie" and "Middle East Blues," penned by Clements and Kahn.

Jack Benny flew to West Africa in a DC-3 dubbed *Five Jerks to Cairo* in October of '43. "Welcome as Benny was, actresses Anna Lee and Wini Shaw were probably even more so; many of the GIs had not seen a girl in more than a year," reported Army Sergeant Ken Abbott for *YANK* magazine. "Benny introduced red-headed British Miss Lee with 'Hey fellas, a woman!

Remember?' Corporal Abe Fass of Brooklyn got the one and only kiss given by Miss Lee."

In Northern Iran, Army Sergeant Frank McDuffie ran the Post Exchange and rationed beer to the soldiers. "One night, he noticed four dogfaces sitting outside one of the PX windows and drinking their beer," reported Sergeant James O'Neill for *YANK*. "It was windy; the air was thick with the dust of Iran that Mac could hardly see their faces. By the next ration night, Mac had moved all the PX supplies out of the storeroom and piled them behind the PX counter.

"Then he dug up a piano somewhere and found a sergeant named Al Delong, who used to play in the clubs around Los Angeles. Delong started rambling on the piano, and in a half hour the room was filled with smoke, beer, conversation and GIs. One of the boys tacked up a sign over the storeroom doorway: DUFFIE'S TAVERN. After a few more ration nights, you could scarcely recognize the place. Delong brought along a few hep artists from the Special Services band and the Tavern really began to jump. Corporal Billy McIntyre, professional comic from Washington, D.C., came over to tell a few jokes and before he was through, he had organized a few amateur talent acts and put on a floor show."

Corporal Bob Crosson headed up the Army Special Services efforts with the Persian Gulf Service Command in the region, putting on stage shows and running a radio station, recreation hall, and dawn-to-dusk intramural sports schedules. Helping out with the musical revues were Sergeant Grady Whittle, a jack-of-all-trades Texan, Werner Erikson, who had learned the ropes while performing in San Valley, Idaho; and Dick Vaus, a western crooner with Boston's Texas Playboys.

Former Berlin actress Marlene Dietrich didn't hesitate to journey to the war zone to entertain Allied troops, knowing full well Adolf Hitler had put a price on her head after she declined his "generous" offer to return to the Fatherland. She wasn't afraid of being killed while venturing so close to the front, but she was concerned about what would happen if she were captured by the Nazis. "They'll shave off my hair, stone me, and have horses drag me through the streets," she recalled in her autobiography. During a flight across the Atlantic, her troupe—which included an unknown comedian named Danny Thomas—assumed they would be going to somewhere in Europe, but once aloft they were given instructions that their destination was Casablanca.

They performed on makeshift stages, truck beds, on the hood of a jeep, virtually anywhere a group of GIs could gather around. But they were still in a war zone, and all too often their impromptu performances were interrupted by air raids as Nazi fighter planes and bombers swooped through and caused some mischief.

LEFT: *Only a few months prior, Army Private Dick Vaus was strumming with the Texas Playboys, but here he's assigned to the Persian Gulf Command as an engineer, though he still performed country music whenever time allowed, after hours.* *YANK* Magazine Photo

"The first thing you learn during a raid is to hide," Dietrich remembered. "Everything else is simple. Three things count: eating, sleeping, taking cover. I was more afraid about my teeth than about my legs. Thank God there was always a GI nearby to give me a shove."

(While in North Africa, Dietrich visited with an old friend, French actor Jean Gabin. She thought he had been killed when a warship taking him to Morocco was sunk by a U-boat in the Atlantic. He survived and joined an armored tank unit of the Free French at Algiers. Dietrich also performed for the French troops there.)

Bob Hope certainly experienced a few air raids during his many USO trips overseas. After a show at Bone, Hope and his troupe moved on to Algiers, where General Eisenhower had set up his command post. During a brief get-together, and after learning that the entertainers had already been through a few hairy situations, Ike assured Hope that he could finally get some peace and quiet in Algiers.

"'We haven't been bombed here for a month and a half. They can't get in, we're so strong here. You'll get a good night's rest tonight,'" Hope recalled the general saying in his book *Have Tux, Will Travel.*

Of course, that same night, while getting some "peace and quiet" at the Aletti Hotel in Algiers, Hope and company were startled awake by . . . an air raid!

"The bombers kept trying to paste the battleships in the harbor, which was just outside the door. And all the big guns and the anti-aircraft guns, the

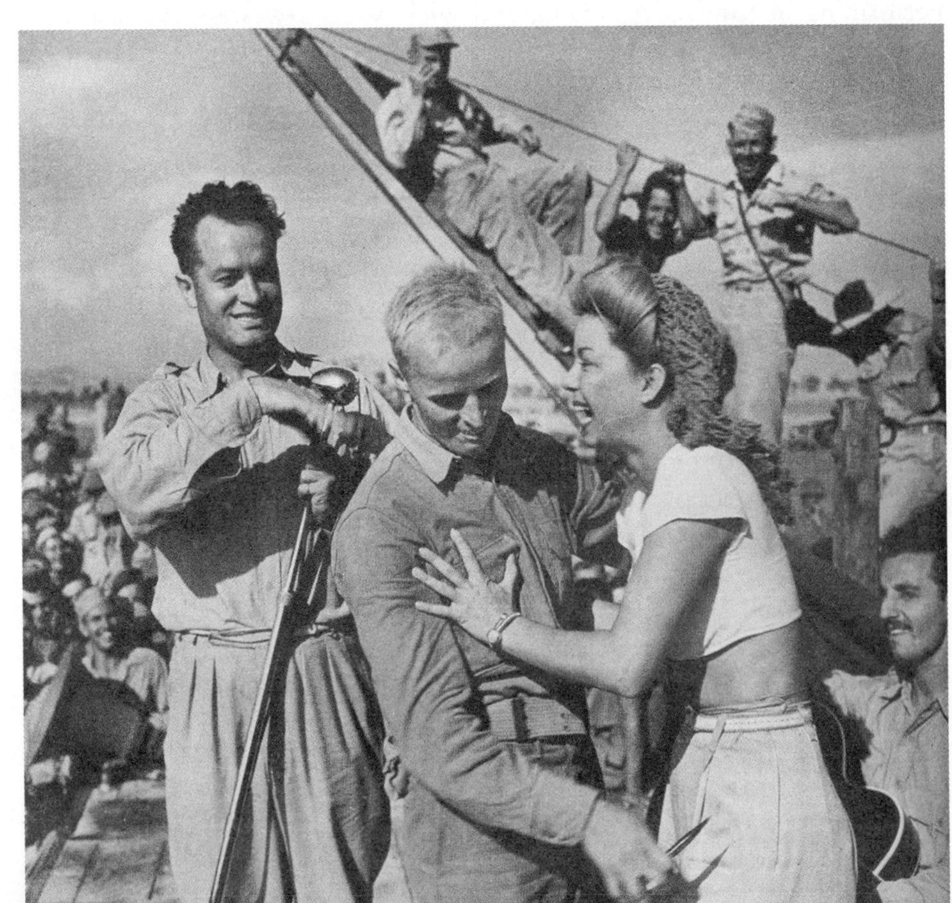

RIGHT: *Comedian Bob Hope looks on as Frances Langford flirts with one lucky GI plucked from the crowd during a USO show in North Africa. The duo also took time out to visit General "Ike" Eisenhower while in Algiers, who assured them that the region was safe from enemy attack. And of course that same night, Luftwaffe bombers attacked warships in the nearby harbor.*
Army Signal Corps Photo

ninety millimeters, were firing. I can't describe the racket," Hope remembered. "But I'll say this, I knew something was going on. The next day I sent Ike a wire and thanked him for the rest. I said, 'I'm glad I wasn't here on one of the nights when you had some action.'"

Humphrey Bogart had starred in the movie *Casablanca*, and he returned to the exotic city when American troops got there. "It's a humorous image, Bogart doing a soft shoe, twirling a cane, and singing 'Thanks for the Memories' with Bob Hope. He did have a fair singing voice but the fact is that his act consisted of reciting speeches from *The Petrified Forest* and other films," wrote his son, Stephen H. Bogart, in his book *In Search of My Father*. "By the time he got to North Africa, Bogie was known around the world, mostly from his gangster films."

He also enjoyed playing chess and frequently sought out a few respectable competitors from among the many soldiers at every compound he visited. When he found a true rival at the game, he would get his name and unit and then correspond with him, continuing to play chess via V-mail.

Song-and-dance man Al Jolson also toured extensively and caught up with General Ike at Algiers, delivering a message from Mrs. Eisenhower: a kiss to take care of himself and a kick on the butt for not writing to her. And yes, Jolson did deliver both messages, physically. The good-natured general asked Jolson to give Mamie a kiss when he got back home—just not too passionately! Jolson also collected messages from homesick soldiers and personally delivered them to loved ones or called to say their boy was doing great.

The British military's entertainment effort was known as the Entertainments National Service Association, or ENSA. "Jugglers, crooners, monologists, violinists, tap dancers, comedians, aging matinee idols or younger ones and girls . . . always girls. By troop ship and truck, by DC3 and Oriental caboose, by jeep and command car, the many ladies and fewer gentlemen of the theater wander into sand and jungle with Noel Coward plays and singing and dancing acts," wrote U.S. Army Private Irwin Shaw for *YANK*. "One of the most successful ENSA productions is a variety show called *Hello Happiness* which has been touring Africa more than three years. After nine months in the Cairo desert, the cast was putting on the last polishing touches before opening. Reg Lever, a well-known comedian, directed and produced the show. It does seem that Africa is more dangerous to actors than to anyone else. All the least attractive types of dysentery, malaria and desert sores seem to hit theatrical companies as soon as they touch the sand of the Dark Continent." Noel Coward, Vivien Leigh, and Danny Kaye were just a few of the many entertainers who toured the British colonies on behalf of ENSA.

Movies Explore Intrigue of the Dark Continent

The quagmire that was North Africa in the late '30s—with the bewildering French factions at each other's throats—and on into the war years with the

Nazis and the Brits thrown into the mix, led to several movies laced with international intrigue, mistaken identity, misguided loyalties, and missed opportunities. Among those were several B films, a stinker or two, and one great classic.

In early January of 1942 the *Hollywood Reporter* announced the casting of an upcoming film project with North Africa as its setting: "Ann Sheridan and Ronald Reagan will co-star for the third time in Warner's *Casablanca*, with Dennis Morgan also coming in for top billing. Yarn of war refugees in French Morocco is based on an unproduced play [*Everybody Comes to Rick's*] by Murray Burnett and Joan Alison."

But soon Reagan was in uniform, and some suspected the studio had thrown his name out there just to keep him in the public eye. Warner tossed the casting net further. The final lineup resembled the melting pot of nationalities in the real Casablanca: American Humphrey Bogart and his main rival, Austrian Paul Henreid, both vying for the attention of Swedish beauty Ingrid Bergman. Supporting players included those two "Mad Dogs and Englishmen," Sidney Greenstreet and Claude Rains, S. Z. Sakall and Peter Lorre from Hungary, and Marcel Dalio and Madeleine LeBeau from France. (Dalio had fled his homeland after the Nazis invaded, and during the filming of this movie he was informed that his parents had perished in one of the many Nazi concentration camps in Eastern Europe.)

Each character became an integral part of the project, making the whole stronger for his or her involvement. One other important role was that of Sam, the piano player: "The [song] plugger: was a short, stocky Negro named [Arthur] Dooley Wilson," reported *Time* in its May 10, 1943, issue. "Warner Brothers, seeking a love theme for Ingrid Bergman and Humphrey Bogart in *Casablanca*, fished 'As Time Goes By' out of the files. Instead of giving the tune to a conventional crooner, Warner picked Dooley Wilson. He is something special. He sings with a sense of mood worthy of a great lieder singer. Dooley gave 'As Time Goes By' everything he had. And when Ingrid Bergman says that no one can sing the song like Sam [Dooley], millions of moviegoers have agreed with her."

Plagued by constant rewrites, the film was destined to be just another of the hundreds of B flicks that Hollywood churned out to keep moviegoers in the theaters week after week. But the fickle finger of fate reached out and plucked this one from the depths of mediocrity right into the middle of world events. "It opened in New York on November 26, 1942, only eighteen days after the Allied armies had landed in Oran, in Algiers and in Casablanca and after newspaper headlines had pushed Casablanca into the public consciousness. The film was also shown at the White House on December 31, 1942," wrote Jeffrey Meyers in *Bogart: A Life in Hollywood*. "A few days later, Roosevelt left Washington to meet Churchill at Casablanca. The film was released throughout the country on January 23, 1943, during the vitally important Casablanca Conference, when the two wartime leaders planned the invasion of Sicily, the bombing of German territory, the demand for unconditional surrender, and the transfer of British forces to the Far East after victory in Europe."

Above: *It didn't start out to be a classic, just another of the hundreds of B movies the studios cranked out, but* Casablanca, *starring Humphrey Bogart and Ingrid Bergman, had a lot of luck and some great timing on its side, released just as President Roosevelt and Prime Minister Churchill met in Casablanca to hash out the Allied war strategy in both Europe and the Pacific.*
Associated Press Photo

Some have called *Casablanca* "the best bad film ever made," while others just consider it bad. But it did win an Oscar for Best Picture, and many critics and fans have voted it a classic that has stood the test of time.

Humphrey Bogart returned to North Africa later in 1943 as Army Sergeant Joe Gunn in *Sahara*, but "Lulubelle" was the "star" of this feature, about a lost American tank crew that is trying to make it to a British unit somewhere in the area but is quickly running out of fuel and becoming ever more desperate for water. Lulubelle is the clankety, sputtering tank that announces its approach at every gully and dune. As the group meanders across the desert, they approach the rubble of an Allied field hospital and pick up a few stragglers. Once again, an international motley bunch—including a British doctor, a French resistance fighter, a black thespian, an African soldier, and an Italian POW—represent the entire world fighting those evil Nazis.

"Since the soldiers are stranded in the distant desert there are no women in the film and no sentimental reunions of soldiers on leave," wrote Jeffrey Meyers in *Bogart: A Life in Hollywood*. "Bogart—stoic and cool—portrays the kind of heroic soldier who would win the war. The tank that wins the battle and rescues the men stranded in the desert symbolizes America's ability to defeat the Nazis and save the Allies."

When Lulubelle is strafed by a German fighter plane, the tank crew gets lucky and shoots it down, capturing the pilot, the sort of tall, blond Aryan that Hitler idolizes. The disparate bunch argues about killing the enemy combatant, but Sergeant Gunn steps forward as judge and jury. No matter how despicably the Nazis might conduct themselves, the Allies will take the upper hand and still win in the end.

The crew keeps running across dry wells, and soon reference to the Bible is made when one soldier states, "You'll have to hit a rock to get water, like Moses." Then, miraculously, as they make a last stand at another dry well, with Nazi soldiers closing in around them who are just as desperate for water, even willing to surrender, a missile strikes the well and it suddenly gushes with water.

The film closes with Sergeant Gunn reading the names of the men who died alongside him and the news bulletin that the Brits have driven back the Afrika Korps at Alamein.

Eric von Stroheim played Erwin Rommel as arrogant and sadistic in *Five Graves to Cairo*, directed by Billy Wilder in 1943. In the film, Rommel brings about his own downfall at North Africa by laying out his war plans to an Allied spy. The spy sends word to "the good guys," who promptly defeat the Africa Korps at El Alamein. (Of all the high-level Germans, Rommel never considered himself a Nazi at heart; in fact, he opposed Adolf Hitler.)

Director John Huston was serving with the Army Signal Corps Photographic Service Unit and had to rely on all his Hollywood wizardry to fulfill a request from President Roosevelt, to make a documentary on the North Africa campaign.

"Anatole Litvak and his crew had shot some pretty good stuff, but the ship carrying the exposed film had been sunk before it could even put to sea. So there was absolutely nothing," recalled Huston in *An Open Book*. "The brass was acutely embarrassed. If it could possibly be kept from him, the President was not to know that the Photographic Services had assigned only one man and his crew to the landings. However, they had the solution: Frank Capra and I would 'manufacture' a North African film and be quick about it. We went out to an Army training base in the Mojave Desert where the terrain looked like Tunisia. We had troops moving up and down hills under fake artillery concentrations—the worst kind of fabrication. We got this trash—now titled *Tunisian Victory*—together. The material was so transparently false that I hated to have anything to do with it." While Huston loathed collaborating on this project, fortunately it was not released for public viewing.

Two other documentaries about the war in Africa, both released in 1943, were *Desert Victory*, done by the British Ministry of Information and featuring the British 8th Army at El Alamein; and *At the Front*, an Army Signal Corps project headed up by Colonel Darryl Zanuck.

In 1943's *The Immortal Sergeant*, Henry Fonda is suddenly thrust into a leadership role after his tough-as-nails sergeant dies on the North African battlefield. Fonda is not sure if he has what it takes to do the right thing in combat, remembering how he couldn't even say what he wanted to say before

BELOW: *Before joining the Navy and heading off for the war in the Pacific, Henry Fonda starred in* The Immortal Sergeant, *about a crusty NCO who keeps remembering all the great times he had with his gal back in England, at the same time second-guessing his decisions in combat.*
U.S. Navy Photo

leaving his girlfriend (played by Maureen O'Hara) back in England. He recalls their times together, shown in flashback, and second-guesses his current decisions at every turn.

On a lighter note, Carole Landis and several other starlets had toured North Africa in late 1942, entertaining the troops. Landis kept a daily journal of their experiences, and after returning to Hollywood put everything together for a book. In 1944 Fox made the book into *Four Jills in a Jeep*, with Mitzi Mayfair, Kay Francis, and Martha Raye in a lighthearted re-creation of their trek from England to the Dark Continent. Other guest stars included Jimmy Dorsey and his band, George Jessel, Betty Grable, Carmen Miranda, Dick Haymes, Alice Faye, and Phil Silvers.

A year after the war was over, the Marx Brothers were planning to do a movie in 1946—*A Night in Casablanca*—but Warner Brothers tried to block the project, even threatening a lawsuit, feeling the movie might somehow adversely effect their blockbuster, *Casablanca*. Julius Henry Marx, the third brother (better known as Groucho) fired off a letter when he heard about the pressure from Warner: "I had no idea that the city of Casablanca belonged exclusively to Warner Brothers. You claim you own Casablanca and that no one else can use that name without your permission. You probably have the right to use the name Warner, but what about Brothers? Professionally, we

ABOVE: *Comedienne and movie star Martha Raye had a heart of gold for the troops and they returned that affection whenever she came around, such as visiting these soldiers in Casablanca.*

During an earlier trip to England and then on to North Africa, Carole Landis kept a journal of her exploits with Martha, Mitzi Mayfair, and Kay Francis, and the four of them reprised their roles for the movie, Four Jills in a Jeep.

National Archives Photo

LEFT: *Comedienne Martha Raye was a tireless trooper for the USO, traveling to wherever "her boys" were fighting even if it meant riding in a tank, in North Africa.*

Office of War Information Photo

were brothers before you were. . . ." He then rambled on about Jack Warner not being the first Jack, nor was Harry Warner the first, either.

The brothers Warner were perplexed by Groucho's letter and demanded to know about the plot of the Marx Brothers movie. Groucho obliged: "There isn't much I can tell you about the story. In it, I play a Doctor of Divinity who ministers to the natives and, as a sideline, hawks can openers and pea jackets to the savages along the Gold Coast of Africa . . . When I first meet Chico, he is working in a saloon, selling sponges to barflies who are unable to carry their liquor.

"Harpo is an Arabian caddie who lives in a small Grecian urn on the outskirts of the city. As the picture opens, Porridge, a mealy-mouthed native girl, is sharpening some arrows for the hunt. Paul Hangover, our hero, is constantly lighting two cigarettes simultaneously. He apparently is unaware of the cigarette shortage."

This rambling only confused the Warners more. They again requested details from Groucho, who became a little testy and quipped, "In the new version, I play Bordello, the sweetheart of Humphrey Bogart . . ." Of course the Marx Brothers proceeded with *A Night in Casablanca*, another of their madcap capers, and it in no way tarnished the stature of *Casablanca*.

Kicking the Nazis in the Boot

From the start of the land campaign for North Africa, the battle-hardened German Panzer commanders and crewmen out-dueled the British. But as American ground forces joined the fight and Allied fighter planes strafed and bombed the enemy armor columns, the "good guys" took the offensive and by May had the Afrika Korps turning tail, retreating toward Egypt.

With Europe's underbelly in Allied hands, bombers took off from North African airstrips and began targeting outposts and vital industrial cities under Nazi control in Italy and Romania, crippling oil refineries, rail lines, power plants, and aircraft factories.

Next stop on the journey to dismantling Hitler's Thousand-Year Reich was to hop the Mediterranean, and get some leverage on the Italian peninsula, and then "boot" the Nazis back to the Fatherland. Allied forces first planned to storm the beaches at Sicily, in August of 1943. Just offshore was Navy special operations officer Douglas Fairbanks Jr., directing a newly formed group of

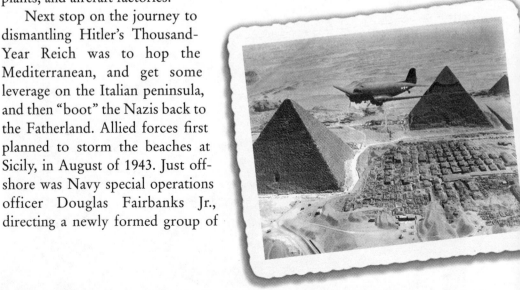

RIGHT: *An Air Transport Command cargo plane flies over the pyramids of Egypt, headed for the North African war front. Loaded down with everything needed to sustain the fight, these transports flew from the East Coast of America and England, and traversed the Atlantic almost daily.*
U.S. Army Photo

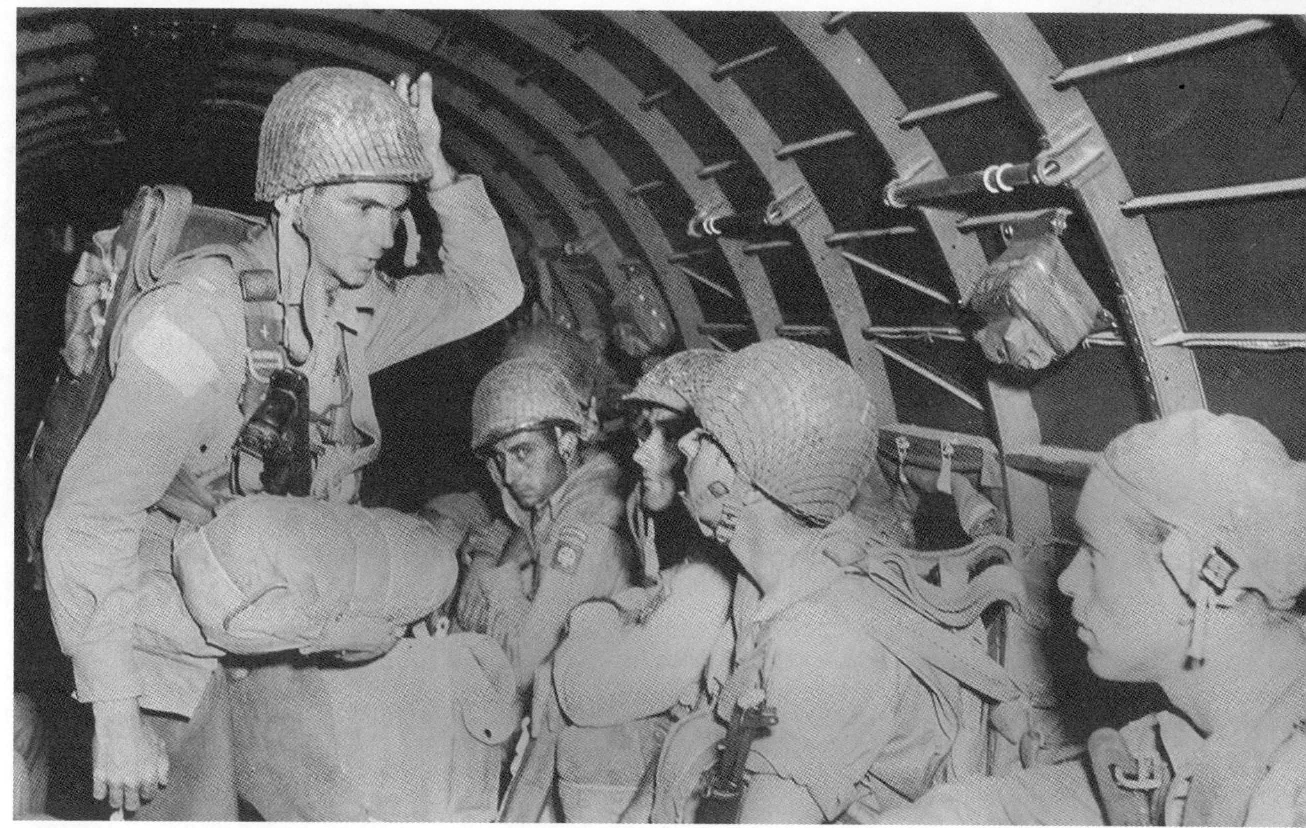

ABOVE: *Paratroopers of the 82nd Airborne go over the mission one last time before jumping at Salerno, in mid-September of 1943.* Smithsonian Institution Photo

commandos known as the Beach Jumpers, tasked with sneaking ashore and marking the beach for assault troops following close behind. While ground operations took place on Sicily, Fairbanks and his Beach Jumpers—which included a small flotilla of PT boats and a destroyer—harassed enemy forces up and down the coast and on tiny specks of islands, such as Elba. (For the swashbuckling Fairbanks, who starred in *The Dawn Patrol* in 1930 and *Gunga Din* in 1939, none of the action in his movies could compare to his real-life exploits, as he found himself frequently under fire with the little known but highly respected Beach Jumpers.)

Jumping onto Sicily were members of the British 6th Airborne Division, which included actor Trevor Howard. Another British actor in the Italian Campaign was Alec Guinness, who joined the Royal Navy and earlier had been ordered to the United States to pick up a new landing craft still under construction. But delays at the shipyard allowed him time to appear in *Flare Path* on Broadway. Once his LST was seaworthy, Guinness and crew headed for the invasion of Sicily, then on to Elba, and then moved off to Yugoslavia to provide resupply to partisans there.

Three weeks after hitting Sicily, the Allies turned their attention to Salerno. From there the American and British forces could push northward and race each other to Berlin. Christopher Milne was with the British Army

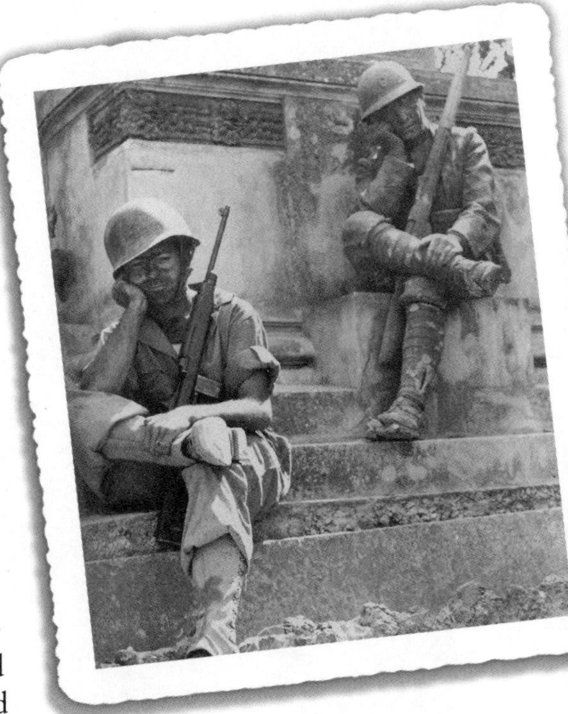
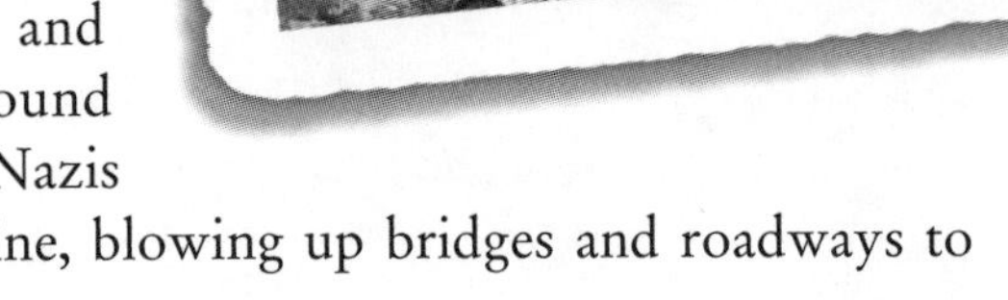

RIGHT: *At a war memorial in Brolo on the island of Sicily, an American infantryman has a little fun during a lull in the fighting, and before moving on to the next big engagement—assaulting the Italian peninsula.*
National Archives Photo

at Salerno. (As a youngster he was known as Christopher Robin, the son of children's author A. A. Milne and inspiration for the Winnie the Pooh series of stories in the book, *When We Were Very Young*.)

The Nazis would not easily relinquish Italy, choosing to give ground methodically, taking up commanding positions along mountain passes and overlooking impassable rivers, such as the Volturno, to watch all the approaches, laying down mortar rounds and machine-gun fire and calling in fighter planes and bombers whenever Allied ground forces attempted to advance. The Nazis first pulled back to the Gustav Line, blowing up bridges and roadways to slow down the Allied pursuit.

Two such killing grounds were along the Rapido River and at the base of Monte Cassino, the Benedictine enclave where German snipers were positioned, waiting to pick off American soldiers. Nazi forward observers called down artillery fire with deadly effectiveness, decimating the Allied ground forces massing in the Liri Valley below.

Every appeal was made for the Germans to evacuate the monastery, and at the same time representatives from the Vatican forcefully asked Allied commanders to spare the historic site. But when the Nazis refused to leave, when they continued to use the vantage point, the Allies had no option but to bomb the abbey, causing an uproar among Italian Catholics. On February 15 of '44, more than two hundred bombers dropped incendiaries on Monte Cassino while artillery guns opened up, leaving it a smoldering ruin.

Allied bomber crews also disrupted rail transports and convoy routes behind German lines, cutting off the Nazi resupply efforts. Among the bomber crews and fighter pilots were future television writer and producer Norman Lear, a radio operator with the 15th Air Force, which would eventually set up its operations at Foggia. Lear would fly fifty-seven combat missions.

BELOW: *"Popping Smoke" to obscure their advance from Nazi gunners, Army Rangers scale the terraced heights at Salerno, Italy.*
Imperial War Museum Photo

Above: *Though relatively new to air combat tactics, black fighter pilots of the 15th Air Force—better known as the Tuskegee Airmen—quickly established a reputation as lethal and efficient against even the best Luftwaffe fighter pilots, over Italy and later on, over northern Europe.* National Archives Photo

Also at Foggia with the 15th Air Force was Marty Allen, grounded because of a perforated eardrum and working with a security detachment. During one harrowing incident at the air base, a B-17, its bomb bay filled with explosives, was being refueled by a tanker truck when a motor overheated and sparked a fire that quickly spread to the plane. Allen saw the fire and ran over, hopped in the truck, and moved it a safe distance away. Then he ran back to the plane, scrambled on board, and put out the flames before they could spread to the fuel tanks or the ordnance in the bomb bay. (After returning home, Allen turned to comedy, developing a manic, wide-eyed, wild-haired shtick. During the Vietnam War he toured hospitals across the United States, entertaining wounded troops.)

Former collegiate and stock theater actor Don Herbert flew B-24s out of Italy, completing fifty-six missions over enemy positions in country, in Yugoslavia and Germany. (After the war he jobbed around Chicago radio stations and in 1951 debuted on television in *Watch Mr. Wizard*, which first aired on Chicago's WMAQ and a year later was the top-rated educational show on television.)

By mid-January of 1944, British and American forces were thrown ashore at Anzio, hoping to bust through the Gustav Line. One of the soldiers in the landing group was Army Private James Arness, who, at six foot seven, towered over most of his fellow soldiers. "When we were on the LCI, [my squad leader] handed me some burlap bags and told me to carry them to the beach, where someone would take them from me," Arness recalled for *American Legion* magazine in January 2003. "I asked what was in them, and he said, 'TNT.' He also told me that I was to be the first one off the boat so they can tell how deep the water was by where it hit me. They figured if I went under, they needed to get closer."

Obviously anyone carrying more than his normal complement of munitions had to be worried about making it to the hereafter in one piece, but Arness and the thousands of other GIs got ashore without a shot fired at them. Instead they got bogged down along the seven-mile-deep beachhead for three months, while enemy artillery guns lobbed shells down with deadly results.

Two weeks later, on the night of February 1, Private Arness was out on a patrol when he was shot in the leg and narrowly missed being killed when an enemy grenade exploded close by. He would require the miracles of penicillin and a year of rehabilitation to salvage the leg.

(Ten years after being injured at Anzio, Arness was discovered for a new television show, *Gunsmoke*. He later credited his combat in WWII for grounding his characterization of Marshall Matt Dillon: "War experience becomes a part of your life," he told *American Legion*. "If I hadn't had that experience, I don't think I would have fit into the character on the show as well. Matt Dillon had a particular aversion to killing people.")

The Allies were logjammed on the beachhead at Anzio and had to endure weeks of heavy pounding from a massive artillery gun perched in an overwatch vantage point. The rail gun was dubbed Anzio Annie—and she had quite a kick to her.

Listening to Sally

"Because of the stalemate, there was plenty of opportunity for the Germans to engage in propaganda aimed at undermining morale," wrote Don Graham in *No Name on the Bullet*. "Radio broadcasts from Rome featured a sexy-voiced female named 'Sally' who taunted American and British troops by promising good food and kisses, and sweetened her message by playing scratchy versions of 'In the Mood,' 'Chattanooga Choo Choo,' and her personal favorite for the soldiers with their backs to the ocean, 'Between the Devil and the Deep Blue Sea.'

"Axis Sally also told lots of lies, and the GIs laughed at her absurdities while enjoying the nightly renditions of 'Lili Marlene,' the great German song that became the anthem of the Americans as well." Axis Sally was actually broadcast out of Radio Berlin and transmitted to Nazi satellite stations such as the one transmitting out of Rome. The real "Sally" was in fact New Yorker Mildred Gillars, a former coed who'd followed one of her professors to Europe, studying music in France in the late '20s and moving to Berlin by 1934 to be closer to him.

A year after the Nazis came to power, Professor Max Otto Koischewitz was in charge of Radio Berlin, and he quickly established Millie on the air as Axis Sally, spewing out propaganda sprinkled with popular songs of the day. The transmissions continued through the war years. Sally broadcast virulent, stinging messages in English, including "Damn Roosevelt! Damn Churchill. Damn all Jews who made this war possible. I love America, but I do not love Roosevelt and all his kike boyfriends."

She also targeted Allied bomber crews and the American and British ground forces crammed onto the Anzio beachhead, promising that it would become their graveyard. The American ground forces suffered heavy casualties

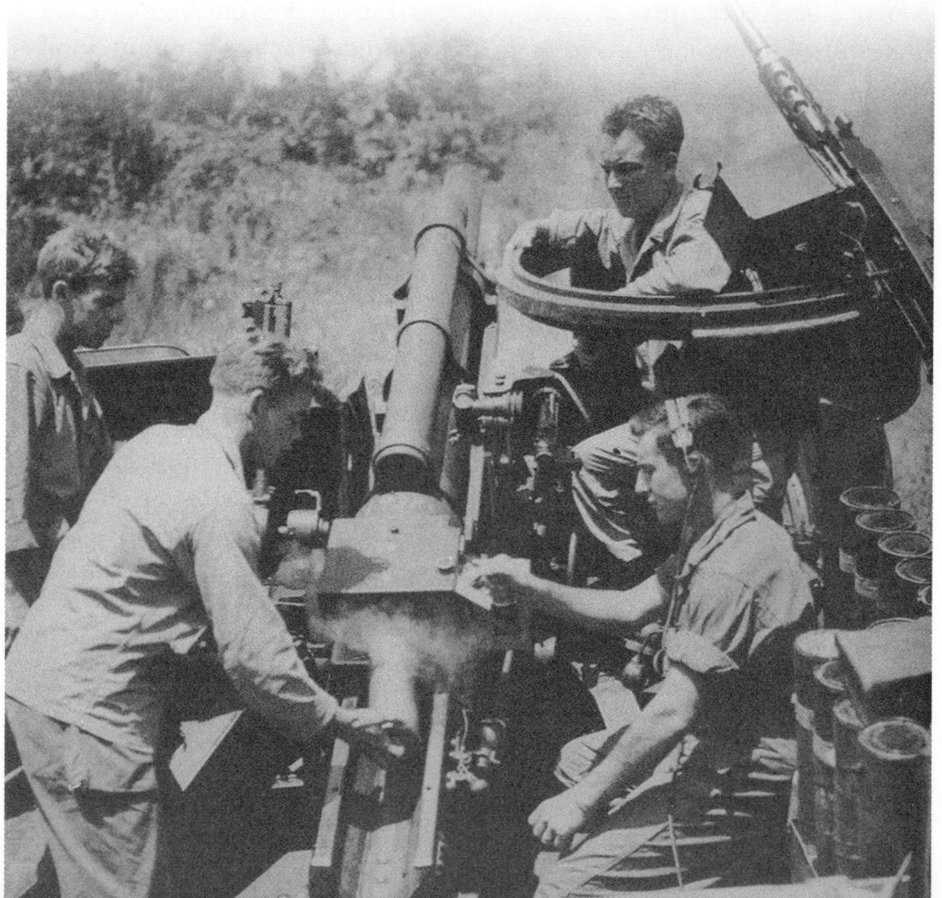

Left: *A 105-mm Howitzer crew from the 5th Army fires on a Nazi overwatch stronghold near the Arno River. Enemy forces, positioned along every mountain pass and river crossing and all avenues of approach, waited for Allied ground forces to maneuver within killing range, then opened up with mortars and machine guns. Taking out those enemy fortifications was crucial to the Allied sweep northward across Italy.*
U.S. Army Photo

at Anzio until reinforcements were called in by May of 1944 and a bust-out was coordinated.

Advancing from Anzio

From Anzio it was on to Rome, but even after the Allies liberated the capital city, there was still plenty of war left on the peninsula. One American wounded in Italy was highly decorated Army Major Lex Barker, who had knocked around Broadway and Hollywood prior to going off to war. (After his discharge in 1945, he returned to Hollywood and worked as an extra on a few films, until he was picked to take over for Johnny Weissmuller as Tarzan in the series based on the books by Edgar Rice Burroughs.)

The Germans retreated quickly to the heavily fortified 150-mile Gothic Line, which spanned the peninsula far north of the Eternal City. The Line was made up of minefields and tank traps and concrete and steel bunkers, where gunners could cut down the Allied forces negotiating the gauntlet below.

Fragmented Nazi units continued to harass the Allied advance, mostly along natural barriers such as mountain ridges scattered along the Apennine Range and swollen rivers, including the Arno and the Po Valley. Mother Nature only made the advance more difficult, with heavy rains in late summer and snow and ice in the winter.

The Italian Campaign would linger to the final days of the war, through April of 1945, with local partisans capturing Benito Mussolini while other Allied units—those that invaded Fortress Europe via the French coast—linked up with the Russians to drive on to Berlin, which continuous bomber attacks were reducing to rubble. The ragtag German forces in Italy finally surrendered on May 2. A frustrated Adolf Hitler admitted that sending reinforcements and valuable munitions to the southern front and to the east depleted his resources against the onslaught from the West, and hastened the demise of his Thousand-Year Reich.

Stars Serve Up Entertainment

As in every WWII campaign, Italy saw intense combat followed by lulls that allowed for a little rest and relaxation before the next skirmish. And as the Allies secured more territory on the Italian peninsula, American and British entertainers made the trek to support the troops. Al Jolson and his pianist and close friend, Harry Akst, first made it to North Africa, then went on to Sicily and skipped over to Italy, performing for large groups of GIs but also seeking out individual soldiers for a little one-to-one comradeship.

Jolson sang all of his standards, including "Brother, Can You Spare a Dime?" and "Give My Regards to Broadway," often within earshot of artillery fire—the rolling thunder that echoed through the mountains and valleys of Italy.

As Burt Lancaster with the 21st Special Services Unit followed the 5th Army across the Med to Italy, he refined his *Stars and Gripes* stage show, often performing close enough to the front lines to hear gunfire and explosions. It was the first form of entertainment for soldiers at Anzio, and then in Rome, before the unit took up permanent roots at Montecatini near Florence. The location quickly became a retreat for thousands of GIs. Other USO shows visiting Italy also stayed at Montecatini, using it as home base as they toured the country. In fact, Lancaster met chorus girl Norma Anderson there when she was called over to replace another performer who became ill. (The two eventually fell in love and got married after returning to the States.)

ABOVE: *Lieutenant General George "Blood and Guts" Patton had a rough exterior but could turn on the charm when the situation required it, such as when meeting Bob Hope and Frances Langford and the rest of their troupe during a stop in Italy.*
U.S. Army Photo

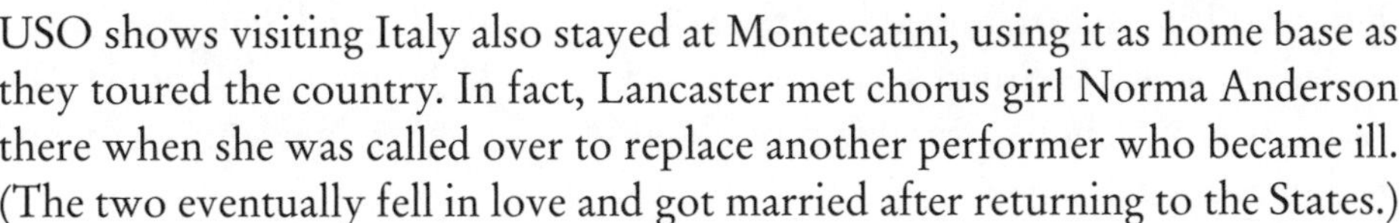

Bob Hope and his troupe got a little too close to the front when they were performing in Palermo for General George Patton's 7th Army. Nazi bombers dropped their payloads perilously close to the entertainers' hotel, and General Patton was concerned enough to order the troupe back to Algiers, safely out of harm's way.

Humphrey Bogart and his feuding wife, Mayo Methot, set aside their differences (he was having an affair with Lauren Bacall at the time) to visit North Africa, Sicily, and Italy from December of 1943 through February on a nonstop tour that could hardly be called a vacation. "Mayo, an old trouper, wrote: 'We slept in blankets on floors, we bounced in jeeps for endless hours over incredibly rough roads, we trudged through mud, and we still did our stuff,'" reported Jeffrey Meyers in the biography, *Bogart: A Life in Hollywood*. "'We wanted to stay in Italy as long as possible because there seemed to be such a terrific need for entertainment there. Usually we were playing to boys who had just left active combat for three or four days' rest.' The tour made Bogart realize how much affection and appreciation he had inspired in his audience, and how closely they identified him with his movie roles. After one show a Chicago gangster, now a soldier in uniform, approached him and discreetly asked for news of the mob."

Bogie would run through some of his better-known movie "tough guy" gangster characters and then conclude the show by saying, "There's nothing I can say, no words to tell you what the folks at home think about you, what a good job you're all doing. All I can say is, good luck and God bless you."

The Italian Campaign on the Silver Screen

In the mid-1930s Mussolini had aspirations of creating a film studio that would rival any of the crown jewels of Hollywood. He even sent his son to Tinseltown to tour the various studios, take notes, make sketches, and return to Rome, to build a sprawling movie complex that would be the envy of Europe.

Cinecitta, or "City of Cinema," spread out over ninety-nine acres near Rome, opened in 1937. It quickly became a glitzy showcase, turning out upper-class portrayals that many Italians considered a slap in the face as they struggled with the turmoil and sacrifices of war. Mussolini wanted his movie empire to rival that of Nazi Germany's, and encouraged budding Italian directors to study from Europe's best. He asked the French government if renowned director Jean Renoir could visit Rome and give a series of lectures on filmmaking. (After finishing his lectures, Renoir returned to France, but his anti-Hitler stance forced him to seek a visa to the United States, where he ended up at RKO Studios in Hollywood. In 1943 he made the movie *This Land Is Mine*, about a French schoolmaster who defies Nazi authority and becomes a local hero.)

"As WWII's battlefield moved to Italy, Cinecitta was bombed by the Allies from above and looted by Nazis on the ground," reported Chris Nashawaty in "Cinema's Paradiso" for *Entertainment Weekly*, in 2002. "By 1944, the studio had stopped film production entirely and was being used as a makeshift refugee camp for Italians fleeing from the south." (Cinecitta was

RIGHT: *The two-headed monster that terrorized Europe—Fascist Italy's Benito Mussolini and Nazi Germany's Adolf Hitler—created massive propaganda machines to pummel the masses at every opportunity. While the Nazis shut down German film studios, purged all Jewish influence, and then churned out pure venom, Il Duce set out to establish a film studio near Rome patterned after and even rivaling anything in Hollywood. It was called Cinecitta, or "City of Cinema," and in fact was used for numerous Hollywood productions after the war.* National Archives Photo

rebuilt after the war and soon some of the biggest Hollywood productions were being filmed there, including *Ben-Hur* and *Cleopatra.*)

During the war years, Italy became the backdrop for several notable films and one great classic: 1945's *The Story of GI Joe*, which relied on correspondent Ernie Pyle's newspaper columns for narration.

Pyle, who was concerned about Hollywood's dramatization of his story, agreed to the project only if he was played by someone who "weighed in the neighborhood of 112 pounds . . . almost anemic." Well-known actor Burgess Meredith got the part. Pyle also didn't want the false ring of a love story added to tug at the heartstrings.

To further add to the film's realism, more than a hundred veterans from the fighting in North Africa and Italy were brought together. "The director—William Wellman—planned to use only these actual combat troops as extras and for all uniformed bit parts," wrote Lee Server in the biography *Robert Mitchum: Baby, I Don't Care*. "'I made actors out of them,' Wellman said, 'and then all the actors had to live with them, drill with them, and learn to be like them.' Actors carried eighty-pound packs all day long and dined on the dreaded K-rations. Wellman was pursuing a physical and psychological realism for *GI Joe*."

Just as important as Burgess Meredith's portrayal of Ernie Pyle was the casting of Robert Mitchum as Lieutenant (later promoted to Captain) Bill Walker. "It was a small part, but Mitchum's one good scene was the emotional and philosophical core of the film," noted Lee Server.

"In a virtual soliloquy, his worn-down lieutenant struggles with little success to find some meaning in all the death and destruction surrounding him, his face a haunted mask of resignation and despair. An intimate and tender scene, its impact increases in retrospect as it serves as Lieutenant Walker's last testament."

Walker was one of the good officers, who cared for his men, who disciplined them as needed, but who was always right there with them in the thick of it.

His death occurs offscreen, but as his body lies on a stretcher outside the aid station, his men solemnly pay their last respects. "The closing sequence then shows Private Dondaro—last seen resentfully digging latrines as punishment for neglect of duty—weeping as he holds his dead captain's hand," wrote Tom Milne in the compilation, *Movies of the Forties*. "Here, at least, we are being 'seduced or manipulated' not cynically but sentimentally."

Movie critic James Agee wrote, "Many things in the film move me to tears . . . and in none of them do I feel that I have been deceived . . . as one usually has to feel about movies."

Tom Milne added, "In fairness to Agee, it must be remembered that in 1945, in the context of Hollywood's insistence on flag-waving and rampant heroism in all war movies, *The Story of GI Joe* came as a breath of honest, clean air with its infantryman's angle on war as a meaningless vista of mud, muddle, and fatigue ending very probably in a wooden cross."

Clyde Jeavons, another writer for *Movies of the Forties*, further stressed about this breakthrough film, "There were no mock heroics, only the hunger, misery, fear, boredom, and weariness of the foot soldiers amidst a confusing nightmare of military maneuvers. The film also dares to show the bodies of dead infantrymen in a low-key finale which was at odds with the euphoria of the time and would account for the wariness with which it was received."

After seeing *GI Joe*, Supreme Commander Dwight D. Eisenhower considered it the greatest war movie he'd ever seen.

Another film about foot soldiers in Italy—the 143rd Infantry Regiment of the 36th Texas Division—that may have been too realistic for civilian audiences was *The Battle of San Pietro*, made by John Huston and released in 1945. This thirty-two-minute documentary followed these soldiers—who had already been bloodied at Salerno and Naples, then on to the horrendous Volturno River crossing—as they assaulted the tiny village of San Pietro at the mouth of the Liri Valley.

Huston recalled in *An Open Book*: "Previous to our first attack I had interviewed, on camera, a number of men who were to take part in the battle.

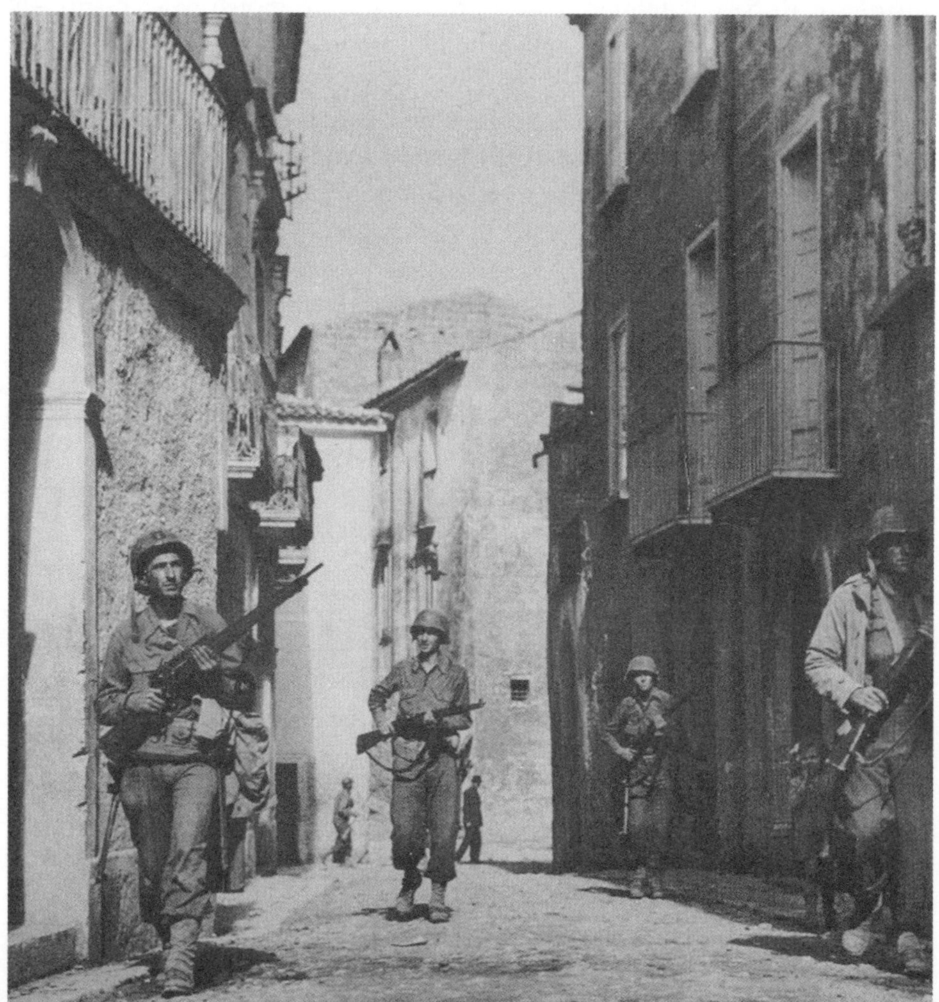

RIGHT: *With the potential for snipers in any window and booby traps in every doorway, American infantrymen proceeded cautiously while cleaning villages occupied by retreating Nazi forces, such as in the village of Caiazzo near the Volturno River.*
U.S. Army Photo

Some of the things they said were quite eloquent: They were fighting for what the future might hold for them, their country and the world. Later you saw these same men dead. I had my cameras so placed that the faces of the dead came right to the lens. In the uncut version I had their living voices speaking over their dead faces about their hopes for the future. Considering the emotional effect it would have on the families of these men, and also how American audiences of the time might react to it, we later decided not to include this material."

Huston's concern that maybe the film crossed into uncharted territory was confirmed when it was screened for senior Army officers. "About three quarters of the way through the picture the [three-star] general got up and left the projection room. It was naturally assumed that he was displeased with what he saw, and it was incumbent upon the rest to show their displeasure also. By the time I got back to my desk, furious complaints had started coming in. The film was classified SECRET and filed away, to ensure that it would not be viewed by enlisted men. The Army argued that the film would be demoralizing to men who were going into combat for the first time."

San Pietro might have been shelved, never to be seen again, if not for the decision of General of the Army George C. Marshall, who saw the film and realized that "this picture should be seen by every American soldier in training. It will not discourage but rather will prepare them for the initial shock of combat."

A few other films set in Italy during the war years included 1944's *Fiddlers Three*, a farcical and far-fetched comedy that follows two soldiers in Rome who time-travel back to ancient times; Roberto Rossellini's *Open City*, released a year after the war ended and featuring resistance fighters in Rome; and *A Walk in the Sun*, based on the novel by Harry Brown, which follows a lone Army platoon at Salerno. *A Walk in the Sun*'s producers had difficulty financing the film and had to scramble for backers. Whether it was known or not, a prominent member of the Las Vegas mob fronted the necessary funds. When filming began, there were a few extra "soldiers" in the platoon, and these reinforcements were a little older and looked a little more sinister than the others. In fact, they were members of the Vegas mob, there to protect their "investment" in the picture!

Dreaming of Being a Movie Star

As a youngster, Sophia Scicolone was teased about being skinny—other kids in Pozzuoli called her *Stuzzicadente,* or toothpick. Because her harbor village had a munitions plant, Allied bombers targeted the area, forcing the villagers to seek shelter in a nearby railway tunnel after the last train to Naples had passed every night.

"The tunnel became the focal point of our lives," she would later tell writer A. E. Hotchner in the book, *Sophia*. "Every night we dragged our mattresses and, in the winter, our blankets, into its pitch-black interior . . . no light, not even a candle, was permitted. No one was allowed near the entrance, where there was some air, because of the possibility that fragments of a bomb, falling in that vicinity, could penetrate . . ."

Eventually, the villagers were forced to evacuate and had the misfortune to make it to Naples, which suffered even worse bombardments. "Naples was the most bombed city in Italy, and when the air raid sirens started wailing it really sounded as if the world were ending." Once again the refugees were uprooted, and they reluctantly returned to the ruins of their hometown and began the tedious process of rebuilding.

"When Pozzuoli's only movie theater reopened, it offered Hollywood movies for the first time. Before the war only drab Italian films had been shown," Sophia remembered. "The Hollywood films took me into a world far removed from the desolate years of my childhood. But it was not the opulence I saw on the screen that overwhelmed me; it was the stars themselves and the roles they played."

She was fascinated by the graceful moves of Fred Astaire and Ginger Rogers, the handsomeness of Clark Gable and Cary Grant, "and above all, Tyrone Power. He was the god of my adolescence. When he appeared in the melodramatic epic *Blood and Sand*, I went to see him twelve times. After I saw Rita Hayworth in *Gilda*, I started to comb my hair the way she wore hers; later I switched to Veronica Lake's hairstyle when one of her pictures captivated me."

As she grew older, her body began to develop . . . and develop a little more, and young Sophia was suddenly a beauty at drama school in Naples. She planned to be a teacher back home but thought maybe she could earn enough from modeling or acting to pay for her schooling. While she was in Naples, though, her drama teacher told her about an American movie being made at the Cinecitta studios in Rome that would require hundreds of extras. Sophia and her mother showed up, and both were selected to appear in the 1951 epic *Quo Vadis*, for which they were paid the enormous sum of 50,000 lire (seventy-six dollars)! But this job led to work in modeling, posing in *fumetti,* or soap opera photos, which would be published in the local newspaper. The pay wasn't terrific, but the exposure led her to Rome's acting community, and she was spotted by movie producer Carlo Ponti, who owned a production company with Dino de Laurentis.

If this were a movie, sixteen-year-old Sophia would then be cast in a blockbuster romantic role and find true love with her leading man. Instead, screen test after screen test turned out disastrously for her. "The cameramen complained that there was no way to photograph me, to make my face attractive, because my nose was too long . . . also, I was too hippy."

Ponti suggested she have plastic surgery on her nose and lose some weight to reduce her posterior, but Sophia insisted she wouldn't change anything about her "look." She continued to get small parts and smaller parts, then bigger ones, and then suddenly, after appearing in 1957's *Boy on a Dolphin*, the world discovered the exotic beauty of the latest Italian bombshell, the poor village girl who had pretended to be the glamorous Veronica Lake or Yvonne DeCarlo or Rita Hayworth, the little "toothpick" who blossomed to become the vivacious Sophia Loren.

"Spooks" of the OSS

"MEN WHO COME TO FIGHT LIVE BADLY, IN PRECARIOUS FASHION, WITH FOOD HARD TO FIND. THEY WILL BE ABSOLUTELY CUT OFF FROM THEIR FAMILIES FOR THE DURATION; THE ENEMY DOES NOT APPLY THE RULES OF WAR TO THEM; THEY CANNOT BE ASSURED ANY PAY; ALL CORRESPONDENCE IS FORBIDDEN."

—*Excerpt from leaflet for French resistance fighters*

BACKGROUND: *An American B-25 bomber completes a mission over Tivoli, Italy, which was a crucial supply depot for the Nazis occupying nearby Rome.* Office of War Information Photo

LONG BEFORE HE BECAME PRESIDENT, FDR WAS INTERESTED in the clandestine world of spooks and shadows, of finding out what the U.S. government's enemies planned to do before they could implement those plans. In 1940 Roosevelt plucked William "Wild Bill" Donovan from New York's legal network to become the government's Coordinator of Information, sending him to London as a liaison and to share espionage efforts with England. (One of the British agents was Ian Fleming, who would later lead a commando raid on Gestapo headquarters in Denmark. The Nazis sanctioned an assassination attempt in retaliation, planting a bomb to eliminate Fleming. Instead, the explosion killed Fleming's wife.)

Eventually the COI became the Office of Strategic Services, or OSS, operating primarily in North Africa and the Mediterranean and from Europe to the Caribbean.

Initially FDR turned to his network of friends for the core of this secret and eclectic group, people he trusted, such as businessman Vincent Astor, publisher Nelson Doubleday, poet Archibald MacLeish, future chef Julia Child, and his own cousin, Kermit Roosevelt. "The famous writer Ernest Hemingway was also utilized by FDR as his personal agent," reported Peter Kross for *WWII History* magazine in July 2003. "Operating from his home in Cuba, Hemingway organized a private band of friends, whom he dubbed the 'Crook Factory,' to conduct espionage operations in the waters off the Cuban coast, looking for German U-boat activity. The Crook Factory proved to be more of a fishing and drinking club than a serious espionage operation, and it was soon closed down."

During the war years, the OSS was involved in numerous secret operations. Actor Sterling Hayden served with an OSS commando unit that was running the German blockade in the Adriatic, clandestinely delivering weapons, ammo, and supplies to Yugoslavian partisans. (When he enlisted in the Marines, Hayden decided to change his name to John Hamilton to avoid the glare of publicity, wishing to be just another recruit at Parris Island. After completing officer training, he was selected for duty with the Office of

Strategic Services.) In Yugoslavia, he worked with Marshal Tito and headed up a group of four hundred partisans operating out of Monopoli.

Hayden was also involved later with the denazification program as Allied forces occupied German territory. He was amazed that "there came squirming into the light millions of anti-Nazis. It was tough, they said, waving handkerchiefs and wringing their hands with joy, to have lived under Hitler. The real anti-Nazis were dead or in exile, or in Auschwitz, [or] Buchenwald."

One of the most important OSS initiatives was providing aid to French resistance fighters, known as the Maquis. They required training in guerrilla tactics, improved weaponry, a steady cash flow, and continued resupply drops. Former French Foreign Legion soldier and, at the time, U.S. Marine Corps officer Peter Ortiz was selected to lead two others behind the lines to link up with the Maquis and coordinate their harassment of Nazi units. Ortiz also assisted in the rescue of any Allied airmen shot down over France, until he was finally captured in 1944. He would sit out the rest of the war as a POW. (After he was liberated and returned to the States, Ortiz served as technical adviser for the movie *13 Rue Madeleine*, starring James Cagney and based on the exploits of Ortiz and his OSS commando team.)

Navy ensign Michael Burke was also assigned to the OSS and was sent to the Med to convince members of the Italian Fleet to switch sides and work for the Allies. By 1944 he too was helping the French resistance groups in the Vosges Mountains. (After he was discharged, Burke worked as a screenwriter in Hollywood, drawing on his experiences for the movie *Cloak and Dagger*, starring Gary Cooper.)

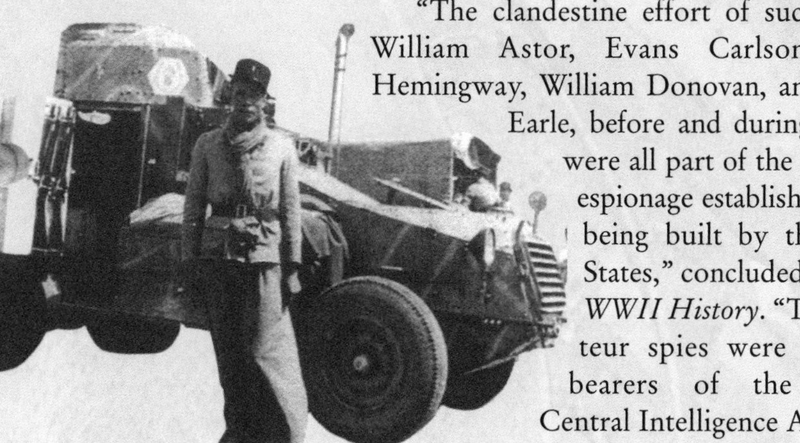

"The clandestine effort of such men as William Astor, Evans Carlson, Ernest Hemingway, William Donovan, and George Earle, before and during the war, were all part of the mammoth espionage establishment then being built by the United States," concluded Kross for *WWII History*. "These amateur spies were the forebearers of the modern Central Intelligence Agency."

Left: *As a commando with the Office of Strategic Services (OSS), actor Sterling Hayden didn't want others to recognize him, so he changed his name to John Hamilton. Operating in the Mediterranean region, he helped deliver guns and ammo to partisan groups in Yugoslavia, and sabotaged German shipping in the Adriatic.*
Marine Corps Photo

Left: *Peter Ortiz was very active with the French resistance effort, helping Allied airmen shot down, training partisan groups such as the Maquis, and calling in resupply drops of food and munitions. He was captured in 1944 and became a POW. (Hollywood spotlighted his war exploits in the movie* 13 Rue Madeleine, *and Ortiz served as technical adviser to the film, which starred James Cagney.)*
National Archives Photo

9. Chasing the Foe Across the Pacific

"OUR SOLDIERS ARE FULLY PREPARED TO REPULSE THIS INSOLENT ATTEMPT. THE JUNGLES WILL RUN RED WITH THE BLOOD OF THE BUTCHERS OF GUADALCANAL."

—Radio Tokyo broadcasting to U.S. soldiers and Marines assaulting New Guinea in December of 1943

EARLY ON IN THE OPENING SALVOS OF THE WAR IN THE Pacific, the Japanese clearly had the upper hand. After severely crippling the U.S. Pacific Fleet at Pearl Harbor, they took out America's air wing in the Philippines, brushed aside an Allied fleet of WWI-era ships at the Java Sea, wiped out the valiant but overmatched garrisons at Guam and Wake Island, and took months but eventually pounded into submission the courageous American and Filipino defenders of Bataan and Corregidor.

The Doolittle Raid on Tokyo was the first whiff of good news—ecstatic, banner headline, shout-it-to-the-world good news—that maybe the Japanese weren't unbeatable after all.

Obviously the United States didn't suddenly flip a switch after the raid and go on the offensive in the Pacific. Strategists in Hawaii were doing their damnedest to track the enemy's movements long before the attack at Pearl. Soon after, Admiral Chester Nimitz formulated the Principle of Calculated Risk, determining that the U.S. Navy would be willing to skirmish with the Japanese armada only if there was a clear shot at inflicting more damage than it sustained. The U.S. could not afford a one-for-one loss of battleships or aircraft carriers. The numbers were weighted too heavily against them to wage a war of attrition.

Nimitz would not have to wait long to see if his Principle had merit, to find out if his battered but not beaten Pacific Fleet could take on the seemingly invincible warships of Imperial Japan. The fate of American freedom would rely on Admiral Nimitz and his untested theory. For a country waging war on two fronts, it was a calculated risk the United States had no option but to pray for.

While Admiral Nimitz arrived in Hawaii and took command after the attack on Pearl Harbor, Army General Douglas MacArthur witnessed firsthand just how unprepared American air, ground, and sea forces were in the days and weeks after December 7.

Ironically, the first major naval battle of the Pacific (not counting the lopsided Allied defeat in the Java Sea) involved exclusively carrier-launched planes. Not even one battleship from either side lobbed any shells at opposing warships in the battle of the Coral Sea, which fell prey to lousy weather, combat exaggerations, guesswork, and good old-fashioned dumb luck. Overeager Japanese pilots reported sinking three American flattops, when in fact only the *Lexington* was lost. The

OPPOSITE: *For the first time in naval warfare history, it was possible for two opposing armadas to do battle, to inflict heavy damage without being in range of the others' big guns. The mighty aircraft carriers, with an arsenal of war planes aboard, could send out waves of dive bombers and torpedo bombers for hundreds of miles, seek and destroy the enemy, and return to re-arm and head out again for more victims.* U.S. Navy Photo

RIGHT: *According to the Japanese, the mighty carrier* Yorktown *was sunk at least every other month of the Pacific Campaign, but such were the exaggerations that led them to believe they truly had a superior advantage on the high seas. Admiral Chester Nimitz's Principle of Calculated Risk ensured that the U.S. fleet not engage the enemy unless there was a clear and decisive opportunity to inflict more damage than was sustained.*
U.S. Navy Photo

Yorktown was damaged but repairable, and the third "carrier" was actually an oil tanker. (In fact, enemy pilots had made so many ridiculous claims that, if the purported damage was all added up, they would have sunk the entire U.S. Pacific Fleet ten times over! This misinformation would cause perplexing strategic problems for Japanese commanders, who erroneously assumed they had a numbers advantage going into every confrontation.)

At Coral Sea the Japanese lost two carriers (one was still afloat but would need months of repairs to return to combat). More importantly, they lost twice as many men as the United States: 1,074 compared to 543. The Pacific's next naval engagement, at Midway, would severely strain the Principle of Calculated Risk and could very well give the victor a decisive advantage in all future naval conflicts. And once again, bad weather and Lady Luck played crucial roles in this devastating and lopsided battle.

One of the carriers at the Battle of Midway was the *Enterprise,* and on board was ordnance specialist Richard Boone, who helped to keep the big guns and anti-aircraft batteries well fed and spitting fire. Later he would return to the States for reclassification as a radio-gunner with Avenger torpedo bombers, then he'd head for the Pacific again. (Once the war was over and Boone was out of the Navy, he used his GI Bill benefits to study acting and debuted on Broadway in 1947 in *Medea.*)

The U.S. Pacific Fleet lost another precious carrier, the mighty *Yorktown,* and a destroyer in the waters near Midway. More importantly,

307 pilots and sailors were killed and 147 planes lost. The Imperial Japanese Navy suffered a much more crippling blow at Midway: 3,500 men killed (many were the same pilots who had bombed Pearl Harbor), 322 planes lost. Japan's biggest toll was in warships: two cruisers, three destroyers, and four mighty carriers lost, taken out of the fight. There was no doubt which side came out on top at Midway, a turning point in the naval campaign in the Pacific. There would continue to be setbacks and losses for the U.S. Fleet, but finally there was some success to build on, and there was no loss in fighting spirit, no wavering in determination.

Dauntless Doug Tastes Early Defeat

With his headquarters in Manila, MacArthur didn't need the steady flow of situation reports he was getting from Washington and Pearl and other garrisons in the region to know that the Japanese were rampaging across the Pacific, the Philippines, and other outposts under attack. He would hear the roar of enemy planes, and he could feel the rumble of their bombs exploding close by, and he could see the destruction and the smoke and the fire and the chaos as Manila was attacked.

After moving his command group to the island fortress of Corregidor, MacArthur felt the frustration of not having viable combat units to go on the offensive. Instead, Dauntless Doug and the Battling Bastards of Bataan and Corregidor—those who weren't already dead, and those who weren't already captured and trying to survive the brutal Death March—braced themselves for the continual bombardment and artillery barrage that would beat them into submission. And when finally he was ordered to withdraw while he still could, MacArthur felt the sting of defeat.

He urged the American and Filipino defenders on Corregidor—known as the Rock—to hold off the enemy attackers for as long as possible, and he promised his Filipino friends he would someday return and liberate their beloved country.

MacArthur and his strategists relocated to Australia and assessed the situation across the region. Japanese forces were threatening every outpost and island chain in the Pacific—from the Hawaiian Islands and the Philippines, the Solomons to the Marianas, and all the many little clusters of dots on the map, like the Marshalls, the Gilberts, and the Carolines. He did not plan to dispatch combat units to repel every challenge, because they simply didn't exist in early '42. Even with a vast mobilization effort, it would be too costly to confront and annihilate the entire Japanese army. Instead, MacArthur planned to secure key landing strips and port facilities and rout the enemy where they posed the greatest threat, but he would ignore other outposts where the enemy was dug in and waiting, allowing them to "wither and die" unopposed.

The goal was to defeat Imperial Japan, not destroy its military down to the last combatant. Still, the battle for the Pacific would be a tough fight, an escalating series of brutal engagements and skirmishes, on the high seas, above the clouds, and down in the swamps, and in the jungles, and on the beaches.

Some described it as opening the gates of hell and plunging into the inferno. Others felt they always had one foot in the grave and the Grim Reaper kept trying to pull them in, but Lady Luck wanted them to stick around a while longer and suffer a little more. Some would say the lucky ones were those who survived the hell in the Pacific. Others would say the lucky ones were those who died, because they wouldn't have to remember it anymore.

ABOVE: *The Japanese were massing in the Solomons, threatening to attack Australia and New Zealand and cut off Allied supply routes in the region. Bougainville became a fierce and pivotal confrontation in the South Pacific, with the newly arrived Marines trying to decimate the entrenched Japanese. For the Marines at Bougainville—"Where the hell is Bougainville?"—it took constant pounding with mortar shells, and inch-by-inch probing of the jungle to fight a tenacious enemy.* Archives Idees et Editions Photo

Serving at Sea and on Land

With Japanese naval marauders lurking out in the vast beyond of the Pacific, prowling silently somewhere in the ocean deep, and launching scout planes aloft to seek out U.S. warships, there were no sanctuaries for American sailors or the soldiers and Marines they transported to battle. Everyone was at risk; everyone faced the same odds against surviving another day and maybe another day after that. Among the many were hundreds from Hollywood and Broadway who served in uniform with the Navy or the Coast Guard.

Former Academy of Dramatic Arts student and Navy radio operator Jason Robards saw the lethality of the Japanese military at just about the same time most Americans were learning about the attack on Pearl Harbor.

Robards was on board the warship *Northampton* as part of the carrier *Enterprise* battle group, more than one hundred miles west of Hawaii, when news of the attack was flashed to all U.S. ships in the Pacific. The next day the group arrived at Pearl, and sailors on board saw the smoldering carnage at Battleship Row. After a quick refueling and replenishing, the battle group set back out to sea for some heavy payback.

Robards would serve in fourteen engagements, including naval skirmishes and troop invasions. During the Battle of Tassafaronga off Guadalcanal, the *Northampton* would be hit by two torpedoes, ripping a massive hole in her port side, causing her to list and then slowly slide into the

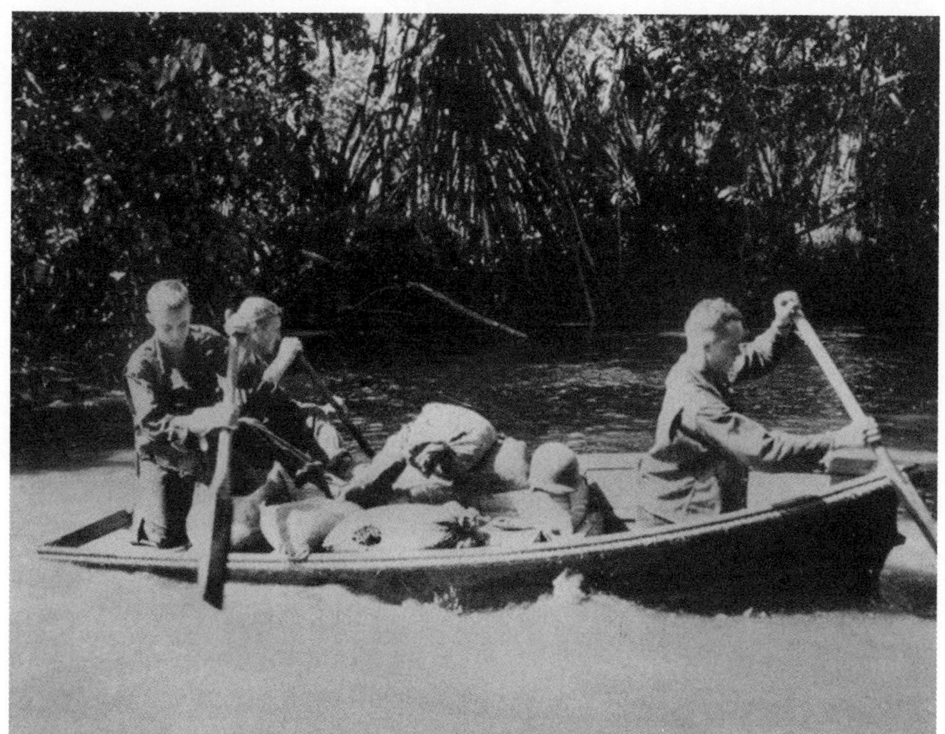

Left: *Some of the jungles of the South Pacific were so dense it was impossible to get through, making air drops and river excursions the only way to resupply the front lines. Here, soldiers of the 32nd Division haul supplies, food, and munitions down the Gira River on Buna, on New Year's Eve in 1942.*
National Archives Photo

deep. Most of the crew, including Robards, survived. (After the war he returned to New York and struggled to make it on Broadway, and went on to a successful film and television career.)

New Yorker Tito Puente played drums with the renowned Machito Afro-Cubans before signing on with the Navy. He saw plenty of action on an aircraft carrier—the USS *Santee*—during three years of engagements with the Japanese. Also on board the *Santee* was big band music arranger Charlie Spivak, who spent time tutoring the eager Puente on swing music styling, rhythm, and syncopation. (Puente would later use his GI Bill to go to Juilliard, and became a fiery salsa musician and bandleader.)

Drama student John Russell was working at Interstate Aircraft in southern California when he enlisted in the Marine Corps. He was eventually assigned to the 2nd Marine Division and sent to Guadalcanal to strengthen the battle lines being held by 1st Division leathernecks. He was wounded and received a battlefield commission for his actions.

Bernard Schwartz had stopped by the Hollywood Canteen prior to shipping out to the Pacific; he was fascinated by the actors and starlets gracing the club that night. He was assigned as a signalman on a submarine tender and then tried life under water as a torpedoman on the sub USS *Dragonette*. (After being discharged, Schwartz would use the GI Bill to attend the Dramatic Workshop in New York. He changed his name to Tony Curtis and soon parlayed his training and good looks into a film career.)

Longtime vaudeville performer Christian "Buddy" Ebsen joined the Coast Guard and was schooled in anti-sub combat strategy, then served as executive officer on the sub-chaser, USS *Pocatello*, in the Pacific. (During lulls he put on variety revues for the men on board. He received his discharge in January of 1946 and headed for the bright lights of Broadway.)

Robert Montgomery had been nominated for Best Actor for his role in *Here Comes Mr. Jordan,* but skipped the 1942 Academy Awards because he was already heavily involved in the war, serving as a naval intelligence officer in a variety of assignments. By 1942 he was in the South Pacific at unheard-of places, such as Noumea and Espiritu Santo, commanding a PT boat. (He would later star with John Wayne in John Ford's *They Were Expendable*, about the valiant daredevils of America's PT boats in the South Pacific.)

Author John Monks, who wrote *Brother Rat* for Broadway and Hollywood, was a Marine captain in the South Pacific.

Martin Robinson had been fascinated with the Old West as a boy, listening to tall tales about his grandfather, a Texas Ranger. He enjoyed Gene Autry movies and imagined himself one day being a singing cowboy. When he turned seventeen he joined the Navy and soon had the perilous job of skippering a landing craft carrying soldiers and Marines to the beaches of South Pacific isles while under hostile fire. (While in the Navy he learned to play guitar and started writing country-and-western songs. After his discharge in Hawaii in 1945, he began to pursue his childhood dream, eventually becoming a popular recording star as Marty Robbins, the singing cowboy.)

Future movie director Robert Altman was only nineteen when he joined the Army Air Corps. As a copilot on a B-24 bomber, he flew forty-six missions in the Pacific.

Below: *They were the "expendables," the swift-moving PT boats with a nasty bite—torpedoes, depth charges, and top-mounted machine guns—dashing in hard to take on anything afloat, launching their deadly "fish" at enemy warships, then turning hard about and scrambling out of danger, while behind them their torpedoes did their damage. Toward the end of the war, John Wayne glorified the exploits of these valiant men in the movie,* They Were Expendable.
National Archives Photo

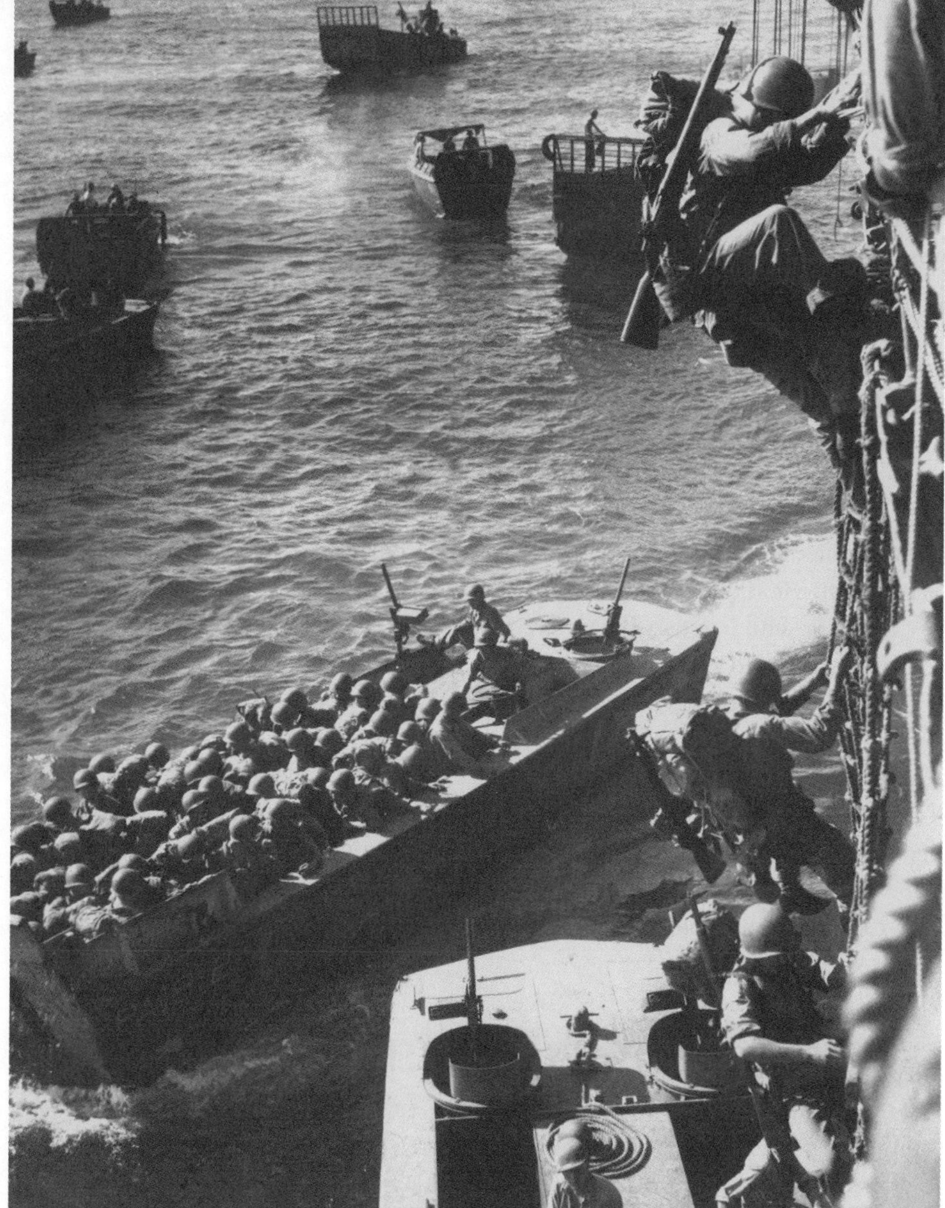

Left: *Amphibious landings were never an easy undertaking for the thousands of soldiers and Marines who jammed themselves onto landing craft that provided little protection from enemy coastal guns, mortars, and machine guns ripping into them. Here the combatants load onto Coast Guard vessels for the perilous journey to Empress Augusta Bay at Bougainville.* U.S. Coast Guard Photo

Lee Van Cleef served in the Navy and saw action on a sub-chaser in the Caribbean, and on a minesweeper in the Black Sea and the China Sea. (It wasn't until after returning home that, because of his sinister look, he was encouraged to consider acting, starting with community theater in New Jersey. Within five years he was cast in numerous films, almost exclusively as the villain.)

Swooping Down from Above

They were the glamour boys, the hotshots of the military, those fighter jockeys who could ruin anyone's day with a burst of fire from their onboard guns. Their brethren in the skies were the rock-steady bomber crews who could withstand a gauntlet of flak from enemy anti-aircraft batteries yet stay on course to deliver five-hundred-pound bombs on target, and the torpedo bomber pilots who could dive down and skim the waves to drop a torpedo on a straight path toward an enemy warship.

Dan Rowan had knocked around Hollywood in 1940, picking up odd jobs but finding nothing to satisfy his acting bug. After war was declared, he joined the Army Air Corps and trained to be a fighter pilot in a Curtiss P-40. He would be assigned to the 49th Fighter Group of the 5th Air Force and deliver a few haymakers on enemy planes. He did get shot down himself but survived and remained in the fight until he was discharged at the end of the war. (He returned to LA and took acting classes, then teamed up with bartender Dick Martin to form a comedy team, performing mostly in nightclubs with frequent successes and setbacks through the years.)

Former child actor Brian Keith grew up fascinated with the Marine Corps and joined the Reserves in 1941. A year later he was activated and on his way to Hawaii, then to the Solomons, where he served as a rear gunner on a Douglas Dauntless dive-bomber, covering its tail against approaching enemy fighters. He and his crew had a few close calls, but obviously Lady Luck was flying with them. (Keith would return to the States and continue flying the rear seats for pilots training on the new Curtiss Helldiver. After the war he drifted back to acting, first in stock theater and radio, then on the newest medium—television—with frequent stints on Broadway and the silver screen.)

Entertainers Endure South Pacific Perils

The glitz and glamour of Hollywood was left behind at the dock as service members with Army Special Services units (and their Air Force and Navy counterparts) loaded onto transport ships already crammed with other soldiers, Marines, and airmen bound for the vast unknown of the Pacific. Their first inkling that maybe it wasn't going to be a pleasure cruise was when they all had to get a series of shots to ward off a host of nasty diseases.

Many stopped off at the island paradise of Hawaii first, for rehearsals in front of appreciative but apprehensive troops staging there, worried about the big fight to come. The performers enjoyed Hawaii's scenery and the serenity, the cuisine, and the culture, and probably some may have thought their assignment in the South Pacific wouldn't be as bad as everyone said it would be.

When it was time to kick off their tour, some made the rest of the journey on another ship across perilous waters; some took air transports to locations they'd never heard of before. None would forget the experience, and no one would mistake Honolulu for Hollandia, or Maui for Makin . . . or heaven for hell.

Left: *"Where the hell am I? And will I ever make it back home again?" wondered thousands of GIs while serving overseas, especially those in the thick of the fighting.*
YANK Magazine Photo

One of the most active troupes in the Pacific was the Army Entertainment Section's Central Pacific Theater, headed up by former British stage actor Maurice Evans. He pulled together an all-star lineup of musicians and actors that would rival any cast in Hollywood or on Broadway. The group put on a musical revue, shortened versions of Shakespeare's *Hamlet* and *MacBeth*, and numerous other shows every year. Some of the members were established professionals, plucked from big bands and radio, movies and theater. Some were still spreading their wings in community theater or college bands and weren't yet discovered, but the experience with Evans would propel many to stardom.

Comic Howard Morris was just a teenager when he took part in the National Youth Administration's radio workshop along with another up-and-comer, comedian Carl Reiner. They would get together again in Hawaii when Evans put together his troupe. (After the war the bond between the two continued when they joined Sid Caesar on his variety show, one of television's earliest classics.)

Werner Klemperer was the son of renowned German conductor Otto

Left: *One of the first rules every recruit learned was "Never volunteer for nothin'!" But when a pretty girl came around and wanted to know how to shoot a really big gun, that rule was quickly forgotten. Corporal George Avram was the lucky recruit who showed actress Dorothy Fay how to brace a light machine gun on her hip and fire it, while she toured the Jungle Training Center in Hawaii.*
Army Signal Corps Photo

Above: *Big-mouthed comedian Joe E. Brown had worked some pretty tough crowds before, but the local natives on Fiji didn't always understand his punch lines. And then there was the time he met up with that tribe of head-hunters, somewhere in the China-Burma-India Campaign.*
YANK Magazine Photo

Klemperer. When the Nazis came to power, the family fled Cologne and made it to Los Angeles, where the senior Klemperer found work with the city's Philharmonic. Following in his father's footsteps, Werner was classically trained on numerous musical instruments. He also studied stagecraft at the Pasadena Playhouse. During WWII he joined the Army as a military policeman, but was reassigned to Special Services and was a natural for Evans's Shakespearean productions. (After the war Werner found work in numerous films, mostly as an aristocratic European. In the mid-'60s he was offered the role that would forever be his alone: Colonel Klink on the popular television show, *Hogan's Heroes.*)

High school comedian and ventriloquist Don Knotts had quite a following around his home of Morgantown, West Virginia, but he couldn't catch a break when he hit the nightclubs and pounded on stage doors in New York. After returning home briefly, he enlisted in the Army and got selected for the Special Services soldier show *Stars and Gripes* in the Pacific; soon he was perfecting his shtick in front of GI audiences and pushing all the right buttons for laughs. (After getting his discharge, he would use his Army connections and stage experience in country bumpkin roles to earn a part as Barney on *The Andy Griffith Show.*)

Peter Lind Hayes had learned his patter as a child doing skits with his mother, vaudeville performer Grace Hayes. As a teenager he was acting on Hollywood film stages during the day and joining his mom for nightclub routines after hours. By 1942 he was in the Army Air Corps and starred, along with a cast of hundreds, in the military revue *Winged Victory*, first on stage and then on film. After the show finished touring, he put together his own variety show, *The Winged Pigeons*. (After he got out in late '45, Hayes teamed up with his wife, actress Mary Healy, and they did a nightclub routine together. They then took their act to television, first with Arthur Godfrey, and then with their own variety show.)

Hundreds of big band musicians ended up in one of the many military bands, enduring marches and patriotic music, but refining their licks and their chops in smaller stage bands. In fact, many of the best military stage groups rivaled their civilian counterparts, with Glenn Miller's leading the parade. Trumpeter Ray Anthony had played with Miller and Jimmy Dorsey, and then joined the Navy and headed up his own band in the South Pacific. Lee Anderson freelanced around the Midwest, playing alto sax on call, and then linked up with the fiery Carlos Molina band when they toured the country. In the Navy Submarine Service band, Anderson arranged the music and took the leadership role. (After getting out of the Navy he kept busy with commercial jingles for radio and television, performed with the Honey-dreamers singing group, and even had a stint as Clarabell the Clown on the children's television show, *Howdy Doody*.)

Ray Bolger was on Broadway, playing Sapiens, the queen's husband in *By Jupiter* (the last collaborative effort of Richard Rodgers and Lorenz Hart), when he left the troupe to join another one, touring the Far East in 1942.

Pianist Claude Thornhill was in constant demand in both New York and LA, writing and arranging big band music, playing on recording sessions with Glenn Miller and Billie Holiday, and performing on Bob Hope's radio show prior to the war. In mid-1939 he made his way back to New York to form his own big band, but three years later he called it quits and signed up with the Navy, playing with Artie Shaw's group. By Christmas of '42, he was playing in Hawaii. He later broke off to form a trio with drummer Jackie Cooper and singer Dennis Day; the group toured nonstop throughout the South Pacific until exhaustion wore them out. (After getting his discharge, Thornhill formed another band, mostly made up of ex-GIs just as eager to play great music.)

Army Sergeant Don Harrison reported for *YANK* on some red-blooded American GIs who actually got along with soldiers from the Land Down Under, all of them together in the South Pacific: "Deep in the jungles of New Guinea, the Aussies and the Yanks are going Broadway with the most unusual flesh show of the global war. It's called 50–50, being composed half of American and half of Australian troops and equally financed by both governments.

"Every soldier of the troupe of 60 has done battle on the fronts of New Guinea. Costumes are tailored to fit the individual and include false busts for the she-males in the chorus."

Noted guitarist Bob Gilchrist headed up a USO camp show that included magician Marty Sunshine, known as Kismet, and Hollywood vocalist Jim Burke. "The group hit New Caledonia, did 60 shows there, then left for Guadalcanal," reported *YANK* magazine. "'When we got to Guadalcanal,' said Gilchrist, 'the men rushed to see if we had any women. Then they wanted to know how the hell three old men like us were going to entertain them. But when we finished our first show, they wanted us to start the whole thing over again.'

"The Canal was their base of operations for five weeks. From there they flew or went by boat to the Russells, to Tolagi, the Floridas, and many other dots in the Pacific. The group did two shows a day. Sometimes bad weather or Jap bombing raids would interrupt. One particular raid came five minutes before the show was ready to go on. That was the raid over Guadalcanal when the Japs lost 94 planes.

"'The Zeroes were falling all over the place,' said Gilchrist, 'like a swarm of bees somebody was swattin' down.' An hour and a half later the GIs scrambled back to their seats and Gilchrist announced: 'The main bout's over. We'll now have the semi-finals.' After Guadalcanal the troupe went to the Fijis. When they arrived in Honolulu they hadn't seen a white woman for five months. 'By that time,' remarked Gilchrist, 'we had a pretty good idea of how the boys out there felt without women.'"

Hollywood Unveils Opening Salvos in the Pacific

The early battles in the Pacific, from Pearl Harbor to the Philippines (including Bataan and Corregidor), to Guam and Wake Island, were bleak for the United States. It would take some time for the U.S. Pacific Fleet to recover from Pearl Harbor and for ground forces to deploy to the region, and until then the Allies would continue to take a beating. Two "last stand" movies fictionalized the lopsided fight for Bataan and Wake Island, with all the good guys perishing at the end. But they hadn't died in vain, at least not if America pulled together for the ultimate victory: the defeat of Imperial Japan (and, oh, by the way, they might as well take care of the two other Axis powers at the same time).

OPPOSITE: *War dogs played a crucial role in the Pacific, sniffing out the enemy, serving as sentries, couriers, tunnel rats, and attack dogs. Hundreds were killed, but they saved many more American lives with their dedicated service, such as these on patrol with the Marine Raiders on Bougainville in late 1943.*
Marine Corps Photo

But there would be hundreds of battles and skirmishes along the way, and Hollywood blurred the truth enough to make combat films palatable for public viewing, and maybe to inspire young men to do their part.

After the filming of 1942's *Wake Island*, Macdonald Carey and several other cast members were so moved, they decided to join the Corps. Carey became an ordnance officer with Air Warning Squadron 3, dispatched to Espiritu Santo, to Bougainville, Mindanao, in the Philippines, and to Manus Island near New Guinea.

"*Destination Tokyo* was the first big-budget submarine movie of World War II combat, and it became a famous and fondly remembered film," wrote Jeanine Basinger in *The World War II Combat Film*. The 1943 movie starred Cary Grant as commander of the submarine *Copperfin*, on a perilous mission to the coastal waters of Japan. His costars in the suspenseful film included Alan Hale, John Garfield, and Dane Clark. Basinger noted, "It lives in people's memories partly because it clearly establishes the dramatic world of the combat submarine. It shows people how men lived in subs and made war. It shows how a submarine works, how it dives, how its machinery functions, and how it defends itself from attack from above as well as from the inevitable crushing danger of the ocean."

Writer Richard Tregaski went ashore with the Marines at Guadalcanal in August of 1942. He documented what he saw in *Guadalcanal Diary*, which was quickly published and snatched up by 20th Century Fox and made into

a movie by late 1943. "As the camera sweeps across the deck [of a troop transport] the universal platoon comes into view," wrote Clayton Koppes and Gregory Black in *Hollywood Goes to War*. "William Bendix plays a taxi driver from Brooklyn who thinks of nothing but his beloved Dodgers; Anthony Quinn represents minority America as Soos Alvarez, who can think of nothing but his girlfriend; Lloyd Nolan is the tough veteran sergeant; Richard Conte is the captain who loves his men; and, Richard Jaekel plays the young soldier facing his first battle."

This cross-section of America became typical of many movies made during the war years—from the bomber crew to the infantry squad, from the men of the silent service on a submarine to the Marines of a recon patrol—always a group of disparate individuals with conflicting views, who set aside their differences to fight as a cohesive whole, and often to die in each other's arms. None of them wants to be where they are, but each understands why he must.

While preparing for the impending battle, and concerned for his untested men, Sergeant Hook Malone (played by gravel-voiced Lloyd Nolan) warns them about the Japs and their underhanded combat skills: "Most of you have never had any experience in the jungle before and the Japs have, plenty. Lemme give you a word of advice . . . keep your mouths shut. Stop yelling your head off. We can beat them at their own game of silence if we try. Keep an eye out for snipers, all the time. If you see a bunch of bananas in a coconut tree . . . shoot 'em down. That makes sense, don't it? And one more thing . . . watch out for booby traps. Don't go around picking up any helmets or anything else the Japs leave layin' around. Just forget about it. You're liable to find it's been rigged up with wirin' and it'll blow right up in your kisser."

The group tries to break the tension with singing, whistling, and dancing an Irish jig, but it all only masks their apprehension.

"Here is the attitude of humor and resignation, the acceptance of the burden the enemy has laid on us," Basinger wrote in *The World War II Combat Film*. "This represents, says the myth, the American pioneer spirit, the ability to go to a strange land and take

RIGHT: *Okay, so not all Marines looked like Hollywood hunks, but when it came to combat, they knew how to get the job done, including this leatherneck on Peleliu, where the fighting was bloody and nasty.*
U.S. Army Photo

hold of it. We show our American character through griping and complaining, but also through singing and praying."

During the filming of *Diary*, Bendix became a "casualty" when he was injured while diving into a foxhole. He wound up with a sprained shoulder, lacerations, and contusions. After a quick trip to the aid station to be bandaged and wrapped tight, he returned to finish the scene.

Later in the movie, during a sustained bombing of the island, his character "Taxi" admits his fears, echoing what thousands of servicemen felt: "I don't know about these other guys but me, well . . . I'm telling you, this thing is over my head. It's gonna take somebody bigger than me to handle it. I ain't much at this praying business, my old lady always took care of that. I don't know as I mean that kind of praying, you know, the Lord's Prayer and things like that. I'm no hero. I'm just a guy. I come out here because somebody had to come. I don't want no medals. I just want to get this thing over with and go back home.

"I'm just like everybody else and I'm tellin' you I don't like it, except maybe I guess there's nothing I can do about it. I can't tell them bombs to hit somewhere else. Like I said before, it's up to somebody bigger than me, bigger than anybody. What I mean is . . . I guess it's up to God. And I'm not kidding when I say I sure hope he knows how I feel . . . I didn't ask to get in this spot. If we get it, sure looks that way now, we're gonna only hope he figures we've done the best we could and lets it go at that. Maybe this is a funny kind of praying to you guys, but it's what I'm thinking and praying."

Maybe it was his unorthodox way of praying, but "Taxi" is one of the lucky few from his squad that makes it through the Guadalcanal campaign.

Another book that quickly became a movie was Robert Trumbull's book *The Raft*, a story of three naval flyboys and the thirty-four days they endured while adrift on a raft in the Pacific after ditching their bomber. Navy Ensign Harold Dixon, who served as the film's technical adviser, endured more than a month in a rubber raft with two other servicemen in the South Pacific.

Although it was released in the middle of the Pacific Campaign, *Behind the Rising Sun* was set in pre-war Japan. It starred Tom Neal as a Westerner who witnesses Tokyo's transgressions against Japan's neighboring countries. This inflammatory film supposedly peeled back the clandestine and despicable treachery of the Japanese in the '30s, fueling the stab-in-the-back feelings Americans felt after the sneak attack at Pearl Harbor. "In mid-1942 Hollywood rushed into release a number of pictures that embellished the stab-in-the-back thesis," continued Koppes and Black. "In *A Prisoner of Japan* the enemy kills 'for no apparent reason other than to satisfy their bloodlust,' said OWI [the Office of War Information]. *Menace of the Rising Sun* described Tokyo's diplomacy as a 'filthy game of treachery' and the Japanese as 'murderers.' *Remember Pearl Harbor* and *Danger in the Pacific* repeated the theme of the 'fiendish, diabolical' enemy. *Pacific Rendezvous* and *Manila Calling* embroidered the espionage theme. It was a rare film that did not employ such terms as 'Japs, beasts, yellow monkeys, nips or slant-eyed rats.'"

In Universal's 1943 film *Gung-Ho,* the Japanese are portrayed as incompetent and inferior to America's fighting men on a dangerous mission led by the dashing Randolph Scott. The movie suggests "that when Japanese troops were placed in an unusual situation they could not adopt new tactics because they are incapable of independent thinking," reviewed Koppes and Black in *Hollywood Goes to War.* "In contrast, when Americans are placed in unusual situations their individualism and common sense will pull them out. It was another version of the inferiority of the Japanese as a race." The Japs' only tactic was to hide in the trees and shoot the GIs in the back, to duck and run, like "yellow-bellied chickens," or to surrender willingly and then kill their unsuspecting American guards. Scott's character cautions his men that they must not let their guard down for even a second, and eventually, despite losing some of their brothers in arms, they do wipe out "those slant-eyed bastards" and accomplish their mission.

Koppes and Black continued: "Then, while being transported out of harm's way on a submarine, Scott talks to his men, both the survivors and the deceased, as he also cautions the American public: 'Our course is clear. It is for us to dedicate ourselves again, our hearts, our minds, our bodies to the task ahead. We must make sure that the peace that follows this holocaust is a just and equitable and conclusive peace. And beyond that to make sure that the social order which we bequeath to our sons and daughters is truly based on the freedom for which these men died.'"

Noted Director Foresees Final Outcome

Navy Commander John Ford was one of Hollywood's most respected movie directors when he was assigned to head up the Field Photographic Branch of the Office of Strategic Services. Much like the Army's First Motion Picture Unit, Ford's group was tasked with documenting the numerous battles in the Pacific and Atlantic, Asia and Europe.

"Most of the people in our outfit—officers and men from Hollywood—were writers, directors, some actors, but mostly technicians, electricians, cutters, sound cutters, negative cutters, positive cutters, carpenters," Ford later reported for the Naval Historical Center.

After pulling together a documentary about the attack on Pearl Harbor, Ford and his crew headed for Midway just prior to the battle there. He later offered his insights on the situation at Midway: "The Marine gunners and our Navy gunners were excellent. I have never seen a greater exhibition of courage and coolness under fire in my life. I was really amazed; I thought that some kids, one or two would get scared, but no. The Marines with me . . . they were kids, I would say from 18 to 22, none of them were older. They were the calmest people I have ever seen. They went popping away with rifles [bolt-action .30-caliber rifles]. None of them were alarmed. I mean, a Japanese bomb would drop through and they would laugh and say, 'My God, that one was close.' I figured then, if these kids are American kids, I mean this war is practically won."

Background: *Near the front lines, medics at an Army aid station in Bologna, Italy, care for the wounded of the 10th Mountain Division and prep them for transport back to a larger field hospital for surgery and recovery.*
Archives Idees et Editions Photo

Wounded Vets Cope

"I don't know what difference it made in me, but I learned one thing: No matter how badly off you think you are, there's always some other guy who's worse off."

—*Comedian and wounded soldier Art Carney*

"Of all the soldiers I met, the GIs were the bravest. Bravery is simple when you're defending your own country or health. But to be bundled off to a foreign country to fight for 'God knows what,' to lose your eyes, arms, legs and return home a cripple . . . that's something quite different."

—*Actress Marlene Dietrich*

COMBAT IS NOT FOR THE FAINT-HEARTED, WHICH IS NOT TO say every soldier and Marine on the front lines was a cold-blooded warrior. They may leave that impression many years later when they're retelling their war stories, with minor embellishments sprinkled in for dramatic effect, but the majority were God-fearing patriots wanting more than anything to survive, yet willing to give their all for their country. Many more have never been willing to share their experiences, locked away forever but never far from their thoughts.

But what many have forgotten is that fear was a constant companion, beside them in the foxhole, lurking behind them in the submarine, pounding on their back during a dangerous bombing mission, screaming in their ear during an enemy artillery barrage. For most it wasn't the fear of death that they worried about, but rather the fear of disfigurement, of returning home less than whole. Some were patched up at the aid station, sewn together, awarded their Purple Heart, and thrown right back into the fight. The lucky ones got sent home with the elusive million-dollar wound—severe enough to get them discharged, hopefully with a monthly disability compensation, but nothing that would cramp their lifestyle—or their love life.

In addition to the doctors and nurses, therapists, and social workers who spent considerable time with each patient, Red Cross and USO volunteers were always around. "Volunteers regularly reached out to soldier-patients in hospitals during the most emotionally vulnerable period of their young lives and visited them at a time when they were separated not only from their families at home, but also from their friends in the military," wrote Frank Coffey in *Always Home: 50 Years of the USO*. "USO workers in hospitals assisted the

Left: *While an Army medic cares for a wounded soldier, local Sicilian villagers watch intently.*
National Archives Photo

wounded in writing letters home and provided much-needed companionship. In addition, USO volunteer artists went to the hospitals, where they would sketch portraits of the wounded GIs to send back to their families."

Entertainers Feel the Sting of Battle

Some were already established stars when they got the call to serve; others hadn't yet made it in show business when the war put their plans on hold; and still more wouldn't even know they were destined for a show business career until many years later. All of these servicemen were wounded or became bedridden from disease, or frostbite, or battle fatigue during the conflict with one of the Axis powers. Some were hurt while in training. Most managed to heal from their injuries or ailments to make it to Hollywood or Broadway after the war.

Desi Arnaz (the Cuban big band leader and husband of comedienne Lucille Ball) was drafted in May of 1943, soon after completing a role in the movie *Bataan*. He was selected to be a bombardier with the Army Air Corps but tore cartilage in his knee while playing sports before he completed his training. He was given a medical profile and attached to the Army Medical Corps at Birmingham Hospital near Los Angeles. While still rehabilitating his knee, he was responsible for putting on shows and entertaining fellow injured GIs. (After getting out in late 1945, he formed the Desilu Production Company with his wife, Lucy; his musical career soared with his own big band; and it all came together when he played Cuban musician Ricky Ricardo on the *I Love Lucy* television show.)

On the *Report to the Nation* radio show, Art Carney impersonated such prominent national and world leaders as FDR, General Dwight D. Eisenhower, Wendell Willkie, and George Marshall. This led to more radio gigs on children's shows, soap operas, thrillers, and others. For *The Man Behind the Gun*, Carney and others spotlighted the very real, very graphic wartime exploits of America's fighting men, "for the purpose of telling you that your boys and their comrades-in-arms are waging our war against Axis aggression." In 1942 the show won a Peabody Award.

Carney was drafted late in the war, joining up with the Keystone Division in mid-1944 after it went ashore at Normandy, France. His brother Ned was with the Navy Reserve in the Dental Corps, while another brother, Fred, was with Army Special Services in Italy. A month later, at St. Lô, the explosion from a German mortar knocked Art down, and he suffered a crippling shrapnel wound to his right thigh.

"'Something whammed me, and I was on the ground with my right leg bent in a funny way,' Art recalled for his biography, written by Michael Seth Starr. "'I moved the foot a little. It was still attached. Nothing hurt much. A piece of shrapnel had ripped into my right thigh, but it just felt numb, and I started hollering 'Medic, Medic!' Never even fired a shot and maybe never wanted to."'

He was first evacuated to England and then returned to the States for nine months of rehabilitation at McGuire General Hospital in Richmond. "Despite being in pain and forced to remain immobile, Carney entertained, and acted as big brother to the other men on the ward," wrote Scott Baron in *They Also Served*.

The injury left Carney with a limp, his right leg shorter than the left. While recuperating he met fellow New Yorker and occupational therapist Rhoda Goldberger, who was tasked with keeping the patients busy.

"Nobody was interested in what I was pushing because Art had them in stitches; he had taken over as a sort of master of ceremonies and he had everybody singing and telling jokes," she recalled for Starr's book. "And he had everybody so happy and busy that they didn't want any part of me. I always wanted to go up there and was delighted to be there because the atmosphere was so great. It was a very happy place to be." (After being discharged, Carney returned to New York and became Jackie Gleason's sidekick on *The Honeymooners* television show, for which he won three Emmy awards.)

Issur Demsky was a drama student at the prestigious Academy of Dramatic Arts in New York, and briefly experienced the bright lights of the Broadway stage in 1941 with a small role in *Spring Again*. It would be the start of a very long acting career, mostly on the big screen, as the dashing leading man with the rugged name to go along with the image—Kirk Douglas. But a year after Pearl Harbor, he put those plans on hold to enlist in the Navy, becoming an ensign on a sub-chaser in the waters off Algiers. In early 1944, while in the Pacific, he was injured when a depth charge exploded prematurely. (Douglas would return to Balboa Hospital in San Diego for five months to heal his internal injuries and for recuperation; then, he was discharged that summer and resumed his acting career.)

Lee Marvin joined the Marines at eighteen and was quickly thrown into the thick of the fighting in the Marianas and the Marshalls. While on a reconnaissance mission on Saipan, his patrol came under fire, and he was nearly killed. He was wounded in the lower back and was lucky not to have been paralyzed. He would spend more than a year at the Chelsea Naval Hospital in Massachusetts before getting his discharge. (He made it to Hollywood and appeared in more than forty movies, winning an Oscar in 1965 for his role as a drunken cowpoke in *Cat Ballou*.)

RIGHT: *Lee Marvin experienced the worst of combat as a Marine in the Pacific, and was nearly killed on Saipan when his patrol encountered the Japanese. He was wounded and almost paralyzed. He would be stabilized and eventually sent to a naval hospital in Massachusetts, where he spent a year in rehab.*
Marine Corps Photo

Future character actor Pat Hingle dropped out of the University of Texas to join the Navy just days after Pearl Harbor. He would serve on the destroyer USS *Marshall*, which ended up being dispatched to the Marshalls.

Versatile comedian Red Skelton was raking in the big bucks through numerous movie roles and his own radio show when he was drafted in early 1944. After basic training and Army Entertainers School (where he probably showed the instructors a thing or two about showmanship), he was assigned to a troop transport in Italy. His job was to keep the servicemen on board occupied during the lengthy journeys at sea and distract them from the constant threat of being torpedoed by a U-boat. Entertaining virtually every day from dawn to way past dark took its toll, and Skelton collapsed from exhaustion. He was shipped back to the States and spent four months on the mend before getting a medical discharge in mid-September of '45. (Skelton returned to Los Angeles to resume his grueling schedule, though at a more manageable pace.)

Al Jolson was on a whirlwind tour of North Africa and Italy when he started to feel ill, but, like a trouper, he continued to perform, knowing that his minor discomforts were nothing compared to what "the boys" on the front lines were experiencing.

What started as malaria quickly turned to pneumonia, and Jolson wound up in a hospital bed with strict orders to cut back, and no more

LEFT: *Red Skelton had his own popular radio show in the early forties and was a frequent headliner at the Hollywood Canteen, here doing his "Guzzler Gin" shtick in April of 1944. At this same time he received his draft notice and continued to do what he did best, but in the Army. Skelton was in such demand that he literally broke down, exhausted. Soon he was back in the States for rehab and recharging of his batteries.*
Associated Press Photo

ABOVE: *Al Jolson was a seasoned song and dance performer when he headed overseas to dazzle the troops in England, here in 1943, and on both sides of the Mediterranean, in North Africa, and Italy. Even after feeling under the weather, the old trouper continued on until pneumonia closed the show and he was confined to a hospital bed, then sent home. After recuperating stateside, Jolson went on another road show—the "Purple Heart Circuit"—stopping at veterans hospitals across the country.* National Archives Photo

overseas tours. Once he regained his strength, Jolson appeared as himself in the 1945 movie *Rhapsody in Blue*, about composer George Gershwin, and then he badgered the USO to send him back out on tour. Reluctantly, the USO arranged for him to perform again, this time making personal appearances on the "Purple Heart Circuit," taking a zigzag trek across the United States, hitting as many hospitals tending to wounded servicemen as he could.

After a hitch with the Navy prior to Pearl Harbor, Jack Warden requested a transfer to the Army, where he served with the 101st Airborne. During a training jump in England, in preparation for the assault on Fortress Europe, his parachute malfunctioned and he shattered his ankle. While going through a year of rehab, he picked up a copy of Clifford Odets's play *Waiting for Lefty*, and it intrigued him enough to check the library cart for others. He had seen some of the soldiers lucky enough to get into Special Services, putting on musicals and serious plays, and contemplated giving it a go as an actor once he got out of the Army. (It took a few years of rejections and odd jobs in New York; then, after joining a repertory group and getting a crash course in theater production, Warden finally broke into television. From there it was on to Hollywood.)

Army platoon sergeant Neville Brand arrived in France with the 83rd Infantry Division a month after D-Day. The Division immediately saw action from France to Luxembourg, and Belgium, and on to Germany. Only a few weeks prior to Germany's surrender, he was injured near the Weser River. Brand was bleeding severely from a gunshot wound to his upper arm, but his unit was taking heavy fire from enemy positions that day and he couldn't be pulled back to safety. "I knew I was dying," Brand later recalled for *TV Guide*. "It was a lovely feeling, like being half loaded!"

A medic eventually got to him and stopped the bleeding, and then got him to an aid station in the rear. Brand was evacuated to a military hospital, where he was stabilized and soon recovered. (After the war, Brand moved to New York. "He found himself associating with actors and writers, and when he heard about the American Theater Wing he enrolled as a student, using his GI Bill entitlements," wrote James E. Wise Jr. and Paul Wilderson III in *Stars in Khaki*. "While at the school he acted in several films for the Army Signal Corps, playing opposite another struggling actor named Charlton Heston.")

Stewart Stern had been born into a movie family—his mother was an actress and his uncle was mogul Adolph Zukor, founder of Paramount Studios. During family vacations to southern California, he often saw his uncle's friends and associates, including Douglas Fairbanks, Mary Pickford, Charlie Chaplin, and Chaplin's wife, Paulette Goddard. With the cinema in his genes, he headed for the University of Iowa to study drama and speech. Soon after graduating, he joined the Army's 106th Infantry Division and endured the freezing cold during the Battle of the Bulge.

During heavy fighting, Stern wound up separated from his unit and was reported as missing. He suffered frostbite from prolonged exposure. Cold ailments were common injuries for servicemen fighting in the northern European conflicts during the winter months. (Stern survived, made it back home, and wound up in New York. He found occasional roles on Broadway, and later headed for Hollywood, where he became an award-winning screenwriter.)

John Russell joined the Marine Corps two months after Pearl Harbor and received his commission nine months later. He was assigned to the 2nd Marine Division, tasked with reinforcing the 1st Marines on Guadalcanal. Like thousands of other servicemen fighting in the South Pacific, Russell came down with malaria and assorted other nasty ailments. He was shipped back to the Navy hospital in San Diego and was informed that he had one of those diseases that would likely come back at the most inopportune times. (It wasn't long after that the good-looking Russell was discovered and signed by Universal/International, going on to star in numerous Westerns and combat films.)

Army Ranger Charles Durning was with the first wave that hit the beach at Normandy and was the only one from his unit to survive an ambush. He was later wounded in Belgium, then patched up in time to participate in the horrific Battle of the Bulge, where he again narrowly escaped death.

His buddies weren't quite so lucky. They were massacred near Malmedy in Belgium. Durning would be injured again during the final push into Germany. "'I was shot in the chest by a bullet, a ricochet,' he recalled. He was once again hospitalized and this last wound ended his war service," wrote Wise and Wilderson in *Stars in Khaki*. "Over the next four years Durning was hospitalized periodically for treatment of both his physical and his psychological wounds. 'The physical injuries heal first,' he noted. 'It's your mind that's hard to heal.'"

(After getting out of the Army, Durning continued with his recovery, taking an acting class to deal with a stuttering problem that he developed during his war experiences. After getting a taste of

BELOW: *The war in Europe was in its final weeks in 1945, and every soldier, on both sides, just wanted to survive to the end. Here an Army medic patches up a U.S. infantryman near the front, in Germany. Future actor Charles Durning was one of the GIs wounded, again, near the closing days of the war.*
U.S. Army Photo

acting, he enrolled at the New York Academy of Dramatic Arts, improved his stagecraft over the next two years, and soon got roles with numerous touring companies. It would take him nearly fifteen years to finally be "discovered" by producer Joe Papp, who would use the versatile Durning in more than thirty productions before he broke into film with a part in *The Sting*, with Robert Redford and fellow WWII veteran Paul Newman.)

Stars Care for the Wounded Warriors

For thousands of wounded service members, it would require months of agonizing physical therapy, subsequent surgeries, and countless hours of soul-searching to piece together whatever they still had left to function with. Some tried to close off the outside world, bitter at what fate had stolen from them—to hell with therapy—and the only "medication" that did any good came in a bottle marked "whiskey" or "gin."

Still a teenager, Sidney Poitier enlisted in the Army and was with the all-black 1267th Medical Detachment at the veterans' facility at Long Island, where he handled service members suffering from psychological injuries, then called shell-shock. (Poitier was discharged in 1944 and took acting lessons with the American Negro Theatre, making his first appearance in *Lysistrata*. Five years after his discharge from the Army, Poitier appeared in *From Whom Cometh My Help*, a documentary produced by the Army Signal Corps. He wound up in Hollywood, earning an Oscar for his acting in *Lilies of the Field* in 1963).

Starlet Joan Fontaine volunteered her services to help the wounded. "I became a nurses' aide, working long shifts at the Good Samaritan Hospital, the Los Angeles County Hospital, and St. John's in Santa Monica. Our training with the Red Cross was thorough and intense," she wrote in her autobiography, *No Bed of Roses*. "We nurses' aides got the bedpans, bed making, bed baths, the serving of meals, pulse and respiration charting to perform. I would come home to Rodeo Drive dazed by the suffering I'd seen that day."

Rick Jason got into acting while stationed near Nashville, when he stopped by the community theater, tried out for a part, and got it. Under the guidance of former stage actor Raymond Johnson, the young soldier was encouraged to make his way to New York and use his GI Bill benefits to enroll at the American Academy of Dramatic Arts. At the close of 1944, Jason was transferred to the convalescent hospital in upstate New York for a unique rehabilitation program for combat servicemen.

"My service record showed that I'd had some experience at horseback riding," Jason recalled in his book, *Scrapbooks of My Mind*. "The post at Plattsburg boasted a large stable, so twenty-two horses were rounded up, shod, and shipped in a boxcar to us. I and three other soldiers were selected to gentle down these animals. We were given two weeks to get everything ready before the first influx of patients, and we spent our share of time getting bucked off and landing on our asses."

The approach was to get the patients in the saddle and get them to care again—first for the horses, then for themselves—and to build up their confidence so they could eventually return to civilian life.

Cheering Up the Boys

Performers on tour, whether stateside or overseas, frequently stopped by hospital wards and aid stations in the field to visit with the wounded, maybe give an abbreviated version of their stage show, and talk with the GIs one-on-one.

"You had to understand that the hospitalized ones wanted no sympathy. If you gave it to them, they'd roll over in bed and ignore you," recalled Bob Hope in *Have Tux, Will Travel*. "So I'd walk into a hospital and if there were a lot of guys in traction I'd say, 'Okay fellas, don't get up.' Then I'd walk into the next ward and say in a loud tone, 'All right, let's get the dice and get started.'"

Frances Langford shared her remembrances from her syndicated column "Purple Heart Diary" with wounded veterans as she toured hospitals throughout the country in 1944.

Leading actor Humphrey Bogart visited wounded GIs at both overseas and stateside hospitals, and formed a special bond with any who played chess. He kept in touch with them and played chess via long distance, letting the guys know they weren't forgotten.

James Cagney was one of the biggest cheerleaders for the troops, and like Bogie, he nurtured a personal bond with them, visiting the patients in hospital wards, drawing pencil and charcoal caricatures on their casts or any available paper. After talking with the individual soldiers and Marines, sailors

LEFT: *Bob Hope and his many longtime sidekicks—including Jerry Colonna, Frances Langford, and Bing Crosby—visited wounded GIs everywhere they went, shown here celebrating with a little Christmas cheer.*
U.S. Navy Photo

and airmen, Cagney would send personal notes to their loved ones or call their family members with a kind word or an assuring message.

Hollywood "hunk" John Wayne "worked from dawn till midnight and past, visiting every hospital he could find, trying his best to meet every wounded man in them," reported Mike Tomkies in *Duke: The Story of John Wayne*. And, typical of the Duke, he did it without fanfare, because it was the right thing to do, not because it would look good in the papers the next day.

One of the luckiest servicemen during the war years was PFC John Farnsworth, who spent three years in the Pacific and was sent home with malaria. When movie star Ginger Rogers planned a dream party for one lucky GI, PFC Farnsworth got picked . . . earning him the envy of every serviceman around the world. Rogers invited starlets Jinx Falkenburg, Barbara Hale, Chili Williams, Lynne Baggett, Dolores Moran, and Gloria DeHaven over to her home in Beverly Hills to help her treat the twenty-two-year-old soldier like he was king for a day.

Hundreds of other wounded servicemen returned to the Hollywood Canteen "confined to wheelchairs or walking on crutches. Bette Davis put together a thoughtful primer to help the volunteers deal sensitively with these men. 'Forget the wounds, remember the man,' she instructed. 'Don't be over-solicitous, nor too controlled to the point of indifference. Learn to use the word 'prosthetics' instead of 'artificial limbs.' Never say, 'It could have been worse.' And when he talks about his war experience, listen, don't ask for more details than he wants to give," wrote James Spada in the Davis biography, *More Than a Woman*.

Hollywood legend Mary Pickford generously opened her Hollywood estate, Pickfair, to wounded servicemen rehabilitating at local hospitals. Her annual lawn parties and Christmas galas attracted many of Tinseltown's luminaries, including singer Dinah Shore and her husband, actor Buddy Rogers, himself serving in the Navy.

Hollywood stars and starlets who visited the military hospitals had the difficult task of busting down those invisible walls, of dishing out a little TLC to patients who often just wanted to be left alone. For many entertainers visiting the wards, seeing those wounded servicemen—many of them still teenagers—was an emotional roller coaster. They were expected to sing and dance and tell jokes and look pretty and smile and fight back the tears, because the last thing any of those American heroes wanted to see was pity. Some stars couldn't deal with it.

"A young woman singer with the USO, on a visit to an Army hospital in Italy, was asked by a wounded soldier to sing 'Abide with Me.' When she began to sing, he abruptly stopped her, and said he did not want her to perform it then but later, at his funeral," reported Frank Coffey in *Always Home*. "Hiding her shock, she tried to joke him out of his morbid prediction, to no avail. A few days later, the soldier, barely into manhood, died; the equally young singer granted his wish."

On one hospital ward, another singer found herself unable to make it through a song she'd sung hundreds of times before. "Finally it came time for Frances Langford to sing. The men asked for 'As Time Goes By.' She got through eight bars and was into the bridge, when a boy with a head wound began to cry. She stopped, and then went on, but her voice wouldn't work anymore, and she finished the song whispering and then she walked out, so no one could see her, and broke down. The ward was quiet and no one applauded," reported John Steinbeck in *Once There Was a War*.

Even that tough old comic, Bob Hope, who'd been to every war front and survived more than quite a few close calls, sometimes had difficulty visiting the boys in the hospitals: "It ought to be clear by now that I'm a softie about such things. My feeling about these matters was underscored when I talked with a boy [who] was badly injured. He was very weak and they were giving him a transfusion," Hope remembered in his book, *Have Tux, Will Travel*. "Walking up to his bed, I said, 'I see they're giving you a little pick me up?'

"His eyes went to the transfusion tube and he gasped, 'It's only raspberry soda, but it feels pretty good.'

"Two hours later a doctor walked up to me in the officers' club. 'Remember that boy who was joking with you?' he asked. 'He just died.'

"I thought about how, in his last moments, he'd grinned and tried to say something light. I couldn't stand it. I had to go outside and pull myself together."

When Woody Herman took his big band on the road, they visited the Percy Jones Hospital in Battle Creek, Michigan, which handled a large number of amputees and nerve injuries. One of those patients was Robert Coate, an Army medic, himself badly injured during the European Campaign. "It [was] a staggering sight to go into a hospital and see only young men, most of whom are either crippled or have lost limbs. About the time I was finally able to move around, Woody Herman's band came to play," Coate recalled for Joan Swallow Reiter in *The Swing Era: 1940–41*.

"Herman played in an auditorium where all of us patients sat. The curtain parted and there was the Herman Herd! They sounded marvelous, great, out of this world. But after about four or five numbers, Herman said, 'I'm very sorry, we have to terminate the program,' and the curtain closed.

"All of Herman's band were just numbly moving around, packing their instruments. I found my man [a friend of Coate's father who was in the band] and asked him what had happened. 'You can't imagine what it's like,' he said. 'From where we were sitting on that stage, we could see two thousand young guys, all without legs and arms.' And he said, 'I don't know how we played even four numbers.'"

When she competed in the Miss America Pageant at Atlantic City, Bess Myerson and the other contestants were sent to the Thomas F. England General Hospital (the former Traymore and Chalfont Haddon Hall hotels), where wounded veterans were being treated. At the time there were nearly five thousand patients at the facility. The girls promenaded on a stage in their swimsuits. Myerson recalled for Susan Dworkin in the book, *Miss America 1945*: "From our vantage point onstage in the lighted hall, we could clearly see the men. On stretchers. In wheelchairs. With nurses standing among them like white candles. We were in the biggest amputee hospital in the world. When we were asked to stay the afternoon and visit the boys from our home states, some girls demurred. They said they needed to rehearse. Or rest. Any excuse not to remain in that sad place. It was not a simple thing to sit down on the beds to talk to those veterans. To see where the sheet dropped, where the leg ended. To reach out to shake a hand and find a hook." (Myerson would go on to win the Miss America title, becoming the first Jewish contestant to wear the crown. She immediately became the sweetheart of the Jewish War Veterans.)

One of the other pageant contestants took the experience even harder. "'They told me there was a young man in the hospital who was a quadruple amputee,' Jeni Freeland recounted. 'He was from Florida and they wanted to take my picture with him. It would really thrill him, they said. So I said 'Okay.' And when I saw him, I was just devastated. He was such a darling blond curly-headed boy. And I was just . . . just overcome . . . it was all I could do to hold back the tears. Whoever was with me, this officer said, 'Turn around and smile at him and don't you dare cry.' So I did. But as soon as we were out of sight, I broke down and sobbed. It was the first time I'd ever seen anything like that."

Up-and-coming MGM starlet Esther Williams liked to pull soldiers on stage and have a jitterbug contest wherever she went. She also made it a point to stay overnight near military hospitals that had swimming pools so she could swim with the boys the next morning. (She had been a top American swimmer in the late '30s, and missed making the U.S. Olympic team only after the 1940 Games were cancelled due to the war in Europe.)

"At Forest Glen, just outside of Washington, D.C., it was different. It seemed more subdued. I

RIGHT: *When the studio brass at MGM strongly encouraged swimming sensation and budding starlet Esther Williams to put together some kind of routine and go out on the road to entertain the troops, she was a little apprehensive. She worked with the wardrobe department and a dance coach and soon she was visiting training facilities, such as the Army Air Corps aviation base in Merced, California, hosting jitterbug contests, pulling reluctant GIs up on the stage or out on the dance floor, twirling and flirting, and flashing a little leg and a lotta smiles.*
Army Signal Corps Photo

got to the pool early, swam a few laps and waited for my new teammates to arrive. As I sat on the steps of the pool, I saw the same boys who danced with me the night before being wheeled to the edge of the pool. Some had no legs, others had one arm. Others had just stumps," she recalled in *The Million Dollar Mermaid*, written with Digby Diehl. "My heart broke. No one had told me that this was a hospital for amputees. Tears welled up in my eyes. The last thing I wanted to do was to embarrass them or hurt their self-esteem. They'd get quite enough of that without me." Reluctantly, Williams agreed to "race" the guys. "I let a whole bunch of them touch the end of the pool before I did. The win belonged to them. They deserved the taste of victory. I hugged all the swimmers and laughed with them. It was such good medicine, not just for them, but for me too."

Hollywood and Broadway Tell the Story

With thousands of wounded and disabled servicemen returning from the war zones, with thousands more dealing with psychological wounds that were just as debilitating, and with their loved ones and friends coping with their difficult transition to some semblance of normalcy, Hollywood turned its attention to this emotionally charged issue.

"World War II-era filmmakers typically went beyond treating permanent injuries as simple badges of honor and began looking at the new lives the veterans would be leading," reported Marty Norden in *VFW* magazine, April 2003. "The best known and loved of these films remains *The Best Years of Our Lives*. It broke ground in a number of ways. Not only was its director, William Wyler, a disabled WWII veteran, but he took the unprecedented step of casting a severely disabled veteran—Harold Russell, who lost both hands in a demolition accident—in a pivotal role."

As a soldier, Russell had been instructing demolitions trainees at Camp Mackall in North Carolina when a defective fuse he was handling sparked a TNT charge. The explosion mangled both hands, and they had to be amputated. He was fitted with hooks and spent months struggling to do the simplest tasks. Russell was then featured in the War Department documentary *Diary of a Sergeant*, concerning a soldier dealing with both the physical and emotional hurdles of learning to use prosthetics. MGM mogul Sam Goldwyn saw the film and cast Russell for the role of Homer Parrish in *Best Years*.

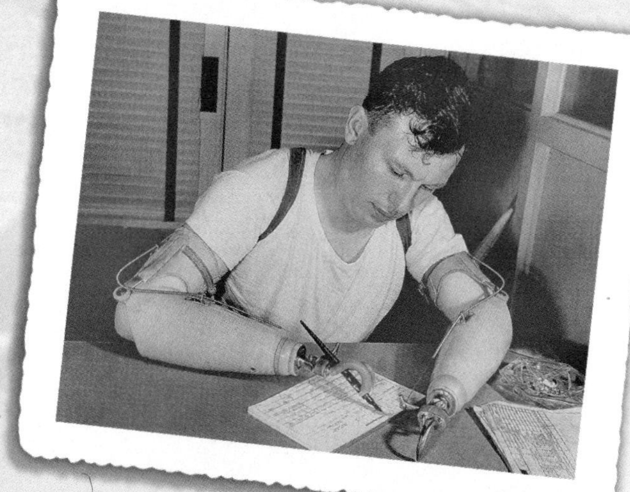

BELOW: *When an explosive charge blew up in his hands, Army Sergeant Harold Russell was left with two bloody stumps and endless months of rehabilitation and uncertainty if he would ever be able to function in the civilian workplace. He was fitted with mechanical hands, then had to learn how to use them. Simple daily routines such as buttoning his shirt, brushing his teeth and tying his shoes suddenly seemed insurmountable, but over time, with continual practice he was able to master the prosthetics. The Veterans Administration produced a short documentary on his rehab, and from that he was "discovered" by Hollywood director William Wyler and starred in the movie* The Best Years of Our Lives, *for which Russell received a Best Supporting Oscar, and a second statuette, for inspiring other disabled veterans.*

Army Signal Corps Photo

"Compared with the other actors, like Dana Andrews and Frederic March, he doesn't have the polish, but there's something really sweet about him," recalled actor Anthony LaPaglia for *Entertainment Weekly* in 2002. "His awkwardness fits the film. When he breaks the windows with his hooks because a group of kids is staring at him, that's one of the all-time great scenes."

The film won the 1947 Oscar for Best Picture, Wyler was selected Best Director, and Frederic March won for Best Actor. The film also won Oscars for screenplay, editing, and music. But what was most extraordinary was the recognition Russell received for his portrayal of a physically challenged veteran. This war hero, with no previous acting experience, who was not dwelling on what he lost, but was just trying to deal with "whatever I have left," won the Oscar for Best Supporting Actor and a second one "for bringing aid and comfort to disabled veterans through the medium of motion pictures."

RKO Studios star Robert Ryan didn't have to go far for his military hitch as a drill instructor with the Marines at Camp Pendleton in California. He trained teenagers and young men to fight for their lives, then saw them ship out to the Pacific, knowing some of them wouldn't be coming back. The hardest thing was to see the wounded Marines returning home, busted up, some of them blind or paralyzed. The healthy ones were still overseas, for the duration. It began to wear on him, and soon Ryan became a pacifist. At about this same time he discovered author Richard Brooks's novel, *The Brick Foxhole*, about combat veterans attempting to cope with civilian life. He even contacted Brooks, wanting to be cast as the lead character if the book ever became a movie. (After getting out in late '45, Ryan returned to RKO to resume his lengthy string of acting roles. A year later, *The Brick Foxhole* was in fact made into a movie, retitled *Crossfire*, with Ryan getting his wish to be cast as the lead. The role earned him an Academy Award nomination.)

Montgomery Clift took on Lillian Hellman's stage play, *The Searching Wind*, portraying Samuel Hazen, a wounded soldier returning home and learning that his family embraces fascist views. *Vogue* magazine wrote about his portrayal: "Montgomery Clift gives the best performance of the season in *The Searching Wind*, Lillian Hellman's controversial play. As the wounded corporal bitter at the appeasing fumblings that have caused him to fight, Clift plays with throbbing self-control and tension of nerves."

A year later Clift accepted a role in *Foxhole in the Parlor*—a play about a former musician who joins the Army but can't handle the intensity of combat and returns home. Even though he received rave reviews for his portrayal of the troubled GI, Monty couldn't save the production, which closed after a six-week run.

Respected Broadway and Hollywood actor Louis Hayward joined the Marines in mid-1942 and was dispatched to New Zealand as a photo officer.

With camera crew in tow, his task was to film wounded Marines during their recovery. Many local villagers had taken in these valiant war heroes, and their rehabilitation included typical farm work, such as shearing sheep, milking cows, tending to crops, and pitching hay. Marine officials felt this type of therapy was more beneficial to the servicemen than staying in hospitals. In addition to giving them a daily "mission" or purpose, the hard work strengthened them physically and mentally and helped them prepare for readjusting to civilian life when they got back home. (Hayward also led a film crew at one of the most harrowing battles of the Pacific, on the island of Tarawa.)

One of the most controversial documentaries about psychologically disabled veterans, this one produced by the Army, was *Let There Be Light*, filmed at Long Island's Mason General Hospital. The movie was completed in 1946 but was suppressed for thirty-five years after it was shown to Pentagon brass.

"'They told me they wanted a film to show to industry, to prove that nervous and emotional veterans were not lunatics. At that time these men just weren't getting jobs. Our purpose was to help them,'" stated John Huston in the biography *John Huston: King Rebel* by William F. Nolan. "It was necessary to obtain footage of actual interviews and psychiatric treatment at the hospital. Huston set up several hidden cameras to record the emotionally disturbed veterans as they discussed their problems."

Huston saw great merit in the film—"this was the most joyous, hopeful thing I ever had a hand in"—and was dismayed when the War Department squelched it.

"They said it violated the patients' privacy, even though all the men filmed had signed releases," Huston explained in an interview with Joseph Persico. "I think the Army was concerned about not destroying the warrior myth. Only a few weaklings were supposed to break under the experience of war. The others were to come out standing proud and tall." (In 1947 a sanitized version featuring actors instead of true servicemen was filmed and released as *Shades of Gray*, a hollow facsimile of the gritty, unglossed original.)

In 1945's *Thrill of a Romance*, Van Johnson played a wounded war hero, Major Thomas Milvaine, with bathing beauty Esther Williams as a local swimming instructor he falls in love with. "*Thrill of a Romance* was a hit, largely because audiences really responded to the chemistry between the two of us," Williams remembered in *The Million Dollar Mermaid*. "Van and I matched—it looked like we belonged together as a couple. He was as much the all-American boy as I was the all-American girl. As World War II drew to a close, we also became icons, in a way, symbolizing the virtues that people loved best about America. Van represented all the young men who had gone off to war for their country, and I represented the girls they were fighting to come home to."

Five years after the war ended, Marlon Brando was cast in his first film role, as a wheelchair veteran in *The Men*. To capture the authenticity of his character, Brando prepared for the role by confining himself to a wheelchair and living with paraplegics at a local Army hospital. After Brando had had time to bond with the veterans, a group of them went down to a local bar for something with a little more kick than just coffee or sodas. Like a caravan, they negotiated curbs and traffic, ignoring the stares from children and the averted glances from other adults passing by.

But when a Salvation Army matron approached, they couldn't ignore her. She seemed disturbed at their condition and lifted up her outstretched arms, looked to the heavens, and shouted out what seemed like an impossible plea: "Oh Lord, grant that these men may be able to walk again!"

And like a miracle from God, Marlon Brando suddenly stood up from his wheelchair—and scared the holy crap out of her!

Hollywood Rallies the Country

Background: *A bevy of Hollywood beauties were enormously popular among GIs during the war, with studios sending out thousands of cheesecake photos every month. Betty Grable and Rita Hayworth, shown here, became official mascots for countless military units around the world.*
Office of War Information Photo

"The practical value of history is to throw the film of the past through the material projector of the present onto the screen of the future."

—*B. H. Liddell Hart,* Thoughts on War, *1944*

"It seemed to me that the film as the most widely disseminated medium should concern itself not only with entertainment—its basic function—but from time to time with the problems of society, the threats to liberty, the miseries heaped upon the minds and bodies of fellow human beings."

—*Edward G. Robinson in* All My Yesterdays

THEY CALLED IT THE GOLDEN AGE OF HOLLYWOOD, WHEN some of the greatest movies of all time were produced. Such classics as *Gone with the Wind* (1939), *Citizen Kane* (1941), and *The Wizard of Oz* (also in 1939) captivated audiences by tugging at all the emotions—laughter and sadness, anger and fear, exhaustion and exhilaration, hope and hopelessness.

But by the mid-1930s, Nazi Germany and Imperial Japan were on a war footing, with clear intentions to occupy and exploit all neighboring countries, then extend their "sphere of influence" further and further until their poison contaminated the entire world. And they had the military muscle to destroy any country that dared to offer up any kind of resistance. This turmoil, especially in Europe, would change the dynamics of filmmaking and the direction Tinseltown would take by the late '30s.

"In 1939 the Nazi menace, long smoldering, erupted . . . [and] one commercial result of which was the loss of many overseas markets," wrote John Douglas Eames in *The Paramount Story*. "Europe had about twice as many cinemas as America, and revenue from them had often made the difference between a movie's financial success and failure." Specifically, "Hitler's invasion of Austria and Czechoslovakia had caused a significant drop in the revenues for Hollywood films from those countries," wrote John Russell Taylor in *Hollywood 1940s*. "The outbreak of war [in September of 1939] made the whole commercial scene in Europe more impenetrable still."

Hollywood profits from Europe would virtually dry up with the Nazi occupation of Poland and France, then North Africa, and the bombing of England, all before the United States got involved in the war.

This loss of overseas profits was a direct result of the Nazi crackdown of literary and cinematic works they deemed subversive: anything that had a pro-Jewish slant or ran counter to the Aryan super race myth they were trying to disseminate to the masses.

Exiles Look for Payback

The Nazi blacklisting forced hundreds of authors, actors, actresses, musicians, directors, artists, and craftsmen to flee to neighboring countries and to flee again when those too fell under Nazi occupation. Hollywood became a safe haven for hundreds of Europe's creative talents.

Many of them arrived with only what they could carry, but all of them brought a heavy concern for family and friends left behind, and they despised the Nazis who had destroyed their homeland's literary, artistic, and cinematic treasures or confiscated them as war booty for the Fatherland. They also heard the rumors that Jews were being rounded up and sent to "detention" camps somewhere to the East. (The Nazis had in fact established numerous concentration camps and five massive extermination camps, with the sole mission to eliminate the Jewish race from all Nazi-occupied territories.)

Many of those European exiles who made it to Hollywood combined that anger with their creative talents to produce movies that screamed at the world to take notice of what was going on in Europe. Renowned French filmmaker Jean Renoir created 1937's *La Grand Illusion*, an anti-war story about a World War I POW camp for German soldiers. Renoir had reluctantly given up his position as one of France's leading directors when the Nazis overran his country and shuttered French film studios. Many of Renoir's associates in the film industry back home thought they could wait out the harassment. They would quickly regret their decision to stand fast.

Berlin cabaret actress Marlene Dietrich may have been the most vocal instigator of anti-Nazi rhetoric, selecting film roles in Hollywood with a pointed message, when she wasn't traveling to the front lines of Europe, thumbing her nose at any death threats and bounties the Nazis tossed her way.

Supporting the Allies

While America tried to stay out of the war, the country did bolster its Allies with ships, planes, and personnel, food and fuel, supplies, and munitions to sustain their fight with the Axis powers. President Roosevelt appealed to Congress and spoke to the American people in his radio-delivered Fireside Chats: "Never before . . . has our American civilization been in such danger as now," FDR cautioned, referring to the agreement among the three Axis powers—Germany, Japan, and Italy—that if the United States made any attempt to block their expansion efforts, such as aiding Britain, China, or Russia, they would turn their combined attention (and potent arsenals) on America, its vast industrial centers, and its natural resources.

"If Great Britain goes down, all of us in the Americas would be living at the point of a gun. The vast resources and wealth of this hemisphere constitute the most tempting loot in the world." In defiance of any threat from the Axis powers, Roosevelt wanted to increase the delivery of ships, planes, and war goods to the Allies. "We must be the great arsenal of democracy," he commanded.

Britain, Australia, and New Zealand were longtime allies of America, and they felt the crush as Germany and Japan threatened to destroy them. Many films coming out of England conveyed underlying messages to the Yanks, but British movie director Alfred Hitchcock wasn't so subtle in the 1940 thriller, *Foreign Correspondent,* in which a U.S. news reporter (played by Joel McCrea) warns, "It's as if the lights were all out everywhere, except in America." He urges the United States to build an arsenal of guns, and battleships and planes to protect those lights. "Hello, America. Hang on to your lights. They're the only lights left in the world."

At the same time, the United States was lending support to Russia and China, and FDR asked Hollywood to jump on the bandwagon and do what they did best for these new allies—using film to get the message out.

Old movie scripts were dusted off and reworked, tossing in Russian names like Ivan and Dmitri, Sasha and Natalie—nothing too long or confusing—or the films were given a Chinese locale, such as Hong Kong or Shanghai, Peking or Singapore, and everyone was dressed in silk pajamas and coolie hats, so no one would ever know it was really filmed on the back lot at MGM or Paramount or down in Chinatown or Little Odessa.

Warner Brothers secured the rights to Ambassador Joseph Davies's memoirs of his duty in Moscow from 1936 to '38. The film, titled *Mission to Moscow* and released in 1943, had U.S. official cooperation stamped all over it, "to help bolster an uneasy alliance, [but] the picture airbrushed out most of the nasty features of Stalin's regime," noted Clayton Koppes and Gregory Black in *Hollywood Goes to War*. "Upon reflection no one believed *Mission to Moscow* rendered Soviet reality accurately. The film became the most notorious example of propaganda in the guise of entertainment ever produced by Hollywood."

Despite the miscalculation of *Mission*, other studios continued to attempt Russian-themed projects, including *Three Russian Girls* from United Artists, Columbia's *Boy from Stalingrad*, and MGM's musical revue *Song of Russia*, to name a few—and not necessarily the best of the bunch.

China fared little better in the hands of Hollywood filmmakers. In fact, *Dragon Seed* became another embarrassing fiasco, despite a rewrite that was signed off on by the Office of War Information, which praised the film during a private screening, saying it "emerges as a document not only of the fighting Chinese people but, by implication, of people all over the world who have united to fight aggression." Despite that praise, critics and audiences recognized *Dragon Seed* as, plainly, a bad movie—not the least of its flaws being the fact that all of the "slant-eyed Japanese bastards" in the Imperial Army were played by Chinese actors, while the roles for Chinese peasants and partisans were given to Caucasian actors and actresses, including Katharine Hepburn.

Fox picked up the story of Catholic missionary A. J. Cronin's work in China in the early 1900s and produced *The Keys of the Kingdom*, which, as originally written, dealt with China's civil strife. The OWI put the brakes on the project and demanded a rewrite, even though the script closely followed the original book.

The OWI then released its assessment of the current situation in the region: "China is today taking her place as one of the four great United Nations of the World. She is contributing immeasurably toward the defeat of our Japanese enemy, and is destined to play an important role in the peace to come. This emphasis on Chinese disunity and internal strife is particularly unfortunate today when it is important to acquaint audiences in all parts of the world with a new and unified China."

The problem with films that spotlighted Russia and China was that true depictions would prompt diplomatic censure and might damage the delicate relationship between the United States and the offended government. But glossing over the internal purges and pretending that everyone "lived happily ever after" was pure fiction, and most audiences would easily see through the smokescreen.

Jingoism, Hollywood Style

Long before President Roosevelt officially declared war on the Axis powers, thousands of Americans were already putting their lives in danger—as pilots volunteering for the American Eagle Squadron of England's Royal Air Force or the Flying Tigers in China; and as Merchant Marines and Navy Armed Guard on board tankers and transports bound for Australia, New Zealand, England, and Russia by way of Murmansk. They were America's earliest war heroes (and its first casualties), and Hollywood rushed to tell their story.

But even for movies on a fast track, the turnaround time from concept to completion could easily take a year or longer, and some of these projects were still in production when Pearl Harbor plunged America into war. And just that suddenly, Hollywood too, like other industries, converted to a war footing.

There was no question the Japanese sneak attack on Pearl Harbor was a devastating—and some might say brilliant—blow to American military might in the Pacific. Virtually every military film coming out of Hollywood immediately after the attack portrayed the Japanese—*all* Japanese—as slant-eyed, buck-toothed, sneaky bastards, while the Germans were portrayed as either good Germans or evil Nazis.

"The Germans really were different from the Japanese, the movies seemed to say. In November 1942 the OWI's Bureau of Intelligence analyzed portrayals of the enemy on the screen, and uncovered distinct differences in the way Hollywood treated the two Axis powers," revealed Koppes and Black in *Hollywood Goes to War*. "German soldiers were generally shown as being efficient and obedient, but rarely 'cruel and barbarous' like the Japanese." (Years later, of course, when the horrors of the Holocaust were revealed to the world, the Nazis' legacy would forever taint Germany.)

In hindsight, many of the movies in early 1942—such as *Little Tokyo, USA*—represented pure venomous hatred for the Japanese, which is exactly what the American public was saying and felt. But FDR appealed to Hollywood to rethink its purpose, which he said was to win the war, not with hatred, but with a unified, unwavering effort.

An Overseer Is Established

The Office of War Information, established in mid-June of 1942, was responsible for "selling" the war. The department ensured that all media—newspapers, radio, and movies—acted in concert to successfully convey a positive message to the American public.

Six months after the office was created, Lowell Mellett, President Roosevelt's liaison with the media, strongly urged the studio chiefs to submit all movie scripts to the OWI for review and approval: "For the benefit of both your studio and the Office of War Information it would be advisable to establish a routine procedure whereby our Hollywood office would receive copies of studio treatments or synopses of all stories which you contemplate producing and of the finished scripts. This will enable us to make suggestions as to the war content of motion pictures at a stage when it is easy and inexpensive to make any changes which might be recommended." While Mellett "strongly urged" studio cooperation, and said it was "advisable" to submit movie scripts for review, it was clear to everyone that without the OWI stamp of approval, movie projects would not be allowed to proceed.

The studios made hundreds of war-related movies during the early '40s, plus a slew of great and maybe not-so-great musicals with military

LEFT: *Radio exec Elmer Davis headed up the Office of War Information, which tightly controlled the "message" that all media released to the public—including reading all printed material, monitoring radio programming, and approving all movie scripts—and then demanding any changes necessary to ensure they stayed within OWI guidelines.*
Office of War Information Photo

themes, and all of these needed OWI clearance which might require rewrites and months of back-and-forth give-and-take. The studios didn't abandon the Western, or the comedy, or the thriller, or the fantasy, sometimes even spinning the genres to include a few nasty-looking Nazis or "slant-eyed bastards," and even these had to be reviewed by the OWI before they were green-lighted.

No matter what the studios churned out for public consumption, the government mandated that all of their movies should inform, influence, or inspire the audience. In fact, the OWI had a specific set of guidelines they strongly urged the studios to abide by:

> Will this picture help win the war?
> What war information problem does it seek to clarify, dramatize, or interpret?
> If it is an "escape" picture, will it harm the war effort by creating a false picture of America, her allies, or the world we live in?
> Does it merely use the war as the basis for a profitable picture, contributing nothing of real significance to the war effort and possibly lessening the effect of other pictures of more importance?
> Does it contribute something new to our understanding of the world conflict and the various forces involved, or has the subject already been adequately covered?
> When the picture reaches its maximum circulation on the screen, will it reflect conditions as they are and fill a need current at that time, or will it be outdated?
> Does the picture tell the truth, or will the young people of today have reason to say they were misled by propaganda?

Some scripts had a hard time answering those questions or demonstrating that they had any redeeming value. Certainly any that didn't conform to government policy would be shelved, or radically rewritten until they got it right, which didn't necessarily mean a true depiction of the American homeland or the fighting front.

"In the OWI/Hollywood vision, the war produced unity. Labor and capital buried their differences for a greater cause; class, ethnic, and racial divisions evaporated in the foxholes and on the assembly line; even estranged family members were reconciled through the agency of war," noted Koppes and Black in *Hollywood Goes to War*.

"No studio was willing to make a film that criticized the war while the bullets were flying," reported Robert Butler in his article, "The Whims of War Films" for the *Kansas City Star*, March 10, 2002. "The resulting movies often caricatured our German and Japanese enemies, while touting the moral superiority of the American fighting man."

All-Star Revues Hit All the Right Notes

If the studios couldn't always get it right when they dove into combat movies, they did manage to rally 'round the flag, generate a huge bounty for war relief and bond drives, and spotlight all their top stars whenever they churned out another in the string of musicals that came out during this era.

"Many of these musicals bore no relationship to the war. Others contained indirect reference. The leading man might be a sailor on leave (*Anchors Aweigh*) or a man who goes overseas into combat while his girlfriend waits back home (*The Gang's All Here*) or a man who joins up late in the conflict to entertain troops (*Cover Girl*)," wrote Jeanine Basinger in *The World War II Combat Film*. "However, a curious link is forged between the musical and combat through the use of World War I in many musical stories . . . either through actual combat or through the device of entertainers going overseas to sing for the troops.

"There appears more than once a scene in which the soldiers who are going to combat are called directly from the theater (where they may be an audience, or part of the performance) to board their warships. Such a scene makes a powerful visual metaphor for the leaving behind of a joyous, peaceful life to enter the life of war."

Warner came through with Irving Berlin's revue, *This Is the Army*, an updated remake of his popular World War I stage show, *Yip, Yip, Yaphank*. The studio then captured the nightly impromptu goings-on at the Hollywood Canteen in a film by that name, starring John Garfield and Bette Davis, along with every available contract player the studio had, who were shown either performing on stage or mingling with servicemen in the crowd.

The studios also spotlighted Broadway's Stage Door Canteen, George M. Cohan, and every American songwriter with a halfway decent collection of catchy tunes. Many musicals had nothing to do with World War II, except to provide an hour and a half of simple joy to the war-weary American public. Once the theater lights came up again, folks could plunge back into the reality that war demanded.

BELOW: *Composer Irving Berlin's WWI-era stage show* Yip, Yap, Yaphank *was dusted off for WWII and hit the stage again, as* This Is the Army, *which became quite a moneymaker for war-relief coffers. The show was then given the Hollywood treatment, starring every available performer, with Ronald Reagan leading the pack.*

Later in the war, Berlin toured overseas, shown here leading a chorus of WACs on Hollandia in Dutch New Guinea, in a medley of his numerous hits.
National Archives Photo

Rationing and Manpower Shortages Hit Hollywood

The war's toll on Tinseltown was never more evident than at the Oscar ceremonies of 1943, held at the Coconut Grove, when the orchestra played the National Anthem and two young servicemen came marching in. They just happened to be two of Hollywood's former movie stars: Alan Ladd and Tyrone Power. After presenting the colors, they spoke, revealing that more

RIGHT: *Tyrone Power was a superstar before the word was invented. But by the 1943 Oscar ceremonies he had set aside his tux and donned his best uniform, as did another GI—fellow actor Alan Ladd. Together they marched in to the awards show, carrying the colors, representing the more than 27,600 film industry stars and craftsmen serving in the military.*
U.S. Marine Corps Photo

than 27,600 of their counterparts in the film community had joined one of the armed forces. Many more would be called up in 1944 and '45, and hundreds more willingly volunteered in local hospitals or went on USO shows around the country and overseas.

"It was hard to fall in love with a young god on the silver screen because so many major American heartthrobs—among them Henry Fonda, Robert Montgomery, Robert Cummings, Clark Gable, and Jimmy Stewart—were off fighting," noted Susan Dworkin in *Miss America 1945*.

And *Variety* reported, "The war-year of 1943 will go down in motion picture history as the year in which studios scoured the country, in an attempt to uncover able young men who could be elevated to high prominence almost overnight."

Just such a performer was the King of Hollywood, Clark Gable: "The change in MGM between the summer of 1942, when Clark finished his last film, and the winter of 1944, when he was looking for his next, was so vast a decade could have slipped through those two and a half years," wrote Lyn Tornabene in *Long Live the King*. "For one thing, more stars than there are in heaven shifted. Many of the male stars were in service, their places taken by Mickey Rooney, who did not go into the Army until 1944; Gene Kelly, who went in the Navy in '45 and was out in '46; and Van Johnson—darling of young ladies known as bobby-soxers—who was 4-F because of a head injury he got in an automobile accident."

The rationing and shortages that impacted every American citizen also affected Hollywood film studios. Several studios cut extravagant banquet scenes out of respect for limited food stocks across the country. Even the Oscars scaled back its grandiose culinary spread during the war years due to

RIGHT: *In April of 1941, the marquee at the Regal Cinema in Chicago featured movies starring Robert Taylor, Cesar Romero, and James Stewart. All three of them would end up in the military after war was declared eight months later. The mass exodus of Hollywood's leading men allowed a new crop of young actors to gain screen time during the war years.*
Office of War Information Photo

rationing. Many stars who lived close by their studios took to riding bicycles or walking because of gasoline rationing, which also forced cutbacks in the filming of car chases and traffic scenes. Miniature cars and trucks, boats, planes, and submarines solved the fuel problem for filmmakers, although many films suffered from the obvious switch. War films, authorized and supported by the military, got all the jeeps and tanks and planes, and all the fuel they required, plus uniformed personnel for battle scenes.

"Film and lumber allotments were cut almost in half after Pearl Harbor, and art directors were ordered to limit the cost of sets to an average of $5,000. The studios received practically no nails at all and each studio was limited to a meager two pounds of hairpins a month," reported Army Private James P. O'Neill in *YANK*. "The film shortage was the toughest to beat. Directors found themselves hamstrung in the number of takes they could shoot. Actors were ordered to come to the sets prepared to face the camera with a polished version of their roles. The restrictions inevitably brought many other changes to the industry. Art directors who once guarded secrets with their lives became real neighborly and borrowed sets from one another."

British film studios suffered the same controls and shortages and the departure of their finest young actors, but they had one additional obstacle their American counterparts didn't have to deal with: "Shooting was continually interrupted by air raids: there were spotters on the studio roof who would raise the alarm upon sighting enemy aircraft, at which the whole cast and crew would evacuate the soundstage to shelter in the storage areas underneath the concrete studio floor," wrote Roy Moseley with Philip and Martin Masheter in *Rex Harrison*. "There they would remain until the all-clear when they would return to the studio floor and try to get back into the momentum of the scene they were filming. An estimated 125 bombs fell in the vicinity of the studio during filming, which was further disrupted by aircraft noise which made sound recording impossible."

Finding a Balance Audiences Would Accept

Dramatizing the early battles in the Pacific was troublesome for writers and directors who'd never been in combat, and who were used to creating cliffhangers where the heroes face fire and fury—they may get burned and they may get nicked, but somehow, miraculously, they dodged certain death to rescue the millionaire's gorgeous daughter and live happily ever after. Now these directors had the daunting task of retelling tales without happy endings. Some directors tried sprinkling on the sugarcoating, but savvy moviegoers—those who listened to the daily radio updates from overseas, and scanned the newspapers with the lists of casualties and the missing, and read the censored letters from loved ones in the fight—immediately spotted the scam and laughed at the farce or simply walked out of the theater.

"Screenwriters, when they attempt to get their teeth into the war itself, are beginning to realize that combat doesn't consist exclusively of one or two handsome American heroes, very much alive, and millions of dirty Japs, very much dead," reported O'Neill for *YANK*. "Instead of just taking a 4-F writer's idea of combat, the studios bring in technical advisers who have been under fire."

The studios still struggled to find that delicate balance between telling a good story and telling one that would ring true with the American public. Maybe it was okay if war movies didn't always have a happy ending—and it certainly wasn't that way in real life for thousands of grieving families. But the movies should at least give them hope . . . hope that the fight and the struggle and their sacrifice weren't wasted. That hope was often offered up at the end of the movie, in a final letter from a son, or the whispered condolences of a preacher, or in the comforting words from someone who has experienced a similar loss.

In the movie *Tender Comrades*, Jo, played by Ginger Rogers, says good-bye at the train station to her husband, Chris, an Army sergeant. He promises to come back safe, saying the odds were great nothing would happen to him. But then late one night Jo gets a telegram and dreads opening it. She goes up to her room where their newborn son, Chris Jr., is sleeping. Tears fill her eyes as she reads the telegram, and she wakes the baby and tells him the news, even if he can't understand. She shows him a photo of Chris Sr. in uniform and says: "Little guy, this is your father. Chris, this is your son. You two aren't ever going to meet. Only through me will you ever know anything about each other.

"Remember him, Son. Remember your father as long as you live. He was a fine man, Chris Boy. He never made speeches, but he went out and died so that you could have a better break when you grow up than he ever had. Not the same break, but a better one, because he did a lot of thinking about you in his own way.

"Never forget it, Little Guy. Never forget it. He didn't leave you any money. He didn't have time, Chris Boy. No mil-

RIGHT: *Abandoning her dancing shoes, Ginger Rogers starred in* Tender Comrades, *about a pregnant wife who had to say good-bye to her husband, an Army sergeant headed overseas. Later she receives a telegram and fears the worst—that he has been killed. In the darkness, she goes up to her room and picks up a photo of her beloved Chris and shows it to their newborn son. She promises to raise him right, to carry on, like all young widows must do, for the good of her baby boy, for the good of the country, for a brighter tomorrow.*
Associated Press Photo

lion dollars, or country clubs or long shiny cars for you, Little Guy. He only left you the best world a boy could ever grow up in. He bought it for you with his life, and it's your heritage . . . a personal gift to you from your dad.

"And one more thing . . . as long as you live, don't let anybody ever say he died for nothing, because if you let them say it, you let them call your dad a fool. You let them say he died without knowing what it was all about. He died for a good thing, Little Guy, and if you ever betray it, if you ever let it slip away from you, if you ever let anybody talk you out of it, or swindle you out of it, or fight you out of it, you might as well be dead too. So hang on to it, Sweetie. Clutch on to it with those tiny little fingers. Grab on to it, Chris Boy. Grab it right out of your dad's hands and hold it high, hold it proud."

Jo kisses her son and places him back in his bassinet; then she looks at her husband's photo and says, "Don't worry, Chris . . . he'll grow up to be a good guy." She turns off the light and walks out into the hallway. She stops at the top of the stairs and a motherly voice tells herself (and tells every war widow watching the movie), "No matter how tough things are, no matter how bad they seem, think of him. You'll come through. Come on, Jo, head up. Take it on the chin, like a good guy, like a soldier's wife should."

That's all that was expected of Jo, and of every American woman who had a loved one in uniform and in the fight overseas.

10. Allied Bombers Hit Fortress Europe

"THE THINGS A MAN HAS TO HAVE ARE HOPE AND CONFIDENCE IN HIMSELF AGAINST ODDS. HE'S GOT TO HAVE SOME INNER STANDARDS WORTH FIGHTING FOR OR THERE WON'T BE ANY WAY TO BRING HIM INTO CONFLICT. AND HE MUST BE READY TO CHOOSE DEATH BEFORE DISHONOR WITHOUT MAKING TOO MUCH SONG AND DANCE ABOUT IT."

—*Army Air Corps Major Clark Gable*

"THE RUHR WILL NOT BE SUBJECT TO A SINGLE BOMB. IF AN ENEMY BOMBER REACHES THE RUHR, MY NAME IS NOT HERMANN GOERING . . . YOU CAN CALL ME MEIER!"

—*Nazi Reichsmarschall Hermann Goering, August 9, 1939*

OPPOSITE: *Like an artist using the clear blue sky as his canvas, the vapor trails of fighter planes curved upward and behind the Flying Fortresses of the 8th Air Force, headed for targets deep inside Germany.*
Army Air Forces Photo

THE AMERICAN FLYBOYS BASED IN GREAT BRITAIN WERE the heroic swashbucklers who flew into battle against the Evil Empire, who beat back the widowmaker and destroyed the maniacal lunatic and his henchmen, rescuing the English damsels in distress and living together happily ever after, in America, of course.

Isn't that how the movie goes? But there's a bittersweet twist to the happy ending, when the dashingly handsome hero gets a phone call in the middle of the night, then reluctantly has to say good-bye to his bride because his country needs him more, needs him again, this time for dangerous missions in the Far East, clandestine, behind the lines, zillion-to-one-shot missions that others have already died trying to accomplish. If he lives through the hell, he promises to come back, but only when the world is safe again. And she vows to remain forever true—foolishly maybe, but that's how the script is written—longing for the day when she can look into his eyes again and tend to his many wounds and pray his desire for wanderlust has been quenched once and for all, so they can grow old together. Doesn't she realize there will always be another mission?

But of course he knows and the audience knows they'll never see each other again. Such are the perils of the American aviators in war movies of that era. The most common injury seemed to be, at least on film anyway, a long-distance lover coping with a broken heart.

The reality of the air war over Fortress Europe wasn't quite so glamorous or romantic or adventurous, although it was just as dangerous.

BELOW: *"Nasty little critters," these P-51 fighters, roaming the skies over Great Britain and the Channel, accompanying the big bombers on their way to missions over Fortress Europe. Fighter escorts were essential to fending off the Nazi fighter planes swarming overhead and diving in and around, menacing the lumbering giants.*
U.S. Air Force Photo

Pounding Ploesti and Beyond

Once the Americans and the British had established bases in North Africa, military strategists laid out plans to cripple the Nazis with overwhelming air power. Waves of B-24 bombers from the U.S. Middle East Air Force would hit rail yards, and bridges, industries, and shipyards across southern Europe. B-17s from the 10th Air Force were dispatched out of India and relocated to the Mediterranean bases.

Though both the B-24 Liberators and B-17 Flying Fortresses were bombers, there was a huge difference in the two, noted Thomas Childers in *Wings of Morning*: "The Liberator was the most modern aircraft in the U.S. air arsenal in 1944. It flew faster, carried a heavier bomb load, and possessed greater range than its sister ship, the B-17. Yet, unlike the graceful Flying Fortress, which had become the glamour plane of the war, the Liberator was an ugly aircraft. Its squat fuselage, stubby nose, and enormous twin vertical stabilizers lent the ship an ungainly, pugnacious look. Dubbed the banana boat, the flying brick, the pregnant cow, and the old agony wagon, it was a plane that, as one of their instructors put it, 'you couldn't form an attachment to.'"

The first mission for the North African-based bombers was to strike the vital oil refineries at Ploesti, Romania, in mid-June of 1942. The Nazis depended on up to one-third of their fuel needs from the Ploesti fields, and so, despite heavy losses from anti-aircraft fire and Luftwaffe fighter planes, the bombing raids to Romania continued through mid-1944.

For Allied bomber crews and fighter pilots based in England, the war against Nazi Germany had been raging since 1939, first with the Brits going at it alone, then as American swashbucklers joined the Royal Air Force in mid-1940 as pilots, navigators, and gunners. They flew Wellington and Lancaster bombers and Hawker Hurricane or Spitfire fighters. Eventually the RAF created the Eagle Squadrons for the Americans volunteering to do their part in the war effort (most of whom traveled to England under Canadian passports to sidestep America's Neutrality Act), long before the United States officially declared war. After American bomber and fighter

RIGHT: *The massive oil fields and refineries at Ploesti in Romania were essential to the Nazi war machine, and once Allied air bases were established in North Africa and later in Italy, bombing missions were slated to cripple the enemy by cutting off their fuel supply. Though Ploesti was heavily defended by Luftwaffe fighter planes and anti-aircraft guns, they had to be neutralized, and perilous bombing runs with massed aircraft had to continue despite the heavy loss of life.*
Army Air Corps Photo

squadrons deployed to England in mid-1942, the Eagle Squadron pilots, with their invaluable dogfighting experience, transferred to the 4th Fighter Group, exchanging their British uniforms for America's Army Air Corps flight suits. (The mighty Fourth became the most proficient Allied air unit in WWII, and much of that success could be directly attributed to the early experience of the ex-Eagle Squadron "swashbucklers.")

Conventional rules of warfare dictated that both sides confine their bombing to vital industrial complexes such as munitions plants, rail yards, aircraft assembly lines, shipyards, and so on. Of special interest to the Allies were the Ruhr and Saar valley regions with their numerous prime targets, including ball bearing plants, synthetic fuel processors, coal and oil depots, and ironworks.

But when Nazi Germany launched its rockets against London and other English cities, intent on terrorizing innocent civilians, the rules changed and Allied bomber crews prepared for some major payback against Germany's largest cities, with Berlin at the top of the list.

Actress Shelley Winters had married an Army Air Corps officer. In her book, *Shelley*, she recalled one night when he opened up about his experiences: " . . . in bed that night he held me and spoke of the war for the first

LEFT: *The rules of civilized warfare were quickly discarded when the Nazis began launching rockets in the direction of Great Britain and sending bombers over London, not to take out war-related industries but merely to terrorize the populace. Thus the bombing campaign of Europe became one of retribution, devastating to the innocent civilians left to search through the rubble for lost loved ones, for prized possessions, for anything worth salvaging.*

As American infantry troops moved into the region, an elderly German from the city that was once Bensheim surveys the damage of her hometown in the final weeks of the war.

U.S. Army Photo

time. 'Shirley, when you're over the target, you drop the bombs. You know they'll kill hundreds of people, maybe thousands. You get sick to your stomach because you may be destroying good people, like resistance fighters, along with the ammunition dumps and military targets. It's the same in life. You just have to do what you have to do. Bombs away.'"

With hundreds of aircraft slated for some missions, it was inevitable that many would not return, shot down by anti-aircraft guns and Luftwaffe fighter planes knifing through the formations. Some bombers crash-landed behind enemy lines; other crewmen parachuted to safety only to be taken prisoner. (Twenty-five thousand American pilots and crewmen would end up in German POW camps.)

While it was never easy to return to their billets after a harrowing mission and see another empty bunk, many of the bomber crewmen joked about their fate and even sang mocking lyrics to the popular tune, "As Time Goes By"—

"You must remember this, the flak can't always miss,
Somebody's got to die.
The odds are always too damned high . . . as flak goes by."

Hollywood's Finest Risk It All

The two most prominent stars to serve with the Army Air Corps and fly those dangerous missions over Fortress Europe were Jimmy Stewart and Clark Gable. They took decidedly different routes to get there and had different reasons for volunteering.

Stewart followed the news about the war in Europe and listened to Edward R. Murrow's radio broadcasts during the London Blitz, when the city was being pounded nightly by Nazi bomber planes and buzz bombs. Sensing the United States would soon be at war, Stewart took flying lessons, intent on joining the Air Corps if and when he was needed. Two months before Pearl Harbor, he took a physical but was found to be underweight. He worked on bulking up, and then Roosevelt declared war, thus opening up the height, weight, and age restrictions, and Stewart joined the Army Air Corps. He trained at Moffett Field near San Francisco, and received additional training and flight experience in New Mexico and Boise, Idaho.

His final stop before heading overseas was Sioux City in Iowa, where he was assigned to the 703rd Bomb Squadron, which would be part of the 445th Bomb Group, slated for duty in England. Prior to heading

BELOW: *It was heartbreaking for other aircrews to observe one of their own succumb to enemy flak from anti-aircraft guns or strafing from Luftwaffe fighter pilots. They looked on helplessly, counting the number of parachutes, thankful it wasn't them, wondering when it would be. This B-26 goes down over southern France.*
Army Air Forces Photo

LEFT: *As one of Hollywood's top actors, Jimmy Stewart could have easily opted for something a little less dangerous, such as touring the country pitching war bonds, or touring military posts and bases to entertain the troops, or making training films, or being a flight instructor. Instead, he yearned to fly, and wanted to be in the thick of the fight, and that's exactly what he got.*

Serving first with the 445th and later with the 453rd Bombardment Group, Major Jimmy Stewart debriefed some of the other pilots after their return from a mission over Fortress Europe. He would lead them on numerous flights, including deep over enemy territory to Berlin, the capital of Nazi Germany.
U.S. Air Force Photo

overseas, Stewart received a cherished letter from his dad: "My dear Jim boy. Soon after you read this letter, you will be on your way to the worst sort of danger. Jim, I'm banking on the enclosed copy of the 91st Psalm. The thing that takes the place of fear and worry is the promise of these words. I am staking my faith in these words. I feel sure that God will lead you through this mad experience. God bless you and keep you. I love you more than I can tell you. Dad."

Stewart and the 445th ended up at Tibenham, England, one hundred miles from London. They had barely fallen into a daily routine when they began flying missions to Germany, including the massive raid on Berlin by a thousand Allied bombers on March 22, 1944. While other bombers had pinups painted on their noses, with nicknames like *Memphis Belle* and *Tallahassee Lassie*, Stewart personally painted the self-mocking logo on his plane, which he dubbed "Nine Yanks and a Jerk."

Stewart would fly twenty combat missions over some of the most heavily defended cities in Germany, including Bremen, Frankfurt, Schweinfurt, and the capital city of Berlin. And on each of those bombing runs Stewart kept with him the frayed and tattered copy of the 91st Psalm his dad had sent him: "He that dwelleth in the secret place of the Most High shall abide under the shadow of the Almighty. I will say of the Lord, 'He is my refuge and my fortress; my God; in him I will trust. Thou shalt not be afraid for the terror by night; nor for the arrow that flyeth by day, for he shall give his angels charge over thee, to keep thee in all thy ways. They shall bear thee up in their hands, lest thou dash thy foot against a stone."

Whether it was thanks to his belief in God, or his father's prayers, or the best wishes of thousands of fans back home, Jimmy Stewart survived while hundreds of other pilots and crew members perished. Tragically, more than 36,000 American pilots and crewmen were killed in the European air war.

(Stewart returned home to Hollywood after the war and starred in the Frank Capra classic, *It's a Wonderful Life*, a movie about small-town America and how one man can make a difference, if he just steps forward and accepts the responsibility to do what's right.)

The attack on Pearl Harbor prompted Clark Gable and his wife, Carole Lombard, to write to President Roosevelt and offer their help in any way he requested. FDR encouraged them to continue making movies and keep up the morale of the American people.

Lombard knew that wasn't enough, and she encouraged Clark to join the military, even though he was almost forty-one. Three days after Pearl Harbor, the movie industry's top stars formed the Hollywood Victory Committee, with Gable as chairman of the actors division. The committee set out to support the war effort, providing entertainers for camp tours and bond drives. The group also established the popular Hollywood Canteen, stocked it every night with a roster of stars and starlets, big bands and singers, and provided meals and a good time for servicemen heading out to the Pacific Theater.

Lombard went out on a bond drive to her home state of Indiana in January, with whistle stops along the way. She cut the trip short, but she never made it back home. Her plane crashed outside of Las Vegas. President and Mrs. Roosevelt sent condolences to Gable, and FDR later honored Lombard as "The first woman to be killed in action in the defense of her country in a war against the Axis powers."

Seven months after Lombard's death, Gable enlisted in the Army Air Corps, accompanied by MGM cameraman Andy McIntyre, who would document his day-to-day activities, first at basic training and then on to gunnery school and officers candidate school. When asked by a reporter how he felt about enlisting, Gable responded: "I'm going in and I don't expect to come back and I don't really give a hoot whether I do or not."

With his training out of the way, Gable received orders to report to the 351st Bomber Group in Polebrook, England, commanded by Lieutenant Colonel William Hatcher. The airmen of the 351st were dubbed "Hatcher's Chickens." Gable and his film crew were given the assignment to produce a documentary on aerial gunners. Tagging along with him was the Little

BELOW: *Clark Gable and his Little Hollywood Group were tasked with making a recruiting documentary about aerial gunners, and flew several bombing missions over Europe to get thousands of feet of footage. On every mission, their flight was attacked by enemy fighter pilots and hit by flak from anti-aircraft guns protecting industrial cities in Germany.*
U.S. Air Force Photo

Hollywood Group, composed of sound engineer Lieutenant Howard Voss, cameraman Master Sergeant Robert Boles, scriptwriter Lieutenant John Mahlin, cameraman Master Sergeant Marlin Toti, and McIntyre.

"Acting as a cameraman for the film unit, [Gable] flew many dangerous missions over Europe. In August 1943, he took part in a huge raid into Germany aboard a Flying Fortress called 'Ain't it Gruesome?' Gable spent the entire seven-hour flight taking pictures, wedged in behind the top turret gunner. Gable's plane sustained five Nazi attacks, returning to base with fifteen flak holes in the fuselage," wrote Warren G. Harris in *Gable and Lombard*. "In another mission over Nantes, France, Gable operated the nose gun while over the target. Nazi fighters came so close that at one moment Gable said, 'I could see the German pilot's features. That guy won't be around very long if he keeps on doing that.'"

Certainly Gable had a fear of being shot down every time he took off on another mission over Europe, but his concern was more acute than what other airmen were feeling, and for good reason. The pro-Nazi radio announcer Lord Haw-Haw was aware of Gable's arrival in England and welcomed him personally to the fight: "Welcome to England, Hatcher's Chickens, among whom is the famous American cinema star, Clark Gable. We'll be seeing you soon in Germany, Clark." Maybe the King of Hollywood hadn't heard Lord Haw-Haw's message, but he quickly learned about it.

He also found out that Nazi Luftwaffe chief Hermann Goering was offering a bounty to any pilot who shot down Gable's B-17. Gable's death would be an emotional setback for the Americans and the British, but his capture would be a propaganda coup for the Nazis, and Gable knew it.

"If I ever fall into Hitler's hands, the son of a bitch will put me in a cage like a big gorilla. He'd exhibit me all over Germany," Gable told others, vowing that if his plane were ever shot down he would not bail out but would remain on board to the end.

Gable flew five combat missions, and his plane was hit by flak or enemy machine guns on every one, but he made it back to England each time, unlike many of the airmen he had become friends with.

BELOW: *Nazi Propaganda minister Joseph Goebbels and Air Marshall Hermann Goering confer at a high level get-together. When the Nazis learned that Clark Gable was assigned to a bomber unit in England and would soon be flying missions over Europe, Goering, the Luftwaffe chief, let it be known that whichever of his fighter pilots managed to shoot down Gable's plane would be an instant hero of the Reich, though thousands of adoring fans around the world would curse the dastardly villain. When he heard about the bounty, Gable vowed to never bail out and be captured; instead, he would remain on board the doomed bomber and perish in the crash.* German Government Photo

"He knew every man who left on the missions, and missed every one who didn't return," wrote Lyn Tornabene in *Long Live the King*. "Sometimes he volunteered to write the saddest of all letters to the widows and families of 'kids' to whom he had become particularly attached, feeling he knew enough about grief to say the right thing."

The Little Hollywood Group wound up with more than 50,000 feet of filmed footage and returned to Hollywood to finish what became the sixty-three-minute documentary, *Combat America*. By the time it was completed, the movie was overshadowed by the similar film, *The Memphis Belle*.

Others Who Flew into Hell

Walter Matuschanskayasky was the son of Russian Jews and hailed from New York's Lower East Side. As a youngster he read Shakespeare and worked at a local Yiddish theater, frequently getting minor stage roles. Four months after war was declared, he joined the Army Air Corps as a radio operator/cryptographer and gunner, and he was eventually stationed with the 453rd Bomb Group at Attleborough, England. "My job was to teach instrumental takeoff to American pilots," he would later tell writer Allan Hunter. "I flew four missions but the rest was general training stuff. Which was good because all those planes were getting shot out of the sky. We always had new personnel coming in." He also recalled mission briefings by Operations officer Jimmy Stewart.

(After his discharge, Matuschanskayasky used the GI Bill to take classes at the New York New School Dramatic Workshop, which included fellow veterans Rod Steiger and Tony Curtis. His first professional experience was as Rex Harrison's understudy for the role of an elderly bishop in the play, *Anne of the Thousand Days*. This led to countless stage and movie roles, including his breakthrough in the movie *The Odd Couple* with fellow veteran Jack Lemmon. By this time Matuschanskayasky had adopted a much simpler name that audiences could remember. He would forever after be known as the lovable mug, Walter Matthau.)

Hollywood actor Van Heflin had a brief stint with a field artillery battery, then was reassigned as a combat cameraman with the 9th Air Force in Europe. James Best went in the opposite direction, starting as a gunner on a B-17, then transferring to the military police before being selected to act in the Special Services play, *My Sister Eileen*, staged by Arthur Penn. Leading man Robert Preston served as an intelligence officer with the mighty 9th Air Force. (After getting out, Preston took on his most memorable role, as Professor Harold Hill for the musical, *The Music Man)*. Another "music man" was British-born pianist and conductor Skitch Henderson, who returned home to serve with the Royal Air Force, then got his United States citizenship and transferred to the Army Air Corps. (Henderson eventually returned to New York and kept busy with radio shows, stage performances, big band recordings, and television shows, including *The Tonight Show* with Steve Allen.)

Some of the GIs who served in England were able to use their talents for the war effort, although it wasn't always appreciated. One man's serenading was another man's caterwauling, especially at "oh-dark thirty" in the damn morning—at least that was the split decision for the soldiers stationed with trumpeter Tommy Zylman in England. The former horn player with the Tommy Tucker Band would wake up early and blare a swing rendition of first call over the unit loudspeaker, startling everyone awake, whether they liked it or not! He also took care of the bugling chores at reveille.

Entertainers Tour the Isles

Tireless traveler Bob Hope was on a tour of Great Britain when he stopped by the Allied air bases with his troupe of entertainers. Before going on stage he found out that the King of Hollywood—leading man Clark Gable—was assigned to the 351st Bomb Group and was most likely among the servicemen and -women there to watch the show. Other celebrities would have gone backstage to see Hope and the others, maybe catch up on news and gossip from Tinseltown, but Gable wanted to be just one of the guys rather than cash in on his fame.

It was showtime, and Hope walked out to center stage and scanned the crowd.

"There were thousands sitting out on a field, Gable tucked in somewhere with the guys. Hope stood up at the mike, trying his damnedest to get Clark on the stage. He couldn't even get him to stand up," wrote Lyn Tornabene in *Long Live the King*. "Hope kept saying, 'Where is he? I know there's a celebrity out there. Where is he?' The guys laughed and some of them shouted, 'Here,' and started to applaud and whistle. Clark smiled and gave half a wave, then put his head down. The applause and whistling went on, it must have been ten minutes. Everybody thought he was great."

Another living legend—Jimmy Cagney—also visited the British Isles to entertain the troops massing there for the eventual jump to the European mainland. "On one occasion in March 1944, he was playing at a bomber station in Northern England during an air raid. Just as the second act of his show got going, the sound of gunfire could be heard coming from fairly close at hand. 'I'm no expert at this sort of thing,' said Jimmy as he walked onto the stage, 'but I think the general idea is to get out of here!'" wrote Michael Freedland in *Cagney*. "Everyone did, and roared with laughter while doing so. They left the makeshift

Below: *For several decades Bob Hope has been associated with his annual USO tour of military installations around the world, always during the holidays. But the tradition started in WWII, and at that time, was a year-round endeavor. Here, Hope mingles with the local lovelies during a Christmas show in England.*
Imperial War Museum Photo

theater just as it was struck by what sounded like a loud explosion. It turned out to be the fuel tank of a crashing Junkers 88 [a Nazi war plane].

"Jimmy quipped: 'Back in the States, I had to fight to get two gallons of the stuff a week. Over here, Hitler sends us a tankful, by special delivery.' The audience was his for the rest of the hour he was on stage."

Dealing with air raids was one of the many hazards of traveling and staying in Great Britain. Broadway legends Lynn Fontanne and Alfred Lunt were appearing on the London stage in 1944 when a Nazi V-2 rocket exploded close enough to rock the theater and damage the interior. Troupers that they were, the couple continued with the show despite the fallen plaster and scenery all around them and the apprehensive audience trying to figure out where the nearest bomb shelter was.

"London wasn't to be as peaceful as [Bing] Crosby thought. He had arrived in the middle of the doodle-bug attacks on the city—jet-propelled flying bombs launched from occupied territory," wrote Charles Thompson in *Bing*. "When BBC executive Cecil Madden, responsible for light entertainment in Allied Expeditionary Forces [radio] programs, called two days later to collect him for a broadcast, he found the crooner standing on his

RIGHT: *Scenic Hyde Park in London was taken over by anti-aircraft guns pointed skyward to fire a blanket of flak whenever radar sites along the southern coast warned of Nazi bombers approaching. During an air raid exercise in August of 1939, more than 20,000 trained gunners and support crews were mustered in London to test their ability to scramble to their positions and be ready for the enemy onslaught. Over the next several years, they would be tested continually, and thousands would perish defending Great Britain.*
U.S. Information Agency Photo

hotel balcony watching the bombs go by. Alongside him was tough-guy actor Broderick Crawford, then a sergeant with the U.S. armed services."

Radio actor Joseph Julian had traveled to England in mid-'42 to play the lead in Norman Corwin's BBC show, *An American in England*. His journal of his experiences, which included the daily bombings of London, was later published in his book, *This Was Radio*. "July 29. Sirens sounded. An alert. Firing was the 'ack-ack.' There were many people in the lobby, in their pajamas and robes, waiting for the all-clear. As I returned to my room some of the flaming flak from the anti-aircraft shells was floating past my window. For the first time, I have a personal sense of danger here.

"July 30. 2 A.M. Siren screamed an alert. Huge flashes in the sky synchronize with the boom of anti-aircraft guns. A young Tommy explains that a few Nazi planes come over every night about this time.

"August 12. Been here over two weeks now. Beginning to penetrate the shell of strangeness and see the English character, traditionally at its best in adversity. Their stiff-upper-lipism is frequently mocked, but there is something so real and rocklike at its core that nine months of daily Blitz couldn't shatter it, and you can't imagine anything that would. The first attacks sent them reeling, but they recovered their national manners and counterattacked with a barrage of courage, wit, and contempt that wrecked Hitler's plan for systematically softening them up. He could have softened them more by leaving them alone."

American actress Bebe Daniels had been a popular movie star in the 1920s before "talkies" were introduced. She easily made the transition, and was bigger than ever in the '30s. She married fellow actor Ben Lyon, and together they journeyed to England for a brief tour. They ended up staying when Lyons accepted an offer with 20th Century Fox, as head of their talent office in London. Even while London suffered through continuous bombings, Daniels and Lyon chose to stay and entertain appreciative British service members and civilians.

British recruit Stewart Granger endured the typical grind of boot camp, but he later recalled in his book *Sparks Fly Upward* that, unfortunately, "the combination of hard training, army cooked meals, forced route marches and sleeping in ditches . . . had proved too much for my nervous stomach. I developed an ulcer and was sent off to a hospital. I felt both guilty and a failure. All that training, all that square bashing and route marching. To be invalided out with a bloody ulcer."

After returning home, Granger was cast in the Gainsborough Studios film, *The Man in Grey*, with James Mason, and recalled what it was like trying to make a movie in London: "All the time I was filming the war was still going on, bombings at night, the sound of the sirens, the ack-ack pounding away, the shouts of the air-raid wardens telling us to fix our blackout, the glow of the fires, thankfully in the distance."

ABOVE: *Popular boogie-woogie singer Hazel Scott was a hit with the guys in uniform, but her heart belonged to only one . . . a pilot with the 454th Bombardment Squadron. As part of her show, she would walk out on stage wearing a cream-colored waistcoat, with the 454th's insignia—a snarling, flying wolf—big enough for all to see, announcing to everyone her loyalty to the guys who dance among the clouds. She got razzed a little by the soldiers and sailors and leathernecks she performed for, but they certainly understood what it was like – and maybe wished they had a lovely lady waiting at home for her man to return safely.*
YANK Magazine Photo

In August of 1942, *Stars and Stripes* reported: "Film stars Merle Oberon, Al Jolson, Patricia Morrison, Allan Jenkins, and Frank McHugh have arrived in London on the first stop of a four-week tour through the British Isles to entertain the American forces.

"Asked where they were going to put on their shows, Jolson remarked, 'We don't care where we work. We'll work from the back of trucks, in mess halls, in huts, in theaters. Wherever we can get a bunch of the fellows together, we'll put on a show.' Besides entertaining U.S. forces, the group will play in several British war industry factories, for the workers during their free time." The troupe experienced nightly bombings that temporarily interrupted—but never halted—their performances.

The next summer another troupe of entertainers took a transport ship to England, rehearsing on board for the servicemen bound for England. Included in the group was stage and movie hoofer Hal Le Roy, who spoke for the group when he said, "It's swell to get over here at last. It's where we want to be. We're anxious to get to work, and fast."

Other members of the group included blues singer Francetta Malloy, comedian Don Rice, mimic Wally West, accordionists Mildred Anderson and Patricia Melville, radio star Hank Ladd, singer and accordionist Elsie Hartley, dancer Limberlegs Edwards, acrobats Dorothy Deering and Brucetta, magician Eddie Cochran, and comedy dance team sisters Dorothy and Helen Blossom, who planned to pull guys out of the audience for a little jitterbugging. They tried rehearsing that on the transport over, despite the choppy Atlantic. "That only made for better jitterbugging," Dorothy joked.

Tragedy in the Skies

With all the traveling that entertainers were doing to get overseas, it was virtually impossible to avoid flying into danger. In fact, it happened more often than they wanted to think about.

BELOW: *Two years after being seriously injured in a plane crash near Lisbon, Missouri's First Lady of Song, singer Jane Froman, hobbled around on crutches, assisted by her husband, Don Ross. Though she would never fully recovery from her injuries, Froman continued to tour and perform for the GIs.* *YANK* Magazine Photo

Jane Froman—Missouri's First Lady of Song—was one of the top female singers of the mid-1930s and well into the '40s, but while on a USO tour to the European Theater, her plane crashed near Lisbon, Portugal. She was seriously injured and would never be 100 percent again. But, like so many troupers who believed that the show must go on, she continued the tour as soon as doctors allowed her to travel again, even though she had to hobble around on crutches and endure severe pain while doing ninety-five shows back to back. (In 1952 Susan Hayward portrayed Froman in the movie, *With a Song in My Heart.*

LEFT: *Popular British actor Leslie Howard, who was cast in the coveted role of Ashley Wilkes in the blockbuster movie,* Gone with the Wind, *shared a few laughs with Royal Air Force pilots. Tragically, he would be killed in mid-1943 when his plane, flying out of Lisbon, was pounced on by Luftwaffe fighter planes and blown out of the sky. Speculation focused on Howard's well-known anti-Nazi views, but also that one of the other passengers had a strong resemblance to Prime Minister Winston Churchill, who had traveled surreptitiously through Lisbon in the past.*
National Archives Photo

Froman dubbed all the songs, and the soundtrack became a best-selling album.)

In mid-1943, a plane departed from Lisbon and headed out over the Atlantic on its way to London. On board were Scottish actress Annette Sutherland, British actor Leslie Howard (who had played Ashley Wilkes in *Gone with the Wind*), and another British citizen and Howard's business manager, Alfred Chenhalls, who closely resembled Winston Churchill. Howard may have been a target for German agents, because he made no attempt to hide his anti-Nazi views, and his movies and radio denunciations had incensed Nazi Propaganda Minister Joseph Goebbels.

The real Churchill had just concluded a mission to Cairo and was returning home as surreptitiously as possible. He had flown through Lisbon on previous trips, and the Nazis were blanketing the area in a concerted effort to assassinate the prime minister. Whether the ruse was intentional or not, Nazi agents in Lisbon spotted "Churchill" and his party boarding an unarmed British Overseas Airways plane. The agents alerted fighter pilots out of occupied France to patrol the area over the Atlantic. As the DC-3 made its way over the Bay of Biscay, in an area dubbed the Valley of Death, eight Junkers fighter planes pounced on it and shot it down. There were no survivors. The real Winston Churchill made it safely back from the Middle East and remained steadfast in Great Britain's war against Nazi Germany.

Of all the terrific big bands of the day—from Benny Goodman and the Dorsey Brothers to Duke Ellington, Artie Shaw, and Harry James, to name a few—tops among servicemen was the Glenn Miller ensemble. A year after Pearl Harbor, Miller was commissioned in the Army and immediately set out to create the best military band ever, recruiting the finest musicians already in uniform. He also coerced a few who were trying to avoid the military as long as possible.

"The band aired radio broadcasts, staged bond rallies, and recorded V-Discs to be sent to the troops overseas. But Glenn's greatest objective was to take the band to Europe to play for the troops there," reported Penny Howard in the article, "Glenn Miller: Morale Booster Extraordinaire" for *VFW* magazine, January 1995. "So on June 18, 1944, he flew to London. The

RIGHT: *In preparation for his band's jump across the Channel to perform for the American troops in northern Europe, Glenn Miller spoke over the American Broadcasting Service in Europe, announcing the news. Tragically, a few months later, while flying to Paris to scout out potential concert halls and outdoor arenas, Miller's plane was lost at sea and he was pronounced dead.*
Imperial War Museum Photo

band arrived several days later aboard the *Queen Elizabeth,* which had been converted to a troopship." The musicians included four trombonists, two drummers, six woodwind players, five trumpeters, two pianists, twenty strings, a French horn player, two bassists, and a guitarist. The entourage also required five vocalists, plus support staff including an announcer, instrument repairers, arrangers, and producers. The group found quarters in London and endured buzz bomb attacks almost from the start. On many nights the band was performing when air raid sirens blared, and they scrambled to the nearest bomb shelter for the night. During the day they toured Allied bases throughout the Isles, did radio shows, and recorded more V-Discs. Finally, fed up with the nightly bombardments, Miller arranged for the band to move out to Bedford. The very next day, a Nazi rocket demolished their old digs in London.

Soon after the liberation of Paris, Miller made plans to invade the European mainland by the end of the year. The band increased its hectic schedule, prerecording eighty-five half-hour shows for radio broadcast while they were scheduled to be out of the country.

"On the foggy afternoon of Dec. 15, 1944, Miller and two others took off in a small plane for Paris," wrote George Frazier in *The Swing Era.* "Nobody will ever know for sure why the normally cautious Miller did not wait for a better day or a bigger plane. Ten days later, on Christmas Day, *The New York Times* reported: 'Major Glenn Miller, director of the United States Air Forces Band, is missing on a flight from England to Paris, it was announced today. No trace of the plane has been found.' None ever was."

Some theorists believe the plane had icing problems and was felled by the bad weather. Others point to a bomber squadron that dumped its remaining bombs over the Channel as it returned to England. One exploded before it hit the water. A navigator on board one of the bombers claimed to have seen a small plane flying in the opposite direction, toward the French coast, just before the explosion. Later the airman checked all flight logs for that day, and the only plane reported missing was Glenn Miller's.

The British Home Front Hits the Screen

Great Britain was America's strongest of allies in WWII, and movies produced on both sides of "the Big Pond" reaffirmed that partnership. Okay, so maybe the United States didn't jump into the fray as quickly as the Brits would have liked, and some British movies in the late '30s maybe got a little preachy, taking potshots now and then at America's isolationist stance.

But by December 8, 1941, the debate was pretty much decided, and the isolationists in the United States got in line to enlist for the duration . . . or they decided it was best just to be quiet for however long it took to defeat the aggressors of the Axis powers. By late 1941, Great Britain had already been in the fight for at least two years, withstanding almost nightly bombing raids from Luftwaffe planes. The gritty Brits' resolute spirit was the theme of several movies in the early '40s.

In MGM's *Mrs. Miniver*, filmed in 1941 and directed by three-time Oscar winner William Wyler, Greer Garson played the title role, "a courageous mother who holds her family together in the teeth of the Blitz, [who] symbolized in personal terms Britain's lonely heroism in stemming the Nazi tide," wrote Koppes and Black in *Hollywood Goes to War*. The film opened with this overview scrolling across the screen: "This story of an average English middle-class family begins with the summer of 1939; when the sun shone down on a happy, careless people, who worked and played, reared their children and tended their gardens in that happy, easy-going England, that was so soon to be fighting desperately for her way of life and for life itself."

Day-to-day life continues until an afternoon flower show is disrupted by a Nazi air raid. Everyone rushes off, some to their homes, others to local bomb shelters, the Royal Air Force pilots to their planes at the base close by.

The bombing devastates the tranquil town, and the next day a service is held at the bombed-out church. After reading from the Bible, the pastor says to his beleaguered congregation, "We in this quiet corner of England have suffered the loss of friends very dear to us." He names a choir boy and the bell ringer and says, "Our hearts go out in sympathy to the two families who share the cruel loss of a young girl who was married at this altar only two weeks ago. The homes of many of us have been destroyed, and the lives of young and old have been taken. There's scarcely a household that hasn't been struck to the heart. And why?" He asks what everyone is asking, praying to God for an answer. "Children, old people, a young girl at the height of her loveliness. Why these? Are these our soldiers? Why should they be sacrificed? I shall tell you why. Because this is not only a war of soldiers in uniform. It is a war of the people, of all the people, and it must be fought not only on the battlefield, but in the cities, and in the villages, in the factories and on the farms, in the home and in the heart of every man, woman, and child who loves freedom.

"Well, we have buried our dead, but we shall not forget them. Instead, they will inspire us with an unbreakable determination to free ourselves and those who come after us, from the tyranny and terror that threaten to strike us down. This is the people's war. It is our war. We are the fighters. Fight it then. Fight it with all that is in us. And may God defend the right."

Right: *Sometimes Lady Luck had more to do with an aircrew returning from a bombing mission unscathed, than even the most devout Christians. Still, it didn't hurt to have God flying in the copilot's seat.*
Air Force Museum Photo

The congregation then sings "Onward Christian Soldiers," and the camera pans upward through the bombed ceiling of the church as a wave of Allied planes roar by overhead, on their way to another mission to Germany.

Mrs. Miniver's message was loud and clear when the film was made in 1941: Britain would stand resolute and endure for however long it took, to hold out however long it took for America to join the fight. Of course, by the time it was released, in mid-1942, America was in fact at war, standing side by side with Great Britain.

The low-key drama would win six Academy Awards in 1942, including Best Actress for Greer Garson, Best Director for William Wyler, Best Supporting Actress for Teresa Wright (the young girl the pastor was solemnly talking about), and Best Film, beating out, among others, the combat film, *Wake Island*.

Ironically, instead of basking in the glory of his Oscar win, William Wyler was serving with the 91st Bomber Group in England when a *Stars and Stripes* newspaper reporter called with the great news. He had won the greatest award of his profession, and although he couldn't be there for the applause, at the time Wyler was busy doing his part to win something much, much more important for democracy. The celebrating would have to wait until he got back to Hollywood.

The bombing of London was both a backdrop and an obstacle to love in *This Above All*, also released in 1942, which won two minor Oscars. On June 1 of that year, *Time* reviewed the movie, stating, "Why should a young, disillusioned, lower-middle-class Englishman risk his life for the upper classes unless he is sure of a new shake after World War II is won? *This Above All* is a remarkably good love story.

"WAAF Joan Fontaine, who has what it takes to play lady-in-a-haystack, quietly meets her man (Tyrone Power) in the blackout, goes

Below: *Prior to every mission, ground crewmen had to prep the planes, patching holes, checking the instruments and gauges, lubricating everything, and loading munitions – from machine-gun belts in the wing guns of fighter planes to the big 500-pounders in the bomb bays of the B-17s and B-24s.*
National Archives Photo

away with him to a seaside resort, where he leaves her, eventually rejoins him for keeps after the Luftwaffe has almost battered his brains out in a London bombing."

Other British and American films centered around England's home front included *Went the Day Well?*, released in 1942, which told the tale of a British town occupied by Nazi paratroopers, an advance guard for an eventual invasion of the British Isles. Robert Taylor and Vivien Leigh starred in the 1940 romantic tearjerker, *Waterloo Bridge*, about a British soldier who meets a young ballerina just as hostilities break out for WWI. She later hears that he has been killed in the fighting, only to find out years later—on the eve of WWII—that he's still alive. Another saga that spanned the two world wars was 1944's *White Cliffs of Dover*, starring Irene Dunne, Alan Marshal, and a teenaged Roddy McDowall. This flag-waving classic cemented the bond between America and England during the war years. *Forever and a Day*, released in 1943, spanned a century, from the era of Napoleon up through the London Blitz of WWII, portraying the British as steadfast and resolute in the toughest of times.

The dilemma facing British actors and actresses on the eve of the impending war was portrayed in the 1940 film, *Return to Yesterday*, with Clive Brook and Anna Lee working together in a small theater group in England, debating whether to stay and endure the Nazi bombing or return to Hollywood.

While stationed in England, real-life American soldier John Sweet gravitated toward the local community theater, which was casting for the Thornton Wilder play, *Our Town*. Sergeant Sweet had no acting experience, but he was good enough to join the cast and was later discovered by a local movie producer searching for an American GI to play an American GI in 1944's *Canterbury Tale*. (After his brief fling with stardom, Army Sergeant John Sweet went off to war. He returned to the States and resumed his previous career as a teacher.)

The difficulties of producing a movie in wartime England were never more acute than on the set of the 1941 comedy, *Major Barbara*, which starred Wendy Hiller and Rex Harrison and was adapted and updated for the screen by eighty-four-year-old author George Bernard Shaw, who wrote the original script more than thirty years prior. *Time* reported on June 2, 1941, "Work on the script began two weeks before hostilities [with Nazi Germany] began. Then there was a shortage of lumber for sets. Half the picture was finished when the bombing of London began. For months, bomb bursts, air-raid sirens, and anti-aircraft fire made it impossible to make more than a few brief shots a day. Some of the cast lived on the set, passed much of the day in air-raid shelters and the night in rescue work. Once, when the company returned to complete a sequence begun on a street in London's East End, the houses had disappeared."

The European Air War on Film

British civilians maintained the proverbial "stiff upper lip" as waves of Luftwaffe planes roared overhead, attempting to destroy the bombers and fighter planes and swashbuckling pilots of the Royal Air Force, their airstrips, anti-aircraft gun batteries, hangars, and fuel pens. Then the Nazis launched V-1 and V-2 rockets from across the Channel, uncertain of exactly where they might land, but fully aware of the psychological damage they would inflict.

The indiscriminant bombing of London and other population centers in the southern reaches was meant to terrorize and demoralize the English. Instead, it steeled them for a prolonged fight. When British high command sent its bombers and escort fighters aloft to retaliate against the Nazis and bomb cities deep inside Germany, local movie studios rushed numerous scripts into production.

After the initial Nazi air strikes, 1939's *The Lion Has Wings* was the first British film to cover the conflict, piecing the story together from newsreels, re-creations, and other feature films and tying it together with narration. Aerial dogfights were staged using British planes, some of them painted with Luftwaffe markings, and a Nazi passenger plane was depicted as an enemy bomber (the producers assumed the general public would never know the difference). Filmmakers made a more subtle deception in their portrayal of

RIGHT: *Blackout conditions for London during the Blitz didn't affect Nazi V-1 and V-2 rockets, which relied only on propulsion to get across the English Channel. As the fuel ran out, they lost trajectory and exploded wherever they came down, often on population centers such as London, sometimes harmlessly in the English countryside, where the only damage might be to a discontented cow or two. Luftwaffe bombers, however, targeted London, terrorizing its citizenry, hardening its resolve to one day defeat the Nazis. Amid all the smoke sat St. Paul's Cathedral.*
National Archives Photo

Left: *The indiscriminate bombing of London and other southern cities in England was intended to demoralize the citizenry, killing thousands of innocent women and children, with many survivors evacuated further north to the countryside, out of harm's way. These children in East London have just survived a night of bombing in September of 1940, and wait outside of what is left of their home for a familiar face to take them in.*
U.S. Information Agency Photo

how the Royal Air Force detected the incoming bombers and was able to get Spitfires aloft to meet them over the Channel. In truth, radar provided the early warning, but not wanting the Nazis to learn about this new technology, the filmmakers implied that a Nazi double agent and spotters along the coast picked up the intruders.

Even worse, because the producers didn't feel the general public would bother to watch a documentary film, they added a flimsy story line, with Merle Oberon and Ralph Richardson among the many who just went through the motions, creating a muddled mess that still wasn't watched.

Actual RAF combat footage was also used to follow the Wellington bomber *F for Freddy* and its crew in *Target for Tonight*, released in 1941. The film begins with the early reconnaissance of the target—an oil refinery—and continues through the planning, the preparation of the plane and the crew, and all the assorted problems encountered on a perilous mission, including crappy weather, damage from anti-aircraft fire, an injured crewman, a sputtering engine, and a blind landing through a blanket of fog.

The crewmen from the bomber *B for Bertie* aren't quite so lucky in the 1942 movie, *One of Our Aircraft Is Missing*. During a bombing mission to hit the Mercedes plant at Stuttgart, their plane is damaged and the crew parachutes over Nazi-occupied Holland, where local partisans take them

Left: *Sometimes bad weather over the target would cancel a bombing mission, but many more were postponed, maybe for hours, and the crew would be on stand by until it was time to go. This Flying Fortress crew wouldn't have to wait long for another flight into hell.*
National Archives Photo

in, but only after being reassured that the intruders are not Nazi spies. Though shot as a docudrama, the film starred many of Britain's best-known actors of the '40s, including Eric Portman, Hugh Williams, and Godfrey Tearle. Peter Ustinov broke into movies with his first role, as a local Dutch Catholic priest. Ironically, the RAF crew is smuggled to a safe house along the coast and has to wait for an air raid—their own British compatriots bombing Holland—to escape to the sea.

Speaking for both his fellow crewmen and his British countrymen, rear gunner Sir George Corbett, played by Godfrey Tearle, thanks their Dutch hostess for risking her life to help them: "Well, my dear young lady, we can't offer you anything except our love, our gratitude, and our admiration for a brave woman and a fearless country. But we can promise you one thing, a growing help and attack which will sweep these Germans from . . ."

But before he can finish, the air raid sirens blare, and the crew is whisked away to a waiting rowboat. They head out to the Channel and are picked up by a British patrol boat. Three months later, the *B for Bertie* crew is back in the air, on another bombing run to Berlin.

BELOW: *Among his many screen roles, British actor Leslie Howard appeared in* First of the Few, *along with one of His Majesty's most well-known servicemen, actor David Niven. The film followed the development of the spunky Spitfire fighter plane and its role in the defense of Britain against Nazi Luftwaffe intruders.* Associated Press Photo

Other films about the British war role over Fortress Europe included 1942's *First of the Few*, about the development of the Spitfire fighter plane, with Leslie Howard and David Niven; and the same year's *Desperate Journey*, which follows a composite aircrew with English pilot Errol Flynn, a Canadian navigator played by Alan Hale, and American crew member Ronald Reagan after they are shot down and taken to a POW camp. "Released near the end of 1942 . . . it is a Rover Boys-go-to-Germany adventure/comedy in which the Germans are dolts, and in which the heroes face serious danger as if it were a lark," Jeanine Basinger commented about *Desperate Journey* in *The World War II Combat Film*. The three heroes plan their escape, steal an unguarded Nazi plane, and make it back to friendly territory. Then Flynn spearheads another bombing mission on a vital German aircraft plant.

Continued Basinger: "Despite some heavy propagandizing about what swine the Nazis are, the film is more a comedy than anything else. It is in the tradition of the Errol Flynn movie—lighthearted adventure with a graceful hero who never loses his sense of humor despite the seriousness and immediacy of the danger."

Completed in the closing months of the war in Europe, *Way to the Stars* went a few years back in time, to the initial volleys of the Battle of Britain, following a young wide-eyed pilot who has grand illusions of aerial heroics . . . until his dreams are shattered by the reality that many of the heroes around him are dying, and he is one of the lucky few. This film, titled *Johnny in the Clouds* when it was released in America, also had a stellar cast, including Michael Redgrave, Stanley Holloway, Trevor Howard, John Mills, and Jean Simmons.

At the end of the 1942 movie *Flying Fortress*, the narrator, sounding very "prime minister-like," states, "We shall bomb Germany by day, as well as by night, in ever increasing measure, casting upon them, month by month, a heavier discharge of bombs, and making the German people taste and gulp each month a sharper dose of the miseries they have showered upon mankind. Once underway our attack will be relentless. We will smash Cologne, Essen, Emden, Bremerhaven, Kiel, Danzig . . . building with increasing fury towards the day when we shall visit upon Berlin itself the complete destruction to which our preliminary raids have been but a prelude, that great day when we will strike with devastating and unconquerable strength at the detested enemy of all the free peoples of the Earth."

Yankee Flyboys Make It to the Silver Screen

American audiences were certainly sympathetic to the British plight, but they would rally behind Yankee flyers, first with the Eagle Squadrons attached to the RAF, then later when Army Air Corps squadrons fanned out across the

LEFT: *The bombing campaign of Fortress Europe escalated to nearly round-the-clock waves of American and British planes. The pummeling of enemy industrial sites, railroads, bridges, and airstrips crippled the Nazi offensive. Carpet bombing leveled entire cities, such as Dresden, when 450 aircraft hit it in just one day, and continued until the city was little more than rubble. Cologne and Berlin also suffered extensive ruin.*
Imperial War Museum Photo

Above: *Flying above the clouds on the long journey from England to deep within Germany was often quite peaceful. But as the Allied bombers approached their targets, enemy fighter planes swarmed in from out of nowhere, and anti-aircraft gunners blasted the skies with flak. These B-26 Martins are returning from a mission, and once again their crews are enjoying the serenity of "dancing on the clouds"—at least until the next perilous mission.*
U.S. Air Force Photo

once-serene English countryside and created their own heroics worthy of the Hollywood treatment. "*International Squadron* [is] the story of an American pilot—Ronald Reagan—who ferries bombers to Britain and becomes so convinced of the justice of the cause he is aiding that he finally joins the RAF," wrote Michael Freedland in *The Warner Brothers*. A similar movie was *Eagle Squadron*, featuring Eddie Albert, Robert Stack, and Leif Erikson as American mavericks who have to tone it down if they want to make it in the RAF.

Twentieth Century Fox used the title *The Eagle Squadron* for a short time for its own production about the RAF. Darryl Zanuck "unleashed his ultimate weapons, his human embodiments of the atomic bomb which would end the war four years later," according to Hector Arce in *The Secret Life of Tyrone Power*. "The double whammy was Tyrone Power and Betty Grable, and the picture Zanuck began preparing in October of 1940 was *A Yank in the RAF*. Zanuck originally called it *The Eagle Squadron*, and it would revolve around an American test pilot played by Ty who enlisted in the British Royal Air Force, 'a cocksure know-it-all, a breezy, brash young guy.'

"To bring the lessons of war tragically home, Ty would be killed in the first German air raid over England. British government officials, who were cooperating in the production, requested that the American be allowed to live. It was then that the final title was settled on," concluded Hector Arce.

Grable's character is an American showgirl and an old flame of the brash Ty Power, who tries to reconnect with her, with mixed results. "*A Yank in the RAF* was a jumble of insipid love scenes; rabble-rousing speeches; frequent logistical montages of roaring airplanes, and the patter of marching feet; and smashing battle scenes. Several critics complained that the intimate scenes got in the way of the spectacular aerial battles filmed over Germany, France, and England—the actual ones."

William Wyler used his talents with the First Motion Picture Unit to document the exploits of the aircrew of *The Memphis Belle* on their last mission before heading home. In fact, their last mission was uneventful, so Wyler had to use film footage from several previously perilous missions, documented by the 8th Army Air Forces Combat Camera Unit, which had flown on some of the most terrifying bombing runs imaginable. Some didn't make it back. But there was one piece of footage they didn't get, and Wyler wanted it: a flak burst.

"I could never get one explosion because how the hell do you know where one's going to explode? Once the cloud is there it's too late. All that flak so close to us, and I could never get the explosion."

A Guardian Angel

Spencer Tracy took to the skies in MGM's 1943 film, *A Guy Named Joe*, the title making reference to the local British children's nickname for the fascinating American flyboys stationed near their village. Tracy played Pete Sandidge, a courageous (his superiors considered him a foolish) fighter pilot who climbs into the cockpit looking to take on the enemy even if he is outnumbered and outgunned.

His girl is Dorinda Durston (played by Irene Dunne), one of the many women pilots who ferried aircraft from the assembly lines to the East and West Coasts or flew overseas, delivering war planes to the Allied units in England. She is worried about his cavalier attitude in the air, certain it's going to get him killed. She tries to confront him, asking him to return home with her.

"When you crack up I'm supposed to sit around wet-eyed like an old man with asthma and mumble prayers for the rest of my life," she fumes. "What a surprise you're going to get! What's fun about knowing you're asking for it every time you take off? You think I like being sick inside all the time . . . waiting . . . being afraid when a telephone rings?"

Realizing how upset Dorinda is, Pete reluctantly agrees to return to the States and become a flight instructor, if she'll also hang it up. But just as they embrace, their good friend and fellow pilot Al Yackey (played by Ward Bond) barges in and says an Allied convoy is being threatened by a Nazi aircraft carrier and they've been tasked to fly out and sink it.

Out over the Atlantic, and just as they spot the enemy flattop, Nazi fighter planes swoop in and severely damage Pete's bomber. He orders his crew to bail out, then he guides the plane directly at the enemy warship and dies in the explosion. His act of sacrifice is witnessed by his good buddy Al, who eludes the Nazi attackers and returns to break the bad news to Dorinda.

The movie turns whimsical, as Pete comes back as a guardian angel for another still very-much-alive, brash young pilot like he used to be. Pete follows the cadet through flight training and overseas, offering subliminal guidance.

Later in the war, dispatched to the Pacific Theater, Al and Dorinda meet again. He's been hoping she has gotten over the past, no longer mourning Pete, but she is still grieving and will never let go of his memory. Al had hoped for something more, and scolds her, but he could easily be talking to anyone wallowing in self-pity: "You're gonna have to get over this, Dorinda. This is just plain darn foolishness sitting around here mourning like this.

You'd rather stay here and moan? But if you're gonna sit and grieve all the rest of your life, why don't you do it right?

"Why don't you get a little tiny room someplace and lock yourself up in it and wear black silk dresses, and put a little white lace handkerchief over your hair and a pasty look on your face? I know a woman back home did that . . . she got just what she wanted too. Folks felt sorry for her for thirty years. You think you're the only guy who got a kick in the teeth? Well, you're not. It's happening every day and it's gonna keep right on happening until this thing's over. And you . . . you can sit here and feel sorry for yourself or you can come out with me and see how nice people are when they're alive."

Meanwhile, Pete and another deceased pilot are killing time in heaven, enjoying the good life and talking about old times, when he is summoned by The General (played by Lionel Barrymore), who tells him he has a responsibility to not just watch what's going on down on Earth, but to seize the opportunity to "pay off to the future what you owe for having been part of the past. Just another way of saying I'm glad I lived, I'm glad I was alive. Now let me give you a hand."

Pete asks the old sage for another chance, and then he heads back down to Earth, to mentor the young, inexperienced pilot during a harrowing mission and to encourage Dorinda to finally move on and start living again.

It was a message thousands of grieving American women needed to hear.

'Celluloid Commandos' Advance Military Training Frame by Frame

"THE TRAINING FILM IS BEING REBORN; IT IS GOING TO ASSUME 'BOX OFFICE' ASPECTS. IT'S GOING TO HAVE PRODUCTION VALUES. AND THESE PRODUCTION VALUES WILL PAY DIVIDENDS IN LIVES SAVED."

—*Private Hal Levy, Member, First Motion Picture Unit 1942, quoted in the unit's magazine*

"IT WAS UNDERSTOOD WHEN I WENT INTO THE ARMY IT WAS TO MAKE FILMS. THEY REALIZED THE IMPORTANCE OF FILM, ALTHOUGH IT TOOK THEM A WHILE TO GET GOING."

—*Lieutenant John Huston, U.S. Army Signal Corps, quoted in* The Cinema of John Huston *by Gerald Pratley*

BACKGROUND: *The First Motion Picture Unit's special effects team created an exact-scale model of Tokyo, and filmmakers used it to make training movies for pilots about to depart on bombing runs over the Japanese city. Chances are that the airmen aboard this B-29 watched such a film to visualize the flight they would make. The special effects unit members continually updated the model as new intelligence reports and photos arrived.*
21st Bomber Command Photo

DOUBT HUNG LOW IN THE AIR, LIKE THE SMOKE AND squalor of death after the silenced sirens at the end of a Nazi bombing raid. No one spoke for a few moments, each man letting the consequences of his decision bear down on his soul. Willfully deceiving the President of the United States, especially in times of war, made even the strongest egoist reconsider his most deeply held beliefs.

Misleading a few British men, however, didn't bother Frank, the group's leader. Theirs was a just cause, and damning a few Union Jacks to professional obscurity to promote popular politics could be considered only collateral damage. The world had seen enough destruction—in lives lost, cities toppled, countries obliterated—to validate, even venerate these actions. Precious cargo had been lost, and Operation C.Y.A. was the only way to recover it and bolster the war effort. These Brits could recover from a bruised ego, but the world might not withstand continued bludgeoning from Berlin. Morale needed a booster shot, and with proper preparation, their plan could provide that. But their efforts would succeed only if the three men worked together under the veil of secrecy. Each was used to calling his own shots, so collaboration would be difficult. War was the glue that bound them together.

The group had few things left to discuss at this clandestine meeting. Orders had already been given. Frank and his underlings, John and George, spoke in hushed tones, analyzing options, synchronizing schedules, and marshaling materials. This crusade would be fought on three fronts: California's desolate Mojave Desert, Florida's sunny center, and North Africa's barren boroughs (a fourth front, foggy London, would be added later). Each campaign had to be executed to perfection, under cover and under deadline pressure. More than their reputations were at stake. Although they'd scripted hundreds of scenes like these, none carried the potential for commendation or condemnation like Operation C.Y.A. If President Roosevelt found out about their ruse—well, they really didn't want to know what would happen.

The men armed themselves with the tools of their trade, special weapons for every possible shot from every potential angle, and said their good-byes. The stealthy travels and furtive fake fighting they orchestrated left FDR in the dark for a time but shined the spotlight on Allied forces desperate for victory in an America clinging to the hope that the sands of the conflict were shifting.

Operation C.Y.A. doesn't appear in any history books, nor is it the title of a film directed by the three men—Frank Capra, John Huston, and George Stevens—involved in the plot. The name represents what the mission might have been called as the three men worked to cover their collective ass as part of the U.S. Army's Pictorial Services. Huston and Stevens headed combat photography units, and Capra led the 834th Signal Services Photographic Detachment, Special Services Division, when catastrophe struck.

Never was the Signal Corps' deficiency in combat photography training more noticeable than when Anatole Litvak's film of the Americans landing in North Africa was lost at sea (the ship transporting the film was bombed and sunk before leaving the harbor). With Litvak's images buried in the deep blue and with no other coverage, Army Pictorial Services head Brigadier General William H. Harrison knew his career could be just as sunk as Litvak's canisters. "The brass was embarrassed," Huston said in Lawrence

Left: *Signal Corps Lieutenant Colonel Frank Capra received the Distinguished Service Medal from General George Marshall on June 14, 1945, one day before he retired from military service. According to Joseph McBride in* Frank Capra: The Catastrophe of Success, *the director became upset when Marshall summoned him to his office. He feared that he was about to be given a new assignment on the verge of his retirement. Instead, the commander awarded him the medal, and read a statement, which said, in part: "He was responsible for the production of a remarkable series of motion pictures at the personal direction of the Chief of Staff which graphically presented the causes leading up to the present war and the responsibility of the Axis powers for those tragic consequences ... The films produced by Colonel Capra under the direction of the Chief of Staff had an important influence on the morale of the Army."*

McBride wrote that Marshall's aide, Frank McCarthy, recalled Capra smiling during the award presentation and asking where the men's room was as they walked down the hall following the ceremony. McCarthy said that Capra was so moved by receiving the award that he went into the bathroom and vomited.

U.S. Army Photo

Grobel's *The Hustons*, "and the president was not to know that only one man and his crew had been assigned to the landings." Harrison had two choices: tell Roosevelt the Signal Corps had no footage of the landings and face sure damnation, or come up with another plan. The Army and the Bureau of Public Relations hatched the idea to fabricate new footage and pass it off as a chronicle of American combat in North Africa. Huston called it "a huge counterfeit operation simply to deceive the president," according to Joseph McBride's *Frank Capra: The Catastrophe of Success.*

Capra and Huston left for the Mojave with camera operator Joseph Valentine, director Jules Buck, and soldiers who had fought in the Tunisian battles. Stevens and cameraman William Mellor filmed tanks fighting in fake encounters in North Africa, and Huston staged aerial skirmishes in Florida, flying in bombers that were "attacked" by other aircraft. Huston said in *The Cinema of John Huston*, by Gerald Pratley, "None of it was very convincing." When the three met in Washington to review the footage, Huston called it "so obviously false that it was just disgraceful," according to McBride.

The images were so poor that the three men decided to approach British filmmakers who were also putting together a movie about the Allied victories in North Africa, obviously with a British slant. Capra and Huston set up a meeting with Hugh Stewart and Roy Boulting, and under the pretense of showing Allied unity, offered to marry their talents and resources, including the faked footage. The three Americans had already heard complaints from Army brass about the British film, *Desert Victory*, which had appeared in 1943 amid critical and public acclaim around the globe and had won a 1943 Oscar for Feature Documentary. The Americans had to produce *something*, even if it was a collaboration with the Brits. Together, the men released *Tunisian Victory* in 1944.

Huston said in McBride's book: "I regarded the whole thing in rather a more frivolous light than Frank did. The whole thing was a fraud and a frost and funny as hell . . . But Frank was undertaking it in all seriousness to make

LEFT: *This waist gunner aboard a B-17 Flying Fortress attacked enemy aircraft over Tunisia. Hollywood directors and U.S. Army officers Frank Capra, John Huston, and George Stevens worked with British filmmakers to create* Tunisian Victory, *a film about the Allied campaign in North Africa. The movie marked the first "good-news" motion picture released in the U.S.* National Archives Photo

a proper picture out of it and finally succeeded in doing what was required. He was very skillful at concealing his deceit." Huston said later in the book, " . . . Frank won't admit this, I'm sure, but my God, it was terrible what we were doing to them [the British filmmakers], putting our fraudulent stuff in with their real stuff."

Some historians disagree with this account. Frederic Krome wrote in "*Tunisian Victory* and Anglo-American Film propaganda in World War II" for *The Historian,* March 22, 1996, that Capra was ordered to Britain when government officials feared they would offend Americans if their perspective was not included in *Africa Freed*, the working title for the *Desert Victory* sequel. Since the invasion of North Africa—called Operation Torch—had been an Allied combined military action, British Minister of Information Brendan Bracken decided that the film should record the American participation. According to Krome, Bracken and Ministry of Information Films Division Head Jack Beddington "worried that without the assistance of U.S. propagandists, the Torch film might not accurately reflect American views." The British consulted with the Office of War Information Overseas Branch's Samuel Spewack and asked that Capra assist on the movie.

Capra was not welcomed with open arms, however. Krome wrote, "The British Army Film Unit, the makers of *Africa Freed*, were reluctant to scrap their nearly finished product." They even later asked him to hand over his material so that they could decide if, and where, to include the footage in their movie. Capra rejected their demand and told Spewack that he would not allow anyone to see his images until he had assurances that a movie would be made cooperatively. The OWI and the U.S. Army agreed with Capra and pressured the British for a compromise. Capra's reputation enabled him to seize editorial control over the film, with even Bracken supporting him rather than his own film unit, Krome wrote. Capra returned home and completed *Tunisian Victory*. U.S. film critics reviewed the movie more positively than British critics, although many thought the movie was released too late after the fighting for anyone to care.

But not all movies made by the military were faked or done in secrecy. Filmmakers strived for accuracy and made movies in obscurity—no individual names were ever listed in credits of a military-produced film—all to further the war effort. From training movies showing soldiers the enemies and teaching them how to fight, to combat documentaries that graphically captured war's gore, some of Hollywood's best dedicated their talents and their lives to the cause.

A War of the People—All People

By the time the United States entered World War II, the efforts to defeat the evil across the seas demanded every adult's attention and energy. Those who weren't in the military fighting the war supported it by building planes, assembling bombs, making ammunition, saving rubber, buying war bonds, or writing to the boys on the front. No one, and no industry, remained immune. Even Hollywood's silver screens and its shining stars found themselves swept up in the conflict overseas.

World War II ground Hollywood's "Golden Age" to a screeching halt. Actors, actresses, directors, producers, writers, set-builders, and makeup artists all joined a cast of thousands serving their country. Some left a world where a "bomb" could hurt a career to one where a bomb could, and often did, kill. Many traded "Lights, camera, action" for "Ready, aim, fire." No one played a bit part in defending U.S. freedom—every role was critical. Unlike on soundstages, however, in a war riflemen used real bullets that shed real blood—blood that spilled across four continents. Nobody walked away from one of these death scenes.

Still, not everyone went off to fight. Some remained on movie sets and in studios, using their talents to recruit, to train, and to personify the war. The military harnessed the might of movie magic by creating special filmmaking units, enlisting the help of some of the studios' best and brightest. The U.S. Army created the First Motion Picture Unit (FMPU), a full-scale movie studio complete with actors, directors, writers, makeup artists, costumers, carpenters, set designers, sound recorders, and prop specialists. The Army's Signal Corps also made training and propaganda films and shot footage in the war's combat zones. Likewise, the Naval Office of Strategic Services solicited help from the day's top writers, directors, actors, and cameramen. The Office of War Information, which oversaw *all* filmmaking within the War Department, also had its own Motion Picture Bureaus, with Domestic and Overseas Branches. All told, the federal government spent $50 million to make hundreds of movies and training films during World War II.

Joining Forces with Hollywood

Left: *The First Motion Picture Unit logo alerted viewers that the movie was a product of the special Army Air Forces unit.*
First Motion Picture Unit Graphic

General Henry "Hap" Arnold commanded the Army Air Forces (the predecessor to today's Air Force) during World War II, and he recognized the power of moving pictures. Arnold had roles as a pilot in two pre-World War I films. So in the early 1940s, when he started to build an air corps to compete with the German Luftwaffe, he realized that movies could be an effective recruiting and training tool for pilots, gunners, and crewmen.

Army Chief of Staff General George Marshall also enjoyed movies, particularly the

Right: *General Henry. "Hap" Arnold had the vision to start an Army Air Forces motion picture unit to make training movies and documentaries. The commander had played in a film years before World War II, and he knew the power of film. He was not afraid to use it to fight the enemy, who was using its own motion picture propaganda to further its control. Arnold is shown above inspecting ice formations on propeller blades at what is now the John H. Glenn Research Field.*
NASA Photo

ones with beautiful women. He regularly went to the cinema at Fort Myer, Virginia, seeking respite from the stress of military life. But seeing beyond the entertainment, Marshall realized that movies represented an excellent mass medium to not only inform but also influence the world, according to McBride. And, like Arnold, he understood that the Army could never train soldiers to be filmmakers, but it could show movie geniuses how to fight with camera shots and gunshots.

The First Motion Picture Unit was born when Arnold approached Jack Warner, whose Warner Brothers studio was known for making pro-military films, to make training movies for the Army Air Forces. Warner asked writer, producer, and director Owen Crump to accompany him to Washington, D.C., to meet with Arnold. Together the three settled on a plan for the unit. According to a short film the unit produced to describe its activities, the motion pictures made would be operational and inspirational while teaching soldiers what they were fighting for, whom they were fighting against, and what they were fighting with.

Recruiting, Retaining Hollywood's Best

General Arnold sent a lieutenant and two sergeants to handle all military issues and paperwork, while Crump set out to staff the new unit. He created an organizational chart that followed a film studio model and counted how many people would be needed for each department and job. Like a good marketer, he passed along the story to the Hollywood trade press, and soon applications poured in from every studio. While some were draft eligible, many candidates were experienced, middle-aged professionals whose patriotism following Pearl Harbor drove them to "enlist" in the upstart studio.

Arnold ensured that these applicants signed up directly for the film unit, which allowed the specialized unit to come together quickly. The military typically does not allow enlistees to join a specific unit, but Arnold knew it was the only way to make his plan work. It wasn't possible for the Army Air Forces to make military men into moviemakers, but he could train these moviemaking experts to be specialized soldiers. The First Motion Picture Unit's "celluloid commandos" began making training films June 27, 1942, with Warner and Crump as two of its officers.

Despite the importance of these films, and totally without consideration of the high-dollar talents of the enlistees, the First Motion Picture Unit ran like almost any other military organization. Members typically attended a basic training camp before being transferred to the film unit, and most earned a soldier's pay: fifty dollars every week. One way the unit differed from military norms, however, was its friendly, casual environment. Soldiers rarely saluted, and officers and enlisted men called each other by first names. The unit did not start out this relaxed, but as civilian "extras" were costumed for roles, real soldiers saluted everyone who walked by, leading to confusion. No salutes and first-name-basis communication became the rule rather than the exception.

Still, some, including Jack Warner, considered rank important. When Arnold recommended that Warner enlist in the Army, Warner said he would, but only if he could be a general. Arnold offered him a commission as a lieutenant colonel, and Warner agreed. He recognized the potential for publicity and animosity—and knew the move would make his older brother, Harry, jealous. When Jack Warner assumed command of the film unit, he said, "Remember men, the enemy is threatening not only our lives but our property," according to an article in *Los Angeles Magazine*'s December 1997 issue.

Warner felt compelled to serve in the military and fight against the Germans largely because he, like many other Hollywood powerbrokers, was of European Jewish descent. American movie studios operated in Europe in the late 1920s and early 1930s, but Warner Brothers had abandoned its German venture by 1934, a year after the Nazis came to power. Warner viewed moviemaking as an obligation of patriotism and made many pro-military films. He was so pro-military and pro-war that he was accused of warmongering in 1941 when a Senate subcommittee hearing examined Hollywood's role in banging the drums for American entry into World War II at a time when others preached isolationism.

But gaining a commission in the Army didn't force Warner to forsake his shrewd business sense. He managed the film unit like his own studio. Warner hammered out deals, including one with fellow Hollywood executive, Hal Roach, to use his vacant Culver City studio. Roach, by this time in his fifties, had left town for active duty and closed the studio that had created legendary comedies like *Our Gang* and *Abbott and Costello*. Warner's deal with Roach allowed the Army film unit to lease the studio for one dollar. The First Motion Picture Unit had 78,000 square feet of soundstages, with some large enough for up to four groups to operate at any one time. Roach ended up making a shrewd business move, too. He found his studio—renamed Fort Roach by the soldiers who served there—in much better condition at the war's end than when he left.

Once the film unit was organized and at home at Fort Roach, Warner returned to running Warner Brothers Studio, believing he had accomplished the mission Arnold gave him.

Training Gains Tinseltown Touch

The First Motion Picture Unit movies were not intended for public release but for military-only consumption. Films focused on subjects ranging from aircraft navigation to gunnery, from medical treatment to survival. The motion picture unit's movies not only educated new troops, but also prepared young men for the horrors and harsh realities of the war.

The Nazis had used film effectively for many years, to advance their anti-Semitism. But the First Motion Picture Unit members had no way of knowing that. What they did know, however, was how to make powerful, moving pictures in ways only insiders could.

If the First Motion Picture Unit ran like any other military unit, it also ran like any other movie studio, but with different goals. The unit had no intention of making the next blockbuster. It attempted, however, to teach soldiers how to bust through enemy lines and defeat the Germans, Italians, and Japanese on every front. To do this, the unit used its veteran-filmmakers-turned-rookie-soldiers to develop training films unlike any others. The unit put the talents of its special effects experts to work. More than one hundred men made an exact-scale model of Japan's main island by using pre-war aerial photographs and reports from military intelligence units. The model swallowed nearly one full floor of a soundstage. The Tokyo replica showed the coastline and thousands of offices, homes, and other buildings. Camera crews mounted their equipment on movable overhead platforms and then soared over the model, filming what bomber pilots could expect to see at 30,000 feet over Tokyo.

These films changed the way the military conducted its briefings. Before such movies were available, an officer faced a large map and used a pointer to indicate routes and targets. Once these new training films landed in Pacific bases, pilots could "see" their mission on the screen and visualize their routes, their targets, and their successes. The special effects crews updated models constantly. Based on the latest aerial photographs, the crews remodeled the replica to show damage to targets.

The First Motion Picture Unit also had a first-rate animation department, headed by Rudolf Ising, according to an October 30, 2002, *Los Angeles*

Left: *The armed forces utilized experienced cartoonists to create propaganda films for both civilian and military audiences. In this movie,* The Fruits of Aggression, *the triumvirate of evil—Hitler, Mussolini, and Hirohito—divided the world.*
National Archives Photo

Times article by Patricia Ward Biederman. Ising was the co-creator of Warner Brothers' *Looney Tunes* and *Merrie Melodies* cartoons. Animators working for the motion picture unit played many roles, with each artist learning fill-ins, layouts, and cels to fully comprehend how an animated film was made. Ising's team included, among others, Frank Thomas, who was a successful animator at Walt Disney Studios before the war. He already had animated the dwarfs in *Snow White*. (After the war, Thomas would animate the memorable spaghetti scene from *Lady and the Tramp*, as well as scenes in *Cinderella*, *Peter Pan*, and *Walt Disney's 101 Dalmatians*.) The team also included Jules Engle, who had created scenes for Disney's *Fantasia* and worked as the key colorist on *Bambi*; John Hubley, an animator for *Snow White and the Seven Dwarfs* (who helped create *Mr. Magoo* after his service in the film unit); and Bill Scott (who later animated characters for *Rocky and His Friends*, co-produced and wrote scripts for *The Bullwinkle Show*, and gave voices to the show's characters, including Bullwinkle, Dudley Do-Right, and Mr. Peabody).

The animators' experiences immediately showed up in their work. In *Training Film 389* (also called *Straight and Level Flight and Effective Controls*), animators explained the complex concepts of thrust, torque, gravity, and drag to would-be flight crews and pilots. The character of Gravity, lounging in a hammock, very much resembled Sleepy from *Snow White*. The plane's pilot looked like a trim Elmer Fudd, slimmed down, perhaps, from basic training.

The animation team developed new characters to teach recruits. One, Mr. Chameleon, showed soldiers how to use camouflage. Another film, *Jap Zero*, taught soldiers how to recognize Japanese aircraft (and was "dedicated to the flyers who are helping to make the total number of Zeros . . . zero"). When the narrator said that the Japanese Zero's fuselage resembled a cigar, the animators literally made that part of the aircraft look like a cigar. This enabled soldiers to remember critical lessons through visualization. The military wanted accuracy in its training films—so much so that a U.S. cargo plane flew the first Zero captured in one piece to California so that the motion picture unit could film the plane performing aerial maneuvers and send the footage to Pacific commanders.

Training films were not limited to fighting and combat, however. The unit also made films regarding soldiers'

Left: *Illustrators played a key role at the First Motion Picture Unit. Producers called on these artists to help explain complex concepts to trainees. Whether it was a class about how an airplane works or a lecture on the use of safety equipment, young soldiers managed to stay awake because characters like Mickey Mouse appeared in films. Military leaders, such as Major General William Porter (right), approved of animation and personally met with Walt Disney (center) to discuss using cartoon characters in military and civilian defense training movies.*
Associated Press Photo

RIGHT: The Fruits of Aggression *showed that even the evil three—Italy, Germany, and Japan—could not hide from Allied attacks.*
National Archives Photo

hygiene. The most famous of these movies was *Three Cadets*. It chronicled the lives of three sexually active young men. The first used a condom. The second cadet did not use a condom, but he went to sick bay out of fear that he had contracted VD. The third cadet did not use a condom and opted to take sulfa drugs stealthily to cure the effects of venereal disease.

The Army Air Force needed a film like *Three Cadets* because many soldiers suffered the effects of sexually transmitted diseases but did not report them. Many chose to self-medicate, as commanders pulled out of training trainees who reported to sick bay, and those men did not graduate on schedule. Many soldiers failed to realize, however, that sulfa drugs caused them to lose hand-eye coordination at altitudes above 10,000 feet. Several pilots crashed planes when the sulfa in their bodies caused them to become disoriented in midair. Although the Army's Chaplain General wanted to scrap *Three Cadets* because none of the men in the movie received punishment, Arnold praised the movie for saving the Army $30,000 for each plane a cadet didn't smash.

BELOW: *In* Three Cadets, *young trainees learned how to treat venereal diseases. The First Motion Picture Unit made the movie when airmen crashed planes because they secretly self-medicated with sulfa drugs to treat their "social" diseases.*
Screen Capture from First Motion Picture Unit Film Photo

The First Motion Picture Unit also had the task of creating recruiting movies. When generals were desperate in 1942, they looked to the unit to make a movie that encouraged young men to enlist. Crump, who had helped Warner organize and command the Motion Picture Unit, wrote and directed *Winning Your Wings*. The military called Army Air Forces Lieutenant James Stewart from active duty to narrate the film.

Not only did the film tout the various positions available on flight and ground crews, it also boasted of the high pay these fliers received: $75 a month while in training, $245 a month for lieutenants, and $430 per month for captains. It showed young men that Army Air Forces training prepared them for life after war by giving them technical experience and teaching them to be alert, to handle men, and to learn courage. Further, it attempted to strengthen America's opposition to Germany by showing images of bombings and Hitler. "The roar of 100,000 motors sing their song, and theirs is a song of freedom. And their wings outstretched in the cause of decency," Stewart said at the movie's close. "Young men of America, your future's in the sky. Your wings are waiting." The movie—shot in only fourteen days nearly around the clock—lit up screens across the nation and earned credit for helping send more

Left: *Actor Jimmy Stewart (third from left), shown with one of his flight crews in New Mexico, had to gain weight to join the Army Air Forces after being turned down for the regular Army because he was too thin. Stewart took a short leave from active duty to work at the First Motion Picture Unit on* Winning Your Wings, *a film credited with bringing in more than 150,000 enlistees into the air corps.*
U.S. Army Air Forces Photo

than 150,000 enlistees to their local recruiting offices. *Winning Your Wings* earned a 1942 Academy Award nomination for Best Documentary.

The unit did not forget the soldier in the field, either. These moviemakers realized it was one thing to learn how to recognize and fight the enemy, but it was another to be captured. The First Motion Picture Unit created one of its most important and memorable movies in *Resisting Enemy Interrogation*, which earned a 1944 Academy Award nomination by effectively showing how five U.S. airmen unknowingly gave information to Nazi interrogators after being shot down. In the movie, no airman intentionally provided information, but each unwittingly offered a tidbit, which, when pieced together by savvy German officers, resulted in catastrophic consequences for the Americans. After the war, Crump ran into two soldiers who told him that had they not seen the movie during the war, they might have reacted like the airmen in the movie when their planes were shot down. *Resisting Enemy Interrogation* was so vital that President Roosevelt sent each man who made the film a personal letter expressing his gratitude.

Combat Cameramen: Courage Plus Craziness

But the motion picture unit was not all about making movies on Hollywood soundstages and back lots. It also trained combat cinematographers who shot and fought the war. Each combat camera crew had seven officers and up to thirty enlisted soldiers. The crew's size depended on which war theater it covered. All combat cameramen had training in motion picture and still photography and camera maintenance, as well as physical training, combat training, and aerial camera training under realistic flight circumstances. These crews typically accompanied airmen on bombing raids, which had high casualty

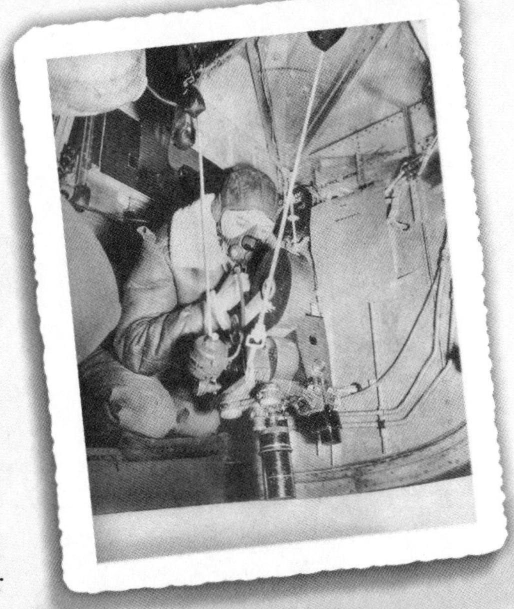

Right: *This combat cameraman aboard a B-24 Liberator depended solely on rubber cords to secure him and his camera to the plane. These photographers had to learn how to shoot film* and *guns, often taking the place of a wounded crewman on a mission.*
U.S. Signal Corps Photo

rates. The combat cameramen's footage was sent directly from the theater of war to theaters in the Pentagon, where top military leaders reviewed battle scenes. Other footage was shown to civilian audiences in newsreels before the feature films. (Combat cameramen shot nearly all of the World War II footage seen in today's programs on The History Channel and The Military Channel.)

Many of these cameramen died shooting footage of battles, and their courage under fire did not go unrecognized. The footage they compiled was used to train other soldiers, who could continue the fight better educated and better prepared. According to Biederman's article, German Field Marshall Wilhelm Keitel said at the surrender: "We had everything calculated perfectly except the speed with which the Allies were able to train their people for war. Our major miscalculation was in underestimating their quick and complete mastery of film education."

Combat cameramen didn't always take themselves seriously, even though they always took their jobs seriously. Norman Hatch, a combat photographer for the U.S. Marine Corps during World War II, said: "The brave ones were shooting the enemy. The crazy ones were shooting film."

FMPU's Famous Face behind the Camera

It's ironic that the most recognized combat filmmaker was a Hollywood legend *in front of* the camera. Arnold selected screen icon Clark Gable to produce a movie on aerial gunnery, hoping the King of Hollywood would inspire others to become gunners. Arnold knew that to bring the most powerful force possible to bear on the enemy, the Army Air Forces needed thousands of men to operate the .50-caliber machine guns that defended U.S. bombers against enemy attacks, because of high casualty rates, especially early in the war. Everyone wanted to be a pilot, and Arnold hoped that Gable's film would show young men that a gunner's life was exciting and lasted longer than ten minutes.

Gable and Arnold first met in 1938 when Arnold offered YIB-17 airplanes from the 2nd Bomb Group for the movie *Test Pilot*. Gable gave little thought to the Army until hearing about the Japanese attack on Pearl Harbor, after which he and his actress wife, Carole Lombard, offered President Roosevelt their help. The President suggested the two keep making movies, but Lombard urged her husband to join the Army. While he considered enlisting, Lombard died when her plane crashed during a war bond tour. Deeply saddened by Lombard's death, Gable announced that he was retiring from Hollywood to join the Army Air Corps.

It was no accident that Arnold telegrammed Gable the day of Lombard's funeral to offer him the assignment to make a movie about aerial gunners. MGM Studios, having already lost many of its stars to the draft, failed to forward the telegram to Gable and told Arnold that the star was mourning his wife and was not able to speak with him. Later that month, however, Gable flew with famed stunt pilot and motion picture unit Colonel Paul Mantz to Phoenix, Arizona, to meet with Army Air Forces Colonel Luke Smith, who in turn encouraged Gable to make the aerial gunners movie. Arnold wanted the film to be in theaters by 1943 to fill the gunners' void. Gable enlisted and later received an officer's commission.

Arnold asked Gable to recruit members for a film crew to fly on combat missions with one of the 8th Air Force heavy bomb groups in Europe. Gable and a friend, cinematographer Andrew McIntyre, trained at the Miami Air Officers Training School, with Gable memorizing class work the way he did movie lines. Gable received no special treatment during his initial training, and he was not an honors student: he ranked 700th out of 2,600 men in his class. He worked eighteen hours a day, seven days a week under the South Florida sun, sweating off ten pounds and pushing his forty-one-year-old body to its limits. Unlike his fellow soldiers, however, Gable had tailor-made uniforms supplied by MGM's costume department. The costumers also kept Gable supplied with extra Army hats, as women would occasionally run off with the one on his head.

After "accelerated" courses in gunnery and photography schools, Gable and McIntyre earned their gunner's wings in January 1943. They were promoted to captains in April. That same month, the two also deployed with their film crew and the 351st Bomb Group to England. By May, Gable had flown his first combat mission, a trip that sent the group's B-17s to Antwerp, Belgium. Gable's crew—McIntyre, screenwriter John Lee Mahin, camera operators Mario Tori and Robert Boles, and soundman Howard Voss—often was called the "Little Hollywood Group" because of the members' experience in filmmaking.

While his movie was supposed to focus on aerial gunners in combat, Gable and his crew began shooting footage in Pueblo, Colorado, before the group deployed. Gable wanted to depict how serious yet eager the airmen were. He continued shooting everything that happened before and during a mission, capturing the pre-mission planning and groundwork, the planes taking off, and the anxious moments experienced by those left behind as they waited for the group's return. He also caught the anguish of the group's first losses, when two planes failed to return from Courtrai, Belgium, on only the second mission. All of the behind-the-scenes footage gave the finished product a realism that had never been shown before.

RIGHT: *Clark Gable (center) probably joined the Army Air Forces in a moment of melancholy following the death of his wife, Carole Lombard. But the King of Hollywood trained with common airmen, first as a GI and then as an officer. Gable received little special treatment from the American military, although German Luftwaffe commander Hermann Goering made him the center of attention when he offered to reward any pilot who shot down the actor's plane. Every mission Gable flew to make his aerial gunner documentary,* Combat America, *faced enemy attacks. This photo was taken after the actor returned from a mission aboard* The Duchess.
U.S. Air Force Museum Photo

Such realism did not come without a price. Gable did not fly "milk runs" or training flights. Luftwaffe commander Hermann Goering had offered to reward any German pilot who shot down Gable's plane, and on each mission he flew, his aircraft was hit by enemy fire. On one mission aboard the plane *Ain't It Gruesome*, Luftwaffe fighter planes attacked, and a 20-mm shell slashed through the plane's bottom. It knocked the heel from Gable's boot and whizzed within inches of his head as it left the plane.

By September 1943 Gable's camera crew had shot nearly ten miles of film, which became *Combat America* and four training movies, including one Gable appeared in, *Wings Up*. *Combat America* was ready in September 1944, well past its 1943 deadline, and obsolete before it was complete. Gable had made the movie for the military, not the masses. As such, its importance and magnificence were eclipsed by *Memphis Belle*, the film that William Wyler, also serving in the First Motion Picture Unit, released the same year. *Memphis Belle* depicted the B-17 Flying Fortress and its crew and graced marquees across America. It was so popular that it was the first American movie *The New York Times* reviewed on its front page, causing other papers to follow suit.

Gable deliberately left his film devoid of special effects and staged scenes because he wanted to tell the true story of the aerial gunners with whom he served and whom he held in high regard. After his return from Europe, Gable continued to request, and was denied, combat orders. He earned a promotion to major in May 1944 and requested and received a discharge on D-Day, June 6, 1944. But he didn't wrap up his movie until three months later.

RIGHT: *The B-17* Memphis Belle *survived 25 bombing missions—the first of its kind to do so. William Wyler documented the plane's history in a film that President Franklin D. Roosevelt ordered placed in civilian movie houses as soon as he watched it. Pilot and Captain Robert K. Morgan named his bird after a girlfriend back home.*
U.S. Air Force Museum Photo

From Fort Roach to the White House

While Gable may have been the most famous motion picture unit member at the time, Ronald W. Reagan would be the unit's most recognizable member today. (A 2nd lieutenant when he was sent to the First Motion Picture Unit, Reagan later became the governor of California and the fortieth President of the United States.) He was called to active duty three months after the Pearl Harbor attack. His poor eyesight confined him to stateside duties, and General Arnold sent Reagan to the motion picture unit. Despite his being a cavalry officer, Reagan's insider knowledge of Hollywood and moviemaking made him a perfect film unit officer. Initially he was given the task of recruiting "behind-the-scenes" crews who were not eligible for the draft. Reagan found himself offering commissions and ranks as high as major to movie directors, some of whom had previously earned half-million-dollar salaries. Reagan served with the film unit and the 18th Army Air Force Base Unit as the personnel officer, the post adjutant, the executive officer, and the commanding officer—often holding two or more positions simultaneously.

Reagan also can be credited with helping to discover Marilyn Monroe. In early 1945, Reagan assigned unit still photographer David Conover to take photos of women working for the war effort, including at the Radioplane Corporation, owned by Reginald Denny, a Reagan friend. Conover photographed *Women in War Work* by shooting images of women on the Radioplane assembly line. He quickly snapped a photo of a young woman with curly blond hair and dirt smudges on her face and proceeded down the line. But something about the young woman struck Conover, and he asked to take additional photos of her off the line. Norma Jean Baker—the future Marilyn Monroe—had been discovered.

Hollywood's Only General

Reagan eventually became the Commander in Chief, but only one of the First Motion Picture Unit's other actors rose to the rank of general. Jimmy Stewart, who as a lieutenant narrated the First Motion Picture Unit's film, *Winning Your Wings*, retired from the U.S. Air Force Reserves in the late 1950s as brigadier general. After his narration stint with the film unit, Stewart flew twenty bombing missions with the Army Air Force over Europe, including France, Belgium, and Germany. Technically Stewart was not assigned to the film unit (he was a bomber pilot), but he aided the unit with several projects.

Stewart's appearance in the recruiting film was not unlike his performance in movies like *Mr. Smith Goes to Washington* or *It's a Wonderful Life*. Despite the leather bomber jacket and aviator sunglasses, the young lieutenant still looked and sounded folksy, as if piloting modern aircraft had not affected him at all. And perhaps it hadn't. Stewart had been in the Army Air Forces for only one year when he made *Winning Your Wings*. In his simple, friendly manner he described the need for 15,000 captains, 40,000 lieutenants, 35,000 flying sergeants, and a total of two million men to keep nearly 100,000 planes flying against the Axis forces. Stewart's manner allowed young men in the audience to see themselves as aviation cadets—making their families proud, kissing their sweethearts good-bye, and successfully completing basic training.

And only Stewart could innocently pull off the scene that promoted how many girlfriends an Army Air Forces flyer could garner: "This isn't a part of the regular training course, but you'd be a chump if you don't include it in your training course. Find out the effect those shiny little wings have on a gal. It's phenomenal," he said as a pretty young woman dumped her dance partner when a flyboy walked in the room.

Stewart earned the highest ranking and most military decorations of any actor to serve during World War II, despite having been rejected by the Army because he was too skinny. He reportedly wanted to serve his country so badly that he stuffed himself with food until he could reach the 148-pound weight limit. Stewart earned the Air Medal, the Distinguished Flying Cross, the French Croix de Guerre, and seven Battle Stars to go along with his two Academy Awards—one for Best Actor in 1942's *The Philadelphia Story* and one in 1984 to honor his life's work.

Gable, Reagan, and Stewart kept company with a litany of other Hollywood stars, directors, producers, and writers who were either assigned to the First Motion Picture Unit or assisted in making military training films or documentaries. Among them were William Holden, Irving Wallace, William T. Orr, Frank Capra, John Huston, William Wyler, George Cooper Stevens, Arthur Kennedy, Stanley Rubin, Stanley Kramer, John Ford, Robert Taylor, Gregg Toland, Gene Kelly, and DeForest Kelley.

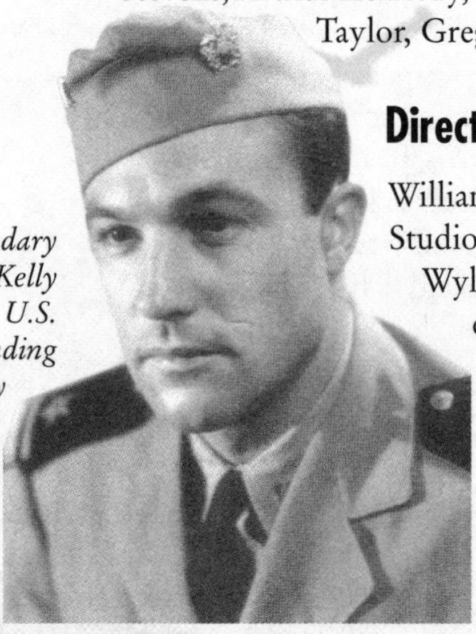

RIGHT: *Legendary dancer Gene Kelly served in the U.S. Navy, spending most of his duty time making naval training films in Washington, D.C.*
U.S. Navy Photo

Director earns Oscar but is AWOL!

William Wyler was the youngest director at Universal Studios, which his uncle, Carl Laemmle, had founded. Wyler won two Academy Awards for films he produced during his armed services tenure, *The Fighting Lady* and *Memphis Belle*. Wyler produced *Memphis Belle* with the film unit in 1943, and Paramount Pictures released the forty-five-minute film in the spring of the following year with cooperation from the Office of War Information.

Despite his professional success, Wyler "just didn't want to miss the war," according to his wife, Talli, in *A Talent for Trouble: The Life of Hollywood's Most Acclaimed Director, William Wyler* by Jan Herman. Talli explained that Wyler didn't want to sit on the sidelines while peers like Frank Capra, John Ford, and John Huston were joining the military. Army Captain Sy Bartlett, a former screenwriter at Columbia, invited Wyler to a dinner party in June 1942 to meet Major General Carl A. Spaatz. (Bartlett had helped the general's aide and head of the Army photography units, Lieutenant Colonel Richard T. Schlosberg, recruit Hollywood talent for the Army.) The general threw the party to celebrate his impending departure for Great Britain, where he would command the 8th Air Force. Wyler said in Herman's book: "General, I don't know where you're going and I don't know what for, but whatever you're going to do I think should be recorded on film." The next day Wyler was a major.

Wyler requested that he and his crew be allowed to fly on bombing runs as early as November 1942. Until then, his only film came from stationary cameras mounted on B-17s that depended on crew members to turn them off and on. The footage was useful only if the film rolled and if the camera didn't freeze in the subzero temperatures. The director did not receive permission to fly on raids until February 1943, when Wyler and his crew began filming bombing missions over Europe.

Despite being asked to film the 91st Bomb Group's missions by its commander, Wyler had little equipment with which to work. With only his Eyemo camera, he began filming at Bassingbourn, taking shots of B-17s and talking to crew members. According to *A Talent for Trouble,* Wyler later learned that his unit's equipment—including two motor-drive Eyemo cameras with lenses, turrets, and tripods, four Eyemos, and a portable sound system—had been lost on its way to Great Britain. Wyler made his films with forty hand-held, 16mm cameras he purchased in England. He was particularly frustrated when John Ford of the Navy's OSS showed up in Europe with a plethora of photographic equipment. He recalled in *Print the Legend: The Life and Times of John Ford* by Scott Eyman: "My equipment had a very low priority. It was coming across on a surface vessel. Suddenly John Ford showed up. . . . He was in the Navy and his equipment was flown over by the Air Force. I don't know how he did it."

The director desperately wanted to film the first air attacks on Germany and implored Colonel Stanley Wray, the 91st Bomb Group commander, to covertly signal him when the raid was about to take place. According to *Stars at War* by Michael Munn, the colonel agreed to have someone call Wyler and ask, "How's the weather in London?" to alert him to the bombing runs. When the crew received the call, they raced to Bassingbourn in a jeep and prepared for predawn departures. The crew filmed attacks on Hamburg, Schweinfurt, and Regensburg.

While working with the 91st, Wyler developed the plan for *Memphis Belle*. In this film, Wyler chronicled the B-17 bomber's final mission—a raid on Wilhelmshafen, Germany's, submarine pens. On bombing runs aboard various aircraft, the director shot much of the footage himself, and *Our Gang*'s bombardier Vincent Evans remembered in *Stars at War* how Wyler walked around the plane's open catwalk in temperatures of 45 degrees below zero. As he tried to aim his lens at flak bursts and Nazi war planes, the tube to his oxygen bottle broke loose and Wyler passed out between the pilots and the plane's nose. Not only was he feeling ill, but the director was angry that by the time he woke up the crew had hit its target and he had missed the shot.

Wyler's crew used handheld cameras inside the plane, and he edited that footage together with film from other missions, such as previous trips on the *Memphis Belle* and *Our Gang*, to characterize all twenty-five of the plane's operations. Wyler flew on five bombing missions over Germany and France, despite being grounded by a general's order. The Air Force feared that his plane could be shot down and the Nazis would capture him. Some of the combat footage was shot by William Clothier, who had not flown on this particular plane, and by First Motion Picture Unit-trained 8th Air Force combat cameramen.

What made the *Memphis Belle*—named after pilot Captain Robert K. Morgan's girlfriend—so special was that it was the first plane of its kind to successfully finish twenty-five missions and return intact and with its crew to the United States. The B-17 Flying Fortress flew its daylight missions through such hazards as anti-aircraft and machine-gun fire and aerial cannons from enemy planes. Wyler edited the film at Fort Roach, and he sent a special request through the Army Air Forces commanders to send the plane and her crew to California. The *Memphis Belle* completed a barnstorming tour across the United States and landed in Hollywood in the summer of 1943 to allow Wyler to complete the film. Although he had shot 19,000 feet of footage, he needed the crew to record voiceovers for the various scenes. Wyler asked screenwriter Lester Koenig to script the movie, and by all accounts Koenig's words verged on poetry. As the movie opened to a pastoral English setting, the narrator said, "This is a battlefront." The scene shifted to airstrips carved from the countryside, and the narration continued, "A battlefront like no other in the long history of mankind's wars." Finally, Wyler cut in footage of a B-17, and the words "This is an airfront" rang out.

According to Herman, when Wyler showed his film to President Roosevelt in the White House's basement theater, the Commander in Chief sat perfectly still and smoked only one Camel. At the movie's end, his eyes welling with tears, FDR told Wyler: "This has to be shown right away everywhere." Wyler even received a recommendation for a Distinguished Service Medal, but the honor was canceled when Wyler punched a Washington, D.C., hotel bellhop and was charged with "conduct unbecoming an officer and a gentleman." The director had been waiting for a cab when the bellhop complained about another patron, describing him as a "Goddam Jew." Wyler

LEFT: *Director William Wyler followed up his successful* Memphis Belle *by shooting a film about P-47 Thunderbolts. Unfortunately, by the time Wyler completed the film the war had ended, lessening the military's and public's interest in combat films.*
U.S. Army Photo

responded, according to *Stars at War*, by telling the bellhop, "You're saying that to the wrong feller." Although the bellhop tried to explain that he'd not been talking about him, Wyler punched him and another Army officer saw the hit and reported him.

After the success of *Memphis Belle*, Wyler decided to make another movie about P-47 Thunderbolts, the powerful plane of the 12th Air Forces 57th Fighter Group in Corsica. The aircraft, according to Herman, was "dubbed 'the seven-ton milk bottle . . .' a rugged, single-pilot fighter capable of matching the Focke-Wulf 190 in air combat at any altitude." The plane also made dive-bombing runs with five-hundred-pound bombs under each wing. Captain John Sturges, who worked with Wyler on the project and later directed *The Great Escape* and *The Magnificent Seven*, said in *Stars at War* that they put Eyemos under the wings, on the tails, and inside the cockpits—all with switches the pilots could turn off and on. Since the planes flew daily missions, Wyler knew he would get powerful air combat footage. But he also wanted images of the planes from ground level. Sturges and Wyler drove to the front lines in the Mediterranean Theater and started filming. Once, they got so close to the action the two dove into a muddy ditch as artillery fire sprayed the area.

Wyler sent the footage and Sturges back to London in late summer 1944, and he traveled to Paris in hopes of being part of the liberation of his hometown, Mulhouse, France. By February 1945 Sturges and Koenig had the first cut of *Thunderbolt* ready for the director's review. The two flew back to Fort Roach, but Wyler had left for Italy, hoping to get some aerial shots of Rome to use as filler in the movie. He flew in a B-25 camera ship in March and made several trips around the city, the coast, and the bombing damage in Corsica. But Wyler got more than footage. He recalled in Herman's book: "I usually flew with the pilot up front. A B-25 is a very noisy plane. This time I got in the waist, where the windows were open, because the cameraman complained about his camera setup. This was a routine flight, no flak, no guns. My hearing just went. I thought it was nothing. A lot of times you step out of an airplane, and you can't hear for a while. But this time I couldn't walk straight when I got off."

Wyler had lost hearing in both ears, including permanent damage to the right ear. He would later receive sixty dollars per month in disability, according to Herman.

BELOW: *Oscar-winning director William Wyler (left) made numerous British friends, among them playwright Lieutenant Terence Rattigan, following the release of* Mrs. Miniver. *Great Britain's leaders, including Prime Minister Winston Churchill, praised the film for showing the depravity of German attacks on London and the countryside. By the time Wyler earned his statuette for the movie, he was serving as a U.S. Signal Corps officer and making military movies.* U.S. Signal Corps Photo

With the war's end, no one was interested in releasing *Thunderbolt*, which did not appear until July 1947. Wyler remarked in *Stars at War* that he had "lost his hearing for nothing."

Wyler earned a Best Director Oscar on March 4, 1943, for *Mrs. Miniver*, which told the story of an English family coming to terms with World War II. He could not attend the Academy Awards because he was busy filming Allied bombing raids. The movie weakened the Americans' opinion of Germany, and Herman reported in the *Los Angeles Times* on February 5, 1998, that MGM studio head Louis B. Mayer bragged about Winston Churchill writing him a letter in which he said *Mrs. Miniver* was very important to the Allies and "propaganda worth a thousand battleships." Coincidentally, Wyler had finished filming but re-shot the ending after Pearl Harbor. He wanted a more moving final scene in which the reverend offers a sermon in a church nearly destroyed by German bombs. According to Munn, President Roosevelt was so moved by the scene he ordered leaflets printed with the text and dropped in German-controlled countries.

(Wyler later garnered two more Academy Awards, for 1947's *The Best Years of Our Lives* and 1960's *Ben Hur*. The former's story line focused on war veterans returning home and settling into life after combat. Wyler understood veterans' issues, particularly those with injuries. The movie also reflects Wyler's newfound concern with human relationships. According to *Stars at War*, his values changed during the war, and the only thing that ultimately mattered to him were these bonds between soldiers, "not money, not position, not even family. Only relationships with people who might be dead tomorrow were important. It's too bad it takes a war to create such a condition among men," Wyler said. He also said that when he went onto the film set, he had no problems making decisions about what the veteran characters would do "because I already knew it in my heart," he said in Herman's book.)

Star Joins Motion Picture Unit, Brother Killed in Combat

Actor William Holden, born William Franklin Beedle, completed his basic training for the U.S. Army Signal Corps before earning a commission in 1943 as a 2nd lieutenant in the Army Air Force. Holden requested combat duty but was given a "public relations" assignment at the First Motion Picture Training Command at Tarrant Field Air Base in Fort Worth, Texas. He appeared in training movies and promoted national support of the war on radio programs. When Holden reported to the motion picture unit at Fort Roach in 1945, he stood at attention for twenty-five minutes while the adjutant dispensed all the unit's rules and regulations. That adjutant was Ronald Reagan. (Holden later served as Reagan's best man at his wedding to actress Nancy Davis, whose maid of honor was Holden's wife, Ardis.)

Holden kept requesting combat assignments but always was turned down. He was discharged in September 1945. Holden's brother, Bob, was killed in action as a Navy pilot flying a combat mission on New Year's Day in 1944, and Holden regretted that his "public relations" schedule conflicted with his brother's duty and they did not get to see each other during the war.

Famous Writer Scripts Training Films

Best-selling author Irving Wallace, who sold more than 200 million copies of his books, was a writer for First Motion Picture Unit and the Signal Corps Photographic Center. Wallace's books include *The Sins of Philip Fleming, The Chipman Report*, *The Man, The Seven Minutes*, *The Prize*, *The Word, The Fan Club, The R Document,* and *The Pigeon Project,* several of which have been made into movies.

Actor Stars in VD Movie

William T. Orr, who went on to produce television shows for Warner Brothers that included *Maverick*, *Cheyenne*, *77 Sunset Strip*, and *F Troop*, served as the First Motion Picture Unit's public relations officer and helped produce training films at Fort Roach. His most notable and notorious role for the unit came as a pilot in *Three Cadets*. Orr played the pilot who self-medicated with sulfa drugs and crashed his airplane, according to his son, Gregory Orr, in a December 12, 2002, *Los Angeles Times* obituary for the producer.

Acclaimed Actor Makes Training Films, Stars in Pearl Harbor Movie

Arthur Kennedy, a Tony Award–winning actor who reportedly was discovered by James Cagney while working on a Los Angeles stage, joined the armed services in 1943. As a corporal in the motion picture unit, he made training films. Kennedy starred in 1943's *Air Force*, which told the story of a B-17 Flying Fortress named *Mary Ann* that left San Francisco headed to Hawaii for a routine training mission on December 6, 1941, the day before the Pearl Harbor attack.

FMPU Producer Earns First Emmy Award

Stanley Rubin worked under Ronald Reagan at the First Motion Picture Unit and helped produce the unit's movies. (Later, Rubin produced the *General*

Electric Theater, which had his former commander as narrator from 1959 to 1964. Rubin earned the first Emmy Award for his movie version of Guy de Maupassant's short story, *The Necklace*.)

Army Signal Corps Makes its Own Kind of Movie

The First Motion Picture Unit was one of several government filmmaking entities during World War II. The Army and Navy had several movie units, as did the Office of War Information. All together, the units spent more than $50 million on War Department films over the war's course, with most of that money being spent on training movies and combat footage.

The Army Signal Corps also had its own filmmaking division. But thanks to Fox executive and Army Lieutenant Colonel Darryl Zanuck's persuasion, the Signal Corps allowed Hollywood to transform boring training and information movies into modern, engaging films. Although Signal Corps officers fought the transition, they didn't stand a chance against Army Chief of Staff General George Marshall, who enjoyed movies and believed them to be a great tool to educate and influence. He wanted the best men to tell the Army's stories, and he specifically wanted Academy Award–winning director Frank Capra to oversee a set of films that explained the events leading up to the war and the causes for the fight.

From Military Math Teacher to Director to Major

Frank Capra had proudly earned three Best Director statuettes before he joined the film unit as a major. He decided to join the Signal Corps only five days after Pearl Harbor, on December 12, 1941. Brigadier General Frederick H. Osborn, the Morale Branch chief, contacted Capra and asked him to make some films ordered by General Marshall. Capra was so excited about his new commission that he dashed to a local Army-Navy store to buy a hat and gold major's leaves. He recalled in his autobiography, *Frank Capra: The Name above the Title,* "I had no idea how to put them on and neither did the tailor."

But it didn't take Capra long to settle into his commissioned officer status. He already had military experience, serving as a math instructor during World War I. And now he was going to do what he did best: make movies. But these movies would be unlike his earlier films, *It Happened One Night*, *Mr. Deeds Goes to Town*, *You Can't Take it with You*, or *Mr. Smith Goes to Washington*. While in the Army,

RIGHT: *When Frank Capra (right) joined the Signal Corps, he admitted to General George Marshall that he had never made documentary films before, but promised him that he would make "the best damned documentary films ever made." In his* Why We Fight *series, which included seven movies, Capra pored over footage from American sources as well as Axis and Allied combat movies.*
U.S. Signal Corps Photo

Capra produced documentaries, beginning with a series called *Why We Fight,* to explain to soldiers why the United States had engaged in military action. General Marshall knew that the average soldier had no idea why he was fighting this war. The fighting seemed far away and the reasons vague. According to Capra's autobiography, Marshall said of American soldiers: "They will prove not only equal, but superior to totalitarian soldiers *if*—and this is a large if, indeed—they are given answers as to *why* they are in uniform, and *if* the answers they get are *worth* fighting and dying for."

Capra faced enormous tests when Marshall ordered him to produce these movies. The filmmaker had to persuade United States citizens to become engaged in war, persuade the Army to integrate its units, and persuade American leaders to form an alliance with the Russians—and he had to please Marshall. As he recalled in his autobiography, Capra told Marshall that his moviemaking experience was limited to feature films. "General Marshall," Capra said, "it's only fair to tell you that I have never before made a single documentary. In fact, I've never even been near anybody that's made one."

Marshall replied, "Capra, I have never been Chief of Staff before. Thousands of young Americans have never had their legs shot off before. Boys are commanding ships today, who a year ago had never seen the ocean before."

Capra apologized. "I'm sorry sir. I'll make you the best damned documentary films ever made."

The director took his assignment—and his promise to the general—to heart. Deep down, however, Capra was disappointed that he was at a desk job and not out shooting combat movies like John Ford. Still, he understood the films' importance, and he wanted the soldiers serving under him to understand it, too. He wrote to the officers in his command in 1942, according to McBride, that "most of you were individuals in civilian life. Forget that. You are working for a common cause. . . . There will be no personal credit for your work, either on the screen or in the press. The only press notices we are anxious to read are those of American victories!"

Capra began work in Washington, D.C., on February 15, 1942, and found a cold reception from fellow Signal Corps officers who regarded themselves experts in military filmmaking. But as Marshall's handpicked officer, Capra wielded great power. The general's aide, Frank McCarthy, recalled in *Frank Capra: The Catastrophe of Success* that Marshall said, "Better let Frank Capra do what he wants, because he knows what he's doing." (McCarthy later became the Hollywood producer responsible for films such as *Patton* and *MacArthur*.) Capra became the commanding officer of the Film Production Section of the Information Division of Special Services, headed by Brigadier General Frederick Osborn. In June 1942 Capra became the commander to eight officers and thirty-five enlisted men in the 834th Signal Services Photographic Detachment, Special Services Division, Film

Production Section—a whole new unit established by Lieutenant General Brehon B. Somervell, the chief of Army Services of Supply, when the Signal Corps tried to take control over the *Why We Fight* series. The next month Capra said good-bye to Washington and its military politics and moved his detachment to Hollywood.

The unit set up at an unoccupied Fox Studio—called "Fort Fox" by the men, but not by Capra. Zanuck offered the studio to the Army at a one-dollar-per-year lease plus renovation costs. Capra sent a memo to his officers in the new unit that stated, according to McBride: "This is a total war fought with every conceivable weapon. Your weapon is film. Your bombs are ideas! Hollywood is a war plant! Hitler has taken over countries on film. Your job is to counterattack and take them back. . . ."

By the time Capra's unit landed in Hollywood, he'd already formulated the basic plans for the series. The director decided to use "found footage," according to McBride's book. He pulled images from newsreels, from Axis and Allied combat and propaganda movies, and even from Hollywood films about war. The limited budget—the first film of the series, *Prelude to War*, cost only $60,974 to produce—did not allow Capra to stage elaborate scenes or do on-site filming. He ended up calling himself the "executive producer" of the films because his unit shot little new material for them. McBride wrote in his book that the Office of War Information added the following at the beginning of each film's public version: "Use has been made of certain motion pictures with historical backgrounds. When necessary for purposes of clarity, a few reenactments have been made under War Department Supervision."

Even with old images and shots from popular movies, Capra found a way to connect the audiences with the films' goals. *Prelude to War* states: "This isn't just a way . . . this is a common man's life-and-death struggle against those who would put him back into slavery. We lose it—we lose everything. Our homes, the jobs we want to go back to, the books we read, the very food we eat, the hopes we have for our kids, the kids themselves—they won't be ours anymore. That's what's at stake. It's us or them. The chips are down."

RIGHT: *Legendary movie producer and U.S. Army officer Frank Capra made outstanding documentaries during World War II. He joined the Signal Corps to make movies specifically requested by Army Chief of Staff General George Marshall, who wanted films that explained to servicemen and civilians alike why America had joined the conflict. Capra won an Oscar for* Prelude to War *in 1943.* U.S. Army Photo

Prelude to War was released to troops on October 30, 1942, shown to defense plants in April 1943, and released to the public on May 27, 1943. When Marshall saw the rough cut of *Prelude* in August 1942 he said he wanted the film shown to the public, and when President Roosevelt saw the movie he agreed that it should be released publicly as quickly as possible. Marshall later ordered that all soldiers be required to watch all films in the series. Capra held up

Left: *John Ford entered the Navy after winning two Oscars. Despite his age (he became a grandfather during his military service), he sought combat action during the war. Ford had no problem finding the fight, landing aboard a warship in time to film* The Battle of Midway, *a movie that recorded the turning point in the Pacific Theater.* Midway *earned Ford an Oscar for Best Documentary.* Associated Press Photo

his promise to produce the best damn documentaries, winning an Oscar for Best Documentary Film in 1942 for his first attempt. Ford also won an Academy Award for his *Battle of Midway* documentary that same year.

Besides *Prelude to War*, which featured animated map sequences by Walt Disney and his staff, the movies in the *Why We Fight* series include *The Nazis Strike*, *Divide and Conquer*, *The Battle of Britain*, *The Battle of Russia*, *The Battle of China*, and *War Comes to America*. The movies were shown to international audiences, although only three films were shown in the United States, according to *War Movies* by Jay Hyams. In all, the 834th Signal Services Photograph Detachment produced seven *Why We Fight* movies and ten other films. The unit released biweekly newsreels and "46 issues of the Staff Film Report, begun in June 1944, a weekly assembly of classified battle, reconnaissance, weapons testing, and enemy footage for viewing by the President, the Joint Chiefs of Staff, American commanders throughout the world, Allied commanders, and the service and command schools," noted McBride.

By April 1943 the Signal Corps was once again fighting to bring Capra's unit back from the Special Services Division. In October the 834th moved back to the Army Pictorial Service. Capra earned the rank of colonel in December and became the commander of the Special Coverage Section, Western Division, where he managed combat photography and worked as the assistant to the chief of Motion Picture Planning and to the Army Pictorial Services' assistant chief (a position he shared with Colonel Charles S. Stodter). Capra's new role allowed him to help George Stevens and John Huston in their war film work. He worked with Allied military commanders to prepare for filming the D-Day invasion on June 6, 1944. Capra had told Stevens that he might have additional help from the unit, but Stevens found himself nearly alone in coordinating the D-Day filming. According to McBride, Capra later wrote Stevens, "I know I haven't given you much guidance or advice as to just what you're supposed to get. . . . Unfortunately I've been so swamped with top-priority work that I haven't been able to pay much attention to what is going on in the Theaters. Stick to it, George, and please know that you have some guys here that are pulling and pitching for you, even though it must seem to you that at times you and your gang are forgotten men." Capra also approved Huston's work in Italy, and he once named it as one of the World War II movie productions he supervised, although he never left his Hollywood office, wrote McBride.

Although Capra retired with the Distinguished Service Medal in 1945, the U.S. Senate Internal Security Subcommittee scrutinized World War II films made by the Army and questioned him about his work on the *Why We Fight* films, particularly *The Battle of Russia*. Senators investigated the director's contact with the Soviets to acquire Russian combat films to use in his documentaries. While most of Capra's file remains classified by the State Department and the FBI, it is known that he sidestepped official methods and went to Russian Ambassador Maxim Litinov to trade American combat footage for the Soviet films. He was never punished for his actions, but he always maintained a distance from *The Battle of Russia* and did not like to be linked with the film. Capra even lied to the investigators about his work on the movie, stating that he'd been in London working on *Tunisian Victory* when *The Battle of Russia* was being made. Clearly this was not true because he already had completed *Russia* before departing for Europe to meet with British producers on the film about the North Africa campaign.

(Capra went on to direct Jimmy Stewart in *It's a Wonderful Life*, Stewart's first role after his service in the Army Air Forces. Capra formed Liberty Pictures with William Wyler and George Stevens the day after V-E Day, but *It's a Wonderful Life* and *State of the Union* failed at the box office, and the movie company dissolved.)

Director Makes Military's Most Compelling—and Censored—Documentaries

U.S. Army Signal Corps veteran John Huston became the only person ever to direct both his father, Walter Huston, and his daughter, Angelica Huston, in Oscar-winning performances, according to the Web site classicfilm.about.com. His career spanned more than fifty years and he directed forty-five films—quite a feat for someone who did not begin directing movies until he was thirty-five.

Huston finished his classic, *The Maltese Falcon*, not long before he volunteered for the Signal Corps. He earned a commission in 1942 and proceeded to make movies for the military, including 1943's *Report from the Aleutians* and 1945's *The Battle of San Pietro*. Huston risked his life to make both films, which found him working on the front lines. "My whole time in the Army was, I suppose, the most compelling experience of my life," Huston said in *The Cinema of John Huston* by Gerald Pratley. *Aleutians* captured the aerial combat as American forces attacked Japanese positions in Alaska's island chain. Although Huston earned an Oscar nomination for that film in 1943, he thought the movie was pure propaganda, and disingenuous. "We were cheering our own boys on," Huston said in an April 16, 2000, article by

Left: *American cameramen documented troop movements and battles in all theaters in World War II, often getting killed or injured doing their jobs. This motion picture photographer captured activity in the Aleutians.*
U.S. Army Photo

Midge Mackenzie in *The New York Times*. "In one of the missions, we said that everybody returned unscathed. Well, very rarely did missions return unscathed." By the time Huston left to film combat in the Mediterranean region, he said he had stopped relating with the military's points of view and started to view things from the troops' perspective, Mackenzie wrote.

Despite Huston's dissatisfaction with the propaganda that he was producing, his time in the Aleutians was both exciting and dangerous. On his first combat photography mission, his plane's brakes froze and the aircraft crashed into two other B-24 bombers on the ground. As crew members fell over themselves to get to exits and run away from the wreckage, Huston shot footage. "I ran around the nose of the plane and began filming the rescue team of four or five men working frantically to get the pilot and copilot out before the bombs went off. I was on my knees filming, telling myself, 'Good man, Huston! You've got nerves of steel.' Suddenly I just began to shake uncontrollably. I put the camera down and ran like hell. I expected the plane to blow all to hell, but the bombs didn't go off," he said in *Stars at War*.

A later mission to Kiska didn't go much better for the director. Japanese Zeros attacked his plane, and he had only his film to shoot. He sat behind the

RIGHT: *Director and Signal Corps officer John Huston filmed many World War II documentaries, including* The Battle of San Pietro *and* Let There Be Light. *Huston also worked with fellow filmmakers Frank Capra and George Stevens on* Tunisian Victory, *a movie about the Allied campaign in North Africa.*
U.S. Signal Corps Photo

RIGHT: *John Huston (left), award-winning director of* Report from the Aleutians *and* The Battle of San Pietro, *visited with military officers in the Alaskan islands. The famed director learned after his first military film that he was making propaganda—not documentary—films. Huston changed course and set about to make movies from a GI's perspective rather than an officer's. With that decision, his films not only became more compelling but also more highly censored.*
U.S. Signal Corps Photo

waist gunner and filmed around him, able to see only what the lens saw. When Huston put the camera down, he discovered that the waist gunner right in front of him had been killed. He quickly traded places with the belly gunner, who took over the waist gun. The combat cameraman engaged in real combat, firing the belly gun at enemy planes.

Huston always seemed to be in the midst of fierce battle. At San Pietro in Italy in late 1943, American troops struggled to gain control of the area from the Germans. The skirmishes were especially difficult, as the Germans maintained machine guns in every nook and cranny of the mountains, mowing down American infantrymen with ease. Huston's film *The Battle of San Pietro* used extensive footage from this fighting (although some fighting was staged later when Huston realized he did not have adequate footage of actual battle scenes), and some Army officers thought the film would hurt the military by making combat frightening for soldiers. The move marked the first time American infantrymen had been shown in combat on screen. *San Pietro* resembled the 1930 classic, *All Quiet on the Western Front*, except that real men, not actors, died in the cold mire. Huston spared no one the repugnant battle scenes.

San Pietro showed patrols that did not return, soldiers sheared in half trying to advance position, and tanks that seldom completed search missions. Huston led his six-man camera crew into the German stronghold, ahead of Allied forces. He ducked between the crew's 35mm handheld Eyemos during the filming, dodging bullets and taking cover whenever bombers descended. In an article written by Midge Mackenzie for *The Guardian* on October 23, 1998, Huston described the scene this way: "The rains had come and all our heavy equipment was in the mire. . . . There had been an attack and the attack had been repulsed, and we went forward ahead of the next attack. And it was quite a day. Numbers of dead. Rain had just fallen, and men were dead behind their machine guns, everything looking very bright. The sun had come out after the rain, Germans were there in force, mortar shells came in, and we dived for cover behind a wall that saved our lives."

A portion of the film's end, in which soldiers placed their dead comrades in body bags as the voices of the dead men played on the soundtrack, disconcerted officers. According to the Turner Classic Movies Web site (www.turnerclassicmovies.com), one general told Huston: "This picture is pacifistic. It's against war. It's against *the* war." Huston retorted: "Well, sir, whenever I make a film that's *for* war, you can take me out and shoot me."

General George Marshall, however, saw the film and wanted every soldier to see it, too. Rather than scaring soldiers, Marshall thought the film would prepare troops for the horrors of war. Marshall was particularly concerned about the effects of shock. Doctors diagnosed an estimated one-third of all early-war casualties as psychoneurotic. According to Pratley's book, Huston said that he "agreed with the few deletions that were made, and it was used as a training film, because as you know, the first few days in combat is when an army encounters a number of emotional casualties and desertions, and the men must be prepared for what they are going to encounter." Marshall also wanted the public to see the movie so Americans would better understand what a soldier goes through during battle.

Huston never forgot the fighting at San Pietro. *San Francisco Chronicle* reporter Judy Stone wrote on May 29, 1990, that years later when someone made a remark about courage, Huston said, "I'll tell you what courage is . . ." and tearfully recalled an American major standing in Italy's frigid Rapido River with dead bodies floating around him while Huston was shooting. The man had lost a hand, but he raised the stump to salute every infantryman marching by. Huston told Pratley, "I learned to have great feeling for the American soldier and his behavior was magnificent. I used to just stand back and wonder when they'd give us an assignment like a frontal assault on positions that were practicably unassailable, and they went forward without questions, without murmur." Producer Michael Fitzgerald said this incident exemplifies how Huston felt about soldiers. "John knew honor and courage when he saw it, and that vision haunted him all his life," Fitzgerald said in *The Hustons.*

But not all accounts of the making of San Pietro match Huston's memories. Lance Bertelsen wrote in the article "San Pietro and the 'Art' of War" in the Spring 1989 issue of *Southwest Journal* that at least two people who were with the director claim he was not there to film the battle and staged parts of the movie. According to Bertelsen, British writer Eric Ambler, who was part of the director's crew, said that he and Huston did not make it to the town until December 16, 1943, the battle's last day. Many soldiers lay dead and the Germans fired off mortar rounds at them, but the two men shot little usable film. Captain Joel Westbrook stated that he helped Huston stage scenes by gathering soldiers, helping them move to predetermined areas for camera shots, and even making sure they threw concussion grenades rather than the fragmentation kind.

Raw footage stored in the National Archives corroborates these stories. Bertelsen asserted that several scenes, including some that appear in the movie's final version, are found on more than one reel. This suggests that Huston set up a scene and filmed it from various viewpoints. "During one sequence, in which a camera continued to roll after the 'action' had stopped, we see a solider in a knit cap come in the frame and attempt to kick a smoking grenade away from the door while the troops stand around watching. Behind the building a second cameraman is visible, and as the soldier who kicked the grenade moves away from the building a third cameraman comes into view on the right. The shots taken from the other two camera angles appear on reels ADC 583 and ADC 587," Bertelsen wrote. Still, the scholar and Westbrook maintain that the film is accurate, even if the footage was not authentically shot during the battle. Bertelsen pointed out that shooting ground combat footage is difficult, if not fatal, and many World War II movies that depict infantry warfare were either staged or shot from a long distance.

Let There Be Light, Huston's third Signal Corps film, dealt with shock and the treatment for and recovery from wartime trauma. The War Department ordered Huston to make the movie to point out how few soldiers were "nervously wounded" and to eliminate the stigma attached to psychoneurotic disorders. Walter Huston, John's father, narrated the film, which followed one group of soldiers being treated at Mason General Hospital on New York's Long Island, interviewing them and showing individual treatments that may have included sodium pentothal (commonly known as truth serum) and hypnotism. Huston even learned how to hypnotize patients and occasionally was asked to help with that treatment when the primary hypnotist, Colonel Simon, was busy.

Huston had been ordered to make a movie that would show America that these soldiers were capable of holding jobs and functioning in society. The movie's opening attempted to explain what happened to these veterans as viewers watched patients with no visible injuries walk down gangplanks:

"The guns are quiet now, the papers of peace have been signed, and the oceans of the earth are filled with ships coming home. Here is human salvage, the final result of all that metal and fire could do to violate mortal flesh. These are the casualties of the spirit, the troubled mind, men who are damaged emotionally. Born and bred in peace, educated to hate war, they were overnight plunged into sudden and terrible situations. Every man has his breaking point; and these, in the fulfillment of their duties as soldiers, were forced beyond the limit of human endurance."

Military police officers seized the 1946 movie as it was about to be shown at the New York Museum of Modern Art, and the military refused to release it publicly until Vice President Walter Mondale signed the orders in December 1980. Huston claimed in a paper by Richard Ledes (presented to the Après-Coup Psychoanalytic Association in 1998) that the War Department objected to the movie because it debunked the idea that war made boys into men and saw them return home stronger, taller, and prouder, as heroes. Huston was quoted by Pratley as explaining the objection this way: "What I think was really behind it was that the authorities considered it to be more shocking, embarrassing perhaps, to them, for a man to suffer emotional distress than to lose a leg, or part of his body. Hardly masculine, I supposed they would say."

But his time at Mason General had touched Huston in a way he likened to religion. "I was very moved to find the men like this, and the actual photographing of them was, by God, practically a religious experience. I felt there what some people feel in church. These men came in from boats in batches of 75 and 100, mute, shaking, with amnesia, blind, with paralysis, as a result of warfare. . . . The original idea was that the film be shown to those who would be able to give employment to reassure them that men discharged under this section were not insane," the director said in *The Cinema of John Huston*.

Capturing History in Living Color

George Cooper Stevens joined the U.S. Army as a major in the Signal Corps in 1943 and later headed the Special Coverage Motion Picture Unit at the request of General Dwight D. Eisenhower. Stevens's unit covered some of the war's most honorable and horrific moments, including the planning of the D-Day invasion from the HMS *Belfast,* the seizure of Hitler's command center in Berchtesgaden, the Allied liberation of Paris, and the release of Dachau concentration camp prisoners.

When Stevens arrived with his film crew in France in the summer of 1944, he lived in a tent like any other GI. Despite its being called the "Hollywood Irregulars," he ran his operation as a military unit, right down to the regulation haircuts he made his men keep. When 2,500 Allied bombers soared over

RIGHT: *George Stevens filmed the travesty and tragedy at the Dachau concentration camp after the Allied liberation. German prison guards attempted to escape by disguising themselves in inmate uniforms. Their full faces provided a stark contrast to the pallid complexions and wiry bodies of detainees. American GIs, horrified by what they saw in the camp, recognized the guards and shot several of them. Freed prisoners bludgeoned numerous other guards.*
U.S. Signal Corps Photo

Stevens's camp on July 25 to attack the Germans at St. Lô—one of the biggest allied raids—his crew shot footage of the seemingly endless flood of aircraft. Cameraman Dick Kent recalled in Michael Munn's *Stars at War*: "The sky was full of bombers coming over everywhere you looked and dropping rows of bombs just ahead of where we were." The U.S. 1st Army forces liberated Coutances by July 28, and French civilians welcomed Stevens and his crew members with flowers, a stark contrast to their devastated town. Despite the liberation, violence erupted. As Stevens set up his personal camera to film images of the ruins, a jeep hit a land mine left by the German Wehrmacht down the road. The blast rattled his camera and sent a shock wave through the GIs. Yet German forces collapsed in Stevens's camera lenses, as Nazi soldiers surrendered with smiles on camera.

By August Stevens and his crew had crossed the Seine on the Army's pontoon bridge and prepared for the Paris liberation. General Eisenhower allowed the Free French to liberate the city on August 23, and the director asked a Free French general to allow him to film his troops' march into the city. Stevens and members of his unit were the only non-French to enter the city on August 25 when the Nazis relinquished control. German Major General Dietrich von Choltitz surrendered Paris, defying Hitler's order to burn the city. Free French Major General Jacques Philippe Leclerc asked Stevens to film his explanation that von Choltitz's submission had saved Paris.

Stevens also shot footage of the Soviet troops meeting up with British and American forces in Torgau on the River Elbe in April 1945. Although the Americans had been prohibited from talking to the Russians, he noticed that the two tenuous allies had spoken to each other, and he started filming. Stevens watched as British soldiers greeted the Soviets and had the cameras rolling when General Emil Reinhardt stomped onto the scene. As much as the British commander wanted to rant, he realized the value of the film and joined the celebration. Although Stevens never believed the feeling between the Soviets and their allies was genuine, the images made for good public relations back in the States.

From Torgau, Stevens and his unit moved to Dachau, a small German town 250 miles to the south. American troops found a scene on April 19 they wanted him to film: one of Germany's oldest concentration camps. Although it was not one of the mass-extermination sites, nearly 30,000 people had been "beaten, starved, tortured, and subjected to medical experimentation," according to Munn. The images Stevens shot shocked him and everyone who saw them. The footage was so atrocious that the American public would not see the film for decades. Munn quoted Dick Kent: "How can one human being do this to another human being? Impossible to think of. How does one justify this mass murder? You just wanted to hate all Germans." Stevens filmed Dachau guards trying to disguise themselves in the black-and-white prison uniforms (their round faces and healthy glow were immediate giveaways). As inmates identified them to the Americans, Stevens captured on tape the execution of 122 guards by angry Americans, and the beating deaths of forty more killed as prisoners bludgeoned them with shovels, makeshift clubs, and gun butts.

Stevens not only directed the black-and-white cameras that covered these events as head of the unit charged with covering European combat, but he also shot his own color motion pictures, which his son found in a North Hollywood storeroom after the director's death. Said son George Stevens Jr. in a 1985 *Houston Chronicle* article by Louis B. Parks: "I knew there was color film, but I didn't know it was so unique. I put a reel in one day in a screening room. I was by myself. Up comes this luminous, vivid color photography. It's at sea, with men on ships, and they're wearing flak jackets and helmets. I realize this is the 6th of June, 1944, and I am seeing this in color—in a way no one has ever seen it except the men who were there that day." Stevens had shot almost five hours of color footage. Over four decades later, these images inspired the way director Steven Spielberg shot the dramatic opening scenes in 1998's *Saving Private Ryan*.

(The elder Stevens retired from the Army as a lieutenant colonel in 1946 and returned to Hollywood, where he directed such movies as *The Diary of Anne Frank* and *Shane*.)

Life in Filmmaking Reflects Army Experiences

Stanley Kramer had moved from set building to directing before he joined the U.S. Army Signal Corps. While with the Corps, Kramer made training films, which provided him with valuable movie-making experience. When Kramer left the Army as a 1st lieutenant, he made independent movies that dealt with topics to which he'd been exposed as a soldier. He tackled issues that included ethnic bias in the military (*Home of the Brave*) and how war affected soldiers throughout their lives (*The Men*, which starred rookie actor Marlon Brando).

Kramer said that he'd faced discrimination in the Army. In his autobiography, *A Mad Mad Mad Mad World: A Life in Hollywood*, written with Thomas M. Coffey, the veteran explained: "In the Army film unit I was assigned to during World War II, I came under the command of a captain who let me know right where I stood. 'I don't like Jews,' he said, 'especially Hollywood Jews. If I were you, I'd get myself transferred out of this unit.' That proved impossible because I had been commissioned directly from civilian life, which meant, for some reason, I wouldn't be allowed to apply for a transfer until after one year. During that unpleasant year, I learned more about the extent of at least one man's hate than I had ever learned growing up in New York's Hell's Kitchen."

Kramer and his crew worked secretly on 1949's *Home of the Brave* to prevent anti-integration pressure groups from causing a disruption. He did not allow visitors to the set, and all actors and Kramer himself came into the studio and left through a back gate. He also insisted they eat meals together during production.

(Kramer later directed the movie classics *High Noon* and *The Caine Mutiny*.)

Naval Photographic Branch Makes Award-Winning Documentaries and Surveillance Films

While the Army was the only armed service to formally organize a movie studio, other armed services made training films using well-known actors and directors as well. Some of Hollywood's entertainment giants served during World War II by creating training movies and documentaries for the U.S. Navy.

Director Chronicles Two Major Sea Battles

John Ford, who had won consecutive Oscars in 1940 and 1941 for *The Grapes of Wrath* and *How Green Was My Valley*, respectively, earned two more Academy Awards as a lieutenant commander in the U.S. Navy. Ford created documentaries for the Navy's Photographic Branch of the Office of Strategic Services—the Central Intelligence Agency's predecessor during World War II—where he earned back-to-back Oscars for *The Battle of Midway* in 1942 and *December 7th* in 1943. Although Ford broke all the rules, he enjoyed playing Navy, according to Ronald Davis's *John Ford: Hollywood's Old Master*. He even gave his yacht, *Araner*, to the Navy in February 1942, and the Navy used the vessel for the next three years to patrol the coast of California for submarines.

Steve Daly reported in *Entertainment Weekly*'s Special Oscar Guide 2003 that in 1941 Ford telegraphed Dudley Nichols, screenwriter for another Ford Navy film, *Informer*, that "awards for pictures are a trivial thing to be concerned with in times like these." Nichols had sent his congratulations to Ford for winning another Oscar. (*Informer* had earned Ford his first Oscar in 1935.)

The Battle of Midway earned its Academy Award for Best Documentary on a Short Subject. Ford shot the footage himself, amid dive-bombing planes, exploding bombs and torpedoes, and sinking ships. He stood in a powerhouse, which is usually the first target of an air raid. Ford, who directed his 16mm camera lens out of a powerhouse window to capture the action, was hit by shrapnel and struck by a block of concrete, according to McBride. He was seriously injured while photographing the fierce fight, but Ford kept the camera rolling. As bombs exploded, the film literally jumped inside the camera, making viewers feel that they are part of the action. Ford shot images of the sailors fighting all around him, and he even captured the American flag being raised amid the combat. "It actually happened—eight o'clock, time for the colors to go up, and despite the bombs and everything, these kids ran up and raised the flag," Ford said in the Davis book.

Eight cans of color film made it from Midway back to the OSS headquarters in Washington, D.C., and Ford and editor Robert Parrish later watched the raw footage behind a locked door with an armed guard. The director told his editor that he wanted to make a movie for America's mothers. "It's to let them know that we're in a war and that we've been getting the shit kicked out of us for five months and now we're starting to hit back," he said in *John Ford: Hollywood's Old Master*. Ford sent Parrish and the film to Hollywood and told him to hole up at his mother's house until he arrived in California, because he was afraid the Navy would learn of the film and try to seize it.

The director put Dudley Nichols on a guilt trip to get him to write the narration. ("We're the ones who are out there getting shot at," Ford told Nichols, according to Eyman.) Parrish and Nichols locked themselves in a cutting room, and for forty-eight straight hours the editor put together images and the writer scripted the text. Ford sent in food and eagerly awaited the finished product. He also issued the order that all services must be represented equally in the film, to keep the branches from becoming jealous of each other. Parrish used footage shot by Ford and Jack Mackenzie Jr., the twenty-year-old son of a Hollywood cameraman. He also included sea action shots taken by Lieutenant Kenneth Pier. Ford stuck true to his style and added patriotic music for the score, including "Red River Valley," "America," "Anchors Aweigh," and "The Marine Hymn."

Ford also played politics in the final cut of the movie, handing Parrish footage of a young soldier and telling him where to splice it into the film. What he had added was a close-up of Major James Roosevelt (the son of President Roosevelt), who had not been at the battle officially. Ford placed the image near footage of the flag-draped American coffins being guided off the PT boats into their watery graves. Although FDR had not been moved by the film up to that point, he watched his son salute the dead sailors and said, "I want every mother in America to see this," according to Andrew Sinclair's *John Ford*. Radio City Music Hall debuted *The Battle of Midway* on September 14, 1942. Soon after, five hundred copies of the film were distributed across the country.

Once Ford was asked to describe the excitement and danger of Midway. He remarked that it was nothing special. "That's what I was getting paid for," he said in *John Ford Interviews,* edited by Gerald Perry. "There's nothing extraordinary about that. I was in this turret to report the position and numbers of Japanese planes to the officers who were fifty feet under the ground, and meanwhile I had a little 16mm camera. I just reported the different things and took pictures. That was what the Navy was for. What else could you do?"

Ford began his Naval service in 1940, when he organized a Navy Reserve unit of nearly two hundred filmmakers, who prepared for combat photography on the front lines in the event America went to war. They also made top-secret reconnaissance films that served to not only survey the landscape but also to deceive. A few years later, Ford's cameras shot images of the Normandy coastline—along beachfronts on which Allied troops were not going to land. The director called this "ippy dippy intelligence," according to the February 26, 1995, broadcast of National Public Radio's *All Things Considered.*

Always the adventurer, Ford wanted to operate with his OSS unit in U.S. territory, although that was strictly forbidden. He broke the rules by sending Parrish and a petty officer to shoot footage at the State Department. What the two ended up with were movies of Marines—who were supposed to be guarding the building—playing cards. Parrish and the petty officer were arrested, however, and nearly faced courts-martial. Ford argued against their detainment, using the film as proof that one of the nation's most essential edifices was not securely guarded. The charges against Parrish and the young seamen were dropped, but not before Ford tried to lobby President Roosevelt to allow the OSS to operate internally. And although FDR refused, the director was not without his sugar daddy. Ford had been given the "official carte blanche" by Major General "Wild" Bill Donovan, the OSS director on May 12, 1942, according to Eyman's book. The document said: "You are hereby authorized to exercise full responsibility relative to the carrying out of the

RIGHT: *Several Hollywood moviemakers earned Legion of Merit awards for their service during World War II. William Wyler, Sy Bartlett, John Huston, and Anatole Litvak each made significant contributions to military training films and documentaries.*
U.S. Signal Corps Photo

projects assigned to you. . . . You are further authorized to direct and control official travel to such points as may be necessary to carry out your said duties." A month later, Ford took himself and cameraman Mackenzie to Midway, leaving Hawaii after hearing a rumor that a battle was headed to that tiny island.

Ford received the Legion of Merit award from Navy Secretary James T. Forrestal for "exceptional meritorious conduct in the performance of outstanding services to the Government of the United States as chief of the Field Photographic Branch, Office of Strategic Services . . . he worked tirelessly toward the preparation and direction of secret motion-picture and still photographic reports and ably directed the initiation and execution of a program of secret intelligence photography."

(Despite winning Oscars for classics and war movies, Ford perhaps is best known for his Westerns, including *Fort Apache*, *She Wore a Yellow Ribbon*, and *Rio Grande*. He won 1952's Best Director Oscar for *The Quiet Man*.)

Cinematographer Tells Pearl Harbor Story His Way

Gregg Toland, who had won the 1939 Best Cinematography Academy Award for *Wuthering Heights*, entered military service in Ford's Office of Strategic Services photographic unit in 1941. By that time, he was in demand as a photography director and had completed cinematography on *Citizen Kane* and *Ball of Fire* earlier that year. He shot Ford's Oscar-winning documentary, *December 7th*, while in the unit. The film actually exists in two versions: the shorter movie Ford and Parrish edited, which the Academy recognized, and a longer version that Toland made on his own design with fictional characters and battle scenes staged on a 20th Century Fox back lot. Linda McCarthy and Jacki Lyden explained on the February 26, 1995, edition of the National Public Radio program, *All Things Considered*, that Toland and Ray Kellogg set up miniatures in a Hollywood studio and blended new shots with official United States government film footage of Pearl Harbor to make the film. Although Ford initially intended to stay in Hawaii with Toland to direct the movie, he left the Islands to fly to Midway.

Toland's *December 7th* features Uncle Sam (played by Walter Huston) and his friend, a wise man named Mr. C (which stands for Conscience) who engage in a conversation about the world on December 6, 1941. Mr. C warns Uncle Sam to be leery of the Japanese living in Hawaii. He tells Sam to prepare for war because these Japanese are disloyal and deceitful. This dialogue infuriated the Navy commanders, who felt the movie was racist and made unfounded attacks against a people to whom no acts of sabotage had been attributed. Ironically, the Navy also objected to the movie showing bravery by African-American and Asian-American sailors fighting against the Japanese.

At the time, military leaders considered the movie "disruptive and unreleaseable," wrote Eyman. FDR even mandated that all future Field Photographic materials be censored. Ford feared retribution on his project, *The Battle of Midway*, which he did not have permission to make and which had not yet been released. (This is when he added images of FDR's son, Major James Roosevelt, to his film despite the fact that the younger Roosevelt officially had not been at the battle.) Ford and Parrish cut Toland's eighty-five-minute would-be documentary to thirty-four minutes, and focused the movie on the efforts to recover and restore Pearl Harbor and its vessels. Although Toland shot the movie, Ford put his stamp on it and earned another Oscar.

The government refused to release Toland's version from its archives until after the Freedom of Information Act was passed many years later. The film was released in a restored form as *December 7th: The Movie* in 1991.

Toland and Ford had worked together on *The Grapes of Wrath* in 1940, and they later made *The Long Voyage Home*. (Because of the acclaim he earned for *Wuthering Heights*, Toland served as cinematographer on William Wyler's *The Best Years of Our Lives*, the director's 1947 Oscar winner.)

Talented Actor Becomes Star Naval Recruit

Robert Taylor, a talented performer who understood both acting and aviation, epitomized the Navy film instructor. Taylor made seventeen naval aviation training films after graduating fourth in his class at New Orleans Naval Air Station and being stationed at Livermore Naval Air Station in 1944.

Entertainer Sings in the Rain and on the Ship

Gene Kelly sang and danced his way through mass-appeal movies while on leave from the Navy during the early 1940s. He'd joined the armed services against MGM's will, but he never saw combat. The Navy stationed Kelly at the U.S. Naval Photographic Center in Washington, D.C., where he starred in training films while on duty until the Navy discharged him in 1944.

Actor Becomes Sailor, then Trekkie

DeForest Kelley, better known as Dr. Leonard "Bones" McCoy in the original *Star Trek* television show and movies, joined the Army and shot a Navy training film at the end of his military career. This launched his acting career when a talent scout from Paramount Studios saw the film and offered Kelley a three-year contract, which started with the lead role in 1947's *Fear in the Night*. (Kelley appeared in the TV shows *Bonanza* and *Route 66* as well as the film *Gunfight at the OK Corral* before *Star Trek* fame.)

Wartime Films, Documentaries Stand Test of Time

The First Motion Picture Unit, its U.S. Navy counterpart, the OSS Photographic Unit, and the Amy Signal Corps made hundreds of movies and shot miles of film that audiences continue to enjoy today. John Langellier, assistant director and chief curator of the Reagan Library, said in Biederman's article: "Every time you flip on the History Channel or the Discovery Channel, and you see World War II from an American perspective, you're watching the work of one of these gentlemen. That's their legacy."

11. Turning Point of the Twentieth Century: The Invasion of Fortress Europe

"YOU ARE ABOUT TO EMBARK UPON THE GREAT CRUSADE, TOWARD WHICH WE HAVE STRIVEN THESE MANY MONTHS. THE EYES OF THE WORLD ARE UPON YOU. THE HOPES AND PRAYERS OF LIBERTY-LOVING PEOPLE EVERYWHERE MARCH WITH YOU."

—*General Dwight D. Eisenhower, Supreme Commander, Allied Forces Europe*

"TWO KINDS OF MEN ARE STAYING ON THIS BEACH . . . THE DEAD AND THOSE WHO ARE GOING TO DIE. GET *UP*! MOVE *IN*! GOD DAMMIT! MOVE IN AND DIE!"

—*Colonel George Taylor on Omaha Beach at Normandy*

OPPOSITE: *The accoutrements of war included simple memorials to the thousands who fell, this one in France.*
U.S. Coast Guard Photo

EVERY FEW DECADES THE ENGLISH AND THE FRENCH and the Germans have to stir things up and get all bloody and entangled in a battle royale and remind the whole world why they really don't like each other much. (Even during lulls in their centuries-old differences, the three keep a wary eye on each other.) True to form, when Nazi Germany's Luftwaffe and His Majesty's Royal Air Force started dropping bombs on each other's homeland, it was the effete French who got caught in the middle. Sure, the politicians in Paris boasted that their massive Maginot Line—a sprawling concrete wall with bunkers and gun emplacements linked by passageways, intended to separate France from the eastern frontier—was built to hold back the Germans. With this pompous assessment, a bumbling underestimate of the Nazi blitzkrieg, or lightning strike, they fully expected to blunt any offensive.

The movie *Reunion in France*, released in 1942, opens with this prologue:

"Paris, May 9, 1940. The ninth night of the ninth month of a war too uneventful to be taken seriously, and too far away to worry about . . ."

Then a French general, speaking at a dinner for the country's industrial and political leaders, addresses the masses via radio broadcast: "Tonight the people of France have reason to be heartened and encouraged. In the north, Hitler's army stands helpless and immobilized before our impregnable Maginot Line. Our soldiers are fully equipped and trained to the point of perfection. And behind them, the people of France are confident and united as never before. It is because of our leaders of industry and of labor that our imperishable republic will not only emerge triumphant but will ensure the freedom of Europe, for our generation and for the generations to come. France is a great country tonight."

With war looming, Madame Michelle de la Becque (played by American actress Joan Crawford) complains to her French paramour: "France is at war, and in times of war, love is a punishable offense. The

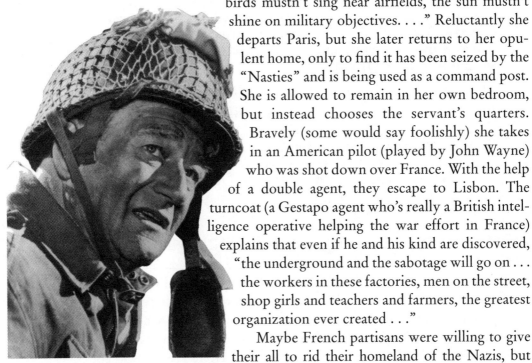

birds mustn't sing near airfields, the sun mustn't shine on military objectives. . . ." Reluctantly she departs Paris, but she later returns to her opulent home, only to find it has been seized by the "Nasties" and is being used as a command post. She is allowed to remain in her own bedroom, but instead chooses the servant's quarters. Bravely (some would say foolishly) she takes in an American pilot (played by John Wayne) who was shot down over France. With the help of a double agent, they escape to Lisbon. The turncoat (a Gestapo agent who's really a British intelligence operative helping the war effort in France) explains that even if he and his kind are discovered, "the underground and the sabotage will go on . . . the workers in these factories, men on the street, shop girls and teachers and farmers, the greatest organization ever created . . ."

Maybe French partisans were willing to give their all to rid their homeland of the Nazis, but when those "Prussian swine" occupied their towns and villages and seized their ports and plundered their treasures, the French leadership barely whimpered, only to have the British send swarms of bombers to drop their incendiaries, to torment the Nazis and bedevil the French common folk. Meanwhile, many leaders fled to French Algiers, splintering into various factions.

ABOVE: *In the movie* Reunion in France, *John Wayne plays an American pilot serving with the RAF, who gets shot down and is taken in by a French madame, played by Joan Crawford. Years later, he returns to France, this time at Normandy in the movie,* The Longest Day.
Associated Press Photo

The true French heroes of the war were those who remained behind as partisans, as couriers, helping downed Allied airmen return to England, photographing Nazi movements and buildups, sending coded messages via shortwave radio, and tormenting the intruders in every way possible. Their inspiration became the peasant girl who rose to command an army—Joan of Arc.

Two movies that reflect this sentiment were 1943's *Cross of Lorraine* and 1942's *Joan of Paris*, the latter about a French waitress, Joan, who falls in love with an Englishman, only to learn he is a wanted pilot trying to find safe harbor. He begs her to escape to Britain with him, but she realizes she must remain behind to help others fighting against the Nazis, and he must continue as a bomber pilot. She promises to wait for him until the war is over, although she knows her decision means she may never see him again.

As her lover escapes across the Channel, Joan is caught by the "Nasties" and is soon executed, just as her real-life namesake was sacrificed. But the movie's message is that there will be others, thousands of other French partisans, continuing the fight, carrying on until the world comes to their rescue.

Another French heroine of the mid-1800s, a simple peasant girl who inspired those seeking impossible miracles, was Bernadette Soubirous of the tiny village of Lourdes. During a visit to a grotto, she saw of vision of the Virgin Mary and a trickle of water began to flow nearby, turning into a stream. Over the next century, thousands of believers—the blind, the lame, the ailing—journeyed to the miracle village of Lourdes in southern France to drink from the healing waters, hoping they might be among the few who would be cured of their afflictions, who would cast aside their crutches to walk again.

In 1943, actress Jennifer Jones starred in *The Song of Bernadette*, with Linda Darnell as the shadowy image of the Virgin Mary. Despite criticism from skeptics and nonbelievers, the aging Bernadette never strayed from her belief in who she saw in that grotto in 1858, and the retelling of her story in the midst of WWII inspired thousands—not just the beleaguered French—to hope beyond hope for miracles.

Sharpening the Point of the Spear

While their efforts to "bomb the Nazis into oblivion" did have its successes—notably, destroying key industrial centers and crippling rail lines—the Allies knew that at some point they would have to launch a ground offensive to penetrate Hitler's impenetrable concrete and steel Atlantic Wall with a razor-sharp dagger, then race across Fortress Europe to Berlin and ultimately to defeat the Nazi empire.

By late 1943 the Nazi blitzkrieg tactics had sputtered to a halt on the frozen tundra of Mother Russia. The vaunted Afrika Korps was in shambles and had retreated closer to home. German artillery batteries in Italy were making life hell for American forces storming ashore, but the tenacious Yanks kept pushing forward and the Germans gave ground, setting up new skirmish lines.

In England, as plans to "jump the Channel" were being argued about, the entire southern coast became a virtual staging area for thousands of men and their accoutrements of war. The Allied forces would include twenty-one American divisions and another twenty-six made up of British, Polish, Canadian, French, Belgian, Dutch, Czech, and Italian troops. They trained by "assaulting" the tranquil cliffs at Dover and the beaches in both directions along the coast, and they waited and they waited until the minutes seemed like hours and the days became an

LEFT: *Okay, so maybe he wasn't the "boogie woogie bugle boy of Company B," but he was certainly harassed about it enough. These two are waiting in England for the big push, jumping the Channel to mainland Europe.*
National Archives Photo

Right: *After endless months of practicing beach landings along the coast of England, dreading another ride in one of those gut-wrenching floating coffins, the thousands of Allied troops bound for the French coast just wanted to get to solid ground, no matter what kind of reception the Nazis had planned for them. Unfortunately, hundreds of GIs died before ever getting to shore.*
U.S. Coast Guard Photo

insufferable hell, and they trained some more, and they pissed and moaned about the boredom, and they trained past the breaking point of ad nauseum.

Many dreaded another excursion in the cursed landing boats bobbing up and down in the surf, lurching from side to side, the floor splattered with vomit sloshing around with the sea water. (In a straw poll of dreaded options, many of the GIs said they would rather storm ashore dodging enemy machine-gun fire and mortar explosions than spend even one more gut-wrenching minute in one of those floating torture chambers! Even jumping out of a perfectly good airplane with tracer bullets streaking across the darkness would be better—or so they thought. The Airborne paratroopers may have had a different opinion about that.)

Jersey boy Jack Lebzelter was one of those paratroopers with the 101st Airborne, doing practice jumps over England in preparation for Normandy. He always told his buddies he would someday be an actor, but they thought it was just bluster. In late May, during a night drop, his chute malfunctioned and he broke his leg. The injury would require a year of rehab and left him with a plate in his leg to stabilize his ankle.

(After his discharge, Lebzelter returned to Jersey. While working in New York as a lifeguard, he would be discovered by actress Margo Jones, who wanted him to be part of her acting studio in Dallas. Lebzelter was soon on his way to realizing the dream he'd told his Army buddies. He changed his name to Jack Warden and soon was appearing on Broadway, in movies, and on television, establishing himself as one of the most recognizable character actors in show business.)

By late spring of 1944 the Allied invasion force was ready for the Channel crossing. The Germans were also ready to repel it, to unleash the fires of hell—with machine guns stitching the sand and the surf, streaking the beaches blood red, and mortars and artillery rounds raining down deadly thunder in very heavy doses, and minefields and ribbons of concertina wire to slow the advance just long enough so every GI had a little time to pick a nice cozy spot in the sand . . . to die. At least that's how the Germans planned the reception, expecting the Allied task force to come ashore, and perish, at Calais.

A Master Stroke of Deception

The Nazis had moved their heavy guns in other over-watch positions along the French coast, but believed the Allies would take the shortest route to attack the European mainland. That is where they planned to repel the onslaught, at Pas de Calais, a mere twenty-seven miles from those cliffs at Dover.

The Allies fed the Nazis' misconception with a major deception campaign. 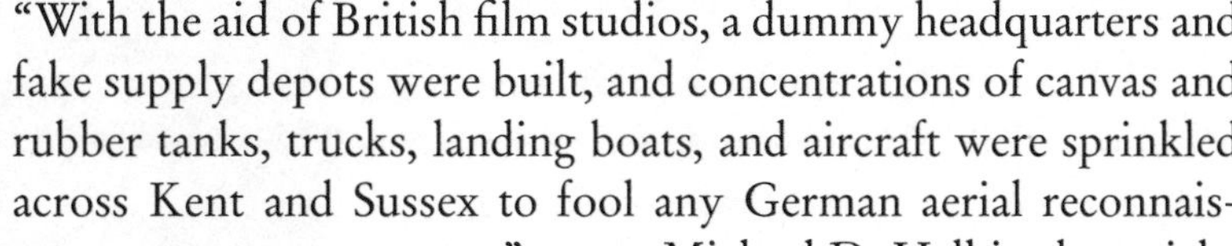 "With the aid of British film studios, a dummy headquarters and fake supply depots were built, and concentrations of canvas and rubber tanks, trucks, landing boats, and aircraft were sprinkled across Kent and Sussex to fool any German aerial reconnaissance," wrote Michael D. Hall in the article, "Deceiving the Reich" for *D-Day* magazine's sixtieth anniversary issue. "Phony airfields were laid out, plenty of radio traffic sure to be heard on the Nazi-occupied Continent was generated, and more Allied reconnaissance sorties and preliminary bombing attacks were made in the Calais area than in Normandy."

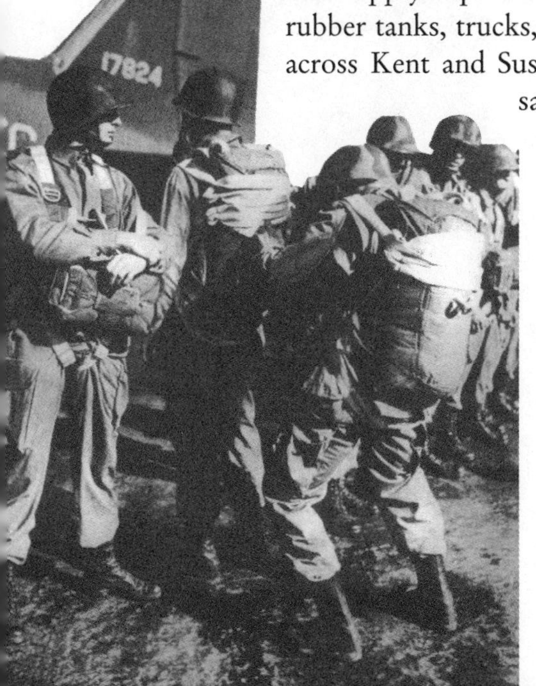

LEFT: *American paratroopers double-check their chutes prior to a practice jump over England. Future actor Jack Warden was seriously injured during a jump and missed the invasion of France, on June 6, 1944.*
U.S. Army Photo

This fictitious invasion task force would be headed up by America's most noted and notorious field commander, George S. Patton, who was called back to England after slapping two battle-weary soldiers at Sicily. Old Blood and Guts Patton was itching to get back into combat and wasn't pleased with his role as a feint, as commander of the fictitious 1st Army Group. He wanted to spearhead the real invasion, but reluctantly understood the importance of duping the duplicitous Nazis.

An Enormous Undertaking

By early June the countdown had begun. Of course, despite all the Allies' planning, Mother Nature would have a hand in limiting the invasion's window of opportunity, dictating when the weather and the tides would be in sync.

For many American soldiers it would be their first taste of battle—three and a half years after the attack on Pearl Harbor and President Roosevelt's declaration of war. They had no idea what they were getting into, and had nothing in their past to measure it against, but they had read what the newspapers were reporting, and heard what the radio broadcasters were saying. Words and phrases like "Monumental and colossal," "A turning point in the war," "A turning point in history," and "The defining moment of the twentieth century" described mighty awesome endeavors for this cast of thousands along the English coast.

The invasion was dubbed a classic long before it even began. Both sides were fully aware of the importance, the implication that was attached to an Allied force of combatants crossing the English Channel to establish a toehold on the mainland and then push inland across France.

The Nazis had constructed the massive Atlantic Wall, thick enough to withstand any bombardment and built to last a thousand years, and they were armed and at the ready to repel any invader and stain the beaches of northern France red. To understate the impact would be foolish. The future of a free and democratic world versus the impenetrable ramparts of the Thousand-Year Reich were at stake. There could be only one ultimate victor.

Late on June 5, after months of rehearsals along the English coastline, the thousands of GIs (and British and Canadian forces) who boarded the five thousand vessels, from battleships to hun-

RIGHT: *There was a narrow window of opportunity to launch the Allied assault on Fortress Europe, with Mother Nature dictating when to go. The troops and equipment were loaded onto the transport ships along the English coast. Meteorologists were tracking a heavy storm moving in, and General Dwight D. Eisenhower knew if he didn't give the order before the storm hit, it might be weeks before they had another chance, and then the Nazis would have more time to prepare for them, more time to find out where the landings would occur.* U.S. Army Photo

dreds of plywood PT boats and landing craft, had mixed emotions. They dreaded those floating plywood "battle wagons," but at least it would be the last time they had to endure the misery. Unfortunately, many would never make it to the English Channel's southern shores.

To cast a little doubt in the minds of the already apprehensive Allied forces massing along England's southern coast, Axis Sally broadcast from Radio Berlin on the eve of D-Day that the Nazis knew they were coming. Her show that night, called "Vision of Invasion," was a dramatization of a worried mom in Ohio who had a frightening dream that her son had been killed when his ship was hit during the Channel crossing . . . by a U-boat? Or a Luftwaffe bomber? A floating mine? Or maybe coastal artillery guns?

It didn't really matter . . . her boy was dead. And she could also hear some of his buddies sobbing . . . but why? It wasn't just because he was gone . . . they knew the odds against them practically guaranteed they'd be joining him real soon in the afterlife. And the Nazis along the French coast were going to do everything they could to send a few hundred thousand more Allied soldiers to join him.

The broadcast had its psychological impact on the invasion force, but it couldn't postpone it. (After the war, Millie Gillars would be tried for treason, not for her lengthy role as Axis Sally, but for that one show she did on the eve of D-Day. She would be convicted and sent to prison until 1962.)

Another Axis propagandist who directed his verbal barbs at the Allies was Lord Haw-Haw—Britisher William Joyce—who turned to fascism as a teenager and left England for Nazi Germany in the late '30s. He was hired by Propaganda Minister Joseph Goebbels to spew Nazi propaganda to the British and then to the Allies when America got in the fight.

At the same time that Allied forces were cramming onto the damnable landing craft, more than 13,000 American airborne troops from the 82nd and 101st divisions loaded up and headed out, intending to drop behind the lines that night to secure key bridges and prevent German reinforcements from rushing toward the beaches at Normandy. But many of the paratroopers jumped miles off course and would be scattered across the French countryside.

Hundreds who descended from the skies would perish, drowning in the surrounding marshlands or cut down by flak and machine-gun fire. Some airborne units suffered a 40 percent casualty rate that first day.

Below: *"Packed in like sardines" was the feeling many Allied soldiers felt, crammed onto transport ships in England, waiting to hit the beach at Normandy, France.* U.S. Navy Photo

An Allied Endeavor

One of the thousands of Allied airborne troops at Normandy was British officer Richard Todd, with the 6th Airborne

Division, and one of the first to jump over Normandy. The 6th's mission was to secure the vital Pegasus Bridge and prevent the Nazis from sending reinforcements to the front. (Todd made it through the mission and survived the war. By 1949 he was starring in motion pictures and was nominated for an Academy Award for his role in *The Hasty Heart*. He would replay his airborne exploits in 1962, when he starred in the D-Day epic, *The Longest Day*.)

Above: *Paratroopers of the 82nd Airborne Division loaded onto glider planes, waiting for their jump behind enemy lines near Normandy, France.* National Archives Photo

Serving with the 508th Parachute Infantry Regiment, assigned to seize the bridge over the Douve, near Brienville, was theater actor William Windom. (He would use his GI Bill benefits to finish college at Fordham and Columbia and would become a theatrical character actor; he also had roles in movies, on television, and on serial radio shows.)

Among the Canadian forces assaulting France was James Doohan, a captain with the Royal Artillery, who injured his hand and leg at Normandy. He later joined the Royal Canadian Air Force and quickly became known as the "craziest pilot" in the service. (After the war he joined the Neighborhood Playhouse in New York. He is best known as Chief Engineer Montgomery Scott—as in, "beam me up Scottie"—on the immensely popular science fiction TV serial, *Star Trek*.)

As the Allied armada approached the fifty-mile Cherbourg to Le Havre crescent, the warships fired their big guns, pounding the coastal defense works, the concrete pillboxes, and the minefields, but they couldn't fully neutralize the Nazi artillery batteries and machine-gun crews, which opened up as the flotilla ventured within range.

On board the destroyer USS *Barton,* which was part of Destroyer Squadron 60, Hollywood leading man Robert Montgomery was serving as operations officer. He had already seen action in the Pacific with the "expendables"—the brave PT boat crews in the Solomons Campaign—before contracting malaria. After a brief stay in the States to recover, he was sent to the Atlantic to direct the offshore gunnery firing on the Normandy defenses. (Destroyer Squadron 60 also lobbed shells at the heavily fortified coastal town of Cherbourg weeks later.)

Another member of the Allied flotilla, with the British Royal Navy, was future leading man Alec Guinness, who piloted one of the flimsy landing craft loaded with soldiers. Fellow countryman and budding actor Patrick MacNee served with the British light coastal forces on board a PT boat at

Normandy. (After the war he appeared on stage and in movies, although he became best known for his role as John Steed in the popular television series, *The Avengers*.)

In all, twenty-four Allied warships and thirty-five auxiliaries were destroyed as they approached the Normandy coast. More than seven hundred of the wooden landing ships were blown apart by German artillery guns and mortars.

Some soldiers jumped over the sides of damaged LSTs but, weighed down with more than a hundred pounds of equipment that was like a concrete anchor they couldn't discard, they drowned before even getting in the fight.

But thousands more GIs made it ashore, then advanced on the enemy strongholds overlooking the beaches at Normandy, an inch at a time. One of those GIs who must have had Lady Luck watching over him was future character actor, Charles Durning. "I was in the first wave to hit Omaha Beach. There were seventy of us that survived that first day at Normandy, but I was the only survivor of a machine-gun ambush,'" he recalled for *Stars in Khaki* by James E. Wise Jr. and Paul Wilderson III.

Working alongside the invasion force to film the joint operation was Marine Corps officer Glenn Ford, in charge of a camera crew, one of many documenting the Normandy invasion. (Ford had appeared in the movie *Flight Lieutenant* in 1942, before joining the leathernecks. Two years after the D-Day landings, Ford was back in Hollywood, starring in the combat film, *Gallant Journey*.)

One of the British soldiers storming the beach was actor David Niven, a member of a Royal Army light infantry regiment, a group of volunteers dubbed Phantom. (At the outbreak of the war, Niven had departed Hollywood to return home and do whatever his country needed him for. He joined the commandos and starred in *The First of the Few* in 1942, followed by *The Way Ahead*.)

FDR Talks to the Nation

Later on that same day, after being informed that the invasion was under way, President Roosevelt spoke to the American people via radio, cautioning that victory was still in question:

"My fellow Americans, in this poignant hour, I ask you to join with me in prayer. Almighty God, our sons, pride of our nation, this day have set upon a mighty endeavor, a struggle to preserve our republic and our civilization, and to set free a suffering humanity. Lead them straight and true. Give strength to their arms, stoutness to their hearts, steadfastness in their faith.

"They will need Thy blessings. Their road will be long and hard. For the enemy is strong. He may hurl back our forces. Success may not come with rushing speed, but we shall return again and again; and we know that by Thy grace and by the righteousness of our cause, our sons will triumph. . . ."

The Inland Advance

After securing the Normandy front, Allied ground forces set out to push the fight inland toward St. Lô and the vital port city of Cherbourg and beyond. As he heard about the invasion, Hitler refused to rush in additional combat units, believing Normandy was a bluff and that the major invasion force would still attack Calais.

ABOVE: *The Germans had plenty of time to strengthen their fortifications all along the French coast, and would not be easily routed. It would require continuous artillery fire, such as this howitzer crew pounding Carentan, France.*
Army Signal Corps Photo

This gave the Allies time to pour additional men, plus tanks, artillery pieces, fuel, supplies, and munitions ashore via Normandy. By the time he realized his tactical error, it was too late for Hitler to do anything but relinquish the region and cajole his remaining units in France to defend to the last, for the sake of the Fatherland.

One of the many soldiers at St. Lô was Private Art Carney, a replacement with the 28th Infantry Division. As a man of many voices on the airwaves, upon enlisting he was hoping to be assigned with Armed Forces Radio. Instead he ended up being sent into battle with the Keystone Division, but it would be a short stint.

"On August 15, 1944, Art had set up his machine gun on Saint-Lô and was filling a canteen with water when, without warning, he was blown off his feet by a Nazi mortar shell," wrote Michael Seth Starr in the biography, *Art Carney*. Shrapnel ripped open Carney's right leg and thigh before he ever had a chance to fire his weapon. "Art was carried off in a stretcher, wrapped in a body cast, and transported to an Army hospital in the English Midlands." (He was sent back to the military hospital near Richmond, Virginia, where he spent nine months in rehab. After his discharge he returned to radio and went on to a stellar career in television and movies, although his brief experience in combat left him with a pronounced limp.)

Among the British troops flooding into Normandy was "Benny Hill of the Royal Electrical and Mechanical Engineers [who] didn't arrive in Normandy until September," reported Richard Hayes for *The Osprey Military Journal* in May 2001. "He was a searchlight operator for the Third Light Anti-Aircraft Searchlight Battery which landed at the famous Mulberry floating harbors." (While he was never a good soldier, Hill's talent for comedy led to his being pulled from duty to join the cast of the British military revue, *Stars in Battledress.* After the war, Hill further developed his acting skills and sense of humor, eventually getting his own long-running television show that relied heavily on bawdy skits with a bevy of buxom beauties.)

The Allies quickly encircled German strongholds such as Saint-Malo. They either pounded them into submission, or the battle-weary Wehrmacht troops there called it quits—out of ammunition, no longer willing to give their all for the Fatherland, knowing they had a better chance of living through the war as a prisoner of the Allies. Paris was liberated by the end of August of '44, and the French toasted the conquering heroes.

During the two-week battle at Rhone Valley, 32,000 German soldiers laid down their arms and surrendered. To hell with the Führer's demand to hold out "to the last man, to the last cartridge." The end was fast approaching, and the defeated wanted to be around for whatever was left of their country.

Below: *After the breakout from Normandy, the Allies swept across France, encountering house-to-house resistance in such villages as Saint-Malo, as Nazi forces were ordered to hold to the last man.*
U.S. Army Photo

The only thing preventing an Allied version of the blitzkrieg was clogged supply lines that could not get munitions and fuel to the advancing units. "In their race across the Seine, the Allied units outran their stocks of gasoline, ammunition, spare parts, and food," wrote Bruce W. Nelan in the article, "Ike's Invasion" for *Time* magazine, June 6, 1994. "To maintain itself in the field, an infantry division required 650 tons of supplies every day. The supply planners assumed that they would not have to support any U.S. divisions north of the Seine until 120 days after D-Day. But within 90 days, sixteen divisions were 150 miles beyond the Seine . . . and had to halt to let supplies catch up."

This delay would allow the Germans to regroup, replenish, and stage a last stand across the German border with France and the Benelux countries: Belgium, the Netherlands, and Luxembourg.

The Southern Push

Two months after the Normandy invasion, another Allied task force invaded southern France along the French Riviera. The operation included 300,000 combatants, with more than 10,000 paratroopers departing from Italy. Prepping the Nazi defenses with a predawn bombardment were 4,000 bombers and fighter planes, plus a naval armada that included more than 130 warships.

"When the invasion of southern France was undertaken in August 1944, [Commander Douglas Fairbanks Jr.] was given command of a six-ship Special

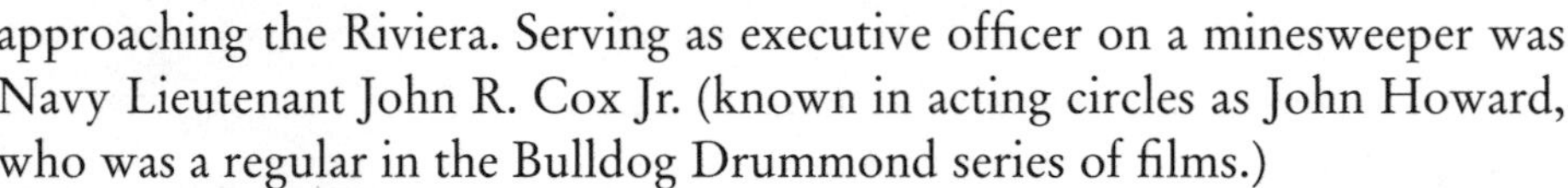

Right: *At Carentan, France, in mid-June of 1944, local villagers erected this simple tribute to a fallen American hero, who died while attempting to rid their country of the despised Nazis.* National Archives Photo

Operations Group—two British gunboats and four American PT boats—conducting a commando raid and diversion near Nice," reported William Van Osdol in *Famous Americans in World War II*. (Following in the footsteps of his father, the swashbuckling actor, Fairbanks took on daring roles both in Hollywood and in real life.)

Clearing the breakwaters of mines was dangerous duty, but vital to secure safe passage for the landing transports approaching the Riviera. Serving as executive officer on a minesweeper was Navy Lieutenant John R. Cox Jr. (known in acting circles as John Howard, who was a regular in the Bulldog Drummond series of films.)

On August 16 of 1944, Cox's ship was clearing mines in the Gulf of Frejus when it was staggered by a mine. As the ship's exec, Cox wrote the battle report, stating, "There was an underwater explosion either directly under the stern or slightly on the port bow. There was a resultant complete destruction and loss of the forward third of the ship up to the middle of the bridge topside." Cox would take over the ship after the commander was killed, along with four sailors, plus another fifteen wounded. (After the war, Cox returned to Hollywood and picked up where he left off, as leading man John Howard.)

As at Normandy, Nazi gun emplacements blasted the wood-sided landing craft as they approached France's southern coast. Still, they couldn't hold off the invasion force, and soon the beachhead of southern France was secured, and additional men and materiel began pouring in to make ready to push inland.

Allied forces could now squeeze the Nazis from both the west and south of France and drive them back, eventually encircling and constricting whatever remained of the once fearsome Nazi juggernaut. By September of 1944, it was fairly evident Nazi Germany would not survive through the next summer.

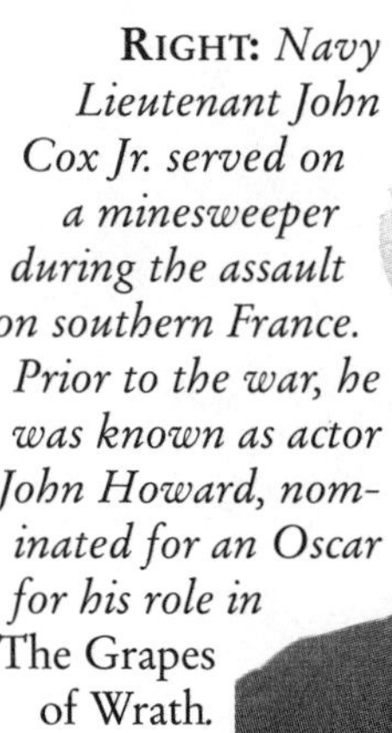

Right: *Navy Lieutenant John Cox Jr. served on a minesweeper during the assault on southern France. Prior to the war, he was known as actor John Howard, nominated for an Oscar for his role in* The Grapes of Wrath. U.S. Navy Photo

Performers Follow the Troops across Europe

After a whirlwind tour of Europe, Josephine Baker was one of the first and the youngest of Americans of the twentieth century to entertain in

France. "Slim and long-legged at nineteen, she races, bare-breasted, onto the stage of the Folies Bergères in 1926 and tears into the Charleston, knees bent, elbows flapping, feet stomping; she bumps and grinds and writhes and shimmies and, from time to time, puffs out her cheeks and crosses her eyes and grins into the camera," wrote Geoffrey C. Ward in the article, "The St. Louis Woman of Paris" for *American Heritage* magazine, November 1989.

At just thirteen, Josephine had run away from the racism she saw in her hometown of St. Louis, had a brief stint with the Dixie Steppers on Broadway, and kept running all the way to Gay Paree, even becoming a French citizen.

"In World War II [she] joined the French Resistance. Her marriage to a Jewish businessman, Jean Leon, brought her to the notice of [Hermann] Goering and the Gestapo, who decided to murder her," wrote Irving Wallace, David Wallechinsky, and Amy and Sylvia Wallace for *Intimate Sex Lives of Famous People*. "Goering invited her to dinner, having arranged to put cyanide in her fish course. Forewarned, Josephine excused herself as the fish was served, planning to drop down the laundry chute in the bathroom to a rendezvous with Resistance workers below. Goering produced his gun and ordered her to eat the fish before allowing her to retire to the bathroom. She managed to reach the chute, slid down, and her colleagues rushed her to a doctor, who pumped out her stomach. After a month of sickness she recovered, but lost all her hair. She always wore a wig thereafter."

Though she avoided a painful demise, Baker tempted fate by serving as a courier for the French underground, smuggling coded messages in her lingerie as she traveled between Lisbon and Casablanca and back to Paris. The Nazis would have shot her on the spot if they had discovered her clandestine activities.

Two other American performers who skirted danger were the comedy duo of Joe and Jane McKenna, who arrived at Normandy a month after D-Day and traveled from one unit to the next, performing for large groups and small. But after taking a wrong turn one night, they got lost and soon found themselves confronted by a German patrol.

Unable to communicate with their captors, the McKennas used pantomime and humorous antics to convince the Nazi soldiers they were just entertainers, not combatants. Still, they were held for nearly two weeks, until they were freed by Allied forces driving hard across northern France.

As city after city was liberated, the Allied forces were smothered with boundless appreciation from the French citizens. One of those American soldiers was jazz devotee Timuel Black, who was later interviewed by Studs Terkel for his book, *The Good War*. "We went from Normandy to Brittany and moved toward Paris. Know how I know they'd retained hope and dreams? They'd buried their jazz records of people like Louis Armstrong and Duke Ellington and Coleman Hawkins. They hugged and embraced us.

They respected something from my own culture so openly, jazz music." With the Nazis routed from France, the jazz records and the movies of Hollywood would once again be enjoyed by citizens young and old.

One of the most popular entertainers among the troops was Mickey Rooney, assigned to the Army's 6817th Special Services Battalion. "He served in France as part of a jeep show under the command of Broadway producer and Army Major Joshua Logan," wrote Scott Baron in *They Also Served*. "Jeep shows were a team of three entertainers who put on shows on the front lines, often under hazardous conditions. On more than one occasion Rooney came under enemy small arms fire."

Rooney explained the concept of the "jeep shows" in his book, *Life Is Too Short*: "Each team was supposed to have a musician, a singer, and an MC, who told jokes. I was the MC for Bob Priester, hometown Hollywood, and Mario Pieroni of San Francisco. Priester sang, mostly Broadway show tunes. Pieroni played the accordion. And I did my old numbers from vaudeville, pieces of Mickey McGuire, bits from my best movies, imitations. God, the troops loved the imitations of their favorite actors: Gable, both Barrymores, Cagney, Bogart, Edward G. Robinson."

Ray Wax was with Army Special Services in France, building makeshift movie screens and stages from packing crates and anything else he could find. "The ingenious Germans had these prefabricated houses. I hit these places and found prefab sections of flooring. I put together six sections and I had a portable stage. Everywhere I went, I could drop down and I had a stage. I put that stage all across France," he told Studs Terkel for his book, *The Good War*. "I put on Dinah Shore. I put on Bing Crosby. These were the live shows coming in behind the men."

One young soldier who approached Ray Wax and asked for help in forming an Army stage band in France was piano plunker Dave Brubeck.

BELOW: *In the movies Edward G. Robinson could handle a Thompson submachine gun while chomping on a stogie and snarling out of the side of his mouth. But near the front lines in France, in August of 1944, it was the boys in uniform with all the firepower, especially after chasing the Nazis back to the Fatherland. When he hit the stage, Robinson reprised his gangster persona and the audience loved it.*
National Archives Photo

"Brubeck was a rifleman, an infantryman," Wax recalled. "When I pulled his [personnel] form, he couldn't move forward [with his unit to the fighting front]. That's what I did with eighteen people in the band. They stayed alive and I had a band."

For many of the former members of the Glenn Miller Band, it would have been easy to call it quits, to pack it in and go home after hearing that their leader had died in a plane crash on his way from England to France. Maybe in civilian life they could have gone their separate ways, but by mid-1944 they were all in the military, and disbanding was not an option. If they no longer wanted to be musicians they could always volunteer for the infantry, or maybe become truck drivers, but they were in for the duration. There was no need for further discussion.

"The loss of Miller, the man who had put the band together and sparked it from the U.S. to England, was a tough blow," reported Army Sergeant Al Hine for *YANK* magazine, October 19 of '45. "The Army put Tech Sergeant Ray McKinley in charge of the outfit and crossed its fingers."

Before leaving England the band recorded two months' worth of radio shows. Then they crossed the Channel for Paris, where they camped out, playing for troops sent to the rear for a little R&R. They also continued to do radio shows on an almost daily basis, playing big band music and pulling in entertainers such as Mickey Rooney whenever they were in the area.

"We had a good singer, Johnny Desmond, and you'll be hearing a lot more of him after the war," McKinley told *YANK*. As for Mac, "I'm going to have my own band again, but I want to wait till I can get a good one. If I get out now and fill up with a lot of young kids, they'll be drafted and then where'll I be? Wait till the Army loosens up and lets out a few of the boys and all the bands will start showing an improvement."

BELOW: *Two months after the invasion at Normandy, Bing Crosby and Broderick Crawford (both on the right), along with Corporals Colin Frampton and Doug Marshall, appeared on the BBC radio show "Mark Up the Map," which followed the Allied advance across Europe. By the end of 1944, Der Bingle had also hopped across the Channel, to entertain the troops.*
War Museum Photo

Time magazine reported from Europe in its March 12, 1945, issue about the growing popularity of the band's new lead singer: "Eager adolescents jam-packed Paris's gilded, rococo Opera House. They had come to hear the shy, Detroit-born, 24-year old Sergeant Johnny Desmond who has been spreading havoc among European bobby-soxers since he first sang over BBC five months ago. Before he enlisted in 1943, black-haired, velvet-eyed Johnny sang with Bob Crosby and Gene Krupa. Then he signed up as a drummer with Glenn Miller's Air Forces Band. Sergeant Desmond, known as "The Creamer," because of his smooth, creamy baritone, was getting fan mail in three languages.

"His 'I'll be Seeing You' and 'Long Ago and Far Away' in phonetic French, make young Parisians jump up and down, squeal 'Bravo!' and clutter up the stage-door alley for a closer look at Le Cremair."

As one of their own, Desmond was just as popular with the GIs, a sentiment they didn't feel toward Frank Sinatra. "By 1945, with his surly bad manners and celebrity disdain for everything outside the orbit of his own desires, Swoonatra had begun to stir up a lot of negative feelings," wrote Don

Graham in *No Name on the Bullet*. "And his disdain for USO shows made him very unpopular with troops in Europe."

France on Film

When the Nazis steamrolled France, they quickly seized the movie studios, shutting down production, looting equipment, and rounding up anyone who had foolishly remained behind. Many of France's top actors and actresses, directors, and writers had already fled to anywhere but their home country, including to London, Broadway, and Hollywood.

Intent on doing whatever they could to rid their country of the Nazi henchmen, many of those expatriates became involved with film projects that continued to tell the French story, about the underground, about living under fascist tyranny. They had to tell the world what was going on in their beloved homeland.

One of those who remained behind was former producer and chief of the Bervia Film Studios, Lucien Viard, who ended up in a Nazi forced-labor camp. (When he returned to Paris, he found his studios stripped bare; he would have to scavenge for cameras, lights, props, and costumes to get back to making movies.)

Actor Claude Dauphin was in the French Army for five years, and he came out of it without a scratch, although he was wounded in a sword fight during the filming of his first role (while on leave from the military) as Cyrano de Bergerac.

"During the German occupation [of France], American pictures were verboten. Just before the Germans came, the French had heard a lot of press agent ballyhoo about glamour queens like Veronica Lake and Rita Hayworth," reported Army Corporal Marvin Sleeper for *YANK*. "It is not strictly true to say that no Hollywood product played in Paris during the Nazi occupation. There was an 'underground' movie house operating right under the nose of Der Kommandant

RIGHT: *French cabaret star and American expatriate Josephine Baker was a sensation in Europe in the thirties and well beyond the war years. She left the United States because of the racism she experienced as a teenager, and became a French citizen, clandestinely working for the underground, passing secret messages during her many trips between Paree and North Africa. Her activities for the partisans were suspected by the Nazis, and one time she suffered food poisoning at a dinner with Nazi blowhard Hermann Goering, who ordered her to eat tainted fish at gunpoint. Fortunately she was rushed to a local doctor and had her stomach pumped, though she did have severe side effects from the poisoning, resulting in all of her hair falling out.*
Associated Press Photo

von Gross Paris. It was a tiny, 100-seat house, and Frenchmen were shelling out the equivalent of $80 American money to get in. The underground movie house was a terrific financial success, and the picture it showed never changed. It was *The Great Dictator*, with Charlie Chaplin starring as Hitler."

Under the threat of certain execution, Parisians dared to view and laugh at this parody, in which Chaplin portrayed a Hitler look-alike as a blustering buffoon. Millions around the world would agree with those French stalwarts and would consider it a dead-on accurate portrayal of the Nazi leader, by this time a desperate, blundering fool.

12. Turning the Tide in the Pacific

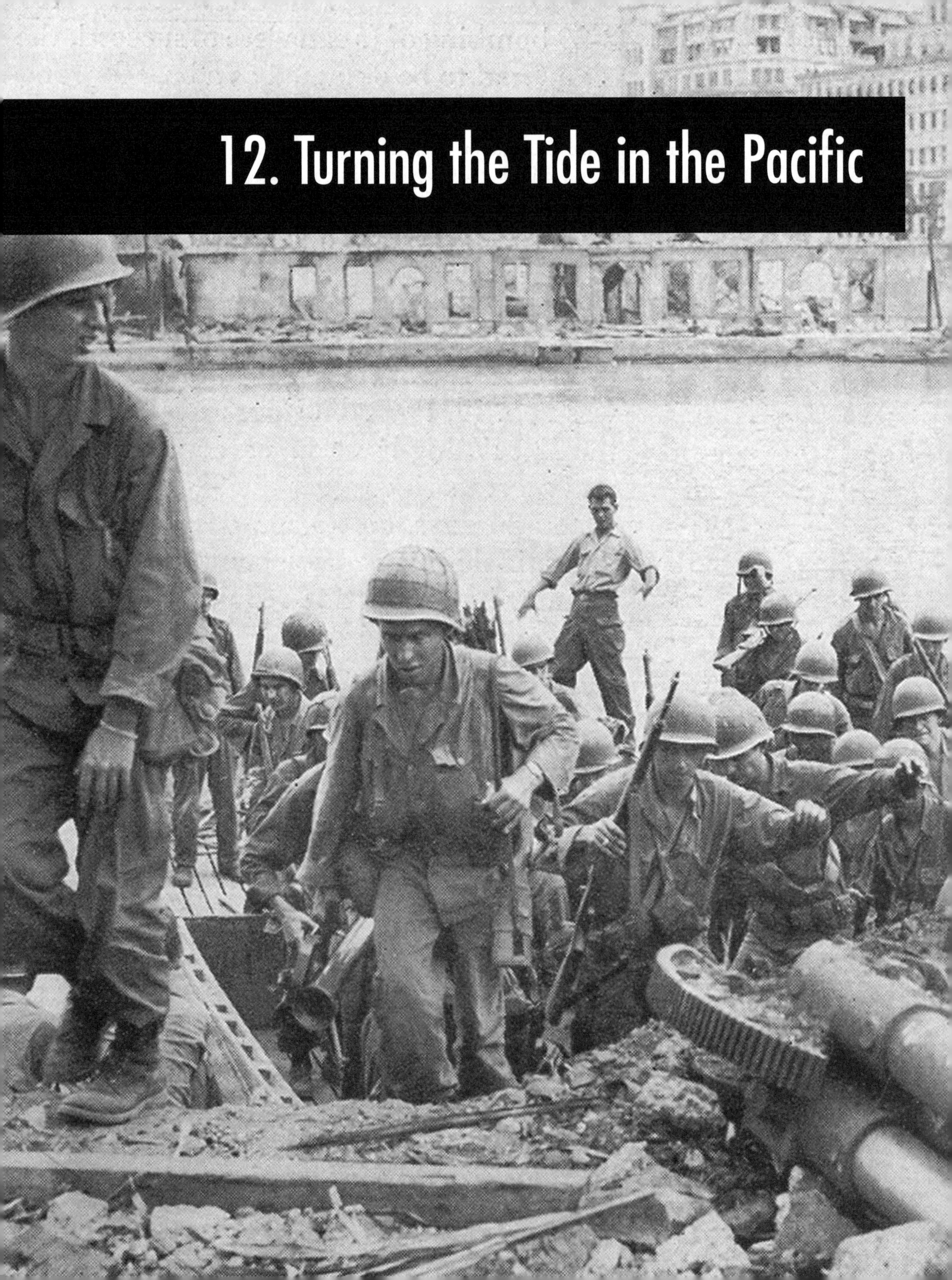

"We expect losses. We expect losses of ships and we expect losses of troops, and we believe they will be considerable. We are taking steps, as far as our knowledge and skill and intent is concerned, to reduce these losses as far as we can, to as low figures as we can. But, we are going to have losses."

—*Vice Admiral Richmond K. Turner,*
Commander of Task Force 53

HOLLYWOOD'S VERSION OF THE JAPANESE FIGHTING man was portrayed as being inferior—mentally, physically, spiritually, and emotionally—to America's brave warriors. But it might be a little difficult to convince the battle-weary U.S. soldiers and Marines that their adversary was inferior. The survivors from the carriers *Saratoga* and *Lady Lex* might have a different assessment of their "slant-eyed" counterparts.

Certainly by mid-1942 the tide had turned in favor of the "good guys" in the war of the Pacific, but not without heavy losses in warships and planes and tanks. And America's greatest loss was also its most valued commodity: thousands of lives were lost, many of them just teenagers.

Statisticians far removed from the front lines could report with great optimism that for every American killed in combat, the Japanese were losing three, or five. "What the hell . . . let's just bump it up to an even ten!" The ratio was even better in the movies.

On film, if a halfwit GI poked his head out of the foxhole to see what was going on, odds were pretty good he'd get shot between the eyes. That one had a message to it—that for everyone else in his squad and any inexperienced troops about to be sent into battle: "Be alert and never let your guard down."

But if the hero's best buddy got shot—probably something slow and painful so he could mutter a few words of encouragement before passing away—that was pretty much a guarantee that at least a hundred of "them yellow-bellied Nips" were going to die. At least that's how it was played out in Hollywood. But for the soldiers and Marines who survived these early battles in the South Pacific, they knew they were facing a formidable foe who would not be easily defeated.

And it would take a lot more men than just John Wayne and Tyrone Power, Robert Montgomery and Alan Ladd to get the job done. Even a hundred more Spencer Tracys leading a hundred more bombing raids on Japan (as Tracy had done in *Thirty Seconds Over Tokyo*) would not be enough.

All it was going to take was everything America had to give.

Opposite:
After months of jungle fighting in far-flung places of the Pacific, Allied troops faced street fighting in Manila in early 1945. Here American and Filipino troops cross the Pasig River, attempting to rout out the Japanese and force them into the countryside where guerrilla forces could finish the job.
Army Signal Corps Photo

The Battles around the Solomons

With Guadalcanal as the centerpiece, the Solomons Campaign became the first major land battle in the Pacific. Perilously close to Australia, the Canal had to be cleared before the Japanese could build an airfield there from which to threaten the Land Down Under. It was at Guadalcanal, beginning in early August of 1942, that the Americans realized they were facing a tenacious foe who would not surrender, who was entrenched and could not be routed easily by heavy bombardment. It would take overwhelming forces, but ultimately, it came down to the lone GI or the Marine squad in brutal close quarters—face-to-face, bloody, and very personal battle—to get the job done.

Sixteen-year-old Donald Yarmy had to exaggerate about his age to join the Marines, but he grew up quickly when he took part in the invasion force at Guadalcanal. Yarmy was shot in battle and, while his wound wasn't life-threatening, he was knocking on death's door after contracting blackwater fever, a nasty disease that had a 90 percent fatality rate. His combat experiences were over, and he was evacuated to a military hospital on New Zealand to fight for his life. Yarmy recovered from his wound and his ailments. (After getting out of the Corps, he turned his attention to a more clandestine sort of service—as Don Adams, Agent 86 on the television series *Get Smart*!)

Another Marine wounded at the Canal was movie star Craig Reynolds. "The matinee idol had been the number-three box office draw at Warner Brothers and the first actor to enlist, long before Pearl Harbor," wrote Frank Sanello in the Jimmy Stewart biography, *A Wonderful Life*. "Reynolds joined the Marines and fought at Guadalcanal. Wounded, the handsome actor spent months recuperating in a veterans hospital. Then he returned to Hollywood. It was a classic case of Craig Who? Warner wouldn't take him back. No other studio would have him. Reynolds ended up finding work as an ice man, driving a truck that supplied huge blocks of ice to housewives."

American commanders would consider Guadalcanal a victory, forever etched in Marine Corps history, but 4,900 young leathernecks were killed there, and none of their family members back home who got the awful news would consider it a victory. Another 4,183 were wounded. Some of those were patched up and sent on to the next battle. Others returned home.

Japanese losses were much heavier, with 25,000 dead—exceeding that eye-catching five-to-one ratio the statisticians in Washington trumpeted. Unwilling to admit their staggering losses, the Japanese High Command reported that they had defeated the U.S. Marines at Guadalcanal and had further inflicted destruction on the remnants of the U.S. Fleet.

From reading the newspaper accounts and hearing the radio reports, the Japanese populace could only assume it would be just a matter of weeks before the Americans surrendered. Then, finally, the entire Pacific could be fully exploited and brought into the Japanese sphere of domination.

Left: *At Cape Torokina on Bougainville, Marine Raiders—notorious as fierce jungle fighters—take a short break, to clean their weapons, restock with ammo and food, and prepare for the next skirmish wherever the Japanese dared to hide out.*
U.S. Navy Photo

The next stepping-stone in the Solomons was New Georgia, followed by "Where in the hell is Bougainville?" But the Japanese obviously understood the importance of this stronghold, and Rear Admiral Miatsuki Injuin warned, "If Bougainville falls, Japan will topple"—although he didn't say it too loudly.

At the same time, the air war heated up over the Solomons, and Allied ships prowling the surrounding waters called "the Slot" sought out enemy transports attempting to land reinforcements and provisions in the area. So many warships, tankers and transports, patrol boats, and submarines were operating in the area that it quickly became known as Iron Bottom Sound, for the vast number from both sides that were sunk there.

Many of the Japanese warships and transports were hit by those American daredevils known as the "expendables"—PT boats armed with radar, torpedoes, deck guns, and depth charges, their crews fearlessly rampaging toward much bigger prey with deadly success. They operated primarily at night, and their philosophy was simple: Strike first, hit 'em hard, then run like hell! Many of the plywood "expendables" couldn't run fast enough and were blown to pieces.

Japanese pilots prowling the skies over the Slot continued with their bad habit of machismo, bloating their successes, claiming they had sunk thirteen American aircraft carriers, twenty-eight warships, and numerous transports and tankers, plus the thousands of men caught on board. (Actual losses were a fraction of that.)

With so many American warships in the region, all of them firing anti-aircraft guns in all directions at enemy planes swarming overhead and at water level, many sustained battle damage—friendly fire—from other warships.

With such a wide array of explosives on board, including torpedoes, depth charges, bombs, and bullets, shipboard mishaps were another hazard. Ensign Kirk Douglas, gunnery officer on board the submarine chaser PC 1139, recalled an incident when sonar picked up the familiar "pinging" that meant an enemy submarine was lurking close by. It was late in the afternoon of February 7, 1943, when the crew went to general quarters to track down the intruder.

"At the point where we had positioned the Japanese submarine, we released our mousetrap attacks. This was a series of little bombs on a rack in the forward part of the ship. The bombs shot off into the water, and we were elated to hear an explosion, because they exploded only on contact. Now we were really excited. I felt like I was in a B movie. It didn't seem real. I couldn't help thinking of it all in dramatic terms," Douglas recalled in his autobiography, *The Ragman's Son*.

"The captain cut back the engines and went slowly toward the site of the explosion. I heard his order over the earphones: 'Release depth charge marker.' This was a green slick on the water to let us know where to drop the depth charges."

But the sailor on deck responsible for releasing the marker instead tripped a depth charge which hit the water and exploded seconds later. "The ship raised up out of the water," Douglas continued with his recollection of the mishap. "People went flying everywhere. I was thrown against the bulkhead, my stomach smashed into the equipment alongside of it. I found myself doubled up on the deck. Torpedo! Torpedo! There was confusion everywhere. But it didn't take us long to realize that we hadn't been struck by an enemy torpedo . . . we had blown up our own ship."

Moving on to Another Piece of Hell

For those Americans tossed into the thick of the fighting in 1943 and '44, there was little time to lick their wounds and maybe enjoy a little R&R, for they were soon to be in battles ten times worse than hell, at a few more unheard-of specks in the Pacific.

Unfortunately, many of the island chains and atolls the United States wanted to seize had been occupied by the Japanese for more than twenty-five years, more than enough time to build concrete and timber fortifications, gun emplacements, and tunnels.

Thus, a deadly lesson the Allies learned early on was that round-the-clock, day after day after day after day of bombardment and

RIGHT: *In addition to fighting the Japanese, U.S. leathernecks also had to battle the elements, including the impassable jungles at Cape Gloucester, in early '44.*
U.S. Marine Corps Photo

shelling would not be enough to kill off the Japanese forces garrisoned on these island fortresses, hiding deep inside mountain caves or underground bunkers. They would simply hunker down and wait out the thunder pounding the hell out of topside, knowing that once the shelling stopped, the invasion forces would soon follow by the thousands. The Japanese also knew that the beachhead would quickly be clogged with soldiers or Marines stumbling over each other, desperately looking for anything to hide behind. And that's when the Japanese tunnel rats would come out of their caves, haul out the weaponry, and open up with mortars and machine guns, cutting down anything and anyone moving on the beach.

Tarawa in the Gilberts chain was the perfect example of just how nasty war could be—and all of it in just four days, beginning with the bombardment from two battleships before dawn on November 20 of 1943, followed by planes from Task Force 50 dropping their ordnance, laying waste to the island.

But out in the surf was a natural obstacle as menacing as concertina wire and minefields: a razor-sharp coral reef that awaited the Marines of the 5th Amphibious Corps, shredding their uniforms and ripping into their flesh just as those damned enemy gunners emerged from the smoldering rubble on Tarawa and stitched the shore with machine-gun fire. Hundreds of brave Marines died right then, right there, before they could make it ashore.

The same fate awaited Marines landing at nearby Betio in the Tarawa Atoll. From his amphibious landing craft, Navy Lieutenant Eddie Heimberger watched as enemy machine-gun fire ripped through the helpless Marines and mortar rounds blew apart other boats, which could only get within five hundred yards of the beach at Betio due to the coral reef. Along with another boat commander, Lieutenant Heimberger guided his vessel closer to shore in an attempt to pick up the wounded Marines in the surf. Though under fire, he scooped up as many of the wounded as his craft could handle and transported them back to the larger ships farther out to sea, making several trips back and forth. He then ordered more landing craft to the area and directed them to pick up helpless leathernecks. (Heimberger was awarded the Bronze Star for his actions at Betio, and was credited with saving dozens of injured Marines that day. Years after the war, he became a well-known movie actor and television star, the popular Eddie Albert.)

Over the next few days, more than 1,100 Marines were killed at Tarawa, and twice that many were wounded, but they had managed to push inland, take out the enemy pillboxes and gun

BELOW: *His mission was to guide landing craft as close to the beach as possible, but when he saw Marines getting killed before they could get to shore at Betio in the Tarawa Atoll, Lieutenant Eddie Heimberger (right) rushed in to pull the wounded leathernecks from the surf and get them to safety. After the war, Lieutenant Heimberger turned to acting and changed his name to Eddie Albert.*
U.S. Navy Photo

emplacements, and seize control of the island—"the most worthless piece of real estate God ever created."

The Japanese, ordered to fight to the death, did just that, with a mere 17 taken prisoner, while 4,836 were killed in the conflict or committed suicide before their positions could be overrun. With Tarawa secured and the airstrips of the Gilberts in Allied hands, the next target was the Marshall Islands.

But after the fiasco of the amphibious landing on Tarawa, the call went out for Navy Underwater Demolition Teams (UDTs), better known as frogmen, to be rushed to the region, with the daunting mission of sneaking ashore at night, before the main invasion force for all future attacks, to clear mines, cut barbed wire, note the locations of all the enemy gun emplacements, mortar pits, and pillboxes, check for any natural hazards, and either radio those known positions or sneak back out to a waiting submarine or patrol boat to report their findings personally.

It was quite a nasty affair, and despite the courageous efforts of the Navy frogmen, amphibious landings were still very dangerous endeavors. And they never got any easier as the war went along.

The Trifecta in the Marianas

Saipan, Guam, and Tinian were the three crown jewels of the Marianas, located due east of the northern Philippines and just 1,500 miles from Japan. Securing the islands would allow Allied bombers—especially the sleek new B-29 Superfortresses—to hit Tokyo and other industrial centers with a devastating firestorm. Although the Japanese garrisons in the Marianas were on their own, with little air cover or naval support, they had been ordered to hold out at all costs, and would not be easily routed. Sensing the importance

RIGHT: *Soldiers of the 160th Infantry Regiment practice amphibious landings at one of Guadalcanal's tranquil beaches, more than a year after one of the fiercest campaigns in the Pacific. They're preparing for the final conflicts of the war against Japan.*
U.S. Army Photo

of the American assault, understanding just how close these three islands were to Japan, the beleaguered commanders decided to rush in two carrier task forces which they felt would be sufficient to handle whatever semblance of naval power the United States could still piece together from its "depleted" fleet. Certainly after the "overwhelming superiority" the Japanese had unleashed at Pearl Harbor, and the Coral Sea, at Midway and Iron Bottom Sound, the U.S. Pacific Fleet couldn't have many warships still afloat and battle worthy. That assessment would prove to be a fatal one.

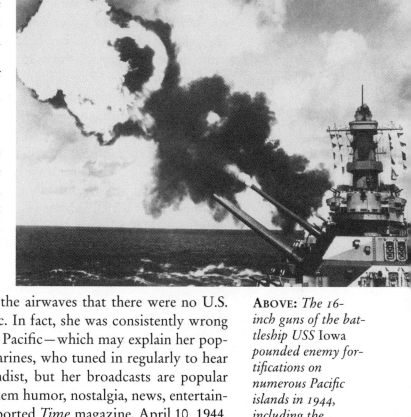

By mid-June of 1944, radio propagandist Tokyo Rose was boasting on the airwaves that there were no U.S. warships still operational in the Pacific. In fact, she was consistently wrong in her reports of the U.S. forces in the Pacific—which may explain her popularity among soldiers, sailors, and Marines, who tuned in regularly to hear her nonsense. "She is a Jap propagandist, but her broadcasts are popular among American listeners: she gives them humor, nostalgia, news, entertainment, and good U.S. dance music," reported *Time* magazine, April 10, 1944. "In a very feminine and friendly voice she murmurs: 'Good evening again to the all-forgetting and forgotten men, the American fighting men of the South Pacific. The 'Zero Hour' to the rescue once again, taking up a few vacant moments you may have to kill.'

"Tokyo Rose's voice is wafted over . . . on a stronger, clearer signal than any provided by U.S. radio. She can usually be heard around 8 P.M. daily, on a 65-minute show designed for U.S. armed forces in the South Pacific."

Rose was actually a collection of female dupes put on the air, but the individual most associated with the role was

ABOVE: *The 16-inch guns of the battleship USS* Iowa *pounded enemy fortifications on numerous Pacific islands in 1944, including the Carolines, the Marshalls, and the Marianas.*
U.S. Navy Photo

LEFT: *When the Japanese occupied the Philippines and seized the radio station in the capital city, they established Manila Myrtle on the air every night between 5 and 6. American troops in the Pacific got a kick out of listening to Tokyo Rose, primarily for the great music and her banter.*
YANK Magazine Photo

American-born Iva Ikuko Toguri, a graduate of UCLA who was visiting relatives in Japan in late 1941 when war was declared. She was trapped in Japan for the duration of the war and worked as a typist at Radio Tokyo. Although she refused to renounce her U.S. citizenship, Iva was selected for on-air duties because she spoke fluent English.

Overseeing the "Zero Hour" was Australian Major Charles Cousens, who was being held by the Japanese and who, because of his broadcasting experience, was ordered to work for Radio Tokyo, writing scripts that had to be approved by Japanese censors. But in fact Cousens, who knew that Allied intelligence officers were monitoring the broadcasts, attempted to surreptitiously slip in vital information about the Japanese. Cousens brought Iva Toguri in on what he was doing and she willingly agreed to go on the air, thinking she was helping her beloved U.S. of A. (After the war, she was arrested by U.S. military police, tried, and found guilty of treason.)

Not only were Japanese citizens lulled into thinking they still had the upper hand and victory was forthcoming, but even Japan's military planners grossly underestimated U.S. Navy firepower in the region. This lack of accurate intelligence reports led the Japanese to send their carrier groups into the Philippine Sea.

What they encountered there was the still very potent U.S. 5th Fleet, which had "only" fifteen flattops and five hundred support ships, including battleships and cruisers, plus all the auxiliaries needed to function as a cohesive and deadly armada.

The two converging forces—the Japanese desperately attempting to prolong the inevitable, and the U.S. Navy determined to sink everything the enemy still had afloat, clearing the seas for the final push to Tokyo—led to one very lopsided outcome, both on the high seas and overhead. By mid-June of '44, the naval flotillas were within striking distance of each other, and on June 19, they launched hundreds of fighter planes, torpedo bombers, and dive-bombers. By this time, the American pilots had honed their aerial skills,

RIGHT: *That little patch of real estate in the vast Pacific is the carrier* Yorktown, *waiting to retrieve its dive-bombers and torpedo bombers.*
U.S. Navy Photo

and the result was what was dubbed the "Marianas Turkey Shoot," with more than three hundred Japanese planes shot out of the skies on the first day alone. Over the next few days, virtually all enemy aircraft were eliminated, three of their carriers were sunk, and three more were badly damaged. The U.S. 5th Fleet suffered two carriers damaged and the loss of one hundred planes.

Left: *Navy fighter pilot Wayne Morris did more than his share to rid the skies over the Pacific of Japanese planes, quickly becoming one of the elite aces of the war. He later parlayed that combat experience into a stellar film career when he returned to Hollywood and climbed back into the cockpit for the movie* Task Force, *with Gary Cooper.*
U.S. Navy Photo

One of those hotshot Navy fighter pilots getting his share of enemy kills over the Marianas was Wayne Morris, flying F6F Hellcats in the Pacific. He was another Pasadena Playhouse alum who set aside a budding acting career to join the military. In 1940, while acting in the movie *Flight Angels*, Morris decided to take flying lessons. A year later, after completing *I Wanted Wings*, he signed on with the Navy Reserve seven months prior to the attack on Pearl Harbor. By late 1944, Morris had flown fifty-seven missions and was recognized as one of the Navy's fighter aces. (After the war he returned to Hollywood, and in 1949 he was back "in combat" as a Navy fighter pilot in the movie *Task Force* with Gary Cooper. It would be one of the forty-seven movies he would make throughout the 1950s.)

At this same time, the battle for Saipan was underway, involving both U.S. Army and Marine forces, who would dish out plenty of punishment but suffer heavy casualties along the way. One of those wounded at Saipan was high school dropout Lee Marvin, serving with the 4th Marine Division's scout sniper recon team. "We went in on Yellow Beach Two. We clawed forward and hit the basic scrub of the beach. Beyond it were those big open fields, thousands of sticks with sake bottles on top. The Japs were using them as artillery markers. They had us nicely pin-pointed. They didn't miss," Marvin was quoted in his biography by Donald Zec. Marvin survived the shelling and machine-gun fire for four days, while many other Marines were killed in the barrage.

Left: *Wayne Morris got his first taste of flying while appearing in the 1940 movie* Flight Angels; *then he joined the Navy Reserve after filming wrapped on the set of* I Wanted Wings, *six months prior to Pearl Harbor. Over the next three years he would get thrown into the thick of the fighting in the Pacific, becoming one of the Navy's top fighter aces while flying an F6F Hellcat.*
U.S. Navy Photo

"We'd just got into one knot, caught dead in an ambush, and Jesus Christ, it was just decimation. We had started out with 247 men, and fifteen minutes later there were six of us. So anyway it was my turn to get nailed. There are two prominent parts of your body in view to the enemy when you flatten out . . . your head and your ass. If you present one, you get killed. If you raise the other, you get shot in the ass. I got shot in the ass."

(Marvin would be evacuated to a hospital ship and then transferred to a naval hospital, where he would rehab for thirteen months. After getting out and bouncing around between various odd jobs, he was doing some maintenance work at the Woodstock Maverick Theater in New York during play rehearsals and overheard the director shouting out orders. He watched as the actors and actresses did as they were told, and it reminded him of a Marine unit. Coincidentally, one of the actors was sick and the director needed a fill-in. Marvin got the part and promptly caught the acting bug. He then used his GI Bill benefits to enroll at the American Theater Wing, appearing in bit parts on Broadway before making it big in the movies.)

A month after the invasion of Saipan, U.S. forces attempted to retake Guam. And near the end of July, they hit Tinian. Naval forces were massed within firing distance, standing nearby for pulling out the wounded, replenishing the assault forces, protecting the approaches, and cutting off any attempt by the Japanese to bolster their holdouts in the Marianas. The Coast Guard attack transport *Cavalier* was one of many auxiliary ships tasked with resupplying the Mariana Islands with munitions and artillery pieces, men, and supplies, and taking on casualties.

On board the *Cavalier* was Chief Boatswain's Mate and First Powderman Cesar Romero, who was one of Hollywood's most recognized stars prior to joining the Coast Guard in October of 1942. The *Cavalier* saw plenty of action and narrowly missed a kamikaze attack but was hit by an enemy torpedo in late January of 1945. Fifty were wounded, and the ship had to be towed to the Philippines for temporary repairs before returning to Pearl Harbor. (Romero returned to the States and toured the country, appearing at war bond rallies before getting back to the business of making movies.)

The Lone Ranger was accustomed to ridding the Wild West of more than a few sinister characters in the long-running series, but actor Lee Powell, who first played the masked man, couldn't wipe out the whole Japanese army by himself when he saw action at Saipan and Tinian. In late July of 1944, while serving with the 2nd Marine Division, Sergeant Powell was killed on Tinian. (He was buried there, but five years later his remains were recovered and he was laid to rest at the scenic Punchbowl Cemetery overlooking Pearl Harbor in Hawaii.)

RIGHT: *Marine Corps Private Lee Marvin served with the 4th Marines as part of a reconnaissance team and would be wounded at Saipan. (Later, back in the States, and while recuperating, he got a small part in a community theater production and used his GI Bill to study acting.*
U.S. Marine Corps Photo

James Whitmore was taking pre-law at Yale before he joined the Marines and caught up with the fighting in the Marianas. He distinguished himself in combat and was awarded with a battlefield commission. (After the war Whitmore decided that he'd like to give acting a try instead of pursuing his law studies. Eventually he became a popular character actor in Hollywood. He also joined a USO show and guided the troupe back to some of his old stomping grounds in the Pacific.)

By mid-1944 and through the closing months of the war, the Japanese forces that were cut off from resupply convoys were running out of food and ammunition and had to resort to using makeshift spears for their weaponry. The final tally for Japan in the Marianas Campaign: 52,000 Japanese had been killed or took their own life, leaving only 6,000 bedraggled and disgraced survivors.

Once the Allies had secured Saipan, they used it as a forward staging area. One of the Navy units preparing for battle there was Torpedo Squadron 99, with Paul Newman serving as a radio operator and rear seat gunner, training other airmen arriving in the Pacific as replacement squadrons.

Newman would soon be on the carrier *Hollandia,* cruising the northern Pacific during the final weeks of the Pacific Campaign. (After getting out of the Navy, he used the GI Bill to attend Kenyon College in Ohio, where he acted in a few theatrical productions. From there he tried summer stock in Wisconsin, then enrolled in the drama department at Yale, where his instructors saw some potential and encouraged him to head to New York. Soon he was getting roles on television and honing his acting skills at the Actors Studio.)

During lulls in the fighting of the Marianas Campaign, Allied forces occasionally watched movies in the evenings. Often the enemy soldiers hiding out in caves dotting the surrounding hills would venture out and watch from a distance, fascinated with the likes of glamour girls Betty Grable and Rita Hayworth and American heroes John Wayne and Alan Ladd.

Every effort was made to send in new movies, but sometimes it was too dangerous for transport planes or ships to come around and so, rather than show nothing, the same movie would be repeated. In the case of one such week in the Marianas, *Going My Way* with Bing Crosby was shown again and again and again—for seven nights straight, with no mercy.

One of those nights an American patrol snuck out and captured some of the enemy soldiers sitting on the hillside. As they all made it back to camp, one of the American translators noticed that the movie was still playing and asked the Japanese captives if they'd like to watch it. No thanks, they politely declined, they'd already seen it seven times and were just as sick of it as the GIs were!

On to Peleliu

Many of the islands in the Pacific had been created by centuries-old volcanoes, rising from out of the sea. Peleliu, part of the Palau central islands, was one such outpost, crisscrossed with caves that the Japanese exploited to turn the entire island into a fortress, with steel-and-concrete-reinforced bunkers, tunnels, and gun emplacements. The beach approaches were littered with mines and imposing dragon's teeth. Here again, prior to dispatching amphibious troops, Allied warships and bombers pounded the island, kicking up plenty of smoke and debris but doing little to reduce the number of Japanese waiting underground for the chaos to stop. And when it did, they scrambled to their positions, lugging mortar tubes and heavy machine guns and ammo belts, waiting for the landing force to get within range, to enter the killing field.

It would take four months of ugly, brutal, vicious fighting for the American soldiers and Marines to claim victory on "Bloody Peleliu." And it was the kind of fighting no one wanted to talk about afterward, the kind no one could ever forget.

Of the estimated 11,000 to 14,000 Japanese on Peleliu at the start, only 300 emerged from the rubble to give themselves up, despite the dishonor their surrender would bring their families.

American losses were also staggering: 278 soldiers and 1,252 Marines killed, with a combined 6,200-plus listed as wounded.

After Peleliu, the Allies ignored nearby Japanese strongholds in the Palaus, as General MacArthur turned his attention to fulfilling his earlier promise to return to the Philippines, the country he loved so much.

Liberating the Philippines

The Japanese had planned to occupy the Philippines immediately after attacking Pearl Harbor. They fully expected their Filipino "brothers" to help rid the islands of the American occupiers and were surprised when they found themselves being attacked and harassed by local partisans who'd found refuge in the hills and jungles of Luzon, Leyte, and Mindanao. Still, with 350,000 Japanese troops in country, the Filipino guerrillas were no match in firepower. All they could do was conduct hit-and-run sabotage tactics.

BELOW: *Pushing inland, fording a river, leathernecks of the 1st Marine Division search out the enemy on bloody Peleliu in 1944.*
U.S. Marine Corps Photo

Above: *These photographers with the 1st Marine Division at "Bloody" Peleliu in September of 1944 did most of their shooting with cameras. Among them, in the middle of the back row, is film star Bill Lundigan, who made his first movie appearance in 1937. There followed numerous Westerns and combat films, including* Salute to the Marines *and* Heading for God's Country *in 1943; then he left Hollywood for boot camp and wound up in the Pacific. After the war, he returned to Hollywood and continued in the movies and on television for the next two decades.*
U.S. Marine Corps Photo

The Japanese prepared for an American assault on the Philippines and positioned their remaining fleet in Lingayen Gulf, hidden among the many surrounding islands, in a last-gasp desperation move they dubbed Plan Sho (Victory). Their strategy was to attack from three directions, hoping to trap and destroy the invasion fleet. But the United States had launched scout planes in every direction and quickly spotted the three enemy battle groups. The combined force of American submarines, PT boats, carrier planes, and warships pounced on the enemy's three-pronged attack force and eliminated four carriers, three battleships, four light cruisers and six heavies, and nine destroyers, killing more than ten thousand Japanese sailors and airmen. Any enemy ships still afloat had barely enough fuel to limp back home to safe harbor.

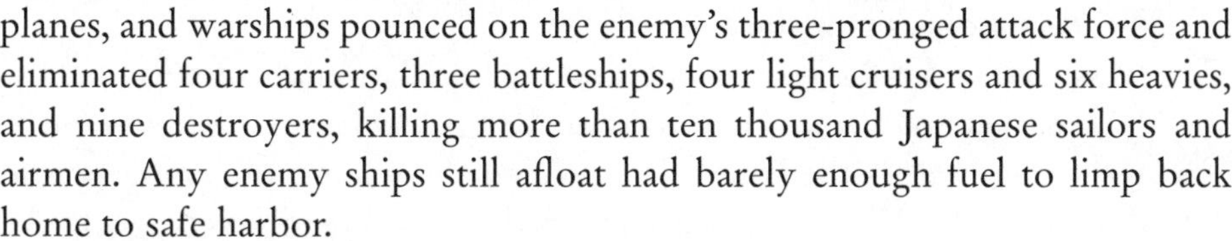

One of the carriers cruising the area was the *Block Island,* with Ensign Logan "Skee" Ramsey serving as a gunnery officer. (His father was CO on the flattop, *Lake Champlain.*) Skee had been studying theater arts at St. Joseph's College prior to joining the military in June of 1942, and was now following in his father's footsteps as a naval officer. (Ramsey would later serve as deck officer on his father's flagship, but by 1946 he had resigned his commission to pursue his acting career again.)

Admiral Nimitz had no interest in retaking the Philippines and wanted instead to plan for the final assault on Japan, establishing a blockade, dispatching his warships within range to unleash their big guns, and stationing his carriers far enough out to avoid coastal gun batteries but close enough to conduct round-the-clock bombing and strafing runs. But MacArthur was insistent that they first fulfill his promise to return and liberate the Philippines before they concentrate on the final invasion of Japan.

On October 20 of 1944, a combined force of 200,000 men came ashore at Leyte in the eastern Philippines. Soon after, Dauntless Doug gave his "I have returned" speech and was welcomed back as a hero.

Controversial actor Lew Ayres had starred in the anti-war movie *All Quiet on the Western Front* and the Doctor Kildaire series of films prior to the war. He had seen the exodus of actors joining the military, and he did some serious soul-searching before deciding what he should do.

"'I thrashed it all out with myself,' he told writer Irving Wallace in a postwar interview. 'To me, war was the greatest sin. I couldn't bring myself to kill other men. Whatever the cost, I decided to remain true to myself,'"

RIGHT: *After his retreat from Corregidor in early 1942, General Douglas MacArthur promised the Filipino people he would someday return. Two and a half years later he fulfilled that promise, landing at Leyte, then continuing the fight to Luzon and Mindanao, eventually retaking Manila and driving the Japanese into the surrounding hills and jungles.*
U.S. Army Photo

wrote Bernard A. Weisberger in *Forgotten Heroes*. "On the official form for claiming conscientious objector, 1-AO classification, he wrote that his personal religious convictions would make it impossible for him to bear arms. He had taken Red Cross training and become an instructor on the MGM lot, and now he begged to 'be of service . . . in a constructive and not a destructive way.'"

The backlash was immediate. The press trashed his "cowardly decision," while thousands of fans jammed the MGM switchboard and wrote scathing letters, demanding Ayres be fired. Theater owners across the country refused to show any of his movies, and MGM shelved the Kildaire project in production, literally killing off the character.

Lost in the firestorm was the simple fact that Ayres was willing to serve in the military—he just didn't want to be on the killing end of the war. "There was to be a Hollywood fairy-tale ending," continued Weisberger in *Forgotten Heroes*. "His military record turned out to be exemplary. He served nearly two years in the New Guinea jungles, where he contracted dengue fever, and in the Philippines, where he landed with U.S. invasion forces in October 1944. By then Ayres had become a chaplain's assistant who had helped calm wounded men under fire. On Leyte, he volunteered to assist in treating civilian casualties during heavy aerial bombardment."

RIGHT: *The retaking of the Philippines began with the Allied landing at Leyte, a relatively uneventful operation compared to other amphibious assaults in the Pacific. Here an American soldier with the 96th Division takes a break at Leyte before the next big push on the sweep toward Manila.*
U.S. Army Photo

Prior to the Leyte landing, Ayres said in an interview with *YANK* correspondent, Army Corporal William Carpenter Good, "I never intend to go back to pictures. I want to continue this work, God willing. It's taken war to give me understanding of men and to find myself."

With a foothold on Leyte, the invasion force pushed on to Luzon and the capital city of Manila. Rod Serling had hoped to be sent to the European Theater, but ended up as a paratrooper with the 11th Airborne Division on the other side of the world. He was wounded by shrapnel from an enemy artillery shell in street fighting in Manila. (After his discharge in 1946, he went to school in Ohio and began writing scripts aired on the school radio station. A few of his scripts were purchased for radio while he was still in college. Once he started writing full-time, his scripts were picked up for television, and by 1957 he had developed the popular *Twilight Zone* science fiction series.)

After the street-to-street fighting in Manila, the 65,000 remnants of the Japanese occupation force fled into the surrounding hills, where they were tracked down by Filipino guerrillas. Small pockets of Japanese remained, with small arms and any other weapons they could carry, such as machine guns and mortars, intent on inflicting as much death and damage as possible until their ammunition ran out. Russell Johnson was flying over Mindanao when his plane was shot down and he was forced to crash-land, breaking both his ankles. (After rehab, he used the GI Bill to attend Hollywood's Actors Lab, appearing in many forgettable sci-fi movies and television shows. He is best known as the Professor on television's *Gilligan's Island.*)

LEFT: *After starring in the anti-war movie,* All Quiet on the Western Front, *about fighting trench warfare during WWI, actor Lew Ayres knew he couldn't go to war in real life and ever kill a man. He requested conscientious-objector status during WWII, but was drafted and served as a chaplain's assistant, working with medics to treat civilian casualties on New Guinea and the Philippines.*
YANK Magazine Photo

All told, 190,000 Japanese troops were killed in the numerous battles in the Philippines. Unknown thousands of Filipino soldiers, partisans, and innocent civilians were killed. The Japanese implemented a "scorched earth" policy as they pulled back, destroying an infrastructure—bridges, dams, water plants, power stations, harbors, industries—that would require years to rebuild.

American forces poured into the Philippines, staging there for the final assault on Japan's home islands. Many new arrivals were fresh from the European Campaign, hardly enthusiastic about taking on the Japanese after dismantling Nazi Germany.

The Navy set up an aviation overhaul depot on Samar Island in the Philippines to patch up its ships and planes. One of the sailors stationed there was Roy Fitzgerald, assigned to off-load planes from aircraft carriers berthed alongside the dock. He also worked as an aircraft mechanic until he was seriously injured and transferred to light duty. He was discharged in '46. (He parlayed his good looks, some acting lessons, and a name change into a successful movie career as the heartthrob actor Rock Hudson.)

Another sailor in the Philippines was Don Rickles, assigned to the USS *Cyrene,* a PT boat tender. (Rickles's future would be in show business, as a wisecracking comic taking jabs at anyone within earshot.)

RIGHT: *After the Philippines were retaken in late 1944 and in the early months of 1945, U.S. troops rushed in and renewed the bond with the beloved Filipino people. During a baseball game at Manila's Rizal Stadium, the 37th Division Band played a rousing rendition of the old standard, "Take Me Out to the Ball Game" for the cheering crowd.*
YANK Magazine Photo

The Final Hurdles

Iwo Jima and Okinawa. Two of the toughest, most godforsaken snake pits ever created on Earth, the worst of the worst. They would become the final stepping-stones of the war, and as each one fell, it would bring American forces that much closer to the ultimate battleground: Japan's home islands.

But even with Japan's air and naval forces in disarray, even with its ground units desperate for food, fuel, and ammunition, these final two confrontations would not be easy. But they could not be sidestepped either.

American planes flying out of the Marianas to bomb Japan passed directly over Iwo Jima, where the enemy had positioned a radar and communications center to alert homeland anti-aircraft batteries and scramble fighter aircraft to intercept the approaching American intruders. In addition, the airstrip at Iwo Jima, once secured, could be used in an emergency for any Allied aircraft badly damaged and unable to limp back home. U.S. fighter planes could also be based there and sent aloft to escort the long-range bombers to Japan and back.

Resupplying the American forces at Iwo Jima and later at Okinawa was the role of cargo ships and transport pilots, one of whom was Hollywood leading man Tyrone Power, flying a Curtiss C-46 cargo plane dubbed *Blythe Spirit.* While assigned with VMR-353 flying out of the Marianas, Power would log more than 1,100 hours in the air. (By January of 1946 he was back in Tinseltown looking to resume his status as one of America's top ten-box office draws.)

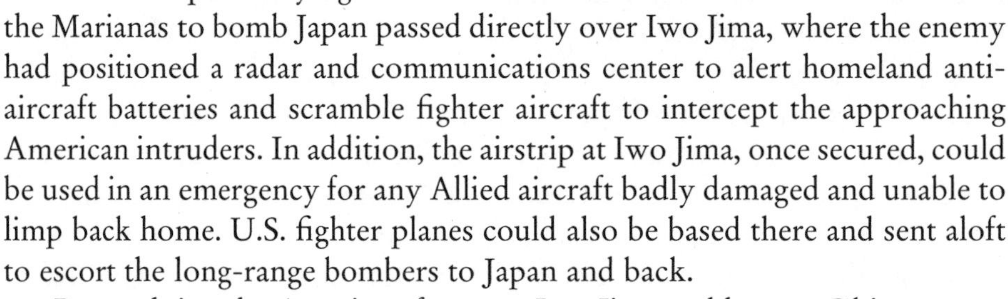

RIGHT: *In a much lighter moment, the crew of the mighty carrier* Enterprise *holds the traditional Neptune party for the "pollywogs" new to the flattop, in September 1944. One of the many sailors on board was ordnance specialist Richard Boone, who was later reclassified as a radioman and gunner for Avenger torpedo bombers.*
National Archives Photo

Like so many other volcanic islands the American forces had to neutralize, Iwo Jima was a catacomb of underground caves and man-made fortifications. After so many casualties at so many other amphibious assaults, U.S. military strategists decided to bomb the hell out of the island, and they pounded it for seventy-four days in a row, day and night. By mid-February of 1945, the island was little more than a wasteland of bomb craters and rubble, and Navy frogmen began attempting to clear the approaches for the main invasion force. But Japanese snipers spotted the frogmen and cut them down—170 of them—in the surf.

On February 19, Navy warships and Army Air Corps bombers and carrier planes again pounded the island.

On the destroyer *Taussig,* torpedoman Rod Steiger had already seen plenty of action in the Pacific, from the naval battle at Midway to the invasion of Iwo Jima. A seasoned combat veteran by the time he got to Iwo, Steiger would have missed the earlier confrontations in the Pacific if he hadn't lied about his age when he enlisted at sixteen. During the engagement at Iwo Jima, the *Taussig* was screening for aircraft carriers attempting to neutralize enemy planes at airstrips in the region. (After his discharge in August

ABOVE: *Future actor Leif Erickson, serving as a Navy photographer's mate, and Navy pilot and fellow actor Tyrone Power chat at Yontan Airfield on Okinawa, in April of 1945.*
U.S. Marine Corps Photo

LEFT: *At Baguio in the Philippines, infantry soldiers were accompanied by an M-7 105-mm howitzer motor carriage, with just enough firepower to do some damage against any entrenched Japanese forces attempting to blunt the offensive, in March of 1945.*
U.S. Army Photo

Below: *Okinawa was a maze of caves and catacombs, reinforced tunnels and rat holes, where the Japanese troops could seemingly pop up out of nowhere, take a few potshots at unsuspecting leathernecks or lob a few grenades, then scamper back into hiding and re-emerge somewhere else. It was a slow and deadly process to locate and secure each opening, one at a time, often sealing off an entrance with grenades or bringing up flamethrowers to burn everyone inside to a crisp. Here a lone Marine crouches down inside a cave opening, watching for enemy snipers in the final weeks of the war.*
U.S. Marine Corps Photo

of 1945, Steiger used the GI Bill to enroll in the Dramatic Workshop of New School for Social Research and spent time at two other acting schools while trying out for stage roles in New York. In the 1950s he made it to Hollywood, and he went on to receive two Academy Award nominations for his acting, finally winning an Oscar for 1967's *In the Heat of the Night.*)

Former big band pianist Eddie Duchin was on board the destroyer escort USS *Bates.* Because he had perfect pitch and was highly attuned at distinguishing sounds, he was trained on underwater detection devices such as sonar, which would be invaluable in hunting down enemy subs. In April of 1945 he was sent to Hawaii, and a month later the *Bates* was sunk by a kamikaze attack near Okinawa.

Thousands of Marines from the 4th and 5th Divisions poured onto the beach at Iwo, scrambling for cover, with little or no hostile fire coming from Mount Suribachi looming above. Maybe, for once, the continuous shelling had done its job and the thousands of Japanese tunnel rats had been eliminated, except for a scattered few. Maybe, but not likely.

Once the beachhead became clogged with seven battalions of Marines, plus tanks, and jeeps, transport ships off-loading crates of ammunition and food, and all the accoutrements they required, those "sneaky little slant-eyed bastards" came out of their rat holes on Mount Suribachi, set up their mortars and machine guns, and rained down a hailstorm of shells and bullets that ripped into bodies and everything else vital to waging war successfully. On that first day that had started so easily—that worst day that ended so horribly—1,854 Marines were wounded and 566 were killed.

Inch by inch the Marines made it off that beach and scratched and crawled their way up Suribachi to plant the American flag. But the battle for Iwo Jima would last another month as the Marines had to check cave after cave for stragglers, roasting them with flamethrowers, tossing in satchel charges to seal the entrances, repelling fanatical bayonet charges. All told, more than 20,000 Japanese soldiers died on Iwo Jima, and more than a thousand surrendered. In comparison the Marines lost 6,821, with 24,000 wounded. The Corps had little time to lick its wounds and assess its remaining combat strength in the Pacific, because four days after Iwo Jima fell, the campaign for Okinawa began.

The invasion of Okinawa was inevitable, and the Japanese knew it was coming, but they had little firepower—warships or aircraft—to stop it. They did have 100,000 soldiers entrenched on the island, ordered to sustain and hold on for as long as possible, to give shipyards back home time to finish new carriers, and submarines, and battleships standing in dry docks. (Exact totals of the enemy forces are blurred, because thousands of Okinawans and Koreans were mustered into service by the Japanese.)

But no one told the Japanese on Okinawa that American bombers were targeting those shipyards on a daily basis, or that many of those shipbuilders were tired of being bombed and had taken their families to the countryside or had just stopped going to work, or that there wasn't enough iron plating or sheet metal on hand to finish the jobs because the metal works had also been bombed.

Japan couldn't even repair the damaged warships returning from the fight in the Philippine Sea or Lingayen Gulf. Nothing was going to be ready in time, en masse, and rushed to the waters near the Ryukyu Islands to help the war-weary holdouts on Okinawa.

The only desperation "weapon" the Japanese still had were kamikaze pilots, willing to plunge their planes into an American warship, willing to sacrifice themselves and possibly improve the odds against their country. An estimated 1,900 kamikaze flights were witnessed over Okinawan waters, with 263 hitting Allied warships.

Former film star and Navy intelligence officer Henry Fonda, on board the seaplane tender USS *Curtis,* survived those cursed kamikaze attacks at Guam, Saipan, and Iwo. It was a stroke of luck that he happened to be off the ship when it was struck by a kamikaze, because the explosion destroyed the berth he normally occupied. (Ironically, three years later Fonda was on Broadway playing the title role in *Mr. Roberts*, as a Navy officer who dies in a similar incident. Fonda would reprise the role for Hollywood in 1955.)

"According to Radio Tokyo, the Kamikaze Corps began its 'death-defying, body-crashing' tactics last October 15th [1944] when Vice Admiral Masabumi Arima flew his plane into a U.S. aircraft carrier, lest 'the traditional spirit of the Japanese Navy be spoiled,'" reported *Time* magazine in its July 16, 1945, issue.

"Thereafter, Radio Tokyo daily intoned the names of 'hero gods,' and Japanese journalists interviewed little boys whose ambition was to grow up and become suicide pilots."

But despite these last-gasp efforts by the kamikazes, the odds against Japan by this time were insurmountable, with half a million GIs ready for the fight, waiting on more than 1,500 warships, comprised of forty aircraft carriers (including British flattops), ten battleships, twenty-three destroyers, and nine cruisers, plus bombers and fighter planes from airstrips at Iwo Jima and the Marianas.

The attack transport USS *Randall* delivered many of the young combatants to the Okinawan shallows. On board was Navy sailor Milton Hines. (After the war Hines went to school on the GI Bill and then toured the nightclub circuit as a comedian, using the catchy name of Soupy Sales.)

Below: *Hollywood leading man Henry Fonda was a Navy lieutenant during the Pacific Campaign, shown here receiving the Bronze Star from Vice Admiral George Murray. Fonda had been an intelligence officer on the seaplane tender, the USS* Curtis. *He would later serve again in the Navy, but this time on Broadway, in the title role of* Mr. Roberts, *and again in 1955 for the movie version.*
U.S. Navy Photo

Right: *On Okinawa, infantrymen from the 77th Division listen to a radio report, announcing the surrender of Nazi Germany on the other side of the world. They had no idea how long it would take for Imperial Japan to fall also.*
U.S. Army Photo

Two other comedians providing diversionary antics for their shipmates on the carrier *Bon Homme Richard* were Marine Private First Class Jonathan Winters and swabbie Shecky Greene. Winters manned an anti-aircraft gun on the flattop and had a ringside seat for the enemy pilots trying their hardest to perish in a fireball near Okinawa. The "Bonny Dick" missed being hit by a kamikaze, although Winters tempted fate every night, sleeping in the munitions magazine, practically daring the widowmaker to take his best shot.

Shecky Greene's "battle station" was belowdecks, manning the soda fountain in the ship's mess. "The bombs would be falling all around and I'd be yellin' below: 'Ya want chocolate and sprinkles, too?" he quipped to James Bacon for the book, *Hollywood Is a Four-Letter Word*. Besides "overdosing" on sundaes and sodas, Greene and Winters imbibed hooch and honed their rapid-fire putdowns during their war exploits with the *Bon Homme Richard*.

Canadian Raymond Burr had appeared on stage as a nightclub singer in Paris and as an actor on Broadway and with the Pasadena Playhouse before the war. During a brief tour of England he met and married Scottish actress Annette Sutherland. (She would later be killed along with British star Leslie Howard when their plane was shot down by Nazi fighter pilots over the Atlantic.)

Burr turned his back on a movie contract with RKO Studios and joined the Navy, American style, making it to the waters near Okinawa, where he would be wounded by shrapnel when his ship was attacked. (He would require several months to recover from his wounds, but by 1946 he was back in Hollywood, appearing in the movie *Without Reservations* with John Wayne, Cary Grant, and Claudette Colbert.)

After a week of shelling and bombardment on Okinawa, Underwater Demolition Team 17 swam ashore while the island was still being pounded. One of the frogmen was Seaman First Class Aldo DaRae, tasked with assessing the landing zone to identify any natural and man-made hazards that might hamper an amphibious landing. A few hours later the team was

Left: *Their bravery was unmatched in the Pacific, these frogmen of Underwater Demolition Team 17, who slipped onto the beach at Okinawa and assessed the enemy fortifications and plotted where the hazards, such as mines and concertina wire, were likely to hamper the amphibious landing a few hours later. During earlier beach landings in the Pacific, U.S. troops were unprepared, and hundreds of soldiers and Marines were killed in the surf and on the beaches. Frogmen were rushed to the Pacific to minimize these losses. One of those frogmen was Seaman First Class Aldo DaRae of UDT 17, shown in the lower right. (After the war, he accompanied his acting brother to an audition, and Aldo was plucked from the crowd and got a part in the movie. He soon got the acting bug and Aldo Ray found steady work, appearing in many movies, usually as the tough guy with the gruff voice.)* UDT Seal Museum Photo

back aboard the *Crosley,* one of the many warships assigned to the Okinawa Campaign.

On the morning of April 1—both April Fool's Day and Easter Sunday—thousands of soldiers and Marines poured onto the beaches at the island's midsection, and met with token resistance. The bulk of the Japanese forces—twenty-nine infantry battalions—were spread out along the southern third of the island, with two more battalions to cover the remaining two-thirds.

Aldo DaRae and the rest of the frogmen from UDT 17 remained aboard the *Crosley,* manning anti-aircraft guns, firing at the kamikazes harassing the invasion force and the warships standing by. (After his discharge from the Navy in 1946, DaRae attended college in Berkeley. Five years later, his brother, an actor, coerced him into going with him to a movie audition in nearby San Francisco. The casting director spotted Aldo, liked his ruggedness and gruff voice, and offered him a secondary part in the film. It was the first of many tough-guy roles for Aldo Ray.)

James Gregory had been president of his high school drama class in New Rochelle, New York, even appearing in summer stock along the East Coast, with a brief stop on Broadway in 1939. But during WWII, he mothballed his acting skills while he was in the Pacific, spending three years in the Navy and the Marines, two endless months in the Okinawa Campaign, and then preparing for the invasion of Japan. (After the war, Gregory became a noted character actor on Broadway, and by the mid-1950s had gravitated to television, appearing in hundreds of shows over the next several decades.)

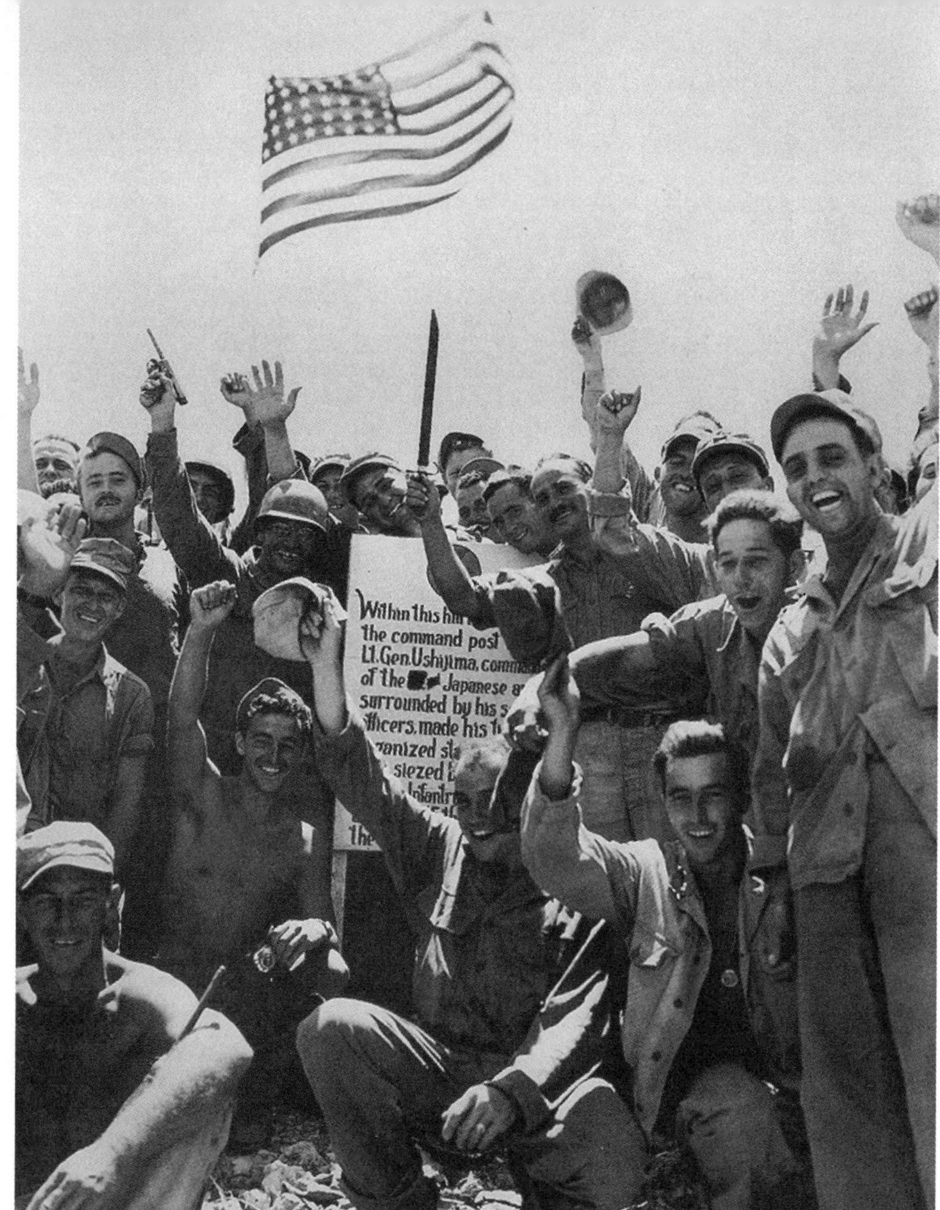

RIGHT: *The fight for Okinawa was long and it was deadly, but on June 21, 1945, soldiers of the 7th Division had finally captured the command post of Lieutenant General Ushijima of the Japanese Imperial Army, little more than a bunker on Hill 89.*
U.S. Army Photo

The Okinawa offensive would take two months of intense, brutal, deliberate combat. The weary Japanese combatants could not prolong the fight long enough for new warships to be built and dispatched to the area, but the battle did exact a heavy toll on both sides.

"The losses were enormous. More people—about 150,000 Okinawan civilians [who were told they would be tortured by the Americans and many committed suicide to avoid such a fate], 75,000 Japanese soldiers, 10,000 enslaved Koreans, and 13,000 Americans—died at Okinawa than were killed as a result of the atomic explosions at Hiroshima and Nagasaki combined," wrote Bruce I. Gudmundsson in the article "Okinawa" for *World War II Presents Pacific War* magazine in 2003. And a surprising 7,400 Japanese surrendered rather than commit suicide, the "honorable" choice.

Left: *Fluent in Japanese, Tad Van Brunt interrogated Japanese prisoners, squeezing them for any information that might prove crucial in future fights. Here on Okinawa, he tries to encourage an enemy soldier to broadcast a plea for the remaining holdouts to surrender.*
U.S. Marine Corps Photo

The death toll among Okinawans would have been much worse if not for the efforts of Frederick "Tad" Van Brunt, who had been raised in Yokohama and Kobe, Japan. His father had a lucrative import-export business that became threatened by the late '30s. The Van Brunts moved to California and Tad earned a scholarship to the Pasadena Playhouse. But after Pearl Harbor, he enlisted and attended the Navy language school in Colorado, specializing in Japanese. After finishing the course Van Brunt could have remained with the Navy, but he chose the Marines instead, remembering seeing them in China when he was traveling with his dad as a boy.

He would serve with the 3rd Marine Division, first at Guadalcanal, where he interrogated Japanese POWs to extract information from them. Later, at Okinawa he talked with the local villagers and convinced them the Japanese had lied about what would happen if the Americans liberated the island. Tragically, thousands committed suicide before they could be reached, afraid of the cruelties they might suffer if captured by the American "savages."

(After returning to California, Van Brunt attempted to kick-start an acting career but appeared in only a few minor roles. He served with the Marines again during the Korean War as an intelligence officer.)

Left: *In the event the Japanese resorted to using mustard gas or other forms of chemical warfare as a last-ditch effort toward the end of the war, American troops deploying to the Pacific in 1945 had to be trained, shown here with a Red Cross dog wearing gas masks.*
National Archives Photo

With Okinawa in their control, the Allies formulated plans for the final push, the invasion of Japan, expected to kick off in late 1945.

Entertainers Follow the Troops

Wherever the GIs went, Hollywood and Broadway stars tried to get to the war zone as soon as they were allowed. Few would consider their tour to the Pacific a pleasure cruise, but they learned to make the best of whatever accommodations were offered, knowing it was still a helluva lot better than what "the boys" had.

And very few performers who spent any time in the Pacific weren't affected by their experiences.

John Wayne was too old to serve, but he did make war movies. For him, it wasn't enough. "He wanted to be out there himself, to go personally and do what he could for the boys fighting the war," wrote Mike Tomkies in the Wayne bio, *Duke*. "In 1944 he went. He spent three months taking camp shows to the Pacific war fronts. He performed as close to the action as he was permitted to get—in mangrove swamps and in twenty-five-foot-high kumi grass. And when he got back to America, he did not launch into rhetorical eulogies about what he had seen. He told it like it was—simply and strongly.

"'What the guys out there need,' he said, 'are more letters, cigars, snapshots, phonograph needles, and radios. And, if you can spare 'em, cigarette lighters. I can't say it strongly enough. Those guys are in a hell of a war. It's not only fighting, but work and sweat. They're where 130 degrees is a cool day, where they scrape flies off, where matches melt in their pockets and bombs take legs off at the hip.

"'I've worked on stages built of old crates, with the guys sitting in the mud and rain for three hours waiting for someone like me to say, 'Hello, Joe.' We've got to do more for 'em.'"

Another of Hollywood's most rugged leading men who toured the region was Gary Cooper, who logged over 20,000 miles with actresses Phyllis Brooks and Una Merkel. According to Hector Arce in his biography of the film legend, Coop remembered one night when there were 15,000 GIs sitting in mud, waiting out a rainstorm for the show. Finally the troupe went on stage and did their show, but the guys wanted more. "'Hey Coop,' one of the young men yelled out, 'how about the Lou Gehrig farewell speech to the Yankees?' The rest of the young men broke into applause."

"'Give me a minute to get it straight,' Cooper replied. He rose and quietly spoke into the microphone. 'I've been walking on ball fields for sixteen years, and I've never received anything but kindness and encouragement from you fans. I've had the great

Below: *Besides winning the Oscar for his portrayal of real-life WWI hero Sergeant Alvin York, Gary Cooper discounted his talents, saying he couldn't dance, sing or play an instrument ... or do anything the "boys" overseas might want to see. But his "ah shucks" attitude changed when a GI shouted out and asked him to reprise the Lou Gehrig speech from* Pride of the Yankees, *another movie he starred in. The reaction was overwhelming, and soon Coop agreed to tour the Pacific, shown here with starlets Phyllis Brooks and Una Merkel during a stop in New Guinea.*
Army Signal Corps Photo

honor to have played with these great veteran ballplayers on my left—Murderer's Row—our championship team of 1927. I've had the further honor of living with and playing with these men on my right—the Bronx Bombers—the Yankees of today.

"'I have a mother and father who fought to give me health and a solid background in my youth. I have a wife—a companion for life—who has shown me more courage than I ever knew. People all say that I've had a bad break, but—today—today I consider myself the luckiest man on the face of the Earth.'

"All about him, Cooper saw young boys crying. They, who were facing possible death, were stunned by Gehrig's simple words and the way an insulated and well-protected movie star had interpreted them. It was a humbling experience. Never before had Cooper felt the magical effect his presence could have on a live audience. He continued giving the farewell speech at every show, invariably receiving the same reaction."

Bob Hope spent many months and logged a lot of miles in the Far East. He had a lot of laughs with the GIs but also experienced a few downers he'd never forget:

"It was in 1944 that we reached Tarawa and did a few shows. While there we saw movies of the Marines landing on Tarawa six or eight months before," Hope recalled in his book, *Have Tux, Will Travel.* "The audience was so quiet we could hear palms rustle. A hundred yards from the theater were rows of white crosses where some of the Marines that we were seeing on the screen were lying. After the picture we got up and walked back to our Quonset hut past that cemetery. Those white crosses reached inside of us and squeezed our guts."

Former Buffalo, New York, radio jock Jack Paar was in the Army, reluctantly, charged with entertaining the guys in his unit however he could. "With our own morale at zero, we set about our morale duties," he recounted in his book, *I Kid You Not*. "Our shows usually consisted of an emcee, a few specialty acts like acrobats or jugglers, sometimes three GIs with balloons tucked in their shirts lip-synching to records of the Andrews Sisters singing 'Beer Barrel Polka' or 'Bei Mir Bist Du Schon,' and a small musical group or just a piano. It wasn't much, but, as the old vaudevillians used to say, they loved us in Guadalcanal and Fiji and Suva and Munda.

"Often we played to war-weary, begrimed men, just back from killing Japs in the jungles, but they always responded to humor. Our role wasn't very heroic, but I can always tell my grandchildren that I played before thousands of armed men and never got shot."

Some of those GIs on Guadalcanal actually pulled double duty, as stretcher-bearers with the Massachusetts National Guard and as musicians who'd been playing together back home for more than a decade. "The band didn't

LEFT: *Hollywood veteran Randolph Scott enjoyed a casual respite with leathernecks at Guadalcanal in early '44, providing them with some new—and maybe juicy—gossip from back home.*
U.S. Marine Corps Photo

RIGHT: *"How come all the good-looking guys get to escort the babes?" Lucky palookas Harvey and Moe Weiss, the boxing twins, walk arm in arm with starlets Mary Elliott, Rosita Moreno, and Frances Fay when the trio made a brief stop at Guadalcanal, in February of '44.*
U.S. Marine Corps Photo

have a chance to play a note during its first six weeks [at the Canal]. During combat the outfit served as hospital attendants, and at Mount Austin its members distinguished themselves as relief stretcher-bearers who carried wounded over a six-mile trail through rugged jungle terrain from advanced positions to first-aid stations," reported *YANK* correspondent Mack Morris in the July 23, 1943, issue.

After the island was secured, the band members had some free time to get back together and perform for the troops, who preferred swing music, not sentimental schmaltz.

Hundreds of big band musicians were in uniform and assigned to one of the many military bands in the Pacific. George "Bob" Crosby, younger brother of crooner Bing Crosby, was in charge of the 5th Marine Division Band that toured the region and experienced all the travails of performing in the tropics. Artie Shaw put together the finest military musicians he could find in the Navy and maintained a nonstop schedule that took them from Guadalcanal and the Solomons to a lot of those little specks on the map no one had ever heard of before, such as Noumea and the New Hebrides. But whirlwind playing, air raids, and sweltering tropical heat and humidity exhausted the band and several, including Shaw, had to be hospitalized in the States.

RIGHT: *George "Bob" Crosby may have been Bing's younger brother, but he was an established big band leader prior to joining the Marines and heading up the 5th Marine Division Band that toured the Pacific, wherever leathernecks staked a claim in the region.*
U.S. Marine Corps Photo

The Claude Thornhill troupe, including former child actor Jackie Cooper and radio tenor Dennis Day, frequently came ashore at locations where mop-up operations were still ongoing and gunfire could be heard in the distance.

Hollywood Profiles the Heroes

In the war of the Pacific, it was very clear that the Americans were the good guys and the

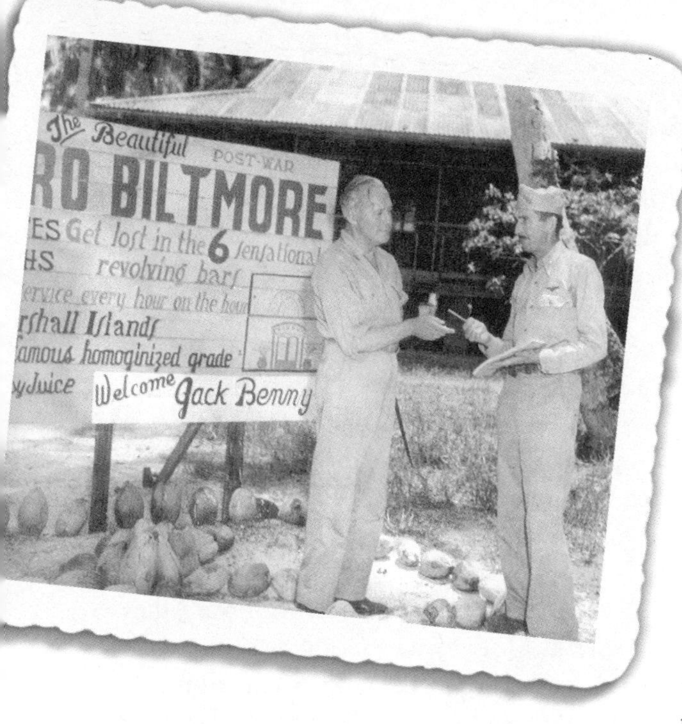

LEFT: *He may have been cheesy and a little bit square, but deadpan comedian Jack Benny was a hit with the GIs during his USO tour of the South Pacific in mid-1944. Of course he wasn't quite as popular as any of the leggy, buxom beauties who tagged along with him.*

Here he talks with Navy Commander W. J. Wicks while staying at the "Majuro Biltmore" in the Marshall Islands.

U.S. Navy Photo

Japanese wore the black hats. Maybe the tales didn't always have a happy ending—certainly not any of the movies about Pearl Harbor, or Bataan and Corregidor, Wake Island and Guam. But it was easy for Hollywood to put a positive spin on the not-so-happy endings, just by promising that the early sacrifices, the lopsided loss of precious lives, only strengthened America's resolve, and total vigilance would ultimately lead to victory.

By 1944 there were a string of movies about American combatants in the Pacific. The documentary *With the Marines at Tarawa* was filmed with the 2nd Marine Division and directed by Captain Louis Hayward. Two of the cameramen for this project were killed in battle. *The Fighting Seabees*, featuring John Wayne as a construction foreman and Susan Hayward as a newspaper reporter, portrayed the unarmed civilian engineers contracted to build airstrips across the Pacific and how they get caught up in Japan's war posturing in the region.

Wing and a Prayer, starring Don Ameche as Commander Bingo Harper and Dana Andrews as his second in command, profiles the sailors on a carrier in the Pacific and the flyboys who launched themselves off the pitching

LEFT: *Tramping through the surf while loaded down with gear was never an easy task, especially if enemy mortar crews and machine-gunners were peppering the landing beach. For troops of the 41st Infantry Division, hustling ashore at Wakde Island, Dutch New Guinea, the first task was to get out of the water, then get out of the line of fire.*

Photo Courtesy of the MacArthur Memorial Museum

flight deck. Even pinup stars Betty Grable and Alice Faye made an appearance in this "man's movie," but it was in the form of the aircrews watching the actresses in the movie *Tin Pan Alley*.

The Fighting Sullivans tells the tragic story of the five Sullivan brothers from Waterloo, Iowa, who lobbied the Navy to serve together, then perished when their ship was torpedoed. Twentieth Century Fox had difficulty casting the movie because many of the younger actors in Hollywood were in uniform or about to depart for battles unknown.

Pride of the Marines, released in 1945, profiles the heroism of Marine Sergeant Al Schmid on Guadalcanal, who was credited with making two hundred kills before being blinded by an enemy grenade. The film, starring John Garfield as Schmid, follows him from civilian life to combat and then back home, where he deals with his blindness.

Even though by 1944 the tide had definitely turned in favor of the Allies in the Pacific—with the naval victories at Midway and Coral Sea two years earlier—Hollywood revisited 1941 and early '42 with such films as *Destination Tokyo*, *They Were Expendable*, and *Back to Bataan*, the last two released after the war with Japan was over and the American public, weary of combat, was ready to move on.

They Were Expendable follows a small band of PT boat crews during the early skirmishes in the Philippines, as they hear the news about the attack on Pearl Harbor, prep for the Japanese onslaught headed their way, and scatter in all directions when their base is attacked. After regrouping and debating whether they should join the ragtag Army at Bataan or continue with what they were trained to do—hit and harass enemy warships—they elect to carry on.

During an intense skirmish between an enemy warship and the two PT boats led by Lieutenant (junior grade) Rusty Ryan (played by John Wayne) and Lieutenant John Brickley (played by Robert Montgomery), several of their crew are killed and injured and their boats become disabled. Later, at a memorial service for their fallen comrades, the men gather in a church and Rusty says a few solemn words:

"A serviceman is supposed to have a funeral. That's a tribute to the way he spent his life . . . escort, firing squad, wrapped in the flag he served under and died for. In war

RIGHT: *In the movie* They Were Expendable, *Robert Montgomery played PT boat commander Lieutenant John Brickley. The film, which costarred John Wayne, spotlighted the heroic men of the Navy's PT boats, the "expendables" stationed in the Philippines in the early days leading up to war with Japan. After the attack on Pearl Harbor and the Philippines, some of the PT crews—those whose boats were destroyed by the Japanese in early skirmishes—wound up enduring the bombardment of Bataan and Corregidor, while other crews managed to continue on, harassing Japanese warships.*
U.S. Navy Photo

you gotta forget those things and get buried the best way you can. Y'all knew Squarehead Larsen and Slug Mahan. They were just a couple of bluejackets who did their job. Did it well. Now they're both gone. Slug, he was always quotin' verse, bits of poetry, so . . . here's one for him. It's about the only one I know:

'Under the wide and starry sky, dig the grave and let me lie. Glad did I live and gladly die, and I laid me down with a will. This be the verse you grave for me. *Here he lies where he longed to be. Home is the sailor, home from the sea, and the hunter home from the hill.*'"

One of the crewmen plays "Taps" on his harmonica and then they all gather across the street at a closed bar and drink to their buddies. A radio is tuned to an armed forces station, playing a sentimental love song, when an announcer breaks in: "WBKR San Francisco. A brief interruption, please. This is tragic news from the Philippines. The white flag of surrender was hoisted on the bloody heights of Bataan this afternoon, 36,000 United States

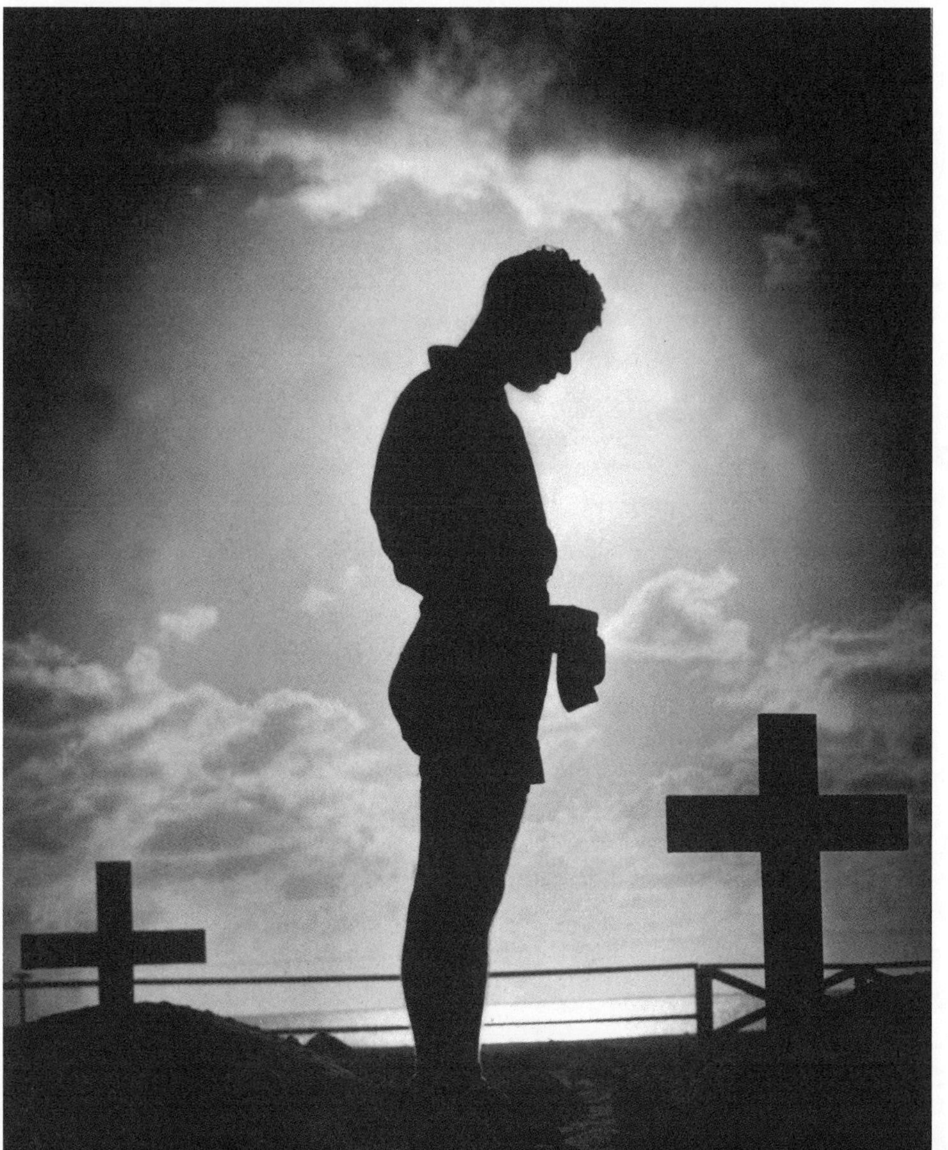

Left: *A simple cross marks the grave of another American hero who died at a godforsaken piece of rock and sand and volcanic ash somewhere in the Pacific. A Coast Guardsman says good-bye to a buddy who wasn't quite so lucky.*

Most of the dead at these temporary grave sites would later be moved to American cemeteries in the Pacific or returned home.

U.S. Coast Guard Photo

soldiers . . . hungry, ragged, half-starved shadows, trapped like rats but dying like men, were finally worn down by 200,000 pig Japanese troops.

"Men who fight for an unshakable faith are more than flesh . . . they're not steel. Flesh must yield at last, endurance melts away, the end must come. Bataan has fallen, but the spirit that made it stand as a beacon to all lovers of liberty will never falter. The white flag was hardly hoisted over Bataan before Jap artillery began slamming away at Corregidor, our last strongpoint in the Philippines."

Both Rusty's final words to his lost crewmen and the radio announcer's plea to stand firm are clear messages to not just the PT boat survivors, but to everyone, that it is going to be a long and bitter fight, with setbacks along the way and the loss of many more brave souls. But still, everyone who loved liberty and freedom must carry on, must see the fight to its ultimate end. That would be the only acceptable way to honor their deaths.

Destination Tokyo follows an American submarine on a seemingly impossible mission, to sneak into the waters off Tokyo, past minefields and sub nets and land commandos, so they can plot the exact locations of key installations there, all for the planned first air strike against Japan, led by the Doolittle Raiders in April of 1942.

Before heading out to sea on their clandestine mission, Captain Cassidy, played by Cary Grant, briefs his men: "I'm sorry your liberty was cut short, but I guess the Navy would've let us have Christmas ashore if this wasn't important. The men who've been with me on previous patrols know I don't believe in fight talks. When a man gives a fight talk I suspect he needs one himself.

"For the benefit of the newcomers . . . you're here because you volunteered. You're well-trained, highly selected men and we're glad to have you aboard. You may be infants in the submarine service but we figure you'll be veterans by the time we make port again. We've had pretty fair luck so far . . . let's hope we really smear 'em this time."

Once out at sea, Captain Cassidy opens an envelope to reveal their destination: Tokyo. On the way, while topside to recharge the sub's batteries, they get strafed but manage to shoot down the Japanese fighter plane. But when they attempt to rescue the downed pilot, he stabs one of the old-timers and kills him.

Captain Cassidy talks with his men about the loss. "Trying to figure out about Mike? Well, ya know, officers and men on submarines are closer together than most branches of our Navy. Mike was with me on my first patrol. He was my friend. I know his family. His wife's a fine, great-hearted woman. I know his kids. I remember Mike's pride when he bought the first pair of roller skates for his little five-year-old boy. They were the finest roller skates that money could buy. Roller skates for a five-year-old.

"Well, that Jap got a present too when he was five, only it was a dagger. Ya see, his old man gave him a dagger so he'd know right off what he was supposed to be in life. The Japs have a ceremony that goes with it. At seven, a Jap kid is taking marches under an army instructor. At thirteen he can put a machine gun together, blindfolded. So as I see it, that Jap was started on the road twenty years ago into putting a knife in Mike's back.

"There are lots of Mikes dying right now and a lot more Mikes will die, until we wipe out a system that puts daggers in the hands of five-year-old children. Ya know, if Mike were here to put it into words right now, that's just about what he died for . . . more roller skates in this world, including some for the next generation of Japanese kids, 'cause that's the kind of a man Mike was."

That said, it is time to get on with their perilous mission and do their part to put an end to Imperial Japan.

Anthony Quinn played Captain Andres Bonifacio, Filipino descendant of one of that country's past heroes, in 1945's *Back to Bataan*. The movie begins with the rescue of prisoners at the Cabanatuan POW Camp and then flashes back to the fall of the peninsula and the nearby island of Corregidor. Rather than surrender to the brutal Japanese, U.S. Army Colonel Joe Madden (played by John Wayne) encourages Bonifacio and many of his followers to flee into the hills and continue to fight, as partisans, holding out until the Americans return. But as the guerrillas are tracked down and killed by the Japanese, the survivors begin to wonder if the GIs are ever coming back, if General MacArthur really plans to keep his promise to the Filipino people.

Only their unwavering faith and the dream of a democratic homeland bolsters their sagging resolve, until MacArthur does in fact return. (The general arrived at Leyte in October of 1944.) By this time the guerrillas have evaded the Japanese patrols for two years and have made it to Tacloban on the island of Leyte, just as the Americans storm the beach and rout the Japanese there.

The film closes with Captain Bonifacio hugging his longtime sweetheart, who has waited endless months for his return. Then American troops—the actual survivors of the Bataan Death March rescued from the Cabanatuan Camp—hobble past the camera as the narrator names real-life heroes of the battles of Bataan and Corregidor and proclaims, "The blood, sweat, and tears have not been in vain. Freedom is on the march again."

Background: *Starlets making the rounds at training camps across the country usually pulled one lucky GI from the crowd and gave him hugs and kisses. Tech-5 John Gunn enjoyed the attention of June Haver and Jeanne Crain during their show at Camp Perry, Ohio.*
YANK Magazine Photo

Pinup Girls Show "T & A" Weapons Don't Refer to Tanks and Artillery

"The pin-up pretties, I am quite sure, were meant
For men in the barracks and men in the tent.
But how can a tent-dweller keep his chin up
When there's no damn place to pin up a pin-up?"

—T-4 Arthur M. Zipser's "Pin-up Problem," a poem published in YANK

"A lot of guys don't have any girlfriends to fight for. I guess you could call us pin-up girls kind of an inspiration."

—Actress Betty Grable, America's top World War II pinup girl

VA-VA-VOOM. OOO, LA LA. PING. OOMPH.

No matter how the GIs sliced it, it was all cheesecake. And in World War II, beauties abounded and pretties were plentiful, at least in the small corners of a soldier's or sailor's world.

Life magazine created the phrase *pinup girl* on July 7, 1941, when it crowned Dorothy Lamour as the first pinup girl. (The *Los Angeles Times* counters that freelance writer and executive editor of *YANK* magazine, Hartzell Spence, coined the term when he told his colleagues that the publication needed photos of beautiful women to entice enlisted men to spend a nickel an issue.) Besides being the first paper dolly, Lamour also earned the nicknames "the Sarong Girl" for her movies in South Seas settings and

Right: *Lovely lady Dorothy Lamour shared her newly debuted publicity photos with a young private at DeRidder Army Air Force Base. Lamour's sarong-clad body appeared in servicemen's bunks and barracks around the world. In an October 24, 1991, interview with a* Denver Post *reporter, Lamour said, "My God, the sarong was like long underwear today."*

Dubbed "the bond bombshell" for selling war bonds worth more than $300 million, Lamour said she wishes movies were censored again. "Why do pictures today have to be so graphic? Do you agree with me? People say it's for art's sake. Well, someday I'd like to meet Art and ask him why he can't leave something to the imagination," Lamour said in the article.
YANK Magazine Photo

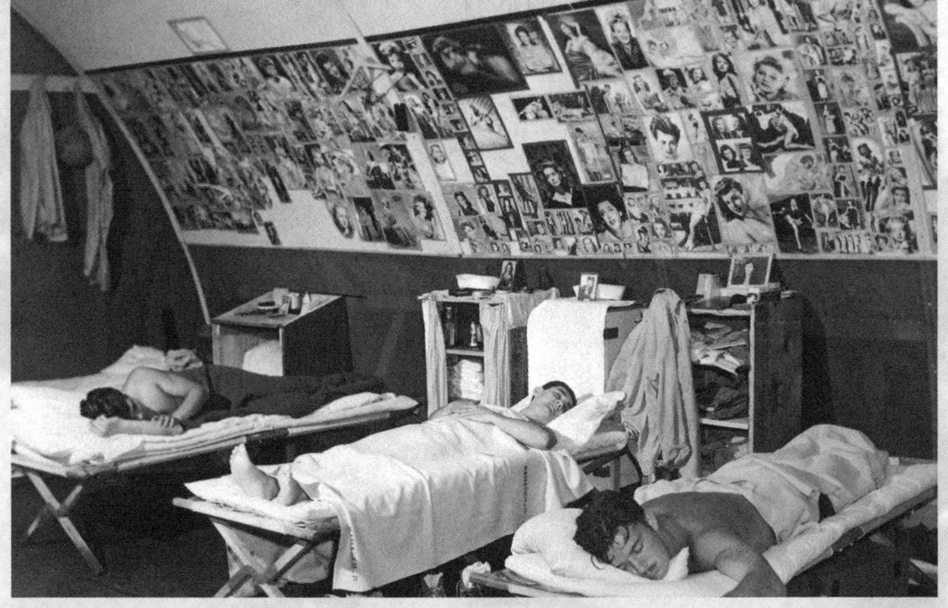

LEFT: *Sailors couldn't wait to return to their Quonset huts to escape wartime weariness. Part of the respite included hours spent staring at starlets, whose pictures decorated nearly every square inch of wall space.*
National Archives Photo

"Bond Bombshell" for selling $300 million in World War II war bonds (which would be worth in excess of $2.7 billion in today's money, according to an article by Marian Zailian in the *San Francisco Chronicle* on November 10, 1991). While the World War I doughboys had to hide their lusty, busty French postcards, fellas from Burma to Belgium displayed paper pretties out in the open.

The U.S. government endorsed pinups, allowing aircrews to decorate planes with nose art copied from seductive poses and permitting the painting of sexy images on bombs, boats, and jeeps. The Army even used Chili Williams, a model from Minnesota, to show GIs how camouflage worked. According to a 1985 *Life* special issue on World War II, soldiers saw a photo of the twenty-one-year-old in stilettos and a sparse outfit made of camouflage material and tree branches with leaves. Officers figured the photo would at least grab the guys' attention. Never before had soldiers wanted to study so much!

Pinups didn't even have to be real women. Joaquin Alberto Vargas y Chavez drew gorgeous women, called Vargas girls, whose sultry yet innocent poses became quite popular with the servicemen, according to a *Los Angeles Times* article by Hunter Drohojowska-Philp on June 23, 2002. Vargas started out

RIGHT: *Air crews personalized their planes, usually by naming them for a special lady and by painting nose art modeled after a pinup picture. Marine Private First Class Handsall W. Sprenger of Louisville, Kentucky, earned the moniker, "Michaelangelo of the Marianas" for his work on B-29s. Often the nose art lacked proper piety and propriety—they showed totally nude women. According to an August 6, 1995,* St. Louis Post-Dispatch *article, when planes too old and too damaged for fighting came home to use as trainers, American women's religious groups expressed outrage over the painted planes. In February 1945, Washington censored nose art, much to the GIs' disappointment.*
National Archives Photo

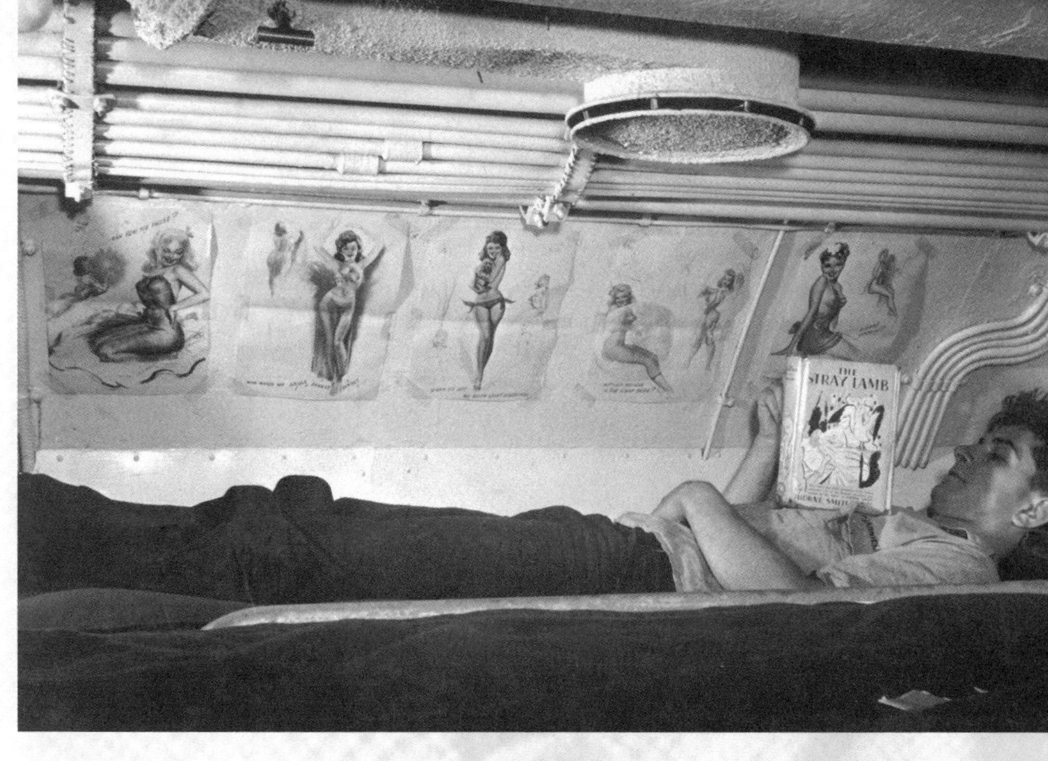

Right: *This sailor aboard the USS* Capelin *based in New London, Connecticut, has limited wall space but discriminating tastes. He decorates his area with Vargas girls, drawings of lovely ladies that appeared in* Esquire.
U.S. Navy Photo

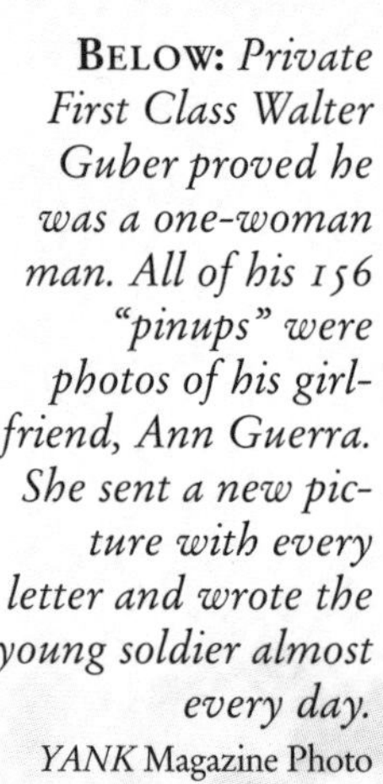

Below: *Private First Class Walter Guber proved he was a one-woman man. All of his 156 "pinups" were photos of his girlfriend, Ann Guerra. She sent a new picture with every letter and wrote the young soldier almost every day.*
YANK Magazine Photo

in Hollywood drawing movie posters after spending several years designing posters and show programs for New York showman Flo Ziegfeld. Vargas drew portraits of many of the Ziegfeld Follies' girls who worked in high heels, feather boas, and push-up bras. Once Vargas was in Hollywood, *Esquire* magazine founder David Smart discovered his unique talent and began publishing the drawings in the magazine. Two months after the first Vargas girl appeared in its pages in 1940, the magazine's circulation had shot up by 100,000.

Cecilia Rasmussen wrote in a June 25, 2000, *Los Angeles Times* story that Vargas claimed he "learned from Ziegfeld the difference between nudes and lewds." But the postmaster general disagreed, and in 1943 he sued *Esquire* for obscenity. Rasmussen's article retold the story of a Navy lieutenant who wrote his congressman to argue that the magazine was "an aid to morale among fighting men." The lieutenant added that he found a young man under his command dead in a foxhole, clutching a picture of one of the Vargas girls. "He had not wanted to risk leaving his picture in the tent for fear the enemy would get it. These boys have so little; they have and hold foremost their memories," the lieutenant wrote. Newspaper accounts of the lawsuit fueled *Esquire*'s sales, and it more than doubled its circulation. The magazine won the case, securing pinups for GIs.

For most GIs the pinup girls were the only American women—or any women—they saw for weeks, often

Left: *Corporal Bernard Butnik and Sergeant Richard Goodbar try to warm up "Agnes" with cola and cigarettes. All they got, though, was the cold shoulder.*
National Archives Photo

months. The models and starlets not only personified the ideal gal the soldier, airman, leatherneck, or seaman wanted to marry when he returned home, they also gave a face to a very complex war that many had entered without fully understanding. They could look into the girls' eyes—once they found their way there—and believe that protecting the buxom beauty and all she stood for was the reason America was at war.

Nearly every unit or ship adopted a lovely lady as its mascot, and thousands of men voted at camps, on bases, and through magazine promotions for their favorite girl in categories such as "Girl to Ride with on a Bumpy African Road," or " Girl We'd Like to Take on a Night Bombing Mission." While there was no such thing as an unpopular pinup, some of the women caught the GIs' hearts and imaginations more strongly than others. And none was more popular than Betty Grable.

Legs Insured by Lloyd's of London

If Helen of Troy had the "face that launched a thousand ships," then Betty Grable had "the gams that launched a thousand sighs." She was undisputedly the most sought-after pinup girl during the war. Grable also was Hollywood's brightest star and the most highly paid woman in the United States in 1945 and 1946, earning $250,000 each year. "Box-office Betty" made 20th Century Fox studios $100 million in the 1940s with her popular movies. Grable was the top movie star from 1942 through 1944, and she remained in the top ten for the next decade. She was not only the girl with the million-dollar legs, but also was the All-American Love Goddess, the straight-shooting yet alluring woman whom any man would like to meet and marry, according to Patrick Agan in *The Decline and Fall of the Love Goddesses*. Her movies included *Tin Pan Alley*, *Yank in the RAF*, *Springtime in the Rockies*, and even *Pinup Girl*.

Grable set the pinup girl standard with the famous photo of her in a white bathing suit, looking over her shoulder, beckoning every serviceman to finish the fight and get home to her, Agan wrote. Her picture found a home near every bunk and aboard every ship. A Quonset hut wasn't a home without the bathing beauty tacked to a makeshift wall. Doug Warren wrote in *Betty Grable: The Reluctant Movie Queen* that Fox still photographer Frank Powolny took that photo (and the last shots of Marilyn Monroe), capturing Grable's essence in one shot. "She tried several bathing suits in different colors, and they weren't exactly right. Finally she put on the white one, and we made a couple of shots. She started to walk away and glanced back over her shoulder. It looked pretty good, so I asked if she could come back and do it again. She struck the pose, and said, 'Is this what you want?' I shot it and that was that," Powolny said.

BELOW: *Mapping never became more popular than when GIs plotted points on pinup queen Betty Grable's "peaks and valleys." Aviators only wished all their targets were as scenic as her million-dollar legs.*
U.S. Air Force Training Center Photo

But even Powolny's memory is fuzzy about how the shot came to be. In a 1982 interview, he said it came from Grable's clowning around, the *Los Angeles Times* reported in the photographer's 1986 obituary. He said: "I asked Betty if she'd like to have a back shot, just to be different. She said, 'Yes,' and began to clown around. 'You want it like this?' she asked, posing. And I said, 'Yeah.' I made only two shots of that pose. It was the second shot that became famous."

No matter the method, by 1942 Fox had received 20,000 requests for Grable's photo every week, making her first in picture requests. The studio mailed out more than five million copies by war's end, earning it a spot in *Ripley's Believe It or Not*. The photo became the second-most popular photo from the era, behind the flag-raising at Iwo Jima.

The bathing suit shot only fueled Grable's fame with the military. Warren wrote that by 1944, one out of every fifteen servicemen belonged to a camp, company, regiment, or unit that had elected the actress as its mascot, dream girl, honorary commander, or some other lofty title. Although she knew she was popular, she had no way of knowing exactly how much GIs adored her. And Grable returned the love. She toured with stateside USO shows, performing at training camps from coast to coast. She even auctioned off a pair of nylons for thousands of dollars to raise money for the war effort.

Unlike some stars, Grable enjoyed being around the men. At the Hollywood Canteen, she jitterbugged with hundreds of servicemen over the years, sharing a laugh and a promise to send a photo. Soldiers at Camp Robinson, Arkansas, sent her 54,000 letters in 1942—and she sent autographed photos to each and every one of them. Grable even posed for a special cheesecake photo in a uniform shirt, pumps, and little else. A grid was imprinted on the picture, and trainees learned how to plot map coordinates using her "peaks and valleys."

While Grable may have inspired the fighting men, she created complications for some women on the home front. Because she exemplified the perfect woman, many men expected to find a girl just like her. They wanted someone who was "pretty, energetic, warm, obliging, and uncomplicated," according to Jib Fowles's *Starstruck*. Many women tried to live up to that standard, only to realize that they would never attain her look. Women found it difficult to be sensuous and still retain the "girl-next-door" image. Other women, however, found Grable to be a "model of the lovable person they would like to become. She was sweet, 'regular'—the girl down the street, a person to trade makeup with," Fowles wrote. It was this universal appeal that made Grable such a star. Once the war ended, the boys returned home and found girls they loved and wanted to marry. Grable's popularity waned, and the pure sexuality of new sensation Marilyn Monroe pushed her aside. Unlike many stars who tried to hang on to their celebrity glory days, Grable told the up-and-coming platinum blonde in *Starstruck*: "Honey, I've had it. It's your turn now. Go and get it."

Although Grable's popularity far surpassed the others, GIs seldom tacked up only one pinup. Other accomplished actresses and aspiring starlets made cheesecake photos that were taped, tacked, stapled, screwed, and glued into and onto any surface a GI could find. Many of these young women's faces greeted the serviceman each morning and bid him sweet dreams at night. Hundreds of beauties became pinup girls, but some of the most famous were Rita Hayworth, Betty Hutton, Jinx Falkenburg, Carole Landis, Joan Leslie, Veronica Lake, Jane Russell, Lana Turner, Susan Hayward, Anne Gwynne, and the government's handpicked Margie Stewart.

The Woman for Whom Technicolor was Invented

Sultry love goddess Rita Hayworth appeared on the cover of *Life* magazine four times, equaled in number of appearances only by President Franklin Delano Roosevelt. The actress, who was born Margarita Carmen Dolores

Cansino, decorated the walls and wallets of GIs across the world. Hayworth's most famous photo featured her posed on a bed in lingerie and appeared in *Life* on August 11, 1941.

A patriot as well as a pinup, Hayworth toured with USO shows and volunteered at the Hollywood Canteen, where she danced for hours with service members. She was second to Grable in popularity, but it was her photo that was pasted to a test atomic bomb and dropped on the Bikini Atoll in 1946, according to *Biography Magazine* in April 2002. GIs at Camp Callan, California, voted Hayworth their "proxy mother" one Mother's Day when their moms were unable to visit. She also earned the title of the "girl we'd like to be cast adrift with" when servicemen voted in a *Life* magazine contest. Some of Hayworth's most famous movies included *My Gal Sal*, *Tales of Manhattan*, *Cover Girl*, and *Gilda*.

ABOVE: *Sultry Rita Hayworth was second only to Betty Grable in pinup popularity. Voted by GIs as "the girl we'd like to be cast adrift with," she volunteered tirelessly at the Hollywood Canteen and was often a serviceman's last jitterbug before battle.*
National Archives Photo

Servicemen "Hot-to-Trot" for "Huttontot"

Lovingly called "Bouncing Betty" for her boundless beauty and energy, Betty Hutton was one of the GIs' favorite girls and Paramount Studio's top blonde. Born Betty June Thornburg, she "could be as sexy as Lana [Turner], as noisy as Judy [Garland], and as seductive as that other Betty, Grable," according to Agan. During the war years, whenever Hutton was not in Hollywood working on her next film, she spent her time traveling across the country with other celebrities selling war bonds. But she never stopped being a star, often posing

RIGHT: *She may have been a little wacky, but Betty Hutton was one of the most popular movie stars ofHollywood's golden era. During a tour of the South Pacific, Bouncing Betty hams it up in a chow hall for swabbies and leathernecks in the Marshall Islands, in December of 1944.*
U.S. Navy Photo

with the mayors of the cities she visited to ensure her photo appeared on the front pages of every major newspaper.

Hutton also entertained troops at the Hollywood Canteen, where she sang "Murder, He Says," her hit song from *Happy Go Lucky*, "about a million times," according to Agan. Bob Hope once joked: "If they would put a propeller on Betty Hutton and send her over Germany, the war would be over in no time," Agan wrote. By 1944 she was receiving seven thousand letters each week from servicemen around the world. Troops voted her the "girl we'd most like to spend a howling furlough with." Her other movie credits included *And the Angels Sing*, *Here Come the Waves*, and *Incendiary Blonde*.

"Jinx"ed with Beauty

Eugenia Lincoln Falkenburg not only earned a high salary as 1941's highest-paid model, but this tennis-player-turned-model also became one of the first beer beauties. Leibmann Brewery, maker of Rheingold beer, named her Miss Rheingold, believing that the company would sell more lager when men noticed the pretty face on the advertisements. Falkenburg, nicknamed "Jinx" by her mother to bring her good luck, began her movie career at age sixteen when she signed a contract at Warner Brothers to make movies such as *The Lone Ranger Rides Again* and *Cover Girl*. She also played in Al Jolson's Broadway comedy *Hold On to Your Hats* in 1940, which led to the Jinx Falkenburg Fan Club and made her an American household name, according to her August 29, 2003, obituary in the *Los Angeles Times* by Jon Thurber.

LEFT: *Turning her backhand to table tennis, starlet and court ace Jinx Falkenburg enjoyed games of Ping-Pong in November 1944 with B-29 airmen in China.*
National Archives Photo

A popular pinup girl, Falkenburg entertained troops at camp shows. Pat O'Brien recounted in his autobiography the story of many of her appearances for soldiers this way: She walked out on stage in a beautiful evening gown, driving the GIs crazy since she looked like "a pinup version come to animated life" and many of the men had not seen an American woman in three or four years. Once the cheering stopped, she'd undo the dress's shoulder straps, and her dress would fall to reveal the tennis outfit she wore underneath it. She would pull a "planted" GI from the front and bring him on stage, telling him that she'd do anything he asked. This caused the men to go wild, letting their imaginations run wild. The stooge told her he wanted to hit tennis balls, and she drove balls that had been autographed by Hollywood's top celebrities into the audience.

Falkenburg loved GIs so much that she married one. Tex McCrary, an Army Air Forces photographer and public relations officer, interviewed Jinx for a story in a military publication. They met again during one of her USO shows and got engaged in 1942. They married in 1945, and the two became the first talk show hosts on radio and on television. *Hi Jinx* earned top ratings on New York's WEAF radio, and the two later hosted NBC's *At Home* on Saturday nights. Falkenburg tackled controversial subjects on her shows, including venereal disease, the atomic bomb, and the United Nations, Thurber reported. As the popularity of the shows grew, the two added a column in the *New York Herald Tribune* to their list of media enterprises.

Falkenburg and McCrary were also political activists. The former choice pinup girl of GIs stationed at the Pentagon worked as a fund-raiser for the Republican Party and was head of the GOP's women's division in 1954. She died in August 2003 at the North Shore University Hospital, which she helped found.

BELOW: *At the quartermaster store on New Guinea in July of 1944, starlets Martha Tilton (left) and Carole Landis (center) get resupplied while on a lengthy tour of the South Pacific with comedian Jack Benny.*
National Archives Photo

A Jill with a Jeep

Actress Carole Landis, nicknamed "the Ping Girl" by servicemen, spent much of her free time touring the world with the USO. The former nightclub singer and dancer who changed her name from Frances Ridste used her time away from the movie studios to bring smiles to the troops' faces. She even wrote a book about her first USO tour, which she had spent with soldiers in England and North Africa. Tinseltown turned the book into a movie, *Four Jills and a Jeep*, starring Landis and Hollywood heavyweights Betty Grable, Carmen Miranda, Martha Raye, Phil Silvers,

Alice Faye, and the Jimmy Dorsey Orchestra. Although critics dismissed the 1944 film as self-serving, Landis missed most of the commentary because she spent much of the year working with the USO on a Pacific tour. The Web site www.glamourgirlsofthesilverscreen.com noted that she returned from the trip very ill with malaria and pneumonia and nearly died.

Landis, who was married to Horace Schmidlapp, committed suicide in 1948 after an affair with married actor Rex Harrison ended, according to her biography on www.lawzone.com. She was only twenty-nine, but left a legacy in films such as *Cadet Girl*, *My Gal Sal*, *Out of the Blue*, and *Brass Monkey*.

ABOVE: *Because there were never enough girls to go around at the camp shows, stars such as stripper Gypsy Rose Lee (left) often "dragged" GIs into the act. Here six guys dressed as gals performed with Lee in Austin, Texas.*
Bergstrom Army Air Force Base Photo

"All-Out Girl" Befriends Troops

GIs honored Joan Leslie with nineteen popularity titles by late 1945, returning her affection for her appearances in defense plants, camps and bases, and the Hollywood Canteen. Ronald Reagan's leading lady in Irving Berlin's *This Is the Army* won everything from "the girl we'd most like to talk to" from the movie cast (regulations forbid soldiers from talking to any civilian actors, according to Garson Kanin's *Hollywood)*, to "the girl with whom we'd most like to go desert happy" by the 3022nd Army Air Forces Base Unit in Indian Springs, Nevada. She also earned the title of "All-Out Girl." Leslie appeared in several patriotic films, including *Sergeant York* alongside Gary Cooper, and with James Cagney in *Yankee Doodle Dandy*.

Pinup Causes Hairy Moments in Defense Plants

Sexy siren Veronica Lake said in Richard Lamparksi's *Whatever Became Of...* that she "never did cheesecake. I just used my hair." So popular was the "peek-a-boo girl's" coif that tumbled over half her face that the War Department asked Paramount Studios to give her a new hairdo because women in defense plants mimicking the style were getting their hair caught in machinery, injuring the workers and the war effort, Agan wrote. The former Constance Ockelman, who had changed her name to Constance Keane before settling on Veronica Lake, made screens sizzle when she starred opposite Alan Ladd in *This Gun for Hire*, arguably her most famous film.

Right: *Appearing without her bullet bra, sexy Jane Russell still captured sailors' attention when she appeared at the San Diego Naval Training Station. Many of these same sailors likely gazed daily at her most famous pinup: Russell scantily clad, posed in a bed of hay. The photo was a publicity shot for* The Outlaw, *which the government censored for years.*
U.S. Navy Photo

She also appeared in *Sullivan's Travels*, *So Proudly We Hail!*, and *Hold that Blonde*. GIs voted her the "girl we'd like most to make our objective."

From Church Camp to Censorship

Buxom Jane Russell struck a chord with GIs but struck out with the Hays Office when she leaned over Billy the Kid in *The Outlaw*, and showed her ample cleavage, and offered to use her body heat to keep him warm. According to a September 15, 1985, article in the *San Francisco Chronicle*, a judge said "her bosom hung over the picture like a thunderstorm over a landscape."

And that was producer Howard Hughes's intention when he designed a bra to create more cleavage and unashamedly promoted the sex appeal of a girl who'd returned early from church camp to take her screen test with him. David Cuthbert of the *Times-Picayune* reported in an October 20, 1997, article that "Russell was mortified by Hughes's blatantly sexual advertising campaign for the movie, which included the catch phrase 'How'd you like to tussle with Russell?'" Censors refused to give the film the government's stamp of approval until 1946, and one legend states that during the movie premiere, an audience member said "Bombs away!" when Russell leaned over and showed cleavage the first time—quite the start to her movie career. She later appeared in *Montana Belle*, *Gentlemen Prefer Blondes*, and *Gentlemen Marry Brunettes*.

Ironically, Russell's friends have said she wasn't a sex symbol at all. According to Cuthbert's article, friend and former Republic Pictures actress Adrian Booth said: "She's the least sex symbol of anyone you could ever know. Jane was a tomboy!" But for GIs that was hard to imagine when they saw photos of the 38–26–36 brunette posing in the hay. And Russell continued to use her voluptuous figure later in life, becoming the spokeswoman for Playtex 18-Hour bras in the 1970s.

Change of Habit: Would-be Nun Becomes "Sweater Girl"

Although the story varies somewhat, talent scout William R. Wilkerson discovered Julia Jean Mildred Frances Turner skipping a high-school typing class and sipping a soda at a Hollywood drugstore, according to Lana Turner's obituary in the *Los Angeles Times* on June 30, 1995. The seventeen-year-old, who enrolled at the Convent of the Immaculate Conception to be a nun but changed her mind when she was asked to cut her hair, earned the title "Sweater Girl" for her small role in 1937's *They Won't Forget.*

And audiences didn't. Turner wore a tight sweater and skimpy skirt for the role, and the men in the audience cheered loudly. According to the *Times* obituary, one movie reviewer said that "she looked like what the average high school boy wished the average high school girl looked like." Turner ushered in the sweater era, a look that was classically stylish yet provocative. It was also a look most young women could afford. The trick, said Kanin, was to purchase a sweater two sizes too small. Her sex appeal landed her roles in numerous other movies, including *Ziegfeld Girl*, *Slightly Dangerous*, and *The Postman Always Rings Twice.*

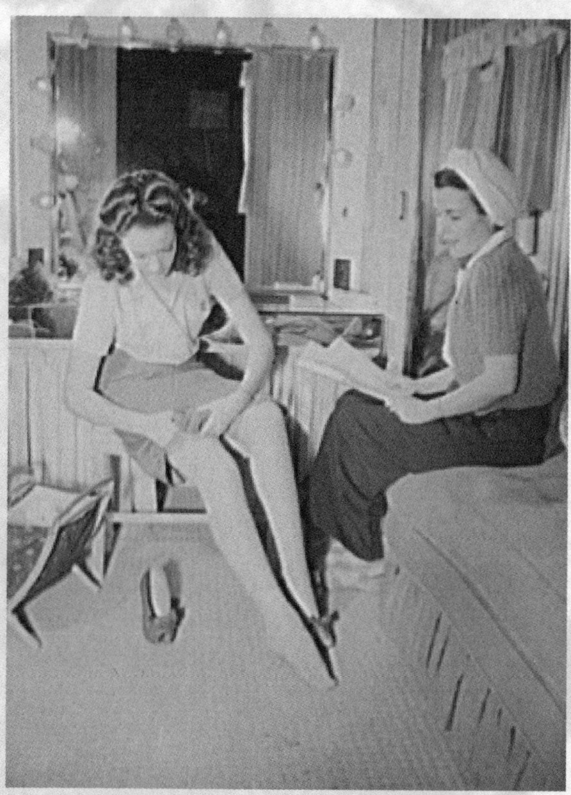

Left: *Lovely Linda Darnell's popularity with GIs never waned—even when she switched from nylons to cotton stockings!*
Office of War Information Photo

In her autobiography *The Lady, the Legend, the Truth: Lana*, Turner wrote that by age twenty she was the "sweetheart of 40 fraternities around the country."

She'd also been voted "the most desirable companion on a desert island" by sailors. She wrote, "The most touching honor of all was the gift of some German shell fragments that British Air Force members sent for my birthday."

Miss Pinup 1944 Entertains Troops

Susan Hayward, the luscious beauty with flame-red hair who torched screens across America, spent many evenings at the Hollywood Canteen performing for servicemen. The actress, born Edythe Marrener, turned a handicap into "a hip-rolling walk" that audiences perceived as sexy, according to Agan. Hayward had been hit by a car on her way to elementary school and suffered two broken legs and a dislocated hip, which failed to heal correctly. Her family was too poor to seek medical care outside of a free clinic. But her meager upbringing gave her the tenacity she needed to succeed in Hollywood, where she won the 1958 Oscar for Best Actress in *I Want to Live*. Other film credits included *I Married a Witch*, *Hit Parade of 1943*, *The Flying Seabees*, and *Deadline at Dawn*.

Swimsuit Model Brings TNT to Pinups

As a top-five World War II pinup girl, Anne Gwynne brought "Trim, Neat, and Terrific" poses to boats and barracks around the world, according to a Web site devoted to her career, www.annegwynne.com. Although she was the top pinup girl for three years, she never surpassed Grable, the era's leading lady of paper dollies. Gwynne got her start when she traveled to Los Angeles with her father, an employee of Catalina Swimwear, which had hired the college sophomore to model bathing suits, according to Lamparski. She quickly earned a movie contract with Universal and a seventy-five-dollar-a-week salary. Studio executives adored her because of her low wages and her eagerness to pose for pinup pictures. None of Gwynne's films were particularly remarkable, although she did earn recognition for her ability to shriek in horror films like *Black Friday*, *The Black Cat*, *The House of Frankenstein*, and *Weird Woman*.

Uncle Sam Picks Pinup Girl

While the Statue of Liberty may have been the U.S. government's first flame, during World War II Margie Stewart became the government's official pinup girl. The Wabash, Indiana, native appeared on at least twenty posters, according to "Issue Girl Friend," by Corporal John Haverstick in *YANK* on July 27, 1945. She was famous for the posters that encouraged Americans to buy war bonds, which was the brainchild of an Army officer who rationalized that if pretty girls could sell soap, they could also hawk bonds.

The government did not seek cheesecake. Instead, they looked for the all-American girl. As Haverstick wrote in *YANK*: "Margie stops short of looking

perfect. The other pinup girls are dream girls in the most unsubstantial sense of the expression. A dream is about the only place most of us are likely to run up against the typical glamour photographer's ideal of a lassie with legs eight feet long, bust 58 inches, waist 20, hips 20, and long, red-gold hair. Margie is a little closer to home . . . she looks like a good girl friend or a good young wife . . . she looks like the dream you not only want to go on dreaming but the one which might continue after you wake up."

LEFT: *Only one woman had bragging rights as the U.S. government's own pinup girl: Indiana's Margie Stewart. She appeared on propaganda posters, promoting everything from war bonds to security. Her poster-girl status later landed her a Hollywood contract.* *YANK* Magazine Photo

Stewart's posters led her to film work in Hollywood, where she landed more than fifteen uncredited roles. She played Marjorie Forrester in the 1944 movie, *Gildersleeve's Ghost*.

Pinups Turn the Tables on GIs

While GIs were busy ranking their favorite pinups, the starlets took a few polls of their own. According to the May 28, 1943, issue of *YANK*, 179 of 213 actresses surveyed at Warner Brothers reported that they would rather date an enlisted man than an officer any night of the week. Sergeants were the enlisted man of choice, with 89 votes. Privates followed with 31 nods, and corporals had 19.

Naturally, hundreds of GIs were more than willing to "volunteer" to date any of the gals willing to oblige. Some even actively pursued the starlets who had written them while they fought overseas. Soldiers, sailors, and airmen returned home looking to date or even marry their pinup pen pals, only to find that the young woman had other love interests and were only acting patriotically by sending them letters.

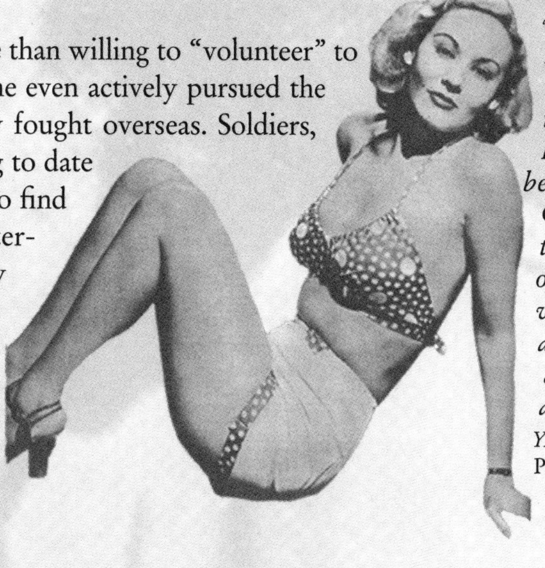

LEFT: *Pat Clark became an enlisted man's dream, but would have been his worst nightmare had he known the starlet's daddy was a major! All eyes might have been on the Warner Brothers' beauty, but the GIs certainly took a hands-off approach whenever the actress made a camp appearance.* *YANK* Magazine Photo

13. The Final Push Across the Rhine

"GERMANS ARE NOT BEATEN UNTIL THEY ARE DEAD OR IN THE PEN. THEY ARE MASTERS OF THE COUNTERATTACK. YOU DEAL THEM A MASSIVE BLOW, BREAK RIGHT THROUGH THEIR LINES AND BANG, THEY ARE SUDDENLY GETTING YOU BY THE THROAT. YOU COULD NEVER TAKE ANYTHING FOR GRANTED WITH THE GERMANS."

—Field Marshal Bernard L. Montgomery

OPPOSITE: *After capturing the German city of Ruhrberg, soldiers from the 2nd Ranger Battalion take a break and check their equipment, ready for the next skirmish, in March of '45.*
U.S. Army Photo

IN THE CLOSING MONTHS OF THE EUROPEAN CAMPAIGN, the Germans had to empty their high schools and raid veterans homes, literally mustering in anyone with a pulse . . . three generations of Nazi fighters with not much fight left in them.

The German replacements thrown into battle in late 1944 and early '45 could sense that Adolf Hitler's vision of a Thousand-Year Reich was in ruins. They had little desire to die for a lost cause. Life, even in a defeated Germany, certainly had a lot more appeal than the other option!

Mass surrenders became commonplace, and in many instances the only reason frontline soldiers continued to put up a halfway decent resistance was because positioned not too far behind them was a German officer holding a machine gun, with orders to fire on anyone attempting to flee or surrender. For the war-weary Wehrmacht soldier trapped between the advancing Allied forces and that rear guard officer with the twitchy trigger finger, it became a deadly game of pick your poison—hope the American taking aim from a hundred yards away was a lousy shot and didn't hit anything vital, or they could lay down their weapon, turn around, and experience the sudden horror of "friendly fire."

Still, the disintegrating Nazi army did have some viable combat-hardened units, with enough firepower and deadly resolve to ruin anyone's day.

With the rapid advance toward the German border, delayed only by clogged roads preventing fuel trucks from reaching the armor units chasing the Nazis into the Low Countries—Belgium, the Netherlands, and Luxembourg, collectively known as the Benelux—Allied forces remained on the offensive until they were ordered to halt and wait while their tanks gulped down hundreds of gallons of precious fuel.

The delay allowed the German forces to regroup and blunt the Allied initiative as it crossed into Belgium, near Mons. Still, the once-mighty Panzer tank divisions were no longer quite as fearsome as they had been rampaging across Poland or North Africa with Luftwaffe bombers and fighter planes screaming overhead, and so, after just a few days of resistance, twenty-five thousand of Germany's elite troops called it quits.

BELOW: *As more and more occupation troops poured into northern Europe, recreation centers and service clubs were set up, for after-hours relaxing and socializing. At an Army club in Belgium, wannabe singer Walt Goldberg gets his shot at "stardom" with his version of "Goodnight Ladies."*
Army Signal Corps Photo

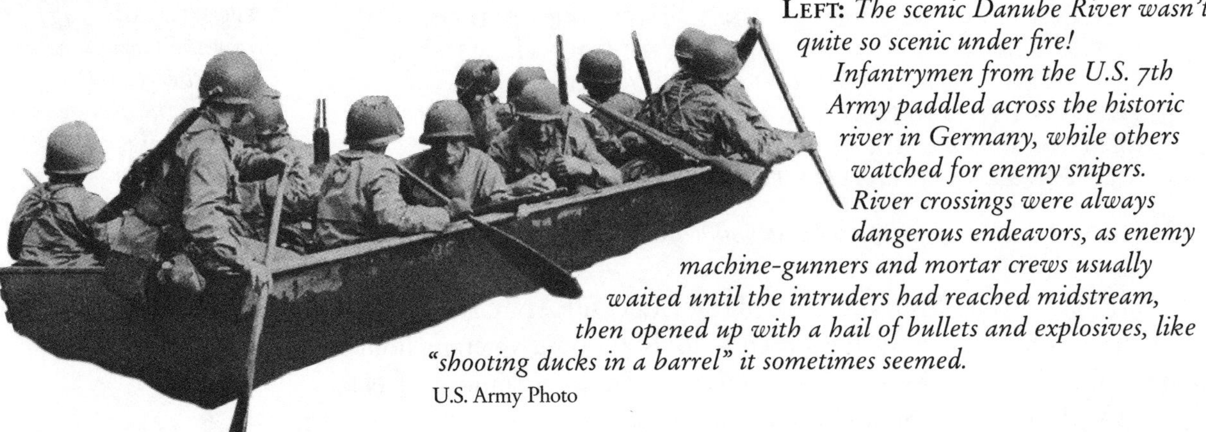

Left: *The scenic Danube River wasn't quite so scenic under fire! Infantrymen from the U.S. 7th Army paddled across the historic river in Germany, while others watched for enemy snipers. River crossings were always dangerous endeavors, as enemy machine-gunners and mortar crews usually waited until the intruders had reached midstream, then opened up with a hail of bullets and explosives, like "shooting ducks in a barrel" it sometimes seemed.*
U.S. Army Photo

Next stop on the Allied "tour" of northern Europe was the German border, breached on September 11 when a reconnaissance squadron of the 5th Armored Division crossed into the Rhineland-Palatinate, followed the next day by the First Army bounding beyond into Trier. But looming directly ahead was the imposing Siegfried Line, Hitler's West Wall, an interconnecting barrier of concrete and steel designed to hold off invading armies. At the same time, the Germans were still holding out in the Netherlands, and they would have to be dealt with and neutralized.

Paratroopers Go to Market

British and American forces had seemed to work together as an awesome cohesive fighting unit that steamrolled over the fragmented Nazi war machine in North Africa, Italy, and France, and now were on their way to doing the same in Northern Europe. Germany itself would be next after that. But in fact, despite their common mission to destroy the Nazis, the Yanks and the Limeys were rivals, competing for the spotlight, attempting to best the other at every opportunity.

For Operation Market Garden, thousands of Allied forces—including more than 16,000 British and American paratroopers—would participate in a daring mission to secure several key bridges being held by the Nazis in Holland. Those bridges were crucial to getting Allied armored and artillery units across canals and rivers so they could continue the push toward Berlin. The Nazis were ordered to hold on to those bridges for as long as possible and then destroy them before pulling back.

By dropping the airborne troops along a sixty-mile zone behind the lines, the Allies hoped they could surprise the Nazis and

Below: *The formula was very simple: If you could play an instrument better than anyone else in your section, then you'd likely get a solo; if you could do the soft shoe, then you might be featured in a dance number; and if you could also sing, you might get your own signature song, or at least team up with a few of the other guys for a barbershop quartet, plus one. For Tony Bennett, he only wanted to sing—solo, duet, chorus, didn't matter—wherever the band needed him, that's where he wanted to be. It was certainly better than anything he'd be doing with his old unit, as replacements for the guys up on the front lines.*
225th Regiment Band Photo

capture those bridges intact. Meanwhile, combined British infantry and armor units would race north toward Nijmegen and Arnhem and reinforce the airborne troops securing those river crossing points, then they would rush everything and everyone across before the Luftwaffe had an opportunity to launch an air strike on the bridges.

Actor Richard Todd was one of the British paratroopers who jumped at Normandy and later into Holland at Arnhem with the 6th Airborne. (He would later jump at Normandy again, for the movie *The Longest Day*.)

Former stage actor William Windom was an American paratrooper with the 508th Parachute Infantry Regiment—the Red Devils—who also participated in the D-Day invasion and jumped into Holland on September 17, then moved on to the Ardennes. (After the war he returned to the theater, on Broadway, and later achieved stardom in the movies and on television.)

The operation in Holland would take three days of mostly house-to-house street fighting. And though the Germans were able to hamper the Allied advance by blowing up train tracks and damaging roads, they could not level the bridges that Hitler had wanted destroyed. Soon Allied forces were "jumping the Rhine River," the last obstacle in their way to demolishing the Thousand-Year Reich.

LEFT: *It was a bold move, dubbed Operation Market Garden, involving paratroopers from the mighty 82nd and 101st Airborne divisions, assigned to drop behind enemy lines in Belgium and secure separate bridges that spanned vital rivers and canals, then hold them intact until ground forces could charge forward and dash across. Nazi garrisons were ordered to hang on to the bridges for as long as possible, then destroy them before pulling back. Though some aspects of the difficult operation failed, the American paratroopers achieved their objective, adding luster to an outstanding legacy.*
Imperial War Museum Photo

LEFT: *An infantryman who gets in the way of a tank is called a "crunchy!"—but for these soldiers from the 60th Infantry Regiment, the tank allowed them to move forward during street fighting in Belgium, in September of 1944.*
U.S. Army Photo

Right: *The perfect ingredients for a tearjerker movie . . . a lonely soldier, a cute kid, and a puppy. The only thing missing is a flirty young coquette looking for love and watching sadly as her brave hero has to go off and continue the fight for freedom! After the liberation of the Netherlands, the entire population—men, women, children . . . and even puppies—came out to say thanks to their American heroes.*
U.S. Army Photo

A Demoralizing Setback

The densely wooded Huertgen Forest was the setting for a stalemate that brought the Allied advance to a jarring halt and carried long into the winter. Those woods would become a killing ground, with no avenue for escape, no foxhole deep enough to protect the helpless, no prayer good enough to shelter the devout or those who had just found religion.

The Germans had set the trap months before, constructing an interlocking maze of bunkers and gun emplacements in the surrounding hillsides and taking up over-watch positions that could order and direct artillery and mortar fire wherever and whenever needed. What made the Huertgen so deadly though, was the damnable German munitions, which didn't always explode when they hit the ground but instead burst high in the trees, splintering them into wooden shards that cascaded onto the ill-protected American infantry soldiers, thousands of whom became impaled on this most primitive of weapons. It was as if the ancient armies of hell had gathered around the perimeter, watching fiendishly as the unsuspecting GIs

Right: *On Christmas Day of 1944, American soldiers of an anti-aircraft gun battery near Puffendorf in Germany watch the dogfight overhead between Allied and Nazi fighter planes.*
U.S. Army Photo

moved within range, walking right into the trap, then raining down spears and arrows and daggers, not forged from molten iron, but splintered from tall timber. The Huertgen Forest quickly became known as "the meatgrinder."

Only a few months earlier, the Americans were hopeful they might be home by Christmas. But now it was late 1944, with winter fast approaching, and they would soon endure the fiercest death toll and the harshest weather of the entire European conflict.

In early November of '44, the Americans countered with their own artillery and aerial bombardment. In fact, by mid-month, more than 4,500 bombing sorties were called in to drop 10,000 tons of explosives on the German lines, laying waste to the once majestic region. Still, by the New Year, the Allies measured their advance not by miles taken, but in yards and feet—and blood.

By February the Huertgen Campaign had finally turned in favor of the Americans, although 30,000 had been killed or wounded in the five months of carnage. Still, there was little time for celebration. The Germans had one more surprise in the works, at another densely wooded killing ground: the Ardennes Forest straddling the border of Germany and Luxembourg.

Left: *The P-51 Mustangs and the brash gunslingers who flew them had a feisty reputation as scrappers, challenging the Luftwaffe's best pilots and knocking the crap out of them. As its ranks were decimated, the Luftwaffe had to rely on new, untested pilots who had little stomach for mixing it up, especially when the widowmaker was always close by. In addition to strafing enemy convoys and rail shipments, repair docks and petrol terminals, the Mustangs, operating out of forward bases in France, also accompanied bombing missions deep within Germany, providing vital air cover to the vulnerable and slow B-17 and B-24 bombers flying out of England.*
Army Air Corps Photo

The Battle of the Bulge

Typically, tanks do not move surreptitiously anywhere. They announce their arrival like a thunderstorm rolling in, starting with a distant

Right: *If it weren't for them damn Panzer and Tiger tanks and German 88s making so much racket off in the distance, the Ardennes Forest might be a serene place for a picnic . . . but not in late 1944, when the Nazis launched a last-ditch offensive that eventually failed, but still cost the lives of hundreds of young American heroes.*
U.S. Army Photo

Right: *While pressing the attack, maneuver elements always have to cover their flanks to ensure the enemy can't find a gap and bust through, then wheel around and attack from the rear. During the Battle of the Bulge, desperate German ground forces attempted to drive a wedge through the Allied offensive and nearly succeeded, until reinforcements were rushed in to plug the opening. Here, ground patrols from the U.S. 1st and 3rd Armies link up near the Belgian village of Houffalize during the Bulge, one of the final campaigns for the splintered and once mighty German army.*
U.S. Army Photo

rumble that builds as the armored columns approach. They sputter and smoke and clank and squeak, and the ground trembles as if to warn all noncombatants to flee while they still can.

In the Ardennes region, the Germans set out to amass two full armies without detection, a seemingly impossible task, staging 200,000 soldiers and supporting Panzer tanks there for a major offensive, a last-gasp desperation move, to turn the tide back in their favor. First, the roads leading into the Ardennes were covered with straw; then, the dwindling number of Luftwaffe planes in the region were sent in on low, ground-hugging strafing runs near the Allied lines to mask the movement of the Panzer tanks and heavy field guns rumbling in at night. By dawn each day, those behemoths would be hunkered down, melting into the underbrush before spotter planes picked them up. The Nazis also curtailed all vital radio communications in the region, knowing their messages could be intercepted, instead using field telephones that required the laying down of miles and miles of cable. They did continue with innocuous radio traffic and propaganda messages to badger and threaten the Allied forces listening in, but they gave no hint of the buildup in the Ardennes.

By mid-December the Nazis were ready to unleash hell against the 83,000 American combatants dispatched along the skirmish line, from Monschau in Germany to Echternach in Luxembourg. The Germans were fully aware of the consequences if this gambit failed; they gave it the lyrical-sounding name, Operation Autumn Mist. Before the sun rose on December

16, two thousand field guns roared to life all along the sixty-mile front. Hundreds of GIs didn't survive the early morning wake-up call. Those American soldiers who weren't obliterated in the opening volley felt the earth erupt all around them. Attempting to dig their foxholes even deeper, but with the ground frozen rock hard with six inches of snow on top, all they could do was pray—not that God had any say as to whose prayers were granted and who was simply SOL that morning.

LEFT: *Directional firing is coordinated by forward observers and a command post issuing grid locations, ensuring that all available weapons—such as this lone 81-mm mortar and heavier artillery pieces—deliver the necessary firepower to the specific target, to make the biggest "impression" on the enemy, in this instance in the dense forest region of Belgium.*
U.S. Army Photo

When the shelling finally stopped, the beaten and bloodied American soldiers poked their head out from the carnage, and checked all their appendages to make sure everything was still attached, and looked around to see who else was still around. But they also braced for the second act. Almost immediately, 200,000 German troops attacked the front, busted through the Allied lines, and drove a wedge aimed at retaking the port city of Antwerp.

The German offensive, led by the Fifth Panzer Army, surrounded the U.S. 28th Division after it fell back and regrouped at Bastogne. Though outnumbered five to one, the Americans—dubbed the Battling Bastards of Bastogne—held on for six days until the 101st Airborne and 10th Armored Divisions could be thrown into the region and a bust-out could be coordinated. To the south, the American 4th Armored and 5th Infantry Divisions were dispatched forward to bolster the American lines.

On Christmas Day the tanks of Germany's 2nd Panzer Division suffered the same problem the American armor units had experienced earlier—lack of fuel to continue the offensive. Less than four miles from the Meuse River, the Panzers became sitting ducks for their counterparts from the U.S. 2nd Armored Division, who were closing in for the kill. Other German units also had to cut off their forward thrust because of lack of fuel.

Among the many American troops caught in the Battle of the Bulge was Mel Kaminsky, a combat engineer charged with the extremely dangerous and deliberate task

LEFT: *"Holy Mary, Mother of God, please watch over me till I get to the other side of this damned pissant river!"*

Another version, for these apprehensive American soldiers attempting to get to the far side of the Moselle near Dornot in September of 1944, might have been, "Holy Mary, Mother of God . . . I promise I'll start going to church as soon as I get back home, if you'll just grant me this one request . . . "
U.S. Army Photo

of clearing mines ahead of the American advance. His unit also constructed portable bridges, often under fire. He would later quip in a February 17, 1975, *Newsweek* article about his WWII experiences, "I was out in the combat engineers. We would throw up bridges in advance of the infantry, but mainly we would just throw up." When the Germans broadcast music sprinkled with propaganda directed at the Americans, urging them to surrender, Kaminsky mockingly sang, "Toot Toot Tootsie, Good-bye" for his fellow GIs. (In later years he would create a black comedy film, *The Producers*, about cash-strapped Broadway hucksters who develop the heavily insured musical "Springtime for Hitler" that is sure to bomb, so they can collect on the policy. By then Kaminsky was better known as comedian Mel Brooks.)

Another combat engineer who wasn't quite so lucky was Dale Robertson. He was wounded in Germany, but he refused to be sent to the rear. (He would later be hospitalized at Fort Bragg in North Carolina. After his wounds had healed, he decided to give acting a try and headed for Hollywood.)

Charles Durning had survived the D-Day landings and was nearly killed when his unit advanced toward the Benelux countries. "'I was crossing a field somewhere in Belgium. A German soldier ran toward me carrying a bayonet. He couldn't have been more than 14 or 15. Even though he was coming at me, I couldn't shoot,'" Durning was quoted in *Stars in Khaki*, by James E. Wise Jr. and Paul Wilderson III. "Durning was stabbed eight times in the arm, right shoulder, and back and was hospitalized. He was released in time to take part in the Battle of the Bulge." There his unit would be ambushed at the Ardennes, and he was wounded again and briefly taken prisoner. (After the war and he was discharged, Durning enrolled at New York's Academy of Dramatic Arts and found success on stage and in the movies.)

Anthony Benedetto was one of the replacement troops assigned to the 63rd Infantry Division and rushed to the front. "The winter months were rough. Snow covered the ground and the front was a front-row seat in hell," he would recall later in *The Good Life*, cowritten with Will Friedwald. "It

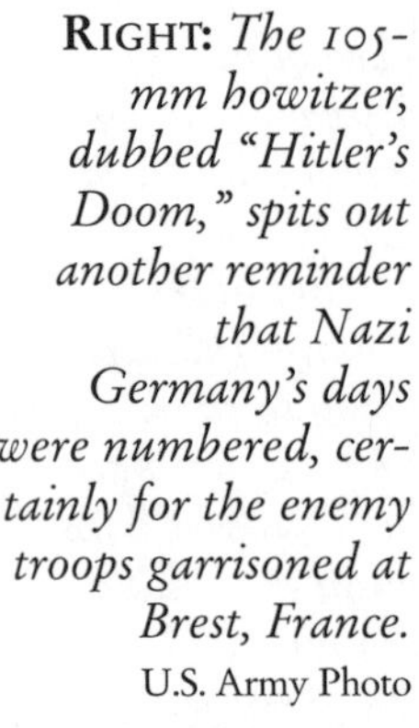

Right: *The 105-mm howitzer, dubbed "Hitler's Doom," spits out another reminder that Nazi Germany's days were numbered, certainly for the enemy troops garrisoned at Brest, France.*
U.S. Army Photo

was an absolutely terrifying spectacle: air battles raging above me, with the roar of the airplane engines and the swirling sound of bombs; and artillery battles all around me, with shells bursting everywhere. I watched as my buddies died right before my eyes. What we were most afraid of were the 88-mm cannons that the Germans used. Those 88s would come whistling right down on us. What a nightmare. Shrapnel flew and hot metal strafed anyone in its path. Nighttime was the worst. We couldn't light any fires to keep warm; we couldn't even light a cigarette, because the glow would be detected by the Germans and give away our position."

Dave Brubeck was deployed to Europe with one of the replacement units that arrived shortly after D-Day. But while his unit was gearing up for the northern Europe campaign, a Red Cross show was performing in the area and needed a pianist to fill in. Brubeck volunteered, and when that stint was over, while his former unit was in the thick of the fighting at the Battle of the Bulge, he was tasked with forming his own jazz band from within the Army ranks. He pulled together the best he could find and they became known as the Wolf Pack Band, one of the Army's first integrated units.

Another soldier who was rushed into the fight near the end of the European Campaign was Italian American Mario Puzo, who would advance with his unit into Germany. (Like many veterans, he later used his GI Bill benefits to go to school, at City College in New York. Ten years after the war he wrote about his experiences as a GI in Germany in *The Fortunate Pilgrim,* which he followed with the classic Mafia saga, *The Godfather.*)

Simultaneously, the Germans attempted diversionary attacks in northeastern France and the Alsace border region, but without the firepower of their Panzer tanks or the air cover from the

LEFT: *The Nazis hadn't yet officially called it quits, but by early 1945 it was very evident the end was fast approaching. Bing Crosby and the Andrews Sisters teamed up to record the well-timed ditty "There'll be a Hot Time in the Town of Berlin," and just as it was climbing the charts and hitting the airwaves, Adolf Hitler checked out, the Russians checked in to Berlin, and the entire western hemisphere—except for the Nazis, of course—finally had something good to celebrate.*

National Archives Photo

RIGHT: *As American and British forces carried most of the burden from the West, Russian troops squeezed in from the East, constricting the Nazis. Many surrendered en masse, with remnants retreating back toward Berlin. At the Elbe River, in April of '45, American and Russian elements linked up and celebrated with hugs and handshakes.*

Army Signal Corps Photo

Luftwaffe, they had little punching power, and the American forces repelled them. Thousands of German soldiers surrendered. By the final week of January, the Allies were ready to continue the final offensive, stampeding across Germany itself to seize Berlin.

Red Army troops were also gaining momentum from the east and, after hearing about the Nazi atrocities done to innocent Russian women and children, they were not in any mood to take any Wehrmacht soldiers as prisoners. German soldiers who had mentally called it quits made every effort to surrender to the Americans rather than face the vengeful Russians. Still, there was plenty of fight remaining all along the front lines as American, British, Canadian, and Russian forces converged from practically all directions.

During heavy small-arms fire along the lines near the Weser River, Sergeant Neville Brand was wounded in the arm but could not be treated because it was too dangerous for a medic to rush to his aid. He was bleeding to death yet could do nothing but wait out the attack. (After being evacuated to a military hospital, Brand was patched up and was discharged in October of '45. He used his GI Bill to study acting and was soon appearing in movies and on television.)

Hitler ordered the destruction of all the Rhine River bridges, but most of his combat units were disintegrating rapidly and his soldiers were more interested in surviving the war than in following orders.

There were still thousands of diehard Nazi combatants who continued to fight for the Fatherland. They fled into various mountain redoubts—including the Harz and Eifel mountains—to fight as partisans. The Allies would neutralize these pockets of resistance during the spring of '45, more token fighting than anything of substance.

BELOW: *It was a long time coming, but once Nazi leaders signed the surrender documents and agreed to all of the penalties, restrictions, and reparations, General Dwight D. Eisenhower, the supreme commander of Allied Forces Europe, announced the end of hostilities. With Ike at Reims, France, for the surrender ceremony was British Air Chief Marshal Sir Arthur Tedder, his deputy.*
U.S. Army Photo

Hitler Takes an Easy Out

Benito Mussolini and his mistress met with a humiliating end in Italy, their beaten and lifeless bodies strung up and put on display for the entire world to rejoice over their demise. Adolf Hitler, living out his final days in his bunker in Berlin, could see that the end was near, and as Russian troops closed in, the Führer decided he would not suffer a similar fate. On April 30 he and mistress (and very brief wife) Eva Braun committed suicide; then their bodies were burned outside the bunker, amidst the rubble and ruin of a grand and glorious city that had once been the crown jewel of Europe.

Hitler was dead, and Nazi Germany's Thousand-Year Reich was both a sham and in shambles. Its legacy in German history would be a black mark, denounced by the entire world for decades to come.

Treasures Lost

Every bit of war news coming out of Europe sent a thunderbolt of electricity through Hollywood's foreign colonies, those clusters of refugees who had fled the Nazi crackdowns, who still had family and friends and associates that had remained behind, who now heard and read about the destruction of so many of Europe's great cities and the near-elimination of their cultural treasures—not only the pillaging of known masterpieces but also the persecution, the silencing of the artists who created them.

One by one, the Allied forces liberated the countries of Europe. It would take years for them to rebuild the great theaters and opera houses, museums and art galleries, some painstakingly brick by brick, but it would never be the same as before. It could never be as it was, for the Nazis had stripped every country of its cultural heritage and smeared it with a black ugly stain. Some of the refugee artists returned to their homelands to rebuild and be part of the next cultural revolution. Others found it too heartbreaking to see the changes that war had caused, none of them for the better.

As a young girl Audrey Hepburn was one of those artists, a ballet dancer, who survived four years under Nazi occupation in Arnhem, Holland. She witnessed her uncle being executed by the Nazis for his involvement with the Dutch underground, and she recalled it and other horrors of war years later. "We saw young men put against the wall and shot. Don't discount anything awful you hear or read about the Nazis. It's worse than you could ever imagine."

The star pupil of the Arnhem School of Music, young Audrey was rarely allowed to dance in public during the war years, but she continued to do "blackout recitals" in secret locations. By March of 1945 she had to remain in hiding, because the Nazis were rounding up all able-bodied women and girls for labor. On Hepburn's sixteenth birthday, May 4, Allied troops liberated Arnhem. "We whooped and hollered and danced for joy," she recalled. "I wanted to kiss every one of them. The incredible relief of being free, it's something that's very hard to verbalize. Freedom is more like

LEFT: *Singer Frances Day toured northern Europe with comedian Will Hay, and toward the end of the war, she paid tribute to the sacrifices of Allied forces and encouraged the audience to join in, shown here presenting a toast during her show in Brussels.* Imperial War Museum Photo

LEFT: *World War II truly was a "world" war involving numerous countries—as combatants, as victims, as conquerors. These West Indian servicemen and -women were invited to speak to the citizens of their home country, over the BBC radio network. (At that time, the West Indies was a member of the British Empire.)* Imperial War Museum Photo

something in the air. For me, it was hearing soldiers speaking English instead of German."

That taste of freedom Audrey Hepburn experienced, finally, was felt all across northern Europe as the Nazi occupiers were driven out, driven back.

The saying "To the victor go the spoils" was never more true than after the Russians were allowed to seize Berlin. They quickly located the command bunker that had protected Hitler, Joseph Goebbels, and other select Nazi leaders as the city was being bombed and slowly choked to death. Among the many personal items seized by the Russians was Goebbels's extensive film collection, including popular American flicks starring Clark Gable, Spencer Tracy, John Wayne, Charlie Chaplin, and of course, the many Hollywood beauties, such as Betty Grable and Rita Hayworth. The Russians sent these movies back to the Great Kremlin Palace for their country's biggest movie buff: Josef Stalin himself.

A Bittersweet Journey

Using England as a jumping-off point, hundreds of entertainers ventured to northern Europe. Some wanted to see "the old country" their parents remembered fondly. Many wanted to see firsthand the joy of life that had always been Europe—the gaiety of gay Paree, the naughtiness of Amsterdam, the festive debauchery of Munich's Oktoberfest.

What they found was a continent staggered by war, cities like Warsaw and Cologne and Berlin reduced to rubble, millions left homeless, scavenging for anything edible, salvaging whatever they could use for temporary shelter. Attempts were certainly made to bring back the performing arts, to bolster

Below: *A year earlier he was one of the top movie stars in Hollywood, teaming up with Elizabeth Taylor and Judy Garland, churning out another Andy Hardy flick. But in April of 1945, he was PFC Mickey Rooney, song-and-dance man for the Army, impersonator of Jimmy Cagney and Clark Gable, to name just two. Army Special Services put together three-man jeep shows that hit the road and stopped whenever they came across American soldiers.*
U.S. Army Photo

morale among the beleaguered citizenry. Cities took their radio stations back from the Nazis and, with the help of Allied communications personnel, plus equipment from U.S. Army Signal and Special Services units and others, were back on the air with news and music, traditional favorites, and current releases from England and the United States.

Entertainers also fanned out across the country to perform for the troops. Mickey Rooney made the trip while the Allies were still making their advance into the Rhineland. "We put on our first show between two Sherman tanks in a Belgian snowstorm, with sixty guys in the audience, three miles from the front, with the sound of howitzers booming in the distance," he recalled in his book, *Life Is Too Short*. "Before we crossed the Rhine, we did about seven shows in one evening, and finished our last show about 3:15 in the morning. Then our guys went off to fight the battle of Remagen about 4:10. At 5:45, I saw many of the men we'd entertained being brought back in, on stretchers, dead or dying."

In show business, timing is everything, and early indications were that Red Buttons was cursed. In mid-1941 he was a burlesque comedian cast for the Broadway show, *The Admiral Had a Wife*, a comical farce set in Hawaii—at Pearl Harbor, specifically—due to open on December 8. Unfortunately, with the real attack on Pearl the previous day, and war declared on December 8, *The Admiral* was sunk before it was even christened. (The unlucky Buttons also happened to be performing at New York's Minsky's burlesque theater the night it was raided.) At the end of WWII, Buttons was sent to Europe with Army Special Services and even teamed up with Mickey Rooney for special shows. Buttons also performed at the Potsdam Conference for President Harry Truman, British Prime Minister Winston Churchill, and Soviet leader Josef Stalin. (After returning to Broadway, Buttons became an immensely popular comedian and actor, performing on stage, television, and in movies, winning a Best Supporting Actor award for *Sayonara* in 1958.)

Army Sergeant Eugene List was a classically trained pianist who was given the honor of performing for the Big Three at Potsdam in an after-dinner concert. "Pianist List angled most of his program for Stalin; some Tchaikovsky, three Shostakovich preludes, folk songs of the Volga, the Caucausus, and the steppes," reported *Time* magazine in its July 30, 1945, issue. "Stalin sprang up, shook List's hand, drank a toast to him, and asked for more."

Anthony Benedetto had already seen action at the Battle of the Bulge and crossed the Rhine River into Germany, but after seeing a USO show with Bob Hope and Jane Russell, sidekick Jerry Colonna, and Les Brown's Band of Renown, he was determined to find a different line of work. "I was in the stands enthralled. It was the greatest thing that ever happened to me. Bob was just fantastic and all the GIs loved him so much for boosting our dismally low morale . . . at that moment he made me realize that the greatest gift you can give anybody is a laugh or a song," Benedetto recalled in his book, *The Good Life*.

With the war in Europe over, some GIs had enough points to go home, but thousands more prepared for redeployment to the Pacific Theater. Benedetto would remain on occupation duty and was assigned to Special Services. "Before the actual surrender there had been a general call put out that anyone who could entertain—guys who sang, danced, played instruments, did imitations or comedy, anything—should report to Special Services. The way I found out about it was pretty funny; I was singing in the shower, and a passing officer heard me. He said to me, 'You've got a great voice. You should get into this band they're forming.'"

Also among the Special Services soldiers in Europe were screenwriter Alan Campbell, Broadway director Joshua Logan, and future movie director Arthur Penn. Benedetto became librarian for the newly formed 314th Special Services Band, put together by Warrant Officer Harold "Lin" Arison, a career Army musician and band director.

"It had been Lin's dream to put together a new band with new music that was on par with what was happening back in the States, a first-class American pop-jazz orchestra," continued Benedetto in *The Good Life*. "Our duty was to do a weekly broadcast of a show called *It's All Yours* over the Armed Forces Network, the title being our gift to American GIs stationed in Germany and to our former enemies as well."

Benedetto ended up singing one or two numbers on each show, crafting his song styling and stage presence. (After the war, there was no doubt he would spend his life in show business. He used his GI Bill benefits to enroll at the American Theater Wing and was "discovered" on the television show, *Arthur Godfrey's Talent Scouts*, placing second to a young female singer, Rosemary Clooney. The two became lifelong friends, though he would be known forever after as Tony Bennett.)

Forgive and Forget? Never!

Hollywood director Billy Wilder was one of the European Jews who had fled the Nazi occupation to continue his screenwriting and filmmaking career in the United States. Remaining in his beloved Austria would have certainly led to deportation to a Nazi concentration camp. (He found out later that his mother, stepfather, and grandmother had all been sent to the Auschwitz death camp, where they perished.) At the end of the war, Wilder was asked to join the Army's Psychological Warfare Division, to return to Germany and help rebuild its entertainment communities.

The one stipulation was that no Nazis would be allowed to have any involvement with German film projects or theatrical productions.

Left: *Future Hollywood movie director Billy Wilder had fled Nazi-occupied Europe because his livelihood as a writer was threatened. Like hundreds of others he made his way to Tinsel Town, learned to speak and write English fluently, then began a prolific and stellar career as one of movie history's greatest directors.*

Near the end of the war, Wilder was asked to return to Europe and oversee the restoration of Germany's cinematic community, barring anyone with Nazi ties. It was a bittersweet task for Wilder, who learned that some of his family members, including his mother, perished at Auschwitz death camp in Poland.

Associated Press Photo

"Wilder was perfect for the job, since he had kept abreast of the bleak changes in his once beloved German film industry and could easily identify people like actor Werner Krauss, who specialized in grotesque Jewish stereotypes in such films as *Jud Suss*," wrote Kevin Lally in *Wilder Times*. Wilder screened hundreds of actors and actresses, writers and directors, technicians and craftsmen, weeding out those with Nazi ties.

For many years, one of the most revered theatrical events in all of Europe was the Passion Play at Oberammergau, which reenacted the final days in the life of Jesus, including the crucifixion. Wilder permitted the event to be performed again, and when he was asked if a renowned German actor, Anton Lang, could reprise the role of Jesus Christ, Wilder said yes, but with one stipulation: The actor, known to have been a member of the Nazi SS during the war, would be allowed to participate only if he was "nailed" to the cross—with real nails!

The Final Days, on Film

Prophetically, in 1944 the Nazis gave the go-ahead for *Kolberg*, a movie portrayal of a dark day in German history. "The film was designed to prepare the entire population to fight to the last man, woman, and child. It was based on the heroic defense of Kolberg by its citizens against the armies of Napoleon in 1807," wrote Jeffrey Richards in *Movies of the Forties*. "By the time the film was available for release in January 1945, almost all the cinemas in Germany were closed. Virtually the only people who saw the film were the garrison of La Rochelle, then completely surrounded by the Allies. A print of the film was dropped by parachute to encourage them in their resistance; they surrendered."

Immediately after the Nazis surrendered, Billy Wilder had the difficult task of convincing the German masses that the Nazi regime truly was evil and had, most notably, formulated the Final Solution to eliminate the Jews and other "undesirables" from Germany and all other occupied lands.

He was given a documentary of the Allied liberation of the concentration camps (and all the horrors discovered there), shot by cinematographers from

RIGHT: *After hearing the news that the Nazis had surrendered, American and British servicemen in London, along with the entire populace, had plenty to celebrate and spent at least the next week doing it. That euphoria quickly spread across Europe.*
Imperial War Museum Photo

the Army's Psychological Warfare Division, along with seized Nazi propaganda footage of massive party rallies and parades, plus those that showed Jewish prisoners being loaded onto railcars, arriving at the various concentration camps, being lined up and shot, standing outside the gas chambers, digging their own graves, and on and on. The Nazis had been meticulous in documenting everything, and now that footage would be turned against them by Wilder, who whittled it all down to a thirty-minute short documentary titled *Todesmühlen* (*Death Mills*).

The film was narrated by noted professor Oskar Seidlin, who spoke for the many who had stood by and done nothing: "They had to die because of the willingness of the German people to follow criminals and madmen, without resistance. At the Party rally at Nuremberg, I shouted, 'Heil!' And then one day when the Gestapo fetched my neighbor, I looked the other way: 'This is not my business.' Do you remember 1933? 1936? 1939? I was there. What have I done to prevent it?"

The finished documentary was screened in Wurzburg and then again in Frankfurt, initially to disbelieving audiences, who reacted with quiet resignation. By early 1946 the film was shown widely in the American zone of occupation.

In his role with the Psychological Warfare Division, Wilder had traveled throughout occupied Germany, meeting hundreds of people, from city officials to lone citizens. To him, a former Jewish refugee, the hypocrisy was everywhere—knowing the fate of his own family, seeing the reels of footage of zealous Nazi followers, the overwhelming support by the masses, from little children to WWI veterans shouting 'Heil Hitler'—and yet, as soon as the war ended, all those Nazi officials and supporters had disappeared.

"I never met a single Nazi. Everyone was a victim, everyone had been a resistance fighter," Wilder recalled in his book, *Wilder Times*, with Kevin Lally. But Wilder knew what everyone else seemed to want to deny, what they wanted to ignore, what they conveniently tried to forget. He would not let them forget.

The Defiant and Unstoppable Marlene

"At work Dietrich was like a soldier. Splendidly disciplined. During the war she was right in the very front line with the ordinary GIs. In Paris I once asked her: 'Tell the truth, Marlene, have you slept with Eisenhower?' She replied: 'How could I? He was never that close to the front line!'"

—*Hollywood director Billy Wilder*

IN BERLIN SHE WAS AN AVANT-GARDE MOVIE STAR, PROvocative, sultry, and mysterious. During the filming of *The Blue Angel*, Paramount Studios in Hollywood offered Marlene Dietrich a seven-year contract, but she declined, not wanting to be tied down to one studio for so long a time and so far from home. Paramount sent a revision to the contract stating she could return to Germany as long as she didn't sign with any other studio. She accepted.

"I set out for America confident that I could return to Germany whenever I pleased," she wrote later in *Marlene*. "I fought for this right not knowing that a powerful, ominous force would be leading my homeland to its ruin and that all my plans would come to nothing."

That "powerful, ominous force" was Adolf Hitler and his National Socialist Party—the Nazis. In 1935 Hitler "invited" Dietrich to return to the Fatherland and resume making films for her country. Instead, she renounced her citizenship and applied to become a U.S. citizen. This infuriated Hitler, and he ordered all of her films banned in Germany. "To give up your homeland and mother tongue, even when forced to by circumstance, is an almost unendurable ordeal," she continued in *Marlene*. (A few years later she did reconsider the Nazi offer to return home, but there was a catch: "She would boast that she had offered to meet Herr Hitler, either to convince him to surrender or to

Background: *At the front, Marlene Dietrich had to grab sleep wherever she could find it—sometimes in the back of a jeep, or in a foxhole, maybe in a crowded tent with a bunch of snoring soldiers. Rarely did she find anywhere approaching the luxury she enjoyed in Hollywood. During a USO tour in northern Europe, she chatted with members of the Women's Army Corps in France, ladies who were more than happy to share their meager accommodations with such a worldly celebrity.*
National Archives Photo

Left: *German-born actress Marlene Dietrich could have been queen of the cinema in her native country, but instead she turned her back on the Nazis, became an American citizen, then toured perilously close to the war front. She feared being captured by the Nazis and humiliated in public, but that didn't stop her from traveling to wherever the boys were.*
Imperial War Museum Photo

Right: *Her signature song was "Lili Marlene," adapted from a poem written by a German sentry during WWI. The song and its many variations became popular with both German and Allied soldiers.*
National Archives Photo

shoot him: 'I am the only person in the world who wouldn't have been searched,'" she stated in *The Girls*, by Diana McLellan. "She had debated calling Hitler directly on the telephone, telling him that she would come and visit him, and then killing him when she got there.")

In addition to her tireless efforts to raise money on bond drives, Dietrich also volunteered to go overseas to entertain the troops, to North Africa, France, northern Europe, and back to her renounced homeland of Germany, even though the Nazis had offered a bounty for her capture.

"She believed that if the Germans took her prisoner, she would be shaved, stoned, and dragged through the streets as a traitor," wrote McLellan in *The Girls*. None of that stopped her from performing perilously close to the front, almost daring the Nazis to come after her.

Ironically, the one song that was beloved by both the Axis and Allied soldiers—"Lili Marlene"—became her signature song as well. By the time she made it to northern Europe, suffering from frostbite, she had altered the lyrics to fit the situation she shared with "the boys," singing it in her performances on stage and on Armed Forces Radio, broadcast to the Allies and to the German masses, announcing her return to Europe:

"When we are marching in the mud and cold,
And when my pack seems more than I can hold,
My love for you renews my might,
I'm warm again, my pack is light . . .
It's you Lili Marlene, it's you Lili Marlene."

V-Discs Bring Harmony to Cacophony of War

"You aren't going to win the war with piccolos."

—*Colonel Theodore Banks*

"This is Captain Glenn Miller, speaking for the Army Air Force Training Command Orchestra, and we hope that you soldiers of the Allied Forces enjoy these V-discs that we're making just for you."

—*Glenn Miller, introducing "Stardust" on V-Disc 65*

JAMES SNATCHED SMALL PIECES OF MEAT FROM HIS PLATE, sopping up the beans and chewing in silence. The wind moaned and caused the door flaps of the mess tent to pop and smack. He was lost in his thoughts, too tired to chew, let alone talk to his buddy, Thomas, standing inches away. And what would he say, anyway, he wondered. He wiped his hands on his field jacket, which was rumpled and rife with mud and sweat, despite the cold temperatures. And then there was the blood. Always the blood. Today it was another man's and not his own, although he feared someday that might not be the case. The ferocious fighting in France had lasted all month, and James's 1st Army Division suffered heavy casualties at the hands of howitzers and German rocket launchers. Nobody really cared that Christmas was only days away. The mood in camp was gloom and doom, not holly and jolly. The day Allied forces would defeat the Germans marked the only holiday GIs could care about.

Background: *Not every recording for V-Disc was musical, although in the case of comedians Bud Abbott and Lou Costello, the cut was certainly lyrical. The duo recorded their famous "Who's on First?" routine for servicemen, teaming up with Brooklyn Dodgers organist Gladys Gooding on the performance for a true at-the-ballpark flavor. The two performed in this photo for soldiers and sailors at New York's Stage Door Canteen in 1942.*
Associated Press Photo

Right: *GI-favorite Bob Hope and actress Jane Russell appeared on* Command Performance *together in 1944. Because entertainers and production crews volunteered their time, studios and record labels ignored contracts, permitting acts to work together at will. It was a part of the industries' efforts to support the war by boosting troop morale. Whenever a top-name act appeared, a military recording engineer was there to capture the moment for V-Discs.*
Armed Forces Radio Services Photo

His eyes held the same hollowness and shared the same despair most men in the unit felt. All fall, with Allied troops closing in on the Germans at every turn and word that Italy had been liberated, the men thought they'd be back in the States with their families for the holidays. But not this December. As the clouds masked the moon, James knew his fighting was not yet finished.

"Silent night,
Holy night.
All is calm, all is bright.
'Round yon virgin, mother and child.
Holy infant so tender and mild.
Sleep in heavenly peace,
Sleep in heavenly peace."

—*"Silent Night," lyrics written in German by Joseph Mohr, music by Franz Gruber, 1818; Army V-Disc 441-A, Navy V-Disc 221-A*

Bing Crosby's crooning over the loudspeaker could not have contrasted the mood in the mess tent more starkly. Even the scratchy sounds from the hand-cranked Victrola couldn't diminish the singer's smoothness. The night really was silent, too dark to shoot any more rounds at the enemy. But it was far from calm and bright. Still, the words and melody of the Christmas classic rang through the camp as a reminder that life beyond the Ardennes Forest was peaceful and normal—or as peaceful and normal as life could be in these times.

James tried to finish his dinner, which by now was cold. The camp food didn't really have much flavor anyway, even when it was hot. And after days of C-rations out on the front lines, he'd grown used to swallowing without savoring. The beef—he guessed that's what it was, although the greenish tinge made it hard to tell—reminded him of a Fats Waller song the REMFs were listening to as he had dragged himself back to camp earlier that day:

"All that meat and no potatoes
Just ain't right, like green tomatoes
Yes, I'm steamin'. I'm really screamin'.
All that meat and no potatoes."

—*"All That Meat and No Potatoes," lyrics by Ed Kirkeby, music by Thomas "Fats" Waller, 1941*

He really shouldn't complain about the food. At least it wasn't frozen, and he hadn't even had to put it next to his torso to warm it up with body heat. Sure, the gravy over the lima beans was lumpy like pudding. But tonight he had lukewarm food, would sleep in a cot instead of a foxhole, and

LEFT: *Soldiers back at mess during the fighting in the Argonne greedily cleaned their plates. Yet even weary, starving soldiers appreciated the ambiance a little music provided. V-Discs were a popular addition—almost like mom's apple pie—to any meal. Here, PFCs William G. Curtis and Donald R. Stratton enjoyed their Thanksgiving Day dinner with the 102nd Infantry Division in 1944.*
Soldiers Magazine Photo

had clean clothes to wear back to the front tomorrow. His night wasn't nearly as bad as the one his buddies out on the line were enduring. And tomorrow night—if he made it—he'd be back in the cold, burrowed beneath the earth's surface, too afraid to sleep.

James dropped his plate and fork into the washtub and walked out of the tent behind Thomas. The Crosby tune had turned him more melancholy than he'd been in weeks, but at the same time filled him with happy memories of Christmases past. Hard to believe one song could do that, he mused.

As the two made their way to cold cots, Bing's baritone rang out over the camp's loudspeaker:

"I'll be home for Christmas
You can count on me
Please have snow and mistletoe
And presents on the tree.
Christmas Eve will find me
Where the lovelight gleams.
I'll be home for Christmas
If only in my dreams."

—"I'll Be Home for Christmas," lyrics and music by Kim Gannon, Walter Kent, and Buck Ram, 1943; Army V-Disc 441-B, Navy V-Disc 221-B

Yes, only in his dreams. And what a holiday James could envision. Snow, with a warm, crackling fire. A wool sweater, not a scratchy uniform covered in dirt and stench and musty, itchy long johns. Laughter, not labored cries. Hot ham and roast beef, not mystery meat and burned beans. Peace. Sweet peace.

Right: *Soldiers crammed every show Bing Crosby held, such as this one in England. Many claimed that in the 1930s and '40s, the smooth baritone was the most popular living American, wrote Gary Giddins in a January 28, 2001, article in* The New York Times. *Crosby's radio show hit 50 million listeners at its wartime peak, according to Giddins, and his near-400 hit singles are unmatched by any performer in any genre. U.S. servicemen named him "the man who had done most for Army morale," in addition to making his "White Christmas" the most requested song for V-Discs. Giddins also wrote that enlisted men did not like Frank Sinatra, whom they viewed as a seducer and a draft dodger. When men returned home from the war, Crosby's popularity skyrocketed, the article claimed, completely overshadowing Sinatra.*
National Archives Photo

> "Hello men. This is Donald Mills. My brothers and I are here in the studio making a few V-Discs for all of you. And we want you to know that we sure hope you have as much fun listening to them as we have in making them for you. Good luck to all of you."
>
> — *Introduction to "You Tell Me Your Dream," V-Disc 452, Navy V-Disc 232*

James fell asleep on the cot next to Thomas's, his head filled with visions of Christmas and the Mills Brothers' tune:

> "I had a dream, dear.
> You had one, too.
> Mine was the best dream
> Because it was of you.
> Come, sweetheart, tell me
> Now is the time.
> You tell me your dream
> And I'll tell you mine."
>
> — *"You Tell Me Your Dream, I'll Tell You Mine," lyrics and music by Charles N. Daniels, Jay Blackton, A. H. Brown, and Seymour Rice, 1908*

Music Lifts Troop Morale

Captain Howard Bronson understood how popular music could lift troops' morale, and as part of the Army's Recreation and Welfare Section, he petitioned

LEFT: *Despite being on the battlefield, soldiers often listened to radio shows over Armed Forces Radio. Programs like* Command Performance *allowed soldiers to send in requests to hear a particular singer, a certain song, or even a "sound" from home. Performers quickly participated in the 30-minute weekly show once they knew a GI had asked for them. Many of these performances were taped for use on V-Discs.*
Archives Idees et Editions

for regular shipments of music to the front lines. He had played with John Philip Sousa's marching band and knew music's significant role during troubled times. According to the Record Collectors Guild, Bronson believed music would lift soldiers' and sailors' spirits and allow them to forget—even momentarily—the rigors of daily life in the war.

But getting music to the troops was not as easy as it seemed, for two reasons. First, the American Federation of Musicians had gone on strike in 1942, and no newly recorded music was available. Old music was nice, but troops really wanted to hear new sounds from home. Second, 80 percent of the shellac 78-rpm records that families and friends sent their favorite servicemen arrived as jigsaw puzzles, because the records could not withstand the package mishandling and harsh conditions. The entertainment troops received through the Armed Forces Radio Service was mostly radio programs that had commercials edited out of the recording.

Making Music, Working Out the "Bugs"

Lieutenant George Robert Vincent, a World War I veteran and sound engineer who designed photograph improvements with Thomas Edison, helped develop ways around both problems that kept new music from the troops. As a member of the Army Special Services division, he met with Bronson to get his approval for a new recording project. Although Vincent received Washington, D.C.'s, approval for the plan in July 1943, he was given no money. But that didn't stop the lieutenant, who then met with Major Howard Haycraft, the Army's fiscal officer. Vincent was so convincing that the bean counter allotted $1 million for the recordings. Next, he pulled in Steve Shoals, a former executive at RCA Victor records, to help him manage the project—which still needed a name.

Legend has it that a secretary suggested the term "V-Disc," with "V" standing both for "victory" and "Vincent." Another story claims Vincent derived the name from Beethoven's Fifth Symphony, in which the first notes—dot, dot, dot, dash—represent the letter "V" in Morse Code. A *YANK* magazine artist designed a patriotic logo for five dollars, and the red, white, and blue label signified a War Department Music Branch. (Shoals returned to RCA after the war and produced records for Dizzy Gillespie before turning his attention to country music. He is responsible for the rise in popularity of the "Nashville Sound," and signed acts like Chet Atkins, Eddie Arnold, Jim Reeves, and a Memphis up-and-comer named Elvis Presley, according to the Definitive Country Music Encyclopedia on www.countryworks.com.)

Vincent then set out to find a way to produce new music for the troops. The American Federation of Musicians (AFM) had gone on strike in 1942 to protest losing royalties on recording sales. Although the musicians earned an hourly rate for their work in the studio, they received no commissions for record sales, nor were they compensated for airplay on radio or jukebox, according to the February 1999 article, "Victory Music: The Story of The V-Disc Record Label (1943–1949)," in *Goldmine* by Chuck Miller. AFM President James Caesar Petrillo warned the four major record companies at the time—RCA Victor, Decca, Columbia, and Capitol—that union members would not make any more recordings after July 31, 1942, unless they were paid royalties, Chuck Miller wrote.

The record companies took two years to agree to compensate the musicians, and the ban was lifted only after the labels and the union reached an agreement. With the help of former RCA salesman Walt Heebner, the Army convinced Petrillo to waive the recording ban so that the troops could receive new music recordings. According to Chuck Miller, Petrillo wrote on October 27, 1943: "This will acknowledge receipt of your letter of October 25th containing the request for permission for our members to make records in connection with your V-Disc project. . . . This is to advise you that the American Federation of Musicians interposes no objections to the making and use of these recordings. . . . This letter also carries with it permission for those members of the American Federation of Musicians, who are desirous of so doing, to volunteer their services for the making of such recordings."

With union permission granted, hundreds of popular musicians volunteered their talents to record songs for the troops. None received any pay for their recordings, but most were happy to play and sing if for no other reason than to hear their own recorded music during the two years of the strike. But the agreement was not without precise guidelines. The recordings could never be used for commercial purposes; in other words, they could never be sold or broadcast on commercial radio. Petrillo also demanded that all V-Discs be destroyed at war's end. Army brass agreed to the conditions and spent the next few years traversing the country recording all types of music in all kinds of venues.

Sergeant Tony Janek, a former Columbia recording engineer turned soldier, often hauled four hundred pounds of recording equipment to concert halls, hotel rooms, radio studios, ballrooms, nightclubs, dress rehearsals for radio shows, films, and plays—wherever musicians made melodies, Chuck Miller wrote. Recording engineers did their best to collect all types of music to match the troops' tastes, including swing and big band, jazz, popular, and country and western.

Once the problem of acquiring new music had been solved, Vincent's unit turned its attention to producing recordings on material tough enough to withstand shipment overseas and adverse conditions on the front lines, from freezing cold to sweltering heat. Shellac, the material records were made of, was neither durable nor plentiful. The Japanese invasion of India and Thailand not only hurt the lac bug population but also decreased the amount of shellac the United States imported. Recycled shellac discs included noises louder than the music. After numerous tests, the Vincent team found that materials called Vinylite and Formvar (a form of polyvinyl from Canada) worked perfectly. Still, not everyone was sold on the new formula; Columbia Records, which produced some V-Discs for the government, refused to use vinyl and relied still on shellac, according to Chuck Miller.

Like a Letter from Home

Production began, and the first V-Disc contained recordings Captain Glenn Miller had made for RCA Victor and Bluebird labels before the strike. On October 1, 1943, nearly two thousand boxes of V-Discs made their way from the RCA Victor plant in Camden, New Jersey, to bases, camps, and ships throughout the world. Each box contained thirty discs, extra steel phonograph needles, song lyrics, and a questionnaire for soldiers. The military also sent out 125,000 wind-up Victrolas over the first few years of the project, according to Chuck Miller, so that every encampment or installation had means to play the new V-Discs. Troops quickly welcomed the monthly entertainment package and the new music it contained. The vinyl records were twelve-inch discs designed to be played at 78 rpm. They also held up to six minutes of music on each side—two more than traditional ten-inch records—allowing for longer songs or jam sessions by bands.

LEFT: *Captain Glenn Miller and his band traveled all over the U.S. and to England performing for servicemen and -women. At his show for the 834th Aviation Battalion, Miller conducted his musicians through crowd favorites like "Keep 'Em Flying," a song recorded after Pearl Harbor that he'd originally called "That's Where I Came In." Miller's career was at its peak when a plane carrying him was lost over the English Channel in December 1944. For troops, V-Discs immortalized Miller's music.*
National Archives Photo

Right: *Glenn Miller's swinging style made him a V-Disc favorite. He appeared on the first record for the GIs, which shipped out to troops on October 1, 1943. No matter the location, hearing the bandleader's music always put the servicemen "In the Mood." Miller's tunes were a taste of home—a melodic reminder of better times they'd had and better times to come.*
U.S. Army Air Forces Photo

Soldiers and seamen everywhere listened to V-Discs before battle. In North Africa, Normandy, and at the Battle of the Bulge, the recordings became part of a serviceman's life—and death.

Troops First to Hear New American Music

Ironically, many of the top tunes from the 1940s were popular with military men long before anyone back home ever heard of them. While some of the songs became classics, it took years for many of them to be heard on the home front, thanks to the musicians' strike. Some of the day's most popular artists appeared on V-Discs: The Andrews Sisters, Count Basie, Perry Como, Bing Crosby, Jimmy Dorsey, Tommy Dorsey, Duke Ellington, Ella Fitzgerald, Benny Goodman, Woody Herman, Lena Horne, Peggy Lee, Ethel Merman, the Mills Brothers, Artie Shaw, and Fats Waller. *YANK* reported in 1944 that thirty-five of the thirty-eight songs on *Your Hit Parade* appeared on V-Discs. The February 1944 kit contained songs such as "Don't Fence Me In," "I Dream of You," "Lazy Bones," "I'm Making Believe," and "Into Each Life Some Rain Must Fall."

Artists gathered in dance halls and theaters in New York and California and invited Janek and other Army sound engineers to record their music. Once

Right: *Soldiers came off European battlefields cold, tired, and hungry. Hearing tunes from V-Discs made them feel a little closer to the United States and the ones they loved. Troops heard new music before other Americans, thanks to a recording industry strike. Since artists made no commercial records between 1942 and 1944, only V-Disc recordings offered new music, and those were available only to servicemen stationed overseas.*
National Archives Photo

the team recorded in a Norfolk, Virginia, hospital when singers performed for patients. Special recording sessions took place at CBS Playhouse No. 3, now called the Ed Sullivan Theater, and NBC's Studio 8H, which is home today for *Saturday Night Live.* In 1943 *Life* photographer Gjon Mili hosted an all-night jam session in his apartment, and Janek and Vincent were there to capture the music. Unfortunately, the apartment's acoustics were so poor that none of the recordings were usable. The troops, and the world, missed out on an all-star band with the likes of Bobby Hackett and Benny Morton on horns, Duke Ellington and Mary Lou Williams on piano, Eddie Condon on guitar, and Josh White, Lee Wiley, and Billie Holiday on vocals. No performer ever received payment for a V-Disc performance, and no one ever turned down the opportunity to record for the troops.

Because of the strike, musicians could work together on the V-Disc project no matter their contract obligations. Typically, only artists on the same record label could work together, but since no commercial records were produced from V-Disc material, anyone could make V-Disc music with anyone else at any time in any location. This brought together incredible talent combinations that can be found only on these military records: Tommy Dorsey and Judy Garland teamed up for "Somewhere over the Rainbow" on V-Disc 335 and Navy V-Disc 159; Ella Fitzgerald and the Buddy Rich Orchestra scatted through "Blue Skies" (for which they forgot the words); and Abbott and Costello performed their legendary "Who's on First?" with Brooklyn Dodgers's organist Gladys Gooding.

The V-Disc recordings even mended a few fences, if only temporarily. Bandleader brothers Tommy and Jimmy Dorsey performed together for the first time in fifteen years in Liederkranz Hall on March 15, 1945, and the Army sound engineers were in New York to record it. The concert was so important that Corporal George Simon arranged the musicians so that the recording would be nearly perfect. He placed brass instruments on one side, reed instruments on the other, and rhythm instruments in the middle. Chuck Miller called the Dorsey duo recording "the hallmark of the V-Disc records." Radio's Bill Goodwin introduced the performance: "Well, fellows, we have two bands making this V-Disc for you. One of them is the former boss of my present boss, a fellow named Tom Dorsey."

The Dorseys and Goodwin joked for a few moments before the combined bands played "More Than You Know," which appeared on V-Disc 451 and Navy V-Disc 231. Every record included musicians' comments and messages directed to the troops as well as music, wrote Amy Duncan in a January 25, 1991, article in *Christian Science Monitor*. The intent

BELOW: *Band leader Tommy Dorsey and his orchestra participated in many V-Disc recordings, including a few with his estranged brother, Jimmy.*
Library of Congress Photo

Right: *Glenn Miller once introduced "Stardust" on a V-Disc with: "This is Captain Glenn Miller, speaking for the Army Air Force Training Command Orchestra, and we hope that you soldiers of the Allied Forces enjoy these V-Discs that we're making just for you," according to a 1999* Goldmine *article by Chuck Miller.*
U.S. Air Force Museum Photo

was to let service members know that they were not forgotten and to bring a piece of the home front to the front lines. But musicians could not say whatever they wanted on the recordings. The introductions were scrutinized, and recording engineers allowed nothing lewd or foul. According to Chuck Miller, Glenn Miller was once interrupted during an introduction by the crash of a music stand. When he responded, "Jesus Christ, what was that . . . ," the engineers immediately censored it. In another instance, as cited in Chuck Miller's article, Crosby admonished guitarist Tony Mottola for missing a note in the opening bars of a song. Crosby said, "Tony, take your &*^% gloves off!", according to the article. The engineers missed it during the recording session but later caught it on playback. All lyrics had to be squeaky clean and not offend anyone. Minor swear words like "hell" and "damn" were not allowed, Chuck Miller wrote.

Jazz legend Fats Waller recorded twenty-two songs for V-Discs, but only nine were deemed usable. Censors thought the other thirteen "too risqué for young GIs' ears," wrote Gregory Spears in a December 23, 1990, article for the *Houston Chronicle*. Waller plied himself with a bottle of Vat 69 Scotch during each session, and the drunker he got, the more suggestive his songs became. His last recordings, made for V-Discs, included "The Reefer Song," an ode to marijuana.

As the wind howled, James's shivering jerked him awake. He pulled the covers over his head and tried to fall back asleep by pretending he'd snuggled in sweet Doris's arms. He hoped—prayed—that she'd still be waiting for him when he returned. But as the months had turned into years he wondered if she hadn't found someone else. He imagined her lying awake, thinking of him, waiting patiently for the day he walked through her door, and the Fats Waller tune he'd heard in camp a few days ago ran through his mind:

"No one to talk with
All by myself
No one to walk with
But I'm happy on a shelf
Ain't misbehavin'
I'm savin' my love for you.

I know for certain
The one I love
I'm through with flirtin'
It's just you I'm thinking of
Ain't misbehavin'
I'm savin' my love for you."

—*"Ain't Misbehavin'," lyrics by Andy Razaf, music by Thomas "Fats" Waller and Harry Brooks, 1929*

ABOVE: *Soldiers had little Christmas cheer, particularly as the war dragged on. Yet music cheered the lonely souls as they decorated a tree with a little tinsel and make-shift ornaments like hand grenades. Bing Crosby's "White Christmas," written by Irving Berlin for the movie* Holiday Inn, *was the GIs' most requested tune of the war, and troops likely wore holes through the vinyl playing the song over and over again on their V-Discs.*
U.S. Army Signal Corps Photo

When members of the Women's Air Corps and Navy WAVES counted responses to the questionnaires sent with each V-Disc box, they found that the troops requested Crosby's "White Christmas" more than any other song. "Stardust" followed at a distant second. Figuring no one could sing the popular Christmas song as well as Crosby, the makers of the V-Discs never included another recording of it. But they offered six versions of "Stardust:" two by Artie Shaw (V-Discs 45 and 560) and one each by Glenn Miller (V-Disc 65), Marie Green (V-Disc 407 and Navy V-Disc 187), Edgar Haynes (V-Disc 681), and the song's writer, Hoagy Carmichael (V-Disc 536).

Crosby Croons for Soldiers and Sailors

Of all performers, Crosby was likely the most popular and one of the most active in the war effort of all nonmilitary entertainers. The crooner was too old and too color-blind to join the armed services, but he took his Kraft Music Hall radio program on the road as a traveling USO show. Crosby often broadcast his performances from naval bases, airfields, and army camps around the United States, Club Crosby President Mark Scrimger wrote in "Bing Crosby's V-Discs." He also used his radio show to promote war bond sales and government rationing. In late 1944, Scrimger wrote, Crosby joined troops on the front lines in Europe, entertaining them with his signature songs. In all, Crosby recorded nearly 110 songs that were included on V-Discs.

War Winds Down, Music Program Follows Suit

Over the years, V-Disc production became increasingly costly, and by February 1944, the sets being mailed to the troops contained twenty discs instead of thirty. At first the cutback allowed the Army to send more boxes

RIGHT: *Crooner Bing Crosby appeared in many USO shows, such as this one with Joe De Rita in 1945; he recorded nearly 110 songs for V-Discs.*
U.S. Air Force Museum Photo

to more overseas locations, but by September 1945 the military decided to cut expenses by including only fifteen records in a kit. A year later the number was reduced to ten. Chuck Miller wrote that by November 1947, the record shipments came only every other month, and May 1949 marked the final shipments of the discs. The final kit featured music by Duke Ellington, Buddy Rich, Tex Ritter, and Sarah Vaughn.

During its six years, the program produced 900 V-Discs with 3,000 different recordings of 2,700 different songs. The military shipped more than eight million discs around the world, and officials did their best to destroy original master recordings and discs in camps, on bases, and aboard ships, as required in the initial agreement with the musicians' union. But collecting the discs after the war proved impossible. Sailors and GIs hid the records in their belongings and brought them home as souvenirs. According to Chuck Miller, FBI agents and provost marshal's officers found veterans in the early 1950s who had smuggled the V-Discs home and seized them. An RCA employee was sentenced to jail when 2,500 of the records were found in his possession. Some of the original discs survive, and these have become popular with collectors. Only the Library of Congress has a complete set of the records, and some of the metal stampers, which are used to press into the vinyl to create the records' grooves, are stored in the National Archives.

Tunes Not Forgotten, Not Gone

One man, retired Navy Commander Ed DiGiannantonio, also held a copy of nearly every V-Disc made. DiGi, as his friends called him, began working with the recording program while he was recovering from being blown overboard from the USS *Vincennes* in August of 1942, according to Duncan. When military officials found out he was a former engineering student at the Massachusetts Institute of Technology, with a ham radio operator's license and experience recording shows for famous musicians, including Artie Shaw, Glenn Miller, and Benny Goodman, they saw he was a natural fit for the program. It's estimated that DiGiannantonio produced five hundred of the V-Disc recordings himself, usually carting nearly two hundred pounds of recording equipment, amplifiers, and microphones everywhere and anywhere musicians played. DiGi, then a lieutenant, kept the V-Discs only because a captain told him to hang onto a set in case of an emergency.

Yet all the time DiGiannantonio had the discs, he recognized their social, cultural, and historical value. He protected them and spent twelve years talking to both military and musical organizations to get the material from the V-Discs released publicly. According to Chuck Miller, a three-cassette V-Disc music series was released in 1990, thanks to DiGiannantonio's efforts. The union granted its permission to sell the music, only after DiGiannantonio promised to pay royalties to the musicians or their estates, Spears wrote. Today the recordings that were mastered from DiGi's personal collection are available on compact discs. DiGiannantonio told Duncan that the tracks are special because the musicians would "be all hepped up to do something for the war cause—it was dynamic. It was live and very vibrant compared to going in and sitting in a studio and doing a normal, routine session." Most of the songs on the new releases include their original introductions. DiGiannantonio supervised a CD line distributed on the Collector's Choice Label that released V-Disc recordings by artists such as Dinah Shore, the Andrews Sisters, Fats Waller, Vaughn Moore, the Mills Brothers, and Guy Lombardo, Chuck Miller wrote. The recordings are readily available through national music retailers and on Internet sites. Other artists' recordings were released on other labels. Today's music consumers can easily find recordings that were previously available only on V-Discs.

DiGiannantonio died of prostate cancer on February 19, 2000, but not before he saw his beloved V-Discs released for new generations to enjoy. " . . . the last thing I'd like to do is give some publicity to the musicians and the record companies and everybody else for their contributions that they gave during World War II for this music. No one has ever said, 'Hey guys, you did a fantastic job and the country thanks you.' It's long overdue," he said in Chuck Miller's article.

"Most of the people who wrote and performed music during World War II wanted to make people feel closer and happier in the difficult time period," DiGiannantonio told Spears. "The music had a lot of feeling, a lot of emotion. It should be heard again—we could use it now."

As the bugler blasted reveille, James rolled over and tried to open his eyes. He felt like the guy in Irving Berlin's song:

"Someday I'm going to murder the bugler,
Someday they're going to find him dead;
I'll amputate his reveille, and stomp upon it heavily,
And spend the rest of my life in bed."

—*"Oh! How I Hate to Get Up in the Morning,"*
lyrics and music by Irving Berlin, 1918

"Oh-dark-thirty" had arrived way too soon. The images of Doris lingered, and he couldn't help but wonder what she was thinking. The battle had raged for weeks, with no end in sight. Gain six inches today, lose half a foot tomorrow. The Germans seemed to be firing every mortar and 88 in their arsenal right at them. He hummed an old song he remembered hearing on the radio. When he'd first heard it, it had a happy sound and made him think of snuggling up to Doris:

"The snow is snowing,
The wind is blowing,
But I can weather the storm.
What do I care how much it may storm?
I've got my love to keep me warm."

—*"I've Got My Love to Keep Me Warm,"*
lyrics and music by Irving Berlin, 1936

Today, however, the wind was blowing the snow, the damp cutting through the tissue-paper walls of the tent like a meat cleaver. Was Doris cold back in Indianapolis? Did she have someone new to snuggle by her side? Or was she worried about him and all that she'd heard about this war? As he slipped into his pants and pulled on his shirt, he started singing:

"The front page of your paper is bound to make you sad,
Especially if you're the worrying sort.
So turn the front page over where news is not so bad,
There's consolation in the weather report.
It's a lovely day tomorrow,
Tomorrow is a lovely day.
Come and feast your tear-dimmed eyes
On tomorrow's clear blue skies.
If today your heart is weary,
If ev'ry little thing looks gray,
Just forget your troubles and learn to say,
Tomorrow is a lovely day."

—*"It's a Lovely Day Tomorrow,"*
lyrics and music by Irving Berlin, 1939

Oh, who was he kidding anyway? He'd already made the guys still in their bunks angry over his singing. Not that he couldn't carry a tune, but how could he be so optimistic? Tomorrow is a lovely day. Humph. He just wanted to see tomorrow. Tomorrow had been but a promise to many of his buddies, splintered, shattered, and scattered by Nazi firepower. Hitler had made this a mean man's war. That reminded him of a tune his granny had played on the old upright when she told him stories about the Great War:

> "I only want to live, but I know I must die.
> The fun I'll have be in the sweet bye and bye.
> Oh, this man's war is a mean man's war for sure.
> Can't think about livin' when you're bound to die.
> Can't think about lovin' when the Heinie's nearby.
> Oh, this man's war is a mean man's war for sure."
>
> —*Song from Tin Pan Alley, circa World War I*

14. The Bombing Campaign over Japan

"THE SIRENS WAILED AT ABOUT 1 A.M. I COULD HEAR THE ROAR OF THE PLANES' ENGINES AND THE WHINE OF THE BOMBS AND COULD FEEL THE VERY EARTH SHAKE. AS I RAN, I KEPT MY EYES ON THE SKY. IT WAS LIKE A FIREWORKS DISPLAY AS THE INCENDIARIES EXPLODED. BLAZING PETROLEUM JELLY, FIREBRANDS, AND SPARKS FLEW EVERYWHERE. PEOPLE WERE AFLAME, ROLLING AND WRITHING IN AGONY, SCREAMING PITEOUSLY FOR HELP, BUT BEYOND ALL MORTAL ASSISTANCE."

—*Tokyo schoolgirl Fusako Sasaki in late May 1945*

OPPOSITE: *After he was captured and taken prisoner, Japanese Lieutenant Minoru Wadda was given the option to be held at a POW camp or to assist American bomber crews, guiding them to his former headquarters for the 100th Japanese Army Division, headquartered on Mindanao in the Philippines. Using a radio headset, he had a bird's eye view of his former compound as it was turned to rubble by Mitchell bombers on August 10, 1945.*
U.S. Marine Corps Photo

JAPAN'S FIRST WARNING THAT JUST MAYBE ITS HOME islands weren't safe from enemy attack was the daring Doolittle Raid in April of 1942, when Mitchell bombers roared off the flight deck of the carrier *Hornet* and hit Tokyo. The attack caused minimal physical damage but dealt a devastating and humiliating psychological blow to the Japanese military's high command. Japan's leaders had gone to great lengths to assure the populace that their country was invincible, protected by a "Divine Wind," but the Doolittle Raid proved that was a fallacy. Now they would have to step up their anti-aircraft defenses, maybe even pull back some naval and aerial forces to ward off any future attacks.

Whatever was done within Japan's territorial boundaries would have a cascading effect on the country's offensive moves across the Pacific. For example, Japan built thousands of anti-aircraft gun emplacements to protect every industrial center around the country, every port complex, rail yard, refinery, and supply depot. But those gun batteries would require thousands more trained personnel to crew them—men who would not be available for combat in the Pacific. Even if women were eventually trained to fire the anti-aircraft guns, they would be pulled away from factory jobs that produced the tanks and ships and planes and bombs and bullets.

Additionally, the Japanese military trained more fighter pilots, not to deploy to aircraft carriers and airfields closer to the fight in the South Pacific, but to patrol the skies over Tokyo and the other major cities, to defend the home islands. Still unsure of where exactly the Doolittle bombers had come from, Japan also dispatched a naval task force to the northern Pacific, near the Aleutians, the only territory any land-based American bombers could have taken off from.

With all the defensive measures taken, the military high command in Tokyo once again assured the populace that no enemy bombers would penetrate Japanese air space, let alone cause further damage. And that promise held true for the rest of 1942 and into mid-'43,

BELOW: *The defense of Japan's home islands would require the valiant efforts of every man, woman, and child, willing to sacrifice their lives for the Emperor. Women trained to use simple bamboo spears would have been no match for the devastating firepower of an Allied invasion force.*
Wartime Japanese Government Photo

RIGHT: *Once air bases were established in the Marianas, fighter planes were deployed there, in order to accompany bombers sent to Tokyo and other key cities. Here a P-51 Mustang prepares for takeoff from a base on Iwo Jima in 1945.*
Library of Congress Photo

but it had little to do with scaring off any American bomber crews. In fact, the Doolittle Raid was a one-time opportunity that probably wouldn't have caught anyone by surprise a second time.

As Japanese ground forces were killed and captured or driven off island after island in the South Pacific, B-24 and B-17 bombers used airstrips closer and closer to Tokyo to launch air strikes on targets that were supposedly impenetrable. But bombing Japan would not be a cakewalk, especially flying through a gauntlet of flak and fighter planes. The toll was enormous, but nothing would halt the bombing—except Japan's unconditional surrender, no matter how long it took to come.

The Allies' deployment of the new long-range B-29 Superfortresses to the Mariana Islands (Tinian, Saipan, and Guam) signaled an upturn in bombing missions to Japan. The sleek, silver Superforts flew higher and faster than other bombers, carried a heavier payload, and were built to bite back, with a full array of machine guns covering all angles to fire on any approaching fighter planes. But the high-level flights—intended to avoid much of the flak being fired at them from anti-aircraft gun batteries—created a problem the Allies had never encountered before.

When 110 B-29s dropped more than a thousand bombs over Tokyo on November 24 of 1944, fewer than fifty of them hit anywhere close to their intended targets. At first strategists thought maybe the problem was caused by cloud cover, but when the bombs continued to stray on subsequent missions through December, even on clear sky days, the problem was identified: a little-known weather phenomenon called the jet stream was causing the bombs to drift off target.

The Japanese knew it was just a matter of time before the Americans figured out the problem and made adjustments, and they dispatched urgent messages to their fighter units throughout the Pacific in late 1944 to search for and destroy the new bomber aircraft wherever they were coming from,

RIGHT: *B-29 Superfortresses based in the Marianas pass by majestic snow-capped Mount Fuji on their way to firebombing Tokyo and other key industrial centers in Japan, from March of 1945 through the end of the war. One of the many crewmen who flew in the B-29s was actor Tim Holt, a bombardier, whose plane was nearly lost on the final day of the war. Future actor Charles Bronson served on a Superfort weather plane, tasked with scouting potential targets prior to each mission.*
U.S. Air Force Photo

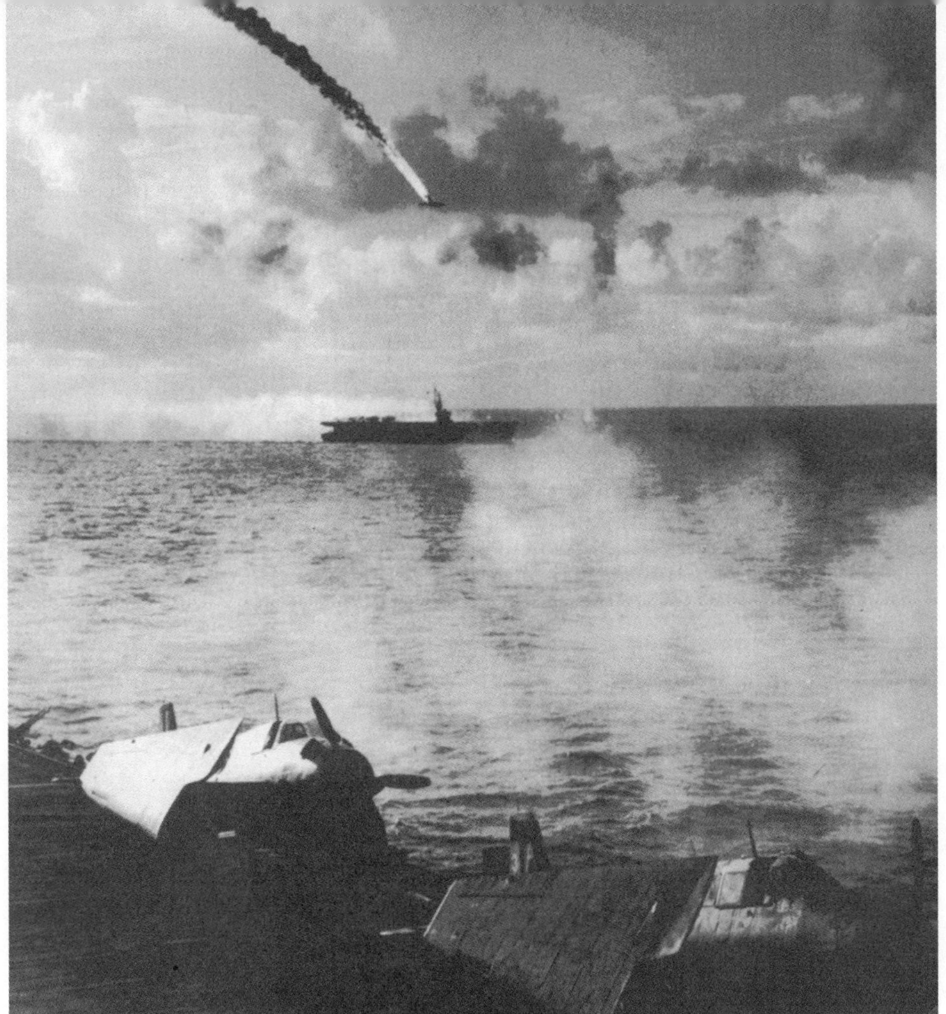

Left: *A crippled Japanese dive-bomber attempts to crash into an American carrier, observed from the flight deck of the carrier* Kitkun Bay. National Archives Photo

somewhere in the Marianas. Within the next month, forty-three of the Superfortresses were damaged and eleven more destroyed.

To improve on his unit's efficiency, General Curtis LeMay, commander of XXI Bomber Command, ordered a new and risky strategy: low-level bombing in single file, with most of the onboard guns removed (leaving only the tail gunner) to allow for bigger payloads, which would be almost exclusively napalm and thermite bombs. And of course, when they were notified, the pilots and crewmen who would be flying those missions thought it would be nothing less than sheer suicide.

But after a trial run to Singapore on February 24 yielded a 40 percent destruction of the target area, the airmen thought just maybe LeMay's strategy would be successful. Two weeks later, the first firebombing mission to Tokyo was scheduled, and even though Japanese radar spotted the oncoming wave of bombers flying "on the deck," fighter pilots sent aloft—many of them inexperienced and not as daring as their brethren who'd flown the early missions to Pearl Harbor, Wake, Guam, and the Philippines—were wary of approaching too close to the bombers, for fear of being shot down by the nonexistent gunners on board.

Right: *A squadron of carrier planes from the USS* Essex *drop their incendiaries on Hokadate in Japan, in the final weeks of the war.* U.S. Navy Photo

The American bomber crews were flying so low they heard the air raid sirens and felt the intense heat as their incendiaries exploded, sending up plumes of fire and smoke, engulfing a large sector of Tokyo. This was the first of many bombing missions to the capital city, making it virtually impossible for Japan's propaganda machine to spin the events in any manner that would be acceptable to the populace. In fact, the continued bombings had a demoralizing effect not only on Tokyo but on other industrial centers such as Osaka, Kobe, and Nagoya, crippling those cities' output of anything to do with the sustained war effort. What firebombs didn't destroy was shut down by worker absenteeism. Japan's entire industrial complex was soon paralyzed.

Normally the laws of war dictated civil and compassionate treatment of innocent men, women, and children, but both the Nazis and the Japanese had tossed aside any semblance of decency when they wantonly, sadistically butchered the Jews of Europe and the populace of China. Pinpoint bombing to take out specific targets was discarded and carpet bombing, the total devastation of entire cities, was approved. The bomber crewmen who flew missions over Japan "were conditioned by their knowledge of the Allied prisoners who had been bayoneted to death, the hospital ships bombed and shelled, the shot-down pilots who were beheaded, the numerous atrocities that had been committed by their enemy," wrote John Vader in the article "Fire Raids on Japan" for *History of the Second World War* magazine, December 12, 1974. "The general mood was expressed in a simple attitude: 'They've only got themselves to blame . . . they started it.'"

Among the many pilots and crewmen who flew the mighty Superfortresses was Tim Holt, who had appeared in several RKO movies prior to joining the Army Air Corps and survived twenty-two missions as a bombardier. His last flight to Japan came on the final day of the war in the Pacific, and it was nearly his last flight ever, as his plane sustained more than 150 bullet holes, lost part of a wing, and crash-landed at Guam. (After returning to Hollywood, Holt costarred in *The Treasure of the Sierra Madre* with fellow veteran Humphrey Bogart, directed by John Huston. Holt was

Left: *Carriers were most vulnerable during refueling and rearming operations, such as the* Enterprise *with its flight deck crammed with Dauntless dive-bombers.*
U.S. Navy Photo

also involved with the rodeo and even became a partner in a touring show, often featured as the headline performer.)

Henry Colman was a B-29 navigator, flying out of Saipan. (He became an early pioneer in television and produced shows that included *The Love Boat*.) Charles Buchinski was a nose gunner with the 61st Squadron of the 39th Bombardment Group stationed on Guam, and flew on a B-29 weather observation plane that frequently scouted locations and visibility over target areas prior to massed bombing missions. (Buchinski later changed his name to Charles Bronson and made it to Hollywood, where he played roles that established his niche: a tough guy not to be ruffled without consequence of pain and suffering to the offender.)

Comedian "Lonesome" George Gobel never got overseas during WWII, but he did joke about his role in the air war against Japan. "'I fought the whole war in Oklahoma,' he explained to a *Tonight Show* audience, wrote Ed McMahon in *For Laughing Out Loud*, cowritten with David Fisher. "'I don't know why you laugh. That's evidently where they needed me or they wouldn't have sent me there.' But then he added proudly, 'We were pretty effective too. Not one Japanese plane got past Tulsa.'"

Hollywood Inspires Flyboys

As the Americans advanced across the Pacific, bombing missions over Japan were conducted nonstop, with the sleek new B-29s leading the pack. Among its other assignments, the Army's First Motion Picture Unit was tasked with producing a training film to prepare the aircrews for flying the gauntlet. With Ronald Reagan providing the narration, *Target Tokyo* utilized the special-effects wizardry of Hollywood to re-create the topography of Japan, specifically the route to Ota, where the massive Nakajima plane factory was producing the new Ki-84 fighter aircraft. "Special effects men were flown to Washington for briefings on every known landmark—cemeteries, rice paddies, factories, geisha joints. From match sticks, piano wire, plaster and cheesecloth, the FMPU's model makers replicated the entire route to Ota," reported Jack Smith in the *Houston Chronicle*, June 5, 1985. "Reagan's voice narrated: 'You are now approaching the coast of Honshu, on a course of 300 degrees. To your left, if you are on course, you will see a narrow inlet.' Rushed to Saipan, the film was chilling to see. 'Uncannily accurate,' the 21st Bomber Command reported. 'It was as if a camera were mounted in the nose of a B-29 and had flown the entire mission beforehand.'"

In *Bombardier*, released in 1943, Pat O'Brien and Randolph Scott are bomber pilots who train young airmen to become bombardiers in New Mexico. Later they relocate to an unknown airstrip in the South Pacific, flying a firebombing mission to Nagoya, Japan. Although Captain Buck Oliver (Scott) and his crew are shot down, they manage to ignite barrels of fuel that will guide the rest of the squadron over the target. The film closes with a night scene of a city in flames as the bombers return to their base. The narrator states: "To put out fire with fire . . . that is the crusade of the bombardiers who are already building a great American tradition. And there are others on the way, a hundred thousand strong."

The early exploits of the American volunteers of the Flying Tigers in China is featured in *God Is My Co-Pilot*, which follows Army Air Corps Colonel Robert Scott, a transport pilot who yearns to do more than just ferry supplies over the Himalayas from India to China. He is allowed to join the elite American volunteers just as the Japanese attack Pearl Harbor. Then, with America officially plunged into war, the Flying Tigers—Americans attached to the Chinese Air Force—are disbanded and rookie Army Air Corps pilots and crews are rushed over to repel Japanese advances in the China-Burma-India Campaign.

Because he is already in the Army Air Corps, Colonel Scott agrees to stay on to teach combat fighter tactics to the untested pilots arriving in country. Many of the Flying Tigers in fact decide to enlist in the Air Corps to remain in China. But on a lone mission, Scott is shot down behind enemy lines and presumed killed in action. After being rescued by Chinese partisans, he returns to his base but is grounded because now he has malaria. His timing couldn't be worse, as his unit is given the daring mission, the "dream mission," to bomb Japan.

Commander Claire Chennault, played by Raymond Massey, gives the briefing to his pilots at a base in Kunming, while Scott stands outside and listens on, wishing he could join them: " . . . over these positions you will encounter heavy anti-aircraft fire. The bombing runs will be due South . . . And now, gentlemen, we start a new and final phase in this war against Japan. Our defensive battles are over. For the first time we have enough bombers to make it hurt . . . and we're going to strike where it hurts most, into real Japanese territory . . . hit 'em hard, and good luck."

As they watch the bombers take off, Chennault tells Scott, "Ya know, Scottie, I'm still a fighter pilot, and I never send the boys up that I don't wish I were going with them, and on this mission more than ever. This is a milestone on the road to Tokyo and the final victory. There's a new Curtiss P-40 out there. It's bigger and faster and better armed than anything you ever flew. It's yours, Scottie, compliments of the old man. Go on. Get in it. Your old group is waiting for you. Take over . . ."

As Colonel Scott flies off to catch up with the bombers and fighters headed for Japan, General Chennault watches with Big Mike Harrigan, the local missionary priest (played by Alan Hale), at his side. As hundreds of aircraft fill the skies, Big Mike recalls the words of an RAF pilot who survived the Nazi bombing of London but died later fighting the Japanese. The words seem to inspire Colonel Scott and the other American pilots as they take the fight to the Japanese homeland: "They who had scorned the thought of any strength except their own to lean on learned at length how fear can sabotage the bravest heart. And human weakness answering to the prod of terror calls, 'Help us, oh God.' In silence that's the silent voice we heard ringing its message like a spoken word . . . 'believe.' 'Believe in me. Cast out your fear.'

"'Oh, I'm not up there beyond the sky, but here, right here in your heart. I am the strength you seek . . . Believe.'"

Prepping for the Final Confrontation

After the collapse of Hitler's Thousand-Year Reich, numerous combat divisions in Europe that were earmarked to return home were instead given the bad news that they would be re-deployed to the Pacific, for the invasion of Japan slated for late in 1945. Allied commanders projected needing more than four million combatants to subdue Japan, with its entire population—including the elderly, women, and children—trained to fight side by side with its men to the bitter end.

As the end became evident, Japan implemented "The Decree of the Homeland Decisive Battle" to train every citizen to repel any invasion force, by any means possible. The role of the kamikaze pilot—honoring the emperor by willingly sacrificing oneself to kill many more of the enemy—was expanded and promoted to include manned torpedoes and suicide boats that could be slipped into the waters and guided to ram into the American warships patrolling nearby. Even small boys had explosives strapped to their chests and were trained to scamper under a passing tank or truck and detonate themselves. Women and girls were trained to hide grenades in their clothing and approach a group of enemy soldiers, maybe offering food or drink; then when the "imperialists" gathered around, they would blow everyone up, including themselves—honorably, of course. Japan's hope was that a sustained effort by every citizen would eventually decimate the enemy ranks and force them to withdraw, allowing Japan to regain the advantage. By May of 1945 the entire country was united in this effort.

The Japanese spin doctors had to work overtime to convince the population that what might appear to be a devastating firebombing campaign by the Allies was actually working to Tokyo's advantage.

Radio Tokyo claimed that the burned and flattened industrial district of the city was slated to be turned into a massive fish pond and rice paddy anyway, to hamper the eventual Allied amphibious landing. By early July, the radio station proclaimed: "The sooner the enemy

BELOW: *Anti-aircraft guns on the American flattop* Hornet *blast away at approaching enemy aircraft, many of them kamikazes, willing to die for the Emperor.*
Department of Defense Photo

comes, the better for us, for our battle array is complete." Few actually heard that broadcast, because by this time many of the citizens of Tokyo were either dead or had fled to safety in the countryside.

The Allied plan was to first seize the island of Kyushu and to make at least one air strip operational soon afterward. From there and from aircraft carriers cruising the coast, the Allies could launch round-the-clock bombing and strafing missions to hit anywhere in Japan.

From the USS *Hollandia,* radioman Paul Newman flew Avenger torpedo planes over Japan. Though he considered his military service "uneventful," Newman was there in the northern Pacific toward the end of the war and did survive a kamikaze attack while he was aboard another flattop, the *Bunker Hill.* (Newman got out of the Navy in April of 1946 and made his way to Hollywood, quickly becoming a fan favorite and Oscar contender. He won the Best Actor Academy Award in 1987 for *The Color of Money*.)

The Allies' plan to attack Japan featured a cordon of warships deployed around the country's perimeter to shell coastal cities and blockade any resupply efforts. This continuous pounding was expected to take four months; then the invasion and assault of the island of Honshu would begin in March of 1946.

But the combined death toll from such an operation was projected to be in the millions. No one on either side wanted to become a statistic, but everyone knew what had to be done.

A Sudden End to the Empire

With the success of the firebombing missions, General Curtis LeMay truly believed the Army and Navy could hold off on the invasion plans and watch while the Air Force pounded the hell out of the Japanese, laying waste to the country and leaving little more than scorched earth. And if that's what it would take for the Japanese to realize the hopelessness of resistance, of refusing to surrender, then LeMay's pilots and aircrews were up to the task of a sustained bombing campaign, of blowing them to kingdom come!

On the other side of the world, German scientists (including those foreigners forced to work for the Nazis) had been rushing to develop long-range rockets and an atomic weapon. But with the collapse of Nazi Germany, those same scientists were recruited to continue their work in the United States, for the top-secret Manhattan Project. Their efforts led to the first underground nuclear detonation, in the desert just north of El Paso, Texas, where they unleashed a force never before imagined.

Soon after the test, President Truman gave the go-ahead to dispatch two of these new weapons to the Pacific. The various component parts for the two bombs, dubbed "Fat Man" and "Little Boy," were loaded onto the warship *Indianapolis* and transported to Tinian in the Marianas for assembly at a secluded part of the island. The two nuclear bombs were actually completely different: Little Boy was a uranium weapon and had never been tested. Nevertheless, it was slated for the first mission. Fat Man was an implosion bomb using plutonium, like those that had been tested in the desert Southwest. It would be the second bomb used on the mission, if it was needed.

The Superfortresses and the aircrews of the 509th Composite Group were given the mission to drop one of the bombs on one of four selected targets: Niigata, Kokura, Nagasaki, or Hiroshima. (The military had initially considered bombing the ancient city of Kyoto, but determined it had more cultural and religious significance to the Japanese than impact on the war effort and thus removed it from the list. Niigata would be a final option primarily because it was so far away from Tinian.) If needed—if the Japanese didn't surrender—the second bomb would be used within a few days on one of the remaining targets. After that, there were no more atomic bombs in the U.S. arsenal, and the countdown would begin for the invasion of Japan.

Below: *B-29 pilot Paul Tibbets of the 509th Composite Group had the dubious distinction of flying the first atomic bombing misson from Tinian Island in the Marianas to Hiroshima, Japan. He dubbed the Superfortress* Enola Gay *in honor of his mom.*
National Archives Photo

During the days leading up to the secret mission, the 509th had a well-known visitor, the singing cowboy Gene Autry and his USO troupe, who stopped off at Tinian after performing on nearby Saipan. In fact, the entertainers observed the hush-hush activity of the aircrews and could only speculate what might be in the works. (Autry was still on the island when the B-29 dubbed *Enola Gay* returned from Hiroshima, and he heard the news. Three days later the performers were back on Saipan, awaiting a transport plane to take them back to southern California.)

"And then came the night of our mission," recalled Harold M. Agnew in the article "A New World, A Mystic World" for *Time* magazine, July 29, 1985. "Our B-29s had a circle with a black arrow in it as their insignia. All the other B-29s had triangles or circles with letters of the alphabet. But the night before the mission, on Aug. 5th, Tokyo Rose came on the radio and said, 'Black Arrow Squadron, we know who you are and what you are, and we are ready for you.' Early the next morning we didn't have black arrows anymore. We had triangles with letters, which I thought was chicken. But it was prudent."

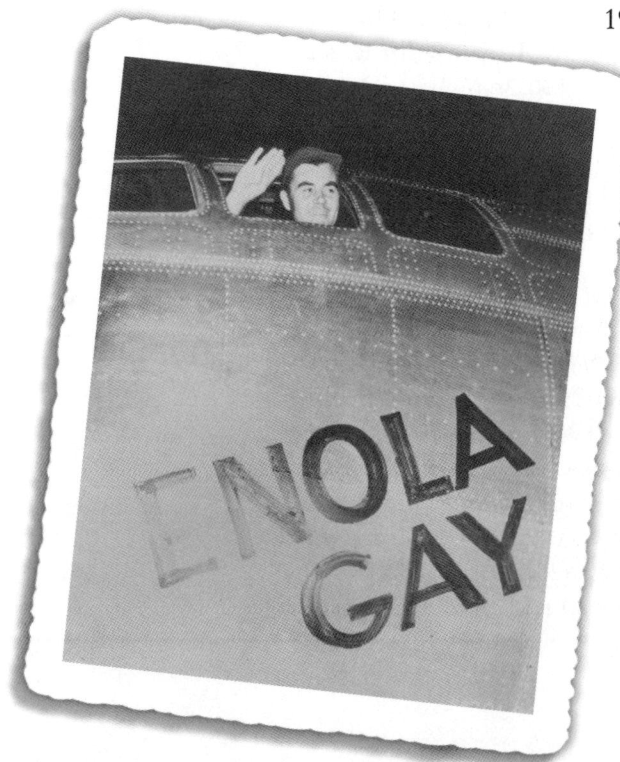

Before "oh-dark thirty" on August 6, several B-29s took off from Tinian, including the *Enola Gay*, carrying the deadly payload and piloted by Colonel Paul Tibbets. Scout planes headed for the target cities and radioed back their observations. Visibility over Hiroshima was good and Tibbets headed there accompanied by two other B-29s, one loaded with atmospheric instruments, the other to photograph the event.

As the nerve center for Japan's homeland defense force and headquarters for the Second Army, Hiroshima was the primary target. Kokura, with its massive steel mills, was the alternate site.

Over the target the *Enola Gay*'s bomb bay doors opened, the bombardier checked his scope, and then released Little Boy. The plane lurched upward immediately, free of the nine-thousand-pound bomb, then it banked hard to the right with its escorts and tried to make it a safe distance away before the blast and the aftershock buffeted the three planes. They circled the city from a safe distance, assessing and documenting the damage, and then headed back to Tinian. Even two hundred miles away they could see the mushroom cloud forming over the devastated city.

The news was slow to reach Tokyo, and when it did, the leadership met the reports with skepticism. The Allies dropped leaflets to warn of more such attacks unless Japan surrendered immediately. President Truman also cautioned the Japanese that there'd be more to come if they didn't capitulate: "If they do not now accept our terms, they may accept a rain of ruin from the air, the like of which has never been seen on this Earth."

Even when it was reported that a single bomb had wiped out Hiroshima, Tokyo Radio announced that it was a cluster of bombs. "The city itself had been full of rumors: a plane had sprayed petrol from the sky and ignited it by dropping incendiaries; the city had been sprinkled with [highly flammable] magnesium powder which exploded when it came into contact with the electric tram wires," reported Louis Allen in "The Nuclear Raids" for *History of the Second World War* magazine, January 9, 1975.

Whatever Japan might have considered doing in response was not done quickly enough. Three days later, the whole scenario was repeated, with Kokura, in the northeast sector of Kyushu, as the target. The B-29 dubbed *Bock's Car* was given the honor of carrying Fat Man, again accompanied by two observer planes. But while everything had gone smoothly for the Hiroshima mission, this one was plagued from start to finish, including a late takeoff, bad weather, problems with the plane's fuel transfer system, and on and on.

As *Bock's Car* approached its target, the city of Kokura was obscured by smoke drifting from the ruins of nearby Yawata, dubbed the Pittsburgh of Japan for its industrial complexes, now destroyed and left as smoldering hulks. The pilot made his approach but called off the run. He tried again from another direction, without success. "Almost an hour had passed since we arrived over the city," recalled Jacob Beser, a crewman on

BELOW: *While Air Force bomber squadrons maintained a rigorous round-the-clock schedule to firebomb Tokyo and virtually every major city and industrial center in Japan, U.S. Army and Marine ground forces were preparing for the final invasion, slated for late 1945. And so when news of the first atomic bombing of Hiroshima was flashed around the world, it immediately caught everyone's attention, in hopes that maybe the end was very near. These GIs at Guam seemed pleased about the news, aware that they would have been part of the invasion force.*
U.S. Army Photo

board both the *Enola Gay* and *Bock's Car,* in a first-person account for *World War II* magazine, spring of 1991.

"Since there was now insufficient fuel to make it back to Tinian and only marginal fuel to make it to Iwo Jima, with the bomb still aboard, we would make one more pass at Kokura, and then, if unsuccessful, we would head for Nagasaki. We began a third pass. At about that time I began to detect activity on the Japanese fighter control frequencies. It was obvious that they were now getting interested in this crazy B-29 milling around overhead."

After a third unsuccessful run over the city, the pilot decided to head to Nagasaki while there was still enough fuel. Kokura was thus spared, but Nagasaki, on the opposite end of the island, was about to experience Armageddon.

"When the news of Nagasaki arrived, the rumor began to spread that Japan too had the atomic weapon but had refrained from using it," continued Louis Allen. "Once the Americans had dropped it, a special [Japanese] naval squadron of six-engined bombers had crossed the Pacific and delivered it on San Francisco and Los Angeles. As this rumor spread, it cheered up those [Japanese] suffering from wounds and sickness, patients in hospitals began to laugh and sing and prayers were offered for the pilots who were supposed to have made the gallant suicide flight." (Obviously Japan didn't have the bomb, and no such mission was conducted.)

As word of the devastation trickled out, heated debate threatened to divide and topple Japan's government, still reeling from the attack on Hiroshima. Even after Emperor Hirohito decided that surrender was the only honorable option, to spare any more suffering by his people, opponents attempted to stop him from broadcasting his decision, attempting to seize the radio station. But the emperor went on the air and announced his decision: "I cannot bear to see my innocent people suffer any longer. It pains me to think of those who served me so faithfully, the soldiers and sailors who have been killed or wounded in far-off battles, the families who have lost all their worldly goods, and often their lives as well. The time has come when we must bear the unbearable. I swallow my tears and give my sanction to the proposal to accept the Allied proclamation . . ."

After twelve years of military aggression in the Far East, beginning with the invasion of Manchuria, the emperor said it was time for the entire country to reverse course and lay down their weapons: "We have resolved to pave the way for a grand peace for all the generations to come, by enduring the unendurable and suffering what is insufferable."

But the radical firebrands in Tokyo were ready to oppose the emperor, willing to fight to the death and allow the entire country to be totally destroyed. That was an unacceptable option for the emperor, who was fully aware that already every major city in Japan was more wasteland than thriving metropolis, reduced to rubble by the prolonged firebombing campaign. And

Left: *Before the world could fully comprehend the magnitude of the nuclear explosion that leveled Hiroshima, Japan, and while Japanese leaders were arguing about what to do next, Nagasaki was leveled (the mushroom cloud shown here), prompting the Emperor to reluctantly give up the fight, to spare his people any more loss of life. Radicals attempted to prevent him from announcing his decision to the country, but everyone knew it was the only option left, short of completely obliterating all of Japan and its people in a protracted but futile battle.*
National Archives Photo

RIGHT: *The war was over but Japan was still simmering—not overtly, but there were undercurrents of militants attempting to rearm to resume the fight. Allied occupation forces were needed to remind the Japanese populace to accept defeat and rebuild the country's infrastructure. Comedian Danny Kaye was dispatched to Japan to bolster the sagging spirits of the American forces, all of them counting and recounting their points, just wanting to get home.*
National Archives Photo

now the Americans had this new weapon. Instead of obliterating a city with two hundred or five hundred or a thousand bombs, they could do it with just one. The emperor could only assume there were more to follow.

The Greatest News Ever

As word of the unprecedented attacks flashed around the world, Americans in uniform were now relatively certain they just might survive the war after all.

Halfway around the world, the Andrews Sisters were performing in Naples, Italy, at a replacement station for GIs wanting to get home but uncertain if that would happen anytime soon. "It was loaded with about eight thousand of the most unhappy-looking audiences you'd ever seen," recalled Maxine Andrews in the book, *The Good War*, by Studs Terkel. "They were hanging from the rafters. All these fellas were being shipped out to the South Pacific. They hadn't been home for four years, and it was just their bad luck. We were trying to get them into good spirits. We were pretty well through with the show when I heard someone offstage calling me: 'Psst . . . psst.' The soldier said to me, 'I have a very

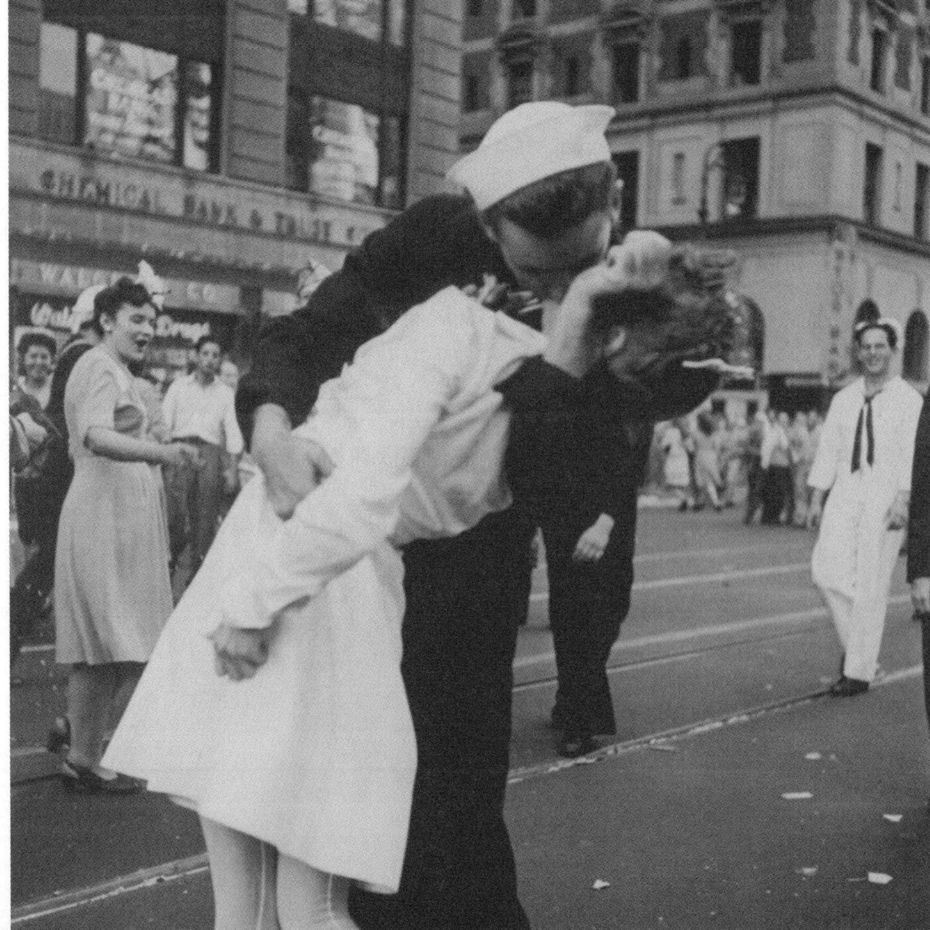

RIGHT: *News doesn't get any better than when it was announced in New York's Times Square that the war was over . . . finally. It was also a pretty good excuse to grab the first pretty girl and plant one right on the ole kisser. (And of course, years later, thousands of sailors and formerly slender gals would claim that they were the ones in the famous photo, though they had no idea what had happened to the one they were kissing.)*
National Archives Photo

important message for Patty to tell the audience.' I started to laugh, because they were always playing tricks on us. I said, 'I can't do it in the middle of the show.' He said, 'You're gonna get me in trouble.' So I took the piece of paper. I didn't read it. I walked out on the stage, saying to myself, I'm gonna get in trouble with Patty, with the CO. Patty said, 'Stop your kidding. We can't read that here. We've got to finish the show.' I shoved the note at her. She finally said, 'All right. I'll go along with the gag.'

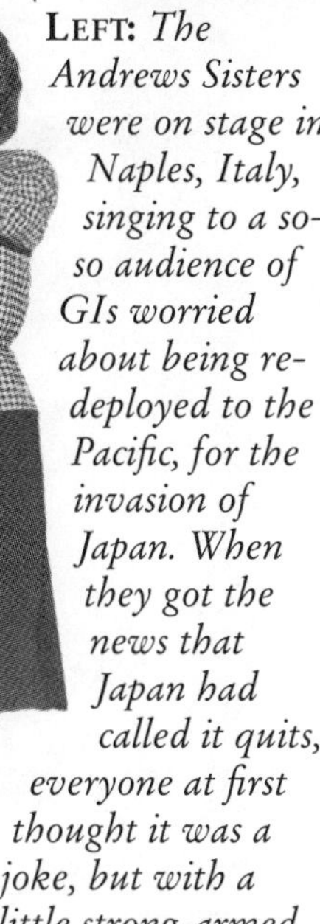

LEFT: *The Andrews Sisters were on stage in Naples, Italy, singing to a so-so audience of GIs worried about being redeployed to the Pacific, for the invasion of Japan. When they got the news that Japan had called it quits, everyone at first thought it was a joke, but with a little strong-armed convincing, the GIs finally realized the great news and bedlam broke out.*
U.S. Air Force Photo

"So she said to the fellas, 'Look, it's a big joke up here. I have a note supposedly from the CO.' Without reading it first, she read it out loud. It announced the end of the war with Japan. There wasn't a sound in the whole auditorium. She looked at it again. She looked at me. I was serious. So she said, 'No, fellas, this is from the CO. This is an announcement that the war is over, so you don't have to go.' With that, she started to cry. Laverne and I were crying. Still there was no reaction from the guys. So she said it again: 'This is the end, this is the end.' All of a sudden, all hell broke loose. They yelled and screamed. We got into the jeep, and all of a sudden it hit us. Oh heavens, if this is a joke, they're gonna tar and feather us. We suffered until we got to Caserta [and our hotel]. They reassured us that the announcement was true."

Some GIs were on board transport ships bound for Japan from the West Coast, combat-ready and accompanied by all the necessary firepower to get the job done when they heard the great news. Thousands continued on, for occupation duty in Japan, to enforce whatever terms would be negotiated in the surrender, to disarm the entire population, to help rebuild Japan.

Transport pilot Tyrone Power had already flown numerous missions in the Pacific when the war ended. He continued for several months more, flying in reinforcements and supplies for the thousands of occupation troops swarming into Japan. During layovers he had time to tour the ravaged country and nearby cities and saw a defeated but defiant population clinging to dignity while

LEFT: *Comedian Danny Kaye and baseball manager Leo Durocher of the Brooklyn Dodgers kept the banter at a lively pace wherever and whenever they felt like creating a little chaos during their tour of the Pacific. A longtime Dodgers fan and Brooklyn native poses for a photo with Leo the Lip, who'd traveled a long way to visit the boys on occupation duty at Atsugi Airfield in Japan.*
National Archives Photo

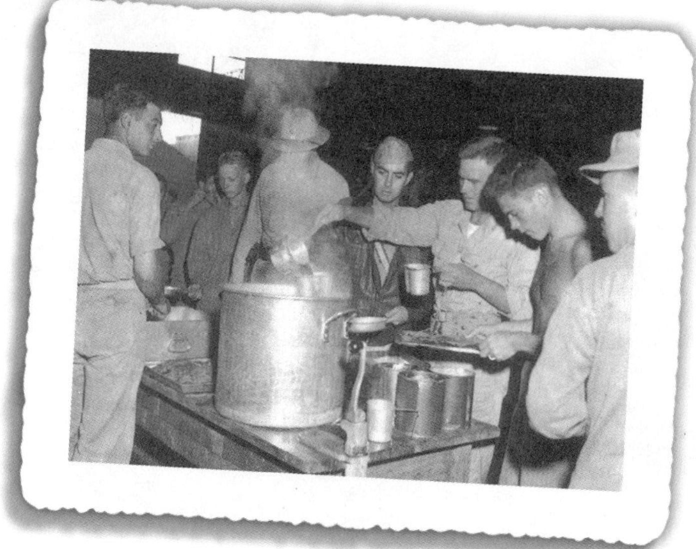

Above: *As news filtered out that Allied troops were massing for a final invasion of Japan's home islands, Marine Corps transport pilot Tyrone Power knew he would be flying daily missions, rushing in reinforcements or dropping supplies. But with the war officially over, and occupation forces fanning out to control the mostly humbled Japanese masses, Power also repositioned with his plane and his unit, to Omura Naval Air Station at Kyushu. Here he waits for a cup of strong black coffee and a hot meal.*
U.S. Marine Corps Photo

working to rebuild their homes. (He returned to Hollywood after his discharge in January of '46 and quickly reclaimed his status as one of the top leading men in movies.)

Jonathan Winters was part of the Marine Detachment assigned to the carrier *Bon Homme Richard*. He was with the earliest contingent of Marines to move into the Yokosuka Naval Base in Tokyo Bay at the end of August in 1945. To relieve the boredom of occupation duty, he did impressions of famous stars, lending each his own twisted vision of insanity. (Six months later he was discharged and began fine-tuning his shtick, first as a radio jock in Columbus, Ohio, then in New York nightclubs, until he made guest appearances on TV and went on to become one of the funniest and most quick-witted comics over the next many decades.)

Gerald S. O'Loughlin was slated to reinforce the Marines at Okinawa but instead was held back to train at Hilo, Hawaii, for the invasion of Japan. His mission changed again when the Japanese called it quits. Then his unit, the 2nd Engineer Battalion of the 5th Marine Division, spent six months on occupation duty at Nagasaki, on the island of Kyushu. (A year after the Japanese surrender, O'Loughlin was discharged from active duty but remained in the Marine Reserve. He used his GI Bill benefit to complete a degree in engineering and enrolled at the Neighborhood Playhouse in New York, where he developed his acting skills. He would be called up again during the Korean War and served briefly with the 2nd Marines. Then it was back to New York and Broadway, and then Hollywood, where he made his mark in the movies and on television.)

Another GI slated to participate in the invasion of Japan was bomber radioman Charlton Heston, who was recuperating from injuries at Elmendorf Air Base in Anchorage. His unit, the 11th Air Force, would be relocated to Okinawa in the months leading up to the invasion, and he fully expected to be on board a B-25 Mitchell bomber again, or maybe the newer, super-sleek B-29s, flying missions over Japan. Those plans got scrapped when the two atomic bombs encouraged the Japanese to reconsider their militaristic attitude about continuing the fight.

Former theater usher Johnny Carson got to the war very late. In fact, he enlisted in the Navy in mid-1943, but with boot camp and then officers training, he didn't get deployed to the Pacific until the closing weeks of the war. "He was en route to the combat zone aboard a troopship when the bombing of Hiroshima and Nagasaki brought the war to a close," wrote Scott Baron in *They Also Served*. "Although he arrived too late for combat, he got a firsthand education in the consequences of war."

Assigned to the battleship *Pennsylvania* two days after it had been torpedoed and limped to Guam for repairs, Carson, "as the newest and most junior officer, was assigned to supervise the removal of twenty dead sailors. He stated that he would never forget the stench of the decaying crewmen."

Jack Paar was pulling radio duty with the "mosquito network" in the South Pacific when the war ended. He had the impossible task of trying to get GIs to do the last thing any of them would consider doing. "The South Pacific was full of troops, all anxious to get home, and I was assigned to assist in a re-enlistment campaign. I wrote and recorded ten one-minute announcements, which were played on the island radio stations, telling the homesick GIs all about the joys of re-enlistment," he wrote in the book, *I Kid You Not*. "I felt a little hypocritical, since under the re-deployment schedule I was slated to leave on the next boat. However, my smugness was ironically punctured by fate." Paar found himself waiting around another six weeks, listening to himself on the radio trying to convince himself and hundreds of other GIs to stick around for another hitch!

LEFT: *Slated to be thrown into the fight late in 1945, for the assault on Japan, Navy junior officer Johnny Carson was instead dispatched to Guam, where he was in charge of removing the bodies of twenty sailors from the battleship* Pennsylvania *after it was hit by an enemy torpedo. It was a grim reminder of the cost of war.*
National Personnel Records Center Photo

The Unconditional End of Hostilities

On September 2, Tokyo Bay was blanketed with American warships, and the members of the Japanese delegation finally realized just how badly they had been duped by their own military commanders, who had grossly underestimated and blatantly underreported the fighting strength of the U.S. Pacific Fleet, which had been far from lying in the shallows at Pearl Harbor, the waters off Midway, or the strait at Iron Bottom Sound near the Solomons. In fact, among the many warships that had been cruising the coastal waters and heaving shells at anything within range were several survivors of the Pearl Harbor attack, including "the *Nevada*, which had been torpedoed and hit by

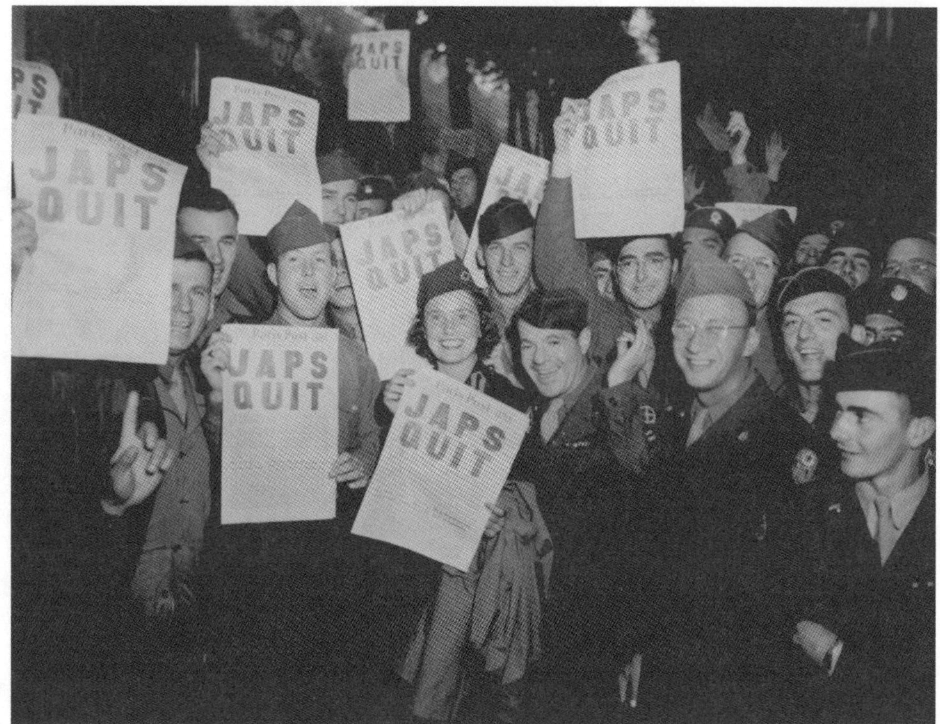

RIGHT: *From New York to London, from San Francisco to Paris, newspapers screamed it as boldly as they could:* JAPS QUIT. *At the Rainbow Corner Red Cross Club in Paris, Allied servicemen and Red Cross workers happily posted the news on August 10, 1945; then it was time for some well-deserved partying.*
National Archives Photo

five 500-pound bombs, the *California;* struck by two torpedoes and a bomb; the *West Virginia,* hit by at least three and perhaps seven torpedoes; and the *Tennessee, Maryland,* and *Pennsylvania,* all three hit but only slightly damaged," reported Thomas Allen and Norman Polmar in *Code-Name Downfall.*

The magnitude of the Imperial Navy's gross miscalculation of the balance of power in the Pacific was clearly obvious at the end of the war. Though still believing they had more warships afloat, Japan in fact only had nineteen destroyers, and no carriers, battleships, or cruisers were fully operational and available to repel the Allied invasion slated for the end of 1945. (Some were in dry dock awaiting repair or still being built, with no possibility of completion.) The Allies (including the British fleet) had twenty aircraft carriers, nine battleships, twenty-two cruisers, and "only" eighty destroyers.

On the day of Japan's official surrender, the skies over Tokyo were buzzing with swarms of Allied bombers and fighters, the same ones that had ignited a firestorm on every major city and industrial center. The surrender ceremony took place aboard the mighty battleship USS *Missouri,* witnessed by General Douglas MacArthur, Admiral Chester Nimitz, and Admiral Bull Halsey. Also on hand was Bataan Death March survivor and MacArthur's close friend, Jonathan Wainwright, along with British commander Ernest Percival.

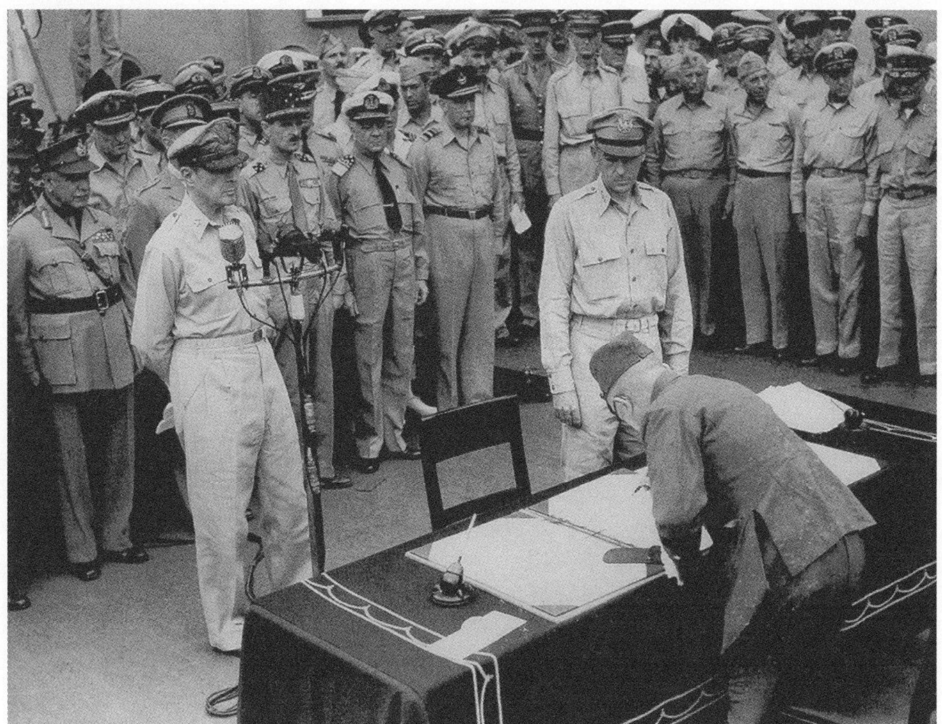

Left: *On September 2, 1945, the formal surrender ceremony took place on the deck of the battleship USS* Missouri *in Tokyo Bay, witnessed by American and British dignitaries, including General Douglas MacArthur, Admiral Chester Nimitz, and Admiral William "Bull" Halsey.*
Imperial War Museum Photo

MacArthur stepped over to the microphone. Speaking by radio for broadcast in the United States, he issued a cautionary message to the entire world: "A new era is upon us. Men since the beginning of time have sought peace. Military alliances, balances of power, leagues of nations, all in turn failed, leaving the only path to be by the way of the crucible of war. The utter destructiveness of war now blots out this alternative. We have had our last chance. If we do not devise some greater and more equitable system, Armageddon will be at our door."

An Afterthought

Over the years there has been heated debate about America's decision to drop the bomb. Certainly it was well known that the Nazis were rushing to develop their own nuclear weapon, while the Japanese had a limited program hampered by minimal funding and lack of vital materials. Both of these Axis powers were desperate by late 1944 to reverse the string of Allied victories, with the invasion of their homelands in the very near future. They lashed out, like caged and wounded animals, frantic to try anything to win back the upper hand. They had already proven with their callous aggressions toward the Jews and other "undesirables" in Europe, the Chinese and Koreans, and the Americans and Filipinos in the Pacific that mass slaughter was an acceptable,

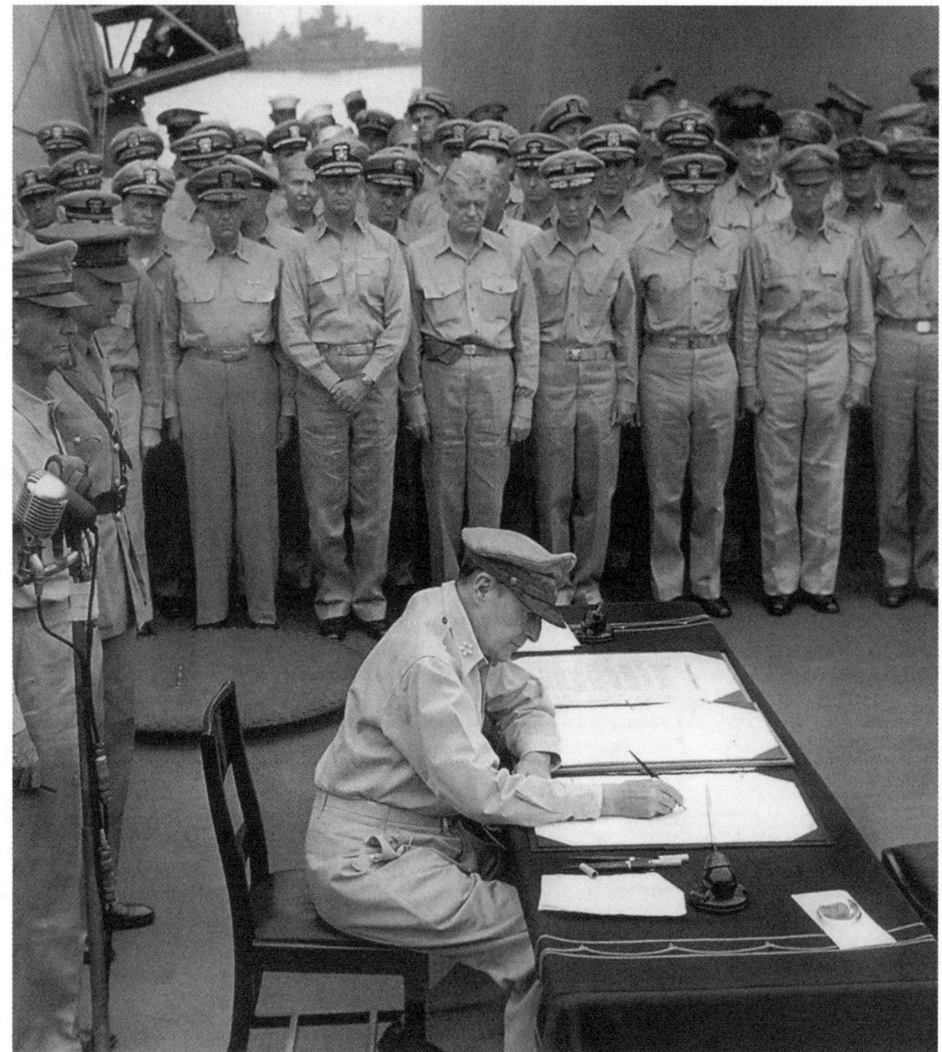

Right: *With numerous American and Allied commanders and strategists looking on, Army General Douglas MacArthur signs the surrender document, officially ending the war in the Pacific.*
National Archives Photo

efficient way to rid themselves of anyone and everyone not of their own kind. Both countries would most certainly have used such a weapon if they had only developed one first. They didn't. America did.

Maybe the detonation of such powerful weapons was payback for the devastation at Pearl Harbor. Quite likely the American strategists determined that using such a fearsome device would end the war, by convincing the Japanese that more such bombs were stockpiled and ready to be unleashed if they didn't surrender immediately. Maybe the U.S. military war planners calculated that wiping out one or two cities would in the long run save more lives—both American and Japanese—than would have been lost during a final offensive campaign for Japan. (Some predictions of that outcome were in the millions of lives lost, on both sides.) But probably no one really understood the impact the atomic explosions would have, not just on

Hiroshima and Nagasaki, not just on Japan, but on all of mankind. At the time, the only consideration was the now, not the distant future.

The United States was responsible for dropping the atomic bomb on another warring nation, the only country in the twentieth century to do so. But it was Nazi Germany and Imperial Japan that plunged the world into a downward spiral that would require such action. Both of the Axis powers learned that when America gets involved in righting obvious wrongs, payback is hell.

15. Returning Home . . . Finally

"HEY THERE, MISTER! YOU'D BETTER HIDE YOUR SISTER, CAUSE THE FLEET'S IN . . ."

From the song "The Fleet's In," by Johnny Mercer and Victor Schertzinger, Famous Music Corporation, 1942

"I'VE SEEN THESE MEN DURING A BATTLE AND AFTERWARD. LONG AFTER THE WAR I SAW THEM AGAIN . . . IN THEIR HOMES, HOBBLING AROUND ON THEIR CRUTCHES, OR SEATED, LEGLESS, HAPPILY SURROUNDED BY THEIR WIVES AND CHILDREN. I'VE SEEN THEM ALL. I'VE LOVED THEM ALL, LONG AFTER THE WORLD FORGOT THEM."

—Marlene Dietrich in her autobiography

WHEN IT WAS FINALLY THEIR TURN TO HEAD BACK HOME, when they had enough points, that mythical, magical number that would allow them to say "Auf Wieder-Bye Bye" and "Sayonara Baby," all that the guys in uniform wanted to do was get home and do absolutely nothing . . . except maybe burn that damn uniform! All the fanfare and the parades and the welcome home posters and banners were more for the folks and the friends who didn't do all the fighting (and the dying) so they could say they did something special "for the boys," all of which only proved they had no idea what these men really thought was "special."

A soft pillow and a blanket that didn't itch or smell like mothballs, real eggs, toilet tissue, an ice-cold root beer float, sleeping in, total silence, warmth, nowhere to be, nowhere to go and no one tellin' 'em to get there fast, Mom's chicken and dumplings, maybe a swig of Dad's secret stash of hooch, a girlie magazine with all of the pages, walking barefoot without those damned combat boots anymore. That's all they wanted. Nothing that cost too much, but all the little simple things that were priceless.

They had gone off and seen another part of the world in all its beauty, in all its horror. They had lived a lifetime of memories they would always hold on to, and coped with the ugliest of nightmares they tried hard to forget.

And when they got home they found the old neighborhood just the way it was—except for the gold star flags in the front windows with the curtains closed. The classmates they knew in high school had gone off to college, gone off to work, gone off to war, and many of them hadn't come back. They too were caught up in the draft, or maybe they had enlisted, knowing it was the right thing to do. But then they had to go off and die in some godforsaken unknown place overseas. Too many of them had gone off and got themselves dead . . . and the only way to know who didn't make it back was to look for the gold star flags in the front window and the heartbroken wives and moms who didn't have much to celebrate when the Nazis and the Japs called it quits and everyone else cheered the boys coming home.

OPPOSITE: *Three years after the war ended, Medal of Honor recipient Audie Murphy—the most decorated American soldier in the war—returned to France, to pay tribute to the thousands of fallen heroes during the conquest of Fortress Europe.*

By then, Murphy was in Hollywood, learning the fickle art of acting at the Actors Lab in Los Angeles, where many more veterans were using their GI Bill to do the same. Though Murphy would eventually star in several movies, mostly Westerns, he never quite chased away the demons that haunted him.

Photo Courtesy of Baylor University

Above: *All they wanted was that "million-dollar wound"—bad enough to get them sent home for treatment and rehab, but nothing too serious, where they might have to sacrifice something vital, like a limb or an eye, or the "family jewels."*
Imperial War Museum Photo

Those who survived combat and came back alive and with all their appendages and vital organs intact were the lucky ones. Many were hailed as conquering heroes. The leathernecks, in particular, could expect the royal treatment: "It was the best time for a Marine to return to the States, since there was a shortage of Marines who had seen combat, and we were very much in demand for dances, social life, and moonlight romance," recalled Art Buchwald in *Leaving Home*. He had spent time on several of those unheard-of islands in the South Pacific, mostly cleaning planes and weapons, trying to stay out of combat and producing a mimeographed newsletter for his unit. "The beauty of being a U.S. Marine during World War II was that when someone saw you in uniform they never asked what you did in the war. They assumed that you were either in Guadalcanal or Iwo Jima. I never once lied or exaggerated my role in the hostilities. It was done for me by people who wanted to believe that I was a hero. Protesting their assumptions did no good, because the more I denied it the more modesty they thought I showed. I had no choice but to relax and enjoy it."

Women Question Their Role

For hundreds of thousands of women, the war had meant tossing aside their aprons and putting on a hard hat, doing a "man's job" and often doing it better. It had meant learning a trade outside the home and getting a paycheck, doing something good for themselves and their family, but maybe more importantly, doing something really great when their country called. But now the men were coming back, and they wanted "the little lady" at home, believing that anyone who couldn't earn enough to take care of his family was less than a man. After surviving the worst of war, they weren't going to tolerate anyone questioning their manhood.

"In the summer of 1944, the War Department published a pamphlet entitled *Do You Want Your Wife to Work After the War?*" reported Doris Kearns Goodwin in *No Ordinary Time*. "The pamphlet tried to impress on its readers that women's roles were changing, but the dominant voices were those that spoke against women's working. Enthusiastic admiration for Rosie the Riveter was replaced by the prevailing idea that 'women ought to be delighted to give up any job and return to their proper sphere . . . the kitchen.'"

Many women were more than willing to be a full-time mom and wife again, but thousands more felt they could juggle home life and work part-time and earn a little extra to get a little extra of the good life everyone was

Left: *They finally earned the magic number, that ever-changing elusive point total that meant they could return home. For these happy GIs it meant boarding a troop transport at Le Havre along the French coast, then enduring another sixteen days or more traversing the Atlantic. At least this time they wouldn't have to zigzag with all the lights blackened out, hoping they weren't torpedoed by a Nazi U-boat. This time there wasn't the apprehension, the uncertainty. This time they knew exactly what they wanted to do . . . they'd only been dreaming about it and talking about it for months, and now, finally, it was actually going to happen. They were finally going home.*
National Archives Photo

talking about. But often when the men came back and reality hit hard, their pride got in the way, and once-perfect marriages were torn apart because of it.

Even without the issue of whether or not to work, women were concerned about what influence the war might have had on the men. "Women's magazines displayed a keen anxiety. The *Ladies' Home Journal* asked the crucial question: 'Has your husband come home to the right woman?' *Good Housekeeping* advised families to give a returning soldier two or three weeks to get over talking and 'oppressive remembering,' and then, if these symptoms persisted, send him to a psychiatrist," wrote Don Graham in *No Name on the Bullet*. "*Recreation* chirpily held that 'Convalescing can be fun.' Hardly any potential problem was overlooked. *House Beautiful* placed its faith in the 'home . . . the greatest rehabilitation center of them all.'"

All the returning veterans wanted was for their wives to be back at home where they belonged, with things exactly the way they were before they left . . . no great leap forward, just take it all back like some very bad dream they suddenly woke up from. But for millions of them, even that was too much to ask for. Life after WWII couldn't be the same, wouldn't be the same as it was, because everyone they knew wasn't doing everything they used to do before.

The Staggering Statistics

While the entire country mobilized to support the war effort, it was the men between eighteen and thirty who did most of the fighting, in unheard-of places they never knew existed, like Tarawa and Tunisia, Saipan and St. Lô, Munda and Monte Rotundo, Bougainville and Bologna. Even men well into their forties and teenage boys who should have still been in school stepped forward to be part of the defining era of the century.

"During the war the American people had contributed a peak total of 12 million men and women to the armed forces, which had a strength close to 10 million at the end of the war," reported Martin Blumenson in the article "America: Troubles at Home" for *History of the Second World War* magazine, February 20, 1975.

"More than one million had become casualties—600,000 were wounded, among them 2,000 paralyzed by wounds severing the spinal cord; almost 250,000 were dead, of whom more than 200,000 were buried on foreign soil—122,000 in Europe, 41,000 in the Mediterranean area, 29,000 on Pacific isles—and about whom more than 90,000 relatives had written the War Department asking that the bodies be brought home; more than 75,000 had been listed as prisoners of war; and 60,000 were missing."

Those numbers were overwhelming, but the primary concern for every American family was their own loved ones in uniform. And that's what brought the war down to a very personal level . . . the triumphs, the tragedies, the homecomings or the heartbreaks, not of thousands, or hundreds, but just one . . . their one.

Bob Hope certainly understood just how precious every GI was, not just to his own family and community, but to the country and to Hope personally. And he knew the sacrifices they had made, for he had seen firsthand what they'd had to endure for the sake of democracy and freedom, and he stated so on one of his radio shows at the end of the war: "I've seen some great acts of achievement in the past few years. I saw a boy in a hospital in Espirito Santos lying in a bed, taking on a quart of blood plasma. This skinny American hero looked up, smiled, saying it feels good. Two hours later they told us that boy died. And there's Salerno and Saipan and North Africa and Guadalcanal, and aircraft carriers that went down dragging Jap battleships and destroyers and Nazi subs and planes along with it. Little jungle clearings and road crossings and creeks and rivers without names, and the achievement of capturing those places took more than perseverance and intelligence. It took blood and missing limbs and blinded eyes and shattered nerves and ruined lives. I'd like to thank every kid in uniform for the honor of working for him." Bob Hope loved the GIs and took every opportunity to let them know that. He continued to entertain the troops for many years after WWII and, sadly, for several more wars to come.

Another entertainer who got a sense of the sacrifices of war was future actor George C. Scott, who as a Marine was assigned to the burial honor guard at Arlington National Cemetery in Washington, D.C. Scott had enlisted in the Corps only weeks after graduating from high school, but it was in mid-1945 and the war in Europe was just ending. By the time he finished boot camp, the Japanese were about to get nuked.

"Previously disappointed about missing out on real-live combat, after watching hundreds of burials and veiled, devastated widows, Scott began to see war in the more brutal light of reality," wrote James E. Wise Jr. and Anne Collier Rehill in *Stars in the Corps.*

Scott remained a leatherneck for four years, until June of 1949, and then studied journalism and drama at the University of Missouri. (He would finally see "action" in WWII many years later, playing the fiery tank commander George S. Patton, a role that earned Scott a Best Actor Oscar award in 1971.)

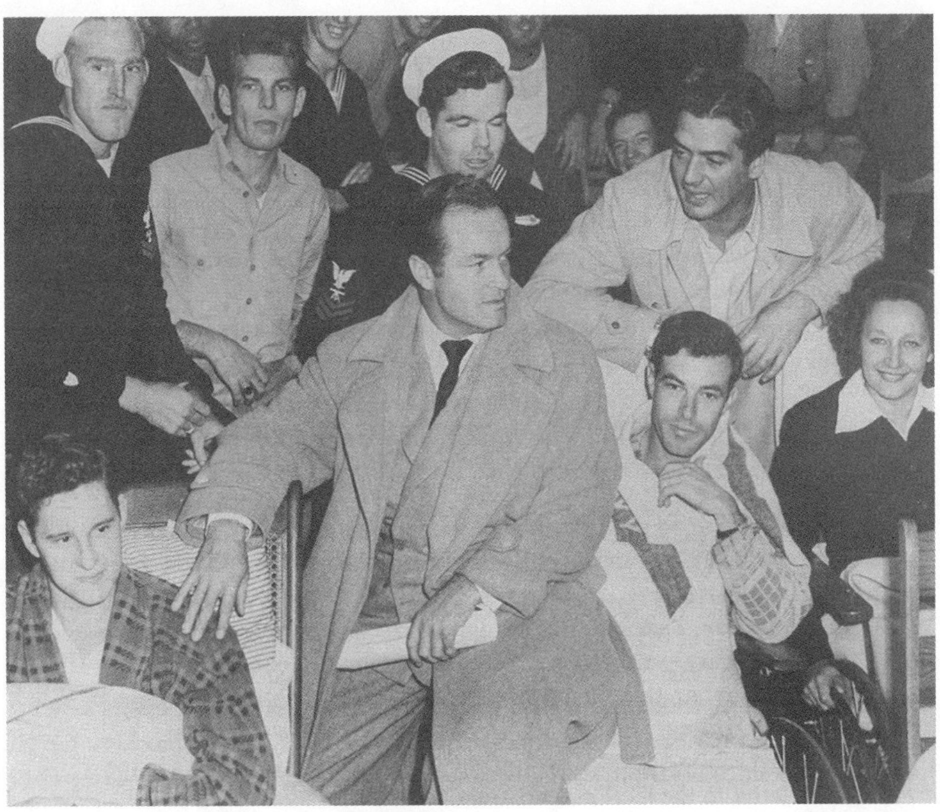

Left: *Bob Hope tried his best to let the boys who were broken and battered know that their sacrifices were not forgotten. He even went on his weekly radio show and told his listening audience just how special these kids were . . .*

Most of them were kids when they left a few short years earlier. They came back seemingly ten years older, having experienced things no one would ever imagine, unable to talk about things they could never forget, second-guessing why they were allowed to live while their best buddy had bought a one-way ticket upstairs.

U.S. Navy Photo

Pursuing the American Dream

Thousands of veterans were able to get their old jobs back. Others went looking for something better, although they weren't always sure what that something better was. Job assistance offices run by the USO, or veterans' groups, church volunteers, and local cities were set up across the country.

Big band leader Horace Heidt used his radio show to help the veterans any way he could. "In 1944, Heidt was featured in a Monday night Blue Network show for Hires Root Beer, a program designed to 'give a break to boys back from the war,'" wrote John Dunning in *Tune in Yesterday: Old Time Radio*. "Here, Heidt introduced two guests—recently discharged veterans—and discussed their war records on the air. He asked employers in areas of the veterans' interest to contact their local Blue Network affiliates with offers of work. A teletype was set up on stage to tick off the job offers as they came in."

The government also did its part to help the returning service members, every honorably discharged veteran with their own Bill of Rights, guaranteeing them a fresh start as they made the transition to civilian life. "The new veteran had the assistance of the GI Bill of Rights, legislation passed by

Congress in 1944 and enacted into law by the President's signature," noted Martin Blumenson in "Troubles at Home." "He could join the 52–20 Club and collect $20 unemployment insurance for 52 weeks. He could have help to purchase a home or start a business. But what attracted him most was the opportunity to complete or continue his education—high school, vocational school, college or university—with a subsidy from the government of $75 a month if he was married, $50 if single, to the extent of his months of active duty. These sums would soon be increased.

"The return of the veterans to educational pursuits would reach flood tide in 1946 and 1947—more than 2.5 million and their maturity, seriousness, application, and success boded well for the country, changed the educational level of the nation, and created a pattern that has lasted."

One who helped his fellow veterans and their families with the transition to civilian life was future actor Rod Steiger, who had served on the destroyer *Taussig* in the Pacific. After getting out of the Navy, he went to work for the Veterans Administration, in the Office of Dependents and Beneficiaries. After that he moved to New York and signed on with the Theater Wing's Dramatic Workshop, which he paid for with his GI Bill benefits.

Literally thousands of former servicemen used their GI Bill entitlements to enroll at performing arts colleges, dramatic workshops, and so on, developing acting and entertaining skills they may never have even considered or been able to afford previously. A few of the many veterans who would use the GI Bill as a springboard to life as a professional entertainer included comedian Sid Caesar, salsa musician and big band leader Tito Puente, and slapstick comedian Milton Hines, better known as Soupy Sales. Among the many budding actors training on the GI Bill were Bernard Schwartz (the future Tony Curtis), Richard Boone, Neville Brand, William Windom, Lee Marvin, Paul Newman, and Walter Matuschanskayasky (later, Walter Matthau).

Hundreds more attended drama schools, performing arts colleges, dance studios, and the like across the country, eventually filling the ranks of entertainers, from community theaters to nationally known television shows, radio programs, repertoire groups, and on and on, doing something they loved and sharing that love every night they went out and performed.

In its December 1945 issue, *Photoplay* magazine noted the large influx of returning actors who had served in the military bumping up against the crop that had dominated the silver screen the previous few years. "During the war an amazing number of men stars burst into being: Van Johnson, Peter Lawford, Robert Walker, Tom Drake, Cornel Wilde, Gregory Peck, John Hodiak, and many more. But already out of uniform or soon to don mufti again are such peacetime favorites as: Jimmy Stewart, Tyrone Power, Robert Montgomery, Henry Fonda, Clark Gable, Ronald Reagan, Lon McCallister, Donald O'Connor, Gene Kelly, Victor Mature, Wayne Morris, and many other golden boys. Yes, it's the problem of whether it is to be the new FF's

Left: *Hollywood actor Tyrone Power had served in the Marine Corps as a transport pilot; then, after the war, he wound up in Japan on occupation duty, writing to his wife, actress Annabella, about his experiences. After returning home to a Hollywood transformed by the war, he wound up competing with a whole slate of new stars—such as Van Johnson, Robert Walker, and Gregory Peck—for roles that previously were his for the taking.*
U.S. Marine Corps Photo

or the old Famous Faces . . . or both! Just to complicate the problem let us add that there are in total 1,500 GIs returning from overseas to the acting ranks. How to get all of them back before the cameras is of course Question Number One . . . and the answer must be Yes!"

While they competed head to head for the almighty dollar, searching for the next blockbuster movie, the various studios around Hollywood were very concerned about the vast numbers of former employees returning from the war. *YANK* magazine writer Private James P. O'Neill reported in the July 27, 1945, issue, "Ten major studios have formulated a plan for the re-employment of the approximately 6,000 former studio workers who are now in the service. The basic plan is this: Every studio will hire a psychologist trained in personnel work whose main job will be to interview each returning former employee and figure out where he'll fit in best.

"Jobs will be adapted to the abilities of disabled veterans. Each ex-serviceman will be given at full pay all the sick leave and vacation time that has piled up in his absence—a fairly juicy slice of the war-boom melon in any man's language."

Drama teachers and coaches became aware of a unique and potentially sensitive problem involving students who were combat veterans. "[Actors] Lab teachers were particularly aware of the possible dangers in the use of affective memory, a key technique in the Stanislavsky method," reported Don Graham in *No Name on the Bullet*. "This technique asked the actor to draw upon a similar event from his own life. The strangulation scene in *Othello*, for example, would require the actor playing Othello to reach back into his own past and re-create an instance when he felt a rage murderous enough to strangle someone to death. Teachers, well aware of yellow journalism news stories about soldiers running amok, were loath to place soldiers and themselves in

Left: *Hollywood leading man Jimmy Stewart had the most distinguished war record among the many actors who had served in the military. In addition to flying twenty combat missions over Europe, he also rose through the ranks, eventually taking command of an American bomber unit in England. Here he receives the Air Medal for his distinguished service.*
U.S. Air Force Photo

Above: *Okay, so maybe his buddies did call him a "hunk of junk," but established actor and Coast Guardsman Victor Mature knew he had the look that could melt a young girl's heart, here receiving his discharge papers in November of 1945 from an adoring fan at the Coast Guard transition office. Mature actually had already returned from the Pacific to tour the country and sell war bonds, turning on the charm in just the right doses.*
U.S. Coast Guard Photo

psychologically dangerous terrain." (Of the 120 students enrolled at the Actors Lab in Los Angeles a year after the war ended, 71 were veterans.)

Some were discovered while still learning stagecraft, plucked for some big-time role in movies; others would have to pound the boards for years before making it on Broadway or getting to Hollywood or breaking in with the new medium known as television.

Well-known actor Melvyn Douglas had served in the China-Burma-India Campaign with Special Services, producing hundreds of musical revues and other stage shows there. After the Japanese surrender he was dispatched to New York to manage the Army's Entertainment Production Unit there, "to prepare soldiers for leaving the Army. Efforts were made to get the servicemen to think about the world they would be returning to and their futures," reported James E. Wise Jr. and Paul Wilderson III in *Stars in Khaki*. While in New York, Douglas was also asked to be involved with a war-related musical, cast almost exclusively with veterans except for Betty Garrett, the female lead. *Call Me Mister* was a hit and went on to do a respectable seven hundred performances. More importantly, this gave the cast a great opportunity to get reacclimated to Broadway and civilian life, and allowed them to showcase their talents for future roles.

Movies Spotlight the Returning Heroes

"Initially, Hollywood 'knew'—as did everyone else in the nation—what Americans would be wanting after the war. The veteran needed advice on how to readjust to civilian life. The civilian wanted reassurance that the veteran was the same human as everyone, his battle trauma notwithstanding," wrote Joseph C. Goulden in *The Best Years: 1945–1950*.

"So Hollywood offered *Pride of the Marines*, starring John Garfield, dealing with a blinded veteran's problems; *Tomorrow Is Forever*, in which Orson Welles played a man so deformed by war wounds that he let his wife believe him dead Welles's character is from the First World War, not the Second World War); *Lonely Journey*, about an amnesiac veteran, exploiting a theme dear to radio soap operas; and *That Man Malone*, featuring John Wayne as an itinerant blacksmith who returned home to find his wife had become a political power. And of course, there was *The Best Years of Our Lives*, about double amputee Homer Parris and two other troubled veterans."

Pride of the Marines portrayed the real-life exploits and travails of leatherneck Al Schmid, who received the Navy Cross for his actions on Guadalcanal, fending off the enemy while manning a machine gun. "The film was, in essence, a two-hour pep talk aimed at all of the country's returning veterans, wounded or otherwise," reported Ted Sennett in *Warner Brothers Presents*. "It told how Schmid, blinded by an enemy grenade after killing 200 enemy soldiers, eventually learned to live with his affliction after many months of bitterness and self-pity. In scene after scene, he is exhorted to find the strength to go on, to learn how to cope with his blindness."

I'll Be Seeing You, released in 1944, dealt with the often ignored ailment of psycho-neurosis, often called shell-shock and today referred to as post-traumatic stress disorder. Joseph Cotten played a discharged veteran coping with the psychological wounds of war, with the always lovely Ginger Rogers faithfully close by, not quite understanding what he is going through. *The Enchanted Cottage*, released in 1945, starred Robert Young as another disabled veteran, his face disfigured by the brutalities of combat, with Dorothy McGuire doing her best to see the goodness hidden behind his resentment at what the war had done to him.

While not a returning-home movie, 1945's *God Is My Co-Pilot* touched on the concerns facing combat veterans wondering how the war was affecting them. Colonel Robert Scott, stationed in the China-Burma-India Theater, talks with Big Mike Harrigan, an American missionary priest there: "Today I killed a hundred men, maybe more. I never killed a man before today, Big Mike. I know I'm a soldier, it's my duty to kill, but I'm wondering . . . will it change me any? Someday I go back to my wife and child, and there'll be millions like us, Big Mike, who've killed men in battle. Will we still be the same men who left them? Or will we be hard and bitter, burned out inside. And will life be the same meaningless thing it is out here?"

Of course, Big Mike says all the right things to assure Colonel Scott that he is only doing what is necessary, that he will be the same warmhearted, loving husband and father he was before. But he can't ignore that Colonel Scott's concerns are the same ones shared by veterans and their families and friends in the closing months of the war and immediately afterward. No one could know for sure what impact the war would have on those who survived it.

"*Beyond Glory* set out to tell a different kind of war story to a 'public perhaps tired of deeds of derring-do,'" wrote Don Graham. "The film explored the problems of a decorated and traumatized soldier [Alan Ladd] who returns to military service by enrolling at the Army Academy at West Point. While there, he is falsely accused of harassing a junior cadet, and in a series of flashbacks and trial scenes his war experience, trauma, and postwar cure are set forth."

And then there's the beloved classic, *The Best Years of Our Lives.* Without question, it's the one movie of the mid-'40s that best profiled the broad range of issues faced by returning veterans. The origin of this, one of the greatest movies ever, began with a photograph.

Two months after D-Day, MGM studio head Sam Goldwyn spotted a black-and-white photo of a group of ragged GIs in *Time* magazine. The men were crammed around the open window of a railcar, and their expressions conveyed every emotion: relief, happiness, apprehension, exhaustion, excitement. The boys were going home, and soon after the photo was taken, they would scatter to all corners of America. Goldwyn instantly realized that very soon there would be a new audience for movies—for MGM movies—and he planned to give them exactly what they wanted to see.

After the D-Day offensive and the continued push toward Berlin, prognosticators were saying that the war might be over by Christmas of 1944. Soon after, millions of servicemen would be returning home, eager to experience everything they'd been missing while overseas, including great American movies again. Goldwyn contacted one of his favorite writers, MacKinlay Kantor, and together they plotted out a story line involving returning vets. Kantor took a year to write the novel *Glory for Me*, which profiled a few GIs and their experiences as they made the transition from the military back to civilian life, with varying degrees of success.

Goldwyn then gave the project to scriptwriter Robert Sherwood and Oscar-winning director William Wyler, both of whom were concerned about how to portray one of the lead characters on film, a shell-shocked veteran who suffered from uncontrollable spasms.

Fortuitously, Wyler happened to see a screening of a riveting twenty-five-minute documentary produced by the Veterans Administration called *Diary of a Sergeant*, which followed a young disabled veteran struggling to readjust to civilian life. What made this former serviceman's story so poignant was that both his hands had been blown off in a training accident, and he was learning to use mechanical prosthetics, with minor successes and many setbacks along the way. But he soldiered on, this true American hero, a humble serviceman named Harold Russell.

Wyler and Goldwyn immediately realized they needed Russell to portray the disabled veteran for their film project, which they'd titled *The Best Years of Our Lives.* Russell agreed, and it became a stellar and memorable portrayal, a rallying cry for the hundreds of other disabled veterans who realized that if Russell could "get the girl" and land a job and do all of the daily requirements of living and enjoying life, despite the loss of both his hands, then they too had to try a little bit harder to make something good from their own shattered lives. For his efforts, Harold Russell, an untrained first-time actor, received the 1946 Best Supporting Actor Award and a special Oscar for inspiring disabled servicemen. He is the only Oscar winner to receive two gold statuettes for the same character.

But just as important were the roles of the two other veterans in the film: an inebriated sergeant and former banker, Al Stephenson (played by Frederic March, who won the Best Actor for this role), who is struggling to reconnect with his wife, Milly, and daughter, Peggy; and a bombardier, Captain Fred Derry (portrayed by Dana Andrews), coping with the loss of a buddy in a harrowing bombing mission to Germany. After spending a night on the town with the two veterans who traveled with him, Fred catches a ride with Peggy Stephenson (played by Teresa Wright):

"What'd ya do before the war, Fred?' Peggy asks him.

"I was a fountain attendant . . . a soda jerk. I was an expert behind that counter. I used to toss a scoop of ice cream in the air, adjust for wind drift, velocity, altitude, and WHAM, in the cone every time! I figure that's where I really learned to drop bombs."

"What'd ya think you'll do now?" Peggy asks.

"I'm not going back to that drugstore. Somehow or other I can't figure myself getting excited by a root beer float. I don't know just what I will do. I'm gonna take plenty of time lookin' around."

Later, frustrated with not finding a job and faced with possibly having to return to that very drugstore he despises, Fred is confronted by his wife, Marie (played by Virginia Mayo), when he brings groceries home to make supper. She's getting all dolled up, planning to eat out at Jackie's Hot Spot.

"I didn't tell ya the money was almost gone because everyday I kept hoping I was gonna land a good job," Fred tells her while getting supper ready. "At last I got it through my thick skull that I'm not going to get one, so we'll just have to forget about Jackie's Hot Spot, and the Blue Devil and all the rest."

"Well, why couldn't you get a job . . . Have you really been trying?"

"Oh sure, I've been all over town . . . all the employment offices. . . . They all tell me I don't know anything. They say I oughta spend a couple years as an apprentice or go to a trade school."

"A couple of years! . . . with you going to kindergarten, and what would I be doing in the meantime?" Marie whines, not certain she wants to wait that long to enjoy the good life.

"You can always help me with my homework."

"Fred? Are you really all right? I mean, in your mind?"

"My mind! You mean you think I've gone goofy?"

"I've been wondering . . . what was Gadowski?"

"Where did you hear about him?"

"You talk in your sleep, Honey. Sometimes you shout something's on fire and you want somebody to get out and you keep saying Gadowski, Gadowski!"

"Gadorski," he corrects her. "Oh, he was a friend of mine, a B-17 pilot, he got it over Berlin."

"Can't you get those things out of your system . . . maybe that's what's holding you back; you know the war's over, you won't get any place until you stop thinking about it. C'mon, snap out of it. . . ."

Just "snapping out of it" seemed so simple to Marie, and to thousands who hadn't experienced combat, who didn't continually wonder why their buddy lost out and they were allowed to carry on. But for the veterans of WWII who returned from overseas, nothing was going to be as simple as they had dreamed it would be. Nothing would be handed to them just because they wore the uniform and had a few colorful ribbons on their chest.

Fred Derry found that out in *The Best Years of Our Lives* when he reluctantly took that drugstore job, and many more veterans shared the humility he had to choke back . . . at least until he got himself fired, stumbled into another opportunity, and (it was implied) dumped the gold-digging Marie for the much more compassionate Peggy. If only every ex-serviceman could be so lucky.

Taking the Bitter with the Sweet

It should have been a fairy tale come true . . . the war was over and the whole world celebrated; manufacturers retooled and churned out washers and dryers, stoves and refrigerators, TVs and hi-fi stereos, cars and more cars. Money was good for those willing to work hard to earn it, and nothing could be harder—at least for the combat veteran—than the months or years of hell they had just survived. Certainly there were thousands of wounded vets who had some mending to do, and thousands more had emotional scars that would never heal. But the vast majority were able-bodied, eager to get back on track, pursuing the American dream.

But while most fairy tales had a happy ending, this one was tinged with bittersweet. The readjustment was a lot harder than those training films had said it would be, and many women weren't quite so eager to "just" be a mom and homemaker again, and those gold-plated jobs were a lot harder to find. Such were the closing chapters of 1945 and on through the end of the decade.

The men and women who lived through the war years survived every hardship and heartbreak that had tested their faith and resiliency but had failed to break their spirit. That is why they've been called the Greatest Generation.

Many were stung by the ugliness of war and allowed it to imprison them, building invisible barriers to ward off the outside world, to shut out any opportunity to live full and enriched lives and do great things.

Others realized that no matter what the future had in store for them, no matter what the obstacles or the challenges or the setbacks, nothing could be

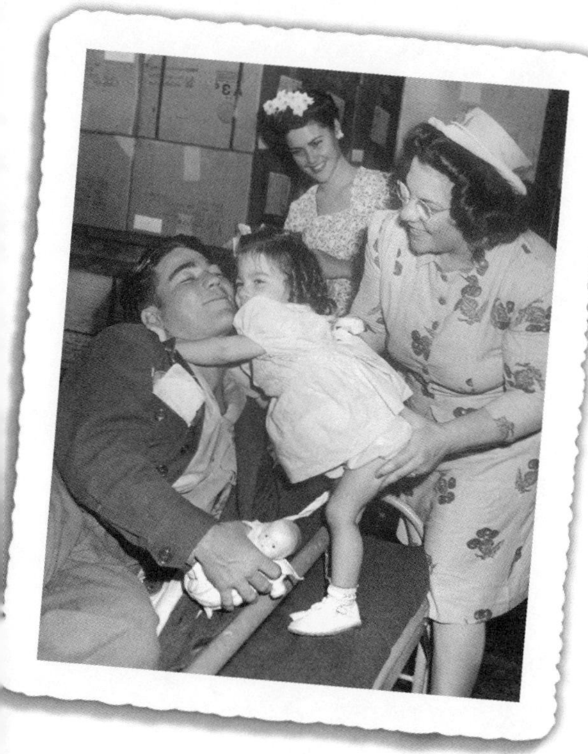

any harder than what they had already endured. Nothing was going to stop them—these forever optimists—from realizing their dreams and accomplishing their goals, of reaching out and taking everything life had to offer, with all the trimmings.

Harold Russell, the double-amputee who starred in *The Best Years of Our Lives,* looked back on those years immediately after the war and said, "'The guys who came out of World War Two were idealistic. They sincerely believed that this time they were coming home to build a new world.'" Wrote Joseph Goulden in *The Best Years*: "'Many, many times you'd hear guys say, 'The one thing I want to do when I get out is to make sure that this thing will never happen again.'" That legacy rings true today. Sure, there have been regional skirmishes and unpopular wars that threatened to divide this country, but nothing that's come remotely close to consuming the entire world. And that is a tribute to the veterans, the men and women of WWII.

Some felt they deserved more than what they got, believing their sacrifice, their service to country, earned them a first-class ticket to Easy Street . . . and they were bitter when they got dropped off along the way. Others expected nothing, but knew an honest day's work would earn them honest wages and that they would one day reap the bounty of that hard work. That was the bitter and the sweet of it all. Such was the fate and the promise and the destiny of America's Greatest Generation.

LEFT: *Many disabled servicemen didn't want to return home to family and friends if they were anything less than whole. Some hid away in veterans hospitals, refusing to accept phone calls, tossing away love letters, unwilling to believe anyone could love a man who was maybe less than a man.*

Others, like PFC Lee Harper, who was wounded in the D-Day invasion, couldn't wait to get back to those he'd been missing, those he'd never seen, such as his little sister Janet, born after he shipped out in the summer after Pearl Harbor. For PFC Harper, the best elixir was the love of his wife and his mom's home cooking, both of them waiting their turn to catch up on the hugs and kisses.
Office of War Information Photo

Bibliography

Agan, Patrick. *The Decline and Fall of the Love Goddesses*, Kensington Publishing Corp, NY, 1979

Agoratus, Steven. "Clark Gable in the Eighth Air Force," *Air Power History*, Vol. 46, Issue 1, Spring 1999, pp. 4–18

Allen, Thomas B. "The Wings of War," *National Geographic,* March 1994

Anderson, Janice. *History of Movie Comedy,* Exeter, NY, 1985

Andrews, Peter. "A Place to Be Lousy In," *American Heritage,* December 1991

Ansen, David. "A Fond Farewell," *Newsweek,* June 23, 2003

Arany, Lynne, Tom Dyja, and Gary Goldsmith . *The Reel List,* Bantam, NY, 1995

Arce, Hector. *The Secret Life of Tyrone Power,* William Morrow and Co., NY, 1979

Atkinson, Brooks. *Broadway,* MacMillan, NY, 1970

Bacall, Lauren. *By Myself,* Alfred A. Knopf, NY, 1979

Bailey, Ronald H. *The Home Front,* Time-Life Books, NY, 1977

Bankhead, Tallulah. *Tallulah, My Autobiography,* Harper and Brothers, NY, 1952

Banks, Scott. "Empire of the Winds," *American Heritage,* April/May 2003

Barnhart, Aaron. "Bob Hope, America's entertainer, dies," *Kansas City Star,* Kansas City, MO, July 29, 2003

Baron, Scott. *They Also Served,* MIE Publishing, Spartanburg, SC, 1998

Barson, Michael. "POPaganda," *Entertainment Weekly,* April 4, 2003

Basinger, Jeanine. *The World War II Combat Film,* Columbia University Press, NY, 1986

"Battle Cry," *Los Angeles Magazine*, December 1997, p. 66

Belton, John. *American Cinema/American Culture,* McGraw-Hill, NY, 1999

——. *Robert Mitchum,* Pyramid, NY, 1976

Bennett, Tony, with Friedwald, Will. *The Good Life,* Pocket Books, NY, 1998

Bergreen, Laurence. "Irving Berlin, 'This Is the Army,'" *Prologue*, Vol. 28, No. 2, Summer 1996

Berlau, John. "Jane Russell Outlaws PC Pose," *Insight on the News*, March 11, 2002, p. 36

Bertelsen, Lance. "San Pietro and the 'Art' of War," *Southwest Review,* Spring 1989, Volume 74, Issue 2

Bessette, Roland L. *Mario Lanza. Tenor in Exile,* Amadeus Press, Portland, OR, 1999

Biederman, Patricia Ward. "Winning the war one frame at a time," *Los Angeles Times*, October 30, 2002, p. E-4.

"Bill Scott, voice of Bullwinkle," Obituary, *Chicago Sun-Times*, December 12, 1985, p. 56

Binns, Stewart. "The Second World War in Color," *History Today*, Vol. 49, Issue 9, September 1999, p. 3

Blumenson, Martin. "The Struggle for Rome," *American History Illustrated,* June 1983

Bogart, Stephen Humphrey. *Bogart. In Search of My Father,* Dutton Books, NY, 1995

Bosworth, Patricia. *Montgomery Clift,* Harcourt Brace Jovanovich, NY, 1978

Bradshaw, Thomas I. and Marsha L. Clark. *Carrier Down,* Eakin Press, Austin, TX, 1990

Breuer, William. *Operation Torch,* St. Martin's Press, NY, 1988

Brokaw, Tom. *The Greatest Generation,* Random House, NY, 1998

Brough, James. *The Fabulous Fondas,* David McKay Co., NY, 1973

Brown, Curtis F. *Ingrid Bergman,* Galahad Books, NY, 1973

Buchwald, Art. *Leaving Home: A memoir,* G.P. Putnam's Sons, NY, 1993

Burns, George, with David Fisher, *All My Best Friends,* G.P. Putnam's Sons, NY, 1989

Burr, Lonnie. *Two for the Show: Great Comedy Teams,* Messner, NY, 1979

Burr, Ty. "Katharine Hepburn," *Entertainment Weekly,* July 11, 2003

Butler, Robert W. "You will remember this," *Kansas City Star,* Kansas City, MO, August 7, 2003

——. "The whims of war films," *Kansas City Star,* Kansas City, MO, March 10, 2002

Byrd, Martha H. "Battle of the Philippine Sea," *American History Illustrated,* July 1977

Callander, Bruce D. "Eight Decades over Hollywood," *Air Force Magazine,* Vol. 79, No. 7, July 1996, pp. 66–72

Capra, Frank. *Frank Capra: The Name above the Title*, The Macmillan Company, NY, 1971

Carney, Steve. "65 Years Later, Invasion Continues," *Los Angeles Times*, October 31, 2003, p. E-38.

Carpozi Jr., George. *The Gary Cooper Story,* Arlington House, New Rochelle, NJ, 1970

Carrier, Jeffrey L. *Tallulah Bankhead,* Greenwood Press, NY, 1991

Cerf, Bennett. *Good for a Laugh,* Hanover House, NY, 1952

Chaplin, Charlie. *My Autobiography,* Penguin Books, NY, 1992

Childers, Thomas. *Wings of Morning,* Addison-Wesley Publishing Co., Reading, MA, 1995

Coffey, Frank. *Always Home: 50 Years of the USO,* Brassey's Inc., Washington, D.C., 1991

Colwell, Robert T., "Radio Luxembourg: It Uses Jokes as Propaganda Against the Nazis," *Life*, March 5, 1945

Comer, John. *Combat Crew,* William Morrow and Co., NY, 1988

Cooke, Alistair. *Six Men,* Alfred Knopf, NY, 1977

Corkery, Paul. *Carson,* Randt and Co., Ketchum, ID, 1987

Crawford, Joan with Jane Kesner Ardmore. *A Portrait of Joan,* Doubleday & Co., NY, 1962

Cuthbert, David. "Soulful Side of a Cinema Sex Symbol, This is Jane Russell," *Times-Picayune*, October 20, 1997, D-1

Davis, Ronald L. *John Ford: Hollywood's Old Master*. University of Oklahoma Press, Norman, 1995

Day, Beth. *This Was Hollywood,* Doubleday & Co., NY, 1960

DeCarlo, Yvonne with Doug Warren. *Yvonne: An Autobiography*, St. Martin's Press, NY, 1987

Descher, Donald. *The Films of Spencer Tracy,* Citadel Press, NY, 1968

Dick, Bernard F. *The Star Spangled Screen,* University Press of Kentucky, Lexington, KY, 1985

Dickens, Homer. *The Films of Katharine Hepburn,* The Citadel Press, NY, 1971

Dietrich, Marlene. *Marlene,* translated by Salvator Attanasio, Avon Books, NY, 1987

"DiGiannantonio, Edmond P." *The Washington Post*, obituary, February 21, 2000

Doolittle, Lt. Gen. James H., and Colonel Beirne Lay Jr. "IMPACT: Daylight Precision Bombing, *American History Illustrated,* February 1980

Dorr, Robert F., "Clark Gable Flew Combat Missions," *Air Force Times*, Vol. 61, Issue 14, October 30, 2000, pp. 42–44

Douglas, Kirk. *The Ragman's Son,* Pocket Books, NY, 1988

Douglas, Mike with Thomas Kelly and Michael Heaton. *I'll be Right Back,* Simon & Schuster, NY, 2000

Drohojowska-Philp, Hunter. "It was all Risqué Innocence; The Vargas girl images were familiar to soldiers and magazine readers," *Los Angeles Times*, June 23, 2002, p. F-53

Dryer, Sherman H. *Radio in Wartime,* Greenberg, NY, 1942

Duncan, Amy. "Victory Tunes from Another War," *Christian Science Monitor*, January 25, 1991

Dunnigan, James F. and Albert A. Nofi. *Dirty Little Secrets of World War II,* William Morrow and Co., NY, 1994

Dunning, John. *Tune in Yesterday,* Prentice-Hall, Englewood Cliffs, NJ, 1976

"During World War II, Star Soldiers Did Celluloid Service," *Los Angeles Daily News*, May 22, 1997

Dwiggins, Don. *Hollywood Pilot: The Biography of Paul Mantz,* Doubleday & Co., Garden City, NY, 1967

Dworkin, Susan. *Miss America 1945: Bess Myerson and the Year That Changed Our Lives,* Newmarket Press, 1998

Edwards, Owen. "'Beverly': Better Than the Bugler," *Smithsonian,* May 2004

Elliott, David. "Rita Hayworth: A pathetic life of fame and desire," *Chicago Sun Times*, December 17, 1989, p. 16

"Evening Report," *YANK*, May 28, 1943, June 18, 1943, and October 15, 1943

Eyles, Allen. *Rex Harrison,* W. H. Allen, London, 1985

Eyman, Scott. *Print the Legend: The Life and Times of John Ford*, Simon & Schuster, NY, 1999

Faris, Gerald. "Rita Hayworth, 'Love Goddess,' of '40s, Dies," *Los Angeles Times*, May 16, 1987

Faulkner, Rob. "Hollywood couldn't fly as high without wild-blue-yonder theme," *Hamilton Spectator* (Ontario, Canada), December 17, 2003, p. G-13

Fein, Esther. "George Stevens, a Son's Tribute," *The New York Times*, May 6, 1985, p. C-13

"Filmmaker John Ford's World War II OSS Work Exhibited," *All Things Considered*, February 26, 1995

"First Motion Picture Unit" documentary, produced by the Army Air Corps' First Motion Picture Unit, 1943

Flanagan, Edward M. Jr., *The Angels. A History of the 11th* Airborne Division, *1943–1946, Infantry Journal Press,* Washington, D.C., 1988
Flint, Peter B. "Frank Capra, Whose Films Helped America Keep Faith in Itself, is Dead at 94," *The New York Times*, September 4, 1991, B-10
Flower, John. *Moonlight Serenade—a Bio-discography of the Glenn Miller Civilian Band,* Arlington House, New Rochelle, 1972
Fonda, Henry, with Howard Teichmann. *My Life,* NAL, NY, 1081
"Forgotten, but not gone," *People*, June 10, 1991, Vol. 35, No. 22, p. 60
Fowles, Jib. *StarStruck*, Smithsonian Institution Press, Washington, 1992
Freedland, Michael. *Warner Brothers—Casablanca*, St. Martin's Press, NY, 1983
——. *Cagney: A Biography,* Stein and Day, NY, 1975
Freeman, Roberta. "Veterans who shot film reminisce Jack Warner started Motion Picture Unit," *Ventura County Star*, November 1, 2002, p. B-1
Friedrich, Otto. "Monte Cassino: a story of death and resurrection," *Smithsonian,* April 1987
Friedwald, Will. "Ocean Crossing," *Vanity Fair,* November 2002
Fussell, James A. "Our Seussical World," *Kansas City Star,* Kansas City, MO, December 11, 2003
Garland, Brock. *War Movies,* Facts on File Publications, NY, 1987
Gibbs, Nancy. "The Greatest Day," *Time,* May 31, 2004
Giddins, Gary. "Bing Crosby: The Unsung King of Song," *The New York Times*, January 28, 2001, p. 21
Gilbert, Julie. *Opposite Attraction,* Pantheon Books, NY, 1995
Goodman, Jack, editor. *While You Were Gone,* Simon and Schuster, NY, 1946
Gordinier, Jeff. "Welles' 'War,'" *Entertainment Weekly*, October 30, 1998, p. 132
Goulden, Joseph C. *The Best Years: 1945–1950,* Atheneum, NY, 1976
Graham, Don. *No Name on the Bullet,* Penguin Books, NY, 1989
Granger, Stewart. *Sparks Fly Upward,* Putnam, NY, 1981
Grauer, Neil A. "The Kid," *American Heritage,* December 2000/January 2001
Green, Stanley. *Broadway Musicals, 1940–1949,* Hal Leonard Publishing Corp., Milwaukee, WI, 1991
Grobel, Lawrence. *The Hustons*, Charles Scribner's Sons, NY, 1989
Hancock, Ralph, and Letitia Fairbanks. *Douglas Fairbanks: The Fourth Marketeer,* Henry Holt, NY, 1963
Harrington, Richard. "Wartime Melodies and Messages," *The Washington Post*, July 3, 1992
Harris, Mark Jonathan, Franklin D. Mitchell, and Steven J. Schechter. *The Homefront: America During World War II,* G. P. Putnam's Sons, NY, 1984
Harris, Warren G. *Gable and Lombard,* Simon and Schuster, NY, 1974
Hastings, Max. *Victory in Europe: D-Day to VE Day in Full Color*, Little, Brown and Company, Boston, 1985
Haun, Harry. *The Movie Quote Book,* Bonaza Books, NY, 1986
Hayden, Sterling. *Wanderer,* Bantam Books, NY, 1963
Henninger, Paul. "Entertaining the Troops: A Human Side of War," *San Francisco Chronicle*, March 12, 1989, p. 12
Herman, Jan. "A Retrospect puts the Spotlight back on the Works of Director William Wyler," *Los Angeles Times*, May 5, 1996, p. 26

——. *A Talent for Trouble: The Life of Hollywood's Most Acclaimed Director, William Wyler*, G.P. Putnam's Sons, NY, 1995

——. "The *Memphis Belle* is the real thing—an up-close look at the people and drama of World War II bombing missions," *Los Angeles Times*, February 5, 1998, p. 16

Heston, Charlton. *The Actor's Life,* E. P. Dutton and Co., NY, 1978

Higham, Charles and Joel Greenberg. *Hollywood in the Forties,* A. S. Barnes, NY, 1968

Higham, Charles. *Audrey: The Life of Audrey Hepburn,* The Macmillan Company, NY, 1984

Hilburn, Robert. "A Slice of American History," *Los Angeles Times*, May 1, 1999

Hyams, Jay. *War Movies*, Gallery Books, NY, 1984

"Invasion of Mae West's Dressing Room," *YANK*, September 29, 1944

"Issue Girl Friend," *YANK*, July 27, 1945

Hope, Bob, as told to Pete Martin. *Have Tux, Will Travel,* Simon and Schuster, NY, 1954

Hope, Bob. *So This is Peace,* Simon and Schuster, NY, 1946

Hotchner, A. E. *Sophia. Living and Loving,* William Morrow and Co., NY, 1979

Hudson, Richard M. and Raymond Lee. *Gloria Swanson,* Castle Books, NY, 1970

Hunter, Allan. *Walter Matthau,* St. Martin's Press, NY, 1984

Huston, John. *An Open Book,* Alfred A. Knopf, NY, 1980

Hyams, Jay. *War Movies,* W. H. Smith Publishers, NY, 1986

Infield, Glenn. *Big Week: The Classic Story of the Crucial Air Battle of WWII,* Brassey's, NY, 1974

Jackson, Arthur. *The Best Musicals,* Crown Publishers, NY, 1977

Jeavons, Clyde. *A Pictorial History of War Films,* Citadel Publishing, Sacaucus, NJ, 1974

Jenkins, Graham, and Barry Turner. *Richard Burton: My Brother,* Harper & Row, NY, 1988

Jensen, Kurt with Mike Clark, and Mike Snider. "100 reasons to toast Bob Hope," *USA Today,* May 29, 2003

Jones, Ken D., and Arthur F. McClure. *Hollywood at War,* A. S. Barnes, Cranbury, NJ, 1971

Julian, Joseph. *This was Radio,* Viking Press, NY, 1975

Kanin, Garson. *Tracy and Hepburn,* The Viking Press, NY, 1971

——. *Hollywood: Stars and Starlets, Tycoons and Flesh-Peddlers, Movie Makers and Money Makers, Frauds and Geniuses, Hopefuls and Has-Beens, Great Lovers and Sex Symbols*, Viking Press, NY, 1974

Katz, Alan. "At 76, Dorothy Lamour still oozes charm," *Denver Post*, October 24, 1991, p. 1-F

Keats, John. *Howard Hughes,* Random House, NY, 1966

Kelsey, Juliett. "Famous and Formerly Enlisted," *Air Force Magazine*, Vol. 82, No. 4, April 1999, pp. 66–71

King, Susan. "History of Hollywood; on the West Coast Front; the studios' approach to winning American hearts and minds in favor of action in World War II are on display at screening exhibit," *Los Angeles Times*, October 22, 2003, p. E-2

Knapp, Ed. "Remember Don Winslow's Great Radio Show?", *Reminisce,* January/February 1997

Knight, Arthur. *The Liveliest Art,* MacMillan Publishing Co., NY, 1957

Kobal, John. *Rita Hayworth: The Time, The Place and The Woman,* W. W. Norton, NY, 1977

Koppes, Clayton R., and Gregory D. Black. *Hollywood Goes to War,* The Free Press, NY, 1987

Kramer, Stanley with Thomas M. Coffey. *A Mad, Mad, Mad, Mad World: A Life in Hollywood*, Harcourt Brace & Company, NY, 1997

Kroll, Jack. "Springing Eternal," *Newsweek,* August 11, 2003

Krome, Frederic. "Tunisian Victory and Anglo-American film propaganda in World War II," *The Historian*, Vol. 58, No. 3, Spring 1996, pp. 517–530

Kruger, Mollee. "Last Waltz on the Way to War: Christmas at the USO," *The Washington Post*, December 25, 1994, C-5

Lamparski, Richard. *Whatever Became Of . . .* , Crown Publishing Group, NY, 1968, 1973, and 1975

"Lana Turner, Glamorous Star of 50 Films, Dies at 75," *Los Angeles Times*, June 30, 1995, p. 1

LaPaglia, Anthony. "Harold Russell," *Entertainment Weekly*, 2002

Lawson, Ted. *Thirty Seconds Over Tokyo,* Random House, NY, 1943

Leaming, Barbara. *Orson Welles,* Viking Penguin, NY, 1985

Ledes, Richard. "Let There Be Light: John Huston's Film and the Concept of Trauma in the United States after World War II," speech given at the Après-Coup Psycholanalytic Association on November 13, 1998. As downloaded on May 27, 2004 from www.apres-coup.org/archives/articles/ledes.pdf.

Lee, Luaine. "Hollywood Went to War in body, mind, and spirit," *Chicago Tribune*, December 10, 1991, p. 2

Leonard, Hal. *I'll be Seeing You: 50 Songs of World War II,* Hal Leonard Corp., Milwaukee, WI, 1995

Leonhard, Robert R. "Overlord: Strategic Compromise at Normandy," *Armchair General,* May 2004

Levine, Justin. "A History and Analysis of the Federal Communication Commission's Response to Radio Broadcast Hoaxes," *Federal Communications Law Journal*, Vol. 52, Issue 2, March 2000, pp. 273–321

Levine, I. E., *Spokesman for the Free World: Adlai E. Stevenson,* Julian Messner, NY, 1967

Levins, Harry. "Sexy Nose Art on Bombers Offended the Bluenoses Back Home," *St. Louis Post-Dispatch*, August 6, 1995

Life Special Issue: World War II, Summer 1985

Lloyd, Ann, editor. *Movies of the Forties,* Orbis, London, 1982

Logan, Joshua. *Movie Stars, Real People, and Me,* Delacorte Press, NY, 1978

Long, Robert Emmet, editor. *John Huston Interviews*, University of Mississippi Press, Jackson, 2001

Longmate, Norman. *The GIs—The Americans in Britain, 1942–1945,* Charles Scribner's Sons, NY, 1975

Maas, Peter. "The Last Great Air Battle," *Esquire,* June 1983

Mackenzie, Midge. "Screen: Huston, we have a problem," *The Guardian*, October 23, 1998, p. T4

——. "An Antiwar Message from the Army's Messenger," *The New York Times*, April 16, 2000

Manchel, Frank. *Cameras West*, Prentice-Hall, Inc., Englewood Cliffs, NJ, 1971

Manchester, William. "The Man Who Could Speak Japanese," *American Heritage,* December 1975

Martin, Mary. *My Heart Belongs,* William Morrow and Company, NY, 1976

Mazzetti, Mark. "The D is for Deception," *U.S. News and World Report,* August 26/September 2, 2002

McBride, Joseph. *Frank Capra: The Catastophe of Success.* Faber and Faber, London, 1996

McLellan, Diana. *The Girls: Sappho Goes to Hollywood,* St. Martin's Press, NY, 2000

McLellan, Dennis. "Film pioneer Hal Roach, comedy king, dies at 100 in Hollywood," *Los Angeles Times*, November 3, 1992

McClelland, Doug. *Hollywood on Ronald Reagan,* Faber and Faber, Winchester, MA, 1983

McMahon, Ed, with David Fisher. *For Laughing Out Loud: My Life and Good Times,* Warner Books, NY, 1998

Melendez, Michele M. "Celebrities in the Armed Forces? Not these days," Newhouse News Service, April 15, 2003

Merman, Ethel, with George Eells. *Merman,* Simon and Schuster, NY, 1978

Meredith, Burgess. *So Far, So Good,* Little, Brown and Company, Boston, 1994

Metro desk. "William Orr, 85, had hit TV shows in 50s, 60s for Warner Brothers," Obituary, *Los Angeles Times*, December 29, 2002, B12

Meyers, Jeffrey. *Bogart. A Life in Hollywood,* Houghton Mifflin Co., NY, 1997

Milland, Ray. *Wide-Eyed in Babylon,* William Morrow & Co., NY, 1974

Miller, Chuck. "Victory Music: The Story of the V-Disc Record Label (1943–1949). *Goldmine*, February 1999

Miller, Joan. "Nazi Invasion," *American History Illustrated,* November 1986

Morella, Joe, Edward Z. Epstein, and John Griggs. *The Films of World War II,* Citadel Press, Sacaucus, NJ, 1973

"Morgan, Robert: Memphis Belle Pilot," Obituary, *The Washington Post*, May 17, 2004

Morrow, Lance. "Not Your Average Joe," *Time,* April 12, 2004

Moseley, Roy with Philip and Martin Masheter. *Rex Harrison: A Biography,* St. Martin's Press, NY, 1987

Munn, Michael. *Stars at War*, Robson Books Ltd., Oxford, 1995

Nachman, Gerald. "V-Discs Bring Back Music of World War II," *San Francisco Chronicle*, December 19, 1990, p. E-3

Nashawaty, Chris. "Cinema's Paradiso," *Entertainment Weekly,* 2002

Nelan, Bruce W. "Ike's Invasion," *Time,* June 6, 1994

Newcomb, Richard F., *Iwo Jima,* Holt, Rinehart and Winston, NY, 1965

Nichols, Major Charles S. Jr., and Henry I. Jr. Shaw. *Okinawa. Victory in the Pacific,* Charles E. Tuttle Co., Rutland, VT, 1955

Niven, David. *Bring on the Empty Horses,* G. P. Putnam's Sons, NY, 1975

Nolan, William F. *John Huston, King Rebel,* Sherbourne Press, Inc., Los Angeles, CA, 1965

O'Brien, Pat. *The Wind at My Back: The Life and Times of Pat O'Brien*, Doubleday & Company, Inc., Garden City, NY, 1964

O'Callaghan, Scott. "The War of the Worlds: Why the Hoax Worked," *Writing*, Vol. 23, Issue 6, April/May 2001, p. 12

O'Connor, Carroll. *I Think I'm Outta Here,* Pocket Books, NY, 1998

Parish, Robert James. *The Paramount Pretties,* Castle Books, NY, 1972

Park, Edwards. "A phantom division played a role in Germany's defeat," *Smithsonian,* April 1985

Parks, Louis B. "Fascinating 'documentary' on George Stevens; a director finally gets his place in the sun," *Houston Chronicle*, November 10, 1985, p. 31

Peary, Gerald, editor. *John Ford Interviews*, University of Mississippi Press, Jackson, 2001

"People," *Time*, 1942

Perrett, Geoffrey. *Winged Victory,* Random House, NY, 1991

Pitts, Michael R., "When Hollywood Makes History," *American Heritage,* March 1989

Pratley, Gerald. *The Cinema of John Huston*, A. S. Barnes and Company, Inc., Cranbury, NJ, 1977

Proeller, Marie. "Vintage Posters that rallied an entire nation during wartime now command attention of collectors," *Country Living*, June 1997, p. 140

Raab, Scott. "Robert Altman (What I've Learned)," *Esquire,* February 2004

Ragan, David. *Movie Stars of the '40s,* Prentice Hall, NY, 1985

Rasmussen, Cecelia. "Vargas' Pinups Inspired GIs, Became Icons of U.S. Culture," *Los Angeles Times*, June 25, 2000, p. 3

Raughter, John. "The Bravest Cowboy," *American Legion,* June 2003

Reed, Rex. *Valentines & Vitriol,* Delacorte Press, NY, 1977

"Reagan Paid His Dues in World War II," *Los Angeles Times,* May 11, 1985, p. Metro 2, Letters Desk

Reagan, Ronald. *An American Life*, Pocket Books, NY, October, 1999

Renoir, Jean, translated by Norman Denny. *My Life and My Films,* Atheneum, NY, 1974

Rickey, Carrie. "Crusading screen legend Gregory Peck dies at 87," *Kansas City Star,* Kansas City, MO, June 13, 2003

Riddle, Amanda. "Singer Brought Troops 'A Vision of Home,'" *The Washington Post*, February 9, 2002, C-3

"Rita Hayworth," *Biography Magazine*, April 2002

Rooney, Andy. *My War,* Times Books, NY, 2002

Rooney, Mickey. *Life is Too Short,* Villard Books, NY, 1991

Ross, Bill D., *Iwo Jima,* Viking Press, NY, 1976

Russell, Rosalind. *Life is a Banquet,* Random House, NY, 1977

Sabulis, Tom. "Jane Russell on bras, Bob Hope, film," *Atlanta Journal-Constitution*, June 16, 1996, L-03

Salaman, Julie. "In Trenches with War Photographers," *The New York Times*, December 7, 2000, E-5

Sanello, Frank. *Jimmy Stewart: A Wonderful Life,* Pinnacle Books, NY, 1997
Sennett, Ted. *Warner Brothers Presents,* Castle Books, NY, 1971
Server, Lee. *Robert Mitchum: Baby, I Don't Care,* St. Martin's Griffin, NY, 2001
Severo, Richard. "Jinx Falkenburg, Model, Actress, Pioneer of Radio and TV Talk Shows, Dies at 84," *The New York Times*, August 8, 2003, B-9
Shipman, David. *The Great Movie Stars,* Crown Publishers, NY, 1970
Sinclair, Andrew. *John Ford*, The Dial Press, NY, 1979
Smith, Jack. "Anecdotal outtakes recall Reagan's military service," *Houston Chronicle*, June 5, 1985, p. 2
Smith, Lynn. "Movies; In supporting roles; When top stars and directors enlisted in the war effort in the 1940s, it was a different Hollywood—and America," *Los Angeles Times*, March 30, 2003, p. E8
"Snapped Famed World War II Betty Grable Pinup, Photographer Frank Powolny Dies at 84," *Los Angeles Times*, January 11, 1986, p. 7
Spada, James. *More Than a Woman,* Bantam Books, NY, 1993
Spears, Gregory. "'40s tunes spun to boost morale on another front," *Houston Chronicle*, December 23, 1990, p. 26
Spreier, Jeanne. "For the War Effort," *Dallas Morning News,* Dallas, TX, June 30, 2001
Squires, Vernon C. "Landing at Tokyo Bay," *American Heritage*
Stanley, John. "Controversial Film on Pearl Harbor Attack Restored," *San Francisco Chronicle*, November 13, 1991, p. E-6
——. "Jane Russell: Her Cleavage Launched a Fabulous Career," *San Francisco Chronicle*, September 15, 1985
Stokesbury, James. "Battle of Attu," *American History Illustrated,* April 1979
——. "1943, Invasion of Italy," *American History Illustrated,* December 1977
Stone, Judy. "Tribute to a Film Maverick," *San Francisco Chronicle*, May 29, 1990, E-1
Summersby Morgan, Kay. *Past Forgetting,* Simon and Schuster, NY, 1975
Swindell, Larry. *Body and Soul: The Story of John Garfield,* William Morrow, NY, 1975
Taylor, John Russell. *Hollywood 1940s,* Gallery Books, NY, 1985
Terkel, Studs. *The Good War,* Ballantine Books, NY, 1984
"The Unquiet Man: Irascible Director John Ford Made Art of of Boozing, Bonding, and Brawling, and it Won Him a Record Four Oscars," *Entertainment Weekly, Special Oscar Guide, 2003*. February 21, 2003, pp. 93–94
Thomas, Bob. "Veterans who did war training films hold 60th anniversary," Associated Press, November 1, 2002
——. *Winchell,* Doubleday & Co., Garden City, NY, 1971
——. *Joan Crawford,* Simon and Schuster, NY, 1978
Thompson, Charles. *Bing,* David McKay Co., NY, 1975
Thurber, Jon. "Hartzell Spence; Coined Term 'Pin-up,'" *Los Angeles Times*, May 29, 2001, B-11
——. "Jinx Falkenburg, 84; Model and Actress Later Pioneered Talk Show," *Los Angeles Times*, August 29, 2003
Tierney, Gene, with Mickey Herskowitz. *Self-Portrait,* Wyden Books, NY, 1979
Tomkies, Mike. *Duke. The Story of John Wayne,* Avon Books, NY, 1971

Tornabene, Lyn. *Long Live the King,* G.P. Putnam's Sons, NY, 1976

Tozzi, Romano. *Spencer Tracy,* Galahad Books, NY, 1973

Trussell, Robert and Robert W. Butler. "Oscar during Wartime," *Kansas City Star,* Kansas City, MO, March 22, 2003

Turner, Lana. *The Lady, the Legend, the Truth: Lana*, E. P. Dutton, NY, 1982

Twomey, Alfred E. and Arthur F. McClure. *The Versatiles,* A. S. Barnes, NY, 1969

Van Osdol, William R. *Famous Americans in World War II,* Phalanx Publishing, St. Paul, MN, 1994

Vermilye, Jerry. *Burt Lancaster: Hollywood's Magic People,* Falcon Enterprises Inc., NY, 1971

VFW Foreign Service, September 1945

Wallace, Irving, David Wallechinsky, Amy and Sylvia Wallace. *Intimate Sex Lives of Famous People,* Delacorte, NY, 1981

Ward, Geoffrey C. "The St. Louis Woman of Paris," *American Heritage,* November 1989

Ware, Susan, editor. *Forgotten Heroes,* G. K. Hall & Co., Thorndike, ME, 1998

Warner, Jack and Dean Jennings. *My First Hundred Years in Hollywood,* Random House, NY, 1964

Warren, Doug. *Betty Grable: The Reluctant Movie Queen,* St. Martin's Press, NY, 1974

"What Goes on in the Entertainment World Back Home," *YANK*, February 25, 1944, June 23, 1944, and July 28, 1944

Wheeler, Richard. *IWO,* Lippincott & Crowell, NY, 1980

Williams, Esther with Digby Diehl. *The Million Dollar Mermaid,* Simon & Schuster, NY, 1999

Wilmington, Michael. "When Hollywood Went to War after December 7, 1941, Pacifist Movies Gave Way to Films that Energized a Populace Bracing for Conflict," *Los Angeles Times*, December 1, 1991, p. 27

Winkler, Sheldon. "The timeless song 'Lili Marlene' became popular with both Allied and Axis soldiers during World War II," *WWII History,* July 2003

——. "The music of World War II provided inspiration and solace to those on the home front and those at war far away from home," *World War II History*, May 2004, pp. 22–27

Winning Your Wings documentary, produced by the Army Air Corps' First Motion Picture Unit, Owen Crump, director, 1942

Winters, Jonathan. *Winters' Tales,* Random House, NY, 1987

Winters, Shelley. *Shelley,* William Morrow and Co., NY, 1980

Wise, James E. Jr. and Anne Collier Rehill. *Star in Blue,* Naval Institute Press, Annapolis, MD, 1997

——. *Stars in the Corps,* Naval Institute Press, Annapolis, MD, 1999

Wise, James E. Jr. and Paul W. Wilderson III, *Stars in Khaki: Movie Actors in the Army and Air Services*. Annapolis: Naval Institute Press, 2000

Yablonsky, Lewis. *George Raft,* New American Library, NY, 1974

Yass, Marion. *The Home Front: England 1939–1945,* Wayland Publishers, London, 1971

Zailian, Marian. "Dorothy Lamour Relives War Years," *San Francisco Chronicle*, November 10, 1991, p. 43

Zeiger, Henry A. *Ian Fleming: The Spy Who Came In with the Gold*, Duell, Sloan and Pearce, NY, 1965

Zierold, Norman. *The Moguls*, Coward-McCann, NY, 1969

Sources from the World Wide Web

"A History of V-Discs," at www.kcmetro.cc.mo.us/pennvalley/biology/lewis/crosby/v-discs.htm

"A Tribute to John Huston," at http://classicfilm.about.com/library/weekly/aa081201a.htm

"Air Force," at www.geocities.com/warmoviedatabase/mairfor.htm

"Anne Gwynne, a favorite cover girl for *Yank*," at www.annegwynne.com/candid/yank.htm

"Betty Grable," at http://history.acusd.edu/gen/ww2timeline/bettygrable.html

"Bing Crosby's V-Discs," Mark Scrimger, at www.kcmetro.cc.mo.us/pennvalley/biology/lewis/v-discography.htm

"Biography of Gregg Toland," at http://entertainment.msn.com/celebs.aspx?mp=b&c=194721

"Carole Landis biography," at www.glamourgirlsofthesilverscreen.com

"Carole Landis biography," at www.lawzone.com/half-nor/landis.htm

"Carole Landis biography," at www.geocities.com/classicmoviestar/carole.html

"Carole Landis biography," at http://users.breathemail.net/birchwood. computers/actresses/CarolLandis/htm

"Clark Gable in the Eighth Air Force," at www.geocities.com/cactus_st/article/article143c.html

"Cinema Five-O: From Hollywood's Egyptian," at www.hollywoodfiveo.com/archive/issue2/cinema/rubin.htm

"Europe and D-Day: Boogie Woogie Bugle Boy," at www.umkc.edu/lib/spec-col/ww2/Dday/bugle_boys.htm

"Famous Iowans," Tom Longden at www.desmoinesregister.com/extras/iowans/carey.html

"Fats Waller," at www.musicweb.uk.net/encylopedia/w/W12/HTM

"First Motion Picture Unit" at wysiwyg://27/http://www.genordell.com/stores/lantern/FMPU.htm

"Frank Capra," on http://en.wikipedia.org/wiki/Frank_Capra

"Frank Capra's 'Why We Fight' Series on the International Historic Films Website," at www.ihffilm.com/francapwhyw.html

"Frank Thomas," at www.toon.com/info/Frank_Thomas.html

"Gene Kelly biography," at www.allsands.com/Entertainment/People/genekelly-biogr_yzn_gn.htm

"George Reeves"at www.celebhost.net/georgereeves/bio.html

"Gregg Toland," at www.twyman_whitney.com/film/celluloid_profiles/toland.html

"Gregg Toland Biography" at www.theoscarsite.com/whoswho/toland_g.htm

"He Hired the Boss," at www.freewebs.com/vbfilms/hehiredtheboss1943.htm

"Hermann Goering," www.spartacus.schoolnet.co.uk/2Wwgoring.htm

"Hollywood's Army: The First Motion Picture Unit, U.S. Army Air Forces, Culver City, California," Master Sergeant George J. Siegel, at www.militarymuseum.org/1stmpu.html

"Howard Hawks," at www.scene360.com/EDITINGroom_Hawks.html

"In the Waiting Room: John Huston's 'Let There Be Light,'" Quentin Turnour at www.sensesofcinema.com/contents/00/6/cteq/light.html

"Irving Wallace," at www.kirjasto.sci.fi/iwallace.htm

"James Petrillo," at www.ieee-virtual-museum.org/collection/people.php

"Jules Engle: Founding Director," at www.calarts.edu/schools/film/faculty/engel_jules.htm

"Jules Engle: Pioneering animator behind early Disney greats," at www.guardian.co.uk/arts/news/obituary/0,12723,1043498,00.html

"Less is More: John Hubley's Animation Revolution," at www.digitalmediafx.com/Features/johnhubley.html

"Lights! Camera! War! Army movie unit gets salute," at http://216.239.41.104/search?=cache:shgJDMTZlogJ:www.s-t.com/daily/05–97/05–23-97

"Marilyn Monroe: The Man Who Discovered Norma Jean," at www.mwsolutions.com/marilynmonroe/m_and_d.htm

"Music, Radio & TV in the '40s," at www.angelfire.com/retro2/ lisanostalgia2/40smusic.html

"Resisting Enemy Interrogation," at http://theoscarsite.com/pictures/1944/resisting.htm

"Stanley Rubin to be Inducted into Daily Bruin Hall of Fame," at www.daily-bruin.ucla.edu/alumni/hall_rubin.asp

"Steve Sholes," at www.countryworks.com/artist_full.asp?KEY=SHOLES

"The Battle of Midway: A Bibliography of Video Recordings," at http://library.nps.navy.mil/home/bibs/midwayvideo.htm

"The Commander-in-Chief: President Ronald Reagan 1981–1989," at www.wpatb.af.mil/museum/history/wwii/rr.htm

"The History Channel Classroom Study Guide: Why We Fight," at www.historychannel.com/classroom/admin/study_guide/archives/thc_guide.0556.html

"The Memphis Belle: A Story of a Flying Fortress," at http://history.acusd.edu/gen/filmnotes/memphisbelle.html

"The V-Discs of World War II," Bob Witek of LovinLife.com at www.wwseniors.com/cgi_bin/artdsp2pl?sect=entertainment&filename=20040308aa

"This Is the Army," at http://history.sandiego.edu/gen/filmnotes/thisisthearmy.html

"V-Discs Boosted Troop Morale During World War II," at www.recordcollectors-guild.org/v_discs.html

"Why We Fight," http://history.sandiego.edu/gen/WW2/Timeline/whywefight.html

"William Wellman: The Wild Man of Hollywood," Sean McCloy, at http://www.iol.ie/~galfilm/filmwest/34wellman.htm

"William Wyler," at www.pbs.org/wnet/americanmasters/database/wyler_w.html

http://Academyawards.20.m.com/profiles/ford.htm

http://awardsdatabase.oscars.org
http://grin.hq.nasa.gov
http://movies2nytimes.com
www.78rpm.com
www.armypictorialcenter.com
www.archives.gov
www.carols.org.uk
www.imdb.com
www.movies.yahoo.com
www.nationmaster.com/encyclopedia
www.obits.com
www.oscars.org
www.turnerclassicmovies.com